BOUNDARIES BETWEEN

Boundaries

THE SOUTHERN PAIUTES, 1775–1995

Between

Martha C. Knack

UNIVERSITY OF NEBRASKA PRESS

LINCOLN AND LONDON

Publication of this volume was assisted by the
Charles Redd Center for Western Studies.

Library of Congress Cataloging-in-Publication Data

Knack, Martha C.

Boundaries between : the Southern Paiutes, 1775–1995 / Martha C. Knack.

p.   cm.

Includes bibliographical references (p.) and index.

ISBN 0-8032-2750-7 (cloth : alk. paper)

1. Southern Paiute Indians—History. I. Title.

E99.P2 K588 2001

979.004'9745—dc21

2001027349

CONTENTS

ILLUSTRATIONS

PREFACE AND ACKNOWLEDGMENTS

This book began in 1973 with my ethnographic research on the household economics of terminated bands of Southern Paiutes in Utah, performed with the financial assistance of a National Science Foundation Pre-Doctoral Research Fellowship and the intellectual guidance of Joseph G. Jorgensen. I asked myself at that time how the interethnic situation I was observing, experiencing, and participating in had come about. I knew, of course, the shallow, immediate causes, having done the requisite preliminary library searches. The ethnographic data on Southern Paiutes were meager compared to those for some other tribes and had not taken long to absorb. The congressional record of Paiute termination sketched their condition a generation before and suggested places I might go to find them today. A handful of newspaper articles decried their subsequent "plight." But none of this prepared me for the human complexity I found in southwestern Utah nor explained to me how it had come to be as it was in any but the most superficial of ways.

When time permitted, between dissertation deadlines, searching for employment, and then keeping it as a junior professor with never enough knowledge, I began to read books and articles on Paiute history. I gradually branched out to the history of the region, the far better known ethnohistory of bordering tribes, and the very ample and carefully maintained Mormon record. I dipped into the newspapers of mining towns and the formal history of the cattle industry and of resource development in the area. In 1986 a small faculty research grant from the University of Nevada, Las Vegas, allowed me to spend two weeks camped on the beach below the United States National Archives Branch at Laguna Niguel in a preliminary search of Paiute materials there.

The following year, grants from the National Endowment for the Humanities Travel to Collections Program, the Phillips Fund of the American Philosophical Society, and the Wenner-Gren Foundation for Anthropological Research enabled me to spend my sabbatical year near Washington DC and do a fairly exhaustive search of the U.S. National Archives records dealing with Southern Paiutes. During that year, Robert Kvasnicka, senior archivist in charge of Record Group 75 materials, Ken Heger, then archivist in the same division, and Constance Potter, in charge of the Archival Reading Room, patiently and generously took me under their collective wing and taught me the arcane mysteries of federal manuscript filing systems, the decoding of seemingly meaningless scribblings on folded letter covers, the finding of lost objects when they were not, as they inevitably occasionally were not, where they should have been. They eased for me the often time-consuming and awkward institutional procedures, for which I thank them wholeheartedly.

Two years later I spent the summer camping near Salt Lake City. The staff at the Church Historian's Office of the Church of Latter-day Saints welcomed me warmly. They indefatigably retrieved endless microfilms and explained yet another distinctive manuscript access system to me without complaint. So too did the staffs of the Utah State Historical Society and the Manuscript Room at Brigham Young University in Provo. I thank them all for their time, expertise, and assistance.

Three years later a fellowship from the Rockefeller Foundation, the award of a junior researcher appointment from the D'Arcy McNickle Center for the History of the American Indian at the Newberry Library in Chicago, and a faculty development leave from the University of Nevada, Las Vegas, enabled me to read further published and rare materials. I benefited not only from the efficiency of the staff of center director Frederick Hoxie and his able assistant, Jay Miller, but once again learned new research tricks under the skillful tutelage of senior librarian John Aubrey. The daily conversations and excitement of this large pool of able scholars of Indian history were a source of intellectual stimulation.

I am grateful for the gracious review of this manuscript by Margaret K. Sobel, Catherine S. Fowler, and David R. Lewis and for their many useful suggestions. The professional skill and meticulous care of the entire staff of the University of Nebraska Press have been of inestimable value in the final preparation of this volume. I must thank David Melton of the University of Nevada, Las Vegas, for drafting the maps and Mary Frances Morrow of the U.S. National Archives for helping me relocate and reproduce many of the historical photographs.

Over the last two decades, many Southern Paiute people have shared their lives with me, offering me friendship and hospitality, and they have spent hour upon hour explaining how things are for them. I have tried to understand not only their words but their meanings. I hope I have succeeded, although any failure is of course mine. I now hope that I can explain to others what I think I have understood.

BOUNDARIES BETWEEN

1

QUESTIONS AND ISSUES

By all the "rules" of history and anthropology, Southern Paiutes would have been expected to disappear long ago. They did not. Today Paiute wives argue with their husbands and then make up. Cousins drive hundreds of miles to visit one another. Clusters of only a few families fearlessly take on the complex regulations of the U.S. government to win legal recognition that they are indeed Indians. Southern Paiutes remain a quietly vital and vibrant society.

Before the arrival of Euro-Americans, Southern Paiutes foraged the arid hills and valleys of the area now called southern Utah, Arizona north of the Grand Canyon, southern Nevada, and southeastern California. They gathered grass seeds for grain and wild plants for leaves and roots, and they hunted, mostly rabbits and other small game. Where water and soil conditions made horticulture possible, they planted a few acres of corn and squashes. In this harsh desert land, where water and food were scarce, they lived in small autonomous communities, shared what little they had with relatives, traveled on foot with all their possessions on their backs, and observed keenly the world around them.

Many theories held by prominent anthropologists have predicted the demise of such small-scale foraging cultures in the face of Euro-American expansion. For instance, in adjacent native California, Alfred Kroeber noticed that small tribes with simple material culture like the Paiutes' vanished historically, while "neighboring tribes—in valleys or on larger streams, more populous, richer, and of more elaborated customs—have usually maintained themselves proportionally better in spite of heavier or at least equal contact with the whites."[1] Julian Steward predicted that such small, structurally simple societies would be driven from environmental resources by the more effective social adaptations of structurally more complex groups with more overlapping layers of sociocultural integration.[2] Leslie White phrased his thought less as competitive adaptation to an ecosystem and more in terms of technological capture of energy from the environment. He thought that cultures that historically consumed only low levels of energy through hand-held technologies, such as those of the Paiutes, would be competitively displaced by high-energy-capturing animal-powered or mechanized technologies, such as those of the incoming Euro-Americans.[3] Yet another prominent anthropologist, Marvin Harris, argued that such economic power undergirds political power, and he predicted that the more powerful would replace or control the less powerful.[4]

Under any of these formulations, Southern Paiutes would have been expected to fall before the more populous, socially more complex, more technologically advanced, and politically more centralized Euro-Americans who entered their land after 1850. Paiutes' survival as a viable and distinct human society contradicts such predictions, and understanding the nature of that survival requires more than a passing accolade to their indisputable toughness as a people or to their stout resistance to cultural destruction. Southern Paiute ethnohistory demands that we reconsider fundamental anthropological assumptions about the role that social complexity, power, and culture play in the dynamics of human history.

Southern Paiutes' interaction with Euro-Americans was in many ways unlike that of other, more familiar native American tribes. Unlike either our contemporary popularized images of Indian history or what actually happened during the nineteenth century on the Great Plains or in the Southwest, Paiute interracial relations were not dominated by warfare. Lacking a centralized political structure to organize large numbers of fighting men, not having economic surpluses to sustain those men for prolonged military ventures, Paiutes were compelled to meet non-Indian immigrants peacefully. Paiutes were never targets of U.S. cavalry campaigns, were never conquered by force of arms, and, perhaps as a result of their nonviolence, Paiutes bargained no treaties with the federal government.

Paiutes' lack of violence does not imply that they were unattached to their homeland and did not feel severely resentful of its loss. For centuries their ability to survive in that land had depended on access to specific sites, most notably springs and other water sources and particular floral and faunal habitats. Loss of only a small number of key water sources meant that suddenly, dramatically, Paiutes' ability to survive on the desert by traditional means had evaporated. Two or three men on horseback with repeating rifles were enough to seize a spring; the cavalry was not needed.

Great Plains tribes experienced well over a hundred years of gradual European exploration and buffalo hide trade; eastern woodlands groups had centuries of beaver trade and encroaching settlement. Comparatively,

Paiutes' domination was historically late, unofficial, local, and instantaneous. Paiutes had no time to familiarize themselves with the newcomers before they were made subject to them. They had less than a generation, often less than a year, sometimes only moments, to devise and initiate strategies of response.

The fact of Paiutes' nonviolence demands that we reach a more complex understanding of interethnic relations than a conflict model's simple duality of white armed conquest against Indian resistance. Southern Paiute ethnohistory exemplifies a variant form of conflict, not death in a few dramatic battles but the daily incursion of imperial mechanisms that ranged from political limitation and economic constraint to casual condemnation of cultural values and evasion of personal contact. Such mechanisms are often invisible to history, and yet these were the subtle stuff of Southern Paiutes' conflict with non-Indians as well as the tools of their self-defense.

Southern Paiutes were not reservation Indians in the classic sense, and they shared few of the experiences of tribes driven under military guard to reserves remote from their homelands. Reservationization was quintessentially an outgrowth of the American expansion westward, a method of clearing indigenous native populations from the land so Euro-Americans could occupy it instead. Presumably, such a need to displace Indians would end once non-Indian settlement had been achieved. Nevertheless, the few tiny and insubstantial reservations set aside for Southern Paiutes were, for the most part, products of the twentieth century and founded long after non-Indians had already become well entrenched in the area. The fact that reservations were by then established at all, let alone at that particular point in time, demands some explanation beyond simple land clearance. Paiute history challenges any assumption that all Indian reservations were a monolithic phenomenon, uniform in purpose, nature, and function.

Contrary to the political rhetoric at their founding, Paiute reservations realistically could not, and some were clearly not designed to, provide a livelihood for the resident natives. The earliest, Moapa, was the most promising because it had several hundred acres of arable land, but even it could not support the two to three hundred local Paiutes. Shivwits was six miles square, had a similar population to support, but had only about a hundred watered acres. The ten acres at Las Vegas were also assigned to two or three hundred people who could at best create a homesite while they procured a living elsewhere. None of the nine small plots eventually designated for Paiute reservations included any mineral, timber, or productive resources other than the land itself. Severe water shortages crippled Paiutes' use of this land for agriculture, industrial production, or even domestic life. Reservations never formed the land base for Paiute society, nor was that society ever contained within them.

Throughout the historic period the majority of Southern Paiutes lived away from reservations. Their society remained dispersed over a large region, as it had always been. Paiutes had to cope with the long-standing challenges of that dispersal, now complicated by additional complex interethnic relationships generated by Euro-American presence. As non-Indian settlements arrogated the best water sources, Paiutes stayed, perhaps in part out of emotional attachment to traditional places and homelands, but perhaps also out of simple lack of alternatives. Not forcibly driven from their lands by military conquest, Paiutes still could not withdraw from the non-Indian presence to some culturally homogeneous reservation refuge. From the earliest moments of Euro-American settlement of Paiute country, communities were racially and culturally intermixed. As towns on the European model were formed, Paiutes became town-dwellers. Paiute society was thoroughly interpenetrated by non-Indian populations. The two groups lived in continuous personal contact with one another throughout the subsequent 150 years of their joint history. Such a situation is precisely the ideal model for which anthropological acculturation theory predicted an absorption of the simpler culture by the more dominant. Nevertheless, Paiute society and culture confounded such predictions by remaining remarkably distinct.

Paiutes were not dominated by federal control and administration to nearly the degree experienced by many native American tribes. Resident in the area last incorporated by American expansion, Paiutes missed many earlier federal Indian policies and were never subjected to their constraints. Although indisputably Indian by culture and ancestry, Paiutes were without treaty-defined federal relationships or trust lands. Thus their legal status remained ambiguous until well into the twentieth century. The extent of federal judicial jurisdiction, educational responsibility, and financial obligations under standard Bureau of Indian Affairs (BIA) programs, for instance, was unclear. Paiutes presaged by nearly one hundred years the problems faced by post–World War II urban Indian populations in more ways than their racially intermixed, nonrural residence pattern. Paiutes' relationship with the federal government was from the beginning obscure.

That federal relationship was not only underdefined but inconstant when in the late twentieth century all federal ties to that portion of Paiutes living in Utah were arbitrarily terminated. Denied legal recognition as Indians for the next twenty-five years, a portion of the Paiute population was cut off from access to federal programs, while other Paiutes, often relatives who were enrolled on reservations in adjoining Arizona, Nevada, and California, retained tribal status. Perhaps more than is true of other native groups, the twentieth-century history of Southern Paiutes is a tangle of the legal conceptualization of "tribe," federal "ward," "trust obligation," and even "Indian." Those shifting definitions constrained and restricted the options politically available to Paiutes as individuals and as an ethnic group at any particular point in time.

Southern Paiute history is theoretically interesting in yet another way. Its structure emulates a classic scientific experiment in which a single sample is divided into separate subsamples and each is then subjected to a controlled variety of external impacts. Southern Paiute culture was an essentially uniform one, but the non-Indian cultures that entered various geographic regions of Paiutes' territory were not.

In the area that became Utah the immigrants were primarily Mormons, theocratically structured and intent on constructing stable residential communities based on irrigation agriculture; they brought their own women and children, coveted land and water, and intended to stay. On the other hand, nineteenth-century Nevada was dominated by a comparatively chaotic, individualistic, secular, and unstable population of miners; overwhelmingly single and male, they wanted specific mineral-bearing rocks and intended to leave the moment they became rich. Northern Arizona and extreme southeastern Utah were eyed by cattle barons and beef cartels; cowboys, the largely mobile, male employees of these absentee investors, wanted grasslands and had no desire to form residential communities at all. Each of these non-Indian groups were culturally distinct. Each wanted to remove for its own profit some specific but different resource from the Paiute landscape. Each had a different social structure, ideological orientation, degree of linkage to extraregional political structures, and duration of commitment. Each constituted a distinctive threat to Paiute life and, most importantly, established its own pattern and mechanisms to deal with native people. Many authors, both scholarly analysts as well as popular writers, have posited that the nineteenth-century loss of control over resources, specifically land, created the condition of twentieth-century Indian society.[5] If this proposal is accurate and adequate, then the differing histories of Paiute groups that suffered different, selective losses to each of these three non-Indian groups should be regionally distinct and have different ends; it becomes a matter of empirical investigation to discover if this was so.

Throughout this investigation of Paiute history my focus will be on what Fredrik Barth called "ethnic boundaries," the interface between Southern Paiute society and culture and those of non-Indians.[6] Earlier acculturation theorists saw contact between cultures as an essentially passive process, a gradual absorption of one or both cultures into the other.[7] Later anthropological advocates saw tribal resistance to such assimilation as praiseworthy and lauded tribes that achieved cultural continuity or, phrased more dramatically, resisted cultural genocide.[8] Despite variable rhetorical intensity, all these phraseologies essentially portray native culture as a static entity, hidden behind a more or less effective barrier, that people attempt to guard from alteration. While such static maintenance may have been the native intent, these theoretical formulations ignore a fundamental anthropological tenet, that culture is a systemically interrelated whole in which one change inevitably generates modification in interlinked aspects. Thus the very act of defense initiates change. The effort to remain a separate entity, shown de facto to have been effective when an ethnic group historically persists as an identifiable unit, inevitably alters the culture of that group, thus changing that which the group defended.

Ethnic boundaries are not static but are creative interfaces in yet another way. Within the very proposition that there are interethnic relations between two societies, we are proposing that they are conjoined into some sort of system. This proposition presumes a linkage between them of some nonrandom order. Those interconnections had to have been created by one or both groups in concert at some point historically after their initial contact. The construction of those interethnic relations must constitute part of Southern Paiute ethnohistory.

If the acculturation model were accurate, interethnic boundaries would in time melt away. All distinctiveness would blur until the two groups had become one amalgam. The very fact that Southern Paiutes have remained an identifiable ethnic group 150 years after non-Indian settlement itself constitutes proof that they have not been assimilated and that they successfully managed to maintain themselves as a unit separate from the incoming societies.

In the process they have inevitably created changes in the structure of their own culture and community, sometimes unintentionally, other times not. They have left behind many of the outward, material elements of precontact Paiute culture. Few, if any, Paiutes today would choose to live off wild foods harvested with handmade tools, eschewing all products manufactured by the international industrial economy. Paiutes, like other desert dwellers, value air-conditioning, washable clothing, rapid automobile travel, and good plumbing. This does not mean that they have "lost" their culture, for culture is not a fixed trait list of material objects or mental patterns. Rather, there is a contemporary Southern Paiute culture, the one of this moment, created by Paiutes of previous generations who selected from among the novel imported goods and ideas, organizations and habits those that seemed useful, advantageous, or beneficial; correspondingly, they dropped older ways that had become relatively laborious, less attractive, or no longer physically possible. The new culture is no less a product of Paiute creativity or less authentically Indian than the old; it is simply a transformation. The re-creation of culture, the ethnogenesis, if you will, is a process that the present and forthcoming generations of Paiutes will continue.[9]

Part of Paiutes' purpose in such cultural restructuring was to maintain their community and to control or at least regulate the interface with other peoples. Paiutes and non-Indians reacted to the presence of an intercultural boundary by constructing mechanisms designed to maintain the distinctiveness of their separate cultures and in so doing assured that there has continued to *be* a boundary. Those mechanisms, predicated on the presence of the other culture and hence a creation of the interethnic boundary, linked the various cultures into a single system. It is the identity and nature of those interlinking mechanisms that will be the focus of this book.

By using the concept of interethnic boundaries I do not want to imply two separate entities in impermeable isolation but, rather, quite the opposite. If there was a regional system, if there were interethnic relations between cultural groups, as I am firmly convinced there were in this case, such isolation was precluded. Paiutes were not "left behind" or "left out" of the history of the region but were drawn into a patterned mesh of interrelationships that tied them in systematic ways to non-Indians. There were, of course, factors that superseded ethnically specific ones that caused events and behaviors along both sides of the ethnic interface, such as world wars, American industrial growth, and the construction of nationwide highways and communication networks. Similarly, at any particular point in time, much of the continuously metamorphosing native culture was not relevant to interethnic encounters per se. Still, a large number of linkages that were created to deal with that boundary, such as tribal councilmen elected to run native communities, missionaries assigned to convert Paiutes, and BIA personnel assigned to manage reservations all became institutionalized within the interethnic system specifically because Paiutes *were* Indians. Such specialists, Indian and non-Indian alike, would have lost their raison d'être had Paiutes lost their "Indianness"; they all had a vested interest in Paiutes' continued ethnic distinctiveness and acted to preserve the interethnic boundary in order to preserve their own roles within the multiethnic system.

This book, then, is about that interethnic boundary between Southern Paiutes and other societies. It was not a static line. It changed shape and position through time and so must be approached ethnohistorically. It was an interface between two, sometimes three or more, societies and was itself an institutionalized structure that linked them together. It was active, not passive; the presence of other cultural groups generated change within the Paiute community as well as along its interface with those others.

Many authors have described such systemic relationships between Indians and Euro-Americans, highlighting the hierarchical nature, political components, and differential economic benefits using a variety of different terminologies. Thomas D. Hall, for instance, explicitly applied Immanuel Wallerstein's insights concerning international ties between "core" and "peripheral" societies in his elegant analysis of southwestern political economy. Eric R. Wolf emphasized the role of mercantile trade in the colonial period to build economic and political relationships across continents on an increasingly global scale. Joseph G. Jorgensen carefully traced the cords of economic self-interest and power that bound what he called "metropolis" areas to reservation "satellites" in twentieth-century America. Richard White summarized the resulting relationships simply as "dependence."[10]

While these and other writers very properly drew analytical attention to the larger historical and regional scope of Indian ethnohistory, they all too often left underspecified the mechanisms through which these larger systems drew local societies into themselves. These interlinkages were often clearly restrictive to and self-defeating for Indians and yet were entered into by native people or established around them. This gap in the theoretical discussion leaves native people appearing to be either helpless pawns before Euro-American power or passive victims with no control over their own history.

Rather than replicating yet again these sound but incomplete theoretical discussions of dependency, world, neocolonial, or metropolis-satellite systems, I want to explore the "middle range" of theory by looking at how those large-scale relationships were actually created and maintained. I want to identify and sharpen our analytical awareness of which specific social and cultural mechanisms composed the hierarchical interethnic relations between Paiutes and non-Indians. It was these localized, empirical structures that had daily impact on Paiute lives; these were the forces Paiutes avoided, rejected, or defended themselves against and in so doing modified their own culture in turn. I want to look at how these mechanisms historically came into existence and were subsequently institutionalized. In this way, I hope to sharpen the visibility of these same processes as they continue to operate today. In other words, I want to bring such concepts as "incorporation within the nation-state" down to the ground and see how such huge historical realignments were actually accomplished in everyday reality.

The ethnohistory of Southern Paiute relations with other peoples was not filled with desperate battles, sweeping cavalry charges, or dramatic winter marches to reservation wastelands. Theirs was a subtle interaction that was grounded in the mundane events of everyday life. Nevertheless, Paiutes were inexorably drawn into a network of social, economic, and political ties that linked them not only to their immediate non-Indian neighbors but also to loci of culture, power, and events at distant national levels. Some of the mechanisms that created and sustained Paiutes' cultural distinctiveness over the years and mediated their interethnic relationships were housed within their own society, others lay within that of the Euro-Americans, and yet others were created along the social interface itself. I want to examine the mechanisms that built and constituted those boundaries between.

2

FROM THE BEGINNING

Sheer walls of red sandstone plunge across Southern Paiute territory, through places now called Zion National Park, Bryce Canyon, Arches, and Canyonlands, slashing their way through southern Utah. Above them, pine-covered plateaus lift to isolated knots of mountains—the La Sals, the Pine Valley Mountains, and the southernmost Wasatch Front. Below, dry plains sweep across deserts only to tumble over the sharp edges of the Grand Canyon into the Colorado River.

For unknown years this land was home to Southern Paiutes.[1] They lived in the southern halves of what are now called Utah and Nevada, a piece of Arizona above the Grand Canyon, and much of the eastern Mojave Desert of California. When Euro-Americans first met Paiutes, the Indians said they had always been there. They saw their lives replicating not only the way of their ancestors but also the form established by the supernatural powers who had set the world into motion at the beginning of time. Their land was lean and chary of its riches, but it did provide support to Paiutes through a series of techniques tested by long experience. Their life required hard work and vigilance; they were vulnerable to threats of drought, accident, disease, and the physical power of outsiders. But it was a way of life Paiutes understood, and they trusted it to carry them safely past any dangers.

Virtually everywhere within this territory, Southern Paiutes could walk in a day's time to some dramatic change in elevation; much of the secret of their success in this arid land lay in their systematic exploitation of that verticality. Stretching more than three hundred miles from south to north, Paiute territory included parts of the Colorado River Valley at only fifteen hundred feet as well as mountain peaks rising over eleven thousand feet. This was no smooth transition but was intercepted by escarpments, local massifs, and even isolated peaks looming out of the desert. Canyons sliced through plateaus to drop without warning to deceptive dry washes that might host torrents after brief cloudbursts.

Map 1. Southern Paiute Territory, 1840 (after Kelly, "Southern Paiute Bands," 554)

The heights were cooler than the lower-lying flatlands, and they also snared passing storms to win more rainfall; the higher the elevation, the more dramatically different the climate. For instance, the valley floor at Las Vegas, only two thousand feet above sea level, baked at temperatures of over 100 degrees day after day for a third of the year, often blazing to 120 degrees in the shade, if any could be found, and cooling overnight to only 90 just before the sun returned. Within sight, the mountains of that valley's western wall stood to nearly twelve thousand feet and sported unthawed snowfields from November until May. The valley averaged five and a half inches of rain in a year, the mountain five times that much.[2]

Each individual altitude zone, drainage slope, soil type, and even angle of sun exposure supported a distinctive variety of plant and animal life. On a single valley side, plant communities might well shift from creosote and cactus, through piñon and juniper, to white pine and spruce. Paiutes learned to harvest an eclectic assortment of nutritious seeds, berries, roots, nuts, leaves, and stalks, each in its own season, from each of these biotic layers. They used not only resources but also their extensive botanical knowledge. They knew, for instance, that plants ripened at lower elevations earlier than at higher, so they stretched the harvest period of useful, food-producing species by following their ripening cycles uphill.

The resource that demanded their most careful husbanding was water. Everywhere Paiute country was arid, in spots true desert. Much of the rain came in winter, drizzling across broad areas over a number of days, but at a season when the dormant plants could not use it for growth; the only benefit lay in its rejuvenation of the uppermost shallow water tables. These winter rains were also undependable; southern Nevada, for instance, often got no rain at all through an entire winter, sometimes several winters in a row.

The short spring and fall were generally dry, but summer brought thunderstorms. Violent winds and lightning accompanied downpours of more than an inch an hour during a season when the ground was so dry that the water beaded up or ran off into the dry washes without soaking below the first soil level. If the storm path happened to parallel a drainage pattern, it could drop enough water to cause dangerous sheet washes that collected in normally dry ravines, turning into flash floods several feet high that shoved debris, boulders, and people before them.

Such summer thunderstorms were isolated; a mile or even a hundred yards aside there might be no rain at all. These cloudbursts left avenues of moisture, but plants were fixed to the ground, and statistically, chances were small that rain would fall on any particular hillside at an opportune point in a specific plant's growing cycle. As a result, desert plants, while often locally lush, produced in spots separated by seemingly barren stretches where their desert-adapted seeds hovered dormant until a luckier year. Even if a patch chanced to fall under a passing summer storm one year, it might well not be equally fortunate another, so the richest blooming of even the same species would shift location through time. For the animals that lived on those plants, whether lowly field mice, browsing deer, or humans, no single place guaranteed a reliable, ample food supply. Paiutes learned to move with flexibility to the most promising spots of any particular year.

Paiutes clearly could not rely on rainfall for drinking water. Perennial streams offered no solution. Southern Paiute country bordered the Colorado River for over six hundred miles along its southern edge, and above it a few mountain massifs were high enough to generate run-off for permanent streams that flowed into it. These were easily counted: the Muddy River near the Nevada-Utah border; the Virgin in southwestern Utah slipping out of what is now Zion National Park; Kanab Creek easing down the eastern side of the Kaibab Plateau; the Paria in central Utah, hiding deceptive quicksand flats; and the San Juan, fed by the high mountains of southwestern Colorado that swung north into Ute country before it slipped into the Colorado River from the east. Between these five rivers lay hundreds of square miles of dry land full of seeds, roots, nuts, and game that Paiutes wanted to harvest; flowing streams were not the solution to Paiutes' daily domestic water needs.

The answer lay in springs. The same underlying layers of sandstone that produced the brilliant red cliffs of Paiute country created numerous impermeable planes that channeled water along until it broke out at a penetrating cliff wall or was pressed up an invisible fault crack. Sometimes the water actually bubbled out as a spring, such as the one that headed the Muddy River. At other times the water lacked pressure to force its way to the surface and hid under a layer of sand; such damp "seeps" were proclaimed by a patch of flourishing greenery, and Paiutes learned to dig down and wait until morning for enough liquid to leak into the hole to support a small family. Where there were no springs, fine sandstone, wind-eroded into shallow basins, might puddle passing rainfall until it evaporated. One such "tank," known as Jacobs Pools, was key to Paiute use of the seed-rich plateau between Kanab Creek and the northern rim of the Grand Canyon, for it held the only water for forty miles in any direction. Paiutes knew the location and condition of every tiny spring, seep, tank, and puddle for miles. Where water was hidden in tumbles of rocks or around the corner of a side canyon, they etched petroglyphs in stone to guide relatives to this life-giving resource.[3]

Although archaeologists assure us that people lived in this area in ways similar, if not identical in detail, to that of Southern Paiutes for well over a thousand years, the first residents whose name we know were the Southern Paiutes.[4] The broad outlines of their culture resembled not only the past in their own area but also that of other Great Basin peoples to the north and west, and it was quite different from that of native California or the Southwest across the Colorado River, where most people spoke dramatically different languages. Most Great Basin people spoke languages of the Numic family in three large, closely related blocks that stretched north and east from the Death Valley area. They all called themselves some variant of the term *nüwü*, "the people," rather than the labels Euro-Americans subsequently placed on them and wrote down. The Western Numic speakers, living along the inner slopes of the Sierra Nevada to Oregon and Idaho, were the Northern Paiutes, linguistically and culturally distinct from the people

Euro-Americans confusingly labeled Southern Paiutes. The middle fan of Numic speakers were mostly Shoshones of central Nevada and Wyoming. The belt of Southern Numic speakers were the Southern Paiutes and Utes, who spoke closely related forms of Southern Numic and occupied Utah and western Colorado.[5]

Many of the cultural features shared between Southern Paiutes and fellow Numic-speakers originated in the very characteristics of the places they called their own. Southern Paiute lands rarely offered a food surplus, let alone abundance. Productive spots were localized and widely dispersed because of unpredictable rainfall. Because no single place provided reliable sustenance, people had to be mobile. They traveled up and down mountain ranges to follow the sequential ripening of food plants, and they traveled out across the valleys to the places most productive that year. Even so, the food they produced was limited, and few people could ever live together; Southern Paiute camp groups of ten to fifteen people were normal, although richer areas, like the Muddy River Valley or along Santa Clara Creek in southwestern Utah, supported larger communities.[6]

The people's movements were far from random; had Paiutes "wandered," as later Euro-Americans mistakenly described their mobility, they would have soon starved. Their movements were based on extensive knowledge of the growth preferences of specific plants and solid familiarity with the seasonal blooming and ripening of each species. Paiutes harvested one plant after the other as each matured. They ate what they needed and sun-dried whatever was left over for winter use. Once one species had ripened and loosed its seeds to the wind, Paiutes moved on to the next scheduled resource, which probably required that they relocate to a place where their past experience and careful observation predicted they would get the best return of food for their time and labor. If drought, plant disease, or insect pests interfered with that anticipated target, they had secondary and even tertiary alternatives in mind, plants that were perhaps harder to collect, less tasty, or less likely to store well.

Over a year each camp or group of camps used an assortment of areas within several days' walk of good water.[7] Because virtually every part of Paiutes' territory offered many different altitude zones in close proximity, their seasonal needs were usually filled in a customary harvest circuit. It was known by all adjacent camps that a particular group of people could usually be found somewhere within that area and that they were harvesting or planning to harvest virtually all its production; hence that zone was acknowledged as "their territory," not in the sense that they owned it or could sell it to others but because their history of customary use had justified their prior rights to its resources. If drought or other prolonged natural disaster stripped all plant foods from a camp group's usufruct lands, and the deer and other game migrated to better browse, a camp might walk into another group's territory. Discretion as well as courtesy demanded that Paiutes search out the local group to ask permission for temporary use of that territory. Such welcome was never refused, for everyone knew that next year it might be they themselves who needed access to additional lands, and those who borrowed undertook the reciprocal ethical obligation to extend hospitality in turn.[8]

Thus Paiutes did not exclusively own or defend land, either as individuals or camp groups. War over land made no sense in Paiute life. To force one's way into another's territory was an unnecessary risk. Those people, with an eye to their own future economic security, would share anyway. Conquering more land than could be used was illogical, since all burdens had to be carried on human backs, and harvests from the far-flung corners of an overly large territory simply made more work in the hot sun. Paiutes accepted pragmatically the nature of their land and found it more sensible to have permeable boundaries than to have private ownership of food resources.

The exception lay in gardens. Along the Muddy and Virgin Rivers and in a few other well-watered areas, Paiutes planted domesticated corn and squashes and transplanted such wild native plants as amaranth, sunflowers, and devil's claw. People on Santa Clara Creek had beans and gourds, too. Fields were small. Women used the same pointed digging sticks with which they uprooted desert plants to prepare the friable loams along permanent streams. On the Santa Clara and other tributaries to the Virgin, they scratched out short diversion channels to spread water for their favorite plants. Nineteenth-century Paiutes in the extreme south, called Chemehuevis, learned from Mohaves to use residual soil moisture left by Colorado River floods to germinate corn seed. Women's work, like their efforts to harvest wild plants, marked the resulting crops as their own. Other Paiutes knew where each family had worked in the spring and generally respected that garden as "theirs." Only a bona fide emergency justified taking crops from someone else's garden; anything less was rude theft and an offensive violation of customary ethics.

This labor, coupled with other obligations on their time, limited Paiutes' gardens to an acre or less. Such small plots could not produce enough to support a family year-round, and Paiutes could not afford to eschew harvesting wild plants in order to guard their gardens from insect or animal pests. They cleared as much land as they had time for in the spring, planted whatever seed they had left after a winter's eating, and left to find food for the summer. In the fall, they returned to harvest whatever had survived. They often treated horticultural crops as a lucky windfall, promptly sharing them around among their kin so that everyone could enjoy this rare treat. Whatever was not immediately consumed was dried for winter or kept for seed. Camp groups in the colder plateaus and mountains of Utah lacked gardens completely and obtained these luxury foods only through trade.[9]

Whether in the low southern area or high above the escarpments of Utah, virtually every camp group's territory provided a slightly different assortment of plants and animals. As a result, each Paiute group's diet was a little different as they made a series of decisions over the year about what, how, when, and where to harvest. Paiutes were primarily vegetarians; they knew how to prepare and use over a hundred species of plants, although no single camp group had all of these locally.[10] Not only were Paiute diets different from region to region, but they also varied seasonally and daily. No single plant was so widespread or so productive as to allow Paiutes to specialize in it alone.

In the low-lying south, from the Mojave Desert across Las Vegas to nearly the current Nevada border, Paiutes harvested desert plants. Ironically, the isolated local marshes provided one of the first foods in the spring as women waded into chilly water to dig up tule roots with their toes and fingers. Men captured lethargic, cold-blooded rattlesnakes and lizards as they emerged from burrows to warm themselves in the weak spring sunlight. Women later lopped off the great flower stalks of the century plant and the tough but edible roots of Joshua trees with wooden digging sticks. By midsummer, mesquite and screwbean trees on the valley floors produced bumper crops of edible seedpods. Women chopped the stiff, fibrous leaves off agaves and roasted the cabbagelike hearts in earthen pits. They cooked the fruit and sun-dried it into cakes for later use. Several kinds of prickly pear cactus yielded juicy red fruits for storage.[11]

All the while, men, women, and children casually picked up desert tortoises; eggs of doves, quail, and sage grouse; and meaty nibbles of lizard, mouse, wood rat, gopher, and chipmunk, as these animals fed on the same plants the people themselves were busily harvesting.[12] Although most of their meat actually came from this smaller game, men made forays into the uplands for the highly desired mountain sheep and deer. They sometimes left their wives and children below so the family could exploit two areas simultaneously. For most of the year, however, the movements of Paiute camps were driven by the sequence and location of plant foods, which provided more food with far greater predictability than the scant and mobile game.[13]

Across southern Utah from St. George, up onto the Kaibab Plateau, and into the Colorado canyon lands farther east, there were no mesquite and screwbean trees or many of the cacti. There, Paiutes substituted nutritious and tasty sego lily, buffalo berries, squawbush, squaw berry, and canyon grape.[14] Instead of desert tortoises and some of the lizards, Paiutes had greater numbers of deer as well as antelope, ducks, marmots, porcupines, squirrels, and chipmunks. Still farther north in the uplands of central Utah, above Cedar City, Parowan, and the upper Sevier River Valley, Paiutes found chokecherries in spring and raspberries, currents, gooseberries, and serviceberries in summer. They replaced the lowland piñon with the local "greasy" variant and fished the high mountain lakes.[15]

All this regional variability rested on the common staples of rice grass seed and piñon. Rice grass ripened in early April or May, depending on the altitude. Women paddled the grass seed into trays, then carried it back to camp in large conical packing baskets on their backs. There they tossed the seeds carefully with hot coals in scoop-shaped baskets, fanning the coals with a constant motion that prevented the baskets from catching fire. They then ground the roasted seeds with a hand-held mano stone against a flat stone metate into flour for a thick oatmeal-like porridge or bread. Depending on the time of year, Paiute cooks flavored these basic recipes with seasonal plants such as wild rhubarb, squaw cabbage, flowers of the Mohave yucca and Joshua tree, and assorted herbs.[16]

In autumn, after quickly harvesting their gardens, Paiutes hurried to the mountains to collect the all-important nuts of the piñon pine. Although not uniformly productive from year to year, groves of piñons could produce enormous amounts of food, more than was needed by any one camp group. Several groups from valleys on either side camped together in the groves along the mountain ridges not only to gather food but also to visit, catch up on news, tell stories into the night, dance, sing, and enjoy one another's company. Piñon was the staple food that had to last people all winter long, so basket after basket load was roasted and carried from the high groves to the sheltered lowland winter camps.[17]

Paiutes also systematically hunted rabbits before winter. After skinning and sun-drying the rabbits whole, Paiute women later pulverized the meat, bones and all, on metates to make a nutritious protein powder that was added to winter piñon stews. They cut the rabbits' autumn-thickened pelts into long, thin, spiral strips. The women twisted pairs of these strips into a heavy rope, pegged it out on the ground, and cross-wove more fur

1. Kaibab Paiute basketmaker, 1873. (Photo by J. K. Hillers, National Anthropological Archives, Bureau of American Ethnology Collection, Smithsonian Institution.)

strips to form tight squares that served as capes during the day and blankets at night.

Paiutes not only gathered food but carefully collected and dried certain seasonal plants for their extensive pharmacopoeia. Among many others, women selected yarrow and desert licorice for stomachaches. They wanted sagebrush leaves for a tea that helped headaches, colds, and intestinal worms and yerba santa for joint inflammation caused by colds and rheumatism. Leaves of manzanita were steeped to relieve fever.[18]

Paiutes found narrowleaf willow among their most important plants, although it was not edible. Women painstakingly wove it into the myriad of basket forms they used every day to gather food for their families. Women stored willow lengths, selectively harvested in September, until winter, when they scraped off the bark and split the wands into flat threads. These they wove into an enormous variety of shapes in carefully selected stitches, tight or open, twined or coiled, to meet specific technological needs—flat gathering trays, cone-shaped pack baskets, paddlelike seed beaters, fan-shaped winnowing trays, tightly woven eating bowls, water jugs sealed with pitch inside and out, women's caps to protect their foreheads from the carrying straps of burden baskets slung on their backs, and cradles to carry their babies in.

Although most Paiutes knew how to make pottery, many preferred not to carry the heavy, fragile objects. They found baskets more practical and convenient for all their needs, including cooking. Since these could not be put directly into a fire, women used an indirect cooking technique. When a basket was filled with stew or porridge, the willow fibers swelled watertight. Meanwhile, women toasted clean river cobbles in the fire to drop into the basket with wooden tongs; the heat transferred into the stew and quickly brought it to a boil.[19]

Women used plants for making other household equipment as well. Piñon pitch sealed water jugs. The coarse fiber of yucca leaves made tough sandals to protect feet from the scorching desert sands. Yucca roots became soap. Cliffrose bark pounded soft for skirts and aprons. Women beat the fiber out of dried milkweed and twisted it into cordage for all kinds of uses: knotted rabbit nets, carrying nets, string belts, trap nooses, or just a handy piece of string. Reeds became mats for house walls or floors. Men sought out rare, straight sections of serviceberry wood for bows. They also used shorter pieces of serviceberry wood, squawbush, or greasewood for arrow foreshafts and set these into longer sections of more readily available reed, which were then feathered. And, of course, both men and women constantly gathered wood for fires.[20]

Because of its specific location, each Paiute group was a bit different in diet and seasonal movements. All groups relied, however, on an eclectic diversity of foods harvested with lightweight baskets and hand-held tools that were carried from one campsite to another throughout the year. Few of these foods produced a bumper crop that Paiutes could store, but those few were critical—rice grass, piñon nuts, rabbit meat. Fortunately, these were fairly reliable, if not in a specific location in a given year, then surely somewhere in a wider range.

Other foods varied immensely. If one failed to produce abundantly or even to appear at all, their very plurality assured that Paiutes had alternatives to which they could and did shift with great flexibility. They had preferences (foods that tasted best, were most easily harvested, or grew in clumps so that walking time was minimized), but they had secondary and even tertiary choices when necessary. Pollen and flower stalks of the ubiquitous sagebrush could be boiled; although bitter and with little nutritional value, still these would keep the family alive until they could walk to a better area. Juniper berries, even if dried and withered, could be softened and the thin layer of fruit nibbled off. If the periodic waves of locusts or cutworms destroyed the green plants, those insects themselves were systematically harvested for their high protein content.[21] Frugal, hard-working, provident, and knowledgeable about the resources of their environment, Paiutes used what they had with great creativity and flexibility, adjusting when they had to.

Paiutes firmly believed that their land was nurturant and productive; they were secure in the knowledge that they could always make a living on their desert if they worked hard, with imagination and persistence. They did not look at their land as a harsh and barren place, as did some other people who came later.

Even with such confidence, Paiutes realized that too many people could not expect to live together, so their camp groups typically were as few as ten to as many as fifty people. This group stayed together during most of the year, moving from where one resource ripened to where the next planned harvest grew.[22] Such a camp group included several families. A man, his wife or wives, their children, with perhaps a grandparent or two, a widowed uncle, or a married daughter lived with a few other families. A young, newly married couple was expected to live near the bride's family for a while, but later they could live with his parents or any of his or her more distant relatives as they were invited, as they chose, or as there were resources available. Households were not really separate from one another, for nearly all of them contained members linked somehow through bilateral kinship to every other family of the camp.[23] The people who lived together were not strangers but relatives, and the kinship system, by defining the rights and duties each expected from the others, glued the families together and made them into a community. The only way a person could justify residing in a particular camp group was to have some kinship tie to someone already there, through either men or women, by blood or through marriage, it did not matter which. There were no strict rules.[24]

Paiutes thought that a marriage created obligations very like those of consanguinity. It bound not only the young couple to each other but all of their relatives to the new affine and those two blocks of relatives to each other through the conduit of the new marriage tie. All those people had a vested interest in the marriage and benefited from its existence; all of them put pressure on and argued with the young people to build and maintain a viable union. In the rare cases when a man felt able to support more than one wife and set of offspring, his polygyny multiplied ties for himself and his children. Affinal ties sometimes outlasted the marriage itself. To maintain these linkages for themselves and to keep the relationships activated for any children, widowed men and women were expected to remarry within the same affinal family in customary sororate and levirate.[25]

Paiutes expected relatives through both blood and marriage to care for one another. At minimum they were pleasant and convivial in the tiny social groups so constantly in each other's company. Relatives joked and teased, picked up errant children and cleaned off scuffed knees, and shared each other's fires in the evening. When a man was lucky enough to bag a deer or mountain sheep, too big for his family to eat by itself, his wife divided it up among relatives. This reduced her labor, for she would not have to sun-dry all the meat and carry it from camp to camp. More importantly, by accepting the gift the recipients incurred an ethical obligation to share reciprocally with the donors whenever they in turn had excess bounty. This was, in essence, a way to store meat *in* other people; it created a form of social insurance by giving each family access to the hunting luck of every hunter in the camp and ultimately rights in every man's kill. When a relative was sick, others shared food or hunted for him. In times of drought, relatives pooled their scant resources so that although all might be hungry, none starved. The worst criticism one Paiute could level against another was that he or she was stingy, not acting as a relative should, violating both kinship and human ethics.

Of course, real human people did not always maintain such ideal, harmonious relationships. Bound to the same few families month after month, Paiutes quarreled with their neighbors, whether relatives or not. Although they closed ranks when challenged by outsiders, bickering within the group was not unknown. When relationships became too strained, or young people simply grew too restless, a family or even an individual moved away. Because kin ties were traced widely and bilaterally and group size was small, in order to avoid incest people often married into other camp groups, so their descendants had relatives in any number of places. Rather than press a dispute until it erupted into open hostility, people often chose to "visit" with these more distant relatives for a season or a year until tempers had cooled and they could reestablish community amity. Camp groups were not fixed membership units but were flexible in composition.

Within this kinship-based camp group, leadership was in the hands of a headman.[26] This figure was most often a man, senior but still active, who, in pursuit of a long life, had learned the landscape in both its routine and unexpected forms, knowing where flash floods would roll or springs still flow after prolonged drought. He shared his knowledge and experience tactfully without infringing on other people's own opinions, experiences, and personalities. Related to many camp group members, he spoke as the senior kinsman to all. In that role he was expected to be generous with his care, time, and material goods. When he grew old, his successor might be a son or other close relative, but with the wide extension of kinship terms and close interrelationships in the camp, most men qualified one way or another. The community often debated which among the many candidates had demonstrated those skills and talents best befitting a new headman.

The community looked for a leader who could offer sound advice on where plants grew under the unique weather conditions of any particular year and knew the habits and habitats of animals large and small. The headman got up early every morning and urged the group to rise and work hard to provide for their families. He made specific suggestions for the day. Every family, and indeed every adult worker, male or female, considered his proposal against their own knowledge of conditions and decided for themselves whether to join him that day or not. Sometimes the group stayed together; other times individuals moved off in several directions to rejoin at the end of the day or at the next campsite. At times a group of men joined the headman in a hunt, and other times they listened to someone else who had an alternative idea. If they did so too frequently, then by that very process the headman's influence was usurped, and the group had chosen a different leader. Without title, rank, ceremonial installation, salary, or special privileges, the headman was simply the man people chose, of their own volition, to follow. Their followership defined his leadership.

In addition to his economic advice, the headman also often settled disputes between camp members over such issues as failure to share food as demanded by kinship ethics, anger at a spouse, or any of the inevitable daily irritations generated in such a tightly knit community. Initially, both disputants mobilized their relatives, claiming their rights as kin for support. Because he was often kinsman to both parties, the headman mediated, serving as a channel for communication between the disputants. He voiced ethical axioms so general that neither party could dispute them and then tried to apply those stipulated tenets to the specific case. He was not attempting to establish right or wrong or the guilt or innocence of either party, or to determine who should be punished. Any such label or punishment would breed resentment and fester in such a tiny community. He possessed no power to force the disputants to accept his proffered solution but could use only his personal influence and rhetorical skill to persuade. He mediated a compromise that both parties could accept as reasonable and proper and that would allow them to continue to live together. If he failed, disputants might activate their numerous kinship ties elsewhere and move to another camp group. This kind of individual autonomy, considered the unalienable right of every adult man and woman, was the ultimate check on the power of the headman. Any authoritarian attempt to force unpalatable, self-interested, unilateral decisions upon people would soon find such a man camped alone, leader of none.

Similarly, when the headman spoke for the group to outsiders, whether belonging to another camp or a different tribe, he did not make decisions or commitments in their name but only expressed the consensus already formed. Should he usurp his followers' rights of independence by making arbitrary statements without their consent, individuals simply failed to feel bound or committed in any way by his public assertions. Paiutes were severely democratic.

The headman was not the only person recognized as having special skills useful to the community. The Paiute system was sufficiently flexible that virtually all unique personal talents were recognized and used for the public good in some situation or another. When they took charge of a community event, these multiple situation-specific leaders were not seen as competitive to the headman in any way. Knowledgeable senior women, for instance, led the women's work parties in daily plant harvesting.[27] Some men and a few women were believed to have obtained special concessions from supernatural beings to give them power over game animals, such as rabbits or antelope, or the power to cure certain types of illnesses that were beyond ordinary herbal remedies. These people were shamans.

If rabbit populations were high in a particular valley, large-scale rabbit drives were held there in the fall. A shaman with power over rabbits was in charge. Particularly among western bands, Paiutes believed that without his spiritual mediation the animals would detect the trap and escape; the mechanical means alone were insufficient.[28] In order to assure success, everyone consented to be under the direction of the shaman, including the headman.

Because the anticipated yield was high but required more labor power than any one camp group possessed, several groups cooperated in the complex choreography of the drive. Each man brought his rabbit net, a tough mesh three feet high and tens of feet long. The men attached their nets to sagebrush end to end in a wide curve across the valley floor. After a ritual of preparation, young men sneaked down to the far end of the valley and returned in a running wall, beating the bushes with sticks to stampede the frightened rabbits in front of them. Sometimes they lit brushfires to further panic the animals. Dashing down valley, the rabbits raced into the waiting nets, became tangled in the resistant mesh, and fell victim to hidden men wielding simple clubs. The meat was divided among those who killed, those who drove, the net owners, and the shaman. Men in lucky positions along the drive line shared with relatives and friends who had been less fortunate. Several such drives might be held on successive days in hopes of harvesting enough meat not only for an immediate feast but also to sun-dry for winter. Because the normal resources of a single area could not sustain this large aggregate population, after the rabbit drive the people broke up again into their separate groups and returned home.[29]

Southern Paiutes believed that the land in which they lived was permeated with beings that had power far beyond the understanding or control of humans. Such supernatural beings were immanent, involved in daily human affairs, and able to contact people. These powerful, invisible beings sought out men and women for friendships through repeated intense dreams in childhood or later in life. Although some people intentionally exposed themselves to supernaturals by frequenting places they were thought to live, overt pursuit of supernatural sponsorship was considered inappropriately aggressive. Some spirit beings offered to persuade rabbits or antelope to sacrifice themselves for human consumption or to come when called to cure a rattlesnake bite or arrow wound. The relationship between a shaman and a spirit being was seen as similar to reciprocal relations between humans, although the fundamental incomprehensibility of the nonhuman member made such partnerships both unpredictable and risky. Not all people who were offered power during a supernatural visitation were willing to venture into a relationship where human ignorance or blunder might incur immortal wrath. Nor was it tactful to refuse a proffered supernatural gift of friendship, so such a visitation created an ambiguous dilemma.

Paiutes were drawn by supernatural offers to cure the numerous illnesses that struck them and their relatives without warning or apparent reason and that were beyond the strength of routine domestic herbal cures.[30] Paiutes clearly conceived various types of illnesses according to physical symptoms and perceived causes. Simple scrapes and ordinary accidents were dosed with tisanes of yerba mansa or perhaps creosote; on the other hand, the ultimate cause for clumsiness in a person normally careful was explained as a brief blindness imposed by a spiritual being. Sudden severe sickness, resistant to secular cures, was attributed to the intrusion of an invisible, supernatural object into the patient's body. Lingering, wasting diseases were diagnosed as the temporary separation of the soul from the physical body, leaving it incomplete and foreshadowing its state after death, that final departure of the insubstantial human essence. To cure any of these illnesses, their cause had to be reversed by mediating the antagonism of a spiritual being, removing the intruded object, or retrieving the lost soul.

None of these causes left visible manifestations subject to human manipulation on a natural level, so the supernatural world had to be accessed. The shaman acted as an intermediary, soliciting through prescribed ritual the assistance of his spirit friend. It was that partner's power and cooperation that effected the cure, acting through the conduit of the shaman's actions. The shaman was not understood himself to be possessed, nor did he enter a trance state. He positioned the patient, chanted, danced, massaged, sucked at the intruded object, called the soul with fragrant smoke of juniper or tobacco, and otherwise enacted the orders of the supernatural power in all-night sessions imbued with the mysterious presence of the unseen. Shaman, patient, and relatives firmly believed that once the true cause of the illness was removed, the patient would return to health, unless again attacked by suprahuman forces.

Even a successful cure left unanswered the question of why this particular patient had been attacked in the first place. Sometimes the answer lay in the supernatural forces whose actions and motivations were by definition beyond human comprehension or in a call from the ghosts of recently deceased relatives for the souls of the living to join them. Other times intentional will to harm seemed the only logical explanation. Who had access to the kind of suprahuman power needed to shoot an invisible lethal object into an unsuspecting victim? Not all people with supernatural partners had openly declared them and used them as shamans for the benefit of the community. Who knew how many others had access to supernatural powers they might employ against their neighbors? People who showed themselves antisocial by grumbling or failing to reciprocate with kin were suspected of such witchcraft. The position of even successful shamans was always ambiguous. By their very success they had demonstrated access to extraordinary powers, so they were careful to follow the ethical demands of their society to avoid the suspicion of misuse of their powerful partnership to cause the illnesses and accidents that befell community members. A string of unsuccessful cures could foment an accusation of witchcraft; the community defended itself by killing the human witch who had instigated the supernatural homicides. Before public suspicions reached such extremes, a shaman often interpreted his or her failure to cure as evidence that the supernatural had withdrawn from the partnership it had originally initiated; declaring their power as weakening, such shamans voluntarily retired from active practice.[31]

Situation-specific leaders such as headmen and shamans were rewarded for their distinctive skills with social prestige but were not economically supported by the community. Conspicuously lacking in Paiute culture was the specialized skill of the warrior. War as an organized struggle of one community against another was extremely rare because there was very little apparent need for it in Paiute life. Ethics of reciprocity and widespread kinship ties made subsistence resources available in times of temporary need when lucky hunters shared their bounty or on a wider basis through travel to a neighboring, more productive territory in case of drought. There was no need to use threats or violence to get food and thereby risk personal injury or cut off future reciprocity.[32] Warfare to enlarge one's territory would only have created the need to guard distant boundaries against retaliation, impractical when seasonal harvests demanded that people be elsewhere. Harvests from a larger than necessary territory simply meant that produce had to be carried farther. Open borders shared among kin were a far more efficient solution to localized, seasonal, unpredictable food resources than would be rigid, exclusive, defended private properties.[33]

Conflict over the theft of personally owned items was also apparently rare within Paiute society. Most men were able to make all their own tools or could easily trade with a relative who did. They all had access to the raw materials, just as women could all go to the willow patches and collect what they needed to manufacture the congeries of baskets they used in their work. Without machined replication, every person's workmanship was distinctive, recognizable, and known. In a community that lived very much in the open, everyone was familiar with everyone else's possessions. If someone showed up with an object not his or her own, it would be immediately recognized. Rather than risk the embarrassment of exposure, it was easier either to take the time to make the object oneself or to ask to borrow it from a relative who was ethically bound to extend the courtesy. The small-scale, interwoven, and public nature of Paiute community life virtually forbade theft.

Although there were no wars over land or conflict over property, Paiute communities were not free of strife. Violations of kinship obligations where everyone was defined by such relationships to everyone else—failure to share meat with a cousin, suspected seduction of someone else's wife, the daily abrasions of constant interaction with the same small set of people —were seen as ethical failures. Such conflicts were probably common, perhaps increased in times of physical or economic stress. It was the obligation of relatives to mend these damaged relationships. If they could not, the group split and used distance and time to heal the anger. They thereby obviated the need for physical conflict, war, and warriors.

Paiute individuals and families moved across geographical space to seek temporarily scarce resources, avoid conflict, visit, celebrate births, and grieve deaths. They traveled along the conduits created by their web of kinship, which stretched across geographical space. In so doing they maintained social relationships with a large number of relatives, meeting their in-laws and friends in turn. If their children became fond of and married these people, they created new kinship ties. The Paiute social nexus of intermarriage and interaction wove physically separate camp groups together. Ideas, idiosyncratic ways of doing things, techniques of making objects out of local materials, and words to describe these unique habits were shared among people who dealt commonly with one another.

The density of such interactions and the corresponding number of shared local customs were highest between adjacent groups, but links of each group to others rippled out until social contacts and subsequent kinship ties declined and finally faded away. Perhaps this social space was interrupted by a physical barrier that made travel rarely worth the effort, such as the Colorado River. Or perhaps the enclosed area provided a reliable assortment of resources for all seasons in virtually any year, making the walk beyond unnecessary. Or perhaps this social sphere included a large enough population pool that a spouse could be found within it and still avoid incest, so that kin ties of consanguinity and affinity closed in upon themselves. For these reasons or others, social contact was much higher within certain geographic zones, kinship ties were predominantly internal, distinctive local habits developed, and minor regional dialect differences marked the people.

Unlike camp groups, known by the names of prominent residents that changed with each generation, these regional groups were named after prominent geographic features, such as Kaibab, from *qaivavits*, "mountain lying down" (Kaibab Plateau), or from their geographic direction from the speaker, such as *tantiits*, "northerners."[34] Anthropologists would later call these geographical zones of social interaction "bands," noting that only very minor cultural distinctions separated them; they described them as "dialect units with political concomitants."[35] Such political concomitants occurred as the leading people, or headmen, of the various camp groups with a common interest in an issue came together in ad hoc gatherings to consult each other and develop a consensual response. This was not a fixed council, and the parties concerned might well vary from issue to issue. No formal political structure, and certainly no hierarchical pyramid of power, tied the component camp groups to one another. The groups composing a band were not an economic unit, either for production or consumption. When people helped each other out, it was not because they belonged to a single band but, rather, because they were individually relatives.[36] Some men were known beyond their own group for their wisdom, knowledge, skill, or shrewdness. Other headmen consulted them, perhaps were convinced by persuasive rhetoric, but nevertheless, those local leaders, and indeed the individual men and women who chose to follow them, retained the right to act on their own interests and understanding of the issue.

Paiutes recognized the fundamental similarities of language and culture that underlay minor band variations. For example, when Chemehuevi band members traveled to Pahrump Valley to trade the stone pipes they carved for tobacco not available in their own territory or carried ironwood knives to Las Vegas to trade for yucca fiber, they recognized people in these places as fellow *nuwuvi*, "people," Paiutes. Cahuilla Indians over the western mountains, from whom they traded bows for yellow basketry grasses, or Mohaves to the east across the river spoke other languages, had different cultures, were fundamentally strangers; they were not *nuwuvi*.[37] Their degree of foreignness marked those Indians as of other tribes, although it did not bar trade, visiting, and occasional intermarriage. With Ute people to the northeast, Paiutes shared a similar language base, although cultural differences developed in time. On the other hand, with Shoshones to the northwest, Paiutes shared many common cultural features, although they spoke different languages.

In the years before the arrival of non-Indian people, Southern Paiutes traveled their desert on foot, gathered seasonal wild plant foods with light-weight basketry, and made small gardens when they could. They hunted wherever they were and saved whatever possible for winter. Each year was different, without a fixed sequence of resources to harvest or campsites to occupy. Camp groups aggregated when rabbit populations or piñon productivity allowed and then redivided into smaller groups. When resources failed, Paiutes visited their relatives elsewhere, perhaps staying a season or years. They socialized with their relatives, married nonkinfolk, and extended the privileges and obligations of kinship to these new affines. Without fixed rules of residence or rigid group membership, they found that intergroup reciprocity and social openness insured greater security than private ownership of property. They traveled lightly, avoiding personal possessions and distinctions of rank based on wealth. Individuals, male and female, were valued for the skills they had to share, whether to hunt, cure, mediate a dispute, or tell a good story on a winter evening. No person was subservient to the dictates of a chief or bound in a social hierarchy; obligations to others were defined by kinship relations, personal friendships, and social ethics. Flexibility and the absence of rigid, culturally defined rules for doing things "properly" as well as the corresponding presence of numerous alternative options enabled Paiutes to meet the varying unpredictable demands of the land in which they lived by means of wide-ranging individual creativity and response. Despite regional band variations, Paiutes formed one native "people." Their way of life was a culture that had supported them through past difficulties and that they trusted would continue to carry them through such new challenges as the future would bring.

3

FATHERS, FUR TRAPPERS, AND TRAVELERS

Long before Paiutes actually saw white men, their lives were changed by Spanish horses from still-distant colonies in Mexico, the Rio Grande, and California. Spaniards, in the person of missionaries, first came to Paiute country in 1776. Although they probably did not directly change the lives of the natives very much, their visits did provide later justification for Spanish claims to territorial suzerainty. Over the next sixty years, itinerant Spanish traders, American fur trappers, and mobile, mounted bands of native allies extracted highly selected resources from the Paiute area for the worldwide European mercantile trade. Not until 1844 did an American governmental expedition initiate a formal U.S. political presence. By then, however, many significant changes had taken place in the Paiutes' world, and their history of interrelations with Euro-Americans had begun.

Probably sometime during the 1600s, horses began to appear in the Great Basin, escaped from Spanish owners and wandering northward.[1] Because the Paiute environment was so sparse, the utility of the horse as convenient transportation did not outweigh its liability as a voracious competitor for food grass seeds and its attractiveness as a docile big game animal. For a long time, Paiutes could not afford horses and ate rather than rode them.

Indians north and east of the Sevier River who spoke virtually the same language as Paiutes and who had, until then, lived in much the same way happened to possess an environment richer in grasses.[2] They captured these feral animals and gradually built up large herds. Possession of horses changed their lives dramatically. Mounted, they had a greater range of travel to find food and could carry larger quantities. Larger groups could live together without overexploiting the environment because they moved on quickly to distant areas. They traveled east to the Great Plains, hunted buffalo, and borrowed many cultural items from tribes there, such as skin tipis and fringed women's dresses. No longer limited to what humans could carry, they could and did acquire more specialized and numerous household items, and they became wealthy. They fought with other tribes for control of pastures and to plunder goods, food stores, and horses. They faced new social problems, such as keeping order in the larger camps, increased intertribal diplomacy, and the military ambitions of mounted warriors, so they expanded and formalized their leadership.[3] Their culture now transformed from that of their pedestrian ancestors and distinguished from their still pedestrian neighbors, these people became known to Euro-Americans as Utes.[4]

Between the emerging Utes and Southern Paiutes stretched a transitional zone, from Utah Lake through Kanosh to Red Lake and Capitol Reef. People there kept a few horses but were not as mobile as the more northern Utes; their groups were also not as large. Some practiced small-scale horticulture like Paiutes. Living along the border, they had extensive political contacts with their Ute neighbors and occasionally intermarried, but Utes often treated them as not quite one of their own. Euro-Americans referred to these people variously as both Utes and Paiutes at different times.

The larger bands of the Utes could mobilize a greater number of adult fighting men than could the smaller, pedestrian camp groups. Their horses gave them the ability to strike quickly from a distance. Specialized warrior leaders provided the organization to attack weaker neighbors successfully. These three factors gave Utes a distinct military advantage over adjacent tribes still on foot.[5] They only needed a reason to turn this potential threat into an actual one.

That motivation was provided by the Spanish market for slave labor, but the conflict began slowly and had pacific beginnings. Until the late eighteenth century, Spanish settlements were limited to the Rio Grande Valley centered at Santa Fe, but in 1769 the first Catholic missions were established on the southern California coast. The Europeans then needed communication links to those new settlements and therefore had to know who and what lay between. In 1776 two expeditions of friars traversed Paiute country from opposite directions.

One party, under friars Escalante and Domínguez, traveled north from Santa Fe into the plateaus of western Colorado before turning west. With Ute guides, they traveled south from Utah Lake along the Wasatch Front to Paiute territory. Staying close to the mountain wall, they crossed several band areas, where they met small groups of people for whom their guides could easily translate. As they approached the Colorado River, there uncrossable, they shifted east toward Kaibab and hence to the ford of the Colorado familiar to their guides, at first called the Ute Crossing but later to be named Crossing of the Fathers in their own honor. Via the Hopi villages and Zuni, they returned to Santa Fe.[6]

The friars had seen some of Paiute country and wrote of native food sources, gathering techniques, settlement patterns, and the occasional small irrigated fields.[7] The missionaries also recorded the cautious way that Paiutes viewed strangers. In contrast to the bold, mounted Utes, the priests called Paiutes "Yuta Cobarde," the timid Utes. When twenty Paiute women gathering seeds first saw the mounted expedition, their instant response was to run; only two were cut off and persuaded to talk to the fathers. Another time five Paiute men initiated contact but carefully controlled the situation to the best of their ability; they hid on a steep cliff face that horses could not climb. One man, very possibly the headman, stood visible while the two missionaries clambered up to talk to him. "At each step we took," they noted, "he wanted to take off. We let him know that he did not have to be afraid, that we loved him like a son and wanted to talk with him. And so he waited for us, making a thousand gestures to show that he feared us very much."[8] Many other Paiutes probably stayed successfully out of sight, for the Spaniards passed through long stretches without noticing any inhabitants at all.

Once reassured of the Spaniards' peaceful intentions, Paiutes throughout the line of travel were friendly and even curious. They shared their small amounts of food and received gifts of knives and beads. On several occasions they led the thirsty friars to water. By the time the expedition had reached the Kaibab area, word of their coming had seemingly spread well ahead of them. There, at a camp of three families, visitors from other camps appeared. The natives fed the expedition, and the fathers preached to them through Ute interpreters. When in exchange a local shaman offered to help cure a sick expedition member, the missionaries reprimanded him for his "idolatries."[9]

The second Spanish expedition in Paiute territory that year was that of Franciscan Father Garces from San Xavier del Bac mission near Tucson headed for California.[10] He crossed the lower Colorado River near the Gila and traveled up the western shore. His Mohave guides led him along their trade trail to the Pacific coast. Garces had no trouble talking to Chemehuevi Paiutes through interpreters as he crossed the Riverside Mountains. He described their clothing and weapons and was much impressed with their fine physiques and fleetness of foot. He praised them as having "much good sense." Like the Utah Paiutes met by Escalante, the Chemehuevi men were well informed about neighboring tribes and described territories for over a hundred miles in all directions, being especially well informed about other Paiutes to the north whom they called "their nation."[11]

The contacts between Paiutes and Europeans during both of these expeditions were peaceful. Especially in the north, Paiutes clearly worried about meeting strangers and tried to avoid contact or to control the situation through a male spokesman. The Spaniards recorded a scattering of observations about the Indians' lives and gave them a few trade objects but mostly talked and asked questions. These Europeans had no intention to establish missions or settlements in the area, and nothing they saw in the landscape enticed them to do so. Paiutes were so few in any one place that the priests only preached once, their lone effort to change Paiute culture or life.

Although the immediate impact of Spanish explorations was probably minimal, the long-term effects on Southern Paiutes were extensive. Escalante made known the Utes' ford of the Colorado River, and that information provided traders with access to the north. Garces opened a route between the New Mexican and Californian colonies. Both of these trails crossed through Paiute territory, and both would soon be used by secular profit-seekers. Further, the fathers provided justification for the Spanish crown's claim to the extensive inland territory between their tiny isolated colonies through "right of discovery." While Spain never significantly utilized its asserted ownership of Paiute country, it did later sign a treaty that, in the eyes of Euro-Americans, transferred that ownership to the United States, a country that would, and did, assert its claims actively.

While Spain and its citizens did not want to occupy the interior basin, they did want to derive a profit from it. Santa Fe was a trade center, extracting resources from the distant countryside through loosely regulated individual enterprise. Traders moved out in all directions to seek native customers and also entertained Indian producers, among whom were Utes, who brought their goods to this center. Of the wide variety of products that figured in the intertribal trade networks, many had no value in Spanish eyes. For such goods as the Europeans did seek (buffalo hides, horses, and always, hopefully, gold), traders offered a wide range of useful and exotic European manufactures—metal pots, needles, and colorfully dyed textiles. In the process, Spaniards introduced a new, invisible element to native cultures, a voracious mercantile system based on the concepts of money and profit. Goods were commodities. Depersonalized and removed from human relations of reciprocity, here even human labor itself became a property to be bought and sold like any other.

The Spanish presence in the Southwest generated many realignments in the relationships of native tribes to one another. Most obviously, some fled overt occupation, such as the Pueblos who sought refuge with Navajos, but there were more subtle changes stemming from the trade relation itself.[12] Colonial governors, who knew how easily commerce could erupt into conflict, tried to regulate trade with natives, but settlers successfully evaded these regulations. Just as Europeans jockeyed with each other for the profits of the Indian trade, so too did tribes juggle one another for territories with resources the Spaniards desired, for routes to Santa Fe, and for profitable middleman positions between Spanish traders and more distant tribal producers.

Active in these intertribal shifts were the Utes. Initially hostile to Spanish colonies, Utes began to trade at Santa Fe sometime after 1700.[13] By 1813, New Mexican traders traveled to Ute customers, penetrating as far north as Utah Lake.[14] Although records are very scanty, the first Mormon settlers in the late 1840s recorded a well-established and regular New Mexican trade into Utah.

Not only did Spanish traders follow Escalante's route into central Utah, but they also tracked Garces to southern California. In 1829 Antonio Armijo proved that wagons were practicable on this route.[15] His brief surviving notes mention Paiutes with small fields both south of the Colorado in what is now northeastern Arizona and north of the Crossing of the Fathers. They gathered seeds and hunted rabbits but offered no hostility; Paiutes were "a docile and timid nation."[16] Like the earlier padres, Armijo reported no Paiutes in places later known to have large populations, such as the lower Virgin River, Santa Clara, and Las Vegas, but he did report them on the lower Muddy River and as far west as the Amargosa River at the current California-Nevada border.

Armijo's route became known as the Old Spanish Trail and stretched directly across Paiute country using native campsites at springs. Each autumn, wagon trains left Santa Fe loaded with wool blankets to trade for horses in California. In the spring they drove the purchased herds back.[17] The impact of this intense, albeit transient, grazing on Paiutes was noted by the first official U.S. exploring party along the Mojave River in 1844: "We were now careful to take the old camping places of the annual Santa Fe caravans, which, luckily for us, had not yet made their yearly passage. A drove of several thousand horses and mules would entirely have swept away the scanty grass at the watering places, and we should have been obliged to leave the road to obtain subsistence for our animals."[18] Not only would travelers be driven away from the trail, but so too would the native people, whose campsites at springs were being usurped and whose own food sources were being fed to horses. Although little documented, this Spanish trade must have seriously disrupted native plant–gathering cycles by expropriating the spring grasses that constituted such an important summer food staple and by forcing shifts in Paiute transhumance patterns away from the trails during the spring and fall.

The Spanish trade affected Paiutes not only in the immediate vicinity of the trails but also those living in remote groups. The large, highly mobile, mounted Ute bands under centralized leadership were also seeking profit. From their home bases in central and northeastern Utah, they rode south across Kaibab Paiute country to Santa Fe to trade hides for manufactured goods. Duplicating the trade Spaniards themselves found so profitable, Utes traveled southwest across Paiute territory to California too. After getting horses through either trade or raid, they recrossed Paiute territory, forded the Colorado, and resold their herds in New Mexico.

Utes knew enough about Spanish concepts of commodity trade to realize that the growing European colonies would pay well for manpower as well as horsepower. They soon turned their military advantages of speed, mobility, and band size against the Paiute camps through which they traveled, seizing Paiutes to sell as slaves in the markets of California and Santa Fe. On foot and with only a few men to defend each isolated camp group, Paiutes were vulnerable. Ute bands selectively captured women and children, reflecting Spanish expectations that these people would be more tractable and less likely to escape. As they whirled into a pedestrian camp, mounted Ute horsemen intentionally intimidated Paiute families into giving up their children, later reported to the Spaniards as voluntary sales. Numerous Euro-American reports declared that unpredictable food resources and periodic famine forced parents to offer children in exchange for cast-off Ute horses to eat or guns to hunt in order that the rest of the family might avoid starvation.[19] This trade became so entrenched that by 1850 there were standard values for Paiute slaves, from $50 to $200 depending on their sex, age, and state of health.[20]

Spanish colonists excused such slave traffic, not on the basis of their own desire for cheap labor but as a humanitarian effort to convert "heathen" Indians. In 1824 colonial California passed a law against the sale of Indians into slavery, but this did not stop the trade; the law could not remove the market for labor, so both Ute and Spanish entrepreneurs continued to supply it.[21] The slave trade flourished throughout the Spanish colonial period and into subsequent Mexican and American ones as well. An American mountain man recalled that along the Wasatch Front in the late 1830s, "it was no uncommon thing in those days to see a party of Mexicans in that country buying Indians," and Kit Carson purchased a Paiute boy from Utes on the Green River in 1843.[22] Despite its technical illegality, the traffic in Paiute slaves seems to have escalated in the 1830s and 1840s.[23]

Thus even before 1820, when American fur trappers began the first regular non-Indian visits into Southern Paiute territory, the European presence to the south had already created significant changes in Paiutes' relations with other tribes. Natives with more ecologically favored homelands had adopted horses, creating the cultural differentiation of Utes from Paiutes, and, by the time of the first European observers, a political boundary had come into being between the two tribes. The Spanish market enticed those Utes to profit from their increased mobility by raiding pedestrian Paiutes. Understandably, their slave raids soured their relations with Paiutes to such an extent that one observer said, "This slave trade gave rise to the civil wars between the native tribes of this country, from Salt Lake down to the tribes in Southern Utah."[24] Even if Paiutes had not previously run and hidden when mounted strangers approached, now they had good reason to fear and to secrete away their women and children.

While written records portray a clear Ute dominance, they do not document other internal effects slave raiding very likely had on Paiute society. Presumably, the removal from any small Paiute camp group of even a few women, the primary plant gatherers, would restrict that group's ability to acquire food. Such loss of major subsistence producers, coupled with periodic flight from food-gathering areas, must have influenced Paiute diet, health, and physical strength in ways that can only be guessed. Marriages between adjacent camp groups, the major means of creating linkages, would necessarily be fewer, thus weakening the network of Paiute society. Ultimately, the selective capture of nubile women hindered recovery from population loss, extending the demographic effect of the raids themselves. If an early Indian agent was at all accurate in his estimate of 50 percent population loss to slavery, then the impacts on Paiute society must have been considerable indeed.[25]

The Spanish and Ute traders were not the sole visitors to Southern Paiute territory in the early nineteenth century. The first American observers were fur trappers in the 1820s who traveled south from the Salt Lake area through Paiute country for pelts to sell at the mobile annual Rocky Mountain rendezvous. They left scant and vague records, however, for few were literate, and even those who could write were reluctant to leave detailed records because their presence in then-Mexican territory was illegal. Peg-leg Smith, for instance, saw the Sevier River headwaters in 1825 but recorded only that he met more resistance from unspecified natives than the number of furs were worth, so he moved quickly to the south across the Colorado.[26]

Two years later, Jedediah Smith hunted south along the Wasatch Front, past the Sevier River to the Virgin. After winding through its gorge on what is now the Utah-Nevada border, he followed the Muddy River to the Colorado, thus traversing most of Paiute territory. Despite his slow trapping along the way, his memoirs rarely mentioned that he saw native groups, and his descriptions were exceedingly brief. The Indians near present-day Beaver, Utah, he called simply "wild," probably referring to their flight from him rather than aggression, for he left a knife as a gift for them on a rock where he hoped they would find it. The Santa Clara he called Corn Creek, implying that he saw native fields there.[27] This was probably the area he later described where "they raise corn and pumpkins, on which they principally subsist," although other trappers and travelers reported these fields as small and assumed that the amount of food from them was correspondingly insignificant. Smith arrived at harvest time and may have seen Paiutes near their fields eating the fresh crops, giving him the impression of a significantly horticultural diet. Smith also observed that "except a few hares, very little game of any description is to be found."[28] Mountain men were meat eaters, and the fundamentally vegetarian Paiute diet was both immediately obvious and unattractive to them. Another who trapped near Sevier Lake in 1827 called Paiutes "miserable Indians" and specified: "Their diet consists of roots, grass seeds, and grass, so you may judge they are not gross in their habit."[29] American trappers, most of whom had adopted and adapted Plains Indian lifestyles, adjudged Paiute culture in general to be "low," "mean," "degraded," and "miserable." They scorned Paiutes' clothing, housing, and general quality of life as well as diet, unlike the Spanish priests, who admired Paiutes' sturdy physical prowess and ingenious skills in coping with the severe desert environment. Such opinions were far more than simply disparaging and dehumanizing stereotypes; they were the forerunners of attitudes later Americans would use to legitimize imposing cultural changes on Paiutes and to justify colonization of their lands.[30]

A trapper who visited Paiute country the following winter was unimpressed with the people and appalled by their food sources. Far from contented farmers, in midwinter he observed, "They food consists of occasionally a Rabbit, with roots + mice, grasshoppers + insects, such as flies, spiders + worms of every kind—Where nuts exist they gather them for food—They also luxuriate + grow fat when they find a patch of clover."[31] On the basis of their diet, simple technology, and scanty attire, he judged them to be "the lowest species of humanity" and said of culturally similar groups in northern Utah, "From their mode of living on roots + reptiles, insects + vermine they have been called Diggers—In fact they almost burrow in the earth like the male [mole] and are almost as blind to everything comely."[32] Despite his disparaging description of Paiutes, his record of Paiute reaction to roaming bands of mounted strangers was more thorough than that of other early Americans:

> *Wading, in the snow, as the sun went down, one dreary evening, a solitary Indian was discovered, whose dwarfish stature + lean, half starved, nakid person, a heap of bones + skin. . . . A single rabbit-skin [robe] hung over his otherwise nakid shoulders—With a rude bow + arrows he was hunting rabbits—He was met by surprise + started, with affrighted visage, to run—But impeded by the deep snow he could not escape, + stood trembling with affrighted visage, in expectation of immediate death[.] They soothed him with presents of awls, beeds and vermilion, + he sat down to contemplate the articles given him—At the request of the strangers he led them to his people. . . . The individual called to his people to allay their fears, for they were greatly terror stricken—All they had in the world was some dried rabbit-meat—The party gave them knives + awls.*[33]

Of the American trappers, only Peg-leg Smith actually caught many beaver in Paiute country.[34] Near the Santa Clara headwaters in 1829, he quickly secured all the pelts he could carry and left for California but made no observations on the Paiutes.[35] The impact of the beaver trade on Paiutes was probably minimal and not long-lasting. Although Paiutes fled at the trappers' approach, there is no indication that they abandoned any areas permanently. Beaver, apparently never very plentiful, were reduced in numbers but not eradicated, for Mormon settlers were irritated by their dam-building habits on the same Santa Clara in the 1850s. The horses and pack animals of the fur trappers surely grazed near campsites and trails, but most trappers traveled in winter, when pelts were at their prime, not in summer, when Paiutes were harvesting lowland grass seeds for human consumption.

Aside from ecological effects, trappers also were a political presence. They occasionally "chastised" natives in northern Utah for theft and to the south fought with Mohaves, but they gave small gifts to Paiutes and had primarily peaceful relations with them.[36] Utes possessed good beaver lands and engaged directly in the fur trade themselves. The presence of American trappers had little effect on the intertribal relations between them and their Paiute neighbors.

Soon yet another group of Euro-Americans followed the Indian trails that the trappers had used. Beginning with an initial trickle in the 1830s, the flow of these immigrants with their wagons and families reached flood proportions in the late 1840s. Many were gold seekers; others came to settle and farm but found little in Paiute country to entice them, so they rolled on to California. Nevertheless, the sheer number of travelers created a far greater impact on natives than had earlier explorers and trappers. Many who arrived at Salt Lake too late in the season to risk crossing the snowy Sierra Nevada to the gold fields chose to turn south through Paiute territory, across the Mojave Desert, and into southern California. Therefore, much of the wagon traffic interrupted Paiutes' busy autumn harvest season or came even later during the period of frugal survival on scant stored foods.

Paiutes reacted to these parties of lumbering wagons and their mounted men in the same way they had to earlier Spanish trade expeditions and American trappers. At first sight, they fled, and women and children hid. The chronicler of the party that gave Death Valley its name recalled climbing into the piñon hills of southern Utah in the fall of 1849: "I heard some pounding noise as I came near, but what ever it was, it ceased on my approach. There were many signs of the rock being used as a camp, such as pine burrs, bones of various kinds of animals, and other remains of food which lay every where about,"[37] but he saw no Paiutes. That same year, another group in Beaver Dam Wash happened upon an "Indian lodge pot on boiling, all their effects in and about the lodge, the Indians having fled."[38] Many immigrant diaries do not mention seeing any Paiutes at all as they passed through the territory, and some, perversely, took even this as a sign of hostility: "We saw Indian signs almost every day, but as none of them ever came to our camp it was safe to say they were not friendly."[39]

Despite such suspicions, the actual contacts immigrants recorded with Paiutes were often friendly or at least neutral. When natives initiated a meeting, they very carefully tried to control the circumstances. Nearly always it was men who attempted to restrict travelers' penetration into the native residential area. In 1850, for instance, a small group of Paiute men came into a wagon camp along the Santa Clara to talk in the evening. "They then disappeared in different directions," the diarist recorded, "but where they went we never knew, for we saw no lodges or wickiups, except some old ones. They were back next morning by daylight. Had no women, no children; they said they had sold them to the Spaniards."[40] Such an assertion may have been less a statement of fact than a politic strategy to discourage any interest on the part of these unknown mounted strangers. The Death Valley travelers did sight a woman one day: "She instantly caught her infant off its little pallet made of a small piece of thin wood covered with a rabbit skin, and putting the baby under one arm, and giving a smart jerk to a small girl that was crying to the top of her voice, she bounded off and fairly flew up the gentle slope toward the summit, the girl following after very close. The woman's long black hair stood out as she rushed along, looking over her shoulder every instant as if she expected to be slain."[41]

Paiutes had good reason for such fear, for not only had earlier Spaniards and Utes raided them, but immigrants habitually handled them roughly as well. Many parties headed west without experienced scouts, trusting to the deep ruts of the roadway to lead them to watered campsites each evening. Frequently, in open desert areas such as southern Nevada, they became lost and thirsty. Many literally captured whatever natives they could lay their hands on and forcibly extracted trail information. They casually recorded, "Saw and caught two Pah Eutahs."[42] The Death Valley party "saw an Indian dodge behind some big rocks, and searching, they found him in a cave as still as a dead man. They pulled him out and made him go with them, and tried every way to find out from him where they were." They kept him in camp overnight, and in the morning "he showed us a small ravine four miles away which had water in it." While they are drinking, "attracted by a slight noise they looked and saw Mr. Indian going down over the cliffs after the fashion of a mountain sheep, and in a few bounds he was out of sight."[43]

Not only were immigrants often thirsty, but they were hungry as well when the deserts proved to be much larger and the road slower than they had been led to believe. Some freely helped themselves to Indian food caches, without thought of the frugal natives they were thus condemning to a winter of hunger. One such group found food stored in rock niches in the barren Amargosa Valley. They took the "balls of a glistening substance looking something like pieces of varigated candy stuck together. The balls were as large as small pumpkins. It was evidently food of some sort, and we found it sweet but sickish, and those who were so hungry as to break up one of the balls and divide it among the others, making a good meal of it, were a little troubled with nausea afterwards."[44] Some travelers evidently felt they could do this with impunity because the Indians were not there to guard their stores. Others felt far less secure from native retaliation or had moral qualms about these thefts, and they encouraged each other to leave Indian property scrupulously alone.[45]

Other intrusions that immigrants could not avoid were made by their draft stock. Mostly oxen, mules, and a few horses, they had already come well over fifteen hundred miles by the time they arrived in late fall or even winter to find but little grass. Travelers' accounts repeatedly mentioned how welcome the seemingly abandoned Paiute cornfields appeared as pasturage. They turned their stock loose on the stubble at night, such as one party in Beaver Dam Wash who "passed over an old corn field and camped on one that had just been gathered, good feed for our animals."[46]

In short, immigrants treated anything they found on the land as theirs to appropriate. They refused to acknowledge Paiutes' private property rights in the fields they had laboriously tended or the wild products they had cached for winter food. Immigrants conceived of the land as empty of meaningful habitation, even when they occupied native campsites, recorded Indians fleeing across the hills in front of them, or kidnapped Paiute people to extort information from them. Most of what the travelers stole was food, for they considered local culture to be too "low" and uninteresting and their own travel arrangements too demanding to collect other objects merely as souvenirs.

On their part, Paiutes sometimes gave small amounts of food to these same immigrants, perhaps receiving a token gift in return, as would seem natural to natives raised on an ethic of reciprocity. Their corn was virtually the only food Paiutes could offer that satisfied Euro-American culinary prejudices. Along Santa Clara Creek in October 1848, a Mormon Church leader "bought some corn of them + made them some presents."[47] The next year another traveler in that same horticultural area "bought about a gallon of corn from an Indian and gave him flour for it. We also gave them some presents."[48] Paiutes harvested corn about October; rarely was its trade recorded later than December, suggesting that native supplies may have been very low or exhausted by that time. The wants of immigrants may very well have reduced the amount of this desirable food that Paiutes themselves consumed.

Not all Paiutes tolerated travelers' high-handed treatment with equanimity or shared their scant stores with generosity; they developed techniques to express their resentment in actions. Contrary to the modern popular television image of cohesive wagon trains in tight linear formations breathing each other's dust, immigrant diaries show that this was actually an exceptional traveling pattern. As draft animals struggled through the deep sand or labored up rocky ridges, a party strung out. When weakened animals dropped in their traces, they were unharnessed and left behind. Their owners trusted that herd instinct would lure them to struggle along after their companions as best they could. Single wagons and loose stock often stumbled into camp out of the darkness well after midnight. Paiutes saw a way to benefit from this typical American traveling style.

Bands along Santa Clara Creek and the Moapa River had gained quite an unsavory reputation by 1849. Unable to attack large parties militarily, they could and did take advantage of stragglers. They attacked lone men who were perhaps nursing a lame ox or searching for a lost horse. Once scattered, no group seemed immune. In 1843 the large semimilitary federal exploring party that first circumscribed the Great Basin, led by John Frémont and guided by Kit Carson, came along Santa Clara Creek. A mule dropped hopelessly behind, and a young wrangler turned back to salvage its metal shoes. A scientist of the party wrote in his diary:

> *Only a mile from camp he was killed with arrows by hidden Indians and thrown into a rapid river. . . . Last night, when he did not return, Kit [Carson] and Alex [Godey] rode back and brought back the first animal for which he had searched, wounded by an arrow. . . . May God have mercy on the Paiutes who fall into our hands now. They lurk like wolves between the rocks along the road. Often we are surrounded by thirty or fifty of them without knowing it. One hears nothing, yet one is watched by a hundred eyes. Woe to him who moves too far away from the party or accidentally remains somewhat behind. . . . We must guard against the Paiutes until we have crossed the Colorado; beyond it the land is free of these wolves of this desert.*[49]

When Paiutes were actually seen rather than feared, their numbers were nearly always in the range of ten men or fewer, not large-scale war parties of "a hundred eyes." Their political and social structure prohibited mobilization of the entire tribe or even a regional band. Rather, the men of a single camp group near the trail seem to have mounted opportunistic efforts to harvest the bounteous resources passing by them.

It was often the animal rather than the man that interested Paiutes the most, for it constituted hundreds of pounds of meat, worthy game for desert dwellers, while the man often escaped to tell the tale. A traveler near the Muddy River in 1848 "discovered that the horse which McMickle brought along was missing + at once detailed 4 men to go in pursuit but they returned + joined us about midnight without having found a trace of him. He was most likely killed + promptly concealed by the Piutes."[50] Rarely did immigrants risk leaving the trail far to hunt for such stock, but even so they often found the dead animal within a mile or two, out of sight up a draw, being butchered by a small group of Paiutes. The natives had noted both Euro-Americans' hesitation to linger in unknown drylands and their fear of venturing out into Indian country; Paiutes did not anticipate pursuit.

Nevertheless, occasionally travelers did follow, as did Frémont to recover some horses stolen on the Mojave Desert west of Las Vegas. A private diarist with the party recorded how they treated the next Paiute camp in absence of any evidence that these Indians had been involved in the theft:

> *Kit [Carson] and Alex [Godey] sneaked like cats, as close as possible. Kit shot an Indian in the back; the bullet went through under the chest, and the Indian was able to run two hundred feet and get behind a rock. In the meantime, Godey . . . passed within a few paces of the rock, from which the wounded Indian shot an arrow close past Godey's ears. Turning, he first dispatched this one, and then he shot the running Indian. Thus he was entitled to both scalps . . . Godey rode into [our] camp with a yelling war cry, both scalps on a rod before him. Kit was somewhat disgruntled because of his bad luck. To me, such butchery is disgusting, but Frémont is in high spirits. I believe he would exchange all [scientific] observations for a scalp taken by his own hand. The women escaped.*[51]

Obviously not utterly intimidated by their long history with dangerous mounted Utes and more recent experiences with equally dangerous mounted Americans, Paiutes did not always wait passively for stock to be left behind. Perhaps in greater need because of the thefts by travelers of native stored foods and seasonal occupations of grass seed lands, Paiutes quickly developed active techniques to harvest livestock. A traveler described one method in 1846: Paiutes were "occasionally a source of great annoyance to those who traverse these deserts, by gathering around their camps in the darkness of the night, and letting fly a volley of arrows at the traveller's horses and mules, mortally wounding or disabling more or less of them, so that they must be left behind when the caravan moves on; and when danger of chastisement has passed, they surfeit themselves on their carcasses."[52]

In anticipation of their attacks, travelers took defensive postures. On the advice of his mountain man guide, an early traveler crossing the northern Sevier River in 1848 wrote, "Here commences the region occupied by the Pah-Eutah Indians. They are said to be a poor, treacherous, and dangerous race of people. Stealing animals at night, and shooting them from the bluff and high points during the day, constitutes their principal mode of annoying the whites."[53] It is significant that travelers rarely feared for their lives directly but worried about being marooned in the unknown desert without transportation.

Paiutes also gained meat when travelers, faced with dire necessity, killed a draft animal themselves. Their hurried butchering left much that Paiutes could salvage.[54] Sometimes a traveler tried to gain political advantage by giving a broken-down animal to the Indians before it had to be abandoned. Frémont himself "gave a fatigued horse to some of the Indians [along Santa Clara Creek] for a feast; and the village which carried him off refused to share with the others, who made loud complaints from the rocks of the partial distribution."[55]

In addition to meat, travelers provided other resources to Paiutes. As stock weakened and deserts stretched endlessly in front of them, most immigrants lightened their loads. They cut down their wagon beds and abandoned their property, sometimes carrying away only backpacks of food.[56] In the Paiute area of Ash Meadows, at the entrance to Death Valley, one diarist said, "Here I had to leave five good linen shirts, boots, hankerchiefs, one coat, friend Adolph's hat, stockings, and buffalo hide, etc."[57] Paiutes could wear such clothing, use the furniture for firewood, and recycle harness leather into any number of objects. The aggregate amount of property thus abandoned must have been substantial, for virtually every traveler recorded jettisoning goods at least once while crossing Paiute country. And yet, although they described livestock skulls and wheel ruts marking the wagon road, few diarists mentioned dumps of goods; watching Paiutes had probably already utilized them. Even when travelers burned their wagons and possessions to deny Paiutes the plunder, the ashes yielded wagon rims, nails, harness buckles, and a wide assortment of metal fittings that frugal Paiutes gleaned. Cut and patiently ground to a point against a rock, these oddments were raw material for the metal-tipped arrows Paiutes commonly used in the 1850s.

The relationship, then, between Paiutes and immigrants was a complex one. Travelers not only exploited Paiute land and seized food stores, possessions, and occasionally persons but also provided a source of meat and extensive castoffs. As one might expect, travelers at the beginning of the immigrant flood in 1848 recorded seeing Paiutes along the trail, both individually and in camps. They also saw Paiutes years later, indicating that natives had not abandoned the lands near the roads, undoubtedly in part because these were their homes but perhaps also because the wagon routes themselves had become resource zones that natives wove into the eclectic, multiple resource cycle of their economy.

This was not an invisible, silent, peaceful symbiosis. As with the Frémont party, fear often marked the relationship between Paiutes and immigrants that in itself led to conflict. When Kit Carson was surrounded by three hundred Paiutes along the Muddy in 1847 "who wanted to come into my camp," he "refused to admit them, telling them that they had killed seven Americans the fall before, that they were treacherous characters who could not be trusted, and that I would not allow myself to be deceived by them. I said further that their objective was to come to me under the guise of friendship and then kill my party; and if they did not retire, I would fire on them. I was compelled to fire, and one Indian was killed. The others withdrew, and we had no more trouble on the road."[58]

Between 1775 and 1850 an increasing number of travelers came to Southern Paiute territory—Spanish padres, New Mexican traders, Ute raiding parties, American fur trappers, federal explorers, and the first wave of California-bound American immigrants. These early Euro-Americans shared certain characteristics. All came on horseback. None came purposefully *to* the Paiute homeland. They either wanted to extract highly specific resources, such as beaver skins or labor, or had goals that lay entirely elsewhere. They were transients who had little interest in this land, and few saw anything that attracted them to stay.

Beyond such similarities, these travelers had different impacts on Paiutes' lives. Ute horsemen swooped down on Paiute camps to capture women and children to trade with the Spaniards for more guns. Although they were motivated by economic gain, they created a newly hierarchical political relationship between the two Indian peoples. With the differential power given by their numbers and the technological advantages of horses and guns, Utes forced Paiute individuals and communities into decisions they would not otherwise have had to make, such as intimidating Paiute parents into giving over children. This strategic balance would significantly affect Paiute society for at least another decade.

Paiutes adopted a defensive response that even the most superficial Euro-American observers noted; Paiutes abandoned their homes, fires, and stores at the approach of any mounted party. If cornered, they denied that their camps harbored any women or children. Only elderly men braved approach under conditions that put horses at a disadvantage, such as rocky slopes. Euro-Americans scornfully called this pattern of behavior cowardice, but when the Utes' slave raiding is taken into consideration, Paiutes' response seems wholly appropriate.

The presence of Euro-Americans altered not only intertribal politics but also native relationships to property. Paiutes had always acknowledged individual ownership of household goods and tools created by personal labor, while game belonged to whoever killed it. Spaniards introduced market exchange in a whole gamut of new commodities, even Paiute labor.

Later, Americans brought their own brand of laissez-faire capitalism for exchanges of beaver pelts, land, and gold. The earliest direct conflict between Paiutes and Euro-Americans over property involved livestock. Non-Indians saw stock as privately owned tools for transportation; they took offense when Paiutes hunted the animals for food.

Euro-American travelers frequently complained of the lack of grass for their stock. Since that same scarce wild grass was a primary grain for the native human diet, the beasts travelers brought with them were obviously competitors for foods already in short supply. At the same time, these domesticated animals were a large, easily approached source of meat in an area where big game was scarce. Paiutes adapted quickly and devised safe strategies to harvest this periodically available meat source.[59]

Paiute stock killing soured their relations with travelers, but this was not the only source of tension with non-Indians. Although Spanish priests had had predominantly amicable relations with Paiutes, contacts with American fur trappers and travelers fifty years later were rife with hostility and frequently flared into violence at perceived affronts. Some historians have argued that the difference was that Americans were coming directly from confrontations with militaristic Plains tribes and then stereotyped those experiences to all Indians.[60] Others attribute trapper propensities toward bloodshed to some inherent, primordial Anglo-American psychological aggression and racism.[61] While Euro-American records of this period did rarely differentiate members of one tribe from another, calling all simply "Indians," this may have resulted as much out of ignorance as racism. Furthermore, the Americans were not as uniform as these interpreters would suggest. Some indeed showed an extreme insensitivity to Indian life and property, free expropriation of food resources, capture of people for information, and indiscriminate slaughter of whatever natives were discovered nearest to a stock raid. On the other hand, there were trappers who described Paiutes' stock attacks as mere "annoyances" and travelers who urged their hungry fellows to leave Indian stores alone on both pragmatic and moral grounds. And surely not all the blame for the increasingly tense relations can be traced to one side of the interethnic boundary line alone. Paiutes' killing of stock, while an understandable response, did contribute to the escalating hostilities.

The complex and variable individual or group motivations are irrecoverable at this point in time. What is clear is that until 1850 Paiutes had little reason to fear that their land would be lost to transient Euro-Americans, but they had a major bone of contention over livestock—horses, oxen, cattle, and mules. Individual wagon trains, operating autonomously beyond the reach of the national society, were roughly comparable in size to local Paiute camp groups. The two groups interacted directly, mediated by Paiute headmen, who lacked power to make unilateral decisions for the natives, and the wagon train captains, who in many cases may have had a great deal more authority within their groups. The resulting interethnic relationship was watchful, fragile, and defensive as both sides sought information about the strange group, new economic resources, or the road ahead. They were equally willing either to exchange gifts across a campfire in the evening or to seize a momentary advantage over the other.

Perhaps the most serious and long-lived threat to Paiute life was not foreseen by either the Euro-Americans or the natives at the time. With the exception of Frémont, Euro-American travelers were concerned with their own affairs, their own profits and interests being elsewhere. Nonetheless, they laid the foundation for national claims to ownership of Southern Paiute territory. In the eyes of Euro-American heads of state, the written travelers' reports constituted "discovery" of lands that would then belong to the nation whose citizens had gotten there first (natives, of course, always being excepted). Spain mapped Paiute land as part of its colonial empire, even though it never controlled the region directly. Its successor, Mexico, transferred this passive title claim to Paiute land to the United States in the Treaty of Guadalupe Hidalgo in 1848.

4

MORMONS MEET PAIUTES

By the early 1850s, Paiutes had met several kinds of transient Euro-Americans, but none of these had intentions to stay, until the Mormons arrived. The Mormons were a highly structured, cohesive, self-defined religious community, members of the Church of Jesus Christ of Latter-day Saints. They declared that religious principles should drive their relationships with Indians, and they subsequently did, at least on some ideological levels. On the other hand, like Euro-American settlers elsewhere, Mormon economic and political relations with Paiutes were shaped by self-interest.

Mormons as an identifiable cultural group originated in the 1820s during the Second Great Awakening, a period of intense religious fervor in the northeastern United States characterized by a plethora of unorthodox doctrines that stressed mysticism, the personal experience of contact with God, rejection of solace through formal ritual, tent revivals, millennial prophecies, utopian communities, visions, and revelations. Although like the other sects in many ways, Mormonism outlived nearly all of them.[1]

Young Joseph Smith proclaimed that an angel named Moroni had directed him to plates of gold divinely inscribed with the history of the New World. He asserted that he translated the "Modified Egyptian" in which they had been written, and then the plates were reclaimed by God. The resulting Book of Mormon related that American Indians were descendants of the tribes of Israel.[2] At least two immigrations of these tribes had been divinely directed to sail west to the New World with seeds, oxen, horses, and elephants to build an urban civilization based on grain agriculture. After his death, Christ had preached to these migrants as he had to the Palestinians and established a flourishing church.

But the people quarreled and divided; the Nephites held to traditional ways, but others, the Lamanites, abandoned farming and turned to hunting and war. Angered, God cursed them and "did cause a skin of blackness to come upon them" in punishment for their rejection of his teachings, but he promised that if they repented and rejoined the faithful, they would once again become a "white and delightsome people."[3] The Book of Mormon described these Lamanites "as led by their evil nature that they became wild, and ferocious, and a blood-thirsty people, full of idolatry and filthiness; feeding upon beasts of prey; dwelling in tents, and wandering about in the wilderness with a short skin girdle about their loins and their heads shaven; and their skill was in the bow, and in the scimitar, and the ax. And many of them did eat nothing save it was raw meat; and they were continually seeking to destroy us."[4] The Lamanites completely wiped out the faithful and progressive Nephites, the Book of Mormon related.[5] Therefore, the Indians that Mormons met in the nineteenth century were the descendants of these Lamanites, cursed by God, heathens, and heretics to the true faith.

This conception of history was not merely abstract theology but, rather, it shaped and permeated relationships between Mormons and Paiutes. In 1859, as Mormons were entering and seizing Paiute country, Brigham Young, then head of the Mormon Church, thundered this very doctrine in the Salt Lake City Tabernacle: "the aborigines of this country are dark, loathsome, ignorant, and sunken into the depths of degradation; . . . When the Lord has a people, he makes covenants with them and gives them promises: then, if they transgress his law, change his ordinances, and break the covenants he has made with them, he will put a mark upon them, as in the case of the Lamanites and other portions of the house of Israel; but by-and-by they will become a white and delightsome people."[6] Their theologically inspired perception of history led the Mormons to anticipate that Indians, including Paiutes, would be nomadic hunter-gatherers, violently hostile to the faithful, and above all heretics, as demonstrated by their visibly dark skin. On the other hand, Indians had been previously selected for visitation by God in the form of Jesus and were redeemable; therefore, they could not be treated indiscriminately. Upon their redemption through devout conversion to Mormonism, it was thought that the dark color of their skin, emblem of God's displeasure, would be literally removed.

Mormon relations with Paiutes were also influenced by their belief that the millennium was imminent. Many pioneer Mormons held that the messiah who would build the Kingdom of God on earth would himself be a Lamanite reconverted to the true faith, for "does not that book [of Mormon] say that the Lamanites are to be the principal operators in that important work, and that those who embrace the Gospel from among the Gentiles [non-Mormons] are to have the privilege of assisting the Lamanites to build up the city called the New Jerusalem?"[7] Early church-sponsored exploring parties avidly queried Paiutes throughout southern Utah about other tribes, but it was reported sadly, "They didn't know anything about any white Indians."[8] Mormon missionaries' fascination with Hopis was only in part because of their concentrated towns and agricultural sophistication, but also because of the unusual, inbred albino minority there, wistfully interpreted as either a remnant population of Nephites or precursors of the millennium.[9]

While Mormon scripture shaped many dealings with Indians on both religious and personal levels, there were other factors at work as well. An important element was the Mormon social structure.[10] Operating without ministers to mediate between the believer and God, all adult male Mormons (although no female members) were ranked as priests, entitled elders, and addressed by one another with the pseudokinship term "brother." Despite such apparent democracy, Mormon church and civil life was extremely hierarchical. Each local congregation, or ward, was under the control of a bishop, not elected by the local membership but appointed for an unspecified period by the centralized leadership of the church. Two appointed councilors advised and assisted him. Where population permitted, a number of wards were joined into a stake under an appointed stake president and his council of twelve advisors.

Above these regional structures were the General Authorities, headed by the president of the church himself. Presidents following Joseph Smith were believed to be chosen by God, who spoke directly through them. The church president was not only the ultimate religious authority but also legal trustee over the real earthly property of the church, which through tithing, members routinely deeding property to the church, and enterprises operated directly by the church rapidly became considerable.[11] The president was assisted by the Quorum of Twelve, men appointed for life based on seniority who as a group held immense power in religious matters, including the appointment of bishops and missionaries. This upper structure, informally but revealingly called "The Hierarchy," could and did demand acts of contrition from members, sanctioned ultimately by excommunication for disobedience to any of the dictates of the church. The ability of this male hierarchy to create and enforce uniform action among the religiously homogeneous settlers had an important impact on the Mormons' relations with Paiutes.

For many reasons, Joseph Smith's Mormon community met hostility first in western New York, then Ohio, Missouri, and Illinois. After Smith's death amid bordertown violence in 1844, one schism followed the charismatic Brigham Young west to find an isolated place where they could live free of secular interference. They arrived in what is now Utah and founded Salt Lake City in 1847. That town became the religious, commercial, and political center of Mormon life from whence settlements spread down the Wasatch Front into Southern Paiute territory within five years.[12]

Generally, American settlement of the West resulted from a random assortment of personal decisions, but Mormons moved in a unified mass under the direction of central church authorities. During the semiannual conferences of church members, in personal meetings in the church office, or even by letter, Brigham Young or his delegate announced that twenty or thirty men would form a party to settle an appointed location. Chosen for particular skills, the men thus "called" sold their farms to fellow Mormons and set out for places as yet unknown.[13] Together with their wives and children and led by a church-appointed bishop, they composed a preorganized community on the march. They arrived at the prechosen site en masse, not in a dribble of individual families over months or years such as built towns elsewhere. The first night they formed a church ward whose leadership surveyed out house lots in a grid pattern the next day. The bishop held land title for the community as a whole, and he distributed the homesites, generally by drawing lots. Farmland beyond was often in a communal "Big Field," fenced and worked jointly. The bishop organized work parties to build roads and construct the all-important irrigation system that served the farms of all church members. The group owned the water, and each man was assessed a labor contribution to maintain the distribution system.[14] They then organized a county and held elections for all offices, from sheriff to judge; the men who filled such positions were necessarily from the Mormon company and often were its senior leaders, resulting in a tight interlocking of clerical and civil offices.[15] Under highly centralized direction, an entire town was operating within a matter of weeks, the land cultivated and streams diverted into irrigation ditches.

The church saw native title to land and water as neither a substantial nor a moral barrier to such occupation. Mormon religious ideology declared that natives were Lamanites, hunters and gatherers, and, perhaps most important, heretics. Settlers argued unashamedly that Mormon occupation would bring both material and spiritual benefits to the displaced natives. Brigham Young himself sermonized, "This is the land that they and their fathers have walked over and called their own . . . this is their home, and we have taken possession of it, and occupy the land where they used to hunt. . . . But now their game has gone, and they are left to starve. . . . It is our duty to feed these poor ignorant Indians; we are living on their possessions and at their homes. The Lord has brought us here and it is all right.

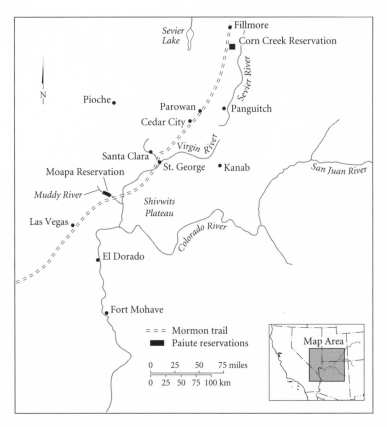

Map 2. Southern Paiute Territory, 1875

We are not intruders, but we are here by the providence of God."[16] Although the federal government claimed sole legitimate authority to acquire land from Indians, Brigham Young declared, "If we should defer our wayside settlement till they [the federal government] had arranged these matters righteously with the 'natives,' how long should we wait? We do not mean to put it into the power of Gov't. to refuse our making settlements . . . to benefit the human family, and ourselves."[17]

Mormons acted quickly. Within four years of their first entry into Utah, they had built Fillmore, halfway down the Wasatch Front. Parowan was the major village in the south, from which Cedar City spun off the next year. Santa Clara, a zone of heavy native occupation, housed an Indian mission by 1854, as did Las Vegas in Nevada the following year. Within seven years the Santa Clara mission had grown into the town of St. George, where Brigham Young established his winter home and seasonally brought the entire administrative apparatus of the Mormon Church into the Paiute heartland. From this first string of villages, others quickly spread. Meadow Valley in the hills north of Santa Clara, Circleville in the Sevier River Valley eastward, and Kanab along the Arizona border in Kaibab band territory were all founded in 1864. Within fifteen years of their first southern settlement, over three thousand Mormons were living in the one hundred miles between St. George and Moapa alone, far outnumbering native Paiutes.[18] In less than a single generation, the Mormons had gained control over virtually all productive areas and major water sources throughout Southern Paiute country.

Paiutes offered little military resistance, probably because of their limited social and technological ability to challenge the Mormon advance. A single wagon train delivering a Mormon community was several times larger than any camp group of Paiutes in the targeted location. That party contained a large preorganized body of mounted men accustomed to unquestioning obedience to a single leader, armed with guns, and potentially more lethal than Ute raiding bands. The only way a Paiute camp could augment its male defense force was to activate kinship ties with adjoining bands, but this took time, negotiation, and cooperation. Paiutes could only sustain such an enlarged group for a short period, because the native economy produced little surplus, especially if men's time was being absorbed in conflict and the resource base had already been reduced by settler presence. Paiutes could match neither settlers' numbers, armament, nor logistics; they were, from the first day, no match for a Mormon immigration in any overt confrontation.

Just as Paiutes had met earlier travelers, they approached these first Mormons cautiously. Historic experience of mounted Ute slave raiders had taught Paiutes to avoid Mormon explorers while observing them from a safe distance. Occasionally, an elderly man, probably the headman whose obligations included dealing with outsiders, initiated contact. For example, Mormons scouting potential settlement sites on the Virgin River told how "one old man came into camp. He said he was afraid of the company. In a little while, other four came and they said they were afraid."[19]

Mormon records insist that after such tentative initial contacts, Paiutes not only failed to dispute their arrival but actively welcomed it, that Mormons were, in effect, invited to take over Paiute lands. The leader of an exploring party wrote the church-controlled newspaper that Paiute headmen from south of Cedar City sought him out in 1852: "They expressed great anxiety to have us settle among them, so they could 'manika' (work) for the Mormons, like the Pah Eeds at Parowan."[20] Similarly, an early Las Vegas settler in a private letter to his wife wrote, "[T]he Cry is winow Mormons, the

Chefe that Lives to the Vagus herde [heard] that we was Comming and Com to meat us. . . . he Preached last knight through the interpreter Said that he was glad that we was amoning [coming] to Live among them and Lern them. . . . he wanted us to Com and Live with them and the Indans wood treat us well he said that his Hart was Warm for the mormons."[21]

It is easy to discount such statements as self-justifications by a religious people striving to assuage their own moral consciences. But Paiutes may indeed have seen some benefits from the Mormon presence, even if those benefits were short-lived and their perceptions naively short-sighted. Many Mormon writers thought Paiutes were motivated by material avarice. They described natives eager for Mormon goods, which no doubt they were. The settlers, however, interpreted this not as an attraction to novel and useful objects but as a frantic desire to alleviate chronic poverty. Their needs were so desperate as to compel Paiutes to work for settlers in exchange for goods with an energy that the Lamanite dogma asserted was antithetical to their very nature. As a Mormon leader near Las Vegas explained, "They are anxious for us to settle the country, and are willing for our cattle to eat their grass, if we will employ them that they may have clothes to wear and food to eat when their grass seed is all used."[22]

While clothes and food were what Mormons usually offered, what Paiutes wanted were guns. Some Mormon parties refused to trade guns or ammunition while others yielded to Paiutes' entreaties for weaponry. The Paiute desire for improved armaments becomes more understandable if we expand our view from a simple Paiute-Mormon duality to the larger context of regional power relationships that existed before the Mormons arrived and that, by their entry, they necessarily altered. Those relations intertwined power between Paiutes, Utes, and their trade partners, the Spaniards. Paiutes may have sought alliance with Mormons to counterbalance regional Ute dominance.[23] In late 1854, Santa Clara Paiutes approached a Mormon missionary,

> *very much alarmed, having heard that some Utah Indians were on their way to steal their children that night. The chief asked if we would help them to fight: I . . . replied that we would if they attempted to steal their children, if it were necessary. I then let them have ten rounds of ammunition for each gun they had. . . . The old chief went aside, and began to preach to the Utahs, as if they were within hearing: he said, they must not come now to steal their children; their white brothers—the Mormons—had come here, and would fight for them.*[24]

Utes not only threatened Paiutes bodily but also claimed the right to move freely over Paiute territory. The Mormons proved useful in contesting that assertion. They recognized that it was in their best interest if territorial claims were held by fragmented and militarily ineffective Paiutes rather than by powerful, mounted, and well-armed Ute bands. Mormon bishops often supported Paiute autonomy.[25] The Utes tried to counter a potential Paiute-Mormon alliance by constructing a political and trade relationship directly with the upper Mormon hierarchy while controlling a position geographically between the Salt Lake Valley and Southern Paiutes. Wakara, or Walker, leader of a mobile raiding band based near Utah Lake, frequently dined with the bishop of Parowan.[26] He asserted to that officer in 1851 that he could speak for Paiutes: "Walker told me that he had visited all the bands of Indians in this country. He had told them that the Mormons were good people and that if they settled on any of their lands, they must not molest them or disturb even a brute of theirs."[27] The next year Wakara publicly beat Kannara, a Paiute headman near Cedar City, for allowing a member of his band to kill a settler's ox.[28] By defending Mormon livestock, a point of contention with Paiutes, the Ute leader sought to curry favor with the immigrants while at the same time exercising dominance over Paiutes.

Thus Paiute and Ute attitudes toward Mormon settlement were rooted each in their own self-interests within a regional power balance, the former seeking to shift and the latter to maintain the status quo. Mormon settlers, who chose to simplify Paiute motivation as either naive hospitality or craven desire for material goods, failed to perceive the complicated intertribal political relationships into which they were intruding.[29] They likewise underestimated the very real, subtle, and complex strategies of Paiute leaders.[30]

Just as Mormons were misled by their cultural preconceptions, so too may Paiute headmen have been. Paiutes' invitation to the Mormons to stay may have been modeled on their own cultural customs. Kinfolk moved from one camp group to another but went home again, carrying with them obligations to reciprocate hospitality to their former hosts. Although we cannot accurately re-create Paiutes' unrecorded mental calculations, they may well not have perceived the unprecedented scale to which Mormon settlement would so soon grow or its intended permanency. By seeking allies against oppressive Utes, Paiute headmen encouraged a historical process they could then neither reverse nor control; as so often in human history, expediency proved a poor foundation for policy and led to unanticipated and undesired results. Even had Paiutes protested and resisted the immi-

gration, in the face of Mormon demographic, organizational, and technological advantages, they could not in all probability have stopped it.

The Mormon leadership immediately set about establishing their autonomy from other American territories by denying that a slave trader's license issued by the New Mexico superintendent of Indian affairs was valid
in Utah. Although this action was couched in humanitarian terms, the
territorial legislature proceeded not to outlaw the Indian slave trade but
merely to regulate it; it can therefore be argued that the Mormons were
merely attempting to control profits.[31] Non-Indians could still purchase
natives, but only under a registered indenture contract that specified educational and clothing benefits. Far from suppressing Ute raids, in 1851 high
church officials issued Wakara a letter of introduction that proclaimed,
"[A]s they [the Utes] wish to Trade horses, Buckskins and Piede children
we hope them success and Prosperity and good bargains."[32]

Like the Spaniards before him, Brigham Young justified removal of
Paiute children from their families not as slavery but as a means to provide
them greater material affluence and religious salvation. He urged settlers in
Parowan "to buy up the Lamanite children as fast as they could, and educate
them and teach them the gospel, so that many generations would not pass
ere they should become a white and delightsome people. . . . I knew the Indians would dwindle away, but let a remnant of the seed of Joseph be
saved."[33] Furthermore, local oral history asserts that settlers had to buy Paiute children for purely humanitarian reasons. One story that recurs in numerous undated settings tells of a Ute slave seller who "took one of these
children by the heels and dashed its brains out on the hard ground, after
which he threw the body towards us, telling us that we had no hearts or we
would have bought it and saved its life."[34]

Contrary to such later traditional accounts, documents contemporary
to the events reveal that Mormons actively solicited children from Paiute
parents. The first recorded instance in southern Utah occurred at the crossing of the Sevier River when an ox of the settlement party leader was killed
after being riddled with arrows. A Paiute man and his son happened to be
in camp begging food at the time, and the bishop "told him it was too late
to cry, but if he would let me have the boy he might have the ox [meat], to
which he readily agreed. . . . The Indian said he wanted to see him dressed
like a white man, on his return."[35]

By buying Paiute children directly this way Mormons undercut the
Utes' lucrative middleman position in the slave trade. In 1855 the missionary Jacob Hamblin described resulting Ute disgruntlement when faced
with a unified Mormon-Paiute block: "Ammon and Other Utahs arrived to

buy children. The Lamanites called a council. I was invited in. Ammon wanted the Piutes to go + bring in children + he would buy them. They refused, + said I had told them not to sell their children. He asked if I had told them that. This placed me in a peculiar situation. I then told him I had, if they did not want to sell their children . . . He said he was not mad with me for telling the Yannawants [local band] not to sell their children to him."[36] Despite Hamblin's encouragement of Paiute resistance to Utes, his own journal revealed that the winter before he had himself bought a Paiute boy for a gun, blanket, and ammunition in order to "make him useful" and that he also bought a girl a mere month after the above incident.[37] The next winter another missionary casually mentioned, "I ministered to the necessities to my red brethren, trading with the[m] rifles +c. for five of their children."[38] These Mormon purchases had reached such an extent that by 1853 each of the one hundred households in Parowan possessed one or more Paiute children.[39]

Settlers' diaries repeatedly cited success in teaching these children to "work" or to "labor" in the Euro-American way in order to become "useful" within the Mormon economy. Even a secondary trade in Indian children developed: "Father kept her five years and let Brother William Pulsipher have her for a span of oxen."[40] Although crass economic motivation was never admitted, the pragmatic labor value of these Paiute children cannot be underestimated for frontier settlements then constructing labor-intensive infrastructure, nor can it be ignored in any explanation of why Mormon settlers continued to remove Paiute children from their native communities long after Utes had been driven militarily from the area.

Mormons contended with Utes not only for control of the slave trade but also over lands in northern and north-central Utah and ultimately for domination within the regional power hierarchy. These conflicting interests burst out in the so-called Walker War of 1853 and 1854.[41] When church leaders ordered abandonment of outlying farms and small villages vulnerable to the angry Ute bands that ranged through the south, Paiutes "had mostly gathered in and were living adjacent to both the Parowan and Cedar Forts" to seek protection and also to avoid being mistaken for hostiles.[42] Although Utes militarily defended their own lush San Pete Valley and Utah Lake areas from Mormon intrusion, they may actually have tried to divert Mormon settlement to Paiute territory. Ute leader Wakara reportedly told Parowan town leaders, "The Mormons were d——d fools for abandoning their houses and towns, for he did not intend to molest them there, as it was his intention to confine his depredations to their cattle, and that he advised them to return and mind their crops, for, if they neglected them, they would starve, and be obliged to leave the country, which was not what he desired, for then there would be no cattle for him to take."[43] Wakara may have viewed southern Mormon settlements in much the same way that he saw Paiute camps, as resource areas from which he could gather profitable tribute through intimidation.

For years Ute raiding parties had exercised violence against Paiutes indirectly to threaten and extort goods from Mormons. This technique was illustrated in January 1853, when the Paiute camp that shared the mouth of Coal Creek Canyon with Cedar City was shot up by mounted Utes and their homes were set afire. "It appeared afterwards from the testimony of one of the Pihedes, that the Utah's had bought one of the Pihede Squaws and the Squaw had run from the Utah's and that made the Utah's mad." The Utes then boldly demanded of the Mormon bishop "to give them some flour, as they were going to leave this point at noon today[.] I told them I would and I sent round the Fort and collected some 75 lb. flour and gave it to them[.] I told them to see that none of their men drove off any of our Cattle or horses."[44] The very next month, nearby Parowan gave yet another Ute band 150 pounds of flour in protection money after they killed five local Paiutes.[45] This Ute technique backfired as it produced a conjunction of Mormon and Paiute interests.

By the end of 1853 Mormon supplies, as well as tempers, were wearing thin. When Utes shot a Paiute at Parowan, the local Indians successfully activated their Mormon alliance. The Mormon leadership

> told the Utes that they must not steal nor kill any of the Piedes; neither their women nor children from that time forth; for so long as the Piedes would do right, we intended to protect them. They had helped us build the fort, and we had promised them protection within its walls. . . . Neither did we intend that they [the Utes] should sponge their living out of us as they had be[en] accustomed to; that we worked for our provisions, and so did the Piedes; and that they [Utes] were no better to labor than we were . . . that we had guns and men who loved to use them; and we would fight sooner than be trampled upon.[46]

It was not until the Mormons defeated the Utes in the north that the southern settlements were freed from such extortions. Paiutes were relieved of Ute slave raids but then faced a firmly entrenched Mormon monopoly; purchases of children burgeoned. A Cedar City man reminisced, "In 1856 I bought an Indian boy papoose, 1 year old, weaned from his mothers breast.

As he grew up he became very useful."[47] Brigham Young's Indian agent in the south, John D. Lee, wrote that he, already with one Paiute boy in his household, "also bought 2 litle girls. . . . They were of the sebee'tes [Shivwits Paiute] Tribe. For the two I gave a Rifle gun + ammunition + a young Horse."[48] Four days later he bought two more Paiute girls for two horses, "amunition, Flour, shirts, Looking glasses +c."[49] The practice continued and was common and widespread.[50]

Mormons rationalized that poverty drove Paiute parents to sacrifice their children for their own short-term economic benefit, without observing that Mormon seizure of the best watered areas for farms and the best grass seed lands for pastures had escalated those needs. Although jettisoning some children might have eased population pressure a bit in the short run, the systematic extraction of girls, whom Mormons favored, must have hampered the native community's ability to recover demographically from the violence that accompanied Mormon settlement. Although Paiute children were no longer taken far away, they were just as effectively lost to the native community. Their life expectancy was short, and those who survived often became marginal individuals in distant Mormon cities.[51]

Having dislodged Ute competition in southern Utah, Mormons set about establishing their own control over Paiutes, often through the manipulation of "chiefs."[52] The Mormons' own lives were so structured by a rigid male hierarchy to which all were obedient that they presumed all people were similarly organized: "of course a chiefs orders are law to all indians."[53] Traditionally, Paiute headmen had contacted outsiders and publicly voiced cultural ideals, such as peace, cooperation, and friendship. Mormons interpreted headmen to be representatives of the group, assumed them to control members' behavior, and took their speeches to constitute firm commitment for the entire band. Mormon settlers proceeded to act on these presumptions, despite headmen's continual denials of such power and despite the frequent events that demonstrated the truth of those denials.[54]

The simplest and most direct method of dealing with headmen was to chide them and demand that they make their followers conform to Mormon interests, such as claims to land and exclusive private property rights in livestock and small goods.[55] Such headmen were denominated "good Indians" and their positions reinforced with rewards, including recognition as leaders, deference, visits, consultation, and treatment as important men.[56] These techniques were easily recognizable within the code of traditional Paiute social relations. There followed material gifts from individual Mormons, as well as from the formal church structure, of guns, ammunition, food, clothes, wagons, seed, tools, and legal title to land.[57] These objects, which might have been interpreted as bribes in Euro-American political structures, here provided a largess that the headman could in turn use to demonstrate generosity to his followers in the traditional manner. In addition to these gestures compatible with Paiute culture, Mormons also used techniques significant within their culture, such as baptism, ordination into the priesthood, and invitation to speak before Mormon congregations.

The Mormons thus shored up the domestic influence of leaders amenable to Mormon interests. They also tried to influence the choice of headmen. As early as the summer of 1855, Brigham Young, accompanied by Pahvant headman Kanosh, "called the Indians together and had a talk and chiefs were elected at Parowan, Cedar City, and Harmony. Those were selected who would work, and all seemed well satisfied."[58] Such intervention in native politics became so common that a Mormon publication complacently generalized, "They have their chiefs, or leading men, who, on the solicitation of the Indians themselves, are frequently chosen by the aid of the 'Big Chief' [head of the Mormon Church] and his white brethren."[59] This may just have been cautious consultation with powerful neighbors to assure they were selecting someone acceptable for interethnic contacts. It may also be an indication of a "shadow" or dual government, the appointment of a "white man's chief" or figurehead completely separate from the real authority structure within the Paiute community itself.

In turn, the Mormons insisted that headmen become the kind of chief they envisioned. This involved going far beyond traditional powers to actual control of the actions of camp group members, ranging from the issuance of orders even to the whipping of dissidents.[60] Clearly, some Paiute men were willing to undertake this augmented role. All the men dubbed as "Big Chiefs" in the Mormon documents, a phrase that implied a hierarchy of native leaders paralleling the Mormons' own, not accidentally were located near principal Mormon settlements—Parowan, Santa Clara, and Fillmore. It was precisely these men who became pivotal to Mormon relations with Paiutes. It served Mormon interests well to augment these headmen's power over the native community, as long as it did not grow so substantial as to negate their own power over the headmen. The very association between Mormons and their chosen Paiute leaders often made it difficult for those headmen to exercise the authority their sponsors expected of them. Paiute culture allowed every adult to determine his or her own opinion on any issue of importance. Those issues increasingly centered on Paiute conflicts with Mormon settlers.

The reasons Paiutes were willing to comply with such apparent corruption of their leaders and intrusions into their political processes may have had less to do with the simple "friendship" presumed by Mormons than with the native conception of what leaders should do. Paiute headmen were expected to lead the people to steady food supplies; Mormon bishops were in charge of the storehouses of tithes, the 10 percent of all personal income and crops donated annually to the church by faithful members. Bishops had authority to issue these goods to Indians, as they had done frequently in the face of Ute intimidation. From even the earliest settlement, bishops controlled a wealth beyond the scope of native production systems.[61] By cooperating with local bishops or even Brigham Young himself, Paiutes need not have been acknowledging white supremacy in wisdom or power or submitting themselves to political subordination; they may have been trying to manipulate Mormon wealth by placing the Mormons under the kind of obligations Paiutes assumed would result: to share reciprocally in exchange for natives' initial gift of the very land Mormons occupied.

Perhaps more than any other, the career of Kanosh illustrates the ideal alliance between Mormons and local headmen.[62] Lionized by local Mormon historians as the "Friend of the Whiteman,"[63] he was head of the Pahvant or, as it was later called, the Kanosh band along the border between Ute and Paiute territories. A well-watered site, it was strategically located directly on the Mormon road about midway between Salt Lake City and St. George. Kanosh adopted sedentary farming and wage work, readily accepted new items of material culture, and openly supported Mormon claims to private ownership of land, livestock, and personal possessions. By 1856 he was described as "the first chief that has made any law among them. He whips for stealing. Not long since he called the tribe together and asked them to tell their feelings. . . . They freed their minds, which cost them 10 lashes on the bare back."[64] In the traditional Paiute model and with accurate understanding of Mormon hierarchical principles, Kanosh shrewdly bypassed bishops lower on the Mormon echelon to form a personalized dyadic relationship with Brigham Young. He exchanged visits and correspondence, polygynously married a ward of Young, was baptized and ordained an elder in the Mormon priesthood, and successfully extracted food and goods from church coffers. He lived in a log cabin built by Young out of federal funds, adopted Euro-American clothes, and cut his hair.[65]

In reward, Kanosh was invited by Brigham Young as the sole Paiute representative to the council that ended the Walker War, and he later signed the Treaty of Spanish Fork that terminated the Black Hawk War. When men of his band were implicated in the killing of federal surveyor John Gunnison, Brigham Young sent Kanosh his own translator to aid negotiations with government investigators. The church deeded a parcel of land directly to Kanosh. At Young's suggestion, Kanosh received a presidential medal.[66]

Paiutes other than headmen were treated quite differently. The Mormons maintained a distinct social distance between themselves and local Indians. Brigham Young was perhaps unusual among frontier leaders in urging his followers to treat "the Indians with kindness, and to refrain from harboring that revengeful, vindictive feeling that many indulge in." Arguing that it was the only way to keep the peace and prevent open warfare with native people, he repeatedly called for fair trade dealings and even declared from the pulpit the then-radical notion that a Mormon "is just as much a murderer through killing that Indian, as he would have been had he shot down a white man."[67]

On the other hand, he saw a fundamental social inequality between Mormon coreligionists and natives. He proclaimed, "Treat them kindly, and treat them as Indians, and not as your equals." He elaborated: "Let any man or company of men be familiar with the Indians, and . . . the more familiar you will find the less influence you will have over them. If you would have dominion over them, for their good, which is the duty of the Elders, you must not treat them as your equals, you cannot raise them up to you. . . . You have been too familiar with them. Your children have mixed promiscuously with them, they have been free in your homes, and some of the brethren have spent too much time in smoking and chatting with them."[68] Church authorities institutionalized this advice on the local level, as demonstrated by the meetings that first established the town of Parowan. When one man was appointed to handle "trade in behalf of the whole camp," settlers were enjoined from giving spontaneous gifts to the natives and were specifically advised "not to run races, box or shoot with the Indians"; in other words, they were not to fraternize.[69]

Like all people, Mormons patterned interaction with others on the principles of their own culture, including intense occupational specialization and hierarchical structure. Management of interethnic relationships for all the settlers became the relegated task of church missionaries. Brigham Young selected and charged these selected few to learn the native language, convert Indians to the Mormon religion, teach them to farm, and act as intermediaries any time there was a crisis of any kind. Nonmissionaries were thus freed of the necessity of relationships with natives and indeed were often ordered not to interfere with the designated missionary program.

In 1854 twenty-five young men were sent to southern Utah as missionaries to the Paiutes. They established New Harmony southwest of Cedar

City and later moved on to Santa Clara Creek in the extreme corner of the territory. The latter especially was a major Southern Paiute population center with many small horticultural fields. The following year missionaries continued southwest to Las Vegas, "The Meadows," where a large spring overflowed onto a pasture oasis along the desert trail to southern California.[70]

Any religious motivation for proselytizing would have remained unaltered since Mormons had arrived in Utah six years earlier, so this sudden onslaught of missionary activity requires other explanation. The Walker War, a conflict that not only broke the power of Ute resistance to Mormon settlement but also demonstrated dramatically the cost of neglected interethnic relations, had just ended. With Ute intertribal domination reduced, direct Mormon control over Paiutes became necessary. Just as the timing of missionary expansion was not random, neither were the locations. All were on the forwardmost wave of settlement and at key watering spots along the route to California. Historian Leonard Arrington has suggested that in the face of an anticipated war with the United States the church planned to establish a string of fortified towns forming a corridor to the coast; amicable relations with the natives along such an escape route would be critical.[71]

Brigham Young's instructions to missionary Jacob Hamblin, put in charge of the Santa Clara mission in 1857, made clear the political as well as the religious task: "Continue the conciliatory policy towards the Indians, which I have ever recommended, and seek by works of righteousness to obtain their love and confidence, for they must learn that they have either got to help us, or the United States will kill us both."[72] Farther west, a senior member of the Las Vegas mission reported success in his strategic assignment: "If the Lord blesses us, as He has done, we can have 1,000 brave warriors on hand in a short time to help quell the eruption that might take place in the principalities."[73] In 1855 Young called Indians "the Lord's battle ax,"[74] a phraseology echoed by missionary David Lewis, who was working with Paiutes: "Ephraim is the battle ax of the Lord. May we not have been sent to learn and know how to *use* this axe with skill?"[75] Federal Indian agents may have been justifiably concerned when they heard natives under the tutelage of Mormon missionaries linguistically distinguishing between "Mormoni" and "Merikats."

Despite its political timing and strategic significance, the Mormon missionary program also had the overt function of maintaining peace. The strategy was to reduce intercultural conflicts by transforming Paiutes into people more culturally compatible with Mormon settlers. Brigham Young charged the Las Vegas missionaries to

*introduce them to the love of truth, the Gospel of salvation and the
way to live as well as to die, and gradually and gently lead them back
to the principles of life, salvation and exaltation in the kingdom of
our God, that they may rejoice in the blessings, privileges, promises
and covenants made unto their fathers [as recorded in the Book of
Mormon]. . . . Visit freely with them and endeavor to instill into
their minds by deeds as well as words that we seek to do them good.
Live with them and seek to raise them to our level instead of sinking
ourselves by condescending to their vile and filthy habits.*[76]

The missionaries put these general instructions into operation by first
establishing a farm—digging ditches, plowing, and planting. Intended to
demonstrate to Paiutes the benefits of improved food supply, this not incidentally also supported the missionaries, separating them minimally from
ordinary settlers. In fact, soon after Harmony was constructed intentionally as an Indian mission, a town meeting relegated Indian affairs to a few
specialists: "consult[ed] the [Mormon] people whither they would grant a
portion of Land for an Indian farm within the limits of our own field: After
some deliberation it was carried unanimously that A portion of Land be
given them and that Said Land and Indians be undr the Supervission of
R. C. Allen [head of the mission] as their head to conduct all thier affairs."[77]
Elsewhere, the missionaries carried their religious and acculturative message into the Indian camps: "Wendsday the 2 [April 1856] I went to the Indians incampment to Show + instruct the Indians how to plant their Corn
and other Garden Seeds."[78]

If Paiutes had indeed altered their own gardening techniques in conformity with the missionary preachings, they would perforce have consolidated their settlement pattern, located permanently along streams, and
ceased movements across the hinterlands, a desirable result in Mormon
eyes, since this would have freed land for non-Indian settlers. Even had Paiutes done this, however, much evidence indicates that the Mormons intended that Indian settlements should remain separate from their own.
In 1857 Brigham Young, president of the church, revealed his vision of continued multiethnic segregation in a letter to the head of the Santa Clara
mission:

*I shall be happy to learn that you have gathered a few more of the
scattered families on the upper waters of the Santa Clara, commonly
known by the name of "Little Jim's band" and had them in one convenient locality for farming and that you purpose building them an-*

other dam there[.] I am informed the distance is not very great from where you have your lower station on the same stream, and that there you have a fort to which you can flee, if necessary: indeed, it would be wisdom if you take your family to live in the lower fort, + go up to the upper farm when necessary.[79]

Missionaries were told that agriculture would enable Paiutes to become self-sufficient, since Mormons insistently described the native economy as producing only starvation and poverty, ignoring the fact that the Indians had lost their most productive food sites and best watered garden lands to Mormon seizures. Transient Ute warrior bands had drained nascent Mormon communities with their aggressive demands for food tribute. The church wanted to avoid any such extractive relationship with their permanent native neighbors adjoining the settlements. Paiute economic well-being would serve Mormon interests well, but only if they would do the work themselves, save their crops for themselves and their families, and in fact farm in the manner of independent yeoman entrepreneurs.

While settlers openly hired Paiutes to aid labor-intensive, initial construction, Brigham Young charged missionaries to do so in the name of acculturation: "in this and all other labor, on the dam +c., use every commendable measure to have the Indians work with you, indeed from the greater number of them, I would expect they would do the greater portion of the work, by this time they should begin to know, their own labor is productive of much good to themselves, in the increase of food and other comforts."[80] It must, of course, be pointed out that by committing time to labor on missionaries' projects for future agricultural production, Paiutes neglected daily hunting and gathering efforts of their own that produced food for immediate consumption.

Missionaries intended to change the Paiute economic base by furthering what they assumed was the new technology of irrigated agriculture, and they siphoned labor from native production tasks; a third leg of their economic plan was to establish a profitable Indian trade. In this, however, they were frustrated. The traditional Paiute economy was geared to subsistence production and allowed for little surplus, either for native needs or to support an expandable consumerism. Further, Mormons found few local products desirable for their own consumption, so by cultural definition Paiutes had "nothing to trade." Quite early the secretary of the Santa Clara mission reported with some embarrassment: "This should be our second report of monthly sales of Indian clothing: but we have sold none + there is no report. Perhaps it would be well to examine some of the causes of this 'dull trade.' . . . the many almost naked [Indians] we find on the Santa Clara + surrounding country have nothing to give in return for this clothing, at present, but they are very willing to work, and perhaps the days are not far distant when they will be taught + capable of producing more than they need to consume."[81]

In order to fulfill their political, economic, and religious functions as specialized intermediaries, missionaries were expected to learn "the Indian" language (there was assumed to be only one, Lamanite). Brigham Young charged the Santa Clara missionaries with "writing down a list of words, go with them where they go, live with them + when they rest let them live with you. . . . you will soon be able to teach them in their own language."[82] In the evenings, missionaries often drilled each other on these word lists.[83]

Nevertheless, actual religious preaching is not as prominent in the missionary records as one might expect. The Santa Clara mission recorded several orations to Paiutes on their Book of Mormon history, but there were far more discussions of a general nature, such as to "manifest to them, that we are their friends, and seek to do them good."[84] Intellectual discussions of deities were less often emphasized than were secular work ethics: "Inculcate upon them the habits of industry, cleanliness, and honesty, as well as the other principles of our holy religion," Brigham Young wrote.[85]

Indeed, missionaries did actively teach the work ethic and respect for Mormon private property rights; the moral precepts most often admonished were those against stealing. Missionaries even appealed to supernatural sanctions to reinforce the cultural values they wished to instill: "Jacob Hamblin told the Indians that if they did not quit stealing the time would come when God would punish them with a bad disease and they would die off like diseased sheep."[86] Indeed, there is some evidence that Paiutes saw missionaries, like their own shamans, as capable of either instilling disease or bringing relief from it.[87] Other Paiutes blamed settlers for their illnesses, directly through spiritual influences rather than indirectly through threats to their food supply: a headman on the Muddy in 1856 reportedly "had heard their was White men on their Land + this Child was groen warse. they Said the grate Spiret was mad becous they alowed white men to Com among them then Said if the Childe Dide that we was all to be kild."[88]

Frontier Mormons believed in the healing power of prayer, especially when performed by a circle of ordained males, accompanied by song, the laying on of hands, anointment with oil, and even speaking in tongues. These behaviors were instantly recognizable to Indians familiar with the ceremonial gestures of Paiute shamans, one of whose primary tasks was also to cure the sick. Mormons believed that a cure would be ineffective unless the patient had faith in the Mormon version of the deity. Therefore, they interpreted any cure to be de facto evidence of conversion. They sought out the sick and actively intervened in search of such proofs: "Many of these Indians I have preached the gospel to . . . have had faith enough to enjoy the gift of healing. . . . many of them have as much faith in the gift of healing as the [Mormon] elders have."[89] Paiutes were soon seeking out missionaries for cures and soliciting their blessings for the dying. The culturally distasteful task of burying the dead was soon shifted onto the willing missionaries.[90]

Missionaries convinced Paiutes that the ceremony of baptism itself had a healing function, which Young seized upon as a mechanism of native pacification and acculturation:

> As regards administering the ordinance of baptism to the Lamanites, I should do it by all means whenever they desire it. Tis true they are ignorant and necessarily have a very poor and imperfect understanding of our principles. Still they will have a still better chance to obtain a knowledge of them if they are baptized and confirmed. . . . I do know that those of them that were baptized in this vicinity and Sanpete have been influenced more or less by the good spirit and have oftentimes been restrained from their hostile excesses thereby.[91]

Long lists of initiates, probably entire camp groups, were baptized after only a few hours of religious instruction through imperfect translation. A typical service occurred on the lower Muddy River in 1855: "Bro[.] Allen + company have baptized about 230 of these Indians since they arrived a week ago." The scene was repeated at Las Vegas: "I preached a little to the Indians after which they went into the water + we baptized 54 of them into the church of Latter Day Saints."[92]

Headmen were specifically targeted for conversion. Young ordered, "Ordain such chiefs, head men, and such as are naturally good, obedient and humble, after having tried their faithfulness, to the Priesthood, as Elders, to preach the Gospel to others of their brethren."[93] In this way Tutsegavits, headman of a Santa Clara band, was in 1862 "preaching to a small band of Apaches [Walapais, sometimes called Walapai Apaches] on the east side of the Colorado, and spreading a good influence among them."[94]

Missionaries' language skills were used not only for religious discourse but also for political purposes, as missionaries mediated between the Mormon settlers and the natives during potential or actual troubles, large and

2. Mormon missionaries baptizing Southern Paiute men near St. George, 1875.
(Photographic Collections, Utah Historical Society, Salt Lake City.)

small. When the government surveyor, Gunnison, was killed in 1853, Brigham Young, in his guise of superintendent of Indian affairs, chose to send missionary Dimick Huntington to Kanosh to identify the killers and recover notes and instruments. Jacob Hamblin negotiated a separate peace for the Mormons with stock-raiding Navajos in 1871 under the very eyes of a federal agent. As late as 1895 Anthony Ivins, then involved in getting Shivwits recognized as a federal reservation, was sent to defuse tensions after a Mormon shot a Panguitch Paiute during a drunken holiday celebration.[95]

Young clearly articulated this political function of missionaries in his 1854 instructions to the Santa Clara mission:

> *If the brethren go amongst them, let them turn in + help the Indians in their work, and show that they feel an interest for them . . . and they will have more confidence in you, and your influence will be much greater over them. In this way we shall be able ultimately to control and govern them[.] [A]s it is now, whenever an excitement arises among them against the whites, they immediate[l]y become unapproachable and we find it difficult to get access to them at all[.]*
>
> *Now if our people were so well established in their confidence and friendship as to control and influence them + more or less, be with them all the time being in their midst at such times. Do you not see that all such excitements could be kept down + we should be able through this agency to have peace + control the natives if this policy could be carried into general effect.*[96]

Not only were missionaries charged to mediate between the institutionalized church and its members and the Paiutes, but they were also virtually the only bilingual individuals allowed by the central church authorities to serve non-Mormons as translators. That included federal officials, who rarely remained in the district long enough to gain even minimal knowledge of the native language. In 1855 an early federal Indian agent complained that "though there are many persons in the Territory who speak the Indian languages, but they are all nominated as missionaries, and I was forced to the humiliating necessity of imploring the clemency of His Excellency, Brigham Young, to permit one of them to remain with me."[97] Not until Paiutes themselves became fluent in English, through local employment and federal schools, did the church lose its monopoly over the interethnic language barrier.

Unlike most American frontiersmen, the Mormons were remarkably open to marriage across the interethnic boundary. Theologically ambiva-

lent, the Book of Mormon declared on the one hand that Paiutes, as Lamanites, were of the House of Israel and hence destined to be saved, while
on the other hand it dictated that their dark skin was a punishment for
heresy, a cause for religious abhorrence.[98] Pragmatically, intermarriage
could generate legitimized entrée to the native community and communication links that could be important during crises. Structurally, Mormon
polygyny accommodated these marriages without denying men more customary, intrafaith unions. Although he did not establish a general policy,
Brigham Young did approve a number of specific, polygynous interracial
marriages, most notably for Jacob Hamblin, Ira Hatch, Thales Haskell, and
Dudley Leavitt, not accidentally, all influential missionaries working with
Paiutes on the Santa Clara.[99] Such alliances required formal church authorization, for when John D. Lee, strongly connected to the upper religious hierarchy, took upon himself to marry an Indian woman, he was promptly
censured by the local church leadership.[100]

All but one of the interracial marriages recorded during the first two
decades in southern Utah were of Indian women to Mormon men; the reverse pairing, Paiute men acquiring non-Indian wives, was simply never
done. Paiutes did not fail to notice this selective directionality, reminiscent
of the systematic extraction of nubile Paiute women by Ute raiders, from
which their demographic sex ratio had not yet recovered. They were particularly sensitive to further loss of women to the newcomers.

One settler on the Muddy River explained that "as for the Squaws they
are very Skirs [scarce] they have but few among them and when there is one
among them that is old anif [enough] to merry they fight for her." Nevertheless, he casually proposed that when "there is a good looking young
Squaw up I shall Join the rough [and tumble?]. I think that one wood com
in good play to me now to Wash my Close + keep my Cabbin cleen when I
git one bilt."[101] The local headman, however, stoutly rejected such suits: "I
did not fetch a squaw home with me. . . . we could not git one if we wanted
one ever so bad. Father Hulit one of our bretern here actuley made an
atempt to git one he had leaf [leave] of Brigham [Young] he Ticked on a
younng Squaw and went to the Chief a bout her he would not concent he
sed he would not ask us for eny of our White Woman and he did not want
to give up eny of his Squaws[.]"[102] Over the next several years, sexual tensions in the area escalated, and Jacob Hamblin urged discretion: "When I
went down I told them that it was a dellicate matter for them to handle and
not to say any thing about it at present. But as they felt very impatient to
take squaws, the young bucks [Indians] had become very jealous of them
and waylaid them to shoot them."[103] Las Vegas elders were far more diplo-

matic than these hot-headed young Moapa men and offered a proposal that would deflect Mormon covetousness from their women: "they say they have no sisters to spare, but they say we ought to have some [women], and if we will only let them, they will take all the women that come here and bring them to us, that is, the travelers."[104] Curiously, one persistent Mohave explanation for their intertribal war of the late 1860s was Paiutes raiding for women to supply to Mormon men as polygynous wives.[105]

After military threats from Utes, Navajos, and other tribes ameliorated over the 1870s and local Paiutes maintained their generally friendly stance, the political motivation for Mormon men to make interracial marriages eased, and such marriages ceased. It had become clear that in the eyes of the Mormon community "the children of these Indian-white marriages carried a certain stigma or were at a disadvantage in their association with the whites."[106] Furthermore, not all Mormon men favored the idea of interracial marriages, even when sanctioned by church authorities; at least one man preferred suicide when ordered to undertake one. Descendants of intermarried missionary men often suppressed genealogical mention of the Indian wife or her ethnic origins.[107]

After the Walker War had determined who would control central Utah, in June 1857 all the Indian missions south of Fillmore were consolidated at Santa Clara under Jacob Hamblin. In the 1860s the Black Hawk War brought new threats from Navajos and Utes of the San Rafael country; Kanab was established directly between those two tribes as a mission. It was there Young sent Hamblin to negotiate with Navajos, resulting in his enigmatic presence at the signing of the 1871 federal treaty at Fort Defiance.[108] By 1880, the mission of Bluff, the first non-Indian village in southeastern Utah, was located exactly where Southern Utes, fleeing Colorado miners and cattlemen, were reviving old conflicts between Navajos and Paiutes in the San Juan Valley. As the tensions and fears of first settlement eased into the routine of occupation, however, the initial missionary zeal waned. Even Jacob Hamblin wrote in a fit of depression, "They [Paiutes] are in a very low, degraded condition indeed; loathsome + filthy beyond description. I have wished many times for the moment, that my lot was cast among a more cleanly people; where there could be found something desirable, something cheering to a person accustomed to a civilized life."[109] The location and sequence of church missions in Southern Paiute country showed that once permanent settlement had been achieved, Paiutes pacified, and Mormon control established, the missionizing effort was abandoned. This indicated that missionary involvement had been driven by political and economic considerations, rather than the theological ones proclaimed.

With the demise of the missionary appointments went most of Mormon interest in Paiutes for the remainder of the century.

Southern Paiutes who lived in the area now called Utah were profoundly affected by Mormon settlement. Unlike earlier explorers, fur trappers, and immigrants, Mormons came to stay. They arrived in large, organized groups, well mounted and well armed. Dedicated agriculturists, they rapidly diverted streams for irrigation, thus effectively controlling the entire area. They used their political control of the territorial government to push out Spanish influence, such as the slave traders. They tried to neutralize Ute power by gifts of food and awards of status to leading chiefs but nevertheless were faced with military resistance. By wrenching loose Ute dominance over Paiutes, they changed the balance of power in the region.

Paiutes, unlike Utes, did not form large groups under military leaders. Rather, they remained in small mobile hunting and gathering camp groups that dealt with Mormons on the local level. Headmen tried to form political alliances with Mormon leaders through the traditional techniques of visiting, exchanging gifts, and verbal support. In turn, the Mormons rewarded native leaders who spoke in favor of settlement. They encouraged Paiutes to rely on agriculture to a greater degree than they had traditionally done and to become sedentary at fixed "Indian farms," thereby abandoning the rest of the territory to Mormon use. They offered intermittent salaried labor as a substitute for the lost subsistence resources of that land. The church assigned missionaries, functionally specialized men, a free-roving ambassador class, to convert natives to their faith, as well as to negotiate the political interface with natives and to spearhead an acculturation program. In addition to efforts to alter general Paiute behavior, Mormons also tried systematically to remove selected individuals, children of both sexes who were bought and raised within Mormon households, and nubile women who were married and brought into the settlements. Otherwise, Paiutes remained socially remote from the new towns, even when those villages were established in close geographic proximity to prime traditional camping sites.

5

PAIUTES MEET MORMONS

The intercultural boundary in southern Utah had, of course, two sides. Not only did Mormon settlers hold views of Paiutes and take actions toward them, but so too did Paiutes have views of and take actions toward the newcomers. Because Euro-Americans held a virtual monopoly on the writing of records during this period, non-Indian actions were far better documented than were Paiute thoughts and behaviors. Nevertheless, it is important to attempt to unearth how Paiutes reacted to the changes that affected their world and, if possible, to understand why they did what they did. Like other people, their response was based on their previous knowledge of their world, the structure of their culture, and their experiences during that specific period.

Historians, like Mormon settlers and the general American nineteenth-century public, expected Paiute reaction to be predominantly hostile, violent, and military. Whether stated in the racist phraseology of the times, that "revenge was sweet and natural to the redman," or in the revisionist late-twentieth-century terminology of proud tribal resistance to invasion of native homelands, the fundamental assumption all too often made was that warfare and hatred were the unavoidable essence of interracial contact.[1] Yet strikingly, early Southern Paiute relationships involved remarkably little bloodshed. Incidents of Paiutes attacking non-Indians, told repeatedly in local oral histories, give the appearance of the anticipated Indian hostility but were in fact a very few events retold precisely because their rarity made them stand out in people's minds for generations.[2]

The first well-documented killing attributable to Paiutes was not of a Mormon at all but of a federal army officer, John Gunnison. Understanding that event requires some preliminary considerations of the federal presence and posture in what became a complex triadic relationship among Paiutes, Mormons, and national representatives. Although the federal government claimed sole control over relations with all Indian tribes, to the exclusion of states, territories, and private individuals, its involvement in Paiute affairs throughout the nineteenth century was minor and transitory. In fact, federal interests in Paiutes appeared often to be an outgrowth of the U.S. government's larger contest with the Mormon Church for power over the Utah territory.

Because of the Mormons' history of persecution and ideology as a "chosen people," Utah settlers aspired to autonomy. In 1849 they declared the nation of Deseret, which continued to maintain its separate legislature long after the territory of Utah was organized under the United States. Federal suspicions of insurrection and political opposition to polygyny and other unique Mormon cultural customs resulted in the U.S. army marching to the mountains overlooking Salt Lake City, which had been abandoned by the Mormons in anticipation of such military action, in 1857.[3] This event fueled an antifederalism that dominated Utah's politics for the remainder of the century, inevitably coloring Mormon attitudes toward federal Indian policy and Indian agents.

Brigham Young's presidency of the Mormon Church and the near universality of church membership among the population of the new Utah Territory made his appointment as governor in 1851 virtually inevitable. In the process he automatically became ex officio superintendent of Indian affairs, thus combining sectarian and political Indian offices. Federal policy presumed Indian agents would be assigned to tribes increasingly confined to reservations, where they could be taught American ideals, sedentary agriculture, and market commerce, goals compatible with Mormon programs. Nevertheless, federal agents were frustrated by the virtual monopoly of control church leaders held. The only non-Mormon among the first set of Indian agents, Jacob Holeman, complained to Washington about Young, his official superior: "No one will dare to oppose anything he may say or do. His power and influence is so great that no officer either of the Territory or the Government, who is a Mormon will dare to disobey his will."[4] He felt "but little can be done for the benefit of the Government or the Indians, under the present organization of the Indian department here."[5]

The agent who replaced Holeman reported what many travelers had already noticed, that Mormon Indian agents and settlers "either accidentally or purposely created a distinction in the minds of the Indian tribes of this Territory, between the Mormons and the people of the United States, that cannot act otherwise than prejudicial to the interests of the latter."[6] Gleefully, Utah folklore still recites the following incident, attributed to an unnamed "Indian chief" everywhere from Las Vegas to the San Juan country. During a Mormon church service, which often featured personal testimonies of faith, the Indian chief "delivered the following sermon: 'Mormon weino [*bueno*, Spanish for "good"]. Mormon tick-a-boo. Make-em water-ditch. Plant-em grain. Feed-em Indians. Mormon tick-a-boo. White man son of a bitch.'"[7] Sources frequently quote Utah Paiutes in the nineteenth century using "Mormoni" as a contrast term to "Mericats"; both of these terms clearly derive from English words and demarcate a conceptual distinction between Mormons and Americans. In contrast, Southern Paiutes living in Nevada, where Mormon settlement was far less influential, called Euro-Americans, whether Mormon or not, *hiko* or *hai-ko*, derived from the native color term for "white."[8]

Federal agents perceived this terminological distinction by Utah Paiutes to be a judgmental one. An army officer investigating potential wagon routes as well as Gunnison's murder explained: "Utah Indians inhabiting the Valleys of Salt Lake, Juab and Fillmore [Kanosh's territory] had been taught that the Mormons were a superior people to the Americans, and that the Americans were the natural enemies of the Indians, while the Mormons were their friends and allies. During my march, I found on the Santa Clara, Virgin, Muddy and Vegas Rivers [all major areas of Paiute concentration] several Warriors who had undergone the same tutelage."[9] Given the separatist tendencies of Mormons and their unauthorized State of Deseret, federal observers perceived courtship of Southern Paiutes by Mormon settlers to be antithetical to the interests of the national government and its citizen travelers. Utah's strategic location, pivotal to the major wagon routes to the West Coast, where gold had recently been discovered, made any recruitment of native mercenaries a major potential threat to national interests.

While non-Mormons were inclined to detect sectarian plotting in such native linguistic distinctions, one cannot overlook the very real difference in the appearance and motivations of the two groups from the Paiutes' perspective. Most settlers were in fact part of the Mormon organization and settled quickly and permanently in large groups. Non-Mormons were, for the most part, transients who had long-term interest neither in the area nor in its natives. These travelers had little reason to cultivate social or political relations with Southern Paiutes.

The distinction between Mormons and national government representatives was further confused when highly placed Mormons filled Indian offices. Non-Mormon Indian agents, suspicious of Mormon intentions and frustrated by sectarian cohesiveness, rarely stayed in Utah long. Then Young, in his roles of superintendent of Indian affairs and governor, assigned local replacements, who were invariably church members. Since he was also appointing Indian missionaries in his capacity as president of the Mormon Church, the distinction between these two classes of men became blurred in the eyes of both natives and settlers; in some cases, they were actually the same men. For instance, in March 1856 Young appointed John D. Lee, his own ceremonially adopted son and already a church Indian missionary, to fill the federal position of Indian farmer for the Paiutes near Cedar City. Young's quarterly accounts listed Lee as drawing a federal salary, as did Anson Call, who was both bishop of Fillmore and farmer for the Pahvants. The BIA central office never received any reports from either of these two men, although it did get regular correspondence from one Peter Boyce, the man Washington listed as farmer to the Pahvants at Corn Creek. Again in February 1852 Henry Lunt recorded in his journal, "At the afternoon's [church] meeting Bro. J. L. Smith [bishop of Cedar City] appointed me as Indian Agent at this point for him."[10] While Young, as governor and Indian superintendent (although not as church president), may have had authority to name Indian agents, surely subordinate churchmen did not.

When the federal government failed to respond to Young's repeated requests for relocation of Paiutes to the Sierra Nevada on the distant California border, he proceeded without authorization to establish three Indian agencies in July 1851. One was for Wakara's militarily important band of Utes, another was for Kanosh's favored group of Pahvants, and the third, based at the Mormon village of Parowan, was for the "southern Indians," presumably all the other Paiutes. The Pahvant subagency was apparently the same land deeded by the church to Kanosh in 1854 and also ambiguously cited as one of the Mormon Church's Indian farms, church-owned missions and demonstration agricultural farms. Other church Indian farms at Harmony and Santa Clara remained under missionary control, but in 1855 federal administration took over the Kanosh land as part of the Corn Creek reserve. Surveyed and mapped as a twelve-mile square, Corn Creek was operated as a demonstration farm by a federal employee for nine years; then, in response to political pressures, it was broken up and sold to local settlers.[11] Surely under such circumstances, Paiutes had reason to confuse Mormon and federal personnel, programs, and policies.

In addition to Indian reservations, treaties were the other cornerstone of relationships between the federal government and Indian tribes nationwide. While treaties often specified trade relations, jurisdictional rights, and third-party alliances, they were also the primary legal mechanism for transferring land title from native tribes to the federal government. That government then delegated title to territories and states or directly to citizens as homesteads. No treaties of any kind were ever finalized between Southern Paiutes and the federal government.

The Mormons, on the other hand, were eager to control land and proceeded independently. Local church leaders made agreements with Paiute headmen that were routinely called "treaties," even though these lacked the authority of law. For instance, the first missionaries who approached Las Vegas conscientiously recorded, "Shortly after we arrived here, we assembled all the chiefs, and made an agreement treaty with them for permission to make a settlement on their lands. We agreed to treat them well, and they were to observe the same conduct towards us, and with all white men."[12] Such agreements involved only nominal if any payments to a few individuals, but Mormons nonetheless chose to interpret them as conferring tribal sale of extensive land areas. Such agreements by private citizens were, of course, in direct violation of the federal Trade and Intercourse Acts, which declared that only the federal government could buy land from Indian tribes; hence they were neither legal nor binding.[13] Such verbal agreements may well have been the origin of the recurrent Paiute belief that they have Indian treaties whose promises have never been fulfilled.

It was in this context of Mormon-federal tension and the eclipse by Mormon Church personnel of routine federal mechanisms of dealing with tribes, such as reservation formation and treaty negotiation, that the first major act of violence between Paiutes and non-Indians occurred. In 1853 John Gunnison and seven of his men were reported killed by a group of mounted Indians along the Sevier River in the Ute-Paiute borderlands of Pahvant country. Gunnison's expedition had been searching for a railroad route to the West Coast.

Youthful headman Kanosh actively cooperated with investigators. Supported and advised by Young's missionary/translator, Dimick Huntington, the Pahvant headman promptly delivered the expedition's notes and survey instruments to the Mormon bishop at nearby Fillmore. Federal investigators took this and subsequent native statements about the attack as de facto proof of Paiute guilt. Kanosh is quoted as testifying that without reason itinerant immigrants from a passing wagon train had killed an Indian whose relatives then had sought revenge on the next white men passing through; they were not even of Kanosh's band, and he had been powerless to interfere with their anger when it fell on Gunnison. After being bribed with horses and following a year of negotiations with both federal and church authorities, Kanosh delivered to the territorial court six elderly men and one woman as the guilty parties, numbers carefully equal to the Gunnison party deaths minus one, for the Indian originally slain.[14]

A number of interesting features appear in this stubborn interethnic confrontation. From the Paiute standpoint, Kanosh was acting as a proper headman to mediate a dispute with outsiders and to mitigate its impact on his group. Native ideology, that individual adults made their own decisions and acted without requiring authorization from a headman, supports Kanosh's assertion that he had no role in the killings. As he had told the investigator, he was powerless. How and why Kanosh selected the particular seven people he handed over to the law, or what inducements he offered to them and their relatives, is unknown.

Both Mormon and federal investigators, however, assumed that a chief controlled his subordinates. Kanosh, therefore, must have approved the murder, was responsible, and shared in the guilt. An elaborate mystification of native band structure emerged from the discussion of this case, in which Kanosh was said to be the "head chief" of the "main band," and other subgroups of Pahvants had subchiefs who, like the Mormon hierarchy, were subject to his command, all of whom were ultimately subordinate to Wakara's band of mounted Utes. Eventually, blame was cast on "renegades" from one of these subbands at Sevier Lake, separated by extensive desert from both the Mormon settlement of Fillmore and Kanosh's camp. Thus the killers were explained both as rebels to Kanosh's just authority and as being a safely distant minor group. Kanosh, having provided scapegoats to federal justice and proved his utility to the settler's interests, was thus exonerated and able to remain the "best liked Indian in the country."[15]

Furthermore, investigators readily accepted the story of immigrant taunts and crimes as activating the "Indian rule of revenge on the next American party found on their grounds."[16] In so doing, they not only stereotyped a hypothetical Indian national character but also suggested that a sharp native distinction between locally resident Mormons and immigrant "Americans" had ossified within two years of initial settlement to such an extent that it was infallible, even when Indians were seething with presumed bloodlust.

Within a few years of Gunnison's much-publicized slaying came the most dramatic accusation against Paiutes for killing non-Indians, the so-called Mountain Meadows Massacre of September 1857. A wagon train of over 110 people was besieged for nearly a week by several hundred entrenched attackers, and all but a few children were killed. Despite immediate Mormon condemnation of Paiutes for the attack, rumors flew that this was not simply another Indian fight but, rather, that local Mormons, and perhaps even the centralized leadership, were fundamentally involved.[17] Eventually, John D. Lee, Brigham Young's agent in charge of the southern

Indian subagency and church missionary, was hanged for leading the attack.[18]

Amid an extremely well documented period, records contemporary to the event are peculiarly scant; nevertheless, later regional reminiscences are uniform to the point of litany. Like the prologue to the Gunnison murder, the wagon party is blamed for actions that justified native retribution, such as putting strychnine in springs near Kanosh's camp and giving poisoned beef to the same Indians for unstated reasons.[19] It is said that Pahvants, again of tangential subgroups and not under Kanosh's leadership, trailed the wagons south through 150 miles of isolated country before attacking them in the far southwestern corner of Utah, just out of sight of Jacob Hamblin's home. Predictably, Mormon sources assert that they tried to save the travelers; Indian statements, while admitting involvement, state that Mormons solicited their participation, provided all leadership, and seized all the booty.[20]

While the objective truth of the matter is probably impossible to establish, sole and autonomous Paiute responsibility appears unlikely for a number of reasons. First, the military strategy is totally uncharacteristic. The only other record of Paiutes digging trenches or engaging in long-term siege tactics against an organized wagon train was at the Colorado River crossing near Needles in August 1858. There, Chemehuevis joined Mohaves, a militaristic tribe that traditionally fought in tight, standing formations, to attack a train bogged down in the shoreline swamps in what was clearly a stock raid.[21] Second, the number of warriors needed for such an attack far exceeded the capacity of local Paiute bands. Secondary records suggest that Pahvants joined men from Beaver, Pinto, Santa Clara, and the Virgin River. No native interband political structure existed that could have recruited such an intercommunity party. Even had food and water sources in the Paiute northland been violated, these other bands had no cause of grievance; Paiute culture contained no obligation to risk one's life for harm done to nonrelatives. Again, either some unproven, universal, primordial Paiute hate of "Merikats" or federally suspected Mormon instigation was offered as motivation for the gathering of the military party.[22] Third, such a coordinated, multiband gathering and lengthy siege would have required an obedience to authority that did not exist in Paiute culture. Men's participation in any event was individually decided and endured only while their personal interests benefited. Fourth, September was the time of the piñon harvest, the busiest time in the Paiute year. It is unlikely that such a large number of men could take time off to march tens and even hundreds of miles from their home territories to take part in such an attack and in doing so risk scarcity and starvation for their families over the coming winter. Fifth, logistical support for such a large party on the march, during the siege, and for their return would require an unlikely level of surplus production. Other family members would have to feed these fighters over an extended period during which they were themselves unproductive. The Paiute economy in late summer could not have done this; it would have required external subsidy. On the whole, therefore, it seems clear that Southern Paiute culture, political structure, and economy could not have produced an action like the Mountain Meadows Massacre without Mormon stimulus and support.[23]

Unlike these high profile killings of Gunnison and the Mountain Meadows party, both noticeably of nonlocal non-Mormons, most Paiute conflicts with Mormon settlers occurred during the major regional intertribal disruptions between 1865 and 1870. Utes in central Utah were being crowded out by Mormon settlement in the northern Sevier River valley. Navajos were under attack by the U.S. military from the southeast and were raiding northwest into Utah for horses, meat, and supplies. Walapais and Yavapai Apaches in the plateaus of northern Arizona were in open warfare with federal cavalry units, driving Chemehuevis and southernmost Southern Paiutes to seek refuge with other bands to the northeast. From all directions except western Shoshone country, Paiutes viewed Indian people fighting for their lives and lands against encroaching whites. They themselves would not escape unscathed amid such turmoil.

Mormon settlers and their descendants viewed the hostilities of this period from a strictly localized perspective. Without causal motivation they saw raiders coming over their horizon to steal their livestock and previously amicable Paiute neighbors inexplicably becoming hostile. They activated militia, consolidated outlying settlements and herds, and built defensive forts. This reminiscence of the events at Panguitch exemplifies the panic that typified the settler reaction:

> [I]n 1864 the Piute tribe of Indian sometimes called Piedes became very hostile and the people had to build a Fort to protect themselves against Indian attacks. In the summer of 1866 they became so viole[n]t + hostile that a war with them became evident, and the settlers were led in the one historic battle (that was fought on Panguitch creek . . .). [This battle consisted of one white man wounded in the ribs and one Indian clubbed to death with an empty rifle.] they left their homes and crops standing and fled from the fear and torture of this band of Indians who were of a low dirty dishonest greedy

type. . . . The crops were left standing when the settlers fled in 1866 but strange to say the Indians never molested either crops or buildings.[24]

Observers who identified the raiders by tribe at all nearly uniformly asserted that these were Navajos, and direct evidence of Paiute guilt was extremely rare. Nevertheless, suspicion persisted that Paiutes, because they were Indians, only "pretended to be friendly."[25] One settler who actually lived along the trail to Navajo country wrote that "the Piedes and the Kibabots [Kaibab Paiutes] on this side of the Colorado river were the thieves, but he believed that the power behind the thrown [throne] was on the other side of the river."[26] The fact that the conflict ended with Navajo incarceration and negotiations by Jacob Hamblin on behalf of the Mormon Church and the federal military with Navajo leaders, not Paiutes, implied that the leadership and the motivation for the raids lay with that tribe. Settlers rarely sought any cause for this outburst of violence by Indians; it simply was their nature. In fact, Paiutes were being crowded not only by Mormons but also by Navajos driven to the northwest, especially into San Juan Paiute lands, by the Kit Carson campaign.

Ethnologists Pamela Bunte and Robert Franklin suggest that San Juan people might have joined forces with Navajos in joint raids into Mormon country.[27] However, Utah Paiutes realized by the mid-1860s that the Mormons were there to stay; prudence and long-term self-interest argued against open hostility. Furthermore, Navajos were traditional enemies who had, like Utes, raided Paiute communities over the last hundred years to supply the Santa Fe slave market. All across southern Utah Paiutes passed on to settlers warning of Navajo presence in order to avoid being themselves mistaken for the raiders; for instance, "Elder John R. Young brings word to St. George at the request of Tutsegavits [headman of one of the Santa Clara bands], that the Navajos are on this side of the Colorado, in considerable force, and in the vicinity of the head waters of the Rio Virgen."[28]

Local Paiutes also served as trackers and guides, retrieving lost stock for settlers. Although Mormons still distrusted Paiutes, they often recruited the local Indians, as in this incident west of St. George in 1868:

An old chief by the name of Beaver Dam Thomas was the head of the tribe which inhabited that part of the country. The trailers talked him into helping them chase the horse thieves. . . . let their Indian helpers have their guns and go on ahead. . . . finally brought back half of the animals. . . . The Indians told a story about how they got the animals from the Navajos but I don't think they had anything to do with it. Our men thought these Indians overtook the herd and brought back the part of them which the Navajos thought would sat- isfy us. We paid the ones who aided us.[29]

Paiutes probably helped recover animals both for reward and to assure whites of their innocence, fearing the violent retaliation of stock owners unable or too careless to tell Indians of one tribe from those of another.

The killing in 1866 of two Mormon ranchers, James Whitmore and Robert McIntyre, in the Kaibab area directly on the route to Navajo country via Crossing of the Fathers exacerbated suspicions of Paiute involvement in the stock raids. The initial raid may have been by Navajos or Navajos and Paiutes together, but a Paiute messenger was the one to bring word to the local settlement.[30] More than a week later, militiamen in pursuit of the slay- ers threatened to hang two Kaibab men caught killing a steer, but they "still persisted in declaring ignorance with what had been done. But, one said he had a dream that Navajos had been here."[31] Acting on information obtained from these Indians, the troop pursued and attacked a nearby camp of Pai- utes without preliminaries, killing between two and nine people. Entering the camp, the militia discovered some fresh sheepskins, clothing, and coin- age that were assumed to have belonged to the two missing ranchers and obtainable by Paiutes through no means other than murder. Whether by accident or from extracted information, the bodies of the two ranchers were found under the snow nearby. Church records related that "whilst those with the wagons were taking up the bodies, the five prisoners [from the attack on the camp] were brought to the place. . . . This meeting was too much for the brethren to stand, so they turned the prisoners loose and shot them on the ground where the murdered bodies lay."[32] Nevertheless, one of the militiamen's descendants revealed another version as told by his family, not of murders of passion but of a chillingly deliberate execution. After ex- plicit promises of safety to induce surrender,

just because they were Indians + Indians had done the mischief never thinking whether they were the guilty ones or not + now the Indians were questioned carefully + they told a Strange Story they said that while they were away on a hunt the Navajoes from over the river came + done the Killing + Stealing + they knew nothing of it until after it was done + now a council [of the posse] was called to decide what they Should [do] with these Indians . . . after much more delib- eration it was decided that they Should be Shot . . . the reason was it

was their land + home. . . . *they [the Paiutes] gathered around Seth
[the narrator's ancestor] clinging to him and pleading that their lives
might be spared . . . but all to no purpose they were shot down like
dogs after promising them their lives.*[33]

These Paiutes may have stumbled on the bodies or taken goods from
the unguarded ranch after the men's deaths, possibilities that seem not to
have occurred to the militiamen. The long-standing Paiute habit of gleaning castoff objects found on the desert, a practice the Mormons had never
protested as long as it was practiced against migrant wagon trains, was here
interpreted as irrefutable evidence of guilt of homicide. The Paiutes may
have simply traded Navajo raiders for the clothing, so highly desirable in
the depth of winter.[34] Similarly, local Indians could easily have discovered
the bodies by watching buzzards and then investigating the source of their
attraction. Although the evidence was indirect at best, the weary militia
standing over the weeks-old bodies incontrovertibly took vengeance
against the nearest available Indians at a level far in excess of the two original murders.

Belying the assumptions made of their guilt, Paiutes subsequently
warned outlying settlers of possible retaliation for that militia action; several camp groups moved toward settlements and voluntarily disarmed. A
month later, local headmen were still protesting Paiute innocence in the
murders, blaming Navajos.[35]

The other killing of Mormons attributed to Paiutes also occurred in
the Kaibab area. In the spring of 1866, the Berry brothers and their families
were traveling around the south end of the Buckskin Mountains, along the
trail to Navajo country, when they were attacked. Although none survived
to narrate details, regional folklore repeatedly asserts that one party of local
Paiutes secretly trailed the family for miles before killing them. Unsup-
ported legend, which could only serve to inflame settler hostility against
Paiutes, detailed that one of the men, tied to a wheel, was "forced to watch
them torture Isabel, who was an expectant mother," even specifying,
"They'd shout and yell and have a good time, and everytime one would hit
her, she'd scream."[36] Most narratives assumed that an inherent bloodthirsty
Indian character was sufficient explanation for these purported events, although one suggests that Berry may have brought it on himself when he
"kicked an Indian off from his place once, and the Piutes just ganged up for
revenge."[37] Unlike the more common stock-raiding incidents, or even the
McIntyre and Whitmore killings, all sources agree that the perpetrators of

the Berry deaths were Paiutes because a tribally identifiable Indian man or, again, a native family had been previously killed by the defenders.[38]

While detailed narratives abound on the Whitmore, McIntyre, and Berry slayings, records give only rare glimpses of what was converse and pervasive Mormon violence against Paiutes. An unusual surviving narrative by Quag-unt, a Kaibab man, told of a white raid on his camp during these years that orphaned him as a seven-year-old child.

> *When I was a little boy I lived in what you call House Rock Valley [between the Kaibab Plateau and the Grand Canyon]. . . . One evening two Indians came to our camp driving some cows that some Navajos had given them to pay for helping drive cattle over the Buckskin [Kaibab Plateau]. . . . Next morning about sun up some white men came close to our camp and began to shoot. Our men got their guns and started to shoot at the white men. My sister and myself ran and hid in the rocks. We hid all day and everything was very still. When we dared to come out we looked around and found all the Indians dead.*[39]

In other cases, settler records themselves describe more clandestine reaction to years of stock raids. One Kanab man narrated: "We found out it wasn't Navajoes doing this [raiding for stock]. We used to go and stay in the fort [at Kanab] and this old Indian would never leave until dusk. We had a business meeting just a few of us. We had a public milking corral and we went down there and dug a hole in the corral and when he came down we knocked him in the head and threw him in that hole and run the cows over it and we never had any more trouble."[40]

Frequently acting on suspicion rather than evidence, not only settlers but also the semi-official militia cavalierly killed Paiutes. In a typical sequence, after the Berry killings the Panguitch town militia head arbitrarily "ordered pickets to bring in all passing Indians for questioning." Two "strange" Indians resisted this sweep, and "a skirmish resulted in which one was killed and the other wounded." The militiaman then "decided to disarm the local Indians and surrounded one of their camps near Panguitch one morning before daylight and took their arms," and another Paiute was killed. Next day the militia raided another camp, where they killed two more natives and seized "many new arrows and a peck of new arrow heads."[41] Possession of this routine hunting gear was viewed as conclusively suspicious and adequate justification for the unmotivated killing of four people.

What was perhaps the largest intentional massacre of Paiutes occurred at Circleville in the Sevier River Valley in 1866.[42] The town was weakly fortified despite Utes from the north taking advantage of the regional unrest to raid for cattle the year before, raids they renewed in April. Two local Paiutes tried to mediate between the Mormons and Utes, but settlers attacked them because they appeared "nervous," and one was killed. Not long afterward, settlers of Fort Sanford a few miles north hastily rounded up an entire camp of Paiutes and then forcibly disarmed, warned, and released them. The next day, when the militia demanded nearby Paiutes come into Panguitch, the Indians justifiably refused. This the Mormons interpreted as "showing plainly that they were in league with the Utes, so the men attempted to disarm them. They showed fight."[43] One of the two Paiutes killed in this affray was a shaman and very likely a community leader. The rest of the camp was warned to stay within an area the whites designated.

These scuffles escalated tensions until the men of Circleville, suspicious now of Paiutes who had been living peacefully with them for years, arrested the entire camp on grounds that unknown Indians had been seen with them and that the Mormons feared possible collusion with hostile raiders. Paiute people often moved between bands to visit relatives or share resources during the spring harvest period, so the villagers' suspicions could well have been misguided. Nevertheless, the Paiute men were disarmed and imprisoned in a church building, separately from the women and children, who were held in a nearby cellar. One Paiute, perhaps trying to intimidate the Mormons, told of a grand alliance between Utes, Navajos, and Paiutes to drive out the settlers; his boasts only made the guards jumpier or perhaps defensively hostile. All the Indian men were gunned down, the later rationale being that the Indians had attempted a break for freedom, and the guards shot in self-defense.[44] Their subsequent actions, however, were clearly not. "The next consideration," a guard recalled, "was how to dispose of the squaws and papooses. Considering the exposed position we occupied and what had already been done it was considered necessary to dispatch everyone that could tell that tale. Three [of four] small children were saved and adopted by good families."[45] The women were brought up out of the cellar one by one, and their throats were cut.

Seventy years later, the descendant of one of these children explained how her family lost all contact with the Indian community after this event:

My Father was a full blood piute Indain[.] his parents were killed by the whites in the spring of 1866 in Circle Valley. . . . he has told my Mother that he knew how [they] killed his parents[.] they were taken

> *out of a cellar and killed. he was a little boy so they saved him and*
> *[James Allred, head of the Circleville militia] sold him or trated*
> *[traded] him for a horse to [P]eter Monsen of Spring City and when*
> *he was a young man he went with some folks to Castel Valley and lost*
> *all track of his people. But he was old enough to know and remember*
> *that he was a piute[.]*[46]

For ten years Paiutes had peacefully shared their country with Mormon settlers. Their cooperation in helping to retrieve stolen cattle was widely known and had been broadly and well documented, as were their frequent warnings to settlers. Paiutes even allowed themselves to be disarmed and incarcerated. Yet despite all this, Mormons continued to suspect Paiutes of collaboration if not active participation in the stock raids, apparently on no other evidence than the deep-rooted frontiersmen's belief that no Indians, no matter what their tribe or circumstances, could ever be anything but hostile. There is no way of telling how many Paiutes died during the five years of intensive stock raiding in southern Utah, nor is there any way of knowing if any or how many were indeed sympathizers, collaborators, or participants in these raids.

Paiutes, on the other hand, learned one sure lesson about their new Mormon neighbors during these years. Despite verbal declarations of religious brotherhood and proclamations of Indians' role in the millennium, Mormons were individually and organizationally capable and willing to flash into violent confrontation upon any perceived threat or slight and wreak havoc and death on the nearest Indian community, which usually meant a Paiute one. Paiutes learned that in violent confrontation with Mormons, they would lose. Outnumbered, noncompetitively armed, and without the economic substructure to sustain prolonged conflict, they had no hope of dislodging the organized white settlements so rapidly entrenched in all their best watered campsites.

Perhaps accepting this military inevitability or the short-term self-interest of alliance with powerful strangers, Paiutes chose an adaptive strategy of peaceful coexistence and remarkable cultural openness. They adopted those features from the novel Euro-American culture that they found pragmatically useful or judged not worth the cost of resistance if settlers should insist. At the same time, they maintained certain native cultural elements to which, by their very act of retention, they demonstrated their emotional attachment. Sometimes those indigenous culture traits were modified to fit the increasingly altered cultural context, and yet they continued to function in meaningful ways within a new multiethnic setting.

One central feature of traditional Paiute culture was the offering of
food and hospitality, tokens that defined and maintained social relations.
Kin expected to have food freely offered if they needed it, without having
specifically to request it; sharing was simply a function of human society,
what friends and relatives did for one another. Paiutes extended generosity,
appropriate in their culture, to early Mormons and explorers, with whom
the natives thereby showed their wish to establish human contact. Some
missionaries, for instance, "called at the 3 wickeups near the mouth of the
Santa Clara, they presented us with some porridge made from seed meal, +
some made of wheat, 'ope' wine, currants and berries all of which we par-
took + were thankful for the good feelings of these Indians towards us."[47]
Paiutes cared for sick whites left behind by their companions, brought
water to lost travelers, and led them to trails.[48]

Of course, natives assumed that such sharing would be reciprocated;
unilateral generosity was not a moral virtue, and relatives who took from
others without opening their own stores freely in return were seen as
greedy, stingy, and undesirable. When the Mormons arrived, proclaiming
their intention to be friends, Paiutes apparently assumed that the same
rules of human relations would apply to them. The conflicting cultural
interpretations of hospitality are clear in this account from the northeastern edge of Paiute country:

> *I was all alone. but with my 2 babys. . . . in the night the indians
> came 6 of them . . . tha [they] said get up you squaw and get us some
> sup[p]er and I was afraid of them. I gave them ther supper and took
> my babys and opend the doore and sad [sat] in the doore I scaird of
> them. . . . in the morin tha came again and orderd ther brakfast. . . .
> I cryed and one indan askd true if i was frade of them I told them I
> wanted my man to came home and tha said pritty soon he come you
> be on frade [unafraid] indain on [no] hurt you. you hipe wyano
> [heap* bueno] we heap liken you. and wen I lurned they could spak
> the naricken [American] language I was not so fraid of them.[49]

The Paiute expectation of open-handed reciprocity led immediately to
one of the major issues of interethnic conflict: Euro-American concepts of
private property, most obviously of land but also of field crops, household
items, and livestock. Like the Mormons, Paiutes farmed, and they agreed
that the labor a person expended to clear land as well as the investment in
seed and the time and effort to tend and harvest the fields made any resulting crops that person's property. They protested when their fields were

threatened. One morning in 1855, the missionaries at Santa Clara were awakened when "some Piedes came to our camp in a great rage saying that our horses had been eating up their wheat." Their claims for damages the agricultural colonists could understand, so "Bro. Steele settled the bill by giving a shirt some corn + flour, his horses having done the damages."[50] The Paiute farmers then tactfully offered to herd the horses for the missionaries, thereby protecting their own unfenced fields in the process.

On the other hand, Paiutes expected these personally owned crops to be shared freely with relatives and friends, not simply consumed alone. Perhaps taking missionary protestations of friendship at face value, Las Vegas Paiute women persistently entered the missionaries' fields but were driven out, "which miffed some of them very much."[51] Finally, in June 1856, when a frustrated missionary chased the women away, "[t]hey were not willing to go + he need[ed] some force such as pushing + some pulling by the hair being very mad which raised considerable excitement among them[.] They went off mad [t]hreatening to kill our cattle. . . . This morning the Indian Chief came in to have another talk[.] He did not want to hurt the Mormons. . . . He did not want to have the squaws hurt or their hair pulled."[52]

Paiutes were told firmly not to enter the field until after the missionaries had harvested the crop but were offered gleaning rights afterward, "at which proposal they were satisfied."[53] As permitted within their own political system, individual Paiutes refused to be bound by the headman's compromise, and standing crops remained a point of contention for years to come.

Paiutes borrowed tools and other personal items from one another, sometimes without asking, because everyone knew that the maker of the item owned it until she or he publicly gave it away. Paiutes very quickly learned the value Mormons placed on material items, because they sometimes offered a reward for finding lost, misplaced, or stolen goods. At the Santa Clara mission in 1854 "A. P. Hardy's knife dropped from the sheath, and one of them finding it came into camp, but concealed it. . . . Bror Hardy had promised some powder, but now being asked through our interpreter if he would give a shirt . . . he now consented to this higher bid, when lo! at once the honest but cunning Indian pulls the knife from his bosom telling us where he found it."[54]

At the Las Vegas mission the return of lost items had become such a specialization that the head of the priesthood "refused to give them anything and gave them to understand through the interpreter that they were not to be paid for doing right and remaining friendly."[55] Meanwhile, Brigham Young ordered the missionaries to do nothing that would "lead on to angry and hostile feelings at every little annoyance caused by their folly, theft, etc. They do not know any better and we should know better than to blame and seek to chastise them for their ignorance."[56] At the same time this letter was being read to the Indians, some boys were in the mission leader's house taking clothing and food. The Indians were chided by missionaries, and native headmen tried to forestall trouble; natives were barred from mission grounds, even chained, without much effect. Finally, the bishop's patience snapped, and he shouted that "he would shoot any Indians that were caught stealing."[57]

Questions of property fomented increasingly aggressive Mormon responses, even from missionaries charged with constructing amicable relationships with Paiutes. John D. Lee seized a Paiute accused of repeated theft,

> *jherk[ed him] down + bound hands + foot, + lashed on the Horse. I collected the Indians + told them that forbearance was no longer a virtue as he neither regarded good talk nor threats, but committed depredations boldly + repeatedly + that I now intended to fetter him hand + foot with Irons + keep him under guard untill the govenor [Brigham Young] Should say in what way he should be disposed off. Some at first objected. . . . Preached to them + told them that if they wished the Great Spirit + us to be their friends that they Must be ours + his, + Must not foster thieves Nor their stolen Property +c.[58]*

Even the moderate Jacob Hamblin related, "If anyone [of the Santa Clara Paiutes] stole, he either paid a price for what he had taken, or was stripped, tied to a tree and whipped, according to the magnitude of the offense. The Indians did the whipping, while I generally dictated the number and severity of the lashes."[59] A settler on the Muddy River was more blunt: "injuns killed a calf the other day we did em up and Blacksnaked [bullwhipped] em I ges they will know better next time made them sing Ki hi Ki hi they have ben good as little pigs since."[60]

Paiutes could not have missed the point. The Mormons repeated their assertion of private rights to property in abstract terms and reinforced their physical arguments with supernatural sanctions. After an interethnic feast hosted by the town of Parowan in 1854, the Paiute headman, Kanarrah,

> *owned that the Pah-eeds had sometimes stolen our cattle, but it was because they were very poor and very hungry, while we were very rich. . . . But they would not steal any more, but be always "tu-o-je*

tik-a boo"—very good, true friends. President [of the settlement] John C. L. Smith thought this a fine opportunity to inculcate moral- ity and industry and made them a speech. He told them that they should not steal or be lazy. If they did they would make the Great Spirit very angry and they would all die off until hardly any would be left. They should quit stealing and should work and be like the whites and instead of dying off they would live and increase and be- come numerous and wealthy.[61]

In the long run it was not property rights to crops and personal items that were the greatest issue of contention between Paiutes and Mormons but claims to livestock. Livestock were the Mormons' most valuable single possession, mechanisms for geographic movement and tools for agricul- tural production. Records are clear that Paiutes saw horses, cattle, and oxen not only as Mormon personal property but also as competitors for the seeds of grasses upon which they themselves depended for food. In April 1868, at the height of the native grass seed harvest season, a Mormon cattle drover taking cattle to southern California for sale was confronted near Kingston Spring on the western edge of Paiute territory: "The Indian leader spoke up: 'The country belongs to the Indians and not to the *hikos* [whites]. . . . It's Injun's water and Injun's grass. White man's cattle eat 'em all up.'"[62] He de- manded three head in compensation before letting the herdsman pass. When Mormon herds reached southeastern Utah in 1883, the Paiute re- sponse was the same. "Mike, the leader of the Piute gang strode over to their camp without a word, his hand menacingly on the stock of the heavy six- shooter on his hip. . . . Before long Mike had subdued his gang sufficiently for the Bluff [town] men to make an arrangement with them for the people of the Mission to put their cattle on the mountain in consideration of fifty dollars, a stipulated amount of flour, and some other things."[63]

More often than being compensated, Paiute protests were discounted, overruled, or simply ignored. Typically, in 1868, as Mormon settlement ex- panded up the Muddy River, natives

demanded that the land occupied by the "Mormons" be paid for. They appeared quite angry, had blackened faces and were armed with bows and arrows. . . . The fact that the brethren were all well armed appeared to pacify the Indians more than any argument. . . . The Indians on the Upper Muddy have some 20 acres of wheat in. They claimed it as their land. The stock of the new comers is running at large and it is highly probable that when this stock will damage the

Indians' wheat, difficulty will arise between the brethren and the na-
tives. . . . The Indians say they will take their squaws and papooses
over towards Pahranegat.[64]

Such withdrawal, a traditional way of dealing with trouble within Paiute communities, was a cultural pattern that, in the historic period, would cost Paiutes some of their best lands and make conquest easy for more aggressive Mormon settlers.

At other times the dislocation of Paiute bands was far from voluntary. During the hungriest time of late winter in 1866, a major stock raid agitated relations with Mormon settlers in the same area. The local Paiute camp, not involved in the raid, fled. A settler recalled, "We determined that they should not return again until they were sufficiently humbled to behave themselves. We knew that they could not sustain themselves any length of time out of the Muddy Valley." The headman, Captain Thomas, opened negotiations and declared that he and "Captain Rufus and other leading Indians were opposed to the stealing but they were unable to prevent it, they fled for fear that the Mormons would kill them." But he also admitted that his group had "been prevailed on" to aid the thieves who were from the north, where Paiutes were being pressed by mining operations. Those Paiutes had cheated them out of their fair share of the spoils and "left them to starve. He said that he and those with him had come to give themselves up, and we might do as we pleased with them, if we would only let the Indians come back to their homes. They were now in a starving condition." He was scolded and humiliated until "the tears ran down old 'Captain Thomas'[s]' cheeks . . . and they throw themselves upon our mercies." The settlers extracted labor as "a good wholesome chastisement for them" before the Paiutes returned to the valley.[65]

Sometimes Paiutes simply moved livestock off their seed-gathering grounds, but Mormons then presumed that they were stealing the animals and reacted unpredictably. Occasionally, as with small property items, they rewarded Paiutes for scouting out the stock, as in this case that occurred near Beaver in 1860: "[T]he Indians would steal his [father's] horses, about once a week, he would hunt for them . . . finally an Indian would come to our place and say, 'I know where horses me bring back if you make a pile of Powder and lead so high.' . . . There was nothing my Father could do, but to Comply . . . they would never fail to bring them when they said they would, those Indians were the Piute Tribe."[66]

On the other hand, Mormons' accusations of stock theft often resulted in whippings. In the same year as the above report, a bit farther south near

St. George, settlers caught an accused cattle thief, and "I suppose his back paid the penalty, *as the custom is,* when they steal, to give them a genteel flogging, and let them live and learn, which is better than killing them, for their motto is 'blood for blood.' "[67] How "genteel" were such punishments is reflected in another report from the early 1860s: "An old Phavant had been found stealing from Samuel Hoyt's store and was to be given a certain number of lashes on his bare back. He was tied to the Liberty pole and the sheriff Byron Warner with a black whip proceeded to adminster thw [the] flogging. The Indian was stripped to the waist. . . . The squaws came from Chalk Creek with their cheeks full of water and amid crying squierted it on the welted ribs."[68] The man died as a result of this beating.

Fearful of indiscriminate settler retaliation against whatever camp group might be unluckily nearest when livestock were lost, Paiute headmen sometimes argued that it was safer for the native community to punish stock thieves themselves. This facet of native leadership was exemplified in 1866: "To-ish-obe, chief of the Muddy Indians, Thomas, Chief of the Indians near the California road, and another chief had met together and decided that two Indians who had stolen horses and cattle were outlaws. Co-quap, one of these had been taken prisoner, and was killed at St. Thomas."[69]

A few of the Mormons understood that this conflict over stock did not stem from innate Paiute avarice or sloth in raising their own food but from settlers' own intrusion into the country. Jacob Hamblin was a perceptive exception:

> *The great numbers of animals brought into the country by the settlers, soon devoured most of the vegetation that had produced nutritious seeds, on which the Indians had been accustomed to subsist. When, at the proper season of the year, the natives resorted to these places to gather seeds, they found they had been destroyed by cattle. . . . Those who have caused these troubles have not realized the situation. . . . Lank hunger and other influences have caused them to commit many depredations. When our people have retaliated, the unoffending have almost invariably been the ones to suffer. . . . This has driven those who were before well disposed, to desperation.*[70]

As early as 1854 in the hills above St. George, a headman voiced the same analysis as Hamblin: "The Mormons are using the water in Pine Valley. You said they would not use it there, only for cutting pine logs. We once could feed our children on Rabbits when they were hungry. Now there are no rabbits for us."[71] Paiutes were undoubtedly desperate as they saw control over their food and water and the very land itself slipping away from them.

That pace of land loss escalated rapidly. The end of active warfare against Navajos and Utes in the early 1870s made the backcountry safe for lone non-Indian herdsmen. Completion of the transcontinental railroad in 1869 made shipment of cattle to eastern markets both possible and profitable. Mormon stock raising expanded rapidly, even to the point of environmental degradation, destroying the very grasses upon which both the livestock industry and Paiute subsistence depended. By 1880 "there was not a single locality west of the Wasatch Mountains from Cache Valley to the basin of the Virgin River that did not exhibit effects of overstocking."[72] Ten years later early tax censuses revealed 400,000 head of cattle grazing the open ranges of Utah, in addition to half a million sheep and uncounted horses. Paiutes who had themselves previous subsisted on the rich seeds of those same grasslands had irrevocably lost their economic base and were forced into other means of livelihood through wage labor for the very settlers who had seized control of their country.

Over the first two decades of Mormon settlement, Paiutes began to distinguish between the behavior of different groups of white men who came among them, in some areas even linguistically demarcating Mormons from other Americans. They had little contact with official representatives of the larger national structure, even with that branch of the bureaucracy that specialized in Indian affairs. No treaties were formalized. A tiny area in Pahvant territory was set up briefly as a reservation, but few Paiutes lived there. Most remained in their traditional band lands, increasingly in daily and direct contact with Mormon towns.

Paiutes were noticeably tolerant of the newcomers among them. Curiously, the two incidents best known, the killing of Gunnison and the Mountain Meadows Massacre, were both of non-Mormons and were far from unambiguous interweavings of complex tensions between Paiute, Mormon, federal, and other interests. Paiutes rarely killed local Mormons, despite the more numerous, constant, and almost casual violences done against them by settlers. Similarly, Paiutes appeared curious about the new culture, especially of technological elements; perhaps their expropriations, the theft that irritated Mormons so much, can even be seen as an expression of their attraction to and open acceptance of these novel cultural items.

Livestock, however, became perhaps the most serious and long-term problem Paiutes had with the settlers, other than the obvious and related permanent seizure of land. Horses, cattle, and other grazing animals ate the plants that grew the seeds so critical to traditional Paiute summer subsistence. As those other foods became increasingly scarce, grazed off, or declared off limits as settlers guarded stock, that livestock itself became an attractive, large-scale food substitute. Mormons defended personal property rights in these freely wandering animals to the point of organized and lethal violence. In so doing, they increasingly demanded that Paiutes submit to Euro-American legal definitions and settler authority structures. Paiutes found those demands enforced with threats, whips, and eventually guns.

6

THE MILITARY,
MINERS, AND MOAPA

Just as trappers affected Paiutes in a way different from that of either immigrants or Mormon settlers, the military, individual miners, and bureaucrats each had an impact on Southern Paiutes in particular ways. Unlike many tribes of native North America, Paiutes never faced officially sanctioned military conquest or occupation. Although they met frequent violence at the hands of Euro-Americans, that violence came from local militia or vigilante posses of settlers, men perhaps actually more hostile to natives than were professional soldiers simply because they stood to gain personally from Indian dislocation. Paiutes felt the backwash of Kit Carson's southwestern campaigns, which drove Navajos to raid Utah settlements. Other military actions against neighboring tribes also altered Paiute relationships with those Indians, but the U.S. military had little presence in Paiutes' own country during the late nineteenth century, and that very tangentially.

Miners, like trappers and settlers, wanted to profit from specific resources of Paiute territory. Unlike Mormons, however, prospectors were neither driven nor restrained by religious dictates. Also unlike the communal agriculturists, miners coveted hard rock outcrops rather than well-watered valleys. Because a major geological boundary virtually coincided with the Utah-Nevada border, and because the Mormon Church forbade its adherents to engage in mining, areas of Mormon settlement were essentially segregated from secular mining towns, and yet both sectors cross-cut traditional Southern Paiute territory. Mining therefore affected Paiute society and history both in different ways and in different places than did Mormon settlement.[1]

A third group intruding into Paiute territory in the late nineteenth century was, like the army, a federal institution—the Bureau of Indian Affairs. It made its first tentative efforts to regulate land title for Paiutes when it declared a reservation at Moapa in extreme southern Nevada but otherwise had little impact on Paiute lives until after the turn of the century.

Long before the actual arrival of Euro-Americans into Paiute country, non-Indian military actions had caused changes in their relationships with nearby tribes. Spanish seizure of southern California intensified the existing conflicts among Yuman-speaking tribes in the Colorado River Valley. Ultimately, perhaps as early as 1828 or as late as the 1840s, the Mohaves allied with Quechans to drive several smaller tribes off the Colorado into tributary valleys.[2] This opened a territory downstream from the Mohaves into which the Chemehuevi band of Southern Paiutes relocated from the Mojave Desert.[3] Mohave tradition relates how they magnanimously allowed their poorer neighbors to occupy the Chemehuevi Valley and to plant cornfields along the western shore and on the lush, seasonally flooded Cottonwood Island. Not unexpectedly, Chemehuevi oral history recalls their own role as more decisive and active.[4]

For years thereafter Chemehuevis visited, traded, and intermarried with Mohaves, borrowing culture traits that then distinguished them from other Southern Paiute bands. In their favorable riverine habitat they expanded their cultivated crops. Their mythology took on the almost map-like, place-specific character of Mohave tales. They learned Mohave styles of battlefield warfare and adopted such weaponry as the "potato masher" war club.[5]

But outside their valley, steamboats probed the lower Colorado, the U.S. army experimented with camels to explore the desert for railroad routes, and gold was found in California. Just before the Civil War, the military mapped a wagon route across central Arizona to ford the Colorado in Mohave country, where the city of Needles was later built. There in 1858 allied Mohaves and Chemehuevis, armed with bows and arrows, raided livestock from an immigrant party.[6] The army response expressed the attitude and policy that would dominate military relationships with the Chemehuevis for years:

> [Y]ou will march against the Mohaves and Pai-Utes who lately opposed your reconnaissance. These tribes, and all others who may assume a hostile attitude, must be brought to submission. . . . There must be no opposition by the Indians to the establishment of posts or roads in and through their country, when and where the government chooses; the property and lives of whites traveling through their country must be secure.
>
> If . . . Pai-Utes decline the combat, then . . . demand the surren-

der of the chiefs who made the attack on your party, and hostages for
their future conduct, or tell them you will lay waste their fields; and
that the troops to be stationed on the river will not permit them here-
after to cultivate their lands in peace.[7]

The army built Fort Mohave just above the Chemehuevis on the eastern
bank of the ford. Several Mohave leaders were killed while incarcerated by
the army, and men sufficiently awed by American power were appointed as
"chiefs" in their place, although many Mohaves refused to recognize their
authority.[8]

While the Civil War drew the military elsewhere, miners discovered
gold at La Paz downriver from the Chemehuevis and at Prescott to the east.
Non-Indian cattlemen pressured Yavapais and Walapais on the plateaus
across the river, and farther eastward Apaches threatened mining expansion. In 1863 the Indian agent for Arizona Territory, trying to forestall a
united regional native resistance, called a conference of representatives of
all the Colorado River tribes, including both Chemehuevis and the cooperative Mohave faction.[9] He negotiated an agreement, never approved by
Congress and hence not recognized as a legal treaty in American eyes, that
allied the Colorado River tribes to the United States against the Apaches. He
also won guarantees that travelers through the region would be free of attack, specifically, "that as mining and prospecting for mines brings Americans in lonely and isolated places in small parties they shall be protected to
the utmost—the main object of their Treaty being to promote the commerce in safety between the before-mentioned Tribes and the Americans."[10] Two years later the BIA established the Colorado River Reservation
on the eastern shore below Parker with the idea that all the tribes of the valley would congregate there.[11]

During that same year of 1865 warfare broke open the relationship between Mohaves and Chemehuevis. Why this happened at this particular
time is unclear, but it may well have been because Mohaves' power was reduced by military occupation and factional division that impeded their
ability to form political consensus. Chemehuevis, still relatively free, attacked; Mohaves pushed some of them back westward into Cahuilla country, but their efforts to drive others north of Cottonwood Island were less
successful. Chemehuevis had returned to the western shore of the Colorado
by 1867; whether they had been driven by American campaigns to clear Indians from southern California or lured by Indian agents eager to expand
their jurisdictions is uncertain.[12]

Despite attempts by Indian agents to broker an intertribal peace, Mohaves again pushed Chemehuevis off the river in 1869. Many fled northeast, and Mormons along the Muddy River thought that "the whole band of Chemehuaves are in our valley" the following winter.[13] A final intertribal battle erupted virtually under the walls of Fort Mohave itself the next spring. The small Chemehuevi camp groups held their own against the more populous and experienced Mohaves, in part because they willingly embraced guns and adjusted their attack strategies to maximize this advantage, while Mohaves stuck to more traditional technologies.[14]

The Mojave Desert was a land of generally tense interethnic relationships in the 1860s. Southern California newspapers reported attacks on freighters, prospectors, mail riders, and a few isolated ranchers by Indians, unidentified but presumed to be Paiutes because of the geographic location.[15] The officer sent to patrol the area declared that the "action of the Chimehuevas is warlike, and appearances indicate the necessity of placing a larger force in the field at an early day to operate against them."[16]

When the end of the Civil War made such an increase in manpower possible, four dozen soldiers were dispatched to keep communications open between field officers fighting Apaches in Arizona and California headquarters, patrolling the entire 150 miles of the Mojave Desert. In 1866 two soldiers were killed by Indians presumed to be Paiutes, and occasionally the desultory patrols had other brushes with natives. Paiutes apparently made only one effort to dislodge the four tiny military encampments but generally found it easier simply to evade the soldiers. In 1868 the mail contractor located a new route farther south that cost him less in stolen stock, so the military posts were withdrawn.[17] Thus direct military occupation of the territory of the "warlike Chemehuevas" fizzled out.

Meanwhile, Walapais, who lived on the high Arizona plateaus below the Grand Canyon, were being pressed by miners and settlers. They considered joining the ongoing Apache resistance and invited Chemehuevis to come along. That would have wedged the Chemehuevis' Mohave enemies, along with the army at Fort Mohave, between two hostile forces. The murder of Walapai leader Wauba Yuma in 1866 caused simmering regional hostility to erupt into open warfare.[18]

Miners, who wanted no disruption of their prospecting, adamantly demanded military action. The *San Bernardino Guardian* supported the war hysteria and derided efforts by the military out of Fort Mohave and the BIA to establish peace: "The troops, it appears, give him ["The Indian"] aid and comfort, instead of scalping him. As long as these wretches are permitted to come into military posts—are fed and protected, it is useless for white men to attempt to occupy any part of the country. As the military act at present, they are a drawback to the miners; prevent the opening up of the country, prospecting, repairing roads, and all the operations of settlers in frontier life."[19]

Prescott frantically petitioned the governor to "issue rations, arms and ammunition to civilians" out of army stores.[20] In response to pleas from "the important settlements at El Dorado canyon," ten troopers were detailed from Fort Mohave. They subsequently saw no action in the two years they guarded those miners, whose population gradually dwindled to two. A military inspector said, "Pi-Utes are ... friendly—make no disturbances."[21] Six soldiers also guarded three white men at Las Vegas Ranch, the owner of which was not incidentally a member of the Arizona territorial legislature. Over these troopers' two-year term of duty the only contact they had with Paiutes was when they hired a man to track one of the army's own deserters.[22]

The main fort saw slightly more activity than did these outlying encampments. In 1867 the fort commander took a Paiute headman, ostensibly as a guide, on his Walapai campaign but candidly reported that this was to "get them in hostility with the Hualapais, whose Country adjoins theirs, separated by the Colorado River, and that I wanted them to know the strength of my Command and how much better it was to be at peace than at War."[23] Apparently he was successful, for sixty Paiute men soon appeared at Fort Mohave to say they would not join the Walapais. Distrusting their promises, for the next year he kept several of these men as hostages "responsible for depredations of any kind committed by any one of his band."[24] The *Prescott Miner* announced this as "Indians Surrendered—Since the late battle with the Hualapaies, the Pah Utes are coming in to save their scalps."[25] Despite such American claims of military supremacy, the Paiutes refused to live on the newly established Colorado River Reservation; they were still actively fighting the Mohaves, and the reserve was in Mohave traditional territory.

Other than a promptly aborted attempt to hire Moapa Paiutes as military scouts against Apaches,[26] these few brief incidents constitute the entire Southern Paiute contact with the United States army. No battles were fought. Paiute territory was never occupied, and no forts were built there. The army never forced Paiutes onto reservations. Whatever short-lived military presence they felt was geographically tangential to the main Paiute territory, restricted essentially to the Chemehuevi areas of the Colorado River Valley and its access routes. Army interest in Paiutes appears to have grown out of campaigns against the Walapais, Apaches, and other Arizona tribes; from concern over supply lines and communications links; and from preemptive obstruction of developing intertribal alliances. The occasional skirmishes Paiutes had with army patrols resulted in few deaths and were minor compared to the far greater carnage inflicted unofficially by citizen settlers. Southern Paiutes' experience with the military was apparently not harrowing.

Furthermore, this minor military contact followed settlement by a decade; it was not a mechanism of conquest to clear land for non-Indian occupation. Mormons in the Utah portion of Paiute territory had intentionally avoided the federal military; unlike the more common western pattern of settler-military alliance against natives, Mormons held the federal government anathema for reasons that related to their own cultural history. The conquest of Southern Paiute country was accomplished by local settler groups in both Mormon Utah and non-Mormon Nevada; the military played a very small role indeed.

Miners were a distinctive Euro-American population moving into Southern Paiute territory in the late nineteenth century, and their influence was both more extensive and longer-lasting than that of the military. Like Mormon settlers, miners wanted resources from the land. Unlike the Mormons, who built an economy based on irrigation agriculture in Utah, Nevada's settlers built an economy on hard-rock mining. The Comstock Lode was discovered far to the north in 1859, and its wealth bought Nevada territorial status two years later. Strips of Utah were whittled off in 1862 and again four years later and added to Nevada. Finally, in 1867 Clark County was separated from the Arizona Territory, and the "funnel shape" of Nevada was completed south to the Colorado River, encompassing a substantial portion of Southern Paiute lands. Silver wealth and Civil War politics got Nevada statehood in 1864, long before its agricultural Mormon neighbor, Utah, which had to wait until 1896.[27]

Nevada's mineral ores were chemically complex and demanded much milling and processing to release the silver, copper, and other minerals they contained. It was not the country for a lone man with a mule and a gold pan to strike it rich. Nevada sprouted massive underground tunnels shored up with heavy timbers, huge smelting plants powered by wood and charcoal, and flumes carrying water miles overland from stream to mill. All this was financed by huge corporations whose fortunes had been made earlier in the California gold fields. An independent prospector still hoped to discover a new strike but to sell out to investors rather than work it himself. The real labor would be done by company employees, paid a salary but without a share or interest in the profits. Once a corporation bought rights to a promising site it imported the entire structure of mine and smelter en masse; a company town of five or six thousand men would erupt within weeks around the tunnel's mouth. If the ore held out, it could become a permanent town; if not, it was abandoned just as quickly as it had appeared in a fluctuating, boom-bust cycle that left ghost towns littered all over the Nevada landscape.

The first such mining town built in Southern Paiute territory was Pioche, located in 1864 in the hills seventy miles north of Moapa. As typical of Nevada mining towns, by 1870 men outnumbered women ten to one, and, out of a thousand people, there were only forty-two families.[28] There were, however, two stamp mills, thirty-two houses of prostitution, and seventy-two saloons.[29] Despite initial technical difficulties, $5.5 million worth of silver and other minerals were produced in the first eight years, and the non-Indian population grew to over five thousand.[30] Despite subsequent decline, Pioche became the Clark County seat and remained the leading town in southern Nevada until the railroad village of Las Vegas superseded it in the early twentieth century.

Restless prospectors from Pioche showed samples of the kinds of rock they sought to Paiutes and hired Indians to guide them to similar outcrops, plumbing natives' intimate knowledge of the landscape in hopes of striking it rich.[31] Indeed, Pioche's own mother lode had been revealed by a Paiute guide to a Mormon missionary. This practice often released the veins of dominance and violence that ran throughout Paiute interrelationships with miners. For instance, in 1874 a pair of miners left town with two Indians "in search of a quartz ledge which the elder Indian informed Newton and Stevens he could show them."[32] Disappointed by the rock, they headed back, but the Indian guide lagged behind, complaining of illness. When the Indian got up in the middle of the night, the suspicious miners felt "satisfied of his evil intentions and feeling certain that he had been playing possum on them for the purpose of getting some advantage, fired several shots at him, three of which entered his body and one struck him in the head. He fell dead directly after the firing commenced, and the Indian boy ran off." The newspaper described this as an "adventure" and mused that the Indian "bore a bad character"; the community considered it a justified homicide. Scouting with prospectors was not only dangerous, but it also brought Paiutes only the short-term advantage of a few days' employment; in the long run, mineral discoveries brought more miners into their country.

Although miners willingly took advantage of Paiutes' geographic expertise, they were unwilling to tolerate any native resistance to prospectors, on whom the prosperity of all mining towns ultimately depended. Any time prospectors in the countryside were threatened, robbed, or killed, their fellows from the towns lashed out with uninhibited violence. The territorial capital, Carson City, was 450 miles northwest of Pioche, so, like other mining towns, it was essentially self-governing. Territorial law officers rarely visited this remote corner, and more rarely still did federal marshals. Civil and criminal law was often handled communally through self-appointed vigilante gangs, especially when it came to Indians.

Because of the nature of their business, prospectors often traveled alone or in pairs, not only across the established trails but also cross-country into every hillside and canyon. Although Paiutes sometimes merely watched,[33] at other times miners' panic was well founded. These Indians had long been in the habit of sniping at lone travelers along the immigrant route, and they continued to threaten prospectors. While prospectors did succumb to water shortage and horse-back accidents, in nearly all cases of death or injury Paiutes were blamed, and miners rode against the nearest Indian camp in retaliation. Although the groups of vigilante miners were less highly structured than parties of Mormons who also attacked Paiutes, the end result was the same. Mormons tended to overlay their attacks with religious pronouncements, while miners were overtly hostile to Indians. Whether these differences resulted in a greater or lesser proportion of natives killed in the mining areas than in Utah cannot be determined.

Paiutes were certainly killed. In a typical incident, a prospector named Rogers was killed west of Pioche. Three weeks later a Paiute named Okus arrived wearing Rogers's clothes. Fearful Paiutes in the Muddy River Valley "pulled up their wheat, some 30 acres and have left for the mountains."[34] Mormon settlers in Panaca, a town between the Muddy and Pioche, captured Okus, and he reportedly confessed. Fifteen armed miners swarmed in "to take vengeance on the Mormons for suffering their friend [Rogers] to be killed by the Danites."[35] Persuaded by the settlers that "it was an Indian murder," the miners dragged Okus behind a horse for ten miles with a chain around his neck, after which he implicated two other men. The miners then tracked Paiutes from an abandoned camp for six further miles, "came upon the Indians, three men, and two women and some children; they killed the men letting the women and children go. Two of these men proved [after the fact] to be the ones indicated by Okus[.] The others had borne good characters; but . . . all shot their arrows very wickedly at the company."[36] Okus was then lynched without trial.

Another time, Indians were murdered in revenge for the deaths of miners who were in fact quite alive. In 1874 a family left Bullionville, near Pioche, to head for the new strikes in Panamint Valley, two hundred miles west. After a few weeks, rumors of their "assassination" by Indians began to circulate, and a local headman, who denied knowing anything about such an attack, was jailed. Federal troops were requested as the local newspaper screamed for immediate action.

> *We think a party should be at once organized to visit the region of the Muddy [the reservation recently established to the south] and ascertain to a certainty the truth or falsity of the terrible rumor. . . . there is every reason to believe that many solitary travelers have fallen victims to the lust for blood which is inborn in Indian nature. Knowing these things, we think it is about time that a measure of retribution should be dealt out to these murdering wretches, the severity of which will give them a lively fear of the vengeance of the whites. We therefore would advocate the immediate organization of an expedition to scour the Muddy country, ascertain the whereabouts of the Castera party, and after that matter has been cleared up then they should turn their attention to the arrest and punishment of those who attacked the Honan [an earlier] party. They are said to be a band of four or five renegade Indians headed by Tempiute Bill, who is notorious for many rascalities, and strongly suspected of other murders.*[37]

Federal troops were sent up from Las Vegas, but a local deputy captured Tempiute Bill. Then "a crowd of men came to the mill from Hiko [another nearby mining town] and demanded the prisoner. . . . the citizens were not to be denied, they were in dead earnest, and in no mood for trifling, and perforce [the deputy] had to give way to superior force."[38] The troop commander took no action. A series of confessions were coerced from Tempiute Bill, during which he was shot in the foot, and he implicated a local man called Johnny.

> *[H]earing that "Johnny" was at the camp in the valley, a number of citizens went down and surrounded the camp. When "Johnny" found that escape was cut off, he went for his gun, but the citizens were too quick for him, and a general melee followed participated in by all the Indians in the camp. The citizens made but short work of them. The time for forbearance was gone by. The result was that some seven or eight Indians were killed; the rest saved themselves by flight. Among the slain was "Johnny," who seemed while living to have been actuated with peculiar animosity against the whites, and took every opportunity of gratifying it by murdering every solitary straggler that might fall in his power. These bloodthirsty savages have had thus a lesson taught them that it is probable the survivors*

*will not readily forget, and for a time, at any rate, will keep from im-
bruing their murderous hands in the blood of the unprotected prospector and traveler. Mob violence we at all times deprecate, but there
are things and occasions when it seems to be justifiable.*[39]

Posthumously, Johnny was declared guilty; Tempiute Bill and another
headman were hanged out of a second-story window without trial. At least
six other Paiutes had been killed in "revenge." All this had happened two
weeks *after* a letter had arrived from the miner family, whose "assassination" had initiated this bloodbath, announcing their safe arrival in San Bernardino. Nevertheless, the editor found the miners' actions "justifiable,"
and the commander of the federal troops reported the killings as "of the ordinary kind that happens on the frontier."[40]

Despite miners' proven violence, Paiutes chose to live in every boom-
town from Ivanpah in the Mojave Desert, through Pahrump northwest of
Las Vegas and El Dorado to its east, to Pioche's suburban mill town of Bullionville. By 1883 the Indian agent estimated that only seventeen of two hundred Chemehuevis lived on the Colorado River Reservation: "the balance
are scattered over the Territory and California working in mines and
Mills."[41] Unlike the miners, these Paiutes had families; they brought women
and probably also children into towns, although sources very rarely mentioned the latter. Paiutes built rather traditional houses that miners called
"wickiups" in separate communities half a mile or so outside town.[42] As
the various mining towns foundered and died, the Indian population "left
for better areas when the miners departed."[43] Paiutes soon found towns a
sufficiently secure environment in which to hold gatherings called "fandangos" by local non-Indians. These resembled precontact piñon harvest
festivals but were now held at various times of the year just for socializing
or for memorial "cries" for the dead.[44]

Both Paiute men and women worked as day laborers at tasks segregated according to Euro-American ideals of the proper sexual division of
labor. Paiute men supplied the support services that miners were too busy
striking it rich to provide for themselves; they chopped firewood, built
roads, manually cut grass for hay, and tended livestock for freight companies.[45] Women found employment even more easily in the heavily male
dominant, woman short mining towns. They performed the manual tasks
of surrogate wives, preeminently washing clothes and cleaning houses.
They did not apparently cook food, however, either privately or in restau-
rants, nor were they employed by the numerous bordellos. They did do
heavy labor never expected of the few Euro-American women, such as car-

rying water from distant sources to the white miners in the pits, just as in farming areas they worked the harvest fields.[46] As early as 1872 a federal explorer said of Paiutes, "From the friendly Indians the ranchmen and miners get more or less assistance in and around their farms and working in the mines and as messengers; in this way they greatly facilitate the early development in this section."[47] Paiutes contributed significantly to the early Nevada economy, doing virtually every kind of work except that very wellspring of Euro-American wealth, mining itself.

Mining companies and other townsmen hired Indians because their labor could be had more cheaply than that of Euro-Americans. Owners of the major mine at Ivanpah explained proudly to their stockholders in 1870, "White labor can be obtained in this region at about $60 per month . . . Indian labor can be had at $15 per month, with rations costing 50 cents per day."[48] Newspaper accounts show the standard Paiute wage in Pioche remained fifty cents per day throughout the nineteenth century. Shortly thereafter, Las Vegas ranchers began paying Indian workers between fifty cents and a dollar a day, still well below the salary of non-Indian hands.[49]

Although Paiutes lived alongside them, miners seemed to know very little about Paiute culture and to have narrowly limited interpersonal contacts with them. Newspapers reported about Indians in town—fights and squabbles, labor disputes, crimes, and even rapes of Indian women by miners. Many such stories emphasized conflict among natives or between Paiutes and non-Indians. Few if any stories described everyday life or routine events. Unlike Mormon sources, the Nevada newspapers recorded a number of Paiutes sick and dying, left alone by their relatives, especially during 1873.[50] In over 150 articles in the Pioche papers before the turn of the century, not a single one dealt with events that occurred in the "Indian Village"; only Indian behaviors on Euro-American turf were observed and deemed worthy of report. Almost universally, writers spoke simply of "Indians," failing to distinguish between Paiutes and Shoshones, who did retain separate camp groups at the town that mushroomed up along their intertribal border.

Mining town sources often overtly misunderstood native customs. Once, when a woman was killed, her death was asserted to be the "Piute custom" in cases of marital infidelity.[51] Further, town-dwelling Indians were openly derided. Women were always referred to as "squaws" and men usually as "bucks." Their behavior was suggested to be genetically controlled, as when marital customs were described as the "mating season of the Indians."[52] Indian men were said to be driven by lust, as when the reason for a street fight was explained: "from what we could learn there was a woman (a squaw), *as there always is*, at the bottom of it."[53] Paiute hostility to Euro-Americans was frequently attributed to "Indian nature" rather than any genuine grievance or damage from political and economic displacement.[54] Indians who were seen as fearsome savages when encountered in the countryside suddenly were less than serious actors in town, objects of ridicule, becoming merely "a buck with a dingy rooster feather decorating his greasy old slouch hat."[55] Newspaper accounts disclose that such descriptive devices were also reflected in actions, as time after time miners were reported standing at the sidelines of Indian activities and laughing or interfering freely whenever they chose. Paiutes certainly did not control and apparently did not act as equal participants in interethnic social contacts within Nevada mining towns.

Paiutes must have obtained some benefits to make such segregation and unequal status tolerable, because they could have left and tried to survive through traditional techniques in the few remaining hinterland areas, despite the threat of periodic vigilante attacks. Some benefits were economic. Paiutes took wage labor to fill the void created in their subsistence cycle after Euro-Americans had usurped native food sources. An early Indian agent saw this expediency: "the Indians are out of grub and running all over the country hunting work where ever they can find it, when they can't get work they beg from the citizens any thing that is fit to eat."[56] Many Paiutes constructed a mixed economy, combining traditional food sources with new ones, as a federal explorer described at Las Vegas in 1872: "They have small farms or gardens, and besides the corn, pumpkins, melons, &c., raised by themselves, obtain scanty supplies from the Vegas ranches for what little work they do."[57] Nevertheless, most town-dwelling Paiutes apparently did some limited hunting and gathering through the nineteenth century, as editorials frequently mentioned the shortage of Indian labor during the fall piñon harvest season.[58] What proportion of the diet came from traditional sources and how much was bought cannot be determined, but the proportion undoubtedly shifted toward purchased foods as access to the countryside became ever more restricted by non-Indian occupation.

Through wage employment Paiute men and women bought novelties unavailable in their own culture. In Nevada, as in Utah, they found that new foods such as wheat flour, clothing, metal cooking pots, and needles made life easier. Unlike in the Mormon zone, in Nevada they could also routinely purchase liquor, and drinking soon became a significant mode of social interaction among Paiutes and between them and non-Indians. In many of the newspaper reports of fights between Paiutes, one or more of the participants was said to be inebriated.[59] In the spring of 1883 a horse race down the main street of Bullionville was attended by drunken miners and Indians. The subsequent brawl resulted in a dog shot, a miner wounded in the leg, and a Paiute, John Findlay, dead, "riddled with a dozen bullets." The inquest held over his body brought in a verdict of "death from gun-shot wounds, at the hands of unknown parties."[60]

Although most of the customers in the saloons were miners who were justly characterized as a hard-drinking lot, they tried to deny Paiutes similar freedoms. The Pioche newspaper editor, presuming an innate and unalterable native hatred of non-Indians, frequently called for a federal ban on the sale of alcohol to Indians, whether on reservation or off: "the proper officers should see that the parties selling liquor should be arrested and indicted and every drunken Indian put in jail. If this is not done the citizens will make a wholesale slaughter some day of the noble red man."[61] The liquor trade continued to find an active native market, and near the end of the century the newspaper was still reporting, "Scarcely a night passes that Indians, both squaws and bucks, cannot be seen reeling past the smelter in a beastly state of intoxication."[62]

The documented beastliness, however, was usually on the non-Indian side. In 1872 "two white men went to the lower end of Meadow Valley . . . and being provided with liquor distributed the beverage among the Indians, and afterwards outraged one or more of the squaws. The Indians were greatly incensed, and the warriors painted themselves and prepared to go upon the warpath."[63] Retaliation was averted through the intervention of the federal Indian agent, in this case. Surprisingly, the newspaper editorialized, "The perpetrators of the outrage deserve punishment," although civil authorities did not, in fact, take action. The press and the miners were united in their conviction that Paiutes, regardless of how clear the justice of their case, should be prevented from taking any autonomous action for wrongs committed against them by any Euro-American.

It was insisted, rather, that the American courts were the sole proper forum for native redress. In a number of cases in Pioche, miners were arrested by town authorities, tried, and given short jail sentences for crimes against native people, most notably for rape.[64] In other instances, Indians were denied a court hearing, as in the case of the Pahranagat Valley man who had to repeatedly herd livestock owned by a non-Indian named Frenchy out of his garden crops. "Mr. Frenchy, it appears, became indignant at the persistent herding, and one day followed a venerable warrior to his wickiup and shot him dead." A non-Indian neighbor filed a complaint of homicide with the justice of the peace in the nearest town, who merely "arranged the matter in private session with Mr. Frenchy on the grounds of self defense."[65]

The converse of that power relationship was that no matter how blatant the offense against him, if a Paiute dared raise his hand against a miner, it was literally worth his life or that of any other Indian caught by white revenge seekers. Sometimes Paiutes in the mining areas cooperated with vigilantes in order to protect themselves from further random violence. After Avote killed a miner at El Dorado in 1893, a number of local Indians joined the manhunt. He "was finally killed by his brother whom the whites threatened to hang unless he procured satisfactory evidence of the murderer's death."[66] The number of recorded incidents after 1865 in which a Paiute intentionally attacked a non-Indian, except when they were alone in a remote area far from town, probably does not exceed half a dozen.

Violence that did not cross interethnic boundaries was of lesser interest to Euro-American newspapers and courts. The number of such reports is far higher than the newspapers' fascination with violence or the novel phenomenon of alcohol would lead one to expect. Indian communities that clung to the edges of mining towns were societies under enormous pressure. The people had relocated physically, had completely changed the routines of their lives, were facing novel material challenges, and were involved in a complex and hostile interethnic social environment in which, suddenly finding themselves a minority, they lacked any control. There were numerous attacks and homicides committed by one Indian upon another, both in town and in the native communities. Sometimes liquor and other times kinship obligations were the reported motivations.[67] Miners treated these matters as internal to Paiute society, and town authorities made no attempt to control, adjudge, or punish the offenders, even when known.

Until well into the twentieth century the issue of jurisdiction over such off-reservation Indians remained legally obscure.[68] While the federal government demanded authority over hostile tribes or those on reservations, others like the Paiutes who required no military suppression and did not reside on a reserve occupied an ambiguous status. In practice, since the earliest days of settlement, Euro-American individuals, without a shred of authority, had habitually seized hostages and publicly whipped offenders. As the initial lawless frontier gave way to a slightly more orderly society, the territories of both Utah and Nevada extended their control over settlers, miners, and Paiutes as well.

As early as 1876, St. George Mormons arrested a headman, accused of attempting a burglary of a church-owned store.[69] Over the next generation, local courts routinely acted as though southern Utah Paiutes were under their authority. An influential Mormon proudly wrote the commissioner of Indian affairs: "I have been careful from the beginning to teach them that they were subject to the law . . . , more especially since one of their number has been arrested at my in[si]stance, tried in the District Court, and sentenced to one year in the Territorial Penitentiary. (For stealing a horse)."[70]

Nevada took a little longer to assert jurisdiction. By 1872 the state legislature had passed a law against selling guns to Indians, and a Pioche merchant was promptly tried and convicted.[71] The Pioche newspaper criticized Mormons for trading guns for Paiute children. When a local Indian killed a Shoshone in 1888, the paper asserted, "Indians are subject to our laws for all crimes committed off an Indian Reservation and it would be well for the Grand Jury . . . to investigate the affair."[72] Although perhaps not the first instance, sixteen-year-old Cochie Segmiller was tried and convicted under Nevada state law for the admitted killing of his employer. The victim was well known to "ma[k]e a practice of intimidating the young Indians to such an extent that they would do his will for fear of him" and had withheld six dollars of honestly earned wages.[73]

Curiously, Indians occasionally actively solicited non-Indian intervention in native conflicts. In 1895 a Paiute killed a Shoshone, and the victim's relatives came to Pioche "for assistance to hunt down Bob, the murderer of [M]ustache Charley last week. They were willing to turn Bob over to the whites if caught, provided the whites would hang him. If any punishment short of this was to be meted out, they preferred to settle the difficulty among themselves."[74] This case was interesting in a number of ways. Since it was an intertribal murder, kinship relationships, the normal conduit for mediation between conflicting parties, probably did not exist. There was the chance of an unresolvable blood feud. Further, the Indians attempted to displace the responsibility for the ultimate sanction onto Euro-Americans, thus removing the guilt for a death, even a just one in their eyes, from the native community. Just as in the case of Mormon missionaries being asked to bury the dead, here too Indians found Euro-Americans useful to handle situations uncomfortable in their own community. If only non-Indians would take over the severest sanctions, then Paiutes wanted to retain their political autonomy in all other instances.

Even though Nevada wanted legal jurisdiction over Paiute behavior, it was not willing to accept native children into local schools. Paiutes, and indeed mixed-blood children, were denied education in the public schools until the 1930s.[75]

In mining areas the impact of Euro-Americans was severe, even though the minerals had not previously been used by Paiutes, and the two populations were not in direct competition for them. Miners did use far more resources than simply the rocks; they used water and wood and had to be supplied by a battalion of ranchers, farmers, and freighters. The miners in the rich Pahranagat Valley were aware of this when they petitioned for a reservation for the local Paiutes: "Our arrival here changed all this [native self-sufficiency]. White men now farm their lands, and our stock destroy their crop of grass seeds; they have no range for Game, we can employ but a comparative few of them, and they are reduced to a very wretched condition."[76]

Another major external force influencing Southern Paiutes, following Mormon settlers, secular miners, and the military, was the federal government in the form of Indian policies executed by the BIA. Although federal impact on Paiutes was minor in the nineteenth century, it would grow in importance in the twentieth.

Miners' posture on Indians was simple. They should go away to reservations where they "belonged" and there be restrained under federal supervision. The Mormon position was more complicated. Much as the farmers wanted unrestricted access to the most fertile lands, unencumbered by native occupation, they were faced with the contradictory need to convert Indians in order to bring about the millennium. That required access to them. Like most Americans by the 1850s, Mormons assumed that reservations were the inevitable native future. The only issue was how far away those reserves would be located and who would be in charge of them.

The BIA, like both miners and Mormons, assumed that Euro-Americans and Indians could not coexist and that some form of segregation was utterly necessary. Euro-American settlers—voting citizens—wanted to be the sole beneficiaries of the West's resources. In 1858, while Mormons were consolidating their control over southern Utah and mining was entering Nevada, the commissioner of Indian affairs asserted the only action "compatible with the obligations of justice and humanity" was establishing "the Indians on small reservations of land, and of sustaining them there for a limited period, until they can be induced to make the necessary exertions to support themselves."[77] These reservations would be far too small to allow Indians support through traditional means, which had required the entire land base. The government would subsidize tools, instruction, and education to induce them to adopt new, more intensive economic methods, although "they are not to be fed and clothed at government expense; but that they must supply all their wants by means of their own labor." Furthermore, these reservations should "isolate the Indians for a time from contact and interference from the whites. They should embrace good lands, which will repay the efforts to cultivate them. . . . By the adoption of this course, it is believed that the colonies can very soon be made to sustain themselves, or so nearly so that the government will be subjected to but a comparatively trifling annual expense on account of them."[78] By 1863 the commissioner of Indian affairs had declared, "The plan of concentrating Indians and confining them to reservations may now be regarded as the fixed policy of the government."[79] Not surprisingly, this purportedly benevolent national Indian policy when applied in Southern Paiute country was, as elsewhere, disrupted by local circumstances, regional interest blocks, and large-scale power structures.

The abstract similarities between this federal policy and that of the Mormons is striking—that Indian lands be cleared to make room for non-Indian settlers, that natives be shifted to an agricultural economy, that Indians be acculturated into a lifestyle comfortable to their Euro-American neighbors, that specialists (whether Indian agents or missionaries) manage Indian relations for the general population, and that this transformation be accomplished as inexpensively as possible.

The earliest reservation for Southern Paiute groups was at Corn Creek in central Utah. In 1851 territorial governor Brigham Young, by virtue of that office automatically superintendent of Indian affairs, acted without authorization from Washington to assign geographic parcels to three subagents. One jurisdiction, called the Parvan Agency, included the Pahvant band, soon to be under the leadership of Kanosh.[80] The leader of a church-sponsored expedition recorded that "these Indians reside upon Corn creek . . . and have there raised corn, beans, pumpkins, squashes, potatoes, +c., year after year, for a period that dates further back than their acquaintance with the whites."[81] Clearly, the entire Pahvant band could not subsist on this two-acre garden but hunted and gathered extensively elsewhere in a complex mixed economy.

Four years later, during the interlude between the Walker and the Black Hawk Wars, the federal subagent at Parvan suggested that "a large number of our friendly Indians, especially of the Utah tribe whose lands the whites have occupied, must be introduced to a knowledge of agriculture . . . to redeem them from their present state of wretchedness."[82] Young promptly suggested four locations near large Mormon settlements: "Corn Creek in Millard county is already occupied by them where a stout beginning is already made. In Iron county I . . . would direct your attention to Coal Creek below Cedar City as the most suitable place."[83] Although the Cedar City site did not become a reality for eighty years, the Corn Creek location, strategically astride the wagon road south, was acted on immediately. The subagent "visited Corn Creek, in company with several gentlemen of Fillmore and the principal men and chieves of the Pah-vantes, and examined the soil and amount of water. Finding the former of good quality and the latter of sufficient quantity to irrigate 700 or 1000 acres, we laid out one township or thirty six square miles." The subagent overlooked the long record of native horticulture and spoke of "introducing a knowledge of agriculture," while the headman said his "heart felt glad" and promised to farm wheat if given some seed.[84] Thus Corn Creek became a reservation through a string of administrative actions totally outside the legally recognized means of reserving lands for Indians: there were no treaty, no act of Congress, and no executive order. Federal funds were subsequently expended there simply by choice of the local superintendent of Indian affairs, who had no legal authority to allocate any lands for tribal purposes.

By spring 1857 the Indian agent reported "at the Corn Creek farm, 95 acres of wheat, 50 acres corn, potatoes, and Squashes. The crops look promising."[85] He listed federal investments in "6 head work cattle, 3 yokes and bows, 3 chains, 3 plows, 1 wagon, 2 harrows, 5 grub hoes, 145 acres of land fenced and under cultivation, 1 addoby house, 2 log houses, 1 corral."[86] Nevertheless, the 1858 harvest did not feed the Indians through the winter, let alone until the next harvest: "the Indians are nearly in a State of Starvation[.] there wheat is all gon[e]."[87] Mormons, reacting to the federal crackdown after the Mountain Meadows Massacre, demanded the exorbitant price of two dollars cash per bushel of wheat. The 1859 crops were "used up by the grasshoppers. . . . the indians appear to be discouraged about the loss of the crop there is but few of them on corn creek the rest are on the hunt," the subagent reported.[88] Contrary to the policy goals of training Indians in agricultural skills and encouraging self-support, the Pahvants were making adobes for a "house with 2 rooms and 1 1/2 story high for the use of the agency," while the subagent did most of the actual farming. In August his report revealed how much he viewed this as a private farm with Indian laborers, rather than a public educational program: "I am now harvesting *my* wheat," he said.[89]

The next year a funding shortage forced cancellation of the planting and in 1861 sale of the farming equipment.[90] The subagent argued, "Corn Creek reservation is yet small, closely surrounded by white settlements, which renders it very nearly valueless as an Indian reservation, because of the Indians continually coming into contact with the whites."[91] On the assumption that Indians and non-Indians fundamentally could not live together, he recommended that all Indians in Utah, Utes and Paiutes alike, be gathered together at the "Winter" (Uintah) Valley into a single, easily managed group.

In 1862 the BIA invested over a thousand dollars to reestablish the farming program it had abandoned the year before.[92] But horticulture was unpredictable, and wisely, Pahvants kept it, like their traditional horticulture, a small component in a more diverse economy of hunting, gathering, and exchange with the newcomers. During the next harvest, Pahvant headman Kanosh persuaded the local Mormon bishop to write "that he with many others has lost their crops, and has no amunition to hunt with. . . . K[a]nosh says he wants some beef, and he say[s] the Indians [to the] North are supplied with beef, and he also wants his share."[93]

Congress ran out of patience with the intermittent efforts at Corn Creek Reservation, which it had never created in the first place, and authorized its sale on 4 May 1864.[94] But since there was no legal description of the land other than the vague topographic boundaries in the original 1855 recommendation, a surveyor was sent west to map the lands so an appraisal could be done. In conformity with his instructions from the secretary of the interior, he attempted to "ascertain, the extent of the tracts of country occupied by the Indians and recognized as their reservations; and . . . include all the arable lands of the valleys in which the reservations are situated, together with a proper quantity of adjacent timber-lands."[95] He laid out a square twelve miles on a side, twice the length of the reservation originally described, thus enclosing four times the land area, none of which actually constituted the Indian farm or campsite.[96] It did, however, include the Mormon villages of Petersberg and Meadow Creek, presumed since 1855 to be outside the reserve. The furious settlers, fearing their lands would be sold along with the Indian lands, petitioned their territorial legislature to force reappraisal from Congress, but by autumn 1869 agents were ready to abandon the reservation.[97]

The government further complicated the Corn Creek situation when it added treaty making to its efforts at reservationization, thus activating both of its major nineteenth-century mechanisms for dealing with Indians. BIA agent O. H. Irish was sent to negotiate a series of treaties to cede a number of western tribal lands. Brigham Young had frequently requested such federal acquisition of title so it could in turn be reallocated to the Mormon settlers who were developing it. At this particular point in time Utes in central Utah were militarily active under Black Hawk, taking advantage of the disruption caused by Navajo raids in the south.

Young, as ex officio superintendent of Indian affairs, invited only Kanosh out of all the southern headmen to join Ute leaders at Spanish Fork and sign a treaty relinquishing all "possessory right of occupancy in and to all of the lands heretofore claimed and occupied by them" except the Uintah Valley. The signers agreed to lead their groups to Uintah within a year and stay there along with "any other friendly tribe or bands of Indians of Utah Territory, to occupy the same in common." Substantial payments were promised to the group, and the headmen were personally bribed with cabins, oxen, wagons, plows, and other agricultural tools. Funds from the sale of Corn Creek and other small reserves were to be used for "construction of improvements upon the said Uintah Indian Reservation or to the purchase of stock, agricultural implements, or such other useful articles as to him [secretary of the interior] may seem best adapted to the wants and requirements of the Indians," in conformity with the standard BIA policy to shift natives to an agricultural subsistence base.[98]

Again that September, Irish gathered six Southern Paiute headmen at Pinto Creek, west of Cedar City. Signers agreed to "hereby surrender and relinquish to the United States all their possessory right of occupancy in and to all of the lands heretofore claimed and occupied by them" as rather inaccurately described by geographic features.[99] Oddly, if not uniquely among Indian treaties, this one simply cross-referenced the Spanish Fork agreement, declaring that these Paiutes "agree to faithfully observe and abide by all of the provisions, stipulations and agreements contained in said [Spanish Fork] treaty and to confederate with the several bands of Utah Indians, parties thereto, and to remove to and settle upon the Uintah Indian Reservation within one year after the ratification of this treaty."[100] They were promised a share in the annuities and other "advantages," including provision for one "head Chief of the Pi-ede and Pah-Ute Tribes" to get a cabin, five acres, and one hundred dollars. Signers were given blankets, clothing, and tobacco.

Through these two treaties the federal government hoped to gain title to much of Southern Paiute land and to facilitate its flow into non-Indian hands, although descriptive inaccuracies would have made this less inclusive than Irish had intended. Although not all Paiute bands were represented, the agreements envisioned moving several onto a reservation where the majority population was not the "friendly" one described at all but, rather, one that had been slave raiding, intimidating, and dominating them for years.

Paiute headmen traditionally had no power to yield ownership of land communally occupied and could not bind other members of their camp group to relocate hundreds of miles away. Certainly, they could not speak or make commitments for camp groups other than their own. These were in no sense "tribal" agreements. Not surprisingly, despite the BIA's decision to sell, "[t]he ParVants, on Corn Creek reservation—wish to remain where they are." The agent feared that the treaty promises might not be fulfilled and recommended that "especially Corn Creek and Deep Creek [the Goshute Shoshone reserve near Great Salt Lake]—be not sold until other locations are selected for the occupancy + use of the Indians."[101]

In fact, the Senate never approved either the Spanish Fork or the Pinto Creek treaties as required by the U.S. Constitution; as far as the United States was concerned, they were moot, and none of the commitments in them were binding on the government. In 1878 Congress passed a law negating the 1864 order to sell Corn Creek and ironically ordered the land, whose title it had never acquired through treaty negotiation, to be "returned" instead to the public domain.[102] Since no other attempt was made to acquire Southern Paiutes' land title, they remained nominal legal owners for another hundred years; pragmatic possession, of course, was an issue of power, and that Paiutes had already lost.

A Utah Indian agent succinctly summarized the condition of Paiutes south of Corn Creek:

These Indians are all extremely poor. For the past two years, the new settlements made in their country have taken up much of the arable land. The miners have taken nearly all the balance, and these influences with the constantly increasing concourse of freighters passing to and fro from this [Salt Lake] City to Southern California, and the Colorado River, have driven off what little game there ever was in the country. Many Indians have perished of starvation, within the past six or eight months. . . . Some of these Indians, to save themselves from actual starvation, have occasionally stolen stock from the miners and settlers. This has led to acts of retaliation, but all these troubles can be quieted by the distribution of a small amount of provisions.[103]

He suggested subsidies as a means of social control, but the commissioner of Indian affairs rejected this strategy because Paiutes were not a federally recognized tribe: "the absence of any Treaty with these Indians, precludes the appointment of any Agents for those localities unless Congress shall make provisions for the same and for their salaries. . . . the Indians could *sustain themselves.*"[104] The Paiutes in Utah had no lands reserved for their use, no treaty relations with the federal government, and no funds budgeted on their behalf. The BIA chose to ignore them for the next thirty years.

Paiutes outside of Utah, however, were more affected by federal reservation policy during the nineteenth century. Nevada miners petitioned the government with standard expansionist arguments: "a rich agricultural and mining locality has been discovered in the Southeastern portion of this State which is being filled up by and with a hardy and industrious population. . . . The prospectors and miners and families now arriving in this Section, desire to inhabit the Vallies and live at peace and without fear of molestation by the Indians."[105] Town officials there worried that cattle ranching interfered with Indian self-sufficiency and asked the BIA for subsistence subsidies for them.[106] Mormon Church leaders wanted Paiutes restricted to small reservations at federal expense.[107]

As a result of these local political pressures, the Indian agent, whose jurisdiction included all of Nevada, was ordered to prepare a report on Southern Paiutes; his two trips 450 miles each way from his base near Reno produced no extant documents. In 1869 a resident agent was appointed to southern Nevada, although he still had no reservation to administer.[108] Reflecting his lack of information and confusion, that agent "recommend[ed] that a reservation be set apart for these Indians of the southeast, whatever be their proper name, somewhere in the Pahranagat valley," which had ample water.[109] Four years later another "selected subject to your approval the only suitable place in this country for a Reservation—what is called the Los Vegas Ranch," the lonely outpost that the military had been helpfully guarding for the legislator-possessor throughout the Walapai war.[110] Yet another agent proposed a single reserve for not only all Southern Paiutes but all Northern Paiutes as well:

> found that there was an absolute necessity to establish an Indian reservation in the extreme southeastern portion of Nevada and from his [Special Agent G. W. Ingalls's] survey and inspection I regard the point the Muddy Valley and I recommend that such reservation be located and that all the Pah-Utes occupying the territory south of line 35 belong to such reservation and special agency. There are large numbers of the Pah-Utes within said territory reaching as far west as Mono, Indio and San Bernideno counties, California, and the sooner they can be gathered upon a reservation the better for the country.[111]

John Wesley Powell, the Colorado River explorer and geologist, suggested sites on the Sevier and Paria Rivers in Utah because of their agricultural potential, water resources, and lingering freedom from immigrant communities.[112] Settlers, miners, and the BIA all assumed that Southern Paiutes could be moved around the landscape at the convenience of non-Indians and often argued that this was for the Indians' own good.

Faced with these diverse suggestions, Special Agent Ingalls, sent to southeastern Nevada to deal with the situation, recommended a large square that ran from the Colorado River north to the springs that headed the Muddy River and from roughly the eastern edge of the Las Vegas Valley to the eastern border of the state.[113] He expected the twenty-four hundred Paiutes from as far east as Kaibab, through Nevada, and south to the Chemehuevis to be brought here. Contradicting the fact that this was less than 10 percent of their aboriginal territory, Ingalls asserted that the "boundaries embrace a much greater area than is actually necessary for these Indians, in fact there is but a very small portion of this territory that is at all suitable for reservation purposes, and that portion is embraced in the valley of the Muddy, it being from one to three miles in width."[114] Blithely ignoring native economic self-sufficiency, which had included partial horticulture (before immigrants had taken so much of their land and its resources), he proposed "making farmers of the Pai-Utes, and thus enabling them to become self-sustaining, and converting them from vicious, dangerous savages to civilized people."[115] In short, Paiutes were to go away and cease to annoy or depend on non-Indian settlers.

The executive order that established the Moapa River Reservation on 12 March 1873 followed Ingalls's recommendation, and the land was removed from the public domain two weeks later.[116] Known variously over the years as the PahUte, Paiute, Southeastern Nevada, and Muddy River Reservation, the lands at Moapa were the first set aside for Paiutes that would actually remain in their hands.

Together, Powell and Ingalls were ordered to locate, count, and learn about the Paiute population planned for the Moapa Reservation. As had both Kanosh during the treaty negotiations at Spanish Fork and also other headmen at Pinto Creek, Paiute leaders again agreed to cooperate with the BIA's schemes for them to leave their homes and relocate. They demanded only "these conditions—that the Government will remove the white settlers therefrom, and will assist them to remove their old people and children from their present to their prospective home on the reservation, and will assist them to become agriculturists, and provide for their maintenance until such time as they can take care of themselves." The government officers found these requests "reasonable and just." Because there was "no" game and "native products are few," they reported, "it would be impossible for the Indians to live on the reservation without assistance. It would be useless to take them there without at the same time providing for their support, as in such a case they would be compelled at once to scatter again over the very country from whence they had been taken."[117]

Over the eight years that the BIA had temporized in establishing a southern Nevada reserve, however, almost two thousand Mormons had displaced Paiute farmers from the only arable land—six thousand acres—within this enormous territory, and four of their towns now occupied the best sites, irrigated by diversions from the Muddy River. The territorial survey in 1871 revealed that they were in Nevada, not Utah or even Arizona as they had thought, and, not wishing to be subject to a secular government and upon the orders of Brigham Young, the Mormon communities had abandoned their holdings en masse and returned to Utah.[118] Cattlemen who provisioned the mining towns around Pioche quickly seized these lands. The government thought to buy out these few ranchers at little expense but realized that "to utilize [that is, farm] the valley as a reservation ... it will be necessary to repair the original canals and drain certain swamps."[119]

The same Pioche newspaper that had begged for a reservation decried one at Moapa as an "outrage" and predicted, "If the Piutes had the Muddy Valley all to themselves they would not cultivate it—the majority of them would be, as they are now, begging and loafing around the streets of Pioche. As a matter of policy an Indian reservation should not be so close to a large settlement of whites as the Muddy is to Pioche." Seventy desert miles, it seems, was too close when it came to Indians; like prisons and drug rehabilitation centers today, reservations were necessary and desirable social institutions but always better somewhere else. The editor continued to reveal the crass economic motivation behind his protest: "[A]nd besides, the Muddy is surrounded by promising mining districts, which are about to be developed. Down on the Colorado river, where no lands have been appropriated, a good Indian reservation can be selected."[120] Disregarding the Paiute farms that long predated the present occupation that had ousted them, he proclaimed that non-Indians had created all there was of value—homes, crops, and irrigation ditches. Surely, he said, the Interior Department, "if properly informed, would not drive off white settlers to make a reservation for savages."[121] Non-Indians, his assumption ran, once in possession of property, should never be dislodged for the benefit of natives.

Paiutes themselves were not too keen on the reservation because, the newspaper argued, they knew they were better off on their own, they resented the infringement on their mobility, and they thought the gifts distributed by the agents were insufficient incentive.[122] Unbothered by the obvious contradiction, the same paper also reported "between four and five hundred Pai Ute Indians, representing 6 different tribes or bands, [had collected] in the Moapa or Muddy Valley on the Reservation. After several days council, these Indians all consented to remain on the reservation, and expressed a willingness for all the other tribes or bands scattered over Utah, Arizona, Nevada and California, to be brought to the reservation in the following season."[123] Even distant "Konosh [*sic*] has signified a purpose to go to the South reservation if we *insist* on his removal to any."[124] He later recanted in favor of Uintah and eventually procrastinated long enough to evade relocation entirely.[125] Coal Creek John, the headman from the Cedar City area, also hesitated and privately told a civilian that "he did not want to go on the Muddy Reservation. That the restraint was irksome to himself and fellow Indians. That they wished to stay w[h]ere they were camped. . . . they thought they could manage better for themselves if they were let alone than such men as the usual class of Indian agents could or would do for them."[126]

Powell and Ingalls found that the solution, proposed in the treaty of Spanish Fork for Paiutes to be sent to Uintah, was untenable. It was "impossible to induce the Pai-Utes to go to the Uintah Reservation, and the Indians of the Uintah Valley are not willing that they should come. Both parties remember their old feuds with great bitterness, and each accuses the other of sorcery, murder, and the stealing of women and children."[127] Paiutes were, however, relatively willing to go to Moapa. The previous winter had been harsh, and "fully *seven eighths* of them have *no means* of procuring employment in mines or on farms."[128] They "would [have] had to be fed or they would have been forced to steal from white settlers or have died."[129]

Paiute cooperation with the BIA's careless plans to restructure their social and political entities may have been rooted in native culture as well as immediate economic circumstances. Camp groups had traditionally coalesced when food resources were rich, using kinship ties to channel fission and fusion. Paiutes apparently perceived sufficient affinity to accept linkage with even distant bands from California, Utah, and Arizona. They did not object to agents' insistence that half the harvest be set aside for bands who might later arrive, as this conformed to their own rules of hospitality.[130] On the other hand, they strictly rejected union with Utes, who were seen as "others," despite their closely related language.

Powell and Ingalls moved actively to forestall speculators by enlarging the reservation to include some timberland to the west. Furthermore, they argued, "An extension of the eastern boundary a few miles will add to the agricultural lands between two and three thousand acres which are very desirable and *necessary* to accommodate all the Indians who have signified their purpose to go on the Reservation the coming season."[131] Their recommendations were approved, and an executive order expanded the boundaries substantially on 12 February 1874.[132]

Shortly thereafter, Pioche commercial interests joined factions within the BIA to pressure for a narrower view of reservation policy than Powell and Ingalls held. By the end of 1874 the agent in charge of Moapa, A. J. Barnes, recommended release from the reservation of any lands that might contain minerals so as "not to interfere with the mining industry of the country." He said that cutting off "the metalliferous territory . . . should not in any manner effect the plan of making this an Indian reservation; inasmuch that all that is necessary for the support of the Indians can be raised in the valley of the Muddy River."[133] In following the strict policy that natives should farm, Barnes never considered that Indians, like Euro-Americans, could participate in the one lucrative industry of the Nevada economy and become miners, or even mine owners, themselves.

Congress leapt at the opportunity Barnes created in order to please constituents. After an unsuccessful bid to abandon it entirely, Congress placed a rider on the BIA's 1875 appropriation bill to reduce Moapa arbitrarily from thirty-nine hundred square *miles* to a mere one thousand *acres*.[134] Those few acres would specifically "not include the claim of any settler or miner."[135] By 3 June 1875 the survey of the reduced reserve was completed, and a month later the secretary of the interior ordered these new boundaries recorded in the General Land Office as an Indian reservation.[136]

The remnant reserve was not in the main part of the Muddy Valley, because Euro-Americans had already taken up all the well-watered land. Not only would it be expensive to buy out established non-Indian interests, but trying to reserve good land for Indians would cause "continual annoyances from encroachments."[137] In other words, the BIA felt impotent to bar any non-Indian who wanted to from seizing any reservation resources.

The single squatter who occupied the abandoned Mormon townsite of West Point upstream, with its old partial irrigation and drainage system, agreed to sell. The local and statewide BIA agents agreed that this site was "the most practicable and economical thing we could do, in the premises."[138] Since the national geodesic grid had not reached this far west, they themselves made an isolated survey of a linear strip of roughly a thousand acres along the river and heaped up rocks to mark the corners. This property had no fences and no trees that could be cut to build them, so range cattle would need to be herded away from Indian farms manually. Mormon settlers had long complained of a local malarial infection. The river itself was so mineral laden that a limey, impervious caliche had built up several feet thick along the river's bottom and banks; the river rode a self-constructed channel above the surrounding land level.[139] When spring thaws or summer thunderstorms drove the river over its banks, water was trapped behind the calcareous natural levee as a brackish swamp choked with alkali. It was these lands to which the BIA proposed all the various bands of Paiutes come and support themselves through agriculture.

During the summer of 1873, investigator Ingalls reported that 750 Paiutes, including people from Shivwits, Kaibab, and Chemehuevi, had arrived, "induced to go[ing] there by promise of cloth, food, tools for farming, and an opportunity to cultivate the soil."[140] Using the old Mormon ditches, he harvested three thousand bushels of wheat off one hundred acres by June. He counted "nearly 1,000 Indians were on the reservation, and *will be again* within the next thirty days, and . . . if aided *will remain*."[141] Clearly, the Paiute population had not simply become sedentary. Ingalls knew what later agents forgot, that Paiutes moved away from places where there were no resources to support them.

Two years later another agent complained that the Moapa Paiutes "have for so long a time been in the habit of receiving blankets, clothing, +c., from the Government [at treaty negotiations and at Powell and Ingalls's meetings, for instance] . . . without any services being given in return, that they believe the Government is bound to provide for them under any and all circumstances." To combat development of what the later twentieth century labeled the welfare mentality, he insisted that he would only "help" them "to become self-supporting by adopting the habits of the white man . . . but [this] was by no means to be considered as a perpetual gift."[142] He did realize that Paiutes could not contribute their time to digging ditches, plowing, road building, and other agency work when they had no food stores to fall back on, so he instituted a wage system. "[W]e give to those at work two yards of Denims at twenty five cents per yard, for each days labor, and while some work better than others, we try to have all work some. By this means all can be clothed and at the same time be taught habits of industry."[143] The agent loaned Indian workers federally purchased shovels and hoes on a daily basis, although many preferred familiar, traditional digging sticks; plowing required agency equipment and teams.[144]

In his late 1873 report Ingalls probably exaggerated his estimate of Paiutes cropping 3,100 bushels from 130 irrigated acres with 200 acres planted to winter wheat. Paiutes, unlike some other tribes in the region, were demonstrating their adaptive reception of new farming customs and other foreign skills; twenty children were learning to read and write in Ingalls's temporary day school.[145] Two years later a new agent was less glowing when he saw only 30 Indian acres cultivated and a total harvest of a scant 200 bushels of corn, 5 of beans, and 10 of assorted vegetables, hardly more than the yield of kitchen gardens. He estimated that Moapa Paiutes got 60 percent of their subsistence from traditional hunting and gathering and only 25 percent from "civilized pursuits." Even relatively little of this was from agency-sponsored agriculture, as he said that forty men and six women, more than 10 percent of the estimated population of four hundred, did wage labor for neighboring non-Indians.[146] Two years later this agent lauded his own success in getting Paiutes to farm 100 acres, their percentage of support from "civilized pursuits" elevated to 60 percent, and the number of off-reservation wage laborers to 75 percent.[147] It is impossible to know how much these statistics were inflated, but even at best, Moapa was too small to sustain the Paiute population by limited agriculture. Cattle owned by non-Indians entered the unfenced reservation to drink at the river and stayed to graze on the crops. Justly skeptical of abject reliance on the newly proffered agriculture, southern Nevada Paiutes continued to do what they had always done before. They compiled a living from a cautious balance of sources, now including not only the plants and animals of remnant unsettled areas but also encompassing the new economic opportunities provided in Euro-American settlements themselves as well as the government programs.

The BIA was not particularly pleased with Paiutes' independent, eclectic economic adaptation. It wanted an isolated, segregated native community neatly out of the way of non-Indians eager to pursue their fortunes in the West, and yet in 1879 the Moapa subagent wrote, "As to the Indians, they are doing well. None of them live on the reservation now. . . . The young men are at work for citizens on farms and at mining camps. Some of the married men work out at times."[148] Faced with the awkward fact of an Indian reservation without any Indians, the subagent sounded a theme reminiscent of both Spanish slave traders and early missionaries as they proclaimed that what they were doing to Paiutes was for their own good: "I am informed the whole tribe are in better condition than they have ever been." In phrases that would be repeated almost verbatim during termination hearings eighty years later, he stated, "They have good clothing and nearly all the men speak good English. They require nothing from the Government only a few tools such as shovels, hoes and axes and when issued should be made to pay for them in work or grain. They are just in the right condition to become self-sustaining, if properly managed."[149]

The number of Paiutes actually resident "on" the reserve continued to be considerably less than the number "belonging" to it or having the right to live there. Distant Paiute bands expected at first to relocate to Moapa never did so. The initial school classes were discontinued after one year, and throughout the 1870s no Moapa Paiutes were tabulated as literate. Many, especially men, learned a bit of English on their own during wage employment.[150]

Nearly all of the available wage work was for non-Indians in off-reservation farming communities and mining towns. Paiute families continuously crossed the permeable reservation boundary to supplement their seasonal hunting and gathering with such wage income. The reservation was little more than a bureaucratic concept. The resident subagent-farmer, who was supposed to provide a model farm for Paiutes to emulate, seems primarily to have simply supported himself. As time went on, however, surrounding non-Indians talked of Moapa as the place where Paiutes "belonged," except those useful for day labor; the Pioche newspaper was beginning to describe any Indians in the countryside as "renegades" from the reservation.[151] Paiutes, on the other hand, saw the reservation as one stop, albeit an old and familiar one, in a wide assortment of rotating camps. In the fall of 1879, the resident subagent reported that the only Indians on the reservation were "the old men and Squaws that never go out to work. they are in great distress about the future and very a[n]xious to know if they can depend on the Government for Grub if their crops should be destroyed. . . . the young men will continue to live out and earn their own living the old men and women take care of home matters."[152] Thus the Moapa Reservation developed almost immediately the age segregation that characterized reserves elsewhere later in the mid–twentieth century, with the middle-aged in their most productive years moving off for wage employment and the aged left to raise their grandchildren in rural poverty.

In 1876 the BIA sent about fifty cattle to Moapa so Paiutes could begin to raise their own meat. A part-time agency employee got the local justice of the peace to issue a state writ, not legally binding on the federal reservation, against the cattle in lieu of federal wages he claimed were due him. Waving guns at the subagent, he and six friends (including the justice of the peace) drove off the stock. The U.S. marshal from Reno, the nearest official having jurisdiction over crimes on federal lands such as Indian reservations, arrested him.[153] While bureaucrats debated whether the cost of bringing witnesses 450 miles to Reno, also the nearest federal court, exceeded the value of the stock, both the Moapa subagent and a part-time blacksmith, the witnesses against the accused, were assassinated, and the case collapsed.[154] This first attempt to use laws and the courts to protect property held in federal trust for Paiutes was defeated by concerted local violence. Federal law enforcement proved too distant, too slow, and too weak to be an effective protector of Paiute interests.

Although the replacement subagent posted the reservation boundaries and warned cattlemen that the reserve was not part of the open range, troubles continued.[155] When Paiutes laboriously handwove willow basketry fences, cattlemen "threaten[ed] to destroy the fence."[156] When the subagent told a Paiute simply to drive trespassing livestock across the nearest boundary, a cattleman "pulled his hair, choked him + threatened to kill him."[157] Non-Indians refused to accept that Moapa was land reserved for Indian use.

Problems beyond disputed range rights remained: scorching summers, lack of timber, and the high cost of freighting in agency supplies. The fact that only one Paiute, employed as a translator, was actually living there, made Moapa awkward to justify, and support for the Moapa Reservation began to crumble within the BIA. "It is my *firm* and *decided conviction*," the agent wrote in 1870, "that the best interests of the Indians and of the government will be subserved by abandoning that reservation and removing the Pi-Utes to the better location."[158] The commissioner of Indian affairs suggested closing Moapa and moving Paiutes four hundred miles north to the Walker Lake Reservation in Northern Paiute territory if there was enough land there for allotments. Despite a full generation's experience to the contrary, he assumed on general principles that Paiutes could not live in juxtaposition with non-Indians and that he could move them across the landscape at will. He ordered the Nevada agent to warn them that "the best lands in Nevada, are all being taken up, and that in the near future the Moapa River reservation will be entirely surrounded by whites, and, therefore, the necessity of their obtaining a permanent home as soon as possible, and use every endeavor to induce them to consent to the proposed removal."[159] The expectation of such an encroachment would hardly be news to Paiutes.

Local mining town newspapers supported the concept of reservationization to achieve racial and cultural segregation. In one of its more benign proclamations, the Pioche paper argued that expanded non-Indian farming in the lower Moapa Valley "forces the Indian to go where he properly belongs . . . where he will have the benefit of the Government aid, such as it is, and plenty of land and tools to work it with."[160] In one of its more rabid moments, the same newspaper advocated, "The Indians should all be placed under military rule; should be kept on their reservation or killed. When an Indian is found off of his reservation he should be killed, for there is no longer a sensible man in Eastern Nevada who believes there is any good Indians until after they are dead."[161] On the other hand, the diaries and memoirs of actual farmers in the lower Moapa Valley reflect a far different opinion: "The Indians did nearly all the [wage] work in the [Moapa] valley."[162] These men found off-reservation Paiutes to be a convenience, as long as they did not try to fence off land or compete for resources.

Paiute views of the reservation can be inferred from their transient occupation; they moved away but also repeatedly returned. In one of the few documents that even purports to express their thoughts, the Moapa subagent summarized for his superior in Reno numerous Paiute criticisms: "They tell me that I am no good Indian man, never give any grub. See Indian heap cry, papoose heap cry, you give no grub, Indian heap hungry, by + by Indian die, maybe so all die pretty soon. White man cattle, horse + govt. cattle eat Indian wheat, barley, squashes, you no keep white man cattle away. You no pay Indian. What good you here. You do nothing for Indian. No have grub. Reservation no good."[163] To the extent that this report is accurate, Paiutes seem to have perceived the federal presence in personalized and pragmatic terms. They viewed the local agent as personally liable for fulfillment of promises made by Powell and Ingalls for tools, for a steady food supply, and for an improved quality of life. In this they were disappointed.

Federal passage of the General Allotment Act in 1887 allowed the BIA to move against a reservation about which so many people had so many doubts. The commissioner ordered Special Agent Henry Welton to go to Moapa. Since the public survey had not reached this far west, the cost of a specialized survey made allotment under the new law too costly, so the commissioner ordered "some *informal division* of the lands amongst them sufficient to prevent quarrels, and to give each family at least an *imaginary* proprietary right in a piece."[164]

Seeing Moapa with fresh eyes, Welton was appalled. Calling the situation "shameful," he wrote, "The Indians have been practicaly *run off* by the Farmer in Chg. [charge] and for *six months* at a time on several occasions, not an Indian has slept on the Reservation."[165] Only thirty-five acres were being farmed, while six Paiute Indians cultivated off-reservation lands that they rented from non-Indians. The Paiutes, he said, "are scat[te]red over the surrounding country for 200 miles in all directions from the Reserve, making their own living, some among the Mormon farmers[,] others in the Mines. . . . they should continue to be selfsupporting and remain in small, desireable numbers among the whites."[166] He promptly fired the subagent for mismanagement and profiteering, sold the few remaining government-owned cattle, and put the money into fencing wire and tools.[167] In some unspecified way he "collected" a council of Paiutes that then "selected" a local rancher "as their Captain and *Trustee*" to oversee the Indians without pay after the reserve was "closed."[168] This man then divided the arable land into twenty parcels, assigning a pair of families to share each.[169] Correspondence within the BIA consistently referred to these assignments as "allotments." Since BIA staff had no further dealings with Moapa for the next decade, the legal status of this land was soon confused with formal allotments under the General Allotment Act. However, no documents specifying federal trust for individual Indians were ever drawn up, as would have been required under that law. Moapa was never officially terminated as a reservation; it was simply administratively abandoned. Moapa Paiutes continued to use it as a part-time residential base, supplementing wage work in the surrounding areas. They exchanged their assigned usufruct rights with each other, inherited them, and traded them over the next generation without any participation by the BIA.

The Moapa Reservation had a short, sad existence in the nineteenth century, and in the end it seems that the lives of Paiutes there differed little from the lives of others in southern Nevada who had no reservations set aside for them. The BIA program was insufficiently funded, poorly administered, challenged by local merchants and cattlemen, and finally abandoned without visible result. Paiutes did what they had done before: they combined marginal small-scale horticulture with a wide range of other resources.

What was happening to Paiutes in areas outside of southern Nevada between 1880 and 1900 is poorly known. The significance of the Kanosh community in Utah dwindled after the Corn Creek Reservation was sold, Kanosh himself died, and Indian affairs were secularized with the removal of Brigham Young as Indian agent. Several Paiute families lived there in log cabins and farmed, sharing a common ditch system with non-Indians coordinated by the Mormon bishop. They hunted and gathered some wild plant foods and worked for wages.

Farther east, the Paiutes on Kanab Creek lived within walking distance of town. John Wesley Powell wintered in Kanab between two of his Colorado River expeditions, and his men visited the Indian camp, traded for native manufactures, and watched round dances. Hopis and Navajos forded the Colorado at the old Crossing of the Fathers and stopped to trade woven blankets for buckskins; Utes passed through heading south.[170] Paiutes supported themselves mostly by hunting and gathering on the still uncrowded plateaus nearby. When Powell suggested a reservation for them, the BIA said they could go to Moapa if they wished.[171] They did not.

Sometime in the next decade, however, this group did relocate away from the permanent stream to small Moccasin Spring, fifteen miles south-west. Why they moved is unclear, but there are hints that Kanab residents wanted the Indians farther from their growing town.[172] The Mormon Church had operated a large cattle operation at Moccasin Spring until over-grazing caused profits to plummet. Local non-Indian oral history asserts that the church guaranteed Paiutes one third of the spring's water for their small gardens, although there is no public document that confirms this agreement was ever put in writing. Those gardens, along with hunting, gathering, and occasional wage employment, provided the Indians' livelihood.

In remote areas of the southern half of Utah, southern Nevada, Arizona north of the Grand Canyon, and the eastern Mojave Desert, travelers throughout the 1870s and 1880s occasionally mentioned seeing two or three Paiute families here and there farming at springs or camping in piñon groves.[173] Military patrols that monitored Navajos after their release from captivity at Bosque Redondo occasionally reported Paiutes along the San Juan River.[174] The numbers of such observations of isolated Paiute camp groups declined steadily over the next twenty years, as non-Indians increasingly controlled even such remote hinterlands for cattle grazing by seizing springs, chasing away Indians, and making an independent native life less viable. Paiutes continued to cluster near Mormon and mining towns as they had from the beginning of settlement. Whether these "Indian villages" were gradually absorbing rural relatives, indeed, whether they were stable populations at all or simply the historically visible section of a complex mobile economy, is simply not known.

After the Chemehuevis' conflict with the Mohaves, these southern-most Paiutes farmed the western bank of the Colorado River and foraged into the higher surrounding hillsides. Non-Indians soon occupied the valley for its agricultural fertility and proximity to transportation routes to Arizona. Chemehuevis offered non-Indians only very occasional, small-scale hostility; they were for the most part open to change and the novel opportunities presented by the Euro-American presence.[175] Long before 1880, Chemehuevis snagged and cut driftwood from the river to sell to steam-boats, worked at mines in the Mojave Desert, and found day labor in La Paz and later the railroad yard at Needles, where they were described as "industrious, naturally intelligent, all wear citizens' dress, and are capable of caring for themselves."[176] They mixed with a non-Indian population of freighters, miners, and frontier brawlers rather than a religiously defined Mormon structure or a selective bureaucratic agency staff; they absorbed the ways of the people around them and had enough social contact for there to be a mixed-blood population by 1890.[177] When the Colorado River Reservation was extended to the California shore in 1874 it incorporated some of their traditional use area. Over the next few years the agent reported Chemehuevis living transiently in that section, but he provided them no federal services, and few Chemehuevis chose to relinquish their independence in exchange for a regulated reservation life.[178]

In the waning two decades of the nineteenth century, Southern Paiutes faced the permanence of the Euro-American presence. Some of these strangers came as tightly organized, religiously based Mormon communities submissive to their own male hierarchical authority. More arrived as individualistic miners seeking personal fortunes amid the rocks. Others were ranchers claiming water holes for their livestock, which then consumed Paiutes' livelihood. All these groups were determined to make the land their own, despite Paiute priority of possession and protests. Each came to take specific but different resources from that land. The Mormons wanted fertile agricultural bottoms and streams that could be forced to flow across their fields. Miners wanted hillsides, but only those with outcrops containing ores of silver, lead, or gold. Ranchers wanted grassy flats where they could fatten their cattle before bringing them into the mining towns to sell. Mormons and cattlemen took directly from the Indians resources previously required for their livelihood; miners displaced some residential sites, demanded safe passage everywhere across the landscape, and funded the prosperity of the other two groups, who produced food for them.

Regardless of which resources each group of Euro-Americans wanted, all insisted on getting their wants free of interference from (and often of the presence of) Paiutes. They all threatened armed violence; it is unclear whether more Paiutes were ultimately killed by the overtly hostile miners and ranchers or by the religious community that asserted a spiritual brotherhood with the Indians. During the 1850s and 1860s this violence was a reality, but by the last quarter of the century open killing had passed into the hands of the official military. Operating only along the fringes of the Paiute world and more concerned with Apache resistance in Arizona, these professionals considered Paiutes unworthy opponents and for the most part ignored them.

Despite the variety of non-Indians who occupied their territory, the effect of their presence on Paiutes was remarkably uniform. Everywhere Euro-Americans seized resources needed for survival—water and food— as their personal and exclusive property. Everywhere non-Indians wanted Paiutes to be under their control and subject to their laws. Paiutes had to retreat, submit, or die.

Both Mormons and miners were discriminatory and separatist. Everywhere Paiutes formed distinct settlements; even while sharing water sources, their homes were apart from Euro-American cabins, on the fringes of towns in an "Indian camp." While welcomed for the labor they would perform cheaply for the settlers, they were not welcomed as friends or equals. Paiutes remained a separate society, living interstitially among non-Indians.

With the pragmatic and practical adaptability that had been the hallmark of Paiutes' native cultural life, they absorbed the new opportunities that these non-Indians brought. While keeping what they could of the old ways, they also took up new styles of clothing, new languages, and new wage labor for the very people who had taken possession of their land.

7

LAND, WATER, AND
THE FEDERAL GOVERNMENT,
1890–1934

The fact that reservations were established for Southern Paiutes was curious, in terms of both purpose and historic timing. As one would expect, reserves had been made at Corn Creek and Moapa during the first wave of frontier settlement; quickly adjudged failures, they were abandoned by the turn of the century. The BIA subsequently reversed itself and over the next forty years set aside eight additional reservations for Southern Paiutes in four states. Since the existence of these reserves complicated the interrelationships between Paiutes, local non-Indians, and various branches of church, state, and federal bureaucracies, it is important to begin by asking why reservations were established at all.

The concentration of native populations onto segregated reservations was not something done by Spaniards colonizing Latin America, by Europeans taking Africa, by Russians settling Siberia, or during the waves of ethnic conquest that constitute Chinese history, and yet it is such a prominent feature of nineteenth-century American policy that many historians never question its inevitability here.[1] When an explanation is offered, reservations are most often argued as a military necessity to control hostile native populations or to make the West safe for Euro-American settlers.[2] A slightly more skeptical interpretation suggests that reservationization and its concomitant treaty making were techniques to clear the territory of native possessors in order to make room for others who coveted the land.[3] All such explanations presume that reservations were an inherent part of the process of Euro-American settlement. Throughout the central Great Basin, however, reservations were essentially a *twentieth*-century phenomenon, not appearing in any significant numbers until *well after* non-Indians had attained effective occupation. There must be additional, less apparent reasons for reservations.

Certainly, the idea that natives must leave the land in favor of Euro-Americans was a popular notion on the frontier itself. The Pioche newspaper reminisced about when settlers entered the Muddy Valley, "an isolated spot, scarcely trodden by the foot of a white man, and built up homes; . . . in answer to an inquiry . . . 'What shall we do with these Indians?' we reply that they may be sent on the reservation now established at La Paz, in Arizona."[4]

Mormons concurred but phrased their agreement differently. Diarists often quoted Brigham Young's 1860s dictum, "It is cheaper to feed the Indians than to fight them," but over two generations Paiutes had shown very little disposition to engage in any such fighting. Increasingly weary of subsidizing the Indian economy, which their own settlements had done so much to disrupt, by the end of the century southern Utah Mormons grumbled that it was not cheaper to feed Indians in the long run. Some bemoaned the loss of pioneer and missionary zeal, but even leaders of the bishopric began to suggest that it was the federal government's responsibility to take on the expense of dealing with the Indians and that it should be doing so on specific reservations.

In southwestern Utah, Anthony Ivins, a prominent Mormon bishop and entrepreneur, championed the establishment of the Shivwits Reservation. Some of the Shivwits band of Paiutes had been living in the high plateau country at the western end of the Grand Canyon south of St. George. In the 1880s the Mohave Land and Cattle Company declared that it had bought the land and water rights to that plateau by giving the Paiutes a few head of cattle. In 1890 Ivins "acquired the interests" of the company and asserted that "ranching could not be successfully carried on, while the Shevwits remained on the land, the right to which they had sold to others. They became insolent, frequently killed cattle for food, and when remonstrated with replied that the country was theirs."[5] Ivins successfully petitioned Congress for a reservation to which the Shivwits Paiutes could be relocated along Santa Clara Creek, site of the early Mormon mission from which Paiutes had long since been displaced.[6]

Ivins voiced a common economic concern. Once the Navajo and Ute raids had ended in the late 1860s, Mormons could and did pasture herds in areas remote from settlements. Nevada mining towns provided a ready market for beef, and stock raising expanded. The desert ranges of southern Utah were stocked beyond carrying capacity long before 1890. The effects of serious overgrazing were visible in many areas, including the disappearance of fragile native flora, the replacement of edible grasses by inedible sagebrush, and erosion.[7] Small camp groups of Paiutes who had retreated to these meager, isolated locations were being crowded out.

After generations of coexistence in towns, increasing white population put stress on land and water resources. In 1891 citizens near Kanosh complained that the Paiutes, who shared a common irrigation ditch, "are in the habit of going to their dam in the night or day and devirting large streams of water and in consequence of said diversion the settlers sustain considerable loss to their groing crops." Paiutes were also routinely accused of shooting Mormons' horses and in general being "a sorce of trouble and annoyance." The idea that Indians' "proper place . . . is at the Uintah reservation" gained popularity, and townsmen asked the government "to have the Kanosh indians removed to their proper reservation."[8]

The land was simply becoming saturated. But whites wanted still more range for cattle, more land for farms, and more water for crops, so Indians who shared the landscape were declared predators. If Paiutes were to be driven away to protect non-Indian private investment and profit, there was a limited number of places left where they could be sent. Reservations here as elsewhere became the answer.

In 1893 the pressure for reservationization that came from population growth and agricultural saturation was compounded when the National Forest system incorporated many of the uplands of southern Utah. Furthermore, in 1906 the Grand Canyon was declared a game preserve and two years later a national park. In 1918 Zion Canyon, in the heart of Southern Paiute territory, was similarly absorbed for tourist purposes. President Theodore Roosevelt, an avid hunter, brought friends and international celebrities to track big game in the Kaibab Plateau; Arizona employed bounty hunters to kill off over six thousand wolves, coyotes, and mountain lions from Kaibab Paiute territory in order to increase the game available for sportsmen.[9] Southern Utah began shifting away from subsistence agriculture toward the recreation-based service industry, which would be its economic foundation in the twentieth century.

Suddenly, both Utah and Arizona began enforcing bag and season limits on Indian subsistence hunters in efforts to preserve deer for sports hunting; on remote hillsides where Paiutes had formerly harvested deer, they dodged game wardens. In 1916 a Kaibab man explained to the commissioner of Indian affairs, "Indians of this trib[e] would like if you would let them Kill Deer of[f] their mountain what they used call it their own, but now it closed. . . . the white people are getting thick and they are holding us from starving in want of food."[10] Hungry natives did not project a picturesque image for the growing numbers of tourists. Bishop Woolley of Kanab, instrumental in the Park Service's purchase of Zion and Pipe Spring, suddenly became a strong supporter of finding a reservation for the poor and starving Indians of his district as long as it was well away from town.

3. Intertribal trade persisted into the twentieth century, as long as Paiutes could produce unique goods to exchange. Navajos traveled to Kaibab in 1919 to trade their blankets to Paiutes for buckskins, a practice that was even then disappearing as Paiutes were made subject to state game laws and deer habitat was absorbed into national forests. The four stone houses were part of the first BIA housing development for Kaibab Paiutes. (Photograph by E. M. Sweet, U.S. National Archives, Bureau of Indian Affairs Records.)

Desire to put Paiutes on reservations was far from universal among non-Indians. Initial reservationization met considerable opposition from local farmers who argued their need for Paiute labor during spring planting and fall harvest. For instance, when Inspector Levi Chubbuck was sent to find lands for the Kaibab and San Juan Paiutes in 1906, he heard "numerous and emphatic declarations that to take the Indians away from Kanab would work a positive hardship on the white people; that they were dependent on the Indians for labor, and that it would be difficult to get along without them."[11] Near Las Vegas the agent reported, "The argument is frequently heard, locally, that the government should let these Indians alone—that they are good workers and can get along very well by their own efforts."[12]

There seemed to be a dispute between those non-Indians who wanted the last remaining Paiute resources and asked that the Indians be removed to reservations and those who did not want Indians themselves taken away from the vicinity because their labor was useful. This apparent contradiction in interethnic relations rested on native participation in the wage labor market, on the presumption that workers would not be competing landowners and producers.

Nevertheless, subtle changes were occurring in the labor market just as outcries for reservations were being raised. There was a noticeable decline in the demand for Indian labor in the first decade of the twentieth century that made Paiutes expendable and vulnerable to reservationization. Some BIA agents thought this was a temporary aberration, the result of a few sequential dry years: "Ordinarily, there is a constant demand for Indian labor, but since the white farmers had fared as badly as the Indians, they were unable to offer employment to any one."[13] Others saw the decline as indicative of a long-term and irreversible economic change. The frontier period was over, and people, as the Kaibab man had said, were "thick" on the land. A special federal agent observed that the rich Santa Clara Valley, where Ivins was trying to get a reservation for Shivwits Paiutes,

> *is now very nearly taxed to its fullest capacity to support its white population. . . . The white people here seem to be loyally and vigorously obeying the divine mandate to "multiply and replenish" for I am sure I never saw more white children, in proportion to population, than may be seen here. This increase is not only pressing the production, but the capacity for production of the valley, and unless better water supply can be developed there must soon come a partial exodus of whites, a fact now fully recognized by thoughtful men here. This condition constantly narrows the opportunities for labor and self support of these Indians. . . . I can, therefore, see nothing ahead for these Indians, except their removal to a better home elsewhere, or, in the main, to be supported by the government, or perish.*[14]

By the turn of the twentieth century, non-Indians saturated remote corners of the Paiute landscape and completed their absorption of land and water. The sons and daughters of settler families began to fill up the labor niches that Paiutes had historically used to supplement their economy after occupation of their lands. As they had before, non-Indians assumed that in the face of competition for resources, it was Paiutes who would have to yield to white priorities. Paiutes would have to move to reservations.

If all the land was already in non-Indian hands, however, it became a question where those reservations would be located. The easiest solution was to double up on already existing reserves: the Pioche paper suggested moving Paiutes to the Colorado River Reservation at La Paz, and the Kanosh townspeople proposed Uintah-Ouray, both conveniently distant. Neither was accomplished. In 1910 a BIA inspector devised a plan that would shape federal treatment of Southern Paiutes for several decades:

> *These Indians are now located remote from civilization where work is scarce, where they are compelled to go anywhere from fifteen to even sixty and seventy miles to secure work, where good land and water, either one or both, is scarce, where advancement is slow and where, at best, they can never acquire a competency and must necessarily remain, for all time to come, more or less of a Government charge. Such propositions are expensive. . . . it would, in my opinion, be well to acquire good land near white settlements, where a water supply for irrigation purposes is assured, and concentrate several bands in one place.*[15]

He knew from persistent Paiute historic patterns of dispersed settlement that they would resist centralization on one reservation, yet he recognized that separate, fully staffed reservations for each small camp group would be extremely expensive to maintain. He similarly argued against BIA schools and use of teachers to supervise the local Indian populace in favor of a less land based strategy:

> *the appointment of some person specially whose sole duty should be traveling from place to place, visiting the different bands and keeping in close and constant touch with them. . . . the personal supervision of a person well acquainted with conditions and having not only an acquaintance with the Indians but their confidence . . . looking to the future establishment of such superintendencies as are actually necessary and avoiding the establishment of small schools, putting, as it were, the Indian business here on a sound business basis for the future, and eliminating or reducing to the minimum, the matter of sentiment.*[16]

As a result of this report, in 1911 the BIA hired a sort of mobile agent based in Salt Lake City who was responsible for all the "Scattered Bands of Utah." The BIA tried a boarding school briefly at Panguitch but soon dropped it in favor of residential day schools at Shivwits and Kaibab, hoping these would lure in several additional small bands. It selected those two reserves for exactly the criteria suggested by the inspector—strategic location near jobs in non-Indian towns, plus arable land and irrigation water for the standard BIA expectation of converting Indians into subsistence farmers. Because arable lands had long since been possessed by non-Indians, the BIA also worried about purchase price.

The beginning of a permanent federal presence in Southern Paiute life was the purchase of the Shivwits Reservation along Santa Clara Creek west of St. George, Utah. In 1890 Anthony Ivins and various prominent southern Utahans complained of the "heavy burden" Shivwits Paiutes placed on local settlers by general begging and by hunting Ivins's own cattle. If they were not placed on a reserve soon, Ivins predicted dire bloodshed and widespread Indian depredations, which contradicted his assurance that "if they could be assisted a little they would settle down at this point and go to work."[17] It is unclear whether it was in his role as mayor of St. George, churchman, or cattle owner that Ivins had already approached Shivwits people about moving to an Indian farm.

Although the commissioner of Indian affairs had just liquidated the reserve at Moapa, he nonetheless appointed an agent to investigate, beginning with finding out who these Indians were. "It is against the present policy to establish any more reservations for the Indians," the commissioner began, "and especially it is undesirable in the case of a small band like this over whom the government could have no satisfactory oversight unless an agency were also established with a regular list of employees, and the establishment of an agency for them is altogether impracticable." If they would not go to Moapa, as Powell and Ingalls had recommended in 1873, or, alternatively, Uintah, he continued, "the best solution to the matter will be found in allotting them lands where they are, or in that vicinity. . . . If with a little aid in the way of implements, tools, seeds, etc., they can make a good living where they are, it is not proposed to make paupers of them by feeding them on a reservation."[18]

Ivins led the investigator to three farms, owned by two struggling Mormon widows and a bankrupt cattleman, for sale on the Santa Clara exactly where Ivins had already discussed a homesite with the Indians. Despite the fact that none of these people held clear legal title, the inspector recommended purchase of their improvements along a six-mile stretch of the valley where a few Paiutes already farmed with the assistance of a local church group. He proposed a mining company's abandoned stone building as a potential schoolhouse. Not unexpectedly, the investigator recommended Ivins be appointed "to look after them occasionally and advise with them."[19]

When the BIA asked for a ten-thousand-dollar appropriation to buy Shivwits, the Senate rejected this "new Indian raid upon the treasury." Funding was only restored after the Utah territorial observer, at Ivins's urging, explicitly "disclaimed any intention on the part of the Indian Bureau or of those who were asking for the appropriation to have a regular Indian agency established for the Shebits with all its attendant expenses."[20] Congress specified that the funds were "for the temporary support of the Shebit tribe of Indians" to purchase land, improvements, tools, and work animals "and for the temporary employment of a person to supervise these purchases and their distribution."[21] The commissioner anticipated that this land would be subdivided into individual allotments under the amended General Allotment Act of 1887. Ivins negotiated to buy the three farms for $2,100, and the secretary of the interior approved the deeds on 27 July 1891. In September his recommendation of thirty-six square miles of public domain for grazing was also accomplished.[22] Finally, one of the previous property owners was put on the federal payroll as a demonstration farmer to teach Paiutes how to use his former land.

In accordance with Mormon habit, Ivins then suggested that Shem, an enterprising and cooperative Paiute already farming in the valley, be recognized as chief of the Paiutes, but the commissioner stated sharply that the government wanted to establish quite a different relationship with the Indians. "You are advised," he summarized concisely, "that it is against the policy of the Government now to either appoint or encourage Chiefs among the Indians. The present policy of the Government is to gradually break up the Indian reservation system, allot the lands in severalty, extinguish the Indian title, destroy tribal relations, deal with the Indians in their individual capacity, and absorb them into the national life as American citizens."[23]

The commissioner, a product of the well-watered East, calculated that the 194 people on the Shivwits census could be accommodated by six or seven miles of river valley in a continuous string of eighty-acre allotments with upland grazing in their off-river portions. Knowing there was not enough arable land, Ivins first suggested allotments a quarter this size but eventually divided the fifty Paiute families informally into four groups, each assigned to share one of the former Mormon farms plus Shem's native one.[24] Thus the BIA established the Shivwits' reservation reluctantly in 1891 as a stage preliminary to allotment. The public survey needed for such formal division did not reach this area until after the BIA had changed its plans, so individual allotments ultimately were not made.

Flush with success at persuading the government to buy several of his neighbors' failed farms, next Ivins tried to convince the BIA that "flocks and herds are the principle source of revenue in this region, and that this branch of husbandry may be made profitable [if] they should have a place where these flocks and herds can be pastured."[25] He offered to sell his own Mohave Land and Cattle Company's property on the Shivwits Plateau, where alleged cattle raiding by Paiutes had generated the initial outcry to remove them to the reservation. Two administrations turned him down before Ivins quit the BIA to join the Utah Territorial Legislature and later the council of advisors to the president of the Mormon Church.[26]

The original Shivwits appropriation had included salaries for both a farmer and a teacher; in 1898 the congressional delegation for the new state of Utah lobbied hard to extend this to $25,000 for a boarding school for Paiutes. Despite its logical placement on the newly formed Shivwits Reservation, city and county politicians objected strenuously to further BIA expansion that would give the Indians a strategic position upstream from St. George on the critical Santa Clara River while they bemoaned the loss of federal largess by removal of Paiute children to the existing BIA boarding school at Grand Junction, Colorado.[27] State legislators suggested a site near Panguitch, claiming it had good land and water and "is centrally located among the indians to be benefitted."[28] At the northern end of the Sevier River Valley, this was actually at the edge of traditional Paiute territory transitional to Ute lands. Since the killing of Paiute headmen at Panguitch Lake and the Circleville murders in the 1860s, Paiutes had had no visible presence in the area at all. Another problem concerned water. Although the proposed 150-acre farm lay directly on the Sevier River, the deed did not mention water, riparian rights not being automatic under Utah state law. Landowners had to own shares in an irrigation corporation that specified acreage to be irrigated; the local ditch company was already in court defending its water title. The farm's owner was jettisoning a property that could soon become valueless. The secretary of the interior waited until 1903 for all title problems to be resolved before releasing the purchase price of $3,950.[29]

Panguitch School had few students when it opened in spring 1904. The curriculum stressed practical manual skills over academic ones and centered on work experience on the demonstration farm for boys and in the cookhouse and laundry for girls. The buildings, designed for a single farm family, were cramped. Although Paiute parents visited the school, the BIA never won the enrollment it had anticipated from bands as far away as San Juan. Most of the thirty pupils were from either Shivwits, 120 miles to the southwest, or Kaibab, 75 miles south. Early high altitude snows often prevented students from returning to the school after helping their families harvest the important fall piñon crop, the school farm was not a noticeable success, and both staff and students experienced health problems.[30]

As attendance dropped, the newly appointed director suggested "use of direct compulsion . . . to put these children in school whether or no" their parents consented. The commissioner of Indian affairs authorized only "moral suasion," stating a preference "to supply the educational needs of these Indians with day-schools" on the Shivwits and Kaibab Reservations.[31] Classes were discontinued at the Panguitch School in June 1908, and Congress gave the property to the state of Utah.[32] The experiment to provide for Paiutes' education through a nonreservation boarding school was over.

Bishop Woolley of Kanab was the next to activate the strategy of getting the government to buy properties that had proven so successful at Shivwits and Panguitch. He bemoaned the "deplorable condition" of the Paiutes in the area to his congressman; in a masterpiece of enlightened self-interest, the Kanab citizen begged that the Indians be moved away from town for their own good so they could become self-sufficient and "not remain a constant burden upon the people [non-Indians] living in that section."[33] The congressman agreed that the government should "purchase a farm, one that *a* white man could make a living on, and one which has a sufficient water right, the Government to hold the title of the same, but grant the use of the land to the" seventy-three Paiutes of the Kaibab band.[34] The Panguitch teacher, then the nearest BIA representative, confirmed the Kaibab Paiutes' condition and mentioned that they were farming a dozen acres at Moccasin Spring, where oral history maintained that they had been "given" one third of the water flow by the Mormon Church. In the Kaibab area, as at Shivwits, "there is no land available except by purchase, all the land for which wate[r] can be obtained having been taken up" by non-Indians a generation or more earlier.[35]

The current commissioner of Indian affairs, unlike his predecessor, who had avoided founding new reservations, held "the opinion that an appropriation might very properly be made to purchase land and other necessaries for them [Kaibab Paiutes]."[36] With his support, the Utah congressional delegation won $10,500 in 1906 "for the support and civilization" of the Kaibab Paiutes, specifically to purchase land and water, along with farm tools and livestock.[37] BIA agent Chubbuck was sent to look for land that fit the standard criteria for a reservation—arable land, albeit with attached water rights, that still was cheap. He was surprised to discover "that instead of these Indians being in a state of starvation, and a burden on the white people of the town and surrounding country, there were abundant opportunities for both men and women to secure employment on the ranches and in the towns in putting up hay, cultivating gardens, irrigating, cleaning ditches, hauling and doing laundry and house work, etc. . . . these opportunities for employment were not being neglected by the Indians."[38]

Indeed, Paiutes' greatest economic problems arose from recent nationalization of the forests and the application of state game laws to them as off-reservation, non-ward Indians. Chubbuck made the radical suggestion that, instead of reservationizing the Paiutes, the Indians be hired as forest rangers and game wardens to administer the public lands they formerly had called their own. Anticipating that his proposal of placing Indians in authority over non-Indians would be rejected, Chubbuck proceeded to analyze over a dozen properties as potential reservation sites and found none, including Moccasin Spring, to be sufficient. Nevertheless, in 1907 the commissioner of Indian affairs, without further specific authority from Congress, asked the General Land Office to remove from the public domain a twelve-by-eighteen-mile rectangle for Indian purposes.[39] This area included Moccasin Spring, already farmed by a non-Indian, along with Pipe Spring, a former cattle base of the Mormon Church itself, some lowland range used by cattlemen from Kanab, and some high rocky plateau above the Vermilion Cliffs. Moccasin was later excluded by virtue of prior homestead occupancy, the town of Fredonia was removed, and Pipe Spring was taken over by the U.S. Park Service in 1923. In addition to the loss of these small but important pieces of property, Paiutes and the BIA faced a continuous battle over the next twenty-five years to pry the Kaibab reserve loose from non-Indian cattlemen and reconvert the land to Indian use.[40]

Although she had never visited the San Juan Paiutes herself, in 1904 the Panguitch School supervisor had been told by a trader at Escalante about a hundred Paiutes who lived "formerly at the head of Pahute Canyon, but as that was included in the Navaho country and was needed by those Indians, they drove off the poor Pahutes, who were thus left without a country."[41] Two years later she reiterated that "their means of subsistence is entirely insufficient." She requested that land along the San Juan River be set aside for them before cattlemen cut them off from the water and that irrigation ditches be constructed "so each family can make a home."[42] The commissioner of Indian affairs recommended that "permanent homes" be found for them before "public lands become scarcer and possibly private lands would have to be purchased."[43] In the same bill that funded Kaibab, Congress appropriated $5,000 to "purchase lands and sheep for the San Juan Pah-Ute Indians."[44]

Chubbuck, searching for land for Kaibab Paiutes, was also charged to investigate sites for a San Juan reserve. Unable to reach the San Juan Paiutes from the north because of the broken landscape and lack of roads, Chubbuck swung south through Flagstaff to reach Navajo Mountain and even then had to rely on local traders for information. He was impressed that "these Indians are not asking Governmental assistance. The greatest of their desires is to be let alone. . . . They claim the territory in which they live (the lower San Juan River country on both sides of the stream) as theirs and deny somewhat aggressively the right of whites or other Indians to locate there."[45] The "other Indians" were Navajos. After they were released from incarceration at Bosque Redondo in the 1860s and encouraged in sheep raising, the Navajos had begun their remarkable historic expansion and population growth. "But vastly outnumbering the Paiutes, the Navajos have gained a strong foothold in that region, and soon the whites will be in there in such force that the few Paiutes will be crowded out and scattered."[46] Chubbuck considered this threat to outweigh Paiutes' wishes for autonomy and recommended that the land between the Arizona-Utah border and the San Juan and Colorado Rivers be "withdrawn from public entry and set apart as a reservation for Indian use, specifying particularly the San Juan Paiutes, and including other Paiute Indians of Southern Utah who have not been provided for otherwise."[47] The area between the San Juan and Colorado Rivers and the Arizona border was withdrawn from the public domain by simple administrative request in October 1907. Mining and oil interests began petitioning almost immediately for abandonment of this San Juan Reservation. The commissioner of Indian affairs repeatedly rebuffed these demands but did allow prospecting.[48]

The few agents to visit this area wrote only of "Indians," failing to differentiate between the two resident ethnic groups. San Juan Paiutes became quite invisible to the BIA, not only because they wanted to be left alone but also because they were using techniques to interact with their Navajo neighbors that were identical to those used by Paiutes farther north in getting along with non-Indians.[49] Many San Juan people became bilingual in Navajo. They openly adopted items of material culture that they found useful, in this case, Navajo clothing styles and hogan architecture. They freely borrowed economic strategies that seemed to work, including sheep raising and rug weaving. Furthermore, they continued to reside in their traditionally small groups, moving frequently to different sites to meet seasonal resource needs to which now were added sheep range. Despite all this borrowing and accommodation, San Juan Paiutes retained distinctive social structures and personal networks that kept them distinct from the Navajos with whom they coexisted.

The nearest Paiute agency, Panguitch, protested the three hundred miles of pack horse trail between it and these Paiutes, so San Juan was added to the Western Navajo jurisdiction.[50] In 1922, with blatant cultural blindness, that agent asserted that "there are no Piute Indians living on the reservation," declaring that they had either died, moved north, or "been absorbed into the Navajo tribe."[51] This BIA misinterpretation combined with mining pressures to get the San Juan Reservation returned to the public domain later that year, from which it soon reemerged as an addition to the ever-expanding Navajo reserve.[52]

Federal relations with various dispersed small bands of Paiutes in western Utah were not handled through land-based reservations. In 1911 Lorenzo Creel was appointed at Salt Lake City to "do such constructive work ... for permanently relieving distress among the Skull Valley and Deep Creek Indians [who were Shoshones] and other scattered bands of Indians in Utah," which included virtually all except the Utes at Uintah and those Paiutes at Shivwits.[53] With energy and initiative, Creel was constantly in the field over the next six years and got land set aside at Indian Peak for Paiutes, consolidated land and water titles for Paiute homesteads at Kanosh and Koosharem, and visited the San Juan country. When he was transferred to Nevada in 1917, the jurisdiction of the Scattered Bands of Utah Agency was broken up, with some Paiute groups assigned to agents at the Shoshone reserve at Goshute and others to Shivwits. Those agents generally handled Paiute matters by correspondence with an annual "circuit ride" around the Paiute areas that they saw as tangential responsibilities.

Early on, Creel worried about a group of about thirty Paiutes living near Indian Peak in the dry mountains along the Nevada border two hundred miles south of his headquarters. Far from the symbiotic wage labor and horticulture complex of Kanosh and Cedar City Paiutes, this band was "nomadic and frequest [frequents] the mining towns [like Pioche, in Nevada] where they procure more or less whiskey. These Indians have no land and as soon as I can make some arrangement whereby they will know definitely where their land is [by legal survey], in addition to the small tract now occupied by them, to which they have only a squatter's right, I hope to be able to improve their condition very materially as [fence] wire and agricultural implements have already been purchased for their use."[54] When the township and range grid survey reached this area in 1915, Creel reminded Washington, "These Indians have a small water right and have made a sort of a home here for many generations."[55] In August an executive order set aside twelve sections from the public domain "for the permanent use and occupancy" of the Indian Peak and Cedar City groups of Paiutes "and such other Indians of this tribe as the Secretary of the Interior may direct."[56]

BIA supervision was so minimal, however, that when a water rights dispute arose with non-Indian cattlemen four years later, the assistant commissioner replied, "The Office knows no Indian lands by the name of 'Indian Peak Reservation'" and asked where it was and what tribe lived there.[57] The following spring, a BIA inspector observed that all the cabins the government had built for Paiutes at Indian Peak were actually outside the reservation in a strip of omitted townships right down its center, as were all the cultivated lands "which they now use and believe to be their property."[58] By the time the BIA got around to ask for the addition of this missing parcel, Congress had, in a general policy snit, forbidden executive order withdrawal of any lands for Indians without explicit congressional approval. A series of temporary executive orders blocked the sale of the strip to non-Indians until Congress finally added it to the Indian Peak Reservation in 1924.[59]

Not only was Congress reluctant to create additional Indian reservations, but the BIA was also still gripped by its policy of allotting small private farms to individual Indians. This philosophy was expressed in the well-known General Allotment Act of 1887, which authorized the breakup of existing reservations into small parcels for assignment, under temporary federal trust, to specific heads of household. For the many Southern Paiutes who had no reservations to break up, amendments to this law opened the possibility for claiming similar sized allotments out of unclaimed public lands, again to be held in federal trust. In addition, special laws in 1875 and 1884 removed the original bar in the Homestead Acts and permitted an Indian "who has abandoned, or may hereafter abandon, his tribal relations" to file for a homestead from vacant federal lands.[60] For much of the Great Basin, especially the thinly populated Southern Paiute areas, the BIA headquarters in Washington recommended that individual Indians claim small parcels of land as public land allotments or homesteads, rather than asking for reservations that would require permanent and expensive agency staffing. The BIA preferred allotments, whose trust files the BIA itself controlled, to homesteads, which were handled by the General Land Office. It also argued that the improvement requirements under the allotment law were more lenient than the standards for homesteads and further that women were allowed to apply.[61]

These options were activated by Agent Creel for the Kanosh and Koosharem bands. Named for the important historic headman Kanosh, the first band was located about halfway between Salt Lake City and St. George.

Federal agents had experimented briefly with the Corn Creek Reservation there between 1855 and 1869. Paiutes had sowed domesticated wheat in artificially dampened areas just as they had previously harvested wild grass seeds, lived part of the year in log cabins, hunted the mountains directly behind them, and traveled at other times to work on Mormon ranches and farms. About 1900, local Mormon Church leaders persuaded six Kanosh men to file for land title under the 1884 Indian homestead law. By the time the BIA agent arrived in Salt Lake, the period legally allowed to "prove up" on these homesteads had expired, and non-Indians were beginning to claim the fifty acres of Indian farms. Creel persuaded the original men to refile their farms as allotments from the public domain and got sixteen more people, including minors, widows, and wives, to claim 160 acres each to make a contiguous block. By 1920 some 2,160 acres were held in twenty-five-year federal trust for members of the Kanosh band.[62]

Eastward near the town of Koosharem in the upper Sevier River Valley, the first BIA inspector found twenty-eight Paiutes and four intermarried Utes living on three homesteads in 1911. Two of these applications had been canceled three years before but had not yet been challenged by local Mormons. Bishop Bagley, the major landholder, had personally agreed to divide the water of Greenwich Creek in half with the Indians, but this had never been formalized by legal title. The Paiutes irrigated small grains and potatoes near their log cabins, fed their own cattle on the alfalfa they raised, and worked part-time on nearby ranches. Together men and women harvested wild piñon nuts for home use and sale and then earned most of their annual cash income by working the sugar beet harvest in Richfield, thirty-five miles to the north, where they lived in tents until early winter.[63] Although the inspector said they were "considered a part of the community," citing their attendance at Mormon church services and conformity to the church taboo against coffee drinking,[64] this was contradicted by the intransigent denial of public school access "owing to complaints of their utter lack of cleanliness," which was "beyond solution."[65]

The BIA gradually increased its presence at Koosharem by fencing the Indians' lands, taking a census, and paying funeral expenses.[66] In 1921 it subcontracted a local Mormon woman to operate a one-room school specifically for Paiute youth, still barred from public education. This segregated school was maintained after the Scattered Bands Agency was closed and jurisdiction over the Koosharem shifted first to the Goshute Agency and then to Kaibab in 1924.[67] Only in 1930 did the sanitary conditions meet the demands of the Koosharem school district; a supervised dormitory-domicile in town was rented so Paiute youths could attended public schools under federal financial subsidy.[68]

Throughout this period the BIA agents who had nominal charge of Koosharem Paiutes seemed to have rarely if ever visited them. Other than schooling, the other major BIA concern was land title, especially to the two homesteads applied for but canceled as incomplete in 1908. Nevertheless, descendants of the applicants had continued to use the land, thinking it their own and sharing it in traditional ways as "[s]mall fields belonging to various Indians are scattered over" it.[69] Local non-Indians spoke of it as Indian land, and the county had never assessed taxes on it. In 1927 the BIA agent recommended that these 360 acres be made into a trust reservation. Inquiry to the General Land Office revealed that two, not just one, of the original Paiute homesteads had been completed, leaving only 120 acres still in the public domain. That parcel was set aside temporarily by executive order in 1927 and confirmed as reservation land by Congress the following year.[70] This torturous bureaucratic compromise resulted in 360 acres held in mixed homestead trust and reservation trust statuses to provide subsistence for seven Paiute families. Most of them continued to work at migrant harvesting in the summers, while one enthusiastic horticulturist, Frank Woody, farmed everyone's land for them while they were gone.[71]

Far to the south along the Colorado River, Chemehuevis were also tangled in the allotment process. In 1906 romantic photographer E. S. Curtis, there to make images of Chemehuevis, wrote to the commissioner of Indian affairs that Chemehuevis lacked title to the tributary valley that carried their name and where they grew some crops using floodwater and ran a few cattle. He was concerned that federal plans for large-scale dam development on the Colorado River would lead local non-Indians to seize the land.[72] The commissioner delegated the investigation to Special Agent C. E. Kelsey, who clearly assumed that the only real policy option was individual allotments, for he asked for clarification whether "the land should be allotted, though unsurveyed, to the Indians, or whether it would be better to ask for its reservation for Indian use and occupancy until it can be surveyed and then allotted."[73]

Kelsey had just been working at Twenty-Nine Palms in the central Mojave Desert where seven Chemehuevi families worked occasionally for wages and kept in touch with relatives along the Colorado but "had a great affection for the place and wished to retain it."[74] Even before visiting the Chemehuevi Valley, Kelsey knew, on the basis of the historical warfare with Mohaves and downriver Yuman tribes, that if Paiutes were sent to the newly founded and already allotted Colorado River Reservation, forty miles south, "this band would find there not only no welcome, but no land. It seems best therefore to take care of them where they already are and have been for centuries." But he knew the river's rampant spring floods slashed out new washes and silted in old ones, so no fixed land parcels could be reliably productive "until an irrigation system has been planned." He suggested a preliminary "setting aside in some manner for Indian use" of seven townships and fractions, "more than actually required by the Chimehuevis," pending his visit.[75]

The commissioner bunched this request and a small parcel at Twenty-Nine Palms, along with seven others for California desert Indians, to "be withdrawn from all form of settlement and entry pending action by Congress."[76] After the secretary of the interior approved the request, the General Land Office discovered a previous 1903 withdrawal of the Chemehuevi Valley lands for a federal reclamation project. Because engineers had not yet chosen the dam site or determined which lands would be flooded, and because "these lands are not desired by the Indian Office as a permanent location for the Indians," the land commissioner saw "no reason why the Indians now residing on these lands should not continue to inhabit them without interference with the work of the Reclamation Service until such time as they are required for construction purposes under an irrigation project inaugurated by the Government."[77] The commissioner of Indian affairs acceded for "such withdrawal to be temporary and not to affect the withdrawal under the reclamation act."[78] Only two years later did the secretary of the interior bother to inform the commissioner that he had thought such a temporary withdrawal for Indian purposes to be redundant and had not bothered to forward it to the land office. At that point the canny director of the Reclamation Service quietly persuaded the interior secretary that "these few Chemehuevi Indians" should more cheaply be moved to the Colorado River Reservation, where a big irrigation system was already under construction, and good land was in abundance.[79] They, along with some seventy-five other Chemehuevi people without land assignments living along the river and in the mountains, would be relocated.

That reservation's superintendent hesitated to accept new residents because his irrigation project was incomplete: "My advice would therefore be to let them alone until we have something definite to offer them," and headquarters agreed.[80] But Fort Mohave Reservation was being allotted, and several Chemehuevis in the old military Hay and Wood Supply Reserve across the river from Fort Mohave told the engineer in charge of relatives in the Chemehuevi Valley twenty-five miles downstream, where they "claim they have lived there a long time and have made improvements, and claim their people have lived there before them"; he innocently asked if he should make allotments to them before leaving the area.[81] Simply told yes, he proceeded to map off 2,040 acres in eight townships edging the river within the mouth of Chemehuevi Wash to thirty-seven Chemehuevi men, women, and children as young as six months.[82] Since the reclamation withdrawal had not been rescinded, the legal status of these allotments remained unclear. Several were soon canceled when the allottees died and heirs did not claim them. Others were denied as unsuitable land. Eventually, the BIA finalized eleven allotments in the Chemehuevi Valley, where several Paiute families made floodwater farms, ran a few cattle, and supplemented their income with occasional forays to town for wage work.[83]

Of the Chemehuevi allotments across from Fort Mohave, all were eventually canceled, but four families remained nonetheless, keeping cattle and small farms in the flood zone of the Colorado. Omitted from their lands was a narrow wedge between the old Wood and Hay Supply Reserve of Fort Mohave and a new military reserve just over the Nevada border. This corridor was contested between the Chemehuevis and non-Indian cattlemen from the desert interior who wanted access to the river. In 1927, after shots were fired, the agent at Fort Mohave suggested that this strip be added to the Chemehuevi reserve in order to forestall non-Indian claims. Five years later the department temporarily withdrew these four township fragments, subject to standing claims of the Reclamation Service.[84] Eventually, several families from Chemehuevi Valley moved to Fort Mohave, and about twenty others received allotments at the Colorado River Reservation.

As early as 1892 a number of still other Chemehuevis were living in a squatter community with Mohaves and Walapais in the Santa Fe Railroad yards in Needles, California. By 1896 over two hundred Indians worked for the Santa Fe and for private businesses around the growing town. A citizen petition attested that "[t]hese Indians, especially the Chemehuevis, are showing a great advance in civilization. . . . They are always willing to work and whenever an opportunity presents itself, they are anxious to make themselves self-supporting." But a business slump cut off many jobs just when a failure of the annual river flood crippled native horticulture. Non-Indians asked the BIA for $50,000 to "help these Indians by enabling them to help themselves" through irrigated allotments, thus relieving the town of their dependency.[85] The commissioner allowed $3,000 for temporary relief "if there is *actual* destitution among these Indians."[86] The agent at the Colorado River Reservation rejected this "kindly offer" on the grounds that "[t]heir most worth[y] traits of character are cheerfulness, contentment and industry. I fear if temporary aid even were given them they would become lazy and dependent."[87] A generation later the Chemehuevis in Needles still lived in wattle-and-daub houses on vacant lots without drinking water, sanitation, or electricity.

In 1924 Needles Chemehuevis requested a small plot of land on which to hold traditional funerals but were told by the BIA to have one of their members file on a homestead that all could use for ceremonial purposes.[88] This plan would have required someone to sacrifice his opportunity for wage work in favor of desert farming without irrigation, under which it would surely be impossible to "prove up," hence guaranteeing inevitable loss of the land again. There were no volunteers.

By 1926 the growing town was pressuring the several hundred Indians to move. The BIA demanded that Indians prove "that they were occupying and claiming the land prior to the allowance of the homestead entries" by non-Indians. A sympathetic new agent at the Colorado River Reservation, C. H. Gensler, collected two Indian affidavits that "they were residents on this particular piece of land many years prior to the date of the first deed I have found any record of." Gensler himself attested that on the arrival of the railroad "Indians were generally camped where the center of the town now is," but they had "from time to time been pushed back" by the growth of businesses and complaints about "the unsightly buildings the Indians have to live in and the insanitary condition of the grounds." Nevertheless, just as Utah Mormons had for a long time resisted reservationization, he said, "The city of Needles wants these Indians . . . [who] are doing a great deal of work about Needles" for the railroad, stores, city street and water departments, wood cutting, errand running, and "at least fifty Indians making and selling native products to the passengers on the trains."[89] He held a meeting with the Indians at which "it was agreed to among them, in view of the fact that certain of these old people had died and that it might be difficult to establish dates of settlements on that particular tract, to withdraw their claims for that part of this land which is now within the limits of the city of Needles" in exchange for forty acres on the edge of town.[90] Congress refused to fund the project. This early urban, wage labor–based, intertribal community never received formal BIA recognition, land, or more than occasional funding.

The urban Indian community in Las Vegas was slightly more successful in gaining BIA recognition. As early as 1870 the first BIA agent in Nevada adjudged "the only suitable place in this country for a Reservation—what is called the Los Vegas Ranch."[91] The ranch house was the old Mormon Fort, built in 1855 near the springs that Paiutes had previously and currently camped around. Even at that time they worked as day laborers for the ranch and continued to do so long after Moapa, fifty miles east across the desert, became a reservation. The ranch eventually came into the hands of Helen Stewart, who employed Paiute men seasonally and encouraged Paiute women to manufacture basketry for sale.[92]

In 1905 the San Pedro, Los Angeles, and Salt Lake Railroad was completed and built a watering station and repair yard about a quarter mile from the old ranch. The town of Las Vegas grew up around the yards and attracted Paiutes from the now depressed mining areas of Goodsprings, El Dorado, and Searchlight as well as from Cottonwood Island, Indian Springs, Pahrump, Manse, and other places throughout southern Nevada and the Mojave Desert.[93] When the Las Vegas Paiute community executed a shaman accused of witchcraft in 1910 and sought revenge for a girl wounded by a miner, non-Indians became worried about natives who had "been let alone to come and go as they pleased, hold their own courts of justice and mete out justice according to the crime."[94] The BIA authorized the Moapa agent to advertise for "land (large or small tracts) suitable for a reservation for the Las Vegas Indians."[95]

Questions of where to locate the reserve revolved around issues of cost, purpose, and fundamental underlying philosophy. The most obvious problem with money was that land around Las Vegas was already selling for $40 to $1,000 per acre. The standard BIA purpose in founding reservations was for Indians to become independent small farmers, but the harsh reality was that "there are no white men making a living from farming, and there is little land suitable for farming purposes in the Las Vegas Valley," the few isolated springs having been long since appropriated by ranchers such as Helen Stewart. The local agent suggested instead that "the reservation should be as near town as possible to enable the government employees in charge to keep a watch on the Indians and their squaws, their work, and the white bootleggers, and be in touch with the white [law] officers," specifically to monitor the relationship between the two ethnic groups.[96]

The philosophical assumption of the right of BIA paternalistic oversight and control often focused on money and alcohol. For instance, one agent recommended that the new land "should be at least three miles from the city limits so as to be without the zone of the city bootlegger and conditions that go with him." He had in mind Moapa, disregarding the fact that at least one enterprising white woman, thrice prosecuted and jailed for it, already had a thriving business there peddling white lightning to Indians and railroad crews alike.[97] He also overlooked the simple fact that Paiutes would never have survived centuries in the desert had they not been perfectly able and willing to walk a paltry three miles to harvest something they wanted. Being free men and women they could easily take the town wages the agent envisioned them earning and buy what they pleased.

The BIA advertised for land. Three of the plots offered were infertile, heavily covered with black alkali and caliche. The fourth was a portion of Helen Stewart's ranch, including a spring and lying within easy walking distance of employment in the town center. The several Paiute families living there showed the inspector the old springs where they had farmed before the arrival of settlers and continuously until Stewart had sold it to the railroad. They asked for their old farm site and for a school, because their children were barred from public education. The inspector knew the railroad would never yield a well-watered section, so he recommended the nearby portion Stewart offered.[98] The Nevada congressional delegation supported the purchase, and after a few technical delays, Stewart sold the BIA ten acres for $500 on 31 December 1911.[99]

Clearly the one hundred Paiutes who called Las Vegas home, or even the half who lived on Stewart's land, could not support themselves by farming ten acres. From the beginning the small size of the purchase indicated that Las Vegas was never intended to be a self-supporting reservation but, rather, a homesite for wage earners reliant on the town for employment.

The Las Vegas community was added to the jurisdiction of the Moapa Agency. Despite the fact that far more Paiutes lived at Moapa and had a working agricultural program there, the Moapa agent immediately argued that the need to control the liquor traffic, supervise the unfamiliar Las Vegas Paiutes, and set up the new school required that he move his headquarters out of the isolated desert valley and into town. The Las Vegas press immediately trumpeted the immanent abandonment of Moapa as a reservation, but its hopes never materialized.[100]

Las Vegas was intended to house an Indian school, which opened in the spring of 1912. Attendance averaged four students a day, fluctuating as high as eight but also down to none as parents found work on distant ranches or left the valley to gather desert foods. The student population never expanded, and the school closed permanently at the end of the fall semester.[101] Still barred from public schools, Las Vegas Paiutes went without elementary education for another generation.

The failure to enlarge the Las Vegas holdings; closure of the day school when Moapa had a school population of eighteen; increasing agriculture, liquor problems, and intracommunity violence at Moapa; and charges of mismanagement by the absentee agent resulted in the return of agency headquarters to Moapa in 1918.[102] The Las Vegas community was rarely visited thereafter by an agent. The town-dwelling Paiutes continued to live transiently in tents and brush dwellings. Their health was poor, with high rates of gonorrhea, tuberculosis, and infant mortality. In the rough railroad town, "girls of immature age are corrupted," and incidents of spouse abuse and intracommunity violence were not rare.[103] In addition, Paiutes faced a threat to the wage labor economy upon which they depended. Just as had happened in Utah with population growth, when the Las Vegas Valley passed to the second and third generation of non-Indians, "the water has now been appropriated and the Indians now have not as good opportunity, as they formerly had . . . now, that the ranches are divided up into smaller tracts, they are worked almost entirely by their owners and there is less market for Indian labor than in the past."[104] By the 1920s Las Vegas Paiutes faced hard times indeed.

Farther north than either Needles, California, or Las Vegas, Nevada, the third town that attracted Paiutes was Cedar City, Utah. In 1907 the superintendent of Panguitch School, looking for students, found about twenty Paiute families at the mouth of Coal Creek Canyon near Cedar City, where they "make their living by doing odd chores for the whites." Although the town welcomed Paiutes as laborers, it segregated their residences and did not allow their children into the public schools because "there is considerable race feeling against the Indians." These Paiutes had "never received any benefits from the Government as far as I can learn," the schoolman wrote, "nor do they want anything whatever to do with the Government now. When I informed them that they were wards of the government and that I was Indian Agent in charge they refused to have anything to do with me, whatsoever." The headman, Captain Pete, informed him that "they were no government Indians, but Mormon Indians, meaning by that that they had joined themselves with the Mormon Church and that . . . they subjected themselves to the Mormon community about them and not to the Indian Department."[105]

Four years later the new agent for the Scattered Bands of Utah discovered that the land the Cedar City Paiutes were living on was "owned by the Mormon Church. This and the necessary water, are given the indians rent free."[106] He suggested buying forty acres for them, but the BIA took no action. By 1920 townsmen were complaining about the unsightly Indian community and threatening to evict the Indian "squatters." A BIA title search showed that in addition to the Mormon Church, several individuals and the city owned various parcels of the land, while "[t]he Indians think that they own the land, believing that their title is that of continuous occupancy."[107] Furthermore, the regional growth of national parks, the highway system, and accompanying tourism led several of the city fathers to view the

Paiutes as a potential tourist attraction, if they "can be taught to make and sell at a good profit baskets, mossasins, gloves and trinkets of various sorts."[108]

With the efficiency, coordination, and obedience to authority that had long characterized Mormon efforts, the local bishop, William Palmer, suggested that the church buy a forty-acre parcel of irrigated pastureland a bit to the north of town as a new home for the Paiutes. He was enthusiastically supported by Anthony Ivins, now a member of the highly influential Quorum of Twelve. The bishop had already convinced the city council to pipe in culinary water, persuaded the church to build houses, interested the Union Pacific Railroad in the tourist potential of an Indian village, and "urg[ed] the Indians to produce what the[y] can in the way of bead work and other trinkets."[109]

Federal interest in acquiring land for Cedar City Paiutes proceeded slowly, tangled in bureaucracy and communications difficulties, while the Mormon Church promptly bought out several properties and at Christmas 1926 physically relocated the Paiutes to the new site.[110] The county Board of Health condemned the old Indian residences and burned them. A BIA inspector wrote, "If the Mormon church wants to look after those Indians I do not see why they are not allowed to do so."[111] The responsible Kaibab agent opined, "It would appear that no further action on our part is warranted."[112]

The BIA in Washington consciously decided at this point to hand over administration of the Cedar City Paiute band to the Mormon Church.[113] After five years, the commissioner of Indian affairs specifically ruled that Cedar City Paiutes were *not* wards of the government and declared that federal funds would no longer be spent on them.[114] Meanwhile, Paiutes registered on the other Utah reserves were increasingly moving to Cedar City for employment and *their* health and school benefits *were* federally funded, creating a dual set of statuses within the Cedar City Paiute community.

The new federal reservations at Shivwits, Kaibab, San Juan, Kanosh, Koosharem, Indian Peak, Chemehuevi Valley, and Las Vegas shared certain features. Although some were isolated and rural and others quite near towns, all were located on lands not particularly desired by non-Indians. Either the soil was extremely poor, there was no water, or they had been already tried by farmers and found uneconomical. Therefore, the lands were either still in the federal domain, as was the case of Chemehuevi Valley, or the federal government could acquire the property at a very low price; the government was not willing to invest much money on reclaiming land for Southern Paiutes.

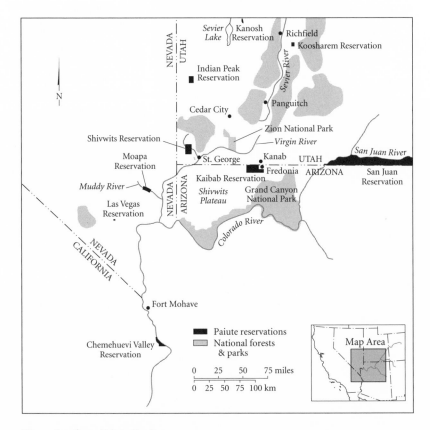

Map 3. Southern Paiute Territory, 1930

The type of land title varied. Although Congress was reluctant to aug-ment tribally owned lands, several of the Paiute plots were held as reser-vations in trust for the associated bands. Both Kaibab and Shivwits were specified as temporary, pending imminent allotment into individual prop-erties. Chemehuevi Valley, on the other hand, was placed directly into allot-ments with a twenty-five-year federal trust period. Kanosh and Koosharem began as individual homesteads, were transformed into allotments, and only later had tribal trust land added to them in a complex mosaic of land titles. The status of the individualized land assignments at Moapa that had been abandoned by the government as a reservation was completely in limbo. In fact, the Las Vegas acreage, ironically only blocks from the down-town area of the raw, booming railroad center, was the only unambiguously traditional reservation of the lot.

Despite the varying forms of land title, the BIA envisioned that all these reserves would operate under exclusive federal control, contrary to the hopes of the local politicians who had urged their establishment. Career civil servants were brought in, men and women whose loyalties were to the national bureaucracy and federal policy. In repulsing a local petition, the commissioner snapped, "There have been so many exploitations of the Indians under the guise of altruism that the Office has felt itself compelled, in almost every case, to retain *all arbitrary authority*, with regard to Indian affairs, in the hands of its duly authorized agents."[115] Those agents often found themselves very much at odds with the local non-Indian community regarding both goals and cultural assumptions.

The BIA also saw reservations as closed corporate communities where Indians could live in stable, permanent, year-round isolation from the prejudices, avarice, and competition of local non-Indians. Federal policy dictated that the BIA would guide Indians benevolently away from native cultures into an acculturated way of life resembling that of the non-Indian majority, into which they would ultimately merge.

The nine Paiute reservations were selected with at least token consideration given to soil quality and water availability so that the Indians could become independent, self-sustaining rural agriculturists. The tiny acreages of the Las Vegas and the church-held Cedar City reserves clearly indicated that these at least were merely living sites, not productive bases; their location near towns, albeit segregated from them, anticipated that wage work for non-Indian employers would continue to be the economic foundation for those Paiutes. But even the largest of the reservations contained far too little arable land to support the enrolled Indian population as farmers. Moapa had the greatest agricultural potential of any, with roughly 600 of its 1,000 acres considered arable, although throughout the early twentieth century there was only enough water for 145 acres. With an enrolled population of 125, this gave only 1.16 acres per person, or 4.6 acres per family, which was totally inadequate for subsistence in this arid area.[116] Similarly, Shivwits looked large on the map, with 26,880 acres, but it had only 60 to 80 acres along the creek suitable for farming. With 100 to 150 people expected to live there, this provided only half an acre apiece, or 2 acres of crops per family.[117] In fact, none of the reservations set aside for Paiute use could possibly support the resident populations by means of the BIA's favorite economy, sedentary agriculture. Even when mixed with open range cattle ranching, as practiced by their non-Indian neighbors, Paiutes could not have supported themselves on these inadequate land bases (assuming they had totally agreed with the BIA program, which they did not).

Inadequate size of the land base was exacerbated by a problematic water supply. All the reserves were arid enough to require irrigation for

4. A council of Shivwits Paiute men was called to talk to BIA inspector E. M. Sweet, who took this photograph as they waited patiently on the steps of the agency school in 1916. He was so impressed with their energy and independence that he wrote on the photo, "instead of multiplying complaints [these men] consumed the entire time enquiring how they might get teams and wagons and farm implements and a tribal herd of sheep and stoves and sewing-machines. This is the year marking the beginning of their larger industrial opportunity—if they be afforded facilities to meet it." (U.S. National Archives, Bureau of Indian Affairs Records.)

crops. Every one of the Paiute reservations suffered water shortages severe enough to cast serious doubts on BIA farm plans.[118] In every case except Las Vegas and San Juan, this water shortage led eventually to BIA threats of or actual lawsuits to wrest water away from non-Indians who had appropriated it before or after the reserves were founded. Conflict over water pitted local non-Indians against the BIA throughout the twentieth century, generating bitter hostility against perceived government interference that then spread from the agents to the Indians they served.

At Shivwits, federal purchase of the established non-Indian farms in 1891 included water rights, which, because Utah was still a territory, had never been formalized into a legal title. Despite the fact that the Santa Clara riverbed crossed the reservation, the Indian lands were denied their due share from the four or five irrigation ditch systems that drained it upstream. After trying to obtain local cooperation for ten years but facing continual water shortages, in 1902 the BIA requested the Department of Justice to file a friendly suit in Utah state courts to "protect the Shebit Indians in their rights on Santa Clara River."[119] Three years later that court awarded Shivwits Reservation water rights for seventy acres with a priority of 1890, based on historic cultivation, a legal limitation rejected by the commissioner's office.[120]

Pragmatically, the water situation changed little as Shivwits was shuffled into the jurisdiction of Panguitch School from 1905 to 1909 with only a field matron on site and thereafter passed to the Kaibab Agency with only a schoolteacher in residence. Inexpensive brush and rock dams diverted water to Indian farms, but these succumbed to flash floods at least four times between 1910 and 1930, each time resulting in loss of a year's crops.[121]

In 1911 the Saint George and Santa Clara Bench Irrigating Company (SGSCBIC) asked for a right-of-way across Shivwits for a canal that would remove virtually all remaining natural river flow. The company wanted Indians to share the costs proportionate to their court-allotted share and to promise not to move near the canal, as "to have the Indians located along the head of the source of supply is almost intolerable."[122] Somewhat evasively, the company assured the BIA that "it has neither the right nor the intention to divert any waters excepting those that it has acquired or may acquire in the future, and that there will always be a sufficient supply in the creek channel for the irrigation of the Indian lands."[123] Because the BIA thought Santa Clara Creek was already fully utilized, neither the local agent nor the irrigation supervisor saw any threat in this phrase toward future acquisition, and both of them recommended approval of the contract. The Washington office insisted on a three-year option to purchase two hundred acres worth of additional water, but it was allowed to expire inactivated.[124]

It was five years later that the indefatigable BIA irrigation engineer, Henry Dietz, discovered that four irrigation companies had water rights prior to SGSCBIC that more than exhausted the normal stream flow; SGSCBIC held only flood rights and had neither capital nor plans to build storage facilities. In short, the company had no water to sell. Sandy soils and a geology contrary to well drilling led him to "strongly advise" against preparation of additional farmlands at Shivwits "prior to the developement of a dependable water supply," which was itself possible only through water storage.[125] Costs of permanent dam construction were "nearly prohibitive for the acreage served," so the pinch-penny BIA policy of periodically rebuilding cheap, temporary, and unreliable brush dams continued for another fifteen years.[126]

Meanwhile, the agent who had negotiated the agreement with SGSCBIC was transferred. Although the new agent was explicitly ordered to "be alive to seize any opportunity" to expand Paiute water rights, he limply replied that he could not "find any record of Indian water rights . . . I presume that the Indians rights are protected."[127] The high turnover rate of agency personnel and erratic local record keeping that would plague Paiute affairs throughout the twentieth century was already hampering the defense of substantial and important natural resources.

Another complication to the water situation at Shivwits grew out of a change in internal BIA regulations. By 1916 the BIA decided that Indians individually should pay for whatever reservation developments would benefit them personally, even when those Indians were in no way involved in the decision to initiate such developments. This would include such expensive items as irrigation construction, despite the fact that Shivwits farmers were not clearing their costs or making subsistence, let alone a profit.[128]

As southwestern Utah continued to grow, pressure on limited water resources escalated. In 1918 several small, local irrigation companies filed suit against the Salt Lake City–based Newcastle Corporation for interfering with their rights to Santa Clara Creek. Hoping to increase Shivwits rights in a more favorable federal court environment, the commissioner agreed to join the suit on behalf of Paiutes, contrary to the recommendations of the Department of Justice, whose fears of a second assertion of state judicial jurisdiction proved accurate.[129] The Shivwits agent feared this "japordising of the rights of these Indians to have the matter settled in the local courts" and cited again the shortage of fertile land.[130]

Just weeks before the case was scheduled in court, yet another replacement agent at Shivwits was horrified to find no record "of the land having been measured."[131] His request for an immediate professional survey of the "scattered irregular patches" of Indian farms was denied for lack of staff, and he was told to rely on the state's maps, which showed 89.2 acres as irrigated. Those maps had been drawn up by the SGSCBIC, hardly an unbiased source, and the company admitted that it "didnot measure the land" but had referred in turn to a state survey from 1910.[132] Since Utah state water law took into account both the acreage under cultivation and the historical date when that land was first tilled, the use of such obsolete and estimated data was significant to the Paiutes' case. When the agent was asked if he thought the 89.2-acre allocation was "fair," without apparently consulting any resident Indians he sealed the fate of Shivwits agriculture: "If we can get this amount, 89.2 acres apportioned to the reservation we will have all we are entitled to and will be satisfied."[133] In 1922 the state court allotted Shivwits Reservation enough water to irrigate 89.2 acres (at 1.49 cubic feet per second) and awarded it the fifth ranked historical priority, behind four large irrigation companies.[134]

SGSCBIC and an electric company proceeded to build additional dams upstream as a major regional drought began. The state water master received complaints that the Indians were tampering with the headgates, while the BIA complained that the reservation was getting as little as half its proper share of water. By late summer 1927, the ditches feeding the Indian fields were totally dry. The irrigation companies established an emergency rotation schedule so that certain users would get all the flow, generating enough pressure to drive their water down the dry ditches to the ends of their fields; those ditches would then go dry for the next week or two. Shivwits Paiutes, however, still got their drinking water from the irrigation ditches; if those ditches flowed only periodically, they would have no domestic water in between. The BIA agent instituted trench warfare against the irrigation company and dug into its canal walls to get water for the Indians. The resultant public meeting called, for the first time, for actual measurement of water used, instead of relying on various farmers' self-reports as previously.[135]

It was in this atmosphere of interethnic competition and tension that BIA agent Edgar A. Farrow, in charge of Kaibab and also now responsible for the distant Shivwits, inquired into the possibility of claiming additional water rights under the *Winters* doctrine.[136] This legal concept grew out of a twenty-year-old U.S. Supreme Court decision that the United States would not have established an Indian reservation without including sufficient water rights to sustain life on that reserve; if those water rights were not explicitly stated, they were implied in the fact of the reservation itself.[137] The BIA irrigation division responded to Farrow's question negatively, arguing that Shivwits Reservation had not been created either by treaty or executive order but rather by purchase, so its legal standing would not support a *Winters* claim.[138]

When the drought eased after five years, a flash flood promptly destroyed the reservation's diversion dam at the same time SGSCBIC wanted concessions to build yet another new dam within reservation boundaries.

The BIA negotiated a cost-sharing agreement wherein the company got its site and handled construction and the Indians got jobs with the Civilian Conservation Corps (CCC), federal subsidies, and free delivery of their decreed water share.[139] Although problems of equitable water division became chronic as soon as the dam was finished, the BIA decided not to press for judicial enforcement of Shivwits contract rights.[140]

At the Kaibab Reservation, water problems were just as prolonged and even more complicated.[141] Unlike the flowing stream at Shivwits, Kaibab's water came from two desert springs, Moccasin Spring and Pipe Spring. Moccasin Spring was located within a privately owned ranch that was judged to have preceded the establishment of the reservation, and even that title was complicated by previous Mormon Church ownership. According to local oral history, the church had "given" the local Indians one third of the water from Moccasin Spring, and the later purchasers subsequently honored this custom, thus establishing for Paiutes a legal water right based on unchallenged use.[142] Their share, one sixth of a second-foot, an amount that fits through a single pipe four inches in diameter, constituted the sole water source for the agency buildings and school as well as the Indians' fields. After years of conflict over non-Indian management of this water at its source, in 1926 the government finally asserted eminent domain rights to four acres surrounding the spring, fenced it in, and took over division of the water between the reservation and the ranchers.[143]

Although Paiutes had another traditionally acknowledged use right to Pipe Spring, non-Indian cattlemen had used it for several generations. Because this was the only water for many miles of public domain range surrounding Kaibab, the cattlemen argued that they needed continued access. For exactly the same reasons the BIA wanted this same water for the tribal cattle herd it was building at Kaibab. Non-Indian cattlemen attempted to buy the spring, but their bid was rejected.[144] Then local non-Indians convinced the National Park Service that the stone fort, built in the 1870s as protection against the Indians (largely stock-raiding Navajos), had historical significance. The Park Service bought the fort from the same family that held Moccasin Spring. The executive order that established Pipe Spring National Monument said only that "the Indians of the Kaibab Reservation, shall have the privilege of utilizing waters from Pipe Spring for irrigation, stock watering and other purposes," a phraseology that did not actually recognize a native water right but suggested instead only a courtesy privilege to use.[145]

When the Park Service hired one of the ranchers as custodian, he expanded water use for campgrounds and other tourist services at the same time that he facilitated access to the spring on behalf of off-reservation cattlemen, including his own family. He repeatedly asserted that there was no water left over for Indians to use. BIA protests over these developments finally compelled a negotiation between itself, the cattlemen, and the Park Service that resulted in an agreement to split the water into even thirds.[146] Accurate division of the water remained a problem for years.

At Kanosh Reservation the Indians' water was delivered through the Corn Creek Irrigation Company, founded in 1887. Oral history describes negotiations by the bishops in charge of original Mormon settlement, working at least indirectly in the name of the church: "early settlers persuaded these Indians to move from their original lands to the lands which they now occupy, with the promise that they would be provided with a water-right."[147] Although twenty shares of water were stipulated for Indian use, the head of the BIA irrigation division noted that "it does not appear that any [irrigation] stock was actually issued to the Indians; however, the general understanding in the community is that the Indians have such a right, and such right is recognized by practically all interested parties."[148] Thus again, Paiutes depended, as they did at Shivwits and Kaibab, on the oral memory, sufferance, and ultimately voluntary cooperation of local non-Indians for access to this critical resource.

Until the 1920s water was ditched in a small but steady flow to the Paiutes' land, estimated as quite close to the 1 percent of the company's water that their shares warranted. With this the Indians irrigated almost fifty acres of wheat, as well as depending on it for their domestic water supply. In 1922, however, as at Shivwits, the company wanted to begin a rotational delivery system. Under this scheme Kanosh Paiutes' shares entitled them to eighteen hours of water once every sixteen days, adequate for irrigation but clearly inadequate for drinking.[149]

The only other source that might provide steady culinary water was Rogers Spring, about a mile and a half away; both Indians and local non-Indians agreed that the Paiutes had ditched and used this spring continuously since at least 1873. In 1924, however, a California woman claimed that she had bought the land around the spring before the turn of the century and thereby acquired all the water rights; she declared that the Indians had only courtesy rights to unused overflow. Two years later a Utah state court opened a window of opportunity in a decision that also involved water use that predated Utah's statehood and its 1903 assertion of jurisdiction; if that use had been continuous but a state water right had not yet been filed for, the claimant was allowed a five-year grace period.[150] On the agent's strong urging, the commissioner authorized him to approach the U.S. district attorney for Utah to have "the rights of the Indians in and to the use of the waters of this [Rogers] spring definitely established."[151] The BIA gathered affidavits, ran surveys, and collected other data preparatory to a lawsuit. The irrigation company, rushing to limit its own legal liability, for the first time issued a stock certificate in the name of the Kanosh Indians for cropland. The U.S. attorney general interpreted the evidence as so strongly favoring the Indians that the government could simply ignore the landowner's claim, and he decided it was "not deemed advisable to institute proceedings to settle and adjudicate water-rights at the present time. It will be time enough when the claimant takes some steps inimical to the interests of the Indians."[152]

The BIA then planned to build a pipeline from Rogers Spring to the Indian community, but it needed to buy up 920 acres of numerous small intervening parcels as a right-of-way corridor. Congress approved these in 1929 as the first tribally held reservation lands at Kanosh.[153] Four years later the irrigation company's rotation schedule, held in abeyance at the request of the BIA, was initiated. So too were town diversions from two small springs that headed on the new reservation land, which Congress had casually acquired without bothering specifically to claim water rights. The BIA did successfully negotiate for these spring rights and proceeded to file for their water for culinary purposes under state law.[154] Only after another fifteen hundred acres were added to the reservation in 1936, however, did the BIA consider investment in irrigation facilities at Kanosh to be economically feasible. It invested in an increasingly efficient system that eventually irrigated 170 acres of garden through cleaning the various tiny springs, rerouting, and lining ditches.[155]

Compared to Kanosh, the water problems at the Koosharem allotments were relatively simple. Paiutes there irrigated about thirty acres of wheat and garden crops with water from tiny Greenwich Creek, a tributary to the Sevier River. In 1911 the agent for the Scattered Bands of Utah had discovered that "[w]hen water matters in this locality were adjusted by the Court, probably no one appeared on behalf of the Indians, and they were not considered or named in the decree. Ex-Bishop Bagley of Greenwich, who was the only white settler on Greenwich Creek, considered that the Indians were entitled to one-half the water. He put in a division-box at his own expense, which division stands to this day."[156] So the non-Indian, who had a downstream position, arbitrarily took it upon himself to decide how much water the Koosharem Indians should get, and then he engineered the physical division. No one interfered; there were no non-Indian neighbors to contest his decision and no BIA yet present to support the Indians, who themselves acquiesced to the situation. The agent saw "a mutual interdependence between them, as their land gives them only partial support, their main support being derived by working for the whites, and the Indians on the other hand being the only labor supply upon which they could depend." Not totally trusting such economic symbiosis to protect Indian water rights amid a competitive agricultural community in an arid environment, the BIA agent pressed Bagley to "formally [convey] this water to the Indians, so that it may become a matter of record."[157] Instead of acknowledging the Indians as owners, however, what Bagley did was give title for half the water to the Mormon Church with the understanding that it was for Indian use.[158]

The BIA installed its own weir and fixed a metal blade in concrete to slice the water flow between the Indian and non-Indian ditches.[159] This did not permanently solve the water disputes. During the deep drought that lasted throughout the 1920s, the Goshute agent, who by then administered Koosharem, discovered "considerable feeling over the division of the water. The Indians, at times, lie in ambush at the weir, for the white men, and the white men carrying their rifles when they go to the weir, and bloodshed is threatened."[160]

Tensions between Bagley and the Indian farmers continued into the 1930s. When Koosharem was shifted to Kaibab jurisdiction, Agent Farrow planned to replace ditch water as the Indians' domestic water source with spring water piped from above the allotments. Bagley immediately wanted "to have you try and work it so we can connect on to it, for we really need it more than the Indians do as they are higher up the stream."[161] When the BIA moved to secure the water right to this spring by buying the quarter section of land around it, Bagley lobbied his congressman to block it; he used the same argument non-Indians near Kaibab had employed—a vested interest based on long prior use "for public stock watering for over fifty years."[162] Nevertheless, Congress approved the small addition as Indian trust reserve in 1937, and drinking water was piped to the Indian homes.[163] Although the BIA offered to build a dam to store the water of Greenwich Creek for all users, it "failed to reach an agreement with the white water users who are to participate in the program."[164]

Like Koosharem, water rights for the Indian Peak Reservation involved chronic squabbling with the few local non-Indians over scraps of water. The issues differed, however, centering on historical dates and the nature of Paiute agriculture.

When the agent for the Scattered Bands of Utah first visited this remote borderland in 1913, he found a dispute already simmering between Paiutes and George Mitchell over the water of Indian Creek.[165] Two years previously Mitchell had filed a desert land claim below the Indians and had successfully filed with the state for all water not used by the Paiutes. He took it upon himself to walk the Paiutes' fields and firmly maintained that they had only 5.5 acres cultivated at that time, while Paiutes equally consistently claimed that they had worked far more before Mitchell moved in.[166] Mitchell watched Indian fields closely to build documentation of prior appropriations under Utah state water law. When Paiutes had added 3.5 acres by 1913, Mitchell complained to the state. Because Indian Peak was not a federal reservation and would not be for another two years, the state officer correctly applied the state legal code uniformly to both parties but also made it clear that he would apply those standards fairly: "You do not set forth in your letter statements which would prove that the Indians have fully developed the rights which they initiated before your application was made. If their original application contemplated the reclammation of more land than was under cultivation at the time application was made, they would have a right to proceed with their appropriation so long as they do so with due diligence."[167]

The responsible agent, at that point from the Goshute Reservation, requested BIA investigation of Mitchell's continued expansion. While admitting himself not an expert, he foolishly wrote to Mitchell: "As I understand the laws of the state, you are intitled to all the water, they were not, at that time, using."[168] Washington censured him severely for offering such an opinion "before referring the matter to the Office. If necessary to go into the courts the Office would prefer to have the matter handled in the Federal rather than the State Court and would want to prepare itself with proper data previous to the bringing of such a suit."[169]

As the regional drought of the 1920s tightened, the U.S. Attorney's Office in Salt Lake City was alerted to a potential court suit, and a BIA engineer was finally sent to collect stream flow data. He found about seven acres planted to alfalfa and food crops near the Indians' residence, along with a tidy stone dam ten feet high and sixty feet long that they had built themselves about twenty years before. He also reported: "On the north fork of the creek, at some distance above the village, the Indians have, or rather, have had at various times, approximately 9 acres in cultivation, while on the south fork of the stream there has been cultivated, at various times, about 10 acres. These areas have been *intermittently cultivated during such seasons as water is available* for their irrigation, which is apparently not oftener than 1 or 2 years out of every 5, as testified to by the Indians."[170] He was clearly describing the same opportunistic farming practiced by precontact Paiutes that shifted freely to hunting or gathering as the availability of rainfall demanded; it was unlike the rigid commitment of Euro-American agriculture to a single method of production at a fixed location. Mitchell saw a short cycle of Paiute farming at Indian Peak over a relatively damp five-year period and assumed this was a point in a longer linear sequence. Paiutes claimed that they had cultivated more land before 1911 than the 5.5 acres, and they very well may have, occasionally and selectively, in the best water years. These two claims were not contradictory so much as stemming from different views of what it meant to be a farmer—whether to take advantage of opportunities and adjust to the realities of the season, or to forcefully expand and ruthlessly fight against an ever resistant Nature.

The BIA investigator estimated that forty acres were arable and that Paiutes had farmed a maximum of thirty acres in any one year. He concluded that "there is normally not even sufficient water here for the use of the Indians and for the irrigation of the fields they now have in cultivation or for the irrigable area within the reservation." He recommended conservatively that the "Indians should be protected in their right to a sufficient supply of water from this stream for the irrigation of all the lands they are *now* cultivating."[171]

The commissioner of Indian affairs initiated a request to the U.S. attorney general that "should he [Mitchell] insist on interfering with the Indians' water *rights* it would appear that appropriate action should be instituted to restrain such interference."[172] Inquiries convinced the U.S. attorney for Utah that "the Indians have superior rights," and he threatened legal action.[173] Mitchell, of course, complained but received a severe response from the commissioner, whose stance was historically significant for Paiutes' subsequent water rights claims:

> The courts have recognized the fact that occupancy and use by a band of Indians, of lands within the public domain establishes a right thereto for the Indians that cannot be displaced by homestead filings, notwithstanding the fact that the lands may not have been formally set apart as an Indian reservation. On the same basis the provision of the State Legislature of 1907, as mentioned in your letter, will not disturb the rights of these Indians to the water of Indian Creek all of which has been used by them and is still needed for the irrigation of the lands upon which they make their homes.[174]

In the face of such a forceful position by the BIA to all the water of the creek and such asserted willingness by the formidable Department of Justice to initiate a lawsuit on the Indians' behalf, Mitchell withdrew. This was one of the very few instances in which the BIA succeeded in carving out Paiute reservation rights from the Euro-American occupancy and utilization of resources that had been allowed to develop. The facts that those non-Indian usages were very recent and that the resource at question involved the BIA's pet project, agriculture, were not insignificant when evaluating the agency's uncharacteristically solid posture.

The water situation at Moapa was very different. Through scorching dry desert summers the Muddy River flowed year-round. Originating in mineral hot springs twelve miles above the reserve, the water was so high in minerals that a thick calcareous deposit had accumulated in the riverbed, virtually impermeable and as erosion-resistant as concrete. Alongside it a natural levy had built up from silt deposited by flash floods generated by summer thunderstorms. As a result, the river actually rode in its self-constructed sluice *above* the surrounding floodplain. The occasional floodwaters could not climb back into the river drainage, so they lay to evaporate slowly in sour, mineralized backwaters.

The federal purchase of Moapa in 1873 specifically included ditches and water rights with priority dates of 1868. As at Shivwits, Koosharem, and Indian Peak, the Paiutes were located upstream from non-Indians who demanded that the reservation yield water rights to them. From the beginning federal agents recognized the importance of "the control of the water privileges . . . there is no chance of escaping trouble and expense, nor is there any means of raising the necessaries of life for the Indians."[175] The BIA made early gestures at irrigation and farming without defining the actual water right. After its tentative land assignments and withdrawal from management of the reserve in 1887, federal concern with Moapa water lapsed entirely.

In 1899 Paiute George Leaye complained of mismanagement of Moapa, and the BIA became aware that the unpaid local trustee it had left in charge was casually using its resources for his own benefit.[176] Markings from the original 1875 Barnes and Bateman survey had long since weathered away or been removed, so in preparation for formal allotment, the commissioner of Indian affairs ordered a new survey in 1901. Surveyor Barber assembled conflicting local oral memories, landmark mentions from the original survey notes, and new measurements, but his resulting map enclosed two recent non-Indian homesteads that had been safely on public domain, according to the old 1881 map.[177] The secretary of the interior and the General Land Office refused Barber's survey.[178] In response, the commissioner of Indian affairs requested two hundred acres to compensate for earlier survey inaccuracies, but this amount was cut in half before being administratively approved and added by executive order.[179] Nevertheless, the confusion generated by the boundary survey question erupted again in 1928, when it was suddenly discovered that Moapa's primary ditch headgates were not built on land actually inside the reserve at all.[180]

Meanwhile, the state of Nevada had made efforts to regularize its water rights records. By his admission the state water engineer had assigned the Moapa Reservation a water allocation without even notifying the BIA:

> no one had made such [a state water] application, but that during the summer of 1906 he had made a reconnaissance of the Muddy River . . . he was unable at that time to secure data relative to the use of water by the Moapa Reservation Indians, only by inquiry of the ranchers adjacent to determine the dates of the Indians priority, which was conceded by the ranchers to have initiated in 1894, to the best of their knowledge, that he, Prof. Thurtell, at that time ran a stadia line around the fields in actual cultivation . . . and found that the Indians had under cultivation 87 acres of land in 1906; that he accordingly awarded them sufficient water for 87 acres of land.[181]

The state assigned Moapa water rights through its own measure of lands in cultivation only three years after the government had reactivated management of the reservation and determined the all-important priority date through word of mouth from competing and hostile water users who had trespassed upon and challenged the existence of the reserve for the last thirty years. The assigned priority dated from this purported use rather than from the 1873 establishment of the reservation and awarded to eighty non-Indians and corporations rights prior to those of the Paiutes. Because the state declared that the normal flow of the Muddy was fully allocated, application for any additional reservation water could only be for floodwaters and would be subsequent to all prior claims; this would have effectually limited Paiute agriculture forever to eighty-seven acres out of the potentially arable six hundred acres and crippled reservation development. It was two years before the BIA became aware of this informally derived, state determination against which the reservation would have to defend itself for the next forty years.

The U.S. attorney for Nevada advised the agent to simply go ahead and use water, "grandfathering" in a state right by five years of unchallenged actual use, to avoid conflict with local non-Indian users, and certainly not to initiate court action. BIA irrigation engineers planned a simplification of the system and drainage for efficiency, while agents documented oral records of irrigation use.[182] Meanwhile, non-Indian corporations bought the off-reservation head springs, planned an electric power plant downstream, and lowered the water table by dynamiting the caliche-lined riverbed, each action affecting Moapa water access and water rights.[183]

The BIA was soon blocked from filing for additional water by the Moapa Valley Irrigation Company, which had claimed this "would seriously injure and be an injustice to all of the owners of water rights in said stream."[184] The commissioner then took the U.S. attorney's advice and ordered that "the entire irrigable area be brought under cultivation as soon as possible, and the necessary water required be diverted from the Moapa River, in order that an unquestioned right by beneficial use may be acquired," through court suit if necessary.[185]

When non-Indian users protested to their senator about the BIA's new survey to replace Barber's rejected one, the commissioner of Indian affairs finally invoked the Supreme Court's *Winters* decision and denied that Nevada had any legal authority to assign any water amount or priority date to the Moapa Reservation. Further, he asserted federal "claims to the waters rightfully belonging to the Indians, sufficient to meet their requirements," not just those lands currently cultivated, and yet he still refrained from initiating litigation.[186] At a public meeting that excluded both Paiutes and their BIA representatives, J. G. Scrugham, then Nevada's state water engineer and later to be its governor and congressman, persuaded the users of the Muddy River to a friendly suit in state court to resolve all outstanding water claims.[187] The commissioner of Indian affairs responded stoutly and without compromise on issues of both jurisdiction and acreage:

> *Relying upon the doctrine laid down in the Winters case . . . , this Office contends that the Indians of the Moapa River Reservation have a prior right to the use of sufficient water from the Muddy River for their needs. . . . If all other parties interested in the waters of the Muddy River are willing to admit the prior right of the Indians to sufficient water with which to irrigate the 625 acres of cultivable land within the Moapa River Reservation, we would then consider the advisability of entering into a stipulation through your office to that effect. We would not desire, however, at this time, by agreement or otherwise, to limit the quantity of water available for the Indians to such an extent as to possibly handicap their advancement or which might prove insufficient for their future needs.*[188]

Without any participation by the federal government, the state court reaffirmed the casual 1906 state administrative allocation of eighty-seven acres worth of water for the Moapa Reservation. Nevada then threatened to seize control of the reservation headgates and arrest the agent if he exceeded this amount.[189] In response, the U.S. attorney for Nevada wrote the most thorough dissertation on federal implied reserved water rights "immune from State control" to appear anywhere in Southern Paiute ethnohistory, and he less than subtly threatened lawsuit.[190] Receiving no reply, he optimistically assumed the state had buckled.

In this he seriously underestimated the importance of water in Nevada politics. Two years later, Scrugham, now governor, issued a formal water certificate to Moapa for only eighty-seven acres. He requested the first investigation of water quality in the Muddy River, from which both Indians and non-Indians had been drinking for years, nominally to protect the sprinkle of tourists to the Lost City archaeological site a few miles downriver. The state report attributed the high rates of bacteria discovered to pollution from reservation irrigation; rumors began to fly through the Muddy Valley that the Indians were about to be moved and Moapa Reservation abandoned. The commissioner of Indian affairs snapped off a very sharp letter to the governor, inviting him, if there was "any further doubt in your mind regarding the exclusive jurisdiction of the Federal Government over the water rights of these Indians," to communicate directly with the U.S. attorney general.[191] Overt state antagonism waned, which is not to say that the fight was over.

The BIA expanded its water management at Moapa with flash flood control, drainage, and redesign of the riverbed. Still more water was needed, and Moapa's small size made independent BIA construction of storage dams for irrigation too expensive per acre to be feasible; nevertheless, this needed to be done soon. The Moapa Valley Irrigation Company had protested that the modest Paiute expansion from 375 to 600 acres of farmland would deprive others of their livelihood, but over the fifteen years before 1929 the state had approved 10,000 acre-feet of new water applications for non-Indian ranchers downstream without public outcry.[192] If Paiutes were not to be crowded out entirely, BIA cooperation with the rapidly developing and increasingly powerful non-Indian regional water storage plans was necessary. Heavily subsidized by federal funding, those plans envisioned completion of a storage dam in Arrow Canyon, just northwest of the reservation, begun in 1935 under the CCC but abandoned for technical reasons. Another associated dam at White Narrows involved the BIA, a local irrigation district, the state of Nevada, and the federal Bureau of Reclamation.[193]

Although BIA irrigation personnel questioned how much of this water would actually flow to Indian lands, it was not until 1944 that anyone asked how this off-reservation development would affect Moapa's legal water rights. In contrast to an earlier commissioner's far more adamant stance twenty-two years previously, the BIA's in-agency attorneys now suggested limply that they should negotiate for a mere four hundred acres of water, using the threat to withdraw from the White Narrows project as political leverage; the commissioner concurred.[194] Following a series of multiparty negotiations between the state, irrigation companies, and the BIA representing the Moapa Paiutes, in 1955 the BIA and the by-then-active Moapa Tribal Council agreed to quantify Moapa's water rights, reduce the estimate of its irrigable land to 546 acres, and install state-approved diversion structures; in return, Nevada recognized federal legal jurisdiction over and right physically to control water within the reservation and further acknowledged a water right for all 546 acres at a rate equal to that received by the rest of the water district.[195]

Those 546 acres were the old 1887 individual land assignments that Moapa Paiutes had voluntarily relinquished in the 1930s and were now held in tribal trust under the management of the newly established tribal council. Federally funded drainage projects had flushed the alkali out of the soil and enabled more than 250 new acres to be cultivated.[196] One member operated this property for the tribe but could not persuade any young man to take up the farm as occupational preferences shifted over the years; by the time the water negotiations were finally resolved, the entire reservation farmland was under lease to a non-Indian.[197]

Chemehuevis farther south had no water works constructed by the BIA, although in 1934 an agent suggested water pumps and systematic water distribution.[198] Like Moapa, their problems arose from regional water developments far beyond Indian lands, in this case the massive federal dam projects to tame the Colorado River. First monumental Boulder Dam and then Parker Dam were built to generate irrigation water for the Imperial Valley and electricity for Los Angeles as well as to control those very floods that made possible the type of farming still practiced by the Chemehuevis. The Bureau of Reclamation simply decided that the Chemehuevi Valley would be one of the zones flooded by the Parker Dam, so native allotments were condemned in the national interest, and monetary compensation was awarded. When floodwaters began backing up across their lands in 1939, only three Chemehuevi families remained to herd a few cattle on the remaining dry uplands.[199] The rest had already left for the Fort Mohave or Colorado River Reservations.

Even the tiny urban reserve at Las Vegas had water problems. The original federal government purchase in 1911 included a small spring, the sole source of water. Although the agent immediately requested wells for additional water so people could raise garden crops, the BIA did not fund drilling until 1932.[200] Water flow was not as high as anticipated because the many other wells throughout the growing city were already lowering the water table. The BIA drinking water well was deepened, two more shallow wells were drilled, and their excess water was impounded behind a small dam; together this produced culinary supplies and enough to irrigate two to four acres of gardens.[201]

Around the Indian community the city expanded rapidly with the construction of Hoover Dam, the wartime military presence, and tourism from legalized gambling, further lowering the uppermost aquifer. By the early 1950s the Indian drinking well frequently dried up in late summer. For another decade the reservation's federal jurisdiction prevented the city legally from connecting Paiutes to the urban water system that flowed within feet of their doorways.[202]

Every one of the Southern Paiute reservations had major conflicts with non-Indians over water. Pragmatic possession of water was necessary if land was to be used to farm, raise livestock, mine, or support an urban life. In addition, by the twentieth century legal water ownership was needed to generate anything of value in this desert area, for Indians or non-Indians alike. Because all the Paiute reservations were declared long after non-Indians had seized water and constructed ditches and in so doing had established vested interests they considered both legally and historically valid, Indians were put in the extremely difficult position of needing to reestablish rights to water. Everywhere they were met with complaints that should Indians get water rights they would deprive non-Indian users of theirs, because all the water was already being used. This argument was contradicted by the constant, new, non-Indian applications that fueled regional expansion.

In some places, such as Kaibab, Kanosh, and Cedar City, local non-Indians condescended to allow Paiutes a courtesy right to a small portion of the water the Indians had used within their precontact territories. Never recognized legally, these folkloristic acknowledgments were often mediated by the institution of the Mormon Church in an unwritten "trust." In other cases, such as Shivwits and Las Vegas, the BIA purchased water rights as part of the land title acquired from prior non-Indian owners. The BIA had to bring suit or threaten suit through the U.S. Department of Justice for six of the eight reservations in order to pry water away from entrenched non-

Indian interests. At both Shivwits and Indian Peak in Utah and at Moapa in Nevada, the BIA faced direct conflict with state water laws and with legal principles over how water should be allocated. At Kaibab the BIA had to challenge another agency within the federal government, the Park Service, and at both Moapa and Chemehuevi, the Bureau of Reclamation. Only at Moapa could the BIA's acquisition of adequate water for Paiutes be considered even remotely successful.

Everywhere else the limited amount of water consequently restricted agricultural use of the small amounts of arable land. Even if Paiutes had wanted to emulate BIA visions of the individual subsistence farmer, they could not have. While Paiutes had about five watered acres per family at Moapa, two acres at Shivwits, and less than one at Kaibab, non-Indian families in the same Virgin River watershed had an average of 19.2 irrigated acres. Those much larger non-Indian farms were judged by a federal report in 1934 to be nevertheless "so small that most of the farmers and their families are obliged to obtain part of their livelihood from outside labor. . . . 73% of the cash income to farm families was from outside sources. In the subareas with the smallest farms the amount of total income from outside sources is even higher than the average."[203] Because Paiutes' reservation lands clearly could not support them either through traditional economic means or through irrigation farming, in the early twentieth century they, like their non-Indian neighbors, relied on wage labor jobs.

Even from the earliest Southern Paiute reservations, Indian agents recognized that they were unable to provide economic support for the native population. At the large Kaibab reserve the agent felt compelled "[t]o encourage the Indians to leave the reservation and seek work that they may furnish themselves with the necessities that the reservation does not furnish."[204] Similarly, at the other reserve with any substantial amount of land, Shivwits, the agent complained,

THERE IS JUST ENOUGH LAND TO KEEP THEM HERE A PART OF THE TIME, JUST ENOUGH TO KEEP THEM FROM HOLDING A JOB THAT WOULD MAKE THEM A LIVING. IF THEY WOULD FORGET THERE WAS A RESERVATION AND THEIR LITTLE PATCHES AND WOULD SPEND THEIR TIME WORKING FOR OTHER PEOPLE ALL THE TIME, AS THEY ARE FORCED TO DO A PART OF THE TIME, THEY WOULD MAKE A GOOD LIVING, HAVE PLENTY TO EAT AND WAIR AND MAKE BETTER PROGRESS THAN IS BEING MADE UNDER PRESENT CONDITIONS. 46 ACRES ACRES [*sic*] IS INADIQUATE FOR THE SUPPORT OF THE MUMBER [*number*] OF INDIANS WHO DEPEND ON THIS LAND. *There is land enough for only two or three families.*[205]

Federal agents generally approved of Paiute wage work. The self-earned income supplied food and support for the aged and infirm who would otherwise be dependent on the agency budget. During the winter of 1912 the Shivwits agent was driven to request funds for "subsistence supplies for destitute old Indians at this agency" because "[t]here is no work here these old ones could do to make any money at this time of the year."[206] Through the 1930s, agents saw a clear inverse relationship between wage labor and agency welfare costs: "If we can work out some plan where all employable Indians can have jobs it will minimize the amount absolutely necessary to relieve widows, orphans, and unemployable members of the Indian communities."[207]

The BIA also approved of wage labor because it saw it as evidence that Paiutes were accepting the Anglo-American cultural values of hard work, ambition, and self-reliance, especially when Paiutes employed the agricultural skills that the BIA was hoping to inculcate. For instance, a Kaibab agent declared that if the Paiutes "were located nearer civilization where they could obtain employment in a farming community, they will learn farming much more rapidly than under the direction of a Government farmer."[208] Actually, Paiute men rarely had much contact with the non-Indian families for whom they worked, because "[w]hen an Indian is employed to work on a ranch, he does not live in the home of his employer, but in his own camp, which is often scarcely more than the shade of a tree."[209] They usually worked under non-Indian foremen, who issued the orders. By 1920 the Moapa agent concluded, "There is no intermingling among the Indians and whites only in a business way. The whites hire the Indian and sell him what ever he needs. There it ends."[210] Because of social segregation, the effectiveness of wage employment as an acculturative process was severely limited.

Gradually, agents came to realize that employed Paiutes were adapting to Euro-American culture in ways that the BIA had not intended. Unlike the idealized wage earner who worked steadily and saved his money, agents saw that "Indian labor is in demand in the summer and good wages is paid, but the money is spent as fast as it is received."[211] Agents were angered when Paiutes mimicked neighboring Westerner role models and spent their money in the saloons so cheerfully operated by non-Indians: "These Indians are very poor . . . not because of their inability to make a good living for themselves and families, but because of them spending a greater part of their earnings for intoxicating liquors, and thereby neglecting their work and losing their jobs with Ranchmen."[212] Paiutes also gambled, both in the old Indian ways and also in the newly learned card games of poker, faro, and blackjack. The Moapa agent chided the "women, who are more addicted to this vice than the men . . . that they must lend a hand in the fields, if they wished to keep from going hungry next winter."[213]

Paiutes got their jobs through direct, individual negotiations; rarely did the federal agent serve as more than a communications contact between the Indian laborers and the non-Indian employers. The categories of jobs Paiutes filled in the early twentieth century closely resembled those they had had in the previous one—men worked at general farm work, road building, timber cutting, and irrigation ditch digging. Occasionally, they rode for large cattle outfits alongside non-Indian cowboys. Chemehuevis mixed farm jobs with mining labor at Needles and Parker. A number of agents noticed that men's agricultural work was markedly seasonal: "The squaws have steady employment the year round washing for the white people. They get from 25 cents to 60 cents per day for putting out a washing."[214]

Paiute men's wages were slightly higher than women's but still below the rate paid non-Indian laborers. In the 1880s the agent at Moapa noted, "[T]here is work for them at from 50 cents to $1.00 per day when ever they will work. They get their pay in money[,] clothing or horses just as they can make their bargain with their employer."[215] The first Kaibab agent criticized Paiutes there because they felt "that they do not have to do a day's work unless they can get their price for it, instead of being willing to work for what they can get. I know men that would employ Indians at $1.50 per day when they can get white labor for $2.00 per day, but the Indians consider their labor equal to that of the whites, therefore the complaint. On the average I think the Indians are well compensated for their labor."[216] During this period the BIA mounted no effort to improve the wages that Southern Paiutes received.

On the other hand, one of the earliest preserved Paiute-written letters was a protest over wages. "Is there any more Slaves should be held in the states any more?" Robert Pikyavit asked the commissioner of Indian affairs. "That Mine Father is working like a slaves of states Utah, only for eat. I could not heardly stand that workes. their he not got any money from. . . . Because my Father doesn't know any things about the Money, and getting old now. He has worked about 7 years, only Just for eat and many other Indians do that at Mormon towns. . . . That slavery working."[217] By the last years of the nineteenth century Paiutes were clearly aware of the value of wages and also of the fact that they were being discriminated against. Despite protests, Southern Paiutes were unable to gain any sort of control over the differential wage scale or pay practices.

Small as it was, this independent source of income sometimes enabled

Paiutes to reject life on reservations and hence escape BIA control entirely. At Cedar City, Captain Pete argued that "if they moved away to a reservation they would not have work, that it would be better to remain and work for the white people and make their living."[218] The Fort Mohave agent was hampered in his efforts to persuade Chemehuevis to come to his reserve: "They told me that they have plenty of work and that they preferred to live in their present location."[219]

When Paiutes did live on a reservation, to get employment they almost always had to leave for the farms, mines, and construction sites of their employers. A Moapa agent made a typical report: "Work in the Cantaloupe crop in the valley being over, quite a number of Indians have returned to the reservation, and are prepareing their lands for fall planting."[220] When Paiute men left for work, they did not travel alone but brought their families with them. At least as early as 1911 Indians seasonally left Koosharem to go to Richfield, where both men and women harvested sugar beets in a migratory cycle that would be replicated for decades.[221] It was this mobility, not the contact with non-Indians or the income, that generated the most tension with the federal agents over wage work.

The agent at Moapa complained, "Many of these Indians spend the greater part of each year off of the reservation, being employed on the neighboring ranches. In fact the influence on the life of these people by government employees has been very slight."[222] Seasonal, migratory wage work specifically conflicted with both of the BIA's primary reservation programs: individual Indian farming and acculturation through education. Wages in those cantaloupe fields south of Moapa were so high that "[b]ut few Indians have staid upon the reservation this summer, and tried to farm their little fields."[223] At Shivwits, Kaibab, and Moapa, the BIA started day schools, but for much of the year there were few children to teach. Koosharem people followed migrant agricultural jobs from April until November, and all Paiutes were busy harvesting piñon for their own use or for sale well through the traditional start of school in September. School attendance was "very much broken," one Moapa agent wrote, and another recommended against the expense of the Kaibab day school "[u]nless these people are fitted out so that they can have a permanent home."[224] Visiting inspectors repeatedly observed that few, if any, of the Indians who were carried on the reservation censuses actually resided there and questioned the continued need for the numerous reserves.

Their own careers threatened, agents consciously tried to lure Paiutes to the reserves in the 1910s and 1920s by creating jobs on the reservations with federal funds. The Shivwits agent hired resident Indians to clean out the irrigation ditches, and at Kaibab he subcontracted Paiutes to cut fence posts and string wire to fence in the reservation cattle pastures. To build the new road across Shivwits, the agent hired four times as many Indian laborers as non-Indians, although he too assumed that the foreman's job, which paid twice as much, would be open only to a non-Indian. When the Koosharem school district finally opened to Indian children on strict stipulation that they be kept clean, the agent hired a Paiute woman from another reservation to scrub their faces and iron their clothes and a Paiute man to drive them to and from school every day.[225] Agents justified these expenditures because they would increase the productivity of the reservations and allow Paiutes to become self-supporting, free of further federal expense. But they knew also that Paiutes simply needed the jobs; a survey engineer justified hiring Paiutes because "the Indians are greatly in need of work, and the money expended at this time will tide them over until harvest."[226] Some agents consciously rotated the few jobs in their budgets among as many needy families as they could. It was Paiutes who built the BIA superstructure on their reservations and provided many essential community services while on federal salaries.

The BIA representatives justified Indian wages not only on economic grounds but also as moral leverage. "Where individuals gamble," the Shivwits agent wrote in 1912, "I would . . . allow them no work of any kind on the reservation for a period of several months."[227] Even the liberal Agent Farrow noted, "[A]fter the last pay day he [the foreman] reported that about 20 of the Indians were drunk, and it was necessary for him to lay them off the road work project for the remainder of this month."[228] Sedentary life was another moral virtue the BIA used jobs to encourage. The Kaibab agent postponed constructing half a dozen two-room stone houses "untill the indians have shown that they are willing to take some work, in earning a living, to indicate that they intend to permanently settle down to live here."[229] As the agent knew very well, the Paiutes were gone precisely in order to work; what he objected to was not any lack of initiative but their transience from his area of control.

Just when the BIA was struggling to encourage Paiutes to be increasingly sedentary, Congress made such residence uneconomical. In 1914 Congress declared that Indians themselves would be liable for all reservation development costs, shifting bureaucratic expenses onto people who had all too often not asked to have their lives managed by the BIA and not been able to participate in the decisions, design, or construction of the projects that generated these demands for federal reimbursement.[230] Paiutes felt helpless before these arbitrary charges. Joe Smith, who signed himself as the Moapa "chief," stated: "In different cases we are being charged with things And alowed to go on to the Amount of our Land. then thretened to take our Lands from us for the Cost of these things."[231] By 1919 $9,000 worth of road construction alone had been billed to the Kaibab Paiutes. Without any form of tribal income, it was impossible to pay off these debts. Nevertheless, water systems, drainage, road construction, bridge building, schools, and even the houses of agents and teachers became billable in an ever escalating series of "reimbursable" expenses.

During the previous year, Congress had funded individual loans for "purchase of animals, machinery, tools, implements, and other equipment" by Indians whose "habits of industry and sobriety may be relied upon to repay the amount expended in their behalf in accordance with the terms of the agreement, which they must sign before the property is delivered to them."[232] Agents on Paiute reservations actively encouraged such contracts. By the end of 1915, for instance, Moapa Paiutes had garnered $950 of individual debts and $625 more pending for teams of heavy plow horses, harness, farm wagons, barbed wire, cultivators, mowers, and hay rakes.[233] At Kaibab, Indians entered into loans to purchase cattle.

Even with such investments in technology the resource base of the undersized and underirrigated Paiute reservations was inadequate. The marginal, subsistence agriculture possible did not produce enough cash for immediate family needs, let alone enough extra to pay off contracted federal debts. By 1917 no payments had been made on any of the Moapa debts, and all were in default.[234] Furthermore, because the life of the equipment was frequently shorter than the term of the loan, the agent often found threat of repossession ineffective leverage, which left him with only one other counterproductive threat under his control: to cancel the debtor's reservation land assignment.[235] A stunningly illogical example of the extremes to which this policy was pursued by the BIA occurred when a train killed a Moapa plow horse owned by Charley Steve under a reimbursable loan contract. After the railroad company lawyers convinced the court that it was not liable, the commissioner of Indian affairs seized the opportunity to teach Paiutes what he saw as the ironclad responsibility of financial obligations; he refused to cancel Steve's one-hundred-dollar debt still owed for the dead horse.[236]

The only means Paiutes had to pay off these financial obligations was through wage employment. This all too often meant leaving the reservation and abandoning the very agriculture the agency was trying to advance. Agents were appalled when Paiutes harnessed their new heavy horses to wagons bought on reimbursable loans and used the technologically improved mobility, provided by the government, efficiently to seek off-reservation jobs.

Paiutes' decision for wage employment over reservation agriculture was a rational one. Alfalfa remained the only practical crop that could be raised on the Moapa Reservation without machinery, which was beyond the budget of either the BIA or the Indians; with hay prices standing at $15 per ton, the average 2.5-acre allotment could produce a maximum of $75 for an entire season's work. If a man's whole family picked cantaloupes for non-Indians down the valley, they could make the same amount in two weeks. Wage work *was* the economically rational choice, and Paiutes made it. Rushing to purchase Model T pickups as soon as they were produced, Paiutes eagerly hit the new highways "to go quickly from their homes to points where work can be obtained."[237]

Despite Paiutes' efforts, the wages they earned in seasonal and intermittent employment barely met their families' immediate needs. By 1924 individual Paiute men at Kaibab, Shivwits, and Moapa had aggregated individual federal debts of over $2,300, most under $30, but a few larger.[238] Too many reservations nationwide were as underproductive as the Paiute ones, and the congressionally mandated policy of charging Indians individually for reservation development costs was rescinded in 1932, but standing debts were not canceled. Paiutes' personal reimbursable debts proved so insurmountable that some were still outstanding in 1954, when Congress finally canceled them as part of the Paiute termination legislation.

By 1930 the federal government had established nine reservations for Southern Paiutes in four states, from Chemehuevi Valley in California to San Juan in eastern Utah. Shivwits and Kaibab were intended to be held temporarily before allotment, while Chemehuevi began as allotments. Kanosh and Koosharem started as individual homestead lands and later had tribal trust lands added.

The BIA considered several of these reserves large and important enough to warrant resident employees, particularly Kaibab, Shivwits, and Moapa. Often those agents were also responsible for one or more of the outlying smaller properties. Sometimes the person in charge was a BIA agent, but at other times the schoolteacher, field matron, or stockman in charge of BIA herds also took care of general administration.

Day schools were attempted at Kaibab, Shivwits, Las Vegas, and Moapa, shifting, combining, and closing at various times with fluctuating enrollments. Efforts were made everywhere to obtain water so Paiutes could farm, but nowhere were land and water resources sufficient to provide subsistence for all the enrolled Indians through agriculture. Southern

Paiutes therefore devised a mixed economy of off-reservation wage labor, some hunting and occasional gathering of wild plants, raising a few crops or gardens on small reservation plots, perhaps owning a steer or two, but always moving from one resource to another across both reservation and nonreservation lands.

Increased tourism during the 1920s demanded that the region be integrated into the national highway grid. One agent noted with surprise that fully one hundred automobiles a day were passing through the Shivwits Reservation along the new state highway that linked Salt Lake City to Los Angeles.[239] This vastly improved transportation system persuaded the BIA to consolidate administration of the numerous Paiute reservations into a single agency in order to save the overhead costs of separate establishments. First the Kaibab Agency on the Arizona border was made responsible for the small reservations at Shivwits and Goshute, as well as tiny groups of Paiutes at Kanosh, Koosharem, and Indian Peak and of Shoshones as far north as Skull Valley above Salt Lake City. Then a more central location at Cedar City or Milford on the railroad line was suggested.[240] Mormon bishop Ivins, so instrumental in the establishment of the Shivwits Reservation, supported the Cedar City option. Oddly enough, it was the BIA that opposed a base in that town, because "the Mormon Church has opened an experiment of caring for the little band of Cedar City Indians I deemed that possibly the presence of headquarters there might in some ways operate to defeat the purpose towards which they are working." On the other hand, Paiutes from Kaibab and elsewhere "have been spending considerable time at Cedar and have gotten into considerable trouble," and Agent Farrow felt obliged to "restrain these infractions."[241]

In 1926 Washington did consolidate administration of all its Paiute reservations in Utah as well as Nevada into a single agency at Cedar City, the one place where there was *no* federal trust land to administer and where the indigenous group of Paiutes did *not* have federal recognition.[242] It was only then that the BIA accomplished the goal first proclaimed in 1910 by the inspector initially sent to learn about Paiutes:

> *to establish a superintendency at some point, or by the appointment of some person specially whose sole duty should be traveling from place to place, visiting the different bands and keeping in close and constant touch with them. . . . the personal supervision of a person well acquainted with conditions and having not only an acquaintance with the Indians but their confidence, could be exerted in the right direction looking to the future establishment of such superin-*

tendencies as are actually necessary and avoiding the establishment of small schools, putting, as it were, the Indian business here on a sound business basis for the future, and eliminating or reducing to the minimum, the matter of sentiment.[243]

8

SOCIAL AND POLITICAL RELATIONS WITHIN AND ACROSS RESERVATION BOUNDARIES

As it had on the original nineteenth-century Moapa Reservation, the BIA tried, on each of the later twentieth-century Paiute reserves, to model a self-sufficient agrarian community under agency tutelage to be separate and isolated from the surrounding non-Indian society. Paiutes, however, refused to sever the ties among the native communities that existed in those dispersed locales. Further, they found that they had to establish a variety of ties with local non-Indians in addition to the economic one. Despite the BIA's persistent efforts, it never succeeded in eliminating or controlling these external Paiute social and political linkages. Nevertheless, the agency was able to mediate and mold them in distinctive ways.

Probably foremost to Paiutes were their connections with other native people living across their now-occupied traditional territory. Besides the nine population clusters the BIA had identified as large enough to administer as reservations, in the early twentieth century significant numbers of Paiute families and individuals resided in numerous other places, either never having left after non-Indians settled or having relocated in search of subsistence, jobs, or peace. Some of these places carried non-Indian names; others were unlabeled springs or hillsides. For instance, in 1920, over 150 Chemehuevis lived off-reservation at Needles, Pahute Spring, and "scattered along the Colorado river from this point [Fort Mohave] to Blythe, California" on both sides of the river.[1] In the years just before and after World War I, the BIA acknowledged the cluster of sixty Paiutes on its Las Vegas reserve but never focused on twice that number who lived as one or two families at outlying places like El Dorado, Searchlight, Goodsprings, Indian Springs, Pahrump, and Manse.[2] North of the Moapa Reservation, two hundred Paiutes were still living in the depressed mining towns of Pioche, Pahranagat Valley, Forty-Mile Canyon, Caliente, Hiko, Panaca, Tippett, Gandy, and Baker.[3] Between the Shivwits and Indian Peak Reservations, Indians lived near Enterprise, Milford, and Modena, as well as Beaver.

In central Utah, Paiutes resided permanently or seasonally near Richfield and Grass Valley, as well as Koosharem.[4] Clearly, Paiutes had not congregated on reservations, as the BIA had been urging ever since 1873, when Powell and Ingalls first recommended that they all be placed at Moapa.

By the 1930s historic mention of such small Paiute isolates was declining for several probable reasons. Some people quietly ended their lives, as did the single, "quite old" man known in Searchlight as Long Hair Tom who "was raised on river 12 miles down from mouth of this canyon and cannot be induced to leave."[5] Sometimes non-Indians brought orphans or others to the attention of the BIA in hopes that they would be drawn into bureaucratic care. The least likely reason for the decline of records was that Paiutes actually moved to reservations, because by the 1970s, at least in Utah, a small but significant proportion still lived separately from the main community clusters.[6]

This apparent shift in the historical record is most likely a product of the BIA's own policy, which increasingly insisted that off-reservation Paiutes were not a matter of federal concern. In 1870 all Paiutes had by definition lived off-reservation, and yet the BIA had defined them as within its jurisdiction, persons to be swept up, relocated, and manipulated into agency control; to a certain extent, local agents, embarrassed by small numbers of resident Paiutes, continued to do so. "Civilized" Indians, in federal parlance, were those "competent" to live off the reservation because they had been successfully acculturated to Euro-American behaviors and customs through agency tutelage. It was presumed that these program graduates would move into the general population, indistinguishable except in physical features from their non-Indian neighbors, free of agency oversight and expense. This was the self-declared goal of federal policy.

By the 1920s it had become obvious that certain Paiutes simply chose not to go to the reserves available or, like the Cedar City and San Juan groups, stoutly told the BIA to stay out of their lives. Therefore, increasingly the BIA squeezed nonreservation Paiutes into its conceptual category of "civilized Indians," despite their brief, marginal, or nonexistent transitional, agency-based acculturation experience. In 1924 the assistant commissioner of Indian affairs told the Colorado River Agency superintendent that off-reservation Chemehuevis nearby, although "technically under your jurisdiction[,] . . . are not subject to the reservation regulations, having separated themselves entirely from the reservation and adopted to a large extent the modes and habits of civilized life."[7] Not only beyond agency control, off-reservation Paiutes were also increasingly not a BIA responsibility. The agent, while actually headquartered at Cedar City, was forbidden

5. Through the first generation of the twentieth century, single families of Southern Paiutes often lived alone in isolated locations, such as this one dwelling at a
tiny spring on the head of Pah-Ute Creek in the eastern Mojave Desert. By 1929,
when this photograph was taken, such outlying settlements were increasingly
abandoned, as Paiutes relocated closer to towns, jobs, and reservations. The car
parked in front belonged to the photographer, probably Frederick S. Rogers.
(Photographic Collections, San Diego Museum of Man.)

to pay school tuition for local Paiutes or mixed-blood children because, although clearly within the BIA's biological definition of "at least one quarter Indian blood," yet still "they appear on no census roll, have no trust property, live like other members of the white community, maintaining a fixed home and in every way deporting themselves as citizens of the community. Under these circumstances, we are of [the] opinion that they do not come within the class of Indians, properly speaking, for whom tuition would be paid by the Government."[8]

Paiute relations with the government were further complicated by the legal conceptualization of Indians as federal "wards." As early as 1831 the Supreme Court argued that the U.S. government had a trust relationship over Indian tribes and hence that individual tribesmen were federal wards. It owed them protection of property, especially land, and tutelage in Euro-American culture.[9] From this it followed that the government did not have these obligations toward Indians who were no longer or had never been wards. In 1925 the U.S. comptroller general wrote a formal opinion that the BIA exceeded its authority and wasted federal monies when it paid the expenses of non-ward Indians. Immediately, the Moapa agent refused to pay a hospital bill for Leo Pete, because "[t]his family does not belong on any of my lists [reservation enrollments] and from the information obtainable from the Indians they have always lived around Caliente. Since the receipt of Circular No. 2145 of October 1, 1925 'Non-ward Indigent Indians' I have not dared to go good for any expense for such Indians as the ruling of the Comptroller seems to preclude payment of and moneys for such Indians."[10]

Non-ward status remained ambiguous. A Paiute could be a non-ward Indian if he had never become a ward by simply not residing or enrolling on a reservation. He could also become a non-ward by adopting the "modes and habits of civilized life." Which specific voluntary actions would constitute proof of acculturation and remove a Paiute from ward status, BIA oversight, and rights on a reservation remained obscure. In 1916 Mary Smith had a five-acre land allotment at Moapa, where she "has never lived . . . for any great length of time." For the next fifteen years she neglected to claim a trust patent but rather had "signified her intention of not returning, stating that the land may be given to any other Indian who might want it."[11] The commissioner of Indian affairs ruled, "Notwithstanding Mrs. Smith's desire to give up the allotment, there is no authority of law under which the allotment could be cancelled and the land made available for reallotment. The fact that the allottee resides away from the reservation and has no intention of returning does not justify cancellation of the selection."[12] Mary

Smith could not, through her own declaration and choice of residence, give up trust property, and hence she remained a "ward Indian."

The very next year the same commissioner decided that a Kaibab Paiute not only could alter his wardship status but did so by simply moving off the reserve. Eight years after the Indian Citizenship Act, Fred Bulletts filed for a homestead on the public domain, declaring he was "a citizen, regardless of his Indian status." The commissioner approved his application, because "[a]bandonment of tribal relations in this case can be accomplished by Mr. Bullets separating himself from the reservation and locating upon public domain land for which he intends to make entry. There is no formal separation in the way of a certificate or written statement certifying to such action, and written relinquishment of rights on the reservation is not required."[13] Discussing a similar California case, the commissioner explained, "[I]t is difficult from an administrative standpoint to provide aid to Indians off the reservation where we have no facilities for the purpose; and our appropriation is intended primarily for reservation Indians. . . . Therefore, we have necessarily adopted the plan of not supplying gratuitous help to ward Indians off the reservation except under unusual circumstances."[14] About the only thing clear about wardship status, however, was that it "cannot be reestablished in the case of an individual who has once ceased to be a ward."[15]

By 1922 a federal district court had ruled that non-ward Indians "who are living off of regularly created Reservations, are Citizens and their children have the same School privileges as the Whites."[16] While the BIA tried to prune its expenses by distinguishing between Paiutes enrolled on reserves but living elsewhere and those with no reservation affiliation at all, states had no patience with such minor differences and tried to avoid all costs for educating off-reservation Indian children. School districts throughout Utah, Nevada, Arizona, and California refused Paiute children access to public schools. When counties developed welfare programs during the Great Depression, they refused all Paiutes payments because they were "taken care of by the government." A Shivwits agent found that even minor state services were denied when he tried to register some birth certificates: "[t]he woman handed them back to me and said she did not handle the Indians."[17]

Although benefits in land, water, and other practical economic opportunities were small on reserves, there was still a mild advantage to reservation enrollment, because states denied Paiutes even basic services. By the 1930s there appeared to be very few Paiutes not enrolled on one reservation or another, even though they might not live there. They lived where they could find jobs, with non-Indian spouses, or simply near old family home places. It is clear that these off-reservation dwellers were not socially cut off from Paiutes elsewhere, including those on reserves; in fact, it was probably all the more important for these people to maintain social contacts, employing a series of both traditional and new strategies and mechanisms.

In the same way that plentiful harvests and sociability had drawn pre-contact Paiute camp groups together, in the early twentieth century Paiutes gathered wherever opportunities would support more than a few of them. At piñon harvest time, groups from Shivwits, Moapa, Cedar City, Kanosh, and Koosharem were often reported at Indian Peak, where there were large piñon groves and little interference from non-Indians.[18] In October 1917 Paiutes from Kanosh, Koosharem, Indian Peak, and Cedar City came to Shivwits for what sounded remarkably like a traditional rabbit drive— "several days of sports and rabbit chasing . . . for the purpose of having 'a good time.'"[19] The following month "[a]ll of the Indians of Southern Utah, including the Shivits, part of the Moapa and part of the Kanab Indians had a gathering at this town of New Castle" while they worked the potato harvest.[20] Every summer through the 1910s there were "Big Times" on the Moapa reserve when "[m]any families come from Shivwits to pick cantel-oupes."[21] Increasingly, non-Indians called these gatherings "powwows" or "fandangos."[22] At them Paiutes socialized, danced, gambled, drank, and talked politics. They used not only the old opportunities provided by natural resources but also the new prosperity of seasonal employment in complex ways, to enjoy life, renew old social ties, and forge new ones.

Paiutes also gathered on less festive occasions. Kin and well-wishers from miles around came to funerals.[23] By the turn of the century if not earlier, Paiutes at Moapa and Kaibab had adopted and modified the native southern California ceremony anthropologists call the Memorial Cry.[24] Held a year or more after a death to give relatives a chance to collect food for visitors, who in turn brought gifts, the dead were honored and remembered, as a somewhat garbled newspaper account described, "with a mournful chant pouring from 300 aboriginal throats for two nights and one day, and the shuffling coyote dance in which that nocturnal prowler is banished to the barren lands."[25]

As they always had, Paiutes continued to travel as families and individuals for resources not available in their own location, but those resources now included jobs and education. They looked for and found work in places they knew; as a reservation agent commented, "these visits are, to my belief, more for social intercourse and in search of labor."[26] For instance, after the BIA had set up its tiny segregated school at Koosharem, "In the win-

6. Drummers and singers at a late summer gathering at Moapa Reservation in 1916 that brought Paiute families from miles around. Use of the notched stick as a musical instrument, Paiutes say, was learned from Northern Utes, along with the Bear Dance that often accompanies it. Use of an inverted washtub as a reverberator is clearly a late historical elaboration. Women in the background right are watching teams of female handgame and card players. (Photograph by E. M. Sweet, U.S. National Archives, Bureau of Indian Affairs Records.)

ter one of the Indians moves in to a vacant lot opposite the school building and makes a camp there where the children live and are taken care of. Different Indian women take turns in caring for this camp."[27]

For many Paiutes this mobility remained a characteristic lifestyle. BIA officials, who held the cultural as well as the professional belief that every person should be associated exclusively with one single place, had difficulty understanding persistent Paiute visiting and the resulting diffuse social network. An inspector at Cedar City bemoaned, "I found visitors from Shivwits, Utah and Moccasin, Arizona. Some of the Indians, in Western Utah, hardly know to what Agency they belong."[28] Another described the life of "a young Indian matron, who with her husband, spent much of their time

roving about among the Indians living south of Cedar City, around Shiv-
witz, Moapa, and [M]occasin, and who returned to their home when she
became too feeble to continue these migrations."[29]

Paiute teenagers were among the most mobile, and they often traveled
alone. Winnie Frank left Kaibab for Shivwits "to avoid attendance at nonreservation school," and John Domingo abandoned Kaibab "to avoid arrest[.] he went first to Cedar City, Goshute Jurisdiction, and then drifted to
Shivwits where he was kept in school."[30] These young people, who had
grown up in very small communities of intensely familiar people, most
often relatives, found the wider social sphere that these visits opened up to
be both exciting and attractive. At multicommunity festivals and funerals
and through family visits and their own individual travels, teenagers found
sexual partners who were not barred by the extensive traditional incest pro-
hibitions against bilateral kin. Even BIA agents were aware of teenagers
forming liaisons that sometimes became permanent: "During the big time
. . . at Las Vegas it was reported that Lola and Lewis Snyder were running
around together."[31] Even widowed adults or those disenchanted with their
current spouses made new social contacts or marriages. Intermarriage
linked the dispersed Paiute communities.

Such ties were hardly new, and the pattern continued. A Kaibab agent
said in 1915, "[F]or years past the Santa Clara Indians[,] the Cedar indians,
the Kaibab Indians and even the Moapa Indians have inter married."[32]
Other agents mentioned that either a bride or a groom moved between Kaibab and Shivwits, Shivwits and Moapa, Chemehuevi and Las Vegas, Kaibab
and Kanosh, and Cedar City with Indian Peak, Kaibab, Shivwits, or Moapa.[33] Such intermarriage, of course, created affinal obligations between the
parents of both the bride and the groom, even though they lived on different reservations. In time it also produced children with grandparents and
relatives in both places. Paiutes had always believed that kinship created obligations between relatives, and they continued to act on those beliefs, even
though many of those behaviors were too subtle to catch the eye of the outside agents who produced the documentation of Paiute life during this
period.

A few of the more visible expressions hinted that Paiutes' kinship expectations had not changed a great deal over the years; only the occasions
and outward tokens of cooperation were different. Women shared child
care so that some of the parents could leave home for short-term employment or to gather piñon. A sharp-sighted agent at Moapa observed that it
was appropriate to offset the expenses of such care: "When one of these Indians who has a child attending the day school wishes to leave home for a

while, he takes the child and *a sack of flour* to a neighbors camp. A few extra children around an Indian camp are not considered a burden."[34] At other times reciprocal care was exchanged, as when Koosharem parents organized their system to supervise schoolchildren in town. Adult sons and cousins worked together on each other's farms in turn, tended each other's herds, and shared information about job openings.[35]

Above all, kin visited one another, re-creating the social familiarity that might eventually transform into new affinal ties. Relatives housed and fed each other when they traveled, and this hospitality expanded, in its most extreme form, into the sheltering of orphans: "The children all went to their parents and friends for the summer . . . and the parents were anxious to have their own children and the orphans that are nearly related, for a last visit" before returning to boarding school.[36] Sometimes orphans were purposefully adopted by childless relatives to care for them in their old age.[37] Married children often lived with their elderly parents, or vice versa, forming extended family households, so agents recorded, "It has not been possible to discover any suffering amongst the old people. Almost all of them are living with their relatives."[38] A person who failed to perform these customary obligations was sanctioned by relatives and affines, who often intervened to break up a relationship that they saw as flawed. Archie Kay at Moapa found this out when "his mother-in-law told him to go away and not come back as he was lazy and would not provide for his wife but ate from the old folks all the time."[39]

When Paiutes' kinship networks drew them to different geographical sites, they became temporarily or permanently members of the local native community. As with precontact camp group membership, they expected to gain access to the resources at those places, even if those places were reservations. Indian agents saw things differently. Should the agency pay for the casket when a non-ward Paiute from Cedar City died at Shivwits?[40] In other cases, agents simply looked the other way, especially when they would not be held accountable for direct federal costs, as when a Shivwits man rode a mare to his relatives' home at Kaibab intentionally to breed her to the heavy plow horse stallion there.[41] At still other times, agents cheerfully counted transient Paiutes to boost their population numbers, to make school enrollments look better, or to boost budgetary requests. Agents drew the line, however, when in-marrying spouses claimed property rights at both their natal and affinal reserves, especially when they wanted scarce farm allotments or pasture rights, or when travelers strained limited agency funds to support the indigent or infirm; then they protested raids against the rights of those Paiutes who "properly belonged" to that reserve.

In the eyes of the BIA, Indians "belonged" if they were on the agency census rolls. In the early days of the reservations, agents had built these rolls by writing down the names of any Indians they found there. Depending on the time of year, who happened to be visiting whom, or the condition of sometimes fragile Paiute marriages, people were included or excluded from these lists who might well call the place home. As agents became more familiar with the names and faces around them, they added to these rolls, with the natural bureaucratic tendency to expand their jurisdiction by including anyone new. As the number of Southern Paiute reservations increased in the late 1910s, agents noticed that some Indians appeared on the census rolls of more than one reserve. This offended not only their limited budgets and the policy that Indians should be sedentary but also their more covert cultural assumption that each person had a single social identity, that each Paiute "belonged" at one and only one reserve. Agents of the various reservations set out to "regularize" the census rolls, to assure that a person did not appear on more than one reservation census, even under different names or spellings. They tried to impose the unitary, permanent identity of reservation enrollment onto a fluid and multifaceted Paiute social space.

BIA headquarters advocated that a "careful examination be made of the rolls of the Indians under your charge to the end that such of them as be found to be carried on the rolls at other schools may be retained in the proper place and double enrollments canceled.... You should ascertain where the Indian or Indians properly belong and permit them to elect at which school they desire to retain their enrollment—such action being in accordance with paragraph 326 of the regulations of the Indian Office of 1904."[42] Agents found the problem extensive. In 1920 a new Shivwits agent considered as dubious 52 of the 113 names on the office census.[43] Agents who could locate no live person corresponding to a listed name queried residents. They might deny knowing the person, perhaps because they knew him under a different name, or she had visited only once as a child and been caught fortuitously in the census sweep, or they were respecting the customary avoidance of the name of someone dead. Agents then sent lists of the remaining names to one another to see if these people were living anywhere else the BIA controlled.[44] They then discovered, "It is frequently the case that Indians are known by different names at different reservations, and Indians of the same name may be found at the different schools"; for instance, the man listed as "Bird" at Shivwits was enrolled as "Bert" at Moapa.[45] Women frequently married more than once; the BIA habitually listed women under their current husband's name rather than their own,

7. Tony Tillohash and family in 1916. Born at Kaibab, this man attended Carlisle Indian School in Pennsylvania, where he worked with linguist Edward Sapir. Returning to Utah, he married a woman from Shivwits and raised his family there, working land assigned to her family while owning cattle maintained at Kaibab. Later in life, he was elected chairman of the Shivwits Tribal Council. (Photograph by E. M. Sweet, U.S. National Archives, Bureau of Indian Affairs Records.)

as they were known in the community. For this reason, women were often duplicated on different lists, and children from their various marriages were enrolled in several places. In frustration, at least one agent posted lists not only of enrolled names but also all known pseudonyms, kinship ties, and physical descriptions.[46]

In the process of "regularizing census rolls" agents found, for instance, that Brig George had a delinquent reimbursable loan at Kaibab, but he was not enrolled there, and so the agent no authority to collect; both Mayo parents were listed there but their children were elsewhere; and Tony Tillohash, boarding school graduate and anthropological informant, had been dropped from his natal Kaibab census but was not listed at Shivwits, where he lived with his wife. Of course, everywhere people had farmland assignments with standing crops, pasture rights, shares in tribal herds, homes, and property on one reserve when they were actually working off-reservation.[47]

Using the more formal and highly structured Plains cultures as a model, BIA officials in Washington told agents that "intermarriage between the Indians of different tribes or reservations does not change their status or entitle them to rights with the tribe or band other than the one to which they belong by blood."[48] They spoke of each reservation as though it housed a separate tribe, in direct contradiction to the fact that all the Southern Paiute reservations were occupied by people of the same cultural entity. Unlike the BIA's perception of identity as a permanent, biologically determined unity, Paiute identity in a community was residential, participatory, optive, and multiple.

Headquarters also reminded agents that, just as regulations required an Indian to chose and submit written selection of tribal identity, when a child's parents come from different reservations "the parents shall indicate in writing the tribe with which they desire the child enrolled and relinquish its rights with the tribe to which the other parent belongs."[49] Contrary to federal regulations, local Indian agents usurped the power to make virtually all these decisions by correspondence and conferences among themselves in which "*we decided* Indian by Indian which should be carried rightfully by each reservation."[50]

In 1917 the Moapa agent optimistically reported, "I believe that our census roll is straight," and three years later the Kaibab agent assured headquarters, "I personally know every Indian enrolled on the Kaibab Census[.] I am sure that it contains no names that should not be carried there."[51] The BIA subsequently assumed that Paiutes had one and only one "proper" place to which they "belonged" permanently by the innate and immutable characteristic of "blood." Nevertheless, adjustment of reservation censuses remained a chronic occupation as the BIA struggled to keep current with births and deaths but even more so with the constant shifting of Paiutes through their fluid social world.

Paiutes retained this social fluidity because they fundamentally disagreed with the agency on the nature of relationships between persons, society, and space. Although they had a strong sense of home and undeniable emotional attachments to places, they also moved in a world that was as much social as geographical. Paiutes did not see communities as bounded spheres enclosing a certain number of people and resources limited exclusively for themselves in the way the BIA was trying to define a reservation. Rather, Paiutes saw a community to be the people who lived in a place at the moment but also those who also had rights to that place through the kinship relationship of their mothers, fathers, grandparents, and great-grandparents, as modified by the life choices and actions of those parents and of themselves. While often based on the wide-ranging bilateral kinship system, biological relationship was not enough; social commitment was also necessary. According to Paiute ethics, people "belonged" and therefore had rights wherever they had active social relationships that they worked to maintain. Every person had many places where he or she could belong, and every community had a large number of potential members, currently living and working elsewhere, who might at any time choose to activate their memberships.

With Paiutes viewing society as a fluid network of people in motion, and the bureau insisting that each reservation had a fixed list of persons who properly belonged in that one place, a compromise was needed. In broader terms, the only concept that the Euro-American legal system provided to fit the situation was "adoption," so the BIA began to interpret the movement of Paiutes from one reservation community to another as adoption of members of one tribe to another. Because the BIA saw memberships as exclusive, it instituted an "adoption" procedure that required relinquishment of membership from the former community.

Paiutes first became aware of these new requirements in cases such as when Achip Benn, Jones Holms, and Charlie Howell, carried on the Las Vegas census (then a subagency under Moapa), wanted to transfer to Moapa itself in 1918. The agent simply filed a pro forma change "since there is no objection by other members to their adoption" and was surprised when the central office rejected it: "applicants for enrollment must furnish sworn statements as to their family history, etc.; and the Tribal Council or Business Committee of the Indians of the Reservation should pass upon such cases and say what they know concerning the rights of the applicants. The proceedings or minutes of the Council meeting should be duly authenticated by you and transmitted with a full report as to the facts in each case."[52]

Southern Paiute political organization had never been highly structured. A great deal of informal discussion and consensus building culminated in a public statement of position at an open gathering of all interested community members. This was not an institution that kept minutes, swore to testimony, or otherwise met BIA regulations. Furthermore, for years agents had discouraged and refused to accept the decisions of these forums whenever they contradicted BIA postures. Instead, the agents had called to their office selected individuals, usually men, whom they knew held compatible opinions, discussed issues with these few, and called the results "the decision of the Indians." This methodology too generated no minutes or other records and would not meet the standards now demanded by Washington for interreservation adoptions.

Yet another mechanism was a general community, or so-called tribal council. This came closer to the Paiute tradition but was now initiated by the agent to discuss an agenda set by him, rather than by the community. The Moapa agent called such a council in the case of Benn, Holms, and Howell, and he reported that this council agreed to the transfer.[53] The agent narrated the Paiutes' rationale: "All the Indians I talk with regarding these Indians and why they voted to have them as one of the tribe say . . . that they voted for them because they wanted more Indians here and that these three were good men; that two of them were married to women belonging here and therefore should be here with their families as one of the tribe and the other (Charlie Howell) because he is a Paiute Indian and has no home and is entitled to some help from the government now that he is nearly blind."[54]

The Paiutes' vote was unanimous, suggesting that the traditional consensus building had been involved in this decision-making process. The Paiute criteria were in-marriage, residence, a record of hard work, known character, and general ethics, not formal, legal criteria. This is particularly interesting since one of the married men was not originally from Las Vegas at all but from the nonreservation community at Pahrump. The blind and dependent man was of mixed racial ancestry and had been raised in the nonreservation mining camp of El Dorado, but Paiutes did not see partial Euro-American ancestry as barring a person from their community; they kept open boundaries. Their own ethical standards held them to obligatory generosity, and this meant helping a handicapped, albeit very distant, relative to the federal rations and welfare support he needed by blanketing him with tribal enrollment. Despite the extremely limited amount of arable land and tiny land assignments at Moapa, Paiutes did not view the reservation as a "limited good," where additional people would threaten the percentage share of those already there. They welcomed the talents and efforts of newcomers, even those desiring land assignments to support their families. In all these ways, Paiute logic contradicted the value system the BIA was trying to instill.

Fanny Adair also asked to be enrolled at Moapa, even though she had been one of the children sold to Mormon settlers in the 1860s: "I am a Piute Indian, sold to Tayler Crosby of Kanab, Utah, when a little girl from Nevada."[55] She had married a Mormon, lived in central Arizona, raised two children by him, and been widowed. Elders remembered how her grandfather had sold her and recited her kinship to prominent Paiutes. She too, along with her mature children, was accepted by a community council and found a land allotment. Moapa Paiutes welcomed back the young widow Nora Lloyd and her three minor children. They enrolled the six children of Grace Samlar, herself three quarters Paiute, after the BIA had tried to fire her Euro-American husband from his stockman's position because of his common law marriage with a "Moapa squaw." They admitted the sixty-five-year-old Sallie Elgin, who had come from a nearby mining town to raise her grandchildren near their relatives. John Quail, who had lived at Moapa for a while as a boy and had a brother there, was accepted back.[56] In every one of these cases, the decision of the council was unanimous. Similar permeability was practiced by all of the other reservation communities as well.

Despite BIA efforts to institutionalize reservation membership decisions to a series of biological equations and legal proceedings, the Paiutes managed to operationalize quite a different set of membership criteria. People continued to move across space and change their community affiliations. They were accepted where they had relatives on either their mother's or father's side or through marriage. They were absorbed whether they had themselves lived on the reserve and contributed to the economy in the past or not. Those who had lost touch with Paiute relatives through historic slave raiding or the Mormon custom of buying Indian children were welcomed back. Members were drawn in from populations that had no federal recognition. The young, nubile, and productive were welcomed, but so too were the elderly and dependent. People of full Paiute ancestry were viewed as community members, as were people of mixed ancestry. Through the early twentieth century, when Indians theoretically had no legal right to define tribal membership at all, Paiutes pragmatically managed to exploit the tiny input the BIA did allow them in order to see that their own open, flexible, and inclusive definitions of community membership were successfully accepted in fact.

Community membership was not the only social structure the BIA wanted to enforce. It also attempted to "regularize" marriage as a single, life-long union under the regulation of authorities external to native society. Agents found some Paiute marital customs praiseworthy, especially the very noticeable gender equality: "in the daily life the father assumes an equal share of the responsibility and care of the children with the mother. The drudgery is not shunted upon the women although they take their equal share." After a divorce, children were often "split" between the two parents.[57]

Nevertheless, agents found a number of other features of Paiute consensual unions culturally offensive. "The marriage custom among the Indians," wrote one early agent, "is to pay the parents for the bride and to commence housekeeping without any further ceremony."[58] Although Paiute custom encouraged girls to marry soon after puberty to men who had already proven their ability to support a family, the resulting disparate ages offended agents whose own culture decreed a more equal age range: "I found at this place [Shivwits] an Indian over forty living with a girl scarcely twelve. The girl was not allowed a say in the matter she having been sold to the man by an old grandmother. I ordered a separation" by sending the girl to boarding school and finding a job for the man in distant Las Vegas.[59] In addition to the lack of religious or political ceremony, the active involvement of relatives in mate selection, and the traditional giving of gifts between affines, the BIA also condemned what agents called the "considerable indiscriminate changing of wives among these Indians. . . . the majority of cases were merely Indian or comomon-law marriages and the changes were made with the consent of all concerned. . . . Divorce is not known except as such is considered by the Indians when separation takes place by common consent or deliberate desertion on the part of one of the parties. The custom of selecting another partner, particularly in the case of the woman, before the old affair is terminated seems common."[60] Although often described as an exchange of wives, implying that Paiute men were the actors accomplishing the exchange, the BIA documented with some outrage native traditions of female assertiveness; women initiated divorce as often as men, and they often wisely located a new partner before severing relationships with the old one.

Not only were BIA officials not fond of Paiute marriage practices, but the reverse was also true: "The Piute has not taken to the white man's idea of marriage."[61] There were a number of reasons for this, but the one obvious to the BIA was its formal difficulty. To buy a state marriage license at Kaibab, north of the Grand Canyon but legally part of Arizona across it to the south, required rigorous travel and considerable expense.[62] Even after the Goshute agent drove a young couple from Indian Peak to the county seat, as with education and other state services, they were refused: "[I was] unable to make arrangements with the Utah authorities for the issueing of [a] license, and in fact they seem to think that the Indian custom is good enough for an Indian."[63] Furthermore, Nevada refused to recognize Indian customary marriages as common-law unions, classifying them as adultery and the resulting children as illegitimate, unable to inherit off-reservation property from their parents.[64]

Just as Paiutes had good reasons for resisting state oversight of their marriages, they also rejected religious sanction. Mormon doctrine distinguished marriage in the local church from being "sealed" in one of the large urban temples by a special ceremony; this latter was believed to unite the couple not only in life but after death as well. Divorce or widowing could not alter this state, and subsequent remarriage (available for the male only) was considered polygyny. This kind of permanence did not appeal to Paiutes. "If an Indian wants a few extra wives," wrote one inspector, "he wants to acquire them in his own way and refuses to be sealed to them for eternity."[65] The Shivwits and Moapa Reservations had non-Mormon missionaries in residence by this time, but even they did not provide a religious alternative. When the Presbyterian at Shivwits, "an irascible old Scotchman," "was requested to perform the ceremony but believing that pagans should not be extended Christian marriage[,] he was so much inclined to stand on a matter of conscience that the couple were taken to St. George" personally by the agent for a civil ceremony.[66]

Paiutes' shifting marital realignments inevitably generated hard feelings within the community. Looking for an ally in the agent, a Moapa woman once wrote, "If he [her husband] does nor pay me I shall take it up and see if I can do some thing with him for leaving me and going with another woman when I am his wife. I shall have him put in jail if I can unless he pays me the $50.00 he spent of mine. . . . If you can get it please sent it down as I need the money and he ran away and left me without any money after he had spent mine."[67] Agents thought that the solution was a "proper" divorce, sanctioned by whichever authority had recognized the marriage in the first place; otherwise, remarriage would result in technical polygyny or polyandry, both marriage forms unacceptable to the BIA, or adultery, a criminal offense. In ruling on a pair of Paiute cases, the office of the commissioner of Indian affairs explained:

> *In the first of these cases, the parties were married according to law and they should be required to resort to the State Courts for a dissolution of their marriage bonds. . . . In the second case, the parties, having been married by Indian custom, might, with some propriety, resort to Indian custom for their divorce. The Office understands that Indian custom divorce consists practically in the desertion of one party by the other, as was done by the wife in this instance; . . . therefore, it is believed that it would be proper for you to recognize him as*

free from the former alliance and at liberty to contract a second mar-
riage, which should be done in accordance with state law. This advice
applies if the parties are non-citizen [ward] Indians. If citizen Indi-
ans, they should never have contracted a marriage by Indian custom
and it may be that their cohabitation has resulted in a common law
marriage, in which event a divorce in accordance with state laws
would be necessary.[68]

Here the BIA was taking for itself authority to rule on the legitimacy of Paiute marriages. Further, it expected Paiutes' social behavior to vary according to their legal status. If enrolled on a reservation and hence wards,
they were allowed the relative freedom of native tradition; those who were
not were expected to meet state statutory requirements.

This simple duality, however, did not encompass the complexity of
many Paiute cases. Shortly after the above ruling, two enrolled Shivwits Paiutes (considered legal wards and not under state jurisdiction) who had
been married on the reservation by a missionary under a license issued by
the agent (not in strict accordance with state law but emulating it) separated. The local state judge did not think he had jurisdiction and refused to
hear divorce proceedings; the agent appealed to the U.S. attorney for Utah
but had received no reply a year later. The commissioner of Indian affairs
tended to stretch state jurisdiction because this would further Paiute acculturation: "the necessity of having, or the believing that they have to obtain
divorces according to State law, engenders in the Indian greater respect for
the marriage ties, which is greatly to be desired."[69] Without any consideration of legal distinctions between state and federal jurisdiction or between
ward and citizen Paiutes, a Shivwits agent proposed "to require all Indians,
when [re]marrying, to obtain a divorce from the Clerk of the nearest
county seat. . . . This would soon put marriage and divorce on a definite basis, and not leave so much to guess work."[70] It would also place Paiutes' marriages, which the Indians saw as a social arrangement between consenting
adults and their affected kin, completely under the power of the BIA; this
was exactly what the reservation agents wanted and the Paiutes did not.

By the early 1920s agents thought they had brought Paiute behavior to
heel. The agent of the Kaibab Reservation, in Arizona, reported that he personally drove prospective couples to the nearest town, "Kanab, Utah (a distance of 25 miles), where a license may be obtained [from the wrong state]
and a minister or justice of [the] peace found to perform the ceremony. . . .
The Indians of this jurisdiction are complying absolutely with the State laws
relating to marriage."[71] To enforce Euro-American marriage customs, other

agents used "more aggressive methods, educative and repressive."[72] The educational methods seem to have been aimed primarily at women, the repressive ones against men.

As part of their larger educational and acculturative program, agents targeted teenage girls with what they called "moral suasion" and practical discussion of the benefits of formal marriage should their children be left orphaned. The often unstated subtext of such persuasion was always the threat to use federally controlled institutions to force Paiute compliance. Agents especially pressured students returning from federal boarding schools such as Lizzie White of Moapa, who "by reason of the educational advantages that she has had should be an example to the Indians of the reservation and is expected to conduct herself as all self-respecting and educated Indians should. In the event of her return to the reservation to resume her relations with Sigmiller, you will require the parties to marry in accordance with the State law, and upon her refusal to do so, you will present the matter to your Indian court."[73]

This preference for the reservation court system was a result of the division of state and federal legal jurisdictions, complicated by Southern Paiute mobility. Under American law, marriage generally fell under state authority, and in the early twentieth century there were virtually no federal statutes dealing with marital relations. Nevertheless, reservation-dwelling Indians were defined as federal wards living on federal trust land and therefore beyond the jurisdiction of state law. Agents repeatedly complained, "There seems to be no Federal law that can be applied and great difficulty is experienced in getting the State Courts to take cognizance of any Indian offense that does not directly interfere with the peace of the community. . . . there is a lack of interest on the part of the [non-Indian] communities which is also agumented by a doubt in the minds of State Officials as to where the wardship rules are to begin or end."[74]

One of the very few federal laws agents could draw on was the Mann Act, the so-called White Slave Traffic Law, designed to prosecute large-scale prostitution by forbidding men to transport women to whom they were unmarried across state lines for immoral purposes. Paiutes lived in four states on eight reservations and many more communities and routinely traveled across state lines for employment. They quickly noticed the jurisdictional weakness created by American-imposed state lines and began "evading punishment by going from one reservation to another."[75]

Agents tried to close this loophole with a test case to show Paiutes that they could not ignore BIA marriage demands. A Shivwits man ran into trouble when he left to pick cantaloupes near Moapa in 1923 accompanied by a woman still legally married to another Shivwits man. This couple was notorious. Two years previously the usually lenient Indian court had judged a substantial twenty-five-dollar fine for their public adultery, and the native community "even accused me [the agent] of taking no action whatever, saying that were it a white man they would have been punished almost immediately," implying that the Paiutes disapproved of this intentional disruption of a standing marriage. As the couple crossed into Nevada, the agent had the FBI waiting, and the U.S. district attorney prosecuted the man under the federal criminal statute.[76]

Agents also demanded changes in other Paiute social organizations beyond the initiation and termination of marriage. Various forms of plural marriage, permitted in Paiute traditional culture as rather rare alternatives, were defined as adultery and prosecuted. The multigenerational extended family households, ones that included dependent junior couples, were criticized, for "Kaibab Indians will not run counter to their relatives," hinting that aggressive kin could exploit the elderly.[77] One young returning student, Thomas Mayo, was chided for "never [having] developed enough energy to establish himself in a home of his own." These extended family households were traditionally and remained most often uxorilocal. In this case, the agent decried that "friction between his wife's relatives was such that he separated himself from her."[78]

In addition to using federal, state, and reservation courts and law enforcement to try to force change in Paiute marital and kinship behaviors, the BIA also wielded the weapon of its own boarding schools. The Shivwits agent hoped to get nubile young Ina off to Riverside School "before spring when her folks will no doubt get the wanderlust and there is all probability of her picking up another man before another year."[79] Although Paiutes continued the traditional kinship obligations to house and support orphans, the Shivwits agent, "fearing she would not have proper care if allowed to stay here," shipped young Elizabeth Cummerall off to Fort Mohave School.[80]

Agents selected Paiute children for off-reservation education for economic as well as social reasons. When her husband died at Shivwits, a woman took her teenage son and two daughters to Kaibab to live with their blind uncle and elderly grandmother, who survived on agency rations; the agent considered the boy "restless and discontented and was having a bad influence on the other children" and shipped him off to boarding school.[81] Eagle Valley John's widow supported her four children and blind parents by taking in washing in Caliente until a warrant was issued on the older boy for "taking a shot at a woman." The city fathers appealed to the BIA: "Some-

body versed in the method of handling Indian Children should have charge
of them otherwise the States Prison is their ultimate end." The BIA took
away all four children and sent them to boarding school.[82] The BIA particularly deemed widowed or divorced men as incapable of child care, presumably because the need to work left no time for home supervision (although
expecting that working women, such as the washerwoman above, would);
men were also thought more susceptible to alcoholism. Two Moapa boys,
age seven and ten, were sent to Sherman Institute in California when the
agent uncovered what he thought were doubly fatal flaws in their home life:
"they have no one to care for them but their father and he is a poor pro-
vider. . . . what he earns goes for whiskey and gambling."[83]

After citing the inadequacy of the reservation economic base, at least
one agent made the improbable suggestion that the total disruption of Paiutes' family structure was for their own good: "The [Shivwits] reservation
has but 47 acres of farm land and the Indians are forced to go away from the
reservation to find work. . . . If the parents would consent it would be better
to send them all to non-reservation schools where they could be cared for
and the parents would then be free to go and find work."[84]

Although some parents were persuaded or pressured by the agency,
other Paiutes remained firmly opposed to boarding schools, especially after
reports of school spanking, a physical punishment abhorred by Paiute culture, began filtering back to the community.[85] If even one relative was willing to approve off-reservation schooling, agents were often relentless in
overriding the opinions of other members of the family. In 1920, after her
mother agreed, a young deaf Moapa girl was sent to a special school in California over the objection of all her other relatives, led by a grandmother,
who feared that "under such handicaps, [leaving] would mean nothing
more than her death, as she could not possibly stand a change of that kind,
without, naturally dieing from home-sickness and sorrow."[86] The commissioner of Indian affairs insisted on her removal, in part because the grandmother was a shaman.[87] Paiute parents also realized that early marriages,
which the BIA was using boarding schools as a weapon to prevent, were an
effective strategy to prevent the agency from shipping their children off to
school: "attempts are now being made to either sequestrate them or marry
them off so as to keep them from being sent away to school."[88]

Over the first third of the twentieth century, the BIA tried to restructure Paiute social organization in a number of specific ways. It wanted sedentary communities on reservations that operated under federal control.
People would belong to just one of these communities, and their names
would be carried on official census lists. Membership would be determined

by a fixed set of articulated rules based on inherited rights by "blood" ancestry. Members of these reservation communities would live in nuclear family households headed by a husband with one wife, who would have married under the authorization of state law. The husband would support his wife and biological children. It was hoped that they would never separate, but if necessary, they would obtain a formal divorce, also through state law, before seeking other marital alliances.

Paiutes blithely ignored or skillfully evaded these BIA demands and continued to structure social relationships in ways they found useful, appropriate, and meaningful. They formed their own marriage alliances without the approval of the agent, church, or state. Their families absorbed relatives that the BIA considered "distant." They maintained ties of kinship and friendship with natives in far-flung communities. They moved from one reservation to another, from one marriage to another, and one job to another without regard to the boundaries the federal agency built to bind them.

The BIA tried to regulate more than just Paiutes' social relationships; it tried to restructure their political relationships as well into an internal community power structure modeled on Euro-American hierarchical authority supported by the threat of physical force. Because Paiutes refused to limit themselves socially to the reserves and for economic reasons could not be pragmatically so restricted, they inevitably had political relationships with people beyond the borders of the federal-trust reservations. As the BIA consolidated its authority over Paiutes, it tried to eliminate, or at least dictate, their interactions with nearby non-Indians, local governments, and enveloping states.

Political issues became readily apparent in situations where a Paiute appeared to violate the cultural or legal standards of American society and perhaps those of Paiute culture as well. The BIA held that violations of the "Big Ten" crimes, such as rape, murder, assault with a deadly weapon, and burglary, if committed by an enrolled Indian while on reservation land, were subject to federal law; other offenses were tried by the Court of Indian Offenses, if available, or, if not, by the Indian agent himself. Indians who were not enrolled on a reservation and were not federal wards were citizens of the states; as such they were "subject to the State civil and criminal laws, can be prosecuted in the State Courts for any offense against the State law."[89] This simple duality was complicated when the commissioner ruled that BIA authority over unenrolled "nonreservation Indians living south of the Moapa River reservation and others contiguous thereto is limited to that of supervision for administrative purposes," but otherwise they were "amenable to the laws of the State."[90]

Efforts to apply this abstract formula proved difficult. In 1920 two Shivwits men, working in the cantaloupe fields south of Moapa, were accused of robbing another Indian worker of $300 after a poker game. The Moapa Indian agent had no jurisdiction over Indians not enrolled at his reserve and none over actions off reservation lands. "If the Shivwits Indian plead guilty in Washington County, Utah" (where Shivwits Reservation was located), a frustrated inspector complained, "they cannot be punished here for an offense committed in Nevada. If placed under arrest and held at Los Vegas, County Seat of Clarke County, Nevada, there is little prospect that the Moapa Indian would appear as a witness against them, since all are Paiutes."[91] Again, "the county officials either flatly decline to act, or undertake action in such manner as amounts to the same thing."[92] So nonreservation Paiutes, and effectively enrolled Paiutes in off-reservation locations, were outside of BIA jurisdiction and generally ignored by state authorities, "let alone to come and go as they pleased, hold their own courts of justice and mete out justice according to the crime."[93]

Homicides were very dramatic examples of political relations between Indians and non-Indians. As had been true in the nineteenth century, in the early twentieth century, when a Paiute killed another Indian, the legal system largely ignored the death even when it occurred off-reservation and before witnesses. For instance, after a Moapa Paiute was killed in the middle of the town of St. Thomas by other Paiutes in 1902, the local newspaper mildly supposed, "No doubt he was killed according to their tribal laws of his own tribe. He is a good Indian now."[94] As had been true earlier, non-Indian assaults against Paiutes were also ignored by the courts, as in 1910, when non-Indian Frank Burns lured two teenage Paiute girls into his cabin at Indian Springs. He got them drunk, they quarreled, the girls ran, and "Burns followed them a little later with a 44 rifle and shot into the tent three times trying to kill them." He hit one girl, who survived, but the assailant "left for the tall timber" and was never prosecuted.[95]

As in the nineteenth-century, when a Paiute killed a Euro-American, the pattern of response was entirely different; the non-Indian community demanded the vigorous exercise of state law. Indeed, frontier vigilante justice flared back to life. Late in 1910 a miner was shot in El Dorado, and the killer was assumed to be an Indian. Posses swept the countryside, and the newspaper demanded that "every Piute who is off the reservation [be] returned."[96] Eventually, a Las Vegas Paiute named Queho was accused of that crime and five additional unsolved and apparently unmotivated murders;

four of these victims had been shot in the back. One of these "victims" later showed up unharmed and bemused, and another was reported to have cheated Queho out of honestly earned wages and been killed in retaliation. Mohave County, Arizona, put up a five-hundred-dollar reward. As official Clark County, Nevada, posses and unofficial vigilante groups scoured the countryside for months, Paiutes lived in fear that these gunmen, like the retaliatory raiders of the frontier settlement period, would be indiscriminate in their questioning of Paiutes or identification of their target. Those fears were probably justified, as one posse member wrote the commissioner of Indian affairs: "We will kill any old Pyute we find if we make a mistake of course we are excusable on the ground of good intentions and a few more or less of his tribe will amount to little."[97] The offended commissioner snapped back, "The fact that Queho is thought by you to be living and responsible for a number of recent murders does not justify one in drawing a conclusion that all Piutes are bad men and that in a hunt for the guilty man one would be justified in killing any Piute that may be found under a mistake of fact."[98] Non-Indians never saw Queho after October 1910. Over the next nine years, he was blamed for twelve murders across the deserts of southern Nevada and California, including the unwitnessed death of a woman at El Dorado gunned down in her living room and two skeletons of indeterminate age found in a cave. Although the reward grew to $2,500, Queho was never captured. In 1941 a desiccated corpse found in a cave overlooking the Colorado River was declared to be his.[99]

This was not an isolated incident. Like Queho, accusations against Tse-ne-gat received widespread press and dramatic law enforcement response. Old troubles over cattle ownership and grazing flared during the years of World War I into what has frequently been declared to be the "last Indian war" in the United States. In extreme southeastern Utah near Allen Canyon, where a small mixed group of Utes and Paiutes lived largely by wage labor for non-Indian ranchers, a Mexican herdsman was shot. Tse-ne-gat, said to be the son of the headman, Poke, and strongly supported by another headman named Posey, had threatened cattlemen encroaching on rangeland used by Indians; non-Indians later saw him with cash and personal property presumed to belong to the deceased. Several Indians signed affidavits naming Tse-ne-gat as the murderer.[100] Nine months later, a Utah posse, without warrants, demands for surrender, or announcement of themselves as law officers, attacked Tse-ne-gat's camp at dawn, "surrounding them in their reservation and shot their children and wounded a squaw."[101] Tse-ne-gat, with twelve to fifteen friends, their wives, and children, fled, cutting telephone lines and firing back at pursuers. National newspapers inflated this two-hour fight to a forty-eight-hour battle and proclaimed the entire town of Bluff "besieged" by "hundreds of circling" Indians; citizens of Bluff dramatized broadly, "The tribe had blood in its eyes."[102] Vigilantes captured nine Paiutes (not including Tse-ne-gat) and imprisoned them in a loft in Bluff, where two were shot "trying to escape." When the BIA agent for the Scattered Bands of Utah arrived, he found Paiutes terrified because "[t]he posse and citizens did not seem to be able to draw the line between combatant and peaceful Indians."[103] He persuaded many to go to the Ute Mountain Ute Reservation for safety. In March 1915, retired general Hugh Scott traveled virtually alone over a hundred miles into the broken country north of the Grand Canyon by auto and wagon and on foot. Noncombatant Paiutes mediated his meeting with Tse-ne-gat, and, convinced of his innocence, Scott promised him a fair trial if he would surrender.[104]

Poke and Posey, accused of shooting at federal marshals, were taken to Salt Lake City for trial in federal court; an out-of-court settlement resulted in their release if they would live on a reservation.[105] Tse-ne-gat was tried in Denver for the murder of the herdsman. Although the federal attorney thought the evidence ironclad, and the Indian witnesses repeated their affidavit testimony before the grand jury, Tse-ne-gat was acquitted. Local Utahans wailed about "fanatical Indian-rights people from far and near" and predicted a large-scale bloodbath by vindictive natives.[106] Tse-ne-gat soon died of tuberculosis, and Poke and Posey led their camp groups quietly back to the Bluff area.

Reservation lands and schools recommended for the Allen Canyon Paiutes and Utes never materialized; they were simply issued some cattle and ignored.[107] Because the interethnic situation remained fundamentally unchanged, frictions with local ranchers over range rights not unpredictably recurred. Eight years later two young Paiute men intimidated and robbed some sheep herders outside Bluff and were arrested under state warrant, but headman Posey stole the sheriff's own pistol in the courtroom and broke them out. A hot pursuit in Model T Fords ensued but quickly shifted to horseback as Posey fled through the late spring snow into the rugged canyonlands. The governor of Utah placed a one-hundred-dollar bounty on Posey dead or alive. Enthusiastic vigilantes chased several camps of Paiutes across hillsides and besieged one group in a cave. As Circleville had sixty years earlier, nearby Blanding "built a bull-pen, a kind of spacious corral with a high barb-wire fence, too high and too closely woven for any human being to get over or through."[108] More than fifty men, women, and children were herded into it. Weeks later, an "official from the outside" found Posey's body alone in a mountain camp where he had died of pneu-

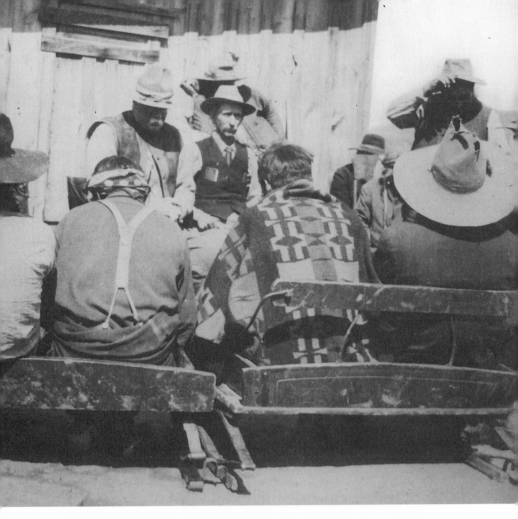

8. Surrender of Tse-ne-gat, 1915. Facing the camera are Gen. Hugh Scott and Indian agent Lorenzo Creel. On the wagon seats, left to right, are headmen Polk and Posey, Jim Allen the Ute translator, then Tse-ne-gat. This and other photographs in the series show no fetters or restraints on any of the Paiutes captured, despite the previously violent pursuit. Persons are identified in pencil on the back of the photograph in Scott's hand, followed by the comment, "Paiutes whipped the Marshall of Utah with loss on both sides. Indians charged with murder. Surrendered to Gen. Scott near Mexican Hat, Colorado, on sole condition he take them to jail at Salt Lake himself." (Hugh Scott Collection, National Anthropological Archives, Bureau of American Ethnology Collection, Smithsonian Institution.)

monia. His two sons were taken out of the Blanding prison pen and forced to dig up their father's body for identification.

Violent interracial conflicts in the early twentieth century followed many of the patterns set previously in the nineteenth. A single Paiute male killed one non-Indian at the spur of the moment, often over wages unjustly withheld and other times over disputed livestock grazing. Large numbers of non-Indians retaliated, often indiscriminately injuring considerable numbers of Paiutes in the process. Local citizens of Utah, Nevada, and California were more than willing to punish Paiutes for killing non-Indians. Posses under the nominal control of local law enforcement officers eagerly pursued the accused, and newspapers whipped up passions, touting the macho nineteenth-century myth of stalwart Indian-fighting pioneers. Although all three of these cases involved crimes committed off federal trust lands by Indians not even registered on a reservation, in each federal marshals were nonetheless involved.

From the other side of the interethnic boundary, Paiutes occasionally tried, albeit unsuccessfully, to activate the state legal structure themselves in cases of murder within their communities. This was particularly true when the cause of death was one not recognized by state law—witchcraft. A Las Vegas shaman, Harry York, lost a succession of patients in 1910, including four daughters of Bismark. The western groups of Paiutes interpreted this not as the result of bad luck, lack of spiritual power, or a particularly contagious disease but as evidence of a Janus-faced shaman who had chosen to use his power to harm rather than cure. Traditionally, once a consensus, including the relatives of the accused, had been reached on a shaman's guilt, several people jointly would remove the threat from the community.[109] Bismark recruited five friends who together confronted York on a trail outside town. Two shot him in front of community witnesses and then carefully buried the body. That night "a pow-wow and big dance was held . . . in celebration of the event, in which there was general participation." There was no effort to keep the execution secret from non-Indians, and the county coroner found the body exactly where the Indians had reported it. When arrested, the five openly related the events, having "not the slightest feeling of guilt, but think they committed a very good act in removing old Harry York from the scene."[110] Non-Indians did not consider Bismark and the other rifleman as a posse protecting their community from a known murderer; instead, they were found guilty of murder themselves under state law. Sent to state prison, the pair were soon released for good behavior.

At least one member of the Paiute community had not agreed with Bismark's action, because Fred Benn shot and killed Bismark when he returned to the community in 1914. The rest of the Paiutes in turn disapproved of Benn's unsanctioned action. In a showcase trial, Las Vegas's leading attorney defended Benn, and ten very prominent citizens sat on the jury, while Paiutes, including eye witnesses, without exception testified against him. The all-white jury found Benn not guilty. The agent feared bad effects from Benn's apparent escape of punishment, not because it might weaken Paiutes' respect for the law but because once freed Benn himself would "be in constant fear of revenge being taken against him by friends of the dead Indian."[111]

The state unevenly subjected Paiutes to its legal system, not only in such dramatic cases as homicide but also in questions of marriage and sexual morality, just as the BIA was trying to regulate those same behaviors. The agency had to ally itself with state law because there was so little applicable federal law in the field of marriage and because some Paiutes had non-reservation status or moved between reserves, effectively divorcing them from BIA control.

This political alliance between the state and the BIA clearly complicated the case of Mericats, who was living openly on the Shivwits Reservation in 1906 with the wife of another man. Mericats's own wife and his paramour had a physical fight on the streets of downtown St. George, after which the latter's husband beat his wife for her adultery. None of the parties acknowledged the authority of the Shivwits Court of Indian Offenses, which nevertheless ruled that "Merycats no do that any more—he do it again arrest him—no do it [if he] stay here—Jake [the second husband] no whip his squaw—mebby whip him [*sic*] a little when he get mad thats all."[112] This warning did not seem to change Mericats's ways. Six years later he persuaded the wife of a Kaibab Indian policeman to run away with him to Kanab, thus crossing a state line. The Shivwits agent was confronted by "Indians here [who] feel that a member of their tribe has heaped insult on injury on their friends the Kiabab Indians. . . . The Indians of this reservation have called on me in a body and have asked me to take this matter up with the Indian Office[.] they request and I recommend that Americats be brought to trial at once."[113] Even though Mericats was enrolled at Shivwits, the woman was not; although Mericats had a history of marital infidelity that made Shivwits Paiutes unsympathetic, the current offense had taken place off-reservation.[114] After wading through the jurisdictional tangle, the commissioner's office passed responsibility to the state: "he could and should be vigorously punished under state law and you should take the matter up and see what can be done to make an example of him."[115] The agent could not interest any of the several county law enforcement agencies in either Utah or Arizona, and the matter was dropped.

Similarly in cases of sexual violence, state exercise of its ambiguous jurisdiction was unpredictable when the victim was a reservation Indian. In 1912 his Moapa mother-in-law accused a young in-marrying man of raping his wife's seven-year-old sister. Statutory rape on a reservation was a federal crime, but the U.S. district attorney pointed to improper collection of medical evidence at the time of the rape and refused to file charges.[116] Four years later, a ten-year-old girl, described as "feeble minded," was raped, and she named the same man as her assailant. She was from Las Vegas and not enrolled on any reservation census; the attack had taken place at a ranch near, but not on, the Moapa reserve. It took two months for the BIA to untangle the jurisdictional issues and conclude that this crime fell under state law. By then the child had died, her family convinced as a result of her assault. The state prosecutor opined that "since the death of the girl, [there is] nothing but heresay evidence, and that it would not be possible to secure a conviction in the District Court. He recommended that the case be dismissed, which was accordingly done." Morally outraged, the Moapa agent seethed, "It is a mockery of justice that the death of the victim should be the means by which the assailant should escape punishment."[117] Supported by Washington, he tried to obtain retroactive state prosecution for the earlier rape but failed. Without legal authority, the county attorney exacted a promise from the man to leave Moapa and not return.[118]

On issues less dramatic than murder, adultery, or rape, the state was willing, if not eager, to exert its authority over Paiutes and often did so without the niceties of jurisdictional examination. Although Nevada was hardly a "dry" state, non-Indians were adamantly opposed to publicly drunken natives and insisted on heavy, systematic prosecution. The Caliente, Nevada, newspaper stereotyped and ridiculed Indian alcoholism: "Three local injuns . . . and a flea-bit, booze-bit warrior from Panaca, gathered beneath the folds of a comrade's wigwam . . . with a deck of cards. . . . bottles of booze were introduced, interviewed and scalped. . . . a declaration of war resulted in which Tom received a seriously cracked cranium and Keno several jagged scalp wounds, it was hoped at first they both would die but it is now feared they will recover."[119] The town sheriff hired a Paiute man to bring in inebriated Indians, the justice of the peace routinely tried and fined them, and the town issued a racially specific curfew.[120] In Las Vegas, too, the state-authorized justices of the peace routinely tried Indians arrested by the town sheriff both before and after the establishment of the reservation there.[121]

Although quick to punish the Indian buyers of liquor, the state was much slower to attack the sources. In 1913 a Las Vegas Paiute girl and two young Mexican boys were lured into the basement of a Chinese restaurant and plied with a pail full of beer. The local newspaper and the Indian agent speculated that this was "presumably with the intention of debauching the girl." The boys' father pressed charges of giving liquor to minors, but the restaurateur plea-bargained a twenty-five-dollar fine. The federal attorney refused to file a charge on the girl's behalf, and she was promptly shipped off to boarding school.[122]

Another behavior the state authorities sanctioned heavily was theft. A teenager in Las Vegas stole a bicycle in 1915, stated in court, "Sure, I steal wheel," and led the sheriff into the brush where he had parked it; the city court sentenced him to thirty days in jail, suspended after one night, purportedly as a moral lesson.[123] Other cases were more complicated, such as the tent and gear of a miner, abandoned while he rode into town for supplies, that were supposedly swept up by one Moapa Paiute and a second nonreservation Indian. The agent found none of the goods in the possession of the Moapa man, and he disclaimed authority over the other Indian, especially since the theft took place off the reserve. Although no evidence was found against either Paiute, the state prosecutor nonetheless complained bitterly about the "deplorable state of affairs when a white man cannot get help and justice in this section from the depredations and plundering of the Indians."[124]

The off-reservation hunting of deer, mountain sheep, and other large traditional Paiute food animals was placed under state regulation early in the century. Southern Paiutes had no treaty-guaranteed rights to off-reservation hunting, indeed, no treaties at all, so the commissioner of Indian affairs could only support this assertion of state jurisdiction over their behavior. The Kaibab Plateau had long been a major deer-hunting area, and buckskins had been exported through intertribal trade well into the twentieth century. Paiutes there petitioned for exemption from state game laws because they still relied on venison for subsistence; they were supported in their request by local communities that feared an Indian welfare burden.[125] Mable Wall of Cedar City complained to the president of the Mormon Church that "these all animal belong to Indian deer fish rabert all belong to Indian they aught have it for nothing White people get rich wont [want] Indin to pay up license for."[126] In 1934 the Cedar City headman, Jimmy Pete, and another man were tried in county court for killing seven deer without a state license. Although they protested that this is how they had always fed their families long before non-Indians had come into the country, they were convicted and served thirty days in jail.[127] Numerous other Paiutes were similarly prosecuted and fined in Arizona and Utah courts.

Gradually, more typically twentieth century issues intruded into Paiute political relations. What political entity had jurisdiction when Bob Russell, enrolled at Moapa, was hit and killed by a non-Indian driver while changing a flat tire at the side of a state highway? Would the driver's insurance pay hospitalization for Russell's wife's broken ankle? The federal district attorney did successfully negotiate a cash indemnity for wrongful death and forced the reluctant insurance company to pay.[128] But if accidents to enrolled Moapa Paiutes a few miles off the reservation were still matters for the federal attorney, and if unenrolled Indians living in nonreservation areas in towns were, as the commissioner said, still under the "administrative" authority of the nearest agent, would this equally hold true for the small number of Paiutes beginning to find their way into the major cities of the West Coast? When Martha Armstrong needed medical treatment in Los Angeles in 1932, the state public health department undertook her care as a matter of routine.[129] How far away did a Paiute have to travel in order to become susceptible to state jurisdiction? There seemed to be no rule as to the distance required or the issues involved and little consistency in the application of state law to Southern Paiutes.

Conversely, if the state was going to assert power to punish Paiute behaviors when off-reservation, such as public inebriation, did consistency not demand that it also extend state benefits to off-reservation Indians, in particular, public school education and voting? Utah was willing to exercise its jurisdiction in the 1920s by sending to state reform schools several Paiute boys whom the BIA had declared "vicious and immoral and dangerous" because of repeated forgery and horse stealing.[130] And yet when the agent sought public education for the far larger number of nondelinquent children, the state superintendent of public instruction refused to distinguish between enrolled and unenrolled, reservation resident or nonresident Paiutes: "The Indians are wards of the [federal] government. Therefore neither state nor local school officials have any legal right to attempt to force Indian children into *our* schools. In other words the state has no jurisdiction over these wards of the government."[131] Only in the growing Las Vegas urban area were the scant dozen Paiute children accepted by the public school system in the 1920s.[132]

When federal law made all reservation Indians U.S. citizens in 1924, at least some Paiutes feared that exercise of that right or even registration to vote would make them liable to auto and hunting licensing laws and property taxes.[133] The Las Vegas newspaper challenged the franchise of reservation-dwelling Indians, and the Utah state legislature blocked native voting until 1956, arguing that reservations, as federal trust lands, were not part of the state.[134]

Inversely, non-Indian employees of a copper company that leased Shivwits lands worried whether their residence on reservation lands jeopardized their voting rights. The secretary of the interior ruled that they had not lost their rights as citizens and could establish a state polling site; and yet, in contradiction, the leased land was not state territory for the purposes of selling liquor to Indians.[135]

State law enforcement authorities were all too often unwilling to make the effort to determine whether any particular Paiute was enrolled on a reservation or held non-ward status. Where the state and the BIA coincided on an issue, most notably in the punishment of public inebriation and the imposition of permanent monogamous marriage, the state and local courts cheerfully exercised jurisdiction, and the BIA overlooked or actively encouraged their dubious authority. Where state jurisdiction would be costly or politically unpopular, such as public welfare or schooling, state officials hid behind the supposed wardship status of all Paiutes and declared them uniformly a federal responsibility.

Federal officers were generally more conscientious in researching their own legal distinctions over whether the parties were enrolled, whether the event took place on reservation lands or not, or whether the action fell under the technical definitions of a federal crime.[136] Despite this scattered application of federal law to an assortment of Paiute actions, by far the most frequent engagement of federal law enforcement authority was for alcohol consumption. Of course, states punished Paiutes when they were intoxicated in non-Indian areas, but none made sale by a licensed saloon illegal; the customer was punished, the capitalist was not. BIA regulations and federal law went to the source and made sale of liquor to Indians illegal long before Prohibition.[137] When such sales took place off-reservation, federal agents had to coordinate with state authorities and prosecute through state courts.

The town of Moapa grew up at the fringes of that reservation during a period of railroad construction; by 1910 it had a population of twenty-five and three full-time saloons that clearly could not have been supported by non-Indians alone. One of these bars was owned by the persistent Mrs. Mc-Kenna. When the BIA coerced six Moapa Paiutes in 1904 to testify that she was their source of liquor, she was charged and convicted in state court. Pardoned, Mrs. McKenna returned to Moapa and reopened her bar. She was arrested for selling whiskey to Paiutes in 1906, imprisoned, and pardoned. She recommenced peddling spirits out the back door of her saloon, which by 1909 was thinly disguised as a restaurant. After the state of Nevada went dry in 1918, McKenna promptly diversified into a general store specializing in alcohol-based patent medicines and wholesale flavor extracts, such as vanilla, which along with "perfume, bay rum, toilet water, etc." became alternate sources for Paiute alcohol consumption.[138]

Saloon owners became more sophisticated and began to plead that "[f]ederal Courts have no jurisdiction when intoxicants are sold them on any but Indian lands."[139] One dealer caught on Kaibab successfully challenged the legitimacy of the reservation itself: "as long as this Reservation was established only by an order of the Secretary of the Interior and not by the President that it really was not a reservation and legally could not be considered so."[140] The conviction rate of BIA liquor cases plummeted in the face of these interjurisdictional tangles as "either [state or federal] court passes the buck back and fourth claiming they have no jurisdiction."[141]

An enrolled Paiute who committed an offense on federal trust land was additionally subject to a Court of Indian Offenses, if one existed, or, if not, to the Indian agent himself acting as prosecutor, judge, and jury. Courts of Indian Offenses appeared through an administrative ruling of the secretary of the interior in 1883 and could be established on any reserve at the discretion of the local agent. He appointed one or more men to try cases involving Indians within the reserve; should one or more of the parties not be enrolled at that reserve or leave the premises, there was nothing they could do. A court session was called by the agent when he thought a case warranted one. Judges had strictly circumscribed powers to punish, and all decisions were reviewable by the agent. The term of office was not fixed, and judges could be removed at any time.[142] The amount of internal community decision making that these courts offered Indians was therefore small indeed.

This was especially true since native leadership had for years been systematically and intentionally undercut. Mormons had tried to subvert cooperative leaders by denominating them "chiefs" and giving them gifts to distribute. Their word was viewed as a group commitment, and decisions were funneled through them; uncooperative leaders were ignored, denied, or occasionally eliminated. When churchman Ivins became the first agent of the Shivwits Reservation in 1891, he promptly called those adult males he thought "entitled to vote" to a council and "explained to them the necessity of choosing a chief." Typical of traditional Paiute egalitarian multicentric leadership, the twenty-four men put forward ten candidates but eventually unanimously decided on Shem.[143] The commissioner of Indian affairs vetoed this action and sharply stated the federal attitude toward native political structures:

[I]t is against the policy of the Government now to either appoint or encourage Chiefs among the Indians.

The present policy of the Government is "to gradually break up the Indian reservation system, allot the lands in severalty, extinguish the Indian title, destroy tribal relations, deal with the Indians in their individual capacity, and absorb them into the national life as American citizens."

You will observe that the advocacy of Chiefs among the Indians is in direct opposition to the policy indicated. It is deemed better for each Indian of that tribe to deal directly with the farmer in charge.[144]

Not only did the BIA discourage native leaders from representing the needs and wishes of the community, but it avoided public meetings, because "these meetings always work to a certain extent to the detriment to the Indians by giving opportunity to Indians who have a semi-political turn to advance propaganda against organized efforts in behalf of the Indians and to increase their discontent."[145]

Despite active Mormon manipulation and BIA discouragement, native leaders continued to function as headmen in both reservation and off-reservation communities. At Kanosh, Peach tried to arrange a land trade with local farmers in 1918. At Cedar City, Captain Pete explained to a BIA inspector why Paiute children were not in school and passed on the community's requests for land title; his successor, Jimmy Pete, solicited prospective employers by mail and coordinated with the Mormon Church for house construction. Kaibab leader William Young, "one of the oldest Indians, and one commonly looked upon by them as chief," presented background information on water usage to a federal investigator and "began his talk as usual 'away back before the white man came.'"[146] Joseph Smith and George Segmiller were "the principal talkers" at a Moapa meeting called in 1901, and twenty years later Smith was principal speaker at another, where he "gave a recital of imaginary grievances from which he thinks the tribe has suffered."[147] When Shem died, "the last recognized tribal chieftain," he was succeeded at Shivwits by Frank Mustache, who was "looked upon as a sort of elder brother," a kinship status that, like traditional headmanship, gave authority to persuade and obligation to protect but not power to coerce.[148]

Perhaps the most dramatic expression of continuing Paiute leadership came during the 1923 pursuit of Posey in distant San Juan country. Peach at Kanosh, Pete at Cedar City, and three other men who signed as "Captains" petitioned Anthony Ivins, then highly influential in the Mormon Church, to intervene in order to assure the safety of Paiutes in that distant territory:

"It is not right to kill woman little children. Reason why I said many of white man not treat right. Because they fire first."[149]

These local leaders performed many of the traditional headman's functions. Headmen had represented the community to outsiders, sought information, voiced native decisions, and explained actions. Just as precontact headmen had led the quest for food, leaders now sought wage jobs for members of the group. They tried to obtain benefits for the entire community, such as better access to water and land; they sought alliances with powerful external groups to protect the larger Paiute society.

Some agents recognized these continuing native leaders and found various ways to work with them. A Shivwits agent said that she, "with the chief and his henchman, arbitrate[d] all difficulties," and at Kaibab, "[f]requently the leading indians discuss the leading questions affecting the indians with the superintendent."[150] More commonly, agents preferred an acephalous, open meeting over private contacts with authoritative men. Unlike traditional Paiute meetings, agents usually called only the men together, excluding women from the information and decision making. The agenda was set by the agent. At Shivwits the agent told how he called meetings to discuss the BIA's agricultural goals "whenever it seems necessary" to him. "The Indians discuss what they want to do," he reported candidly, "and the Superintendent instructs them how to do better farming." When the BIA wanted a body to legitimize transfer of a person from one reserve roll to another, it called a validating "council." A BIA inspector gathered the men of Moapa together to chastise them for overdue reimbursable accounts and embarrassed them individually by discussing each man's financial status in public. In short, as an inspector candidly observed, "These community meetings have had the effect of bringing the Indians into closer contact with the desires of the Department."[151]

Unless the BIA had such a "desire," agents discouraged public gatherings lest the Paiutes "unify by some fancied or real grievance."[152] Similarly, agents denied publicly that indigenous headmen were leaders. As one agent said disdainfully, "[T]he Indians began to think that . . . they could run the reservation; giving orders to the policeman and judge."[153] Headmen might become loci of competitive power within the reservation, a core of resistance to the BIA's will.

Shamans too were potential sources of influence independent of the BIA, which actively suppressed them not only for religious reasons but clearly for political ones as well. The shaman Monkey Frank, brother of leader William Young at Kaibab, "is gaining a very strong hold over the school children. . . . he is making every effort to make them think back to the old uncivilized days; he is a menace to advancement and a general nuisance around the Reservation." The agent wanted to send him back to Moapa, "his proper Reservation."[154] When Nora, the aunt of a deaf girl, protested sending her away to a special school, the Moapa agent discounted her opinions because she "is an old 'Hag' a female 'Medicine Man' of the most troublesome type, always haranguing against the government, agent, etc. and trying to get the Indians to do the opposite than is recommended by the Employees. Also the worst one to try to keep up the old traditions and customs of burning everthing belonging to any Indian who dies, killing the horses of the deceased etc. etc. She belongs over in Utah so I told her to leave and never come back."[155]

To replace the indigenous authority of community councils, headmen, and shamans, the BIA established Courts of Indian Offenses at Shivwits before 1905 and at Moapa in the early 1920s. Unlike the ideal U.S. court system, in which a judge dispassionately decided an issue based on the facts of sworn testimony by witnesses, the agent revealed that in the Shivwits system, "the Judge, Policemen [Indians] and the Superintendent go to one side and the Judge and police make a decision with out the aid of the Superintendent. If it is any thing like a fair conclusion, it is final. If not the Superintendent might make a suggestion."[156] The degree of agency control of these court proceedings was evident in a Moapa agent's report: "I instigated an investigation which disclosed all the facts which will be presented below in the Indian testimony before the Indian Court." Because he thought the judge was a friend of the victim (a condition rather hard to avoid on the small Paiute reservations), he arbitrarily changed the structure, telling the defendant ad hoc to select someone to represent him on the bench, and then the judge and the advocate picked a third Paiute to hear the case. It was the agent, not the judges, who then charged witnesses with "the necessity of telling the truth and being absolutely fair in their testimony." It was the agent who acted as defense attorney, prosecutor, and court recorder: "I questioned each witness and took down the substance of their testimony." When the triumvirate declined to adjudge guilt but negotiated a mutually agreeable fine, the agent asked the commissioner of Indian affairs to support his veto of the decision.[157]

Even when Paiute judges escaped such obtrusive agency supervision, Indian courts differed widely from model U.S. courts. A single set of minutes of the Shivwits court survives from the period after the agent left to operate Panguitch School and the reservation was left under the loose supervision of the resident Presbyterian missionary. The proceedings closely resembled a community meeting. Judges discussed housing construction, school access, and locations of possible wage work, interwoven with long family histories of those involved in the case at issue, an extramarital liaison. They considered the entire life history and character of the parties, not just the "facts of the case," and debated mild reproofs rather than rendered judgments.[158] A non-Indian observer of another meeting of the Shivwits court confirms this image of the proceedings.[159] A letter from Moapa judge Lincoln Silver to Lizzie Segmiller illustrates the moralizing style of these mild reproofs: "you have already lived with four men on this reservation, that you must came back and marry Ben according to law or you cannot live on the reservation any more nor come here. . . . It is hoped that you will appreciate this letter and begin living now as you know you should and is right."[160] Broadly cast issues, importance of general character over specific events, consideration of diverse opinions, and avoidance of unambiguous decisions of guilt were all features of traditional Paiute egalitarian political structure. Like traditional headmen, Paiute courts had little power to punish even in a case of overt guilt; furthermore, the relatives of the accused would be aggrieved against the judge and his relatives. Compromise, conciliation, and the oratorical skill to direct consensus formation, all traditional skills of a Paiute headman, were still the best strategies for Indian judges.

Agents selected men to be judges whom they considered "good," progressive, conformable to agency programs, and thus "worthy" of the salary of $7 per month. If judges were to have their decisions accepted by the community, they had to be men it respected. Not surprisingly, judges were often the sub rosa headmen, those who used their negotiating skills to be effective judges and community leaders simultaneously. The long-standing judge of the Shivwits Court of Indian Offenses was Shem, the man Ivins's early council had unanimously chosen as "chief."[161]

The Courts of Indian Offenses withered away at Shivwits in 1921 and Moapa four years later.[162] By 1926 both reserves were under the jurisdiction of the Kaibab Agency, where the officer preferred councils he chaired directly. Having now centralized authority over all Paiute reserves and eliminated all structures of local self-government, it was ironic that within a few years this same agent was touting the reform policy of the new commissioner of Indian affairs, John Collier: "It is planned to build up on each reservation an organization whose Indian representatives will be asked to and required to assume a large part of the responsibility for the community and industrial schemes."[163]

Paired with reservation courts were Indian policemen, appointed by the BIA to regulate political relations within Paiute communities. The BIA expected them to maintain order on the reservation, seize offenders (physically if necessary), and deliver them to the agent. Which particular Paiute behaviors would constitute punishable offenses were, of course, defined by BIA regulations, so in fact, policemen became the enforcement extension of agency policy.[164]

What Southern Paiute policemen actually did varied from this BIA plan. The first man was hired at the suggestion of the commissioner of Indian affairs in 1902 to patrol the still-disputed boundaries of the Moapa Reservation.[165] Policemen subsequently mediated between the BIA agent, with whom they worked most closely, and other residents, explaining official demands and often unofficially suggesting ways to avoid them. When a new agent at Moapa refenced a pasture for his own horse, he gave the old wire to the policeman to sell. He in turn gave it to Emily Day, who gave it to Swain, who had originally installed it years ago and to whom, by native conceptions of right, it properly belonged.[166] In 1920 Moapa police were told to make sure that all Paiute men worked on their farms "on all suitable days and times."[167] When the city of Las Vegas demanded that the agent do something about the physical conditions at its urban reserve in 1927, he charged the Indian policeman to enforce a regular "clean-up day."[168]

Paiute policemen were caught in a contradiction. They represented the BIA, which paid their wages, but they were also members of the community. In small groups of fifty to a hundred people, policemen were kin and friends, certainly well known to the people they were charged to censure. When a behavior, such as personal assault, was offensive to both Paiutes and the BIA, the police were eager and effective. During this time, however, the BIA was imposing constraints on native marital behavior, gambling, and drinking, and it wanted to send children to school, none of which were popular with Paiutes. When policemen tried to enforce these regulations, they earned the wrath of relatives, friends, and neighbors, people among whom the policemen, unlike the agent, had to live; on these issues they were understandably less keen. In suppression of drinking, the Kaibab agent complained of "the practical uselessness of the Indian Police in obtaining evidence in these matters as well as any other that runs counter to the wishes of the Indians."[169] When the Moapa agent tried to clamp down on gambling, he found that the "police and judge on the reservation are no good whatever and will not do a thing[,] telling me they see no harm in it."[170] The Kaibab agent found native police "of little use" as truant officers as they did not want to offend parents by removing their children to school.[171] Agents saw as subversive this stalwart Paiute insistence on the rights of policemen as individuals still to hold personal opinions and to maintain their social connections: "The police service among the Paiutes is very poor and the judge will decide all cases in favor of the greatest numbers or to please his friends, without any regard to justice. The police will make arrests only where the majority of the indians are in favor of the arrest, in other cases he will throw up his job and leave the place."[172]

The persons of federal agents were shielded by their power and their frequent geographical distance, so the policemen bore the brunt of native resentment against agency policies. It was the policeman who was stabbed with a knife by the furious man at Moapa and another whose haystack was torched.[173] It is understandable why agents sometimes found it hard to locate men willing to serve as police and also why those who did were so often also identified as "chiefs" or headmen, those especially tactful negotiators, talented mediators, and civic-minded community members.

Interaction with federal officials subjected Paiutes to demands that they conform to Euro-American expectations of farming, labor, and childhood education; that they submit to state courts and law enforcement over monogamy, formal marriage ceremony and divorce, hunting licensing and seasons; that they defend their behaviors to BIA agents, federal marshals, and courts. In addition, by 1918 they had become enmeshed in U.S. foreign policy, specifically, the involvement of the United States in World War I. All Indian men between the ages of twenty-one and thirty-one had to fill out registration cards. Enrolled members of reservation groups, considered federal wards and not U.S. citizens, had their cards held by the BIA agent, who forwarded censuses to local draft boards to confirm exemptions; nonward Indians, considered U.S. citizens, had their cards forwarded directly to local draft boards and were placed in the draft pool. The agency for the Scattered Bands of Utah conducted its first census of much of the Paiute population specifically for draft purposes, and Shivwits and Moapa updated theirs. Officials interpreted Paiute mobility as evasion of registration. When Paiutes asserted their need to go into the mountains for the fall piñon harvest, the agent threatened that registration "must be done, evenif we have to use the military to run them down."[174]

Southern Paiutes, like other Indians across the Great Basin, were worried by the demand to register.[175] Along with native judge Lincoln Silver, Emily Workie wrote letters to a former field matron whom she considered a friend and to a visitor associated with national lobbying groups and asked for draft exemption for the men of Moapa. Their letters, expressed from within the compelling web of kinship obligations, show utter alienation from the war and suggest that they understood it in class terms:

We do not want go to the war. The're not very many mens folk here.
only a few mens. Nearly all of them are married and farming. . . .
When german come into the United States and every body have to
fight. and we have to fight to. help our boys and sister and mother and
our country. We know that. Now we not feel like to go and like to stay
on farm. . . . the officer [recruiter] came to the town to get mens. he
say are you ready now. the man say no, not yet, and he go to the other
man. . . . Nearly all White boys are willing to go. be cause the[y] are
so many of white poeples million million million of White poeples.
the[y] dont care to die. the[y] care for money Wast[e] then the[ir]
own body. . . . the[y] have lot money all way . . . million million dol-
lars so the son are fighting for that. and help there mother and sister
father keep german away from that[.] Indians here got not thing no
money no storys [stores] no money in bank and no not thing. the[y]
care for there own body.[176]

The lobbyist friend replied that registration was the law, and they had
to comply, but she reassured them that men with dependents would probably not have to serve.[177] The commissioner of Indian affairs said also that it
was a military matter over which he had no power, and he tried to divert
Paiutes into the war production effort: "tell the Indians not to worry about
this matter but to go ahead and raise bigger and better crops this year than
they have in the past."[178]

Pete, headman at the nonreservation community in Cedar City, expressed many of the same concerns as the more southerly reservation leaders. He vaguely hinted at resistance: "our Trib[e] is very few. . . . White Boys
where the[re] are lots of them. . . . if They are going to get some of the Indian Boys to war They going to be Trouble among Some of tribe . . . For
them to go way off cross the Ocean if it was on our country be better. Indian
aint go[t] no money [to] leave mothers & babys."[179] The agent replied to his
letter with a hard-line threat that his group, not being reservation enrolled,
"are considered as citizens and are required to comply with the Draft Law
as any other persons regardless of color and if your Indians fail to do this
there will be trouble a plenty for all of you."[180] Another agent Pete contacted
responded with more tactful propaganda: "I do not think that those boys
who work on a farm and have families will ever have to go. It is however,
quite likely that young [legally] unmarried men who have always layed
around and not worked and do not know how to farm will be drafted."[181]

In the mining town of Pioche, long known for its history of interethnic
tension and hysterical overreaction, rumors ran rife that "[t]he Indians are

said to have been supplied with arms and poison by a white man, suspected of being a German or of having pro-German sympathies, and incited to attack Indian agents and settlers." The local paper declared the rumor ridiculous, that the only Indian within sixty miles was a single woman supporting her three children by taking in laundry and doing "a lot more work than some able bodied men we know of"; she was undoubtedly much too weary at the end of a day, the paper opined, to carry around grenades in her laundry basket.[182]

The BIA, as a branch of the federal government, responded to national mandates to increase food production for the war effort. Although wartime budgets did not allow for the extension of irrigation works or the subjugation of additional lands, local agents felt duty bound to persuade Paiutes to produce food staples rather than cash crops, threatened withholding of benefits such as part-time jobs if they did not, and facilitated bulking of harvests for collective marketing. When Moon planted half his land at Kaibab with alfalfa, the customary and most lucrative crop on that reserve, the commissioner of Indian affairs himself wrote that Moon's action "is looked upon with grave displeasure by the Office, and that a repetition of the offense will result in the land being taken away from him and assigned to somebody else who will cultivate it in conformity with instructions."[183] Such farm effort constituted the most direct involvement of Southern Paiutes in the events of World War I. By its end, agents reported that none of the Paiutes belonging to any of the reservations either had been drafted or had enlisted voluntarily.[184]

When federal reservations were established during the first quarter of the twentieth century, Paiutes were entwined with structures beyond their own communities that became more numerous and extended outward to form ever larger and more complex webs. The small amount of usable land and still smaller amount of water for it drove Paiutes into wage labor and hence into off-reservation relationships with non-Indian ranchers, farmers, and other employers. Although BIA agents tried to restructure native ethnic identity by enrolling them on a single reservation, Paiutes continued to visit and live with relatives elsewhere. Some lived enough of the year on the reservation to be recognized and enrolled, giving them ward status under federal law; others lived all or most of the time off-reservation and hence were defined legally as non-ward Indians, subject to state law. Even on the reserves, agents increasingly insisted that Paiutes seek state permission for marriages and then used state authority to force those marital relations to be permanent or with only infrequent and formal divorce; Paiutes evaded these demands unless caught and forced to abide by them. State law tried to limit Paiutes' hunting in location, method, and quantity. The state inconsistently claimed the right to punish Paiutes for various violent acts against each other or against non-Indians; it was more consistent in its prosecution of Paiutes for public inebriation and minor property crime. Federal law claimed the right to control a wide range of Paiute behaviors, including such personal habits as drinking and gambling. During World War I off-reservation Paiutes were drawn into U.S. foreign relations because they were subject to draft registration, and on-reservation dwellers were subjected to wartime agricultural restrictions.

Paiutes reacted to these diverse agency, state, and federal assertions of power with many of the same techniques that they employed against the demands of miners, Mormon settlers, and even slave-raiding Utes. Masters of passive resistance, Paiutes practiced evasive nonconformity. They understood the structure of the federal hierarchy and protested to local agents as well as to Washington when they were pressured in ways they believed were incorrect; without any pragmatic leverage or power to alter policy, these protests were usually unsuccessful. Eschewing physical force, Paiutes buckled to agency and state pressures when forced to do so; whenever possible, however, they quietly went their own way. They visited relatives and traveled looking for jobs, despite demands for sedentary agriculture. They married by personal agreement and restructured their marital relationships as they saw fit. Headmen continued to mold Paiute public opinion, even when the agency refused to recognize "chiefs." These men of leadership skills effectively got themselves appointed as judges and policemen under the new structures established by the BIA. Young men went piñon harvesting when it was time to register for the draft. This kind of avoidance of confrontation was strongly rooted in Paiute culture and custom; it served the people well throughout the early twentieth century. Paiutes maintained their own social and political structures in subtle ways, unseen, unrecognized, and unacknowledged by non-Indians from beyond the boundaries of the Paiute community.

9

THE GREAT DEPRESSION
AND WORLD WAR II

During the first quarter of the twentieth century, federal Indian policy and bureaucracy drove the new programs and imposed novel constrictions on Paiute life, but during the second quarter, the national and international economic and political upheavals of the Great Depression and the subsequent world war were the forces that restructured the Paiutes' world.

By 1929 the period of BIA land expansion in the Southern Paiute area was essentially over. Nine years earlier, progress in the systematic rectangular survey of the globe had revealed that one of the inevitable wedges cut through the center of the lands at Indian Peak. Not included in the reservation's original legal description, this slice nevertheless contained all the land Paiutes actually lived on and all the water. A quick executive order tucked this parcel into the reservation.[1] Similarly, in 1932 the old military Hay and Wood Supply Reserve across the Colorado River from Fort Mohave was administratively shifted to the reservation for Chemehuevis.[2]

Increasingly, Congress was more reluctant to commit federal resources to Indian affairs than was the executive branch. In 1919 Congress severely curbed the BIA by demanding explicit congressional approval for any additions to reservation lands, cutting off the more flexible executive order format.[3] The commissioner decided not to expend his limited political capital to try to win lands for Chemehuevis in the town of Needles or for Paiutes in Cedar City. When the Moapa agent declared the purchase of two hundred acres along the northern reservation boundary to be *"the most important question pretaining to this unit"* because the main irrigation ditch crossed it, Congress denied funding.[4] The San Juan Reservation was lost to the same congressional urge to reduce involvement in Indian affairs.[5]

There were increasing political pressures to cancel even long-established reserves, especially those with low populations and high administrative overhead costs. The inadequate arable acreage and irrigation water on all the Paiute reserves made them particularly vulnerable to congressional budget cutting, because this lack of resources drove enrolled Indians to leave in order to earn a living. Shivwits, one of the largest on the map, was typical. It supported only two family farms, plus a few kitchen gardens. Such limited agriculture did not permit Paiutes to generate enough cash to pay off their accumulated reimbursable loans. "Reimbursable property sold to the Indians of this reservation are a DERTIMENT to them," the agent explained. "The teams [of heavy draft horses purchased] keep the Indians poor trying to feed them, tools and other machinery issued or sold to them, while of benifit to them, they did not or do not have sufficient use for them to warrant their going in debt for them."[6] Fully three quarters of the debt charged against the reservation accounts was for road and bridge construction that benefited primarily non-Indians traveling to Los Angeles; nevertheless, the BIA considered selling all of Shivwits's nonirrigated lands in order to pay off this debt. In order to prevent such major inequity, the commissioner did combine Shivwits with Kaibab Reservation in 1922 to reduce administrative costs and avoided selling off any lands.[7]

Unable to continue to increase the Paiute land base for political reasons, the BIA was forced to intensify use of existing lands to support a greater number of people. The World War I demands for food production, coupled with completion of the Union Pacific Railroad south from Salt Lake City to the West Coast through the heart of Southern Paiute territory, enabled Moapa Paiutes to experiment with new crops. They found radishes required prohibitive amounts of hand labor, asparagus succumbed to the alkali, lettuce rotted before it could reach market, and carrots and onions had unreliable prices, but their steep-walled section of the Muddy Valley gave wind protection at the right time of year for setting cantaloupes, which became their best field crop.[8]

At Shivwits, the BIA distributed peach and nut tree seedlings, which provided lucrative crops for Mormons downstream, but in the years it took them to bear, irrigation availability was erratic. To try to escape the limits of chronic water shortages, the agency experimented with dry farming at Shivwits, Kaibab, and Kanosh, using new hardy grain varieties, special plowing techniques, and erosion controls, but the timing was bad. While the early 1920s were a period of unusually high regional rainfall, as soon as the demonstration fields were initiated a massive drought struck that would grip the Southwest for the next ten years. Only at Kanosh was dry-land wheat farming even a moderate success.[9]

Not only did the lack of land and water limit Paiute agriculture, but so too did Paiutes' extreme lack of capital. Elsewhere agriculture was becoming mechanized, but Paiutes were locked into labor-intensive methods.

Agents criticized Moapa Paiutes for growing alfalfa rather than more profitable wheat and yet themselves documented how the Indians still laboriously used hand-thrown wooden flails to husk what little grain they grew and blankets to winnow it. As late as 1938 they were still using horses to plow, plant, and harvest, while their non-Indian neighbors had moved on to tractors and threshing machines.[10]

When members of the Kanosh community requested a BIA loan of $500 that year to buy draft horses and harness, they were turned down.[11] Two years later Shivwits people asked for the release of $900 of tribal funds to invest in new tractor technology to be shared communally; the commissioner replied, "The tribal funds of this tribe are not available for expenditures of this type, except upon specific authorization by Congress."[12] Paiutes could not seem to get past the bureaucratic blockade to gain the finances they needed to make their agriculture competitive.

Another way to intensify use of available lands, in addition to new crops and technologies, was to expand into the mixed cattle production almost universally practiced by nearby non-Indians. Most of Shivwits Reservation was covered with thin piñon and juniper forest but at such a low altitude that in summer the scant grass burned off; Indian Peak, already leased to non-Indians, had summer range but was snowy and exposed all winter, as was Kanosh. The BIA toyed with ideas of developing cattle herds, trailing or trucking them from one reservation to the other in a seasonal cycle. Whether this creative, logistically intricate BIA plan was ever even discussed with Paiutes is unclear, but it certainly was never put into operation.[13]

It was at Kaibab that cattle became "the one really big industrial movement in the jurisdiction."[14] Local ranchers had already been using the range when the reservation was originally declared, and the BIA had avoided confrontation by declaring that Indians had no "need" for the pasturage and continuing to lease it out. In the early 1920s the more stalwart and creative Agent Farrow looked at the mere twenty-five acres that were irrigable with spring water and declared Kaibab to be cattle country. He began first by reestablishing Indian usage of reservation lands and then employed a variety of means to get livestock into Paiute hands. He began with rent funds from non-Indian cattlemen to pay for cross-fencing and then systematically pried loose the Kaibab range from lease holders one by one.[15]

The prolonged drought of the late 1920s thinned out even the normally lean desert grazing. Regional cattlemen reported half to as much as 90 percent of their herds dead of starvation and dehydration several years in a row. That portion of Kaibab so far reclaimed for tribal use could not support the small herd the BIA had provided, so Farrow sold off 40 percent of it and intensified efforts to dislodge remaining non-Indian leaseholds.[16] That remaining parcel, however, contained the only reliable water between the Kaibab Plateau range in the national forest to the north and the rim of the Grand Canyon to the south, so it also controlled practical access to those extensive public domain rangelands. Cattlemen fought, recruited political support in Washington, and in 1933 won a compromise agreement that awarded them permanently one third of the water from the crucial Pipe Spring. Another third went to the national monument that had been sliced out of the reservation in 1923. Not until 1937 did the Kaibab range begin to recover from the drought and lease-induced overgrazing.[17]

Even after Kaibab was cleared of non-Indian cattle, the 350 Indian-owned head exceeded the safe carrying capacity of the drought-reduced range. Paiutes culled the tribal herd, sold calves at rock bottom prices, instituted the first systematic branding ever used in the area, and began a program of careful range recovery and management with the technical assistance of the BIA forestry division.[18] With funds from the Federal Emergency Relief Act, the tribe bought twenty-five purebred Hereford cows and bulls that were in turn loaned to individual Paiute cattlemen, their rent to be paid in calves. Other tribal livestock were dispersed to individual Paiutes in exchange for labor setting fence, cleaning out water seeps and tanks, and riding herd.[19] By the time the drought eased in 1931, the Kaibab stockmen's organization, begun eight years earlier and reorganized in 1935, demanded that the remaining tribal herd be shifted into individual ownership. The last 142 tribal cattle were sold to Paiutes in 1937.[20]

Three years later Indian-owned cattle at Kaibab, among the region's best bred, numbered eleven hundred head. Several men owned one hundred or more cattle, and every family had at least a few. The following year, the tribe took out $20,000 in loans to further expand these herds.[21] Despite BIA range specialists' determination of a carrying capacity of 1,080 head, the new purchases exceeded this by 60 percent before 1943. Driven by high wartime beef prices, Paiutes stretched the limits of the reserve. The unpredictable arid climate chose the summer of 1944 to deliver only 40 percent of normal rainfall. Overgrazing became "acute," and Paiutes again sold down their herds.[22]

The scant and erratic rainfall through the 1920s and 1930s not only made ranching and farming difficult but also complicated Southern Paiute relationships with non-Indian neighbors and states. As both Indians and non-Indians strained their water supplies, rights to water became more contentiously defended throughout the area. Low rainfall also led to use of previously ignored minor water sources and incipient conservation techniques. Many such techniques were feasible only with the labor subsidies of federal Depression-era programs, including the Federal Emergency Relief Administration (FERA), Civilian Conservation Corps (CCC), Emergency Conservation Works (ECW), and National Youth Administration (NYA).

One of the early CCC projects in Nevada was the flood control dam in Arrow Canyon above Moapa; however, the project was abandoned when the foundation developed cracks.[23] The CCC also constructed a subsurface system of tiled drains to take flood and irrigation water off the southern half of the Moapa Reservation and return it to the elevated river. This work reclaimed 100 acres in 1941 and another 150 the following year, more than doubling the cropland then in production.[24] CCC crews built a solid new diversion dam at Moapa in 1937. This reliable structure impounded more water than the old but required the purchase of sixty-four acres from the state to assure that the dam footings, diversion canal heads, and flood zone were within reservation boundaries.[25]

A new non-Indian irrigation dam near Shivwits, partially constructed with CCC labor, shared its stored water with Paiutes. When an ECW labor camp was located on that reservation, the federal program piped in spring water that relieved Paiutes from drinking from the river for the first time, despite years of unsuccessful agency requests to fund precisely that development.[26]

In southern Nevada CCC crews also cleaned out the one spring on the Las Vegas Reservation to improve its flow. Drinking water also became a critical issue at Kanosh when the drought-ridden local irrigation company instituted a rotation system that threatened Paiutes' access to their culinary source for weeks at a time. The BIA did go to Congress and won a 920-acre addition to "surround their present holdings with all protection possible against further controversies relative to the title and use of water from Rogers' Spring."[27] The nearby town of Meadow, Utah, claimed water of two springs on this addition that were so minor they had never been named on the grounds that the congressional action had not specifically reserved this water, but the BIA successfully asserted a *Winters* water right. To save seepage losses, the BIA invested in a cement lining for Corn Creek, the reserve's main irrigation supply, and piped the tiny flows of Little Cottonwood Spring and Oak Spring.[28] Similarly, at Koosharem the BIA piped culinary water, cleaned springs, and sealed irrigation diversion structures to increase efficiency during the 1930s.[29]

By far the most intensive water development took place at Kaibab. With only one-third rights to the two major springs, the only other possible water sources were a few very minor springs and what were called "seeps," damp patches that did not produce water flow but would ooze out enough moisture to supply one or two cows every morning. Over a series of years Agent Farrow patched together range lease money, CCC funds, and even Paiute labor traded for the liquidated tribal cattle herd to capture dozens of these tiny sources and make distant range areas usable by livestock. Paiute CCC crews bulldozed dirt check dams across dry washes to capture runoff from seasonal cloudbursts. The cattlemen's association scheduled herds into the high plateau uplands to graze winter-dead grass while using snow-banks for water.[30]

Not only did Depression-era federal programs create needed water development and conservation work on the various Paiute reservations, but they also funded other resource improvements. The CCC constructed roads and bridges, the ECW fenced the external boundaries of Shivwits and Indian Peak for the first time, and the FERA got fifty head of cattle to Shivwits.[31]

While it would seem that such fundamental and benign infrastructural construction would be noncontroversial, problems did develop with local non-Indians. The northern boundary fence of Shivwits cut across a box canyon where off-reservation cattle drifted for protection in bad weather. Because reservation cattle could not reach this area, the BIA offered a land exchange. When local cattlemen further demanded a public driveway paralleling the state highway across the reserve, the BIA counterproposed compensatory acreage. Cattlemen violently opposed what they phrased as unwarranted "expansion of the Indian farm at Shem," and they lobbied county commissioners and congressmen. The negotiated resolution eventually involved the agent with no fewer than five cattle associations plus the county. By May 1937 the non-Indians had their fenced driveway across the reserve and the northern canyon shelter, and the reservation got from Congress 1,280 acres of public land in exchange.[32]

Because Kanosh had begun as individually held homesteads and allotments with occasional opportunistic additions, in order to fence it for cattle or develop a rational canal irrigation system as the BIA wanted to do in the 1930s, 3,160 additional acres were needed to fill out gaps and holes within the tract. Local opposition ran high. Again, low Indian resident populations told against Paiutes, as non-Indian landowners protested: "they have been allotted about as much public domain as is allotted for 80 to 90 White families in the same area."[33] Such an argument omitted to mention that non-Indian stockmen and even corporate cattle empires in the arid West rarely if ever owned the land on which they ranged their herds; homestead and privately owned land simply controlled water rights to springs or snaked down a streambed, while by the 1930s actual range, formerly on the free public domain, was largely in national forests and federal grasslands, accessible through grazing permits at rates well below land tax. Indian ranchers were virtually excluded from these off-reservation lands and limited to whatever pasturage could be found within trust-reserved properties. Congress gave Kanosh the land.[34]

Other Depression-era federal programs resulted in Paiutes losing land rather than gaining it. The Bureau of Reclamation proposed a dam at the narrow mouth of Shivwits Canyon that would have flooded all the Paiute farms and homes and suggested casually that the Indians could be relocated.[35] Fortunately, this plan was discarded on technical grounds, but the Chemehuevis were not so lucky. Their valley was flooded when the federal government built Parker Dam across the Colorado River in 1938.[36]

Paiutes gained access to small amounts of basic resources like land and water during the Depression, but much of their self-support came from off-reservation wage work, not subsistence farming on the reserves. The year of the stock market crash and the beginning of the Great Depression, the assistant commissioner of Indian affairs questioned whether the various Paiute reserves were even worth the cost of developing: "Would it not be better for the Indians merely to utilize the land as a home and depend primarily upon outside employment for their support?"[37] As the regional economy constricted and realigned over the next decade, such dependence on wages made life increasingly difficult for Paiutes. For the last three generations they had most often worked for local non-Indian ranchers and farmers, but the prolonged drought reduced southwestern agriculture, and recovery was delayed by the banking and financial crisis of the Depression. Another major economic change was the massive introduction of federally funded public sector jobs. By the beginning of World War II a very high percentage of Paiute households had shifted to federally funded employment for their major source of cash income.

The ten-year drought of the 1920s eroded Paiutes' usual source of agricultural employment. Farmers cut their labor costs to the bone, hiring fewer and fewer days of supplemental labor. Even at peak seasons, "the temporary nature of it makes it unsatisfactory as the unemployed time consumed all of the results of the employment leaving the Indian always poor. As a general proposition permanent employment cannot be had."[38] Drought-ridden farmers reneged on mortgages, local banks foreclosed and themselves folded, and only then did the Great Depression hit, taking down the stock market and major urban financial institutions, thus compounding the already-existing regional crisis. By 1930 the Paiute agent wrote, "The labor situation in this locality is and has been the worst we have had for years."[39] Three years later he reported that jobs had dwindled until "there has been very little employment outside" the reservation.[40]

Unemployed Paiutes, like workers across the country during this economic emergency, needed rations. "Labor conditions have been so desperate in the region," the agent explained, "that it has been necessary to give aid to practically all of the Indians in this settlement [Las Vegas]. This is unusual as in normal times only the old and ill required any help, and this only occasionally."[41] By 1934 need had exceeded BIA funds. The Red Cross stepped in, but recipients under this program, unlike the familiar BIA system, had to "return some labor if they were able to work," and Paiutes "were dissatisfied with the arrangement."[42]

Again, like people across the country, Paiutes were unable to meet the demands of creditors. For decades the federal government had actively encouraged Paiutes to take out loans for agricultural tools and equipment. By 1938 individual Paiutes owed $13,000 in federal reimbursable debts, none of which had had payments made on them at all for more than two years, and 70 percent had stood for over twenty years.[43] Washington threatened to seize equipment and livestock or garnish probated property. Local store owners who had extended credit to Paiutes demanded that the BIA collect for them, although it had no power to do so. The stores began insisting on cash, which Paiutes, like other people at this time, had rarely and in small amounts.[44]

To minimize such debts Paiutes hunted and gathered wild foods. They may have even increased their collecting during the Depression, because the BIA actually noticed it for the first time in decades. In 1942 home consumption of piñon, game, and other "traditional foods" was reported to be 5 percent of the gross tribal product at Kaibab, 7 percent at Shivwits, and 17 percent at both Kanosh and Koosharem.[45] An inspector observed that "the Paiutes of Kaibab and Shivwits have learned [!] to eat what they can get, being able to subsist on a strictly vegeterian diet when it is necessary, but on account of the great number of rabbits that inhabit the country, they are usually able to supply themselves with meat with very little effort. It is a great misfortune that there are so few rabbits in the Moapa country, for rabbits often stand between Indians and hunger."[46] Paiutes hunted not only rabbits but also deer, over which the state claimed regulatory authority. Paiutes protested demands for state licenses to hunt the game of their own traditional territory and were arrested.[47] Paiutes' efforts to minimize food costs put them in direct conflict with the legal restrictions instituted over previous decades.

Paiutes also moved to geographic areas they had not occupied in years looking for jobs. "The nomadic habits of many families," Agent Farrow huffed, had become "exaggerat[ed] by present unemployment conditions."[48] Public schools reported Paiute children applying for admission as far away as Tippett, Nevada, and Gandy, Utah. Unneeded by reduced cattle operations of the Pahrump Valley, men moved to the town of Shoshone, on the far side of Death Valley, to work in the borax mines. Gypsum mines, newly opened along the railroad line near Las Vegas, were unlike the old precious metal mines of Pioche and would hire Indians; furthermore, they paid $5 a day, far better than the usual ranch wage of $3, but it was exhausting, dusty, choking labor in the desert sun.[49] Reacting to economic changes they could not control, Paiutes, as they had so often in the past, found new types of work and new employers, and they developed new skills.

Some of those employment opportunities were in the growing towns, and Paiutes became increasingly urbanized. Almost all Indian Peak people had moved to Cedar City, where there were "so many money jobs running after them it has been hard to get them to do their own farm work and their crops have been neglected."[50] In southern Nevada the "little reservation at Las Vegas is becoming of more importance as the town grows," wrote the agent, "as many Indians come there and live, making it their headquarters most of the time."[51] The new federal highway between Salt Lake City and Los Angeles followed the Old Mormon Trail route across both Shivwits and Moapa. Paiutes found construction wages at $3 to $5 a day, twice the rate of harvest labor.[52] Tony Veno saw opportunity and was the first Paiute to apply for a federal loan to open his own business; he wanted to build a gas station and garage at Moapa.[53]

Paiute women contributed to family budgets during the hard economic times of the 1920s and 1930s by commercializing their old skills of basket making and buckskin tanning. Tourists along the new highways supplemented the older market of local non-Indians, occasional anthropologists, and museum buyers, but the demand was not large. As early as 1927 the agent noted, "[T]he markets are glutted and the time required for the work makes it necessary under the present economic conditions for a price to be placed upon these products that is out of proportion to their value, hence they degenerate into curios and the number of purchases is limited."[54] By the middle of the Depression, baskets of materials laboriously gathered from the wild, prepared, and handwoven into multiple-colored patterns routinely sold for $2 or $3. Despite such low prices, Paiute women raised at least $300 through basket sales in 1935, a significant addition to scant family income.[55]

Paiutes exploited growing tourism in other ways, too. M. R. Harring-

9. Ethnologist Samuel Barrett of the Milwaukee Public Museum purchases baskets from Shivwits Paiute women in 1916, while the man on horseback holds other offerings, and friends watch from the background. (Photograph by E. M. Sweet, U.S. National Archives, Bureau of Indian Affairs Records.)

ton, the Los Angeles–based archaeologist, hired Paiutes for his Gypsum Cave and Lost City excavations in the Muddy Valley; when he staged a pageant to dramatize the life of ancient residents, Paiutes from Moapa played the Anasazis. As making westerns became a major industry in southern Utah, Kaibab Paiutes rented out their reservation for scenery and hired on as extras. The highway to the northern rim of the Grand Canyon passed near Kaibab; Paiute girls became maids at motels.[56]

Paiutes were so assiduous in their search for employment, the Kaibab agent complained, that half the adult men visited the reserve only occasionally. Paiutes bought cars, which extended their travel for jobs; two thirds of Shivwits families had one by 1932. Automobiles, unlike horse teams, which could be turned loose to graze and support themselves, cost money for fuel and repairs, demanding further cash and escalating the need for employment. Some agents criticized car ownership as "causing the Indian to dissipate his funds."[57] Paiutes like Mabel Wall, however, valued automobile-facilitated mobility for the off-reservation wage labor on which they subsisted: "We Indians go round the country [to get work] then what We do when they catch with out [state driver's] license. . . . What will Indian do or leave their car home and go on foot and you know what Indian ar[e] poor an[d] have no money. . . . Well it's all right for White people to pay taxes on anything they got. the Indian people got nothing."[58]

To meet Paiute economic need in the face of plummeting off-reservation job opportunities, agents plundered their budgets for wage funds. Agent Farrow justified the one-thousand-dollar addition to his 1932 budget for the combined Paiute reservations in Utah: "Labor conditions and general depression ha[ve] changed so many self-supporting Indians into rationers temporarily that it will not be possible for us to give the necessary assistance without additional funds. . . . every possible means [are being] used to provide work and subsistence for Indians in other ways than direct issue."[59] He hired Kaibab and Shivwits men to cut and set fence posts at twenty-five cents apiece; a consortium of Shivwits men headed by Tony Tillohash then capitalized on this experience, getting a county contract to fence roadsides. The agency hired men to repair flood-damaged roadways, clean irrigation ditches and springs, and install erosion controls.[60] Nine months of Shivwits payroll records from 1933 and 1934 show that an average of 15.5 men were employed at that one reservation who earned an average of $18.11 a month.[61] Farrow conscientiously rotated these jobs so his small funds could benefit as many families as possible and timed his projects when off-reservation employment was unavailable. Very little of the work the agency could generate to construct, maintain, or improve reservation infrastructure conformed to Euro-American concepts of appropriate female employment; only three of the twenty-eight Paiutes on salary at Shivwits in December 1933 were women.[62]

Even with funds thus husbanded, Paiutes' need for jobs exceeded the BIA's means. For the first time, major federal funding for Paiutes arrived from programs not designed specifically for Indians, such as the CCC and the ECW. These federal "relief" programs funneled moneys through BIA channels and provided scores of Paiutes with jobs in the 1930s. The aggregate amounts were substantial; in FY 1935, Moapa Reservation alone received $12,000 in federal wages from these programs.[63] Relief jobs also paid more; the six Shivwits men working for the ECW planting trees in the national forest in April 1933 earned $30 a month, plus room and board, well above agency rates.[64]

These federal jobs gave Paiutes more than just cash, important as that was; they also widened Paiutes' range of experience. Four Cedar City boys traveled to Uintah-Ouray and worked out of the CCC camp for Utes there. Seven men applied for the leadership training program at Fort Apache. Five young Shivwits men went to the CCC camp in Charleston, North Carolina, although they did not stay long.[65] Mobility and visiting had always been important in Paiute life, but now this travel was on an entirely new scale.

Not all federal officials saw employment as the best adaptation for Paiutes to the economic conditions caused by the Depression. The ECW camp at Kaibab was reputed among federal officers to be a major source of liquor, still denied to Indians long after the repeal of Prohibition in 1933.[66] A federal consultant blamed reduced Paiute farming on relief jobs, rather than seeking a cause in nationwide economic conditions or the lack of a profitable market. Julian Steward traced federal jobs to "largely more cars, more gas for trips, more canned goods, more candy. It has meant immediate not deferred, compensation. . . . Farming, with its slow progress, and low initial returns will have been dealt a serious blow."[67]

As the Depression deepened and economic benefits became more competitive, federal jobs also became an issue of conflict between Paiutes and non-Indians. When the Moapa agent got the lucrative job assisting a federal survey of the Muddy Valley for an Indian, "I was criticized by many white people for getting an Indian this job. These people said we had money on the reservation for the Indians."[68] In later years federal relief efforts, especially the WPA, were channeled through state and county agencies. Local elected officials were reluctant to spend their limited resources on Indians and incur such hostility from non-Indian voters. As with public education and health benefits, it was easier to "take the stand that the Indians, being federal charges, must be relieved through federal funds."[69]

Paiutes were well aware of the shift in employment from private local employers to federal jobs. "They cut me off WPA," Joe Pikyavit wrote. "Got to work on CCC now. Hard. Sometimes [used to] make $56 a month—hard work though. Wont let Indians work on WPA. Used to have in their minds to give work to Indians—women wash, iron, men work in fields,—but forget now."[70] Stewart Snow and Tony Tillohash, writing for the Shivwits Tribal Council, recognized how the Depression had restructured their economy by 1940: "For the past six years we have depended largely on the various Federal Relief Agencies. Our farms have been somewhat neglected."[71]

Despite Paiutes' best efforts to find employment, the agency's commitment to part-time jobs, and numerous federal programs, by 1935 the BIA reported that only two families out of all those at Kaibab and fourteen at Moapa were self-supporting; all the families at Kanosh and at Las Vegas depended on federal Depression relief programs for income. Every household at Koosharem depended on direct rations for subsistence, and all those at Shivwits and Cedar City were partially supported by federal largess.[72] Such grim Paiute dependency on federal subsidies continued through the early years of World War II, unaffected by the economic recovery that much of the rest of the country experienced. Not only did Paiutes find employment scarce, but suddenly they no longer had the regional monopoly on unskilled labor that they had so long enjoyed. In the mid-1930s the federal government built Hoover Dam across the Colorado River just outside Las Vegas. That sleepy desert railroad and ranching town instantly became a construction camp, drawing non-Indians from all over the country desperate for jobs. A federal observer saw that Paiutes' "chance for employment has grown increasingly *less* with the great influx of people from all over the country seeking jobs at Boulder City and Hoover Dam."[73]

The mixture of ethnic groups became more complicated. In the mid-1920s Japanese, Koreans, and other people of Asian origin were being squeezed out of California by the Alien Land Act. A few families began labor-intensive, competitive vegetable farms in the Muddy Valley that were very much resented by the established non-Indian population. The BIA encouraged Paiutes to compete with them, introducing cantaloupe, asparagus, radishes, and other novel crops to Moapa, but by 1930 Paiutes were more often employed by rather than outmarketing the immigrants.[74] In 1931 an elderly Indian was convicted of killing his "Japanese" employer in a fight over wages. Nevada senator Patrick McCarran's suggestion to use men of Japanese ancestry interned in California during World War II to reduce the cost of the proposed White Narrows Dam outside Moapa, rather than to hire local Indian labor, would have put Paiutes and Asian-Americans in direct competition for scarce jobs.[75]

Paiute relations with these settlers of Asian origin quickly broadened beyond simply employment. In 1925 a Moapa man wanted to lease his unused allotment "to a Jap," but the agent refused to approve it, in part because Indian water rights there were still under dispute with the state. He also feared a worsening of already tense interethnic relations if there were "a few Japs almost in the center of the Indians [as it] would mean that they (the Japs) would be after The Indian Women and that *would* mean trouble too."[76] At least one Paiute girl bore a child by an itinerant Filipino harvest worker.[77]

10. Moapa Paiutes found jobs such as this seasonal work harvesting radishes on a non-Indian farm in Logandale in 1940 increasingly hard to find. The wage was three cents a dozen pulled, and men, women, and children all worked to earn the family's income. (Photograph by Arthur Rothstein, U.S. National Archives, Photographic Collection, no. 75-N-Carson-320-M-1.)

Elsewhere the regional ethnic composition was becoming more complex as well. Koosharem people had long relied on summer employment in the sugar beet fields near Richfield; during the Depression Navajos began appearing this far north in pursuit of migrant harvest labor. Within a decade they replaced Paiutes in the fields and became the focus of Mormon Church efforts for educational access.[78] In the late 1930s Mexican migrant laborers began to harvest the potato fields west of Cedar City and eventually displaced Paiutes from this sector as well. By World War II southern blacks had migrated into Las Vegas and formed a distinctive neighborhood just across the railroad tracks from the Indian community. Interracial conflicts between the two populations were marked.[79]

Not all the major changes in Paiute lives during this time period were economic. Several communities developed new internal political structures prior to formal tribal councils and in so doing began to change their external relationships with states, the BIA, and other federal entities. A few of the more sensitive agents had recognized the subtle leadership of the Paiute communities and had contacted focal individuals or held periodic general councils or referenda. These informal and flexible structures still lacked legal standing or any acknowledged relationship with external political bodies, but Washington was increasingly reluctant to proceed, particularly with land-use decisions, without some formal mechanism of native approval. For instance, in 1933, when the Paiute agent wanted to establish a CCC camp at Shivwits to secure much-needed jobs, the commissioner of Indian affairs, John Collier, refused to approve the measure "without securing the consent of the Indians."[80] Some representative body had to be found.

By the end of the year the Shivwits Business Committee had been established, two men and a secretary who met at the discretion of the agent. How these individuals were chosen and by whom the agent did not report, although he did suggest condescendingly that the committee was "unhampered by any written regulations that might confuse the minds of the Indians." Its functions were wider than the name suggests, including "domestic relations, school matters, control of irrigation, and the general community economic problems." Despite the critical importance of water issues during that time and perennial "domestic" disputes, in six years the agent said the group "never functioned due to a lack of economic problems of a tribal nature," probably because he himself retained tight control over all financial decisions.[81]

Kaibab Paiutes too developed new organizations in the 1930s. The agent was committed to clearing non-Indian grazing leases from reservation pastures to make room for Indian herds, and he found it politically useful to present the lease cancellations both to non-Indian cattlemen and to the Washington office as the Indians' choice. Beginning in 1932 he systematically called meetings of Paiute cattle owners, a specialized subgroup of male tribal members, whose majority votes he presented as the decisions of the whole tribe.[82] These informal discussion sessions grew into the Kaibab Cattlemen's Association, whose written constitution was approved by the BIA in 1935. This body, to which all tribal stock owners automatically belonged, set grazing fees and regulations, owned and managed the tribal cattle herd, and over the next decade took over range improvement responsibilities. Although limited in powers, this was the first organization of natives that the BIA recognized as holding any powers over Kaibab resources; in other words, it acknowledged the association as a political entity. Along with an Indian judgeship reactivated in 1941, the cattlemen's association managed Kaibab affairs for years after other Paiute groups organized formal tribal councils. Perhaps its most dramatic action was the abortive 1942 attempt to adopt San Juan Paiutes en masse because they "are not getting along too well with the Navajo Indians" among whom they were living.[83]

In 1934 Congress passed the Wheeler-Howard Act, which authorized each reservation-based Indian group to form a tribal council.[84] Once the BIA had approved the written constitution, the tribal council would legally represent the Indians to the federal government and other external agencies. The law assumed that each reservation population was composed of one tribe and, correspondingly, that each native tribe resided on one reservation. This simplistic model clearly did not fit the Southern Paiute situation. The formation of such tribal councils would ossify the already artificial division of a fluid Paiute society into rigid, separate entities.

The law called for a majority vote of enrolled adults on the preliminary question of whether or not to form a tribal council at all. If the vote was positive, a general meeting would select a committee to draft a constitution. The resulting draft, after it was accepted by the local agency, was forwarded to the BIA in Washington, which often demanded changes such as quorum requirements, grounds of removal from office, or other formalities that had been overlooked.[85] The draft was then returned, and if a majority of the voting reservation members accepted it, it was forwarded for final acceptance by the secretary of the interior in the name of the president.

BIA agents presented this Wheeler-Howard Act process to Paiutes in public meetings over the spring and summer of 1934. Response varied. At Shivwits the agent had "little hope of effective organizations until something can be done to change the economic status. . . . Shivwits . . . have very little to look forward to on account of the limited amount of water available for irrigation. It is believed that the possibility of making a living on the reservations must [a]ffect the possibility of organization to a large extent."[86] Nevertheless, the Shivwits Paiutes were among the first to accept the provisions of the law, and they assigned their business committee to draft a constitution. That body immediately asked to take over management of a standing gravel extraction lease and other tribal businesses, but they were told they would have to wait for the formal election of a council. Calling themselves the interim "Tribal Organization," they negotiated with the county for highway right-of-way in 1936.[87]

In contrast with such vigorous enthusiasm was the cool reception at Cedar City. The BIA had no structured relationship with those Paiutes, who lived on church-owned land, so it used Mormon Church missionaries as intermediaries. "I hope you will find it convenient," suggested the BIA regional supervisor, "to interview Mr. William Palmer for the purpose of making the law clear to him in the hope that he may be able to get the Indians at Cedar City to see the advantages of the law so that when the time comes to vote they will not vote against the law."[88] The first balloting on whether to consider forming a tribal council in May 1935 saw only two votes cast out of thirteen eligible voters, well below the 30 percent participation required by law. Nevertheless, the secretary of the interior ruled that since "the majority of the votes cast was in favor of the act, the Office shall hold officially that they have not voted to exclude themselves" from the Wheeler-Howard Act.[89]

Often the men and women first elected to the tribal councils had also been on the constitutional committees. They were middle-aged or older and invariably married, and BIA boarding school educations in their earlier years had given them some familiarity and skill with bureaucratic structures. Every one of the first elected councils contained at least one woman in a position other than that of secretary.[90]

Southern Paiute Votes to Accept Provisions of the Wheeler-Howard Act

RESERVE	DATE	ELIGIBLE VOTERS	ON-SITE YEA	ON-SITE NAY	ABSENTEE YEA	ABSENTEE NAY	CONSTITUTION APPROVED
Cedar City	5/35	13	2	0			——
Chemehuevi							6/70
Indian Peak	11/34	11	7	0	0	0	——
Kaibab	11/34	51	28	5	11	1	5/51
Kanosh	5/35	25	14	11	0	0	12/42
Koosharem	5/35	17	14	0			——
Las Vegas	5/35	22	10	2	0	0	11/76
Moapa	11/34	84	42	3	16	0	4/42
San Juan							1986
Shivwits	11/34	40	27	2	7	1	3/40

Sources: E. A. Farrow to F. A. Gross, 3 January 1935, USNA, BIA, Indian Organization Division, General Records; E. A. Farrow to F. A. Gross, 11 January 1935, USNA, BIA, Indian Organization Division, General Records; F. A. Gross to commissioner Indian affairs, 18 January 1935, USNA, BIA, Indian Organization Division, General Records; E. A. Farrow to John Collier, 20 May 1935, USNA, BIA-CCF; E. A. Farrow to commissioner Indian affairs, 12 May 1935, USNA, BIA-CCF; J. C. McCaskill, Memorandum to assistant secretary of interior, 4 August 1942, USNA, BIA-CCF; Oscar Chapman to C. C. Wright, 2 December 1942, USNA, BIA-CCF; Elmer R. Rusco & Mary K. Rusco, "Tribal Politics."

The Paiute tribal councils dealt with a wide range of social issues. The first Moapa Tribal Council soon accomplished a unanimous voluntary surrender of individual land assignments to the tribe "in order that their land can be developed as a unit and their water rights protected."[91] The first ordinance this council passed authorized a tribal court. Within a year the novice council had established tribal control over reservation grazing resources and was negotiating complicated right-of-way agreements with a regional electric company.[92] Everywhere tribal councils had to defend water rights and develop land-use plans.

While tribal councils elsewhere were increasing their involvement in reservation management, Indian Peak differed. Perhaps because the group was so small, composed virtually of one extended family, they chose not to form a council and continued to operate through traditional kinship mechanisms. Wartime production stresses brought federal inquiries "why these Indians owning 10,000 acres of good grazing land are not in the livestock business."[93] Until a few years before, the reservation had been leased to non-Indian sheepmen, but the Paiutes refused to renew the lease, only to see management of their own affairs removed from them. "Since the Indians involved are not organized [under a Wheeler-Howard Act tribal council], . . . since the Indians are not in a position to use the range [because they owned little livestock], and in view of the fact it is essential that full use be made of Indian forage resources during the war," the BIA overrode the Paiutes' decision, advertised, and proceeded to lease the reservation.[94]

In addition to tribal councils, Kanosh, Shivwits, and Moapa formed corporate business charters under the Wheeler-Howard Act as well. In this legal form a group could own and manage property, take out loans, and operate businesses as a whole.

The Wheeler-Howard Act established a revolving credit fund that could be loaned out to recognized tribal councils and business corporations. The special agent assigned to help write constitutions clearly linked council formation and loan credit in his work at Moapa: "[t]rusting that the enclosed Charter can be readily reviewed, approved, and discussed . . . in order that an election date might be set so that the Indians can ratify same in order to obtain immediate credit to finance their farming program this season."[95] The Moapa agent hoped "a date can be called for this election as early as possible for we are going to be in dire need of the credit funds to operate this [farm] project with this coming spring."[96] The new Moapa Tribal Council, along with those at Kanosh, Shivwits, and Kaibab, each promptly took out substantial federal loans. In every case the profitable agriculture and economic self-sufficiency that the Indians had desired and the BIA had promised failed to materialize.

Kanosh was a case in point. Even before they drafted a constitution, the people of Kanosh applied for a five-hundred-dollar loan, asking to expand farming on their new lands with familiar draft horse and harness technology. The BIA insisted that they form an interim legal entity, the Kanosh Cooperative Association, and then loaned it $1,200 for a highly mechanized wheat combine, tractor, and plows. The eight families of the group assessed themselves $2 a month each from their externally earned wage income to pay off the loan. Since most of these wages were from BIA irrigation projects paid at $16 per month, this was a substantial commitment.[97]

During the 1930s the BIA had invested over $50,000 to buy up land between the original allotments for which Kanosh Paiutes had voluntarily returned title to the group. An irrigation system was planned to serve the consolidated 7,700 acres. The BIA praised Kanosh plans to expand their wheat farming as "very progressive."[98]

Good rainfall and markets in 1942 enabled the new Kanosh Tribal Council to withdraw a second loan application, but a loss of 75 percent of their wheat crop in 1949 forced resubmission of this request for $25,000. They wanted to put all their land in wheat, using their entire water allotment for fifty-five acres and dry farming the rest, a high risk strategy; the BIA disapproved. Federal soil conservation and farm management specialists persuaded the Kanosh people to rotate legume crops to build the soil, contour plow to protect from wind erosion, set aside marginal lands for a few head of cattle, and introduce alfalfa for feed.[99] Once the association agreed to these practices and the tribal council promised that none of the reservation would be used by non-Indians, the BIA approved their loan. Ten thousand dollars was advanced for immediate debts and expenses to be repaid after 1955. Although the group owned land and machinery assessed at more than $30,000, individual families averaged only $500 a year in cash income, although all were self-supporting and none on welfare.[100]

Long accustomed to operating on their own initiative with only rare visits from distant Indian agents, the Kanosh people found the strictures of federal oversight that came with this loan, especially formal accounting procedures, onerous. They were immediately chided for "irregular practices" that were "contrary to the regulations set up in your loan agreement with the Government. For example, you sold certain products of the farm, collected the money and paid such money out without clearing through your bookkeeper or the fiscal channels of this office. Also, some of your transactions were not properly authorized by your own Committee."[101] In 1951 the Indians made a creative but verbal agreement to take in non-Indians' cattle on excess lands to generate cash for their loan payment. Because they had agreed that non-Indians would use no part of the reservation and they had not notified the agency first, the BIA busily issued federal seizure warrants on the cattle for trespass and then tightened its oversight.

By 1953 the Kanosh Paiutes were still not rotating crops, and they had not bought the cattle that the BIA had insisted on. The BIA staff in Washington concluded, "[T]his is a loan that should never have been made. . . . apparently the Kanosh Band is incapable of adhering to agreements. . . . we are now concerned with the protection of the financial interests of the United States."[102] That concern was real. The 1951 harvest was a net loss of $2,680, and the following year a hailstorm and invasion of insects, normal farming disasters, resulted in a crop loss of 60 percent and an operating deficit of $5,580 for the Kanosh Cooperative Association.[103]

The BIA area director considered liquidating the loan, "sale of assets and/or leasing the tribal land."[104] Contrarily, BIA agricultural specialists urged the Kanosh Tribal Council to activate the remaining $15,000 of their loan for cattle purchases. The Indians thought that the herd this could buy would be too small to make a difference, argued that rainfall was too unpredictable for the elaborate crop rotation plan and soil improvements the government wanted, and decided "they could not afford borrowing" more.[105] They faced spring planting in 1953 with an operating capital of only $400 for seed and to carry the farm through harvest. Only two families were now self-supporting, four were on welfare, and income through agriculture had dropped to $200 per year, 60 percent less than when they had taken out their federal loan.[106]

Shivwits followed a similar pattern. The first action of the new tribal council was a fifteen-hundred-dollar loan application for a tractor and other farm equipment that they easily paid off. Under their new business charter in 1946, they asked for a more ambitious $10,000 to mechanize and convert all the arable land to a cooperative. Shivwits Paiutes had an extreme disparity in income distribution, and more than three quarters earned less than $200 per year, but the BIA approved the loan because "the development of this reservation will not result in material wealth due principally to the shortage of water on irrigable lands. Definitely it will increase the reservation income and equitably distribute such income to all members of the tribe."[107] The tribe bought out the only individually owned cattle herd and assumed management of seventy acres, planting eight acres to fruit trees, a long-term investment, and rotating the rest between grain and alfalfa as immediate cash crops. In the 1947 crop year the Shivwits Agriculture, Livestock and Range Enterprise lost $930, the following year over $1,100, and by 1949 was described as "practically broke."[108] Even though the loan was interest-free and they had five years before repayments began, they realized they could never repay the loan this way. In November 1949 the tribal council leased the entire reservation to a non-Indian for the $2,000 due annually on the loan. The tribal cooperative never farmed Shivwits again.

In 1952 Kaibab Paiutes formed Kaibab Tribal Herd Enterprises and applied for a fifty-thousand-dollar federal loan to buy Herefords to pasture on part of the tribal lands. In the first year, with no payment due and using free tribal pastures, they made a net profit of $200. The situation changed by 1953, however, when they lost $13,200 and the following year showed another loss of $6,500. In August 1955 the enterprise was liquidated and produced a three-year overall profit of $6,000 after all the cattle were auctioned.[109]

At Moapa, too, Paiutes applied for a fifteen-thousand-dollar federal loan the same month their tribal constitution was approved to buy up-to-date machinery and seed and to cover the operating expenses of the Moapa Paiute Farming Enterprise, which was to farm the entire reservation cooperatively. While food crops were in high demand during the war, the farm expanded the cultivated acreage, operated at a profit, and paid off more than half its loan. By 1952, however, irrigation-induced alkalinity and water logging had reduced the arable fields to only two hundred acres. Unable to meet its loan payments, in 1953 the Moapa Paiutes leased the entire reservation to a local dairy.[110]

Kanosh, Shivwits, Kaibab, and Moapa Paiutes were each lured by federal loans and promises of an economy based on market agriculture; each group found the reality far less glittering than the hope. On none of their reservations was the land sufficient to support the resident population, not even with the interest-free loans, mechanized methods, and a booming wartime economy. In each case their efforts ended in financial disaster; in half, Paiutes completely lost control of reservation lands to non-Indian lessors in order to meet federal loan obligations.

In part the blame lay in the insufficient size of the usable land base and water supply, but part also lay in the federal goals. Commissioner Collier's Indian New Deal provided funds to develop rural, agricultural economies in hopes that they could support Indians at a level somewhere above desperate poverty. In much of the West, and certainly in the southeastern Great Basin, the regional economy was rapidly moving away from reliance on subsistence agriculture into activities such as tourism and casino gambling. None of the federal programs available to Paiutes through the Depression and World War II enabled them to prepare for this future; rather, they were encouraged to re-create the agriculture that had already proven maladaptive in the arid West.

The military aspects of World War II, in contrast to the economic influence on markets, had relatively little impact on Southern Paiutes. A small number served in the armed forces, and some benefited from the high salaries of wartime industries in major urban areas. Arvilla Benson wrote to a friend in Cedar City, "About frist time I ever seen Salt lake, 'Gee' It was Big City I am planting [planning] on working over there."[111] Yetta McFee found work in a laundry in that same city while her husband got a job in one of the munitions depots nearby. Lila Frank left the harvest fields of the Muddy Valley and followed several other Paiutes from Cedar City and Kaibab to Los Angeles in 1942, hoping to find work in the booming defense industries. Young women from Shivwits and Kanosh used the commercial sewing training they had gotten through the NYA during the Depression to get work from parachute, military uniform, and other defense contractors in Salt Lake City. By 1943 so many members elected to the Shivwits Tribal Council were "employed away from home and while [war-time] gas rationing remains" that it met only in occasional special sessions.[112] Instead, during World War II Paiutes stretched out to regional urban areas in response to the opportunities of industrial employment. They gained metropolitan experience rarely available to previous generations.

On the other hand, Paiutes apparently had less luck with local defense industries, as there is no record that any worked at Nellis Air Force Base or Basic Magnesium, Inc., the large defense-related plant just east of Las Vegas. High wartime agricultural prices and the draft and enlistment of local non-Indians did create an ample agricultural labor market in Paiute areas. Employers such as the major sugar beet refinery in Richfield, which had never hired Indians, solicited Paiute workers for the first time, and Shivwits Paiutes found "plenty of work" bringing the crops in during the war.[113]

During the eventful decades of the Great Depression and World War II many Southern Paiutes continued to live on or near reservation residential cores. Even bolstered with federal Depression-era job programs and development loans, those reserves were just as inadequate to support the growing Paiute population as they had been earlier in the twentieth century. Driven by the lack of a viable reservation economy and in reaction to events taking place far beyond their region and certainly out of their control, Paiutes extended their economic and social networks during these decades, becoming more cosmopolitan as they ventured into major West Coast urban areas for employment. It was usually the young adults, best educated, energetic, and in their most productive years, who left the native community. Their leaving was rarely permanent, however, as they continued to believe that their homes lay in southern Utah and Nevada; they returned there, bringing with them new skills and experiences.

10

LAND CLAIM
AND TERMINATION

In the ten years after World War II, two major events significantly changed the relationship between the federal government and Southern Paiutes, along with their ties to other non-Indian groups. During the mid-1950s, congressional conservatives forced severe limitation of federal involvement in Indian affairs. Instead of its previous active management of Indian resources and social life, the BIA was ordered to withdraw rapidly from Indian life with the goal of terminating all relationships between tribes and the federal government, other than those available generally to non-Indian citizens. This so-called termination policy threatened not only to change but also to remove the relationship between Indians and the specialized agency that had long dominated the existence of all reservation tribes. That threat became reality for Southern Paiutes in Utah.

The second major event that impacted Paiute affairs during this decade was their claim against the federal government for illegal seizure of their land. This was done under a new law that some historians have argued was preliminary to the termination process, a way of clearing federal liability before the government eased out of Indian affairs.[1] Over the years many tribes had tried to sue the federal government for land lost without due process transfer of title, unfulfilled treaty obligations, and other federal violations of tribal rights, but the U.S. Constitution required that the federal government, because of its own sovereignty, had to explicitly consent to be sued in each case individually. Congress, accustomed to the streamlined efficiency developed during the flood of wartime legislation, was weary and wary of bills for such individual legislation. In August 1946 it passed the Indian Claims Commission (ICC) Act, which gave carte blanche to "any Indian tribe, band, or other identifiable group of American Indians residing within the territorial limits of the United States" to file any and all claims within four years and set up an independent judiciary board to hear them.[2] Once the commission had heard evidence, adjudged the claim's validity, and established a monetary compensation, all Congress then had to do was authorize payment.

Even before the ICC was appointed, in December 1946 William Palmer, the Mormon churchman who had engineered the relocation of the Cedar City Paiutes and elbowed the BIA out of their lives, personally visited the commissioner of Indian affairs to argue his view of their claim. He asserted that the government had never fulfilled various "oral agreements" made by Brigham Young when he was ex officio Indian agent for Utah Territory. The commissioner responded that none of the treaties negotiated by Agent O. H. Irish with Southern Paiutes had ever been approved by the Senate, so under the Constitution they were not legally binding. This meant, of course, that the U.S. government had never acquired Southern Paiute territory from its aboriginal owners but had nevertheless sold homestead titles and transferred land to non-Indians as well as retained a fair portion itself for national forests and parks.

Palmer also lobbied local civil authorities and the hierarchy of the Salt Lake City church. The BIA agent responsible for Utah and Arizona Paiutes knew that Palmer was "very active" in persuading Paiutes to hire the firm of Boyden and Wilkinson as their claims attorneys.[3] Ernest Wilkinson had helped draft the ICC legislation, and his partner, John Boyden, had been formerly on staff at the Department of Justice, but these were not the arguments Palmer used with the Cedar Paiutes: "I said that you [Wilkinson] are a Mormon and a member of the Stake Presidency there [Salt Lake City,] they [Paiutes] said they would like you for their Attorney. I am authorized now to speak for the Indians in securing your assistance."[4] Just as Mormon churchmen had formerly directed Paiutes' choice of headmen who would mediate interethnic boundaries, so too from the beginning the church hierarchy wielded its political influence with Washington and molded the selection of the lawyer who would advocate Utah Paiutes' claims for lands lost during the predominantly Mormon settlement of their territory. Furthermore, the local church hierarchy tried to position itself between the Indians and their attorney.

By this time BIA supervision of the various small Paiute reservations in Utah and Arizona was very loose, having become a subsidiary charge to the overworked agent at Uintah-Ouray aided by only a single, very low ranking employee entitled "farmer" at Kaibab. As the deadline for filing a claim approached, the farmer appeared before the Kanosh Tribal Council and held meetings at Cedar City, Indian Peak, Kaibab, and Koosharem. He "informed the group that Boyden and Wilkinson, attorneys, were handling claims for other tribes and that they would handle the claims for this tribe if the tribe wanted them, which would probably be best as these people were well posted on Indian affairs."[5] Accepting the recommendation of both local Mormons and the BIA, these five groups contracted Wilkinson and Boyden's firm to pursue their ICC claims on the standard contingency basis.[6]

The chairman of the Shivwits Tribal Council, Tony Tillohash, suspected the distant Uintah-Ouray Agency of "various malfeasances, including an attempt . . . to solicit business for Mr. Boyden."[7] He could only persuade two others of the five-person council. Lacking the unanimity Paiutes preferred in public decisions, the council avoided voting on a formal resolution for a claims contract; the three men, including Chairman Tillohash, proceeded to contract with the Washington-based firm of James Curry, who had been representing Moapa Paiutes for four years. When the BIA refused to approve what it interpreted as a contract for "individual claims that the Indian Claims Commission cannot adjudicate," the Shivwits Tribal Council in a rare divisive vote hired Curry less than two weeks before the legal deadline to file a claim.[8]

On 10 August 1951 Wilkinson filed a land claim for the five groups of Paiutes in Utah and Arizona, plus representatives of unaffiliated off-reservation Paiutes. It asked compensation for unlawful seizure of Southern Paiute tribal territory by the United States and its citizens. Curry filed a separate claim on behalf of his clients, the three Shivwits men and Moapa, for compensation for the same territory. Because the land and presumably the evidence was the same in the two claims, the ICC joined the two cases. The Chemehuevis had yet a third attorney, but he defined the lands they claimed separately.[9]

The key to a successful ICC claim was proof by a tribe that they had held exclusive occupation of a clearly defined area "from time immemorial" until some specified date, when it was lost to federal malfeasance. William Palmer began collecting Paiute place-names in the native language, but attorneys realized that more professional research and documentary evidence were required.[10] They hired a series of major figures in Great Basin anthropology to testify as expert witnesses in the Southern Paiute cases. Omer C. Stewart investigated for the tribe, and Julian Steward, Robert Manners, and Robert Euler, for the government defense. Alfred L. Kroeber testified for the Chemehuevis, and Harold Driver, for the federal side in that case.

Among the first government challenges was whether Kanosh community members were really Southern Paiutes with rightful participation in this case, rather than in the Ute one that had already been decided without them. Kanosh territory was along the geographic border between Paiutes and Utes; their leaders had historically allied themselves with groups in each direction; they had sometimes used hide tipis, braided their long hair, and kept a few horses, although not as many as Utes. As many historical records referred to them as Utes as called them Paiutes. Tribal consultant Omer C. Stewart traced the ancestry of every individual in the BIA census records and proved sufficient genealogical connections to include Kanosh people in the Paiute litigation.[11]

The ICC held preliminary hearings in January 1951, when a number of elderly Paiutes testified; their early participation was most fortunate, as the case would not be settled for another fourteen years, by which time many had died. Major scholarly evidence was heard in December 1956, cross-examination took place in September 1961, and final arguments were heard in December 1963. The Chemehuevi case was presented in July 1955 and September 1961.[12]

The government tried to block the Paiute case on two preliminary points. First, it claimed that Southern Paiutes did not constitute a distinct Indian tribe in the legal sense and hence were not qualified to sue. It argued that groups across the Great Basin were culturally too similar to one another to be distinguished, but A. L. Kroeber used old data gathered in the 1930s, long before the ICC cases arose, and detailed statistical coefficients of similarity to disprove the identical assertion in the Northern Paiute case.[13] The government cited the linguistic similarity with Ute to argue that Southern Paiutes were just a branch of that larger tribe, but its own witness in the Ute case had specified significant cultural differences, certainly in historical times.[14] Anthropologists had always treated Southern Paiutes as a separate tribe, recognizing Chemehuevis as a distinguishable but clearly related subgroup. When it was pointed out that the government's own senior expert, Julian Steward, had done precisely this in his major monograph for the premier federal research institution, the Smithsonian, thirty years before, argument over Paiutes' distinctiveness folded.[15]

The second government argument pivoted on the question of what a tribe actually was, in contrast to other forms of organization. Government witness Julian Steward insisted that, theoretically, in order to be a tribe a group had to have a single, coherent political structure that possessed land. If only subgroups, such as bands or camp groups, held the land, then only they would be entitled to claim ownership; the aggregated Southern Paiutes were therefore an inappropriate entity to sue in this case. Tribal attorneys reminded the commission of Kroeber's discussion of landholding units across native North America that it had already accepted, as well as its own rulings from cases in New England and Puget Sound that recognized aggregate land possession by politically autonomous, but culturally united, native groups.[16] The ICC found that the Southern Paiutes were a tribe within the meaning of the claims legislation and allowed the case to proceed.[17]

Robert Manners's ethnohistorical testimony for the government minimized Paiutes' territory and questioned the exclusiveness of their use; his interpretation of historical sources was systematically and scathingly rebutted by tribal witness Omer Stewart.[18] The government position crumpled without reply, and it initiated settlement negotiations for both the Southern Paiute and Chemehuevi cases. Although the ICC never issued judgment on federal liability, Southern Paiute territorial extent, or the value of the land when lost, the government negotiated a seemingly arbitrary $8.25 million as compensation for loss of Southern Paiute land to the U.S. government and subsequent owners.[19]

Notified of events by mail, 220 of the enrolled 241 Southern Paiute adults came to a series of meetings with attorneys in October 1964. Although the bulk amount was dazzling, the per acre settlement was less impressive—about twenty-seven cents per acre. Paiutes were warned that if they rejected the negotiated compromise there would be further delay and no guarantee that pursuit of their case to a final judgment would win more. Within a few hours, Paiutes unanimously accepted the settlement by secret ballot.[20] At a similar meeting in November, only one of the 131 adult Chemehuevis voted against the settlement. Eventually, the monies were divided between Southern Paiutes ($7,253,165) and Chemehuevis ($996,835) after they had agreed to the stipulation that "entry of final judgment in said amount shall finally dispose of all rights, claims or demands which the petitioners have asserted or could have asserted with respect to the subject matter of these claims, and petitioners shall be barred thereby from asserting any such right, claim or demand against defendant in any future action. . . . all parties hereby waiving any and all rights to appeal from or otherwise seek review of such final determination."[21] Congress authorized the funds in October 1968 to be "advanced, expended, invested, or reinvested in any manner pursuant to a plan agreed upon between the governing body thereof or by the members thereof" who appeared on a specially prepared tribal roll.[22]

Ironically, the chairman of the ICC who signed the final papers in the Southern Paiute land cases in 1965 was Arthur V. Watkins, the very man who ten years previously had represented Utah in the U.S. Senate and chaired the Indian Affairs Subcommittee. From that position, he had single-handedly trumpeted the termination policy to which the Southern Paiutes of Utah had, while their land claim was being heard, fallen victim.

"Termination" in Indian affairs refers to a policy of ending all federal relations with Indian tribes based on tribal aboriginal occupation, treaties, and political linkages between sovereign tribes and the U.S. government. It would end, for instance, Indian-specific educational and health programs and the trust status of reservation lands. The termination policy denied that tribes as such had meaning, power, or significance and insisted that only individual persons of Indian heritage exist. Their rights within the United States were to be indistinguishable from those of other citizens; Indian people were to have no unique cultural, political, or historical rights defensible in law. Oddly enough, termination policy itself never became a law, approved by a majority of Congress; rather, it was expressed as congressional "intent" in Joint Resolution no. 108: "it is the policy of Congress, as rapidly as possible, to make the Indians within the territorial limits of the United States subject to the same laws and entitled to the same privileges and responsibilities as are applicable to other citizens of the United States, to end their status as wards of the United States, and to grant them all of the rights and prerogatives pertaining to American citizenship."[23]

This change in Indian policy arose from many sources. There was budget-cutting pressure in the prosperous 1950s to reduce any extraneous agencies from their wartime high number. Congress had been told for over eighty years that the purpose of the BIA was to acculturate Indians into the American mainstream; many thought that four generations was time enough. Joseph McCarthy reigned in the House Un-American Activities Committee; he suspected that John Collier's programs to operate reservation economies communally under tribal councils lurked on the thin edge of Communism. Further, as a congressional task force later admitted, termination policy was "triggered by pressures of private 'interests' seeking to acquire Indian lands, [and] was initiated with little concern for the well-being of the affected tribes."[24]

Termination policy's strongest proponent and sponsor, arch-conservative Republican senator Arthur V. Watkins of Utah, introduced Joint Resolution no. 108 and led the floor fight for its passage. As chair of the Joint Subcommittee on Indian Affairs and possessor of considerable seniority, he assumed the mantle of Congress's Indian "specialist." He declared that termination was "freedom" legislation and that prosperity would come automatically after Indians were "liberated" from the "yoke" of federal supervision in order to compete "equally" within the American economy.[25]

Of the 109 reservation groups terminated from federal administration between 1954 and 1958, only 2 were large, the Klamaths and the Menominees; the others were tiny, averaging only ninety persons each.[26] Clearly, Congress selectively targeted the small and politically weak, those having few economic and human resources to mount a successful defense. The first hearings held under the termination policy concerned the four Paiute reservations in Utah—Kanosh, Koosharem, Indian Peak, and Shivwits; they were the second group actually dropped from federal administration.

In 1947 Congress demanded that the BIA prepare a list of tribes ranked according to how soon they could be released from federal supervision. Estimates were based on "degree of acculturation," economic resources, tribal willingness, and, ironically in a plan purportedly to "stand Indians on their own feet," willingness of the states to take over supervision. Southern Paiutes did not appear in even the bottom-most BIA category of preparedness.[27]

In 1952 the BIA surveyed the services it was providing every tribe and their relations with county and state governments; it ordered every agent to construct a plan that would shift administration to tribal and local governments. Moapa and Las Vegas were the only Southern Paiute reservations rated as "ready" for self-management; they were never terminated. Shivwits, Kanosh, Koosharem, and Indian Peak were judged not ready; they were terminated within two years.[28]

As late as the end of August 1953, when the regional BIA superintendents met for "discussing and complying with House Concurrent Resolution 108," they made absolutely no mention of Paiutes.[29] In December the head of the BIA Land Division asked the interior solicitor to confirm trust dates of allotments of "groups involved in the withdrawal program"; he made no query about allotments at Kanosh or Koosharem.[30] The BIA list of documents forwarded to Congress in January 1954 made no mention of Paiutes, indicating it had planned no imminent legislation on their termination. Nevertheless, when Chairman Watkins released his schedule of hearings for the spring congressional session on 25 January 1954, the bill to terminate Utah Paiutes appeared first.[31]

Why Paiutes were among the first tribes to be terminated rests largely in an unfortunate conjunction of geography and congressional politics. When a congressman sponsors legislation involving cost, either financial or political, he customarily demonstrates to his colleagues the willingness of the electorate to tolerate the charges by getting his home state to accept them first. Utah's senior senator was the leading advocate of termination. In Utah the very large Uintah-Ouray Ute tribe had used funds from several successful land claims to hire a staff of lawyers; Watkins left the Northern

Utes alone. The only other Indians in the state were six tiny groups of Paiutes and Shoshones; these were proposed jointly for termination.

Paiutes were also made vulnerable by internal and fortuitous events. An Indian Peak man was involved in a local court case in 1949. His family, supporting him as was proper in Paiute kinship ethics and being virtually the group's entire tiny enrollment, voted to hire a defense attorney with one sixth of the trust account generated by years of reservation leases to non-Indian sheepmen. The Indian commissioner refused to approve release of the funds on grounds that tribal monies could not be used to benefit any particular individual. In desperation, the Indian Peak membership unanimously passed a resolution to sell the reservation, on which none of them had lived for some time, and to divide the money; the man's relatives then planned to pool their shares to meet attorney's fees.[32] Indian Peak's request gave Watkins the opening wedge he needed to claim that Paiutes, *in general*, "wanted" to be terminated from federal supervision.

Although Southern Paiutes were politically vulnerable to termination because of the customs of congressional politics and some of their own actions, BIA records showed that they clearly did not fit its concept of a tribe qualified for removal from federal supervision. The 1952 survey of reservations specified Kanosh as "most nearly ready of our Paiute Bands, they still are not ready for Bureau withdrawal." One in ten adults spoke no English, and two in ten could neither read nor write. Of the six families enrolled, only two were self-supporting, one through cattle kept on the reservation, the other through outside wage labor. Annual family income averaged $2,000, less than half the $4,200 earned by local non-Indians. Even if all reservation resources were fully developed and well managed, the agency estimated that only half the population could be supported at a level comparable to the regional non-Indian norm; the other half were "surplus" and would have to leave to make a living elsewhere. Income was so low, the agent anticipated that once the reservation was removed from federal trust status and became taxable private property, it would "probably be lost for non-payment of taxes."[33]

Likewise, fully fifteen of the twenty-four enrolled Shivwits families were judged "surplus," beyond what the land could possibly support. Ten percent of the adults could not read or write, none of the families were self-supporting (five depended totally on welfare, and the rest were partially dependent), and family income averaged only $1,200, less than a third that of local non-Indians. The tribal council had been inactive for several years, so there was no local community self-government, and the tribal court was discontinued. There were no income-producing enterprises, the farming cooperative had failed, loan repayments for cattle were in arrears, and the entire reservation was under lease. The agent predicted, "If the land is fee patented they will soon lose it."[34] The two smaller reserves had similar conditions.

Actual federal expenditures on the four Paiute reservations in Utah were minimal. The BIA provided no schools, health clinics, or law enforcement services. Irrigation development had nearly ceased. The major expense was the tuition subsidies paid under the Johnson-O'Malley Act that got Paiute children into public schools. Supervision of allotment lands at Kanosh and Koosharem was minimal; the other two reserves needed legal assistance only in arranging annual leases. On-site supervision was by the low-ranking BIA farmer from Kaibab who was required to visit the four outlying Utah Paiute reservations at least once a year. His supervisor, at Uintah-Ouray 450 miles away, budgeted a total of 126 man-hours a *year* to oversee each of the Utah Paiute reservations.[35]

In the two years between this survey and Paiute termination, the BIA instituted no new development programs to help Paiutes build the independence and self-sufficiency it claimed were its goals.[36] A number of meetings were held to extract Paiute consent to termination, giving the impression that Paiutes fairly uniformly wanted to be free of federal interference in their affairs but did not want to lose the governmental assistance programs on which they had come to depend. The BIA reported somewhat snidely that "they are not willing to accept full responsibilities of citizenship such as land taxation"; at the same time, its own documentation showed that Paiutes' income was so low that land taxes would be a crushing additional burden and would inevitably result in loss of the land.[37]

Not surprisingly, the BIA's report to the congressional hearing in February 1954 reflected conditions virtually identical to those in its internal survey two years before, the one in which agents concluded that Paiutes were unready for termination.[38] Nevertheless, in trying to persuade his colleagues to support his pet termination policy, Senator Watkins denied all the facts of history and of the federal government's own documented records and presented a summary of Paiute interethnic relations that can only be characterized as fantasy:

> *[Paiutes] have been obliged to enter the communities surrounding them. Fortunately these people recognized their problem and have successfully attacked it and have fully integrated themselves into the communities around them. They have had the kind assistance of the religious and civic organizations and though they are not rich, pros-*

perous people, having valuable resources upon which to fall back in the event of adversities, they are an ambitious, deserving people who should and will prosper once the yoke of Federal supervision is removed. . . . This then may very well be the first group of Indians to seek and obtain the full rights and privileges to which they have shown the competency and ability to enjoy and to which they are most certainly entitled. They should be complemented on their progressive approach in welcoming and seeking this freedom rather than lying back and objecting to the same as is being done by other equally advanced Indian people throughout the Nation.[39]

With a uniquely twisted form of logic, the congressional committee decided that because Paiutes were costing the government so little, that is, precisely because they were so neglected, that they were therefore already independent of federal services and ready for termination.

The subsequent bill required only "consultation" with Paiutes, which the commissioner of Indian affairs himself said "does not mean that Indian consent must necessarily be obtained before terminating a particular Federal trusteeship. As trustee, the Federal Government must make the final decision and assume the final responsibility."[40] Nevertheless, Senator Watkins held a meeting with Paiutes in April 1954 at Fillmore, just north of Kanosh. Not all Paiutes attended. For instance, the Shivwits Tribal Council, 140 miles to the south, noted, "[W]e have no money. We just can't go. This all."[41]

An Indian Peak man remembers himself as the only person who challenged the senator's presentation of the presumed positive benefits of termination. He also recalls his questions being rebuffed and his pleas of lingering poverty as justification for continued federal trust status being ignored by the senator.[42] Twenty years after the meeting a woman recalled that the senator told them "straight out" that they would be terminated whether they liked it or not. Although BIA records assert that it repeatedly assured Paiutes that there was no connection between termination and their still-pending land claim case, Paiute oral history equally consistently reports informal threats that the land claim would be lost unless they accepted termination.[43] Without money for gas to get to meetings, let alone to hire legal counsel, with long experience of the BIA overriding native leadership and using meetings to dictate its own decisions, some Paiutes recall that the authoritative senator's plan seemed inevitable, and, overwhelmed, they did not protest, "because we didn't know how." But Paiutes' opinions were mixed, because others remember their thoughts differently: "It is OK to be under the government, not to have to pay taxes and all, but they push you around. . . . it is good that the government cannot push you around and that you are on your own, even though the reservation must now pay taxes."[44] Most Paiutes listened to the presentation and went home to talk it over by themselves, never realizing that the senator would report their traditional-style noncommitment as definitive approval.

The BIA held local meetings on each reserve and at Cedar City, which some Paiutes later interpreted not as an attempt to make participation convenient but as "divide and conquer." Paiute oral history remembers that termination was presented as a fait accompli at these meetings, although it is somewhat vague on whether these meetings were held before or after the bill became law in September 1954. Meanwhile, in Washington the secretary of the interior assured Congress as early as February that three of the four Paiute groups had accepted termination and by July 1954 that all had.[45]

As the bill proceeded through Congress, it became obvious that Paiute public opinion was divided on the termination issue. Certain members of the Kanosh Tribal Council telegraphed the congressional committee expressing opposition, but they were later outvoted by the enrolled membership at a special meeting. Jimmy Timikin, authorized spokesman for Koosharem, telegraphed at the last minute to oppose the legislation: "we wish to have more time to learn from our people which we believe our people are Intitled to."[46] Without personal financial ability and unable to use tribal funds, no Paiutes appeared at the congressional hearing in Washington in February 1954. Claims attorney Wilkinson did attend but specifically disclaimed representing Paiutes in any way on termination, only wanting assurance that his pending ICC case would not be affected. An oil company that wanted to lease Kanosh lobbied for termination. The National Congress of American Indians wavered, approving termination in general as long as the Indians involved were fully informed. Only the Association of American Indian Affairs unambiguously opposed Paiute termination, as it did the general policy of unilaterally severing the historic political linkage between tribes and the federal government.[47]

Although the bill did not require Paiute consent, local, county, and state governments were required to accept the handover of Indian affairs. The Uintah-Ouray Agency solicited the county commissioners and mayors near the Paiute reservations and won their endorsements of the termination bill.[48] As early as April a BIA specialist began to design a "rehabilitation" plan for Koosharem people "by the Richfield community through its official committee, namely the L. D. S. [Mormon] Church Committee."[49] Utah was more than willing to put the 46,390 acres of Paiute land onto its tax rolls in exchange for social assistance obligations to approximately 175 people.[50]

Paiute termination became Public Law 83-762 on 1 September 1954. It ordered the "termination of Federal supervision over the trust and restricted property" of the Kanosh, Indian Peak, Shivwits, and Koosharem Paiutes, both as tribes and as individuals, and for "a termination of Federal services furnished such Indians because of their status as Indians."[51] Each group had to compile final enrollment membership lists within six months; people omitted had a sixty-day appeals period or would automatically lose legal status as Indian persons. Listed members then had to decide whether to transfer reservation land and other tribal property to a corporation licensed and operated under state law, hand over management to a private trust agent, sell it and divide the proceeds, or subdivide it among themselves. The secretary of the interior strongly disapproved of that option under American law that came closest to the model the BIA had used for tribal property, joint tenancy in common, saying this was "not a good one because the title complications that would arise would be endless. It would be a very unfair thing, and it might appear to be fair at the beginning but it certainly would result in endless confusion."[52] Paiutes had a maximum of two years to accomplish these real estate transactions.

Incongruously in legislation purported to free Paiutes so they could manage their own affairs, Congress retained for the government the potentially lucrative subsurface rights under the reservation properties for ten years, and the secretary of the interior and his subordinate bureaucrats alone held the power "to issue rules and regulations necessary to effectuate the purposes of this Act." The BIA arranged trust management of minors' shares, disposed of federal physical property, calculated capital gains taxes, and assured standing leases and rights-of-ways for non-Indians. In the long term, far more important to Paiutes was the transfer of reservation water rights to each group or its individual members.

The government graciously canceled its outstanding Paiute debts, long considered uncollectable anyway; these amounted to some $17,000 in recent tribal loans to Kanosh and Shivwits and about $40,000 in reimbursable irrigation development charges made over the last thirty years, often without the request or even approval of the Paiutes themselves. Only superficially redundant of the 1924 Indian Citizenship Act, the provision that assured Paiutes equal political rights with other U.S. citizens effectively stripped them of all rights of self-government won by their Wheeler-Howard Act constitutions.

The termination of these four small Paiute reservations in Utah ac-

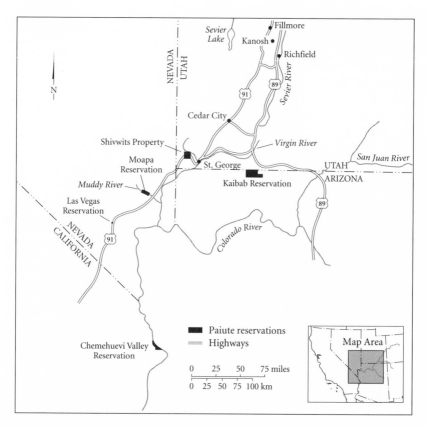

Map 4. Southern Paiute Territory, 1955

complished federal withdrawal and served federal policy and political concerns. It provided few safeguards for the Paiutes, however, and lacked most of the benefits that later became routine in more politically visible terminations, such as those for the Menominees of Wisconsin or Klamaths of Oregon. Paiutes, poor, few in number, and geographically separated from one another, were furthermore given very little time to arrange the complete reorganization of their political and economic lives. Over their heads hung the repeated warnings written into the law; if they did not accomplish the demanded actions by the scheduled deadlines, the BIA bureaucracy would proceed unilaterally without their consent.

The BIA promptly allocated a fifty-thousand-dollar budget to fund a three-person staff who would oversee termination, more money and personnel than it had invested in Paiutes in years. The field office that opened in Cedar City, home to a group not technically terminated, was the first BIA presence at that central location in over a generation. When the staff tried to delegate much of the work to Paiutes as a learning experience, they were naively surprised to find Paiutes "bitter and confused."[53]

The first assignment was preparation of a final membership roll. Committees of Paiutes checked the last BIA censuses, removed the deceased and added recent children, justified their decision-making criteria to federal officials, and held general meetings to gather information about off-reservation members. The BIA then double-checked to its own satisfaction before publishing preliminary lists on 15 April 1955 with a sixty-day deadline for appeals. The only such requests, nine from Shivwits, were ruled to be too late, so the final termination roll in the *Federal Register* in April 1956 replicated the earlier lists.[54]

BIA staff members at Cedar City were under the impression that they had two years after this final enrollment to complete the termination process, but Washington only then informed them that the deadline had been set by the date the law passed. Not until 29 May 1956 did tribal leaders learn that all plans for the dispersal of tribal property, appraisals, transfer of water rights, sale of land if necessary, and legal arrangements had to be completed by 15 August 1956, less than three months away, and that all BIA administrative assistance and funding would cease two weeks later.[55] Amid the subsequent flurry of activity, it is not surprising that Paiutes got the impression that they were "pushed out." BIA records show at least thirteen meetings with Kanosh Paiutes in that last year, eight with Koosharem, five with Indian Peak, and fifteen scheduled with Shivwits, although a quorum of the tribal council appeared only for five.[56] In addition, the subagency tried to contact each Paiute individually.

Relying on verbal promises from both Watkins and the BIA agent, Kanosh people initially wanted to farm their land as an agricultural cooperative after they were relieved of the financial burden of their outstanding federal loan.[57] They boldly asked for an additional six hundred acres of public domain, arguing that if this surrounding unfenced land were ever bought by non-Indians it would worsen interethnic relations; further, this would consolidate their land into a single block for water and other developments. Senator Watkins introduced the bill that transferred this six hundred acres to Kanosh so the group would be "in a more favorable position to carry out their responsibilities under the terminal legislation."[58]

Then several of the fractional heirs to nine of the original allotments whose titles were still clouded by BIA failure to probate the properties became intimidated by the technicalities involved in forming a state corporation and decided to sell their land on the open market rather than return it to the Kanosh cooperative. As pressures intensified, long-standing resentments within the Kanosh population shattered their egalitarian plans. The one man who owned cattle and had been using all the range land was publicly criticized. The three families who had used all the arable land to dry crop wheat were accused of unjust profiteering. Others demanded equal share of tribal resources. In May 1956 Kanosh ideals of cooperative use of the land fell apart.

Through what the BIA euphemistically described as "guidance and persuasion," Kanosh shifted to an alternate plan that divided the land into parcels of equal value. The twenty Kanosh shares of Corn Creek irrigation rights would go to the four active farmers, who represented major kinship blocks. Enrolled members retained "life estate" in their homes at the townsite and in the drinking water the BIA had piped in from Rogers Spring. Range and dry wheat land, including the new six hundred acres Congress had just added, was sectioned into forty-two pieces, one for each member of the group.[59]

The nine allotments whose ownership had fractured the original plan were advertised for sale by the BIA upon the owners' request on 10 July 1956. Two days later the area office realized that the pipeline carrying domestic water to all Kanosh homesteads crossed these properties, but the advertisements had not specifically reserved the right-of-way or the water right. With only a month to wrap up Paiute affairs and despite the history of rancorous disputes over water in the Kanosh area, the BIA proceeded on the dangerous assumption that any buyer would willingly concede these privileges to the Indians. Fortunately, the issue became moot, because only one bid was received during the week the land was on the market. Since this was not considered competitive bidding under federal regulations, the allotment land was "allowed to pass into unrestricted status on September 1st by operation of law," returning it to the public domain without the windfall profit owners had hoped for.[60]

Like Kanosh, the people of Koosharem thought that the land should go to those who were using it but that others should share the overall value. With their history of individual allotments, they initially suggested division into individual parcels. But there was water for only forty acres, so they proposed that the two active farmers get the arable land, along with the group's half share in Greenwich Creek. Other members could camp there, using the spring water the BIA had piped in within the last twenty years. The remaining individual allotment, along with the joint reservation land, was advertised for sale in July 1956. The biggest remaining problem was that the Mormon Church had held title to their stream rights for the last eighty years and would not release it to individual Indians but only to the U.S.

government, which would, of course, not accept trust obligations for Indians it was terminating.[61]

Indian Peak people reiterated their wish to sell but asked that a five-acre cemetery be reserved for them. The commissioner firmly declared that the BIA could retain no trust obligations and suggested instead that the sale contract specify "an easement which will give members of your band and their descendants the right to visit and care for graves, the right of interment, and the right of ingress or egress, to a described tract that is now th[e] cemetery site."[62] This was how it was handled when Utah, already owner of two school sections within the reserve boundaries, purchased the Indian Peak Reservation for a game preserve several years later.[63]

Fundamentally opposed to the whole termination process, Shivwits people resisted forming a single plan, and the BIA interpreted the resulting diversity of opinion as factionalism. People living and working off-reservation, including the tribal council chairman, accepted termination with resignation and supported liquidation of the reservation's assets and division of the proceeds. The predominantly elderly members who lived on the reserve reluctantly and conservatively proposed a joint corporation or trusteeship under the Mormon Church. The Paiute tendency to avoid public contention and insist on unanimous decisions produced meeting after meeting without a quorum. As late as mid-July 1956 Shivwits Paiutes still did not have a plan; continued avoidance would only, under the termination law, empower the BIA to make decisions for them unilaterally.[64]

Bypassing the log-jammed tribal council, Shivwits Paiutes held a general meeting of all enrolled members and made a last-minute decision to sell the land, keeping only the eight hundred acres of arable bottomlands and all the water rights; these would be placed under a commercial management contract. With only weeks remaining before BIA withdrawal, the 26,680 acres of upland were advertised. In the one week that bids were open, Shivwits got no offers that met the federal appraisal, so the complete acreage and water rights were retained and contracted for professional management.[65]

Finding such a manager, as well as someone to perform the legislatively mandated probates of allotment estates at Kanosh and Koosharem and to hold trusteeship of subsurface rights in all four areas, was a problem. The BIA found bankers reluctant to take on the job "unless funds are available to pay for their services. Since it appears that no minerals are now being produced and none are known to exist on any of the Indian lands, the tribes would hardly be able to defray these costs." The probates, too, went begging because of "the extremely low value of the estates."[66] Handling Paiute financial affairs simply did not pay.

Two months before the deadline for federal withdrawal, the commissioner's office in Washington itself persuaded the Walker Bank of Salt Lake City, which held management of the lucrative properties of the Palm Springs Indians in California, to take on the Utah Paiutes.[67] Bureau personnel set about rather desperately convincing all four Paiute groups to contract with this one company. Eventually, Walker Bank managed the property and minors' trust accounts for all four bands, oversaw subsurface mineral rights, arranged the sale of Indian Peak and sections of Koosharem and Shivwits, leased Shivwits land, and got Koosharem water and land rights transferred.[68]

Within two years Shivwits Paiutes petitioned the BIA to break their contract with Walker Bank. They complained it was too far away and treated them as it did its other customers, waiting for them to come or write to it instead of sending its representatives to the reservation, the kind of outreach Paiutes had been accustomed to from the BIA and the Mormon Church for years. When Paiutes did pool money for gas to Salt Lake City, they felt their representatives were offered incomprehensible words in sharp, brisk, too-short business meetings.[69] Further, the bank made decisions without Paiute approval; the BIA pointed out that this was precisely the management service they were paying the bank for, that trusteeship was not a partnership, and that the choice of the distant bank had been their own when tribal procrastination had left virtually no other alternative. After the bank contracted a lease of their former reservation that Paiutes felt did not protect it from overgrazing, some Shivwits members, no longer a tribal council or legally incorporated, negotiated another lease themselves; the bank sued them.[70]

At this point, if never before, Paiutes must have realized the fundamental lie that lurked within Senator Watkins's promise of freedom through termination. Control over Paiute affairs by government agents had been merely transmuted into control by profit-driven private enterprise; the Paiutes continued in a subordinate structural position that had not altered their powerlessness at all.

Not only did the BIA arrange for Paiutes' economic resources to be handled, but it also managed their human resources as well. Part of the termination programming was vocational training.[71] Without debate Congress accepted an amendment to the Paiute termination bill for "language training, orientation in non-Indian community customs and living standards, vocational training and related subjects."[72] Not a single senator questioned why such funding was necessary if Watkins were correct in asserting that Paiutes were "ready" for termination and the secretary of the interior correct that they "have in general attained sufficient skill and ability to manage their own affairs."[73]

Southern Paiute vocational education was contracted to the University of Utah Extension Division as part of a larger project for Northern Utes. The university's preliminary survey revealed that Paiutes' first need was English language skill, then familiarity with non-Indian culture and lifestyle, and finally vocational training. Nevertheless, none of the $150,000 included in the contract covered the first two needs but only eighteen-month to two-year programs in auto body repair, auto mechanics, welding, cosmetology, and clothing construction. The BIA subsidized tuition and housing.[74] It clearly hoped that this training would lead to "permanent relocation" of the declared "surplus" populations of the Paiute reserves. The BIA chief of relocation was thrilled when 65 percent of Paiute adults inquired into the program, less thrilled when only twelve actually went to the Salt Lake City campus and four of these immediately returned, and decidedly unimpressed when none finished their selected programs.[75] The university wanted to extend its contract, arguing that it simply took awhile to convince Paiutes of the value of schooling, but the BIA pointed out firmly that the deadline for federal funding of any Paiute affairs was passed and commented sweetly that the Indians were welcome to continue their education at their own expense should they so choose.[76]

Simultaneously, twenty-two Paiutes, including several who had tried the university program, enrolled in the BIA's own urban Relocation Program in Los Angeles, a nationwide effort to encourage Indians to move off reservations. In this program too, the BIA subsidized housing for people who attended semiskilled vocational training at various established institutions. Four Utah Paiutes completed their training in industrial sewing, auto mechanics, and candy making, and two subsequently found urban employment; virtually all the others returned to their home communities.[77]

Fifteen years later, none of the people who had enrolled in either the Los Angeles or the Salt Lake termination-related programs reported careers or even significant short-term employment in those fields in which they had been trained.[78] By funding education, Congress had saved its conscience, but the goal to integrate Paiutes with the non-Indian community through employment was a failure. What these programs may have done was to drain off precisely the most ambitious, active, and best-educated adults from the native communities at exactly the moment when Paiutes faced the challenge of restructuring their entire relationship with the federal government and with the surrounding non-Indian communities. Certainly, Paiutes were encouraged to pursue their individual interests just when the group, if it was to remain a group, critically needed coordinated decision making and long-term planning.

On 27 February 1957 the secretary of the interior proclaimed that "all federal restrictions on the property . . . and individual members" of the Shivwits, Indian Peak, Kanosh, and Koosharem groups of Paiute Indians in Utah had been "removed."[79] The headline of the BIA press release that day proclaimed that these Southern Paiutes had been "given full autonomy."[80] The Cedar City BIA office closed. The Utah Paiutes had been terminated.

They were also angry and frustrated. Shivwits people had fractious dealings with the Walker Bank. Kanosh people remembered being offered a waiver of wheat production quotas by Senator Watkins. In 1956, pressed for cash to meet land taxes, they tried to activate this promise, but the controlling county soil district denied responsibility for the senator's statements and refused to be bound by them. The Indians appealed to their traditional bureaucratic mediator, the BIA, which replied that now they were a terminated tribe; they would have to extract fulfillment of the senator's political promises on their own.[81] In 1958, when the county road crews knocked down a fence at Shivwits, the Paiutes did not know where to direct their complaint; the BIA had always mediated such matters before.[82] In these and hundreds of other daily encounters Paiutes found themselves suddenly naked before the labyrinth of state and local bureaucracies that had grown up while they had been shielded by the BIA's arrival in the early years of the century. They no longer had the simple option of forming personal dyadic relationships with individual BIA agents or neighboring non-Indian employers. Paiutes were enmeshed in a multilayered, impersonal world. They found that they had to cope with numerous non-Paiute institutions and do so from a position of relative powerlessness, borne of their inexperience, small numbers, and lack of political and economic influence.

The indisputably political origin of Utah Paiutes' termination becomes clear when their conditions are compared with those of Paiutes in Arizona and Nevada who were not terminated. Kaibab Paiutes were never even threatened with termination and yet in many respects were far better candidates. They had rangeland and relatively successful individual and tribal cattle herds. The BIA rated reservation resources as adequate to support the population and considered no families as "surplus," although it saw the need for further irrigation development, sanitation improvements, and soil conservation. If terminated, however, the agency suggested that Kaibab people would not successfully compete with non-Indians, not for lack of resources, water, capital, education, or political inexperience after generations of federal control of decision making but rather because of an undefined psychological lack of self-confidence. As it had said of Utah Paiutes, the BIA reported that "most" Kaibab people "wish to be released from wardship without assuming any of the responsibilities of citizenship" and evaluated Kaibab as "not ready" for termination.[83]

Moapa was both isolated from non-Indian state and county institutions and economically restricted. Only four hundred acres were cultivated, enough, the BIA thought, to support six families, although not even those six were making a living from reservation resources; the entire reserve was, like Shivwits, under lease to non-Indians. The BIA considered fifteen (71 percent) of Moapa's families "surplus," midway between Shivwits's and Koosharem's rating. Local off-reservation employment was limited to agricultural work at very low pay, so that average family annual income was only $1,600. Educational levels were well below local non-Indian averages, and distance from schools made access difficult. Relations with neighboring non-Indians were tense. All twenty-eight reservations in Nevada were administered out of Carson City, four hundred miles to the north, so Moapa's federal supervision was minimal. In sum, Moapa Paiutes differed very little from Utah groups on economic and social measures. They were, like them, adjudged "not ready" for termination, and yet no legislation was proposed to end their federal relationship.[84]

The Las Vegas community was quite another matter. Like so many of the tribes actually terminated, Las Vegas was tiny in size and population. None of the twenty-six families were supporting themselves on the ten-acre tribal land; they all worked for wages, garnering family incomes of about $2,400 per year. The city had grown around them, and huge casino hotels nearby pumped ever more water from the aquifers, sucking the water table below reach of the BIA well drilled in the 1930s. The original well on the Paiute property, with a single hand-pump spigot, was the only source for drinking and bathing water, and it went dry every summer. Paiutes lived in two trailers, in twenty-seven self-constructed houses, or in the open; all shelters were described as "extremely sub-standard," and "from a public health point of view none . . . [were] habitable."[85] Nine outhouses constituted the sanitation system; several lacked doors, and all drained into the ground. Health conditions were summarized as "loathsome."[86] In the midst of a city known worldwide for neon displays, there was no household electricity; in the midst of a desert with 115-degree summer heat, there was no air conditioning. Garbage, old car parts, and trash were thrown into the

11. Las Vegas Paiute community, 1955. The contrast with the non-Indian section of town, visible in right and left rear, is startling. (U.S. National Archives, Bureau of Indian Affairs Records.)

dry wash alongside the railroad tracks because the city garbage service would not collect on the reservation. Roadways were unpaved.[87]

When BIA agencies were charged to survey conditions and develop a termination plan for every reservation in 1952, the Nevada agent felt unable to make a proposal for the Las Vegas community, because it was so under-developed that equalizing the quality of life there to that of the surrounding non-Indians would be prohibitively difficult. The agency recommended acquiring right-of-way access to city streets for the land-locked property and then immediate sale.[88]

The Las Vegas community was gaining an unsavory reputation with both the BIA and the city. Just across the railroad tracks was an increasingly segregated African-American district, known as the West Side, with escalating racial tensions. "Strange Indians," not enrolled with local reservations, came to Las Vegas for work and gravitated to the Paiute community, where they found temporary shelter until they could find a job and housing; there were often as many of these multitribal, transient, "urban" Indians living there as there were Paiutes and Chemehuevis. The BIA, with no resident agent and law enforcement personnel no closer than Carson City, gratefully tolerated the extrajurisdictional intrusion of Las Vegas city police until Public Law 83-280 transferred law enforcement openly to the state of Nevada, and hence the city, in 1955.[89] Those police reported alcohol-related brawls, assaults, and spouse abuse averaging twice a week, a huge amount for so small a population; juvenile and solicitation arrests were constant.[90] Policemen's complaints drew the attention of social workers, who were appalled by conditions in this pocket of poverty only blocks from the major tourist attractions on which the city's entire income depended. The mayor called the Paiute area a threat to public health and investigated dispersing the Paiutes into low-income housing facilities around town.[91] The BIA then balked. The Las Vegas Reservation was federal property; although responsible now for law enforcement, the city could not legally provide social services, city water, and sewers and certainly could not cavalierly sell the property and move the Indians. That was a federal matter, the BIA proclaimed; then the federal government better do something about it, the mayor snapped back.

A bill similar to the Utah one was put before Congress in 1954 that suggested omnibus termination of eight small Nevada reservations, including Las Vegas. The BIA head of termination planning said, "Las Vegas Colony is a hobo jungle, and a menace to the whole community." He thought it "futile to pursue the fiction that the continuation of Bureau activities offers any prospect for Indian betterment."[92] The commissioner of Indian affairs accepted that "the encroaching industrial developments and the adjoining railroad and highway make unrealistic the development of the existing colony lands for residential purposes."[93] He supported sale of the property and relocation of the people to federal low-income housing. This bill was defeated, as was its reincarnation in the following Congress, because the Nevada state legislature refused to accept jurisdiction over the various reservation groups. The Las Vegas Paiute Reservation was not terminated from federal administration.[94]

It was long after Utah Paiutes were terminated and no longer recognized as Indian tribes that the ICC negotiated the 8.25-million-dollar settlement of the Southern Paiute suit against the federal government in 1968. Congress released funds from the U.S. Treasury in October and arranged disbursement.[95] For the terminated groups in Utah who had not been involved with the BIA in a dozen years, those funds were channeled through the Utah State Board of Indian Affairs.

For the first time since their termination amid rhetoric of freedom and promises of future prosperity, the BIA area office in Phoenix felt compelled to look at the Utah Paiutes' situation. Their survey discovered that Paiutes were still "in a poverty status. They are under-employed, they work as menial laborers and for low pay. . . . They lack job skills and job opportunities and are unable successfully to compete in the non-Indian community."[96] In fact, only one third of household heads had steady jobs, another third were intermittently employed, and the rest were unemployed. Nearly half worked at seasonal agricultural jobs at subminimum wage, so that average annual family income was about $2,000 for Koosharem people and $3,000 for Kanosh and Shivwits populations, far below the regional standard. The agency said their houses were "generally deplorable. Poor construction, lack of sanitation facilities, overcrowding, and absence of modern conveniences are typical."[97] This bland statement hid the reality of households averaging nearly five persons crowded into fewer than four rooms. Half the houses had no running water, and only a quarter had indoor bathrooms. Many used wood stoves both for cooking and winter heat. The survey revealed the utter failure of termination to deliver on the politicians' promises: "There is little participation in the activities of the non-Indian community and little active interest by that community in their participation."[98] Utah Paiutes remained an isolated community, segregated from the non-Indians among whom they lived and for whom they worked, but with whom they had no substantial human contact. In other words, after the withdrawal of the BIA, Paiutes' social interrelationships with non-Indians remained as they had been for generations; their economic situation was unchanged; and politically they were ignored by both federal and state officials.

In order to get their share of the federal land judgment fund, Paiutes had to organize administrative structures that the BIA would accept as responsible and legitimate. Each separate historic reservation group plus Cedar City formed such a planning committee. These all promptly voted for division of the money equally so that families could improve their houses, buy cars and school clothes, pay their debts, and otherwise meet immediate personal needs. State and federal bureaucrats refused to accept these plans; they urged reservation groups to set aside a portion of the money for land development and all groups to invest in businesses that would provide long-term jobs and corporate profits. Moapa responded by voting some of their share to pay off their federal loan, take their land out of lease to non-

Indians, and set up a tribal farm that would hire some of their many unemployed men.[99] Kaibab elected to distribute only 15 percent to individuals, hold back an equal amount for a tribal loan fund, and use the rest for land and human resources development.[100] Las Vegas and the Utah groups insisted on straight per capita distributions, for the BIA's less-than-subtle threats of retaliatory termination held little terror for them.[101] For recognized groups, shares due minors were administered by the BIA through U.S. Treasury trusts until the children came of age. Because the BIA could not handle minors' shares for terminated groups, they were placed in trust with banks and overseen by trust committees composed equally of Paiutes and local non-Indians.[102]

In 1971 most Paiute adults received $7,522 from the land claim suit against the federal government, an amount three times the total average annual income of a Paiute family. This payment was final federal compensation for tribal lands lost to non-Indian occupation since the 1840s. Despite BIA expectations and Paiutes' promises extracted before the funds were released that they would use these monies to erase personal debts, improve housing, and develop businesses, the temptations of wealth greater than they had ever before possessed deflated many people's best intentions. An independent anthropological survey of Utah Paiute communities three years later found few visible signs of this large influx of capital. Half a dozen families had new house trailers, the only form of housing affordable in this price range. Like the scatter of new cars, some of the trailers had been purchased on mortgages rather than outright, and when subsequent wage labor did not sustain the level of claims-induced temporary wealth, several were repossessed by banks. Only one family had started a business, but that effort was already struggling and soon failed. The land claims monies had quickly dissipated, moving through Paiute hands into those of non-Indian car dealers, businessmen, and banks, with little lasting impact. Settlement of the Paiutes' land suit made no structural change in their socioeconomic position in the region.[103]

Despite the promises mouthed by the BIA and politicians in the 1950s, termination did not produce freedom and prosperity for Utah Paiutes. The distant, occasional interference of BIA agents and the intermittent subsidy of irrigation, soil conservation, and land development programs were gone. But then, so too was the land. Indian Peak had been sold outright, and most of Koosharem and Kanosh went for delinquent taxes; only the Shivwits Paiutes retained land, albeit through the impersonal management of a corporation. Utah Paiutes were no longer recognized as Indian "tribes," as far as the U.S. government was concerned. Nevertheless, they remained a distinctive people, isolated in geographically bounded communities, marked as well by their poverty, distinctive economic niche, and unique historical past. They continued to cling together as a social entity, encapsulated by the active rejection, or at minimum the uninterested neglect, of the surrounding non-Indian population, state agencies, and the federal government.

11

NEGLECT AND REINSTATEMENT, 1955–1995

During the two generations since the termination of the Utah groups from federal administration, but certainly not because of that termination, Paiutes' lives and communities in Utah, Arizona, Nevada, and California have changed greatly. The Utah groups regained federal recognition as an Indian tribe and created a new governing structure. All of the groups have struggled to overcome poverty, isolation, and political invisibility, to become economically more prosperous and socially viable. They have sought participation in the economic boom that swept Utah on a wave of tourists and Nevada on a tsunami of population growth. Sometimes with the aid of the BIA and sometimes without, they are trying to make their futures more promising than their pasts.

After the BIA turned its back on Utah Paiutes, it did only one brief follow-up study in 1968.[1] That survey, along with a local college survey in 1970 and my systematic community survey of five years later, all documented conditions essentially identical to those reported in the congressional termination hearing a generation before.[2] Nevertheless, the state and local governments, which had assured Congress at termination that they accepted responsibility for Paiute welfare, saw no reason to give Paiutes more attention, services, or concern than they did the rest of the population.

After termination and the distribution of land claims money, Utah Paiutes remained poor. Although they had relatives living from Los Angeles to Salt Lake City, most lived in a handful of medium-sized rural towns across the southwestern quarter of the state. There they were distinctly segregated, forming pockets of poverty on lands generally leased or owned by the Mormon Church.[3] Paiutes' income averaged one third lower than that of non-Indians working in the same regional economy.[4] Paiutes' unemployment rate was ten times the local average, and most of the jobs they obtained were still menial labor, often seasonal and unreliable agricultural harvest work. Competition with non-Indian workers was difficult when their average education was only six and a half years in an area where the general labor force had graduated high school, so young people could gain scant marketable job experience.[5] A quarter of Paiute families relied totally on state welfare for subsistence, six times the general rate in the area. Paiute houses were crowded, with 64 percent more people than the average non-Indian house, because Paiutes so often sheltered grandparents, unmarried daughters with children, cousins, and distant relatives. All these people crowded into smaller than usual spaces, often only a single room or house trailer. Many still lacked domestic water or sewers, although most had recently gotten electricity. Refrigerators were still a novelty for many Paiute housewives.

In the face of these economic constraints, Utah Paiutes demanded that group membership be validated not by blood quotient, possession of heirloom artifacts or traditional skills, or even use of the language, which by then only the elderly employed for conversation; instead, membership was acquired through daily participation in community life. That participation required investment in and constant reinforcement of what they defined as distinctively "Indian" social relations. Strong ethical values required relatives, whether they lived in the same town or in one of the other Paiute residence clusters, to "help each other out." This both maintained the native social network and also required an inordinate proportion of households' small incomes for auto repair, gasoline, and telephone bills in addition to loans, reciprocal labor, and outright gift giving. Nevertheless, this culturally demanded cooperation ameliorated Paiutes' collective poverty.[6]

In contrast to this richly involuted web of assistance and obligation that linked the Paiute community, contacts with non-Indian neighbors and institutions were minimal; virtually no personal friendships crossed the interethnic boundary. The Mormon chapel, built as a mission station in Cedar City in 1956, was the only non-Indian institution active within any of the Utah Paiute communities. Paiutes told of exploitation and discrimination, based on remembrance of historical as well as perceived personal experiences. Paiute communities were social and economic enclaves surrounded by quite separate non-Indians.

Politically, however, Paiutes were not isolated. The Utah Paiute termination legislation passed civil and criminal jurisdiction to the state and counties.[7] Public Law 83-280, another effort to reduce federal involvement in Indian affairs in the mid-1950s, shifted reservations in Nevada, including both Moapa and Las Vegas, to that state's jurisdiction.[8] The BIA claimed insufficient funding for a resident police officer at the Kaibab Reservation, so in 1955 the Fredonia, Arizona, police agreed to be cross-deputized as federal special deputies and stand on call, but they would not make regular patrols.[9]

The rapidly growing gambling center of Las Vegas was increasingly embarrassed by the visible Paiute poverty only a few blocks up Main Street from the crowds of tourists in "Glitter Gulch." The Chamber of Commerce photographed the cabins constructed of scrap and documented the lack of sewers, unmaintained outhouses, "loathsome" health conditions, and absence of electricity for food refrigeration in the blazing summertime heat or for light at night. City police complained of vandalism by Indian youths and solicitation of Paiute women by servicemen from the nearby air force base. Even before obtaining legal jurisdiction, city police frequently entered the ten-acre reservation to quell drunken disturbances.[10] Hoping to disperse the distinctive residential Paiute community, the city proposed opening its low-income housing projects to Indians. Failing to win Paiute cooperation, it then complained to the U.S. attorney general that the "Indian Village" was a public nuisance; Department of Justice research found "no known supervision of the colony by the Indian Service."[11]

Even those reservations under nominal BIA management suffered neglect and economic stagnation during the postwar years. Arguing wartime gasoline shortages, in 1944 the Carson Stewart Indian School near Reno asked that Moapa be transferred from its jurisdiction to the Truxton Canyon Agency, closer but across the unbridged Colorado River. Five years later Moapa was transferred back to the Carson Agency.[12] Unable to decide who should do what for Moapa Paiutes, the BIA did little beyond a few minor irrigation improvements. Kaibab, the other major land-based reserve, also "merely existed."[13] There the tribal council acquired its first physical home in 1970 through a federal program that accepted Paiutes' construction labor as their portion of a cost-sharing grant. On the other hand, ten thousand acres of reservation land was once again leased to non-Indian cattlemen, and schoolchildren were bused to Fredonia after third grade. The only method Kaibab people had to support themselves was short-term wage labor for non-Indians. Similarly, San Juan Paiutes from south of Navajo Mountain trekked to central Utah for seasonal harvest jobs.[14]

Increasingly, Paiutes were openly dissatisfied with the conditions of their lives but did not necessarily see return to a 1920s-style federal relationship as the only possible solution. While terminated Utah Paiutes generally wanted and expected "help," at this time there was little, if any, public discussion of return to BIA supervision as the answer to their socioeconomic woes.[15] They did, however, seek other allies. First and foremost was the local Mormon Church leadership, so long dominant in the Paiutes' interrelationship with non-Indian society. They also turned to the state of Utah, to which termination legislation had delegated their welfare a generation before. Further, in the late 1960s the federal "War on Poverty" crossed boundaries of race and ethnicity, so national agencies outside the BIA, unlimited by federal Indian laws, became involved in the affairs of Utah Paiutes.

In 1970 people from the state junior college in Cedar City initiated a Volunteers in Service to America (VISTA) project to survey Paiute needs. They were surprised by the resistance from local church leaders. The VISTA volunteers were informed in no uncertain terms that Paiutes resided on church-owned land and that no programs not directly sponsored by the church could use its facilities or enter its land. The Mormon chapel contained the only large rooms in the community. Access was controlled by the church-assigned, non-Indian mission head, who also happened to be president of the local John Birch Society. He declared VISTA to be a Communist organization and asserted that "nothing could be done on church property unless through the church."[16] VISTA was denied permission to build a playground for Paiute children. The church withdrew its financial support for Paiutes to rent the college gym for their annual basketball tournament. A VISTA program coordinator reported, "[T]he landowner has blocked several of the attempts of the Indians to qualify for federal programs on what, seem to me to be purely ideological and not rational or religious reasons."[17] The Cedar City Mormon Church was clearly angered when its long-exclusive missionary program met competition from "outside agitators" for influence over Southern Paiutes.

Unable to gain meeting space within the Paiute community, VISTA set up its programs in a nearby state-run elementary school. Paiute mothers quickly activated their interfamilial networks of exchange to car-pool their children to the prekindergarten Head Start classes, which turned out to be VISTA's most popular project. Men responded to the voter registration drive and, perhaps most importantly, to numerous informal conversations about accomplishing goals for themselves. When the enthusiastic young strangers left Cedar City after three summers, they left few visible remains.[18] But for the first time in a full generation following abandonment by the BIA, twenty years during which Paiutes dealt with non-Indians only through the single church structure, someone had appeared who asked Paiutes what they thought they needed and told them that they could change their own lives. This was an exciting message that Paiutes young and old considered very seriously.

Almost incidentally, one of the VISTA interns had written to the Native American Rights Fund (NARF), a group of Indian civil rights attorneys in Boulder, Colorado. In late 1971 NARF's response team investigated ways to improve Paiutes' housing and the unpaved roadway. While NARF believed "there may be a basis for a law suit in Cedar City in that the Indian village is being denied equal city services," it lacked a client, "enthusiastic plaintiffs who would be able to withstand political and religious pressures" to pursue the case.[19] VISTA reluctantly agreed that "the majority of the Indian People feared that such action may . . . cause 'hard' feelings. . . . The Cedar Band People are very much intimidated by the white community and are extremely concerned about their relationship to the L.D.S. Church."[20] It was a year before Yetta Jake courageously asked NARF to draft a complaint to the U.S. attorney general. Despite unequal "protection of the laws" and of "public facilities," the letter cautioned, "we strongly believe that the institution of such litigation would jeopardize the safety and economic standing of us, our families, and our property" and requested federal intervention.[21] NARF continued to monitor Utah Paiute events and acted on the Indians' behalf at several key junctures in the restoration of federal tribal recognition.

Without a client complaint and an active lawsuit, NARF could not act, so the Utah Division of Indian Affairs (UDIA) stepped in to assist Paiutes in general community development. That office successfully persuaded the Mormon Church to sell fourteen acres of the Cedar City property, but the church would do so only directly to the individual Indians and asked a price of $62,000 that was clearly beyond the Paiutes' means.[22] Bruce Parry, head of the UDIA, issued press releases to raise sympathy for the Paiutes, but his tone became increasingly manipulative: "Currently, *we* are organizing the five Southern Paiute Bands into a tribal organization. . . . *Our intention* is to have the land declared a State Indian Reservation, which in turn will make the tribal organization eligible for certain programs administered by the federal government."[23] NARF began to suspect the UDIA of bureaucratic empire building and cautiously suggested, "If the Indians and the State of Utah have different ideas as to what this land will be used for, assuming it is acquired, the State may not be working in the best interests of the Indians."[24]

In August 1970 the college-based advocates who had brought in the VISTA program organized the Cedar City Indian Development Council (CCIDC). This nonprofit corporation of local non-Indian businessmen and churchmen used small-scale fund-raisers such as dinners and sale of "Indian" piñon nuts and venison jerky for projects to improve the physical condition of the Paiute residential area. Their funds were insufficient to mount any substantial projects.[25] Members of CCIDC were aware of the historically different reservation groups that composed the Cedar City native community and self-consciously structured the Indian participation to represent the five "bands" (Kanosh, Koosharem, Indian Peak, Shivwits, and Cedar itself). This soon embroiled the CCIDC in what non-Indian members interpreted as Paiute "factionalism" and "lack of unity," the efforts by politically active Paiutes from different residential areas, kinship groups, and political persuasions, expressing their autonomous opinions.[26] In short, while giving a nominal nod to variations internal and fundamental to Paiute community structure, non-Indians found it preferable to deal with an amorphous, homogeneous group, just as in pioneer days they had linguistically amalgamated all under the generic term "Indians" and had tried to generate a single hierarchical "chiefly" leadership. Although the CCIDC deteriorated within two years, and several Paiutes were demoralized by what they saw as yet another failure of non-Indian promises, CCIDC did foster incipient community activism among Utah Paiutes.

A second incorporation actually by native people was to have greater impact. In 1972 the governor of Utah was looking for a representative for the south on his advisory board for Indian affairs. He contacted Scott Urie, head of the Mormon Indian mission in Cedar City, and Judge Reed Blomquist, long interested in Richfield Paiute issues of legal termination and land claims. They recommended McKay Pikyavit, the Kanosh man who had actively led his group's quest for inclusion in the Northern Ute land claim and subsequently the Southern Paiute one. From a family that had campaigned in the 1930s for access to public schooling and had made extraordinary efforts to see that all their children were educated, Pikyavit had completed several college-level business courses and aspired to manage his own company. In the state board he found political alliance with forces independent of the Mormon Church, which had long dominated the state of Utah and Indian interethnic relations there. Supported by Parry and the federal Economic Development Administration (EDA), Pikyavit quietly incorporated the non-profit Paiute Tribal Corporation (PTC) under state law in July 1972.

The PTC charter stated that its organizational purposes were to "receive, manage, invest, and expend for the benefit of the members of the Paiute nation in Utah . . . such monies and properties as may be received or acquired by the Corporation" and to "represent said bands for purposes of qualification for benefits under any acts of Congress or statutes of the State of Utah which recognize special status for Indian communities and Indian tribes."[27] It was to be, therefore, both a recipient for grants and also a pseudotribal government. Five trustees would represent the historical residence or reservation areas of Kanosh, Cedar City, Indian Peak, Shivwits, and Koosharem. Each of the initial members was middle-aged or elderly, came from a large kinship cluster, and for the most part had been educated at a BIA boarding school. Pikyavit, however, was the sole incorporator and signatory. He said he had proceeded without the broad knowledge or participation of other Paiutes in order to avoid false hopes should his efforts fail; other Paiutes later suspiciously criticized this independent action as attempted self-aggrandizement and clandestine self-benefit.

By autumn the PTC had applied for an EDA grant of over half a million dollars to construct four buildings, one at each of the Paiute residence areas (except the unoccupied Indian Peak). These would be sites for native businesses such as Pikyavit's own or would produce rental income. The centrally located Cedar City building would house corporate offices. Parry, Urie, and Blomquist lobbied Utah congressmen and EDA officials, and the full amount was awarded in November 1972. This substantial amount of capital, with its promise of an income-producing resource, instantly put Utah Paiutes into a completely new financial league. All earlier efforts to improve Paiutes' welfare had been completely under the control of non-Indians and non-Indian institutions, whether the church, the BIA, or even VISTA and the CCIDC; all these efforts were designed to mitigate the superficial symptoms of poverty, but never before had plans attempted to alter the underlying cause of that poverty, the Paiutes' historically produced lack of economic resources.[28]

Initially, the PTC used the one room in the Cedar City Indian community that was large enough, the Mormon chapel, where they opened and closed meetings with prayers and hymns and remained under the pervasive missionary influence. Feeling no confidence in their ability to cope with the technical convolutions of construction and large-scale money management, the Indian trustees voted to form an advisory committee of non-Indian businessmen. Although local Mormon missionaries, such as Urie and Blomquist, predominated, Parry and a representative of the University of Utah Extension Division also sat on the advisory committee. The Indian board immediately delegated the task to write by-laws to these advisors. In the resulting structure, each of the five Paiute "bands" or settlement areas was represented by a "band chairman" after the model of the old BIA tribal council structures; Pikyavit was overall corporation chairman. Each band representative had a four-person, non-Indian advisory committee. Without defining or advertising the position, the board promptly hired another missionary as business manager and corporate planner, despite his lack of credentials or business experience. The degree of continuing church influence was very clear.[29]

Even though plans for a Shivwits building were dropped, the higher-than-anticipated bids by the EDA-selected contractor forced plans to be further cut back. Pikyavit advocated elimination of the office section in the Cedar City building, designed for tribal headquarters. The federal government would not release funds for construction there as long as title to the land it would rest on was not controlled by the PTC; missionary members of the advisory board persuaded the Mormon Church to release five acres of its Cedar City property to the corporation, enough for the building and a parking lot. The Kanosh building was scaled down to a purchase and renovation, rather than new construction. Blomquist got Richfield to donate a parcel of land in town near the Paiute residential area, but Pikyavit, who had moved his family over from Kanosh, later managed to trade this parcel for land out near the county airport, arguing that it had better industrial, if not commercial, potential.[30]

As construction began in 1973, few Paiutes qualified for the highly paid technical jobs. The federal Manpower training program subsidized apprenticeships for two young men at Cedar City, and a few got part-time laborers' jobs. Less than a third of the Cedar City salaries went to Paiutes, and in Richfield, they won about half the work. Many Paiutes once again felt cheated at what they had taken as non-Indian promises of instant and immediate prosperity through the "development" of the corporation.[31]

By late 1974, the PTC was having difficulty finding occupants for its completed buildings. Pikyavit moved his company into the Richfield structure, which he had targeted for himself from the beginning. The centerpiece building in Cedar City stood empty for so long that the planner leased it himself for the cost of insurance payments to try to start a beadwork cooperative, much as missionary William Palmer had in the 1930s. This failed because the few active beaders could not provide a sufficient variety of goods for sale, there were no funds to advertise to tourists beyond the easily saturated local market, and Paiutes distrusted plans made externally. The corporation considered leases to a mushroom-growing company, lumber yard, and skating rink, but the Cedar City building was only permanently occupied years later by the reinstated tribal government.[32]

Pikyavit's company, ensconced in Richfield, never achieved financial success, and within two years his non-Indian partner disappeared into a cloud of rumors about missing money; Pikyavit lost political credibility and the chairmanship.[33] Paiutes, long accustomed to living personally on financial shoestrings, were always suspicious of those with access to communal money, especially if they saw any evidence of more-than-average wealth. With the larger blocks of funds from land claims cases and now federal grants, this distrust escalated, fueled by a smattering of incidents that seemed to confirm those suspicions. It was very hard to find people willing to serve for very long on the committees that oversaw minors' land claim funds because of the constant bitter rumors of mismanagement. Paiute popular opinion was confirmed in 1979 when the wife of the long-term Las Vegas chairman was convicted in federal court of embezzling funds from the lucrative tribal cigarette sales.[34] The chronic Paiute distrust of anyone trying to lead development efforts made many people reluctant to step forward and often reduced the courageous few to anger and bitterness when their personal characters were attacked, even in the absence of any wrongdoing.

In addition to pursuit of its commercial enterprises, the PTC addressed the pressing housing shortage in the native residential areas. In August 1973 a major Salt Lake newspaper feature on Paiute poverty in Cedar City embarrassed the town into offering half of its federal block grant for new Indian houses. To meet federal requirements, Cedar City Paiutes formed a housing authority; it had the same officers as the PTC and held joint, if logically separate, meetings.[35]

The ownership of the land on which the houses would sit remained a question. In a complete reversal from the BIA's early refusal to invest on lands the government did not own, the government now refused authorization unless the beneficiaries of the project either individually or communally owned the land. In 1971, while the Mormon Church stonewalled the VISTA program, the UDIA asked for a formal lease to the Indians of its Cedar City property. The church officials "refused to do this because they felt their verbal understanding with the Indian People was sufficient."[36] They preferred the control inherent in allowing Paiutes to live there only at church sufferance, in constant fear of incurring church displeasure.

Only when it became clear that federal funding would be lost did the church finally agree to long-term lease of specific lots. Government requirements satisfied, the block grant repaired several existing Paiute residences and built two prefab houses. The Paiute housing authority rented them on a sliding scale adjusted to income. Since federal guidelines required water mains and sewer lines, which were still lacking in the community, the town cooperatively extended these onto church property in return for a portion of the house rental fees in lieu of taxes.[37]

The Paiute Housing Authority then applied to the Department of Housing and Urban Development (HUD) for twenty-five additional houses to be spread among all the Utah Paiute residential clusters. Since the Paiutes only actually owned the former Shivwits Reservation, and it was under agricultural lease, most of the houses had to be put on nontribal properties. Small blocks of federally owned lands under the Bureau of Land Management (BLM) were found in various nearby towns. As families moved into these new houses, the Paiute community became more dispersed than it had been for several generations, reversing the fifty-year trend toward centralized, exclusive, segregated clusters.[38] In contrast, when Moapa and Kaibab Reservations won similar grants, they could build on their own lands. Enrolled members who had been squeezed out by the housing shortage came home to live; within a decade Moapa tripled its resident population, and Kaibab swelled, exacerbating already serious employment problems.[39]

While Utah Paiutes were finding new political allies in the UDIA, forging new organizational ties among native residential groups, and restructuring relationships with the church and local towns, events were occurring on the national level that would dramatically affect their future. On 22 December 1973 the Menominee tribe, whose disastrous termination in the mid-1950s had been well publicized, was restored to federally recognized status.[40] The legal precedent thus established could then be followed by other terminated groups, including the Southern Paiutes of Utah. It is unclear how much of their subsequently successful restoration movement was generated by grass-roots Paiute sentiment and leadership; several external agencies that had recently become active in Paiutes' affairs figured prominently in the effort, specifically, the UDIA and NARF.

While the Menominee bill was still working its way through Congress, Parry announced to the PTC board that he already had sought out and won the support of Utah congressmen for reinstatement of the Paiutes; it was only then that he asked the corporation board, as though it were a tribal council or political body, for a resolution of tribal intent authorizing him to proceed on their behalf. He circulated petitions for individual Paiutes to express their support of the proposition, and most did sign. Parry opened contacts with the BIA Phoenix area office. About a year later one member of the PTC board, acting as an individual, asked Salt Lake City Indian attorney Larry Echohawk, kinsman to a director of NARF, for advice on how the Paiutes could regain federal Indian status. Echohawk began to lobby the Utah congressional delegation.[41]

In early 1975 the UDIA held a series of public meetings near Paiute residential clusters to discuss plans for legal reinstatement as an Indian tribe; non-Indian town governments and the CCIDC were actively interested, and the BIA was represented by the man who later headed the restored Utah Paiute Agency. Parry emphasized the benefits of BIA programs to recognized tribes, especially in the areas of social services and employment. Although some elders remembered actually receiving very few such benefits before termination and drew attention to the grim state of current Paiute reservations in Arizona and Nevada, the Utah Paiutes were swept up by the hope that these new promises would be fulfilled and voted overwhelmingly to try to regain federal tribal status.[42]

The BIA area office in Phoenix reasoned that if the four former Paiute reservation groups, which it now called "bands," were readmitted separately, they would each be too weak to be effective in bureaucratic competition for program funding. It used the precedent of the PTC, itself a creation of non-Indian organizational efforts, to argue that the Utah Paiutes should be readmitted as a single unit. Bands would retain autonomy regarding their own resources and internal issues, but external relations and tribally owned resources would be jointly managed. The BIA-drafted restoration legislation dictated that tribal councils would be elected by majority vote of those members over eighteen years of age. Further, the BIA proceeded to usurp the power of self-definition of membership that had been delegated to tribal governments by the Wheeler-Howard Act of 1934; it asserted that membership would require 25 percent Paiute "blood."[43]

The BIA Phoenix office lost its legal assistant, Mary Sloan, who had been spearheading the Paiute case, to Echohawk. His firm, together with NARF, drafted the final legislation. Paiutes formed a restoration committee to coordinate data, communications, and lobbying efforts. Republican congressman Dan Marriott, closely tied to the Mormon Church, became their strongest supporter. In his speech that introduced the restoration bill to the House of Representatives, he declared termination a moral wrong done to socioeconomically unprepared Paiutes. Arch-conservative Republican senator Orrin Hatch could only be persuaded to lukewarm support after his own series of regional town meetings revealed opposition from non-Indian constituents over possible restoration of reservation lands; he only agreed to sponsor the bill in the Senate if Paiutes, unlike other tribes being rerecognized, were provided with no land.[44]

At tightly orchestrated congressional hearings, tribal attorneys argued that Paiutes had been unjustly terminated in 1954 because they had never qualified under the BIA's own criteria. The UDIA pleaded that Paiutes had to regain tribal status in order to qualify for much-needed Indian-specific federal programs. Older tribal representatives said that they had not understood what termination meant at the time, had resisted it, had naively believed Senator Watkins's promises, and had suffered years of poverty produced by that termination. Younger Paiute leaders anticipated that restoration of federal tribal recognition would produce a resurgence of lost native language, culture, pride, identity, and unspecified prosperity.[45]

A state legislator spoke against any grant of federal BLM or Forest Service lands because they were of such "great value to the public," specifically, to his southern Utah rancher constituents. He proposed to "give the people an education and let them go out and move in the private sector," perhaps inadvertently repeating the federal proposal on termination twenty-five years earlier.[46] Senator Hatch tried to present himself as the beneficent patron of Paiutes so they could regain "the great Indian heritage," while avoiding alienation of his conservative allies by suggesting any federal benefit to a small minority group. Hatch actually said that a grant of "enormous land claims in Utah" to Paiutes would foment a racist backlash and civil violence. He presented his own legal brief into the record; rather than seeing such lands as compensation for those that had to be sold off upon termination, Hatch argued that in the acceptance of their 1970 land claim settlement, Paiutes had waived all rights to any tribal land.[47]

Congressmen easily accepted many of the provisions in the draft legislation. Leery of Indian activists' alertness to treaty rights issues, they specifically denied that any treaty provisions would be restored, which was irrelevant, since Utah Paiutes had never had a treaty approved. Responsive to southern Utah constituents, Congress denied restoration of any native hunting and fishing rights but neglected to block claims to wild plant collecting. Utah retained the civil and criminal jurisdiction it had assumed since termination under Public Law 83-280. The only real stumbling blocks were the legal identity of the Cedar City Paiutes and land.

Because the Cedar City group had never been recognized by the federal government, they could not be, and had not been, specified in the termination legislation. The BIA admitted it had "always" known about the Cedar City population (hard to ignore, since agency headquarters had been located there for a generation). Indeed, it even virtuously, if somewhat disingenuously, asserted that *if* any Cedar Paiutes had applied for BIA services over the years since termination, these *should* have been granted.[48] Not terminated, Cedar Paiutes technically could not be restored with the other groups by Congress but would have to be recognized for the first time, which involved a different administrative procedure. Were the Cedar group removed from the restoration legislation, it risked rejection by that BIA acknowledgment procedure and would lose its position in the new collective tribal entity. Tacitly, the BIA and Congress overlooked this technicality by changing the name of the legislation from "restoration" to "federal recognition" of a Paiute trust relationship, so that the four former reservation enti- ties plus the Cedar City group could be treated together. Further, it was agreed to assume that all five groups met the BIA's criteria for restoration (existence as an identifiable community, continued self-regulation, contin- ued residence in a traditional area, use of native language, possession of a tribal culture, deteriorating socioeconomic conditions as a result of termi- nation) without the normal investigation. The PTC's record of "performing governmental functions" was accepted as proof that Utah Paiutes retained a self-governing political organization.[49]

The second issue, land, proved to be far more difficult. Paiutes, the UDIA, NARF, and tribal attorneys had all argued that the solution to Paiutes' well-documented poverty was to place productive resources in the hands of the tribe, specifically, quality land. They faced a Congress, however, that was politically reluctant to increase the Indian land base and had recent precedents in the Siletz tribal recognition without any lands at all and the huge Alaska claims settlement without any federal trust provisions. Hatch persuaded Marriott to introduce a bill that lacked any promise of land. A federally recognized, albeit landless, Paiute tribe simply needed access to the BIA's economic, health, and educational programs, Hatch assured his colleagues: "I have great confidence that if we respect their cultural heritage and their desire to improve by helping them . . . , that before long, we will witness this tribe contributing to the strength of America."[50] Democratic president Carter was less sanguine. He thought that giving tribal recogni- tion without any pragmatic means to alter the dismal socioeconomic con- ditions could only produce a tribe chronically dependent on federal aid. He threatened to veto unless lands were included.[51] The bill was amended to allow for selection of up to fifteen thousand acres of "available federal lands," replacing those lost at termination.[52] This property, along with any accompanying water and mineral rights, would be taken into federal trust and carry legal status as a reservation. So too would previously owned par- cels, including the former Shivwits Reservation and Mormon Church land deeded to the PTC in Cedar City. The tribe, working with the BIA and coor- dinated by the secretary of the interior, would identify these additional lands, subject to congressional veto.

Congress assumed that the estimated agency operating expenses of half a million dollars a year for a recognized Utah Paiute tribe would come out of the general BIA budget. The House (with only twelve nays) and the Senate (by voice vote) approved the bill.[53] President Carter signed the law, which recognized the five groups of Utah Paiutes as once again an Indian tribe, on 3 April 1980.[54] As a result of processes completely external to the

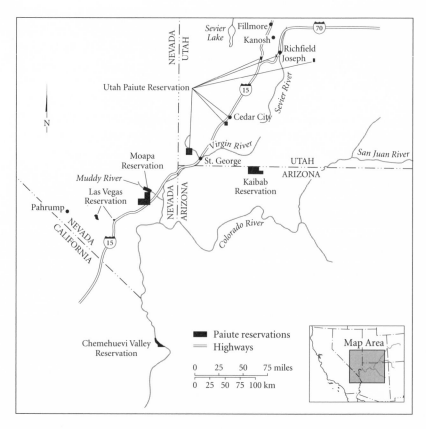

Map 5. Southern Paiute Territory, 1995

Paiute community but to which it was subject, this law created an amal-gamated tribal unit out of five entities that Paiutes had verbally and to some extent socially distinguished. The law excised a sector from the continuous web of Paiute kin and politically separated it from the other "tribes" of Kai-bab, Moapa, Las Vegas, and San Juan Paiutes.[55]

Utah Paiutes hosted a spring powwow to celebrate their restoration to federal tribal status and then got down to work. In May 1980 they elected a constitution committee cum interim tribal council. It took up offices in the Cedar City building constructed by the old PTC economic development grant. Only after they had again been congressionally recognized could the BIA open an agency in Cedar City. From the same town that had been BIA headquarters in the 1930s when it refused to recognize the local native com-munity and from where it had administered Utah Paiute termination in the 1950s, the BIA began to rebuild relationships with the newly structured tribal government.

The Utah Paiute constitution was approved on 8 October 1981 under the authority of the Wheeler-Howard Act.[56] This latest of Paiute constitutions formalized a dual-level structure in which an overarching "federally recognized sovereign Indian tribe" called the Paiute Indian Tribe of Utah encompassed five semi-autonomous "bands" of Shivwits, Indian Peak, Cedar City, Koosharem, and Kanosh Paiutes. Each band elected its own council every four years to manage band properties and internal matters. The band council candidate who received the largest number of votes was chair and also represented that band on the tribal council. A second election by the total tribal membership chose the tribal chair from among the five band representatives. This structure reified the geographic distribution of Paiutes, evolved from the rather haphazard location of BIA reservations during the early 1900s that had only loosely reflected native social groups and was more the result of cheap available land and the location of jobs in non-Indian towns. By choosing equal representation for the five bands, Paiute voters consciously overlooked the significant population disparities between contemporary groups, several of which were small enough virtually to assure some families with permanent council presence.

Members over the age of eighteen could vote and those over twenty-one run for office. Criteria for membership were carefully specified. The 503 members of the five bands enrolled at the time of restoration became the base population of the tribe, along with their descendants who had at least one quarter Indian ancestry. If people of different bands married, in conformity to long-standing traditions of bilateral affiliation, children could be enrolled in the band of either the mother or the father. Elaborate adoption procedures opened membership to full-blood Indians of any tribe who lived in the area, but other rules tightened membership definitions along the lines the BIA had long urged. A person could not be a Utah Paiute and belong to any other Indian tribe at the same time, including Kaibab or Moapa. A person could belong to only one component band and could not shift membership freely, either to gain access to better resources or as a form of political protest; both strategies had been common as little as three generations earlier. The tribe, not the BIA, took on the responsibility of monitoring tribal rolls, keeping track of the one allowable affiliation of recognized members.

The tribal council also assumed the right to tax bands' income from their properties, although not income of individual members. The tribal council claimed power to establish a trial court and court of appeals in which appointed judges would try violations of council-approved ordinances. Foremost, the council could manage tribal lands, minerals, and other resources. Use of those resources could be assigned to bands or individuals or be operated by the tribe at large.

Travis Benioh became the first tribal chair under the new constitution in October 1981. Members of the first council were mostly in their twenties, far younger than those who had led in the previous decade; three of the five were women, even unmarried women. Although these young people were better educated and more experienced dealing with non-Indian institutions, skills needed and appreciated by the community, most came from culturally traditional families. They soon developed into a professionalized managerial elite whose personal behavior and values, which enabled them to be effective dealing with non-Indian bureaucrats, alienated to some extent their constituents, neighbors, and kin. In fulfilling the roles for which they had been elected, they began to meet personal criticisms based on older traditions of interpersonal relations, which confused, angered, and frustrated them.[57]

The council immediately began gathering data to support requests for federal health improvement programs, for preschool and high school tutoring programs to stem the dropout rate, and for grants to build new or repair present housing. The tribal council and its committees very carefully balanced project funds among the bands, arguing for equal division by location rather than apportionment by population or documented individual need.[58]

For the first five years, however, the tribal council focused on selection of the congressionally authorized fifteen thousand acres of "available public lands" to replace those lost on termination. Nearly two thirds of the land base of Utah is managed by the National Forest Service, BLM, National Park Service, and other federal agencies; the full fifteen thousand acres for Paiutes would constitute less than 1 percent of those federal holdings.[59] Nevertheless, Senator Orrin Hatch, who publicly bemoaned that Paiutes "have been so destitute they haven't had the pride necessary to continue the great Indian heritage," took the position that the "joy" to come from "the sheer recognition of their existence" was sufficient for them; he refused to consider providing pragmatic resources for Paiutes to accomplish their renaissance.[60] In this he reflected his constituents' opposition to "giving" land to the Indians. Cattlemen feared loss of lands they leased for grazing, mineral companies feared loss of potential coal or oil revenues, and chambers of commerce feared loss of vague and as yet unrecognized development potential. To counterbalance this opposition, the BIA hired an out-of-state consulting firm to develop a land plan and to liaise between the council, various federal agencies, and interest groups.[61]

The tribal council and the consultants first proposed a parcel near each population area for homes, with the balance of the land to be tribally held, revenue-producing property. Because Cedar City had the largest Paiute population, spread somewhat north when HUD houses had been provided in the 1970s, they suggested a plot of federal land in the hills behind Parowan that had scenic tourist attractions and was on the road to the major regional ski resort. The town leaders of Parowan mounted a fierce campaign to defeat this tribal choice. The council decided to avoid a politically dangerous confrontation and dropped their first selection. Similarly, they backed away from choices near Kanosh and St. George when these too met with local opposition. South of Richfield they considered land with all-weather access off the interstate highway at Joseph, but the parcel was uphill near the town's drinking water well, and the town complained vociferously about public health impacts. Only the federal promise of new water treatment facilities persuaded Joseph to remove its objections.[62]

Greater controversy erupted when the council selected as its revenue property 9,520 acres of national forest land with known coal resources. Senator Hatch sputtered, "I never for the life of me thought they would ask for millions of dollars (of coal land)."[63] Only 160 acres were leased to Coastal States Energy Corporation, but the company had not developed them. Coastal States knew that the entire parcel was due for public sale within six months and planned to acquire the estimated 149 million tons of coal for itself. Reviving arguments that non-Indians had voiced throughout Paiute history, the company's allies on the Sevier County Commission declared that providing such real economic resources to Paiutes would not only take away values that non-Indians needed for regional development but would actually be detrimental to the Indians themselves: "This will provide revenues so they don't have to become self-sufficient and they can just sit there and live off the royalties. We think that is adverse to the long-term effect on the Paiute people."[64] Paiutes repeatedly assured the company that they would not interfere with mining because they hoped it would generate tribal income, that they would not change the lease, and that they would simply take over the federal portion of the royalty payments. Utah's governor asked the company to remove its opposition, and the tribe even offered to pay fees to the county despite legal immunity from state taxation.[65]

Resisting such persuasion, the company lobbied Washington against the Paiute choice. It found a receptive audience in President Reagan's secretary of the interior, James Watt, well known for his strong favoritism for private corporate development of public lands and limitation of federally reserved holdings. Prodded by Coastal States and supported by Secretary

Watt, the Forest Service asked for and won an opinion from the Interior Department's solicitor, who stated that national forest lands had already been designated for a federal purpose and thus did not constitute "available public lands" in the sense intended by the restoration legislation.[66]

This ruling interfered with another parcel Paiutes had eyed at the south end of Fish Lake, also on Forest Service land. They argued that it was a traditional campsite during the fishing season, that people were occasionally buried there, that Paiutes had held a Memorial Cry for the dead and hosted a Ute-style Sun Dance there in the 1930s. Although the tribe asked for the Fish Lake site on the basis of the American Indian Religious Freedom Act, which guarantees native groups access to materials and places necessary to sustain traditional practices, the religious connection to this specific site was not deemed strong enough to outweigh the solicitor's opinion. The Forest Service refused to release land at this popular recreational lake but did negotiate two weeks of guaranteed, albeit nonexclusive, Paiute use.[67]

Once national forest lands were excluded and the tribe withdrew from political confrontation with non-Indians over lands of value, all of which were long claimed in this well-developed regional economy, there was no revenue property available for the tribe. Despite two years of tribal negotiations in more than two hundred meetings with federal, county, and local agencies, despite the political support of the governor, national Indian organizations, NARF, and the local Committee for Paiute Self-Determination, which all favored grant of revenue lands, when Congress finally approved the Paiute land plan in 1984 there were only 4,770 acres, less than one third the original authorization. That acreage was residential, some near enough to highways to have some commercial potential, but none near existing jobs for Paiute workers. Although the federal Office of Management and Budget made no protest against half a million dollars annually to expand the BIA and Indian Health Service bureaucracies to serve Utah Paiutes, it refused to support any financial compensation for the unallotted acreage that might provide a nest egg for Paiutes' own economic development. Only with the firm public support of Senate Indian Affairs Committee chair William Cohen and the lobbying of presidential advisor Edwin Meese was $2.5 million finally included, interest from which would support tribal council operations and economic development projects.[68]

The tribal council discussed truck stops to utilize interstate highway access and small-scale commercial sewing houses to continue projects of the old PTC. They won federal funding for high school tutoring, preschool, home repair, and wellness programs, but these, like most social programs, soon suffered budget decimation during the Reagan years. One of their major diplomatic achievements was persuading the Mormon Church to hand over title of the Cedar City residential area to the restored Utah Paiute Tribe.[69]

Although the Utah Paiute restoration was perhaps the most dramatic event in the years after 1950, other Southern Paiutes were active in their own affairs as well. Far to the southeast, the little-known San Juan Paiutes leapt into public awareness when they sought federal recognition as a tribe. In the 1870s Mormon and federal explorers had visited their campsites in the washes and at springs between the Colorado River and the Hopi villages.[70] Small in number, with little to trade, and offering little military resistance to non-Indian expansion, they were bureaucratically ignored. In the early 1860s U.S. military campaigns drove Navajos northwest into San Juan country with their sheep herds. Paiutes refused to leave and lived interspersed with these new people. They learned their language, sheep raising, and some outer cultural forms, such as clothing styles and hogan architecture, but they intermarried mostly among themselves and kept their own beliefs. They saw themselves and were seen by Navajos as a separate people.[71]

Unlike Utah Paiutes, previously recognized, terminated, and restored by Congress, San Juan Paiutes had to meet the federal standards for previously unrecognized Indian tribes. In 1978 Paiutes living at Navajo Mountain and farther south at Willow Springs on the Navajo Reservation initiated the recognition process.[72] The first issue was whether they had remained a socially and culturally distinct group continuously over the years since "time immemorial." Paiutes declared they had, but the Navajo tribal government challenged this. It argued that the BIA had carried Paiutes on the Navajo Reservation census for years, their population had counted in calculations for Navajo funding, and they had been served by the Navajo programs; they had been, in effect, absorbed into the Navajo tribe. Five years later, when the investigating BIA acknowledgment team decided that San Juan Paiutes were indeed a separate Indian tribe, based on anthropological and ethnohistorical evidence, the Navajos sued the BIA.[73]

This bizarre turn of events was rooted in the 1882 reservation set aside for Hopis "and such other Indians" as the government might see fit to settle there. Hopis had always considered this land theirs, but Navajos expanded onto it with BIA complaisance. By the twentieth century several generations of Navajos could make the claim that, like Hopis, this was their "traditional" use land and that their religious beliefs and practices were interwoven with these places. The BIA, Congress, and the courts had been unwilling or unable to untangle the intertribal claims and vested interests. San

Juan Paiutes were now recognized as a third tribe with aboriginal interests and proceeded to ask for an equal part of this joint use area. The Hopi tribal government gleefully supported San Juan acknowledgment against its traditional Navajo opponent and promptly hosted a celebration upon San Juan recognition.[74]

Unlike other newly recognized Indian tribes, San Juan Paiutes were given no reservation, because their homeland was part of the still-pending Navajo-Hopi land dispute. In 1992 the federal district court that was overseeing that intertribal dispute said it had no authority to award any land to San Juan Paiutes and passed the question of a reservation for them back to Congress.[75] San Juan Paiutes, with their own tribal government but without lands, were removed from the jurisdiction of the BIA's Navajo agency and added to the responsibilities of the new Cedar City office.[76]

At Kaibab Paiutes had organized a tribal government in the 1950s, about the time when Utah Paiutes were being terminated from federal relations.[77] In 1970 the BIA provided a building for tribal headquarters directly across the road from the Pipe Spring National Monument enclave. While Utah Paiutes spiraled into a morass of neglect, Kaibab Paiutes used a third of their land claims judgment funds for tribal enterprises. Combined with grant monies, they initiated ambitious plans for housing, agriculture, employment, and community services.[78]

Their plans went beyond the BIA's concepts of agriculture and cattle raising; primarily because of lack of water, by 1977 the 120-acre agency farm had shrunk to 5 acres of gardens and by 1984 to a single plot. Although the tribe retained rights to one third of the nine hundred cubic feet per minute flow of Moccasin Spring, a tribally funded study showed they were actually receiving less than seventy cubic feet per minute. Non-Indian landholders who claimed the remaining water right said it was the Indians' own fault for not maintaining ditches and reservoir walls, clearing brush, and removing debris; the tribe blamed BIA management and funding. Although the BIA had made several attempts to build a tribal herd early in the century and had dislodged non-Indian cattlemen from reservation pastures, by 1985 only seven Paiute households owned cattle, and the tribal herd was reduced to four head plus two symbolic bison.[79]

Kaibab Paiutes followed the regional economic trends away from marginal mixed desert agriculture toward the one business that boomed in the Southwest—tourism. They had within their reservation boundaries the Pipe Spring National Monument. Once an intrusion that cost them the loss of major water resources, Pipe Spring now lured more than thirty thousand tourists to the reservation every summer. The monument's presentations praised stalwart Mormon pioneers who had built a stone fort surrounding the spring to protect it and themselves from Indians. Paiutes persuaded the monument to allow them to build an interpretive nature trail to explain native use of the land. Tribal hopes of a coequal partnership in historical presentations or in operation of the monument, or even financial benefit from craft sales or a tribal museum, remained unfulfilled.[80] They did, however, build a forty-unit campground as an overnight haven for recreational vehicles passing to the Grand Canyon's north rim.

Other aspects of their federal relationship benefited Kaibab Paiutes more. Federal housing subsidies in the 1970s enabled members to return to the reserve, and the population grew from 130 in 1972 to over 200 ten years later. This exacerbated an already critical employment situation.[81] A few men worked at the lumber mill outside Fredonia, and a few others ran their own cattle, but the tribal government was the largest employer. From a staff of one in 1972, twelve years later it had thirty.[82] Coupled with BIA jobs and several hired as cultural interpreters at the national monument, virtually every household at Kaibab had one member or more dependent on federally funded employment by the mid-1980s. Then BIA, tribal, parks, and other service sector federal jobs were severely cut back by Reagan-inspired federal budget restructuring. By various reports, unemployment rose to a grim 36 to 70 percent of the adult population.[83]

Moapa people had a rather different experience in the late twentieth century, shining for a while as the entrepreneurial example for all Paiutes. In the early 1960s they had leased virtually all their agricultural land to non-Indians and had no native businesses and little local employment. Then they hired a professional business planner who convinced them to stretch beyond the traditional BIA vision of an agricultural, land-based economy, which had repeatedly proven a failure, and reach instead toward light industry and commerce. He advocated initial small, uncomplicated enterprises that risked little money and could be run by inexperienced tribal members, rather than hiring non-Indian experts for a quicker profit. Investing in the people who had conquered basic management and financial skills, that cadre could "graduate" to a second, larger-scale operation with perhaps higher risks and greater profits, while a new set of novices took over the first, in a gradually escalating pyramid.

In 1968 the tribe refused to renew its land lease. To the contrary, they contracted with their former lessee to dig out his dairy yard and packaged and marketed the resulting "Kaibab aged steer manure," soon a mainstay of Las Vegas gardeners. With the profits from this sweat-equity project they set up a small convenience store, the first on the reservation, the profits from which were invested in a few heavy-duty commercial sewing machines. The tribe was soon producing specialized leather cases for electronics, such as citizen band radios. Using nonfederal funding and tribal money, they constructed their own headquarters and community center and then turned their experienced young construction crew onto a HUD-subsidized housing project.[84]

Then in 1978 the Moapa Paiutes launched their most ambitious effort. Mobilizing $2.5 million in simultaneous grants from the BIA and the Departments of Labor, Energy, and Agriculture, coupled with a large commercial bank loan, they hired an Israeli consultant who trained people in modified hydroponic crop production; the tribe then enclosed fifteen acres in greenhouses. Exploiting their ever-present sunshine, extremely long growing season, and nearby market for luxury foods in Las Vegas hotels, they went into the business of growing premium tomatoes.[85]

On the wave of this carefully constructed chain of success, Moapa Paiutes approached the Nevada congressional delegation and asked for seventy thousand acres of public lands adjoining the reservation. The tribe argued that this land had historically been part of their native use area and had actually been in the reserve before the 1875 reduction to a thousand acres.[86] The secretary of the interior recommended against the proposal, but Congress was impressed with Moapa's recent enterprises and added the land to the reservation in 1980.[87]

On a hot afternoon in September that same year disaster struck. One of the brief, localized summer thunderstorms that sweep the Nevada desert passed overhead and for less than one minute hurled golf-ball-size hail through the greenhouse glass at Moapa. Within hours, unshielded tomato plants had shriveled and died. With almost half a million dollars in tribal debts and now comparatively minor sources of income, banks refused further loans to restock. The greenhouses were repaired under insurance but then stood empty and gradually fell into decay; the tribal business planner drifted away.[88]

Trying to capitalize on its newly expanded land base, the Moapa Tribal Council tried to lure non-Indian industry in hopes of lease income, royalties, and jobs for their members. The new parcel, while large, had only a few dirt roads across it, no known source of water, and no electricity or other infrastructure; the tribe could offer few financial compensations when Nevada commercial taxes were so low and businesses preferred locations where their employees lived, in Las Vegas. The only offer came from a brothel. Under Nevada state law, legalized prostitution was a county option, and Clark County, which enclosed both Moapa and the resort city of

Las Vegas, refused brothel licensing. In 1982 the Moapa Tribal Council accepted a bid offering income and construction of a road, small-plane landing strip, and power lines but pointedly lacking the then-standard "Indian preference in hiring" clause. The BIA vetoed the council's business agreement, and in turn the tribe sued the agency in federal court. Two years later, after both district and appeals courts upheld the BIA's oversight powers as specified in the Moapa tribal constitution, the council abandoned its effort.[89]

By 1985 the gambling renaissance was sweeping Indian reservations across the country. Pressed by unemployment as high as 83 percent and desperate to stimulate their economy, the Moapa Tribal Council became the first tribe in Nevada to try Indian bingo. They hired a non-Indian contractor who claimed to have both experience operating games and the capital to pay off winners. The large Las Vegas casinos were cool and noncooperative but did not expect much of their clientele to bother to drive sixty-five miles out to Moapa to play a game that they could more easily play in town. The tribal subcontractor turned out to be less well funded than he had represented. After only two weekends Moapa bingo was struggling to meet employees' paychecks and closed within a month.[90]

Stifled with debts from the tomato business and now bingo, Moapa Paiutes tried to exploit the new land's geographic connection with the interstate highway. By 1992 the tribal convenience store had moved out to a trailer at the intersection. Teenage Paiute employees sold soda to desert-blistered tourists and seasonally sold Fourth of July fireworks. Moapa's run of bad luck was still not finished; in the middle of the afternoon of 28 June 1995 the storage trailer of fire crackers was ignited by a welding torch spark and exploded.[91]

Las Vegas Paiutes, on the other hand, reversed their situation, which through most of the twentieth century had been so predominantly dismal. They converted the reservation's legal immunity from state law, which had long denied them public school access and police protection, into a benefit. In the early 1970s a tribe in Washington state won a case in the Supreme Court that allowed them to sell cigarettes without charging state tobacco taxes, thus undercutting the price of off-reservation competitors.[92] In 1975 a non-Indian approached Las Vegas Paiutes and asked to rent an abandoned building on their urban reserve for cigarette sales, offering to share the profits. Only blocks away from the busy downtown casino center, the dollar per carton savings attracted consumers, and more than three quarters of a million cartons were sold the first year. As they lost market share, non-

Indian competitors pressed the state to regulate, intimidate, and eventually sue the concessionaire and the tribe, although they were unsuccessful.[93]

When the lease expired, the tribe refused to renew but instead bought a trailer, improved road access for customers, and went into business for themselves. Cigarette profits bought two and a half acres of land that gave Las Vegas Paiutes legal street access for the first time. The tribe incorporated a construction company that built a community center and tribal headquarters on that land in 1981.[94]

With nearly 150 enrolled members and a little over twelve acres, Las Vegas Paiutes could easily justify a request for more land, especially if it was envisioned as not just a housing site but as a base for enterprise and job development. Like Moapa, Las Vegas Paiutes could display recent success when they approached the Nevada congressional delegation for surplus federal land. With local, county, and state support behind the tribe, Congress added 3,800 acres to the Las Vegas Paiute Reservation with almost no debate in 1983.[95]

This property did not adjoin the historical central urban location but was an undeveloped parcel of BLM land twenty-five miles northwest on the slopes of Mount Charleston, straddling both sides of a major federal highway. The mountain had long been a cool summer retreat for urban dwellers, and the city edge was moving in that direction at more than a mile per year. Tribal development was initially slow. Some members, squeezed out of the tiny downtown reserve, brought in house trailers. The council considered leases for light industry, but water lay deep below this high alluvial fan, and wells were expensive.[96]

Nearly ten years later, after hiring a professional business planner, Las Vegas Paiutes announced plans for a golf course on the new property. A water right for 289 acre-feet came with the property, but the irrigated golf course and associated buildings would require 44,000 acre-feet, and known water sources in the valley were already overcommitted. The Clark County Water District and the state of Nevada filed suit against the tribe when it boldly announced it would simply overpump its water right.[97] An out-of-court compromise was negotiated but promptly upset when the tribal business manager calmly announced that this was only the first of five projected golf courses, several casino resorts, a theme park, and an artificial lake that the tribe planned to construct on the property. Local, county, and state governments and landowners raced to court; the tribe snapped back that such non-Indian opposition was racially motivated. Negotiators worked amid mounting hysteria and achieved a compromise. The tribe got water for a hotel and two golf courses. This would take all of the tribal water rights,

12. Non-Indian leisure-time sportsmen arrive to play golf at the Las Vegas Paiute Resort, 2000. (Photograph by Martha C. Knack.)

1,500 acre-feet of state water, 500 acre-feet from the city's allocation, and a plan for "artificially recharging the basin." The city would run water mains out to the reservation.[98] Las Vegas Paiutes had won a very considerable extension of their initial water right. They had clearly learned the benefits that large-scale corporate investment could bring to confrontation politics. The tribe took out $13 million in bank loans and began construction. This ambitious project established the Las Vegas Paiutes as the big-time entrepreneurs of the Paiute world.

Farther to the south, economic changes generated major political dissension within the Chemehuevi community. Back in 1939 the flooding of their valley had seemed a disaster but had turned into a blessing by 1980. Over those forty years the Chemehuevi community was fractured by issues of "blood quantum" resulting from interracial intermarriages and differences in cultural backgrounds, experiences, and community commitment.[99] In the late 1980s the issues shifted visibly from sociocultural to politico-economic ones, although these were still divided in a classically

Paiute way along kinship and personal ties. As had other Paiutes, Chemehuevis learned to access federal grants in order to develop the same artificial
lake that had inundated their land. They built a marina, restaurant, store,
and five mobile home parks along its shore and looked toward prosperity
in service industries for non-Indian leisure-time travelers and affluent re-
tirees.[100]

But the Indian gambling boom promised greater profits for a property
this close to Las Vegas and to its spin-off city of Laughlin. Suddenly, the per-
quisites of tribal council office exceeded just being a rare reservation job to
become a previously undreamed-of base of power. The 1988 council quietly
negotiated with a casino corporation for hotel and gambling concessions to
be protected by reservation status from the legal restrictions of California
state law. When some tribal members opposed this move, the council exploited the underspecified procedures of the Chemehuevi government,
which rested largely on customary practices and cultural ethics, to close
council meetings, restrict circulation of minutes, and limit information.[101]

Tensions escalated as the scheduled 1992 council election approached.
People found out that five candidates had been barred, and only the three
incumbents would appear on the ballot. Dissidents accused the council of
nepotism and profiteering. They convinced a California congressman to
get the U.S. civil rights commissioner to visit the reservation; he saw council
conduct that he thought violated American ethics-in-government standards, and, although lacking jurisdiction, he requested investigation by the
Department of Justice.

Three days before the election, an unofficial vote by about a quarter of
the tribal membership chose a dissident tribal council. Within hours the
FBI, with helicopters and SWAT teams, raided the current tribal council
chair's home and seized documents. The chair and entire tribal council fled
the reservation. The irregular dissident council seized power, although the
BIA refused to recognize it. The council in exile, whose term of office was
now expired, accused the dissidents of "terrorist overthrow of a legally constituted government."[102]

After several months, both factions petitioned the BIA for a new election, to be held under new registration rolls, not for offices this time but to
amend the tribal constitution. Tribal officers would, for the first time, be
subject to recall, and there would be a bill of rights.[103] In April 1993 the
Chemehuevis elected the first tribal council under their new constitution.[104]

Severe cuts to the BIA budget during the Reagan administration erased
housing, health, and educational subsidies along with the on-reservation

jobs they had supported. Paiute reservations were hit hard. In 1987 the Kaibab Tribal Council had been able to protest a uranium-mining lease on BLM lands fifteen miles south on the grounds that it would disturb traditional cultural values. Three years later Kaibab itself negotiated for an eighty-million-dollar plant to incinerate one hundred thousand tons of hazardous industrial sludge annually within the boundaries of the reservation. Mounting unemployment pressed the tribal council to this desperate risk in exchange for over a million dollars a year in lease and tax fees and 150 jobs carrying an Indian preference in hiring. Reversing their earlier support of uranium mining, the local non-Indian public protested Paiute industrial development as damaging to the tourist economy. Curiously enough, it was national environmental groups who feared for air quality, groundwater, and public health should the plant operate under federal, rather than more stringent Arizona, laws. The Kaibab Tribal Council cautiously passed off the decision to a plebiscite, which voted in favor of the contract by a two-to-one margin. The nationwide Council of Energy Resource Tribes (CERT) then criticized the BIA for allowing Kaibab Paiutes to make their own decision and for not exercising its responsibility to protect Indian land. Five months later, the tribal council canceled final negotiations with the incinerator plant. It refused to state publicly why, but it may have been because of these external pressures, hardened internal opposition, or growing suspicion of the corporation.[105]

Kaibab Paiutes then experimented with gambling, as had people at Moapa and Chemehuevi. They hoped that tourists to Pipe Spring National Monument and the Grand Canyon would be their clientele but soon discovered that these recreational travelers were too intent on getting down the road to see the next sight. Paiutes found that they were their own best customers, merely redistributing their own incomes around to each other. The tribal casino could not profitably meet salaries and their share of state-managed oversight fees. At the end of the 1996 tourist season, Kaibab Paiutes became the first tribe in Arizona to close its casino, $50,000 in debt.[106]

By the late 1990s the various Paiute communities had weathered the federal cutbacks of the previous decade. While recovering from the nadir of the Reagan years, economies were still precarious. Each Paiute population was still small and geographically separated, although telephones and fax machines linked them now. In July 1982 Paiute leaders formed a Paiute Chairman's Conference to discuss issues and strategies common to all the reservation groups, realizing that each alone had only small political influence in its respective state or in intra-agency competition for BIA and other federal benefits. The following year the BIA agency for Utah Paiutes consolidated with jurisdictions for Kaibab, Moapa, Las Vegas, and San Juan so that all the recognized Paiute tribes in three states, except the Chemehuevis, were served by a single office.[107]

Paiutes' hopes had been buoyed by federal recognition of the Utah and San Juan groups, but they still have won very little real control over their economic future. Las Vegas, Moapa, and Chemehuevi Paiutes lie in the shadow of the fastest growing city in America, awash in expansionist prosperity, and yet only the Las Vegas community was close enough to reap benefits from that growth. Paiutes have left behind nineteenth-century visions of self-sufficiency through reservation-based agriculture; they never had land or water enough, and the national economy has moved beyond the family farm. When Utah Paiutes lost their bid for coal lands, Paiutes were again without exploitable land-based resources. Each group has begun to explore corporate enterprise, large or small. They have learned the intricate techniques of grant and program applications outside of the BIA. Even with the heavy federal subsidies of the 1970s, initial Kaibab, Moapa, and Utah Paiute efforts to construct local industries collapsed from undercapitalization, inexperience, remote location, and the layered encrustation of bureaucratic regulation and delay.

Paiutes' greatest economic successes have been where they joined the regional shift toward upper-middle-class tourism—hotels, marinas, recreational vehicle parks. Just as their frontier-era ancestors had harvested reusable remnants from passing wagon trains, these latter-day Paiute efforts have only been successful where the Indian community lay directly on highways to more distant destinations; only fifteen miles off the direct route to Grand Canyon, the Kaibab casino was too far from the beaten path to survive. Such a tourist-oriented industrial base commits Paiutes to constant daily interaction with non-Indians and indeed makes Indians' success dependent on their skill in those interethnic relations. Their future will show how well they can manage to design patterns of human relations compatible with the fleeting contacts of the tourist industry, so diametrically opposed to the dense, life-long commitment of Paiutes to each other within their own communities.

12

BOUNDARIES AND TRANSITIONS

Over the last 150 years, the several originally autonomous bands of Southern Paiutes have been transformed into an ethnic group embedded within a nation-state. While much of the content of Paiute culture has changed, particularly in material things, Paiutes themselves have remained a distinct people. Their society, like all human groupings, did not simply happen, the historical fossil of an aboriginal past lingering into the present. Neither have they been absorbed to become indistinguishable from the whole, even though their group has always been dispersed and for a century and a half been mixed amid non-Indians. Anthropologists' acculturation and sociologists' assimilation theories would not have predicted this continued distinctiveness and cannot explain it.[1]

Scholars debate whether ethnic groups like the Southern Paiutes are analytically defined from the inside, the result of self-identification, or from the outside, as they are seen by others.[2] The first proposal goes astray because it shifts logical levels. Ethnic identity, like all self-identification, is an individual mental process, rather than a social phenomenon. It is the person who thinks of himself or herself as a member of an ethnic group; furthermore, writers generally leave this key concept of identity undefined and without any way to measure its presence or absence empirically. This approach takes for granted the existence of a social group with which that individual can then identify, even though it is the very presence of that social entity that has to be explained. This is not to say that such personal identification is not real, compelling, and important but simply that it is subsequent, rather than causal. Societies do not just happen or come into being because individuals think they are there, imagine them to be, or wish them to be so; societies are built in a real and empirical sense.[3] Clearly, Paiutes' history has demonstrated how they have built, rebuilt, and maintained their society through the years, even when surrounded and indeed flooded by the more numerous, more highly structured, and politically and economically more dominant Euro-American society.

As ethnic groups are maintained, of necessity they create boundaries of contact with others. Such boundaries differ from the interiors of those societies. Cross-cultural frontiers are created by the societies on both sides of the boundary to distinguish a division between them, not allowing the duality to dissolve into unity.[4]

In looking at the 150 years of known Southern Paiute ethnohistory, the first fundamental reality was their successful ability to remain a recognizable group. Although they lived surrounded first by neighboring tribes and later by non-Indians among whom they were by far the numerical minority, and although they openly accepted a great deal of Euro-American material culture, Paiutes have remained a distinct people. Their communities were segregated neighborhoods at the geographical edges of non-Indian towns. Their social networks only marginally encompassed non-Indian people. Their economic position was clearly different from that of non-Indians, and their political life was isolated from the regional power structure. Even when baptized into the prevailing religion, their congregations were separate, designated missions by the denomination to which they belonged. These interethnic boundaries were structured, ordered, systematic, and repeated in area after area of Paiute territory. The boundaries were not accidental. People on both sides worked to maintain their separate community structures. Nevertheless, they each created and institutionalized mechanisms that linked their group to the other into a single, systemic whole.

A second characteristic of Southern Paiute interethnic boundaries was their immediacy. Paiutes met ethnically different people largely through face-to-face relations with individuals they lived near and knew. These were not abstract enemies seen across a dusty battlefield or faceless elements of an urban mass but named persons, neighbors, employers, and coreligionists. Even where Paiutes had reservations, they could rarely live totally within a native community on those lands, interacting solely with a federal Indian agent. Driven by the inadequacy of land base, water, and capital, Paiute families dealt directly with nonnative others throughout their history. Their interethnic relations consisted of direct conversations over whether they could work for this farmer, whether their daughter could marry that man's son, whether they could sing in the same church or speak at the same town meeting.

The men and women who asked and answered such questions were not isolated individuals but members of larger societies and products of their own cultural upbringings. They were molded by their cultural past as well as their situational present. They were subject to the observation of their peers, censure of their own societies, and sanctions of law. Over time they were influenced by the still larger regional and national growth of economic markets, the technology of transportation and communications, the fluctuations of droughts and rainfall, the worldwide crises of financial depressions and world wars. It is only in the total context of these several native and nonnative cultures and the shifts of history that we can understand the real human contacts that constituted Southern Paiute interethnic relations.

Those relations grew not only out of the internal social integrity of each society separately but also from a series of mechanisms that crossed the boundary between themselves and others, linking together the separate ethnic groups into a more complex regional and ultimately national system. Euro-Americans, accustomed to an economy of occupational specialists and a political structure of hierarchical control, instituted specialized mechanisms to deal with Indian people. Paiutes, on the other hand, accustomed to economic and political egalitarianism, applied to the novel historic situations preexisting mechanisms that were embedded within generalized institutions. The very underspecified flexibility of Paiute culture became itself a major technique for managing their relationships with others across intercultural boundaries.

The U.S. government applied the same techniques it used for dealing with Indians elsewhere rather stiffly and automatically to Southern Paiutes. Those mechanisms featured treaties, special agreements made with Indian tribes but no other ethnic group; reservations, specially designated locations for native communities; laws and legal definitions that applied to Indians alone; tribal councils, limited self-governments unlike any other structure under American law; and preeminently the Bureau of Indian Affairs, the specific bureaucracy that, for almost one hundred years, shared with the military the task of managing federal Indian relations—to maintain the peace, restrict native land use, and manipulate Indians' cultural behavior until it was compatible with non-Indians' expectations.

Mormons, reluctant products of the larger Euro-American culture, similarly negotiated unofficial treaties for land access, set aside church-managed Indian "farms," and designated special Indian missionaries. These missionaries were charged to learn the natives' language, mediate the peace, teach them agriculture, and convert them to the faith. That peace was most often threatened when settlers insisted on their own private ownership of cultivated land, domesticated livestock, and material goods. If Paiutes challenged these claims, settlers reacted with anger, whips, and guns.

In such disputes missionaries stood between settlers and natives, as they did between Indians and non-Mormon travelers and federal officers. Ironically, over the century that BIA agents competed with Mormon religious leadership for suzerainty over Paiutes in Utah, both groups created and appointed a hierarchy of specialized agents to deal with these natives, freeing ordinary non-Indians from routine daily interactions with them. Buffered by such specialists, settlers quickly ceased to notice and record in their diaries and other records the subtle distinctions they had initially tried to demarcate by such terms as Pah-Utes, Piedes, and Pahvants and simply noted generic "Indians."[5] By the end of the 1860s, settlers had largely allocated relationships with natives to designated intercultural specialists, whether Indian agents or missionaries.

In contrast, Paiutes employed the existing features of their generalized hunting and gathering culture to cope with the challenges brought by the newcomers. Flexibility was the hallmark of Paiute response. Camp headmen stepped out to meet the strange travelers and tried to establish personal relationships through the same kinds of gifts and exchange of information that they used with each other. When the livestock of immigrants ate off the grasses along the routes of travel, Paiutes shifted their household economies toward other seasonal foods and other campsites in remote areas, as they had in cases of drought or prairie fire. When steel knives and iron cooking kettles could be obtained through trade or from the jetsam of the roadways, Paiutes abandoned stone blades and the laborious boiling of food in baskets with hot stones. They crafted broken wagon rims and loose nails into metal triangles for new and improved arrowheads. They treated their culture as a pragmatic tool to manage relationships with other groups and with the changing landscape. That culture was not a rigid body of traditions to be clung to for the sake of habit. Paiutes had never been able to afford that type of tenacity in an environment that was so unpredictable of rainfall and resources, even more so now as strangers crowded in and took over many of the best places.

In thus absorbing exotic traits into their culture, Paiutes were not losing their own. The creative result was not a reduced or fraudulent culture but rather the continuing product of experimentation, adaptation, and adoption, a generative rebuilding of their way of life as their lives were changed by forces beyond Paiutes' control.

Paiutes' response was shaped by the small scale of their society. Local camp groups had a limited population and were distant from others. Unlike Mormon settlers, they could not call on a regional hierarchy to send in supplies or reinforcements. Recognizing such limitations, Paiutes crafted interaction strategies that could be accomplished by small groups, particularly by people who knew each other well through kinship and a lifetime of joint activity. When strangers on horseback arrived, Paiute women and children sought hiding places while a headman or elder stepped out to investigate. Paiutes trailed along behind wagon trains looking for slow, lame stock rather than attacking the whole group of travelers; they shouted insults from hillsides rather than ambushing them. Individual men approached evening camps to seek herding jobs, as later single families asked ranchers for work.

Southern Paiutes had been a dispersed people long before Euro-Americans arrived. They had linked their small camp groups together in an intricate and flexible system. A person could justify residence in a camp through any one of a wide variety of bilateral kinship and affinal ties. Every man and woman kept social networks open with gifts, visits, reciprocal exchanges, attendance at funerals, and assemblies around temporarily rich food sources. As non-Indian settlement forced natives to realign how they made their living from the land, Southern Paiutes constantly rebuilt the social networks that constituted the Paiute community. Kin continued to visit, but now from one reservation to another, despite BIA agents' urging to settle in one place where they "belonged." As visitors they joined in the work of their hosts, played, gambled, and mourned the dead. They married, divorced, relocated, and remarried. Children then had relatives in many places and hence had many homes. With the new technology of letter writing, horses and wagons, later cars and telephones, and now e-mail, these contacts were even easier to maintain over greater distances because travel and communication were faster. Paiute life is still a web of people that stretches to include new places, mends to seal the loss of old ones, expands to incorporate the children of interracial marriages, heals to close the loss of the dead.

The specific processes of Paiutes' cultural and social flexibility through which they managed interethnic relations varied with the particular point in time and the group with which they were dealing. Long before the arrival of the first Euro-Americans, Utes, who had sufficient grasslands to support horses, adopted them. With the range and speed these animals gave, Utes traveled to Santa Fe to trade, bringing with them Paiute children, whom the Spaniards wanted for labor. Those Spaniards had only fleeting encounters directly with Paiute groups in the form of itinerant traders and priests, who spent a day bartering here or preaching there before heading on to California. American fur trappers were narrowly interested in the specific harvest of beaver, fairly rare in Paiute country. Seeing relationship with natives as a necessary but tangential aspect of their work, trappers found that they could scorn Paiutes and largely ignore them.

Early wagon travelers were a self-selected group who wanted merely to get through Paiute country to go somewhere else, but they came through year after year in large numbers. Their diaries spoke of dealing generically with Indians, not differentiating Paiutes from the more aggressive tribes that they had met earlier on the Plains. When one Paiute or two asked for food in exchange for herding stock, travelers welcomed their services; when Paiutes stole, shot into camps, or hunted down slow draft animals, travelers met this violation of their claimed private property with collective force. When Paiutes complained about the damage draft animals did to their own summer grass seed harvests, travelers discounted their own culpability as insignificant or immaterial.

Groups as different from one another as Utes, Mormons, miners, and the American military used organized violence, the technological advantage of rifles, and mounted patrols to subordinate Paiutes. Utes raided Paiute camps for female children to sell as slave labor to Spaniards. Mormons drove transient Spanish traders out of the territory with laws and guns, broke the might of the Ute raiding bands, and then proceeded themselves to buy Paiute children freely in a system of indentured servitude. Paiutes, freed of intimidation and raids by their neighboring tribe, suddenly were made subject to the still greater dominance of coresident non-Indians.

Miners too welcomed Paiutes as workers, as long as they lived separately; any native attempt to limit prospectors from ranging freely across their land initiated violent confrontation with ad hoc vigilante parties. Southern Paiute history shows that organized warfare, while dramatic for film makers and popular history, is neither necessary nor inevitable in Euro-American relations with native tribes. The military's minor presence on the fringes of Paiute territory employed such arrogant strategies as kidnapping band leaders as hostages for natives' "good behavior" and demanding they reside within sight of fort commanders. It was groups of local settlers, both farmers and miners, who fomented most of the violence. Mormon communities lashed out in the few instances when an isolated rancher or his livestock were killed, nearly always during regional conflicts with larger, neighboring tribes; settlers then inflicted retaliation far in excess of the original crime randomly on local Paiute men, women, and children discovered nearby. The hierarchical organization and obedience to authority that characterized both the military and Mormons contributed to the success of violence as a strategy of interethnic relationship and assured its recurrence, in the form of citizen posses, until well into the twenti-

eth century. The end result of these local forms of interethnic conflict produced results that were largely identical to formal military conquest—
Euro-American dominance over land and its resources, native impover-
ishment, extensive cultural reorientation, and imposition of legal control
by the nation-state.[6]

The federal government's mechanisms of dealing with Paiutes included nominal efforts at treaty making and reservationization. Treaty negotiations with selected leaders, primarily from the transitional Ute/Paiute
groups, involved at least some input from native headmen but failed Senate
approval; treaties were not a substantial element in Paiute ethnohistory.
Reservations too played a minor role in Paiute relations during the nineteenth century at least. Because Southern Paiutes did not resist non-Indian
arrival with organized, large-scale warfare, the national military was never
sent to drive them onto reservations. Furthermore, because both mining
and agricultural communities wanted Indian labor to help build their own
infrastructures, settlers did not need, and indeed actively resisted, removal
of Paiutes to reservations. Early reserves at Corn Creek and Moapa were
small, the first quickly sold and the second virtually forgotten before the
turn of the century. While they existed, reservation agents were charged
with showing natives the economic advantages of sedentary irrigation agriculture, mirroring the Mormon missionary program, in order to reduce
and segregate native use of land by concentrating their communities under
non-Indian control, thus freeing other lands for nonnative residence in
hopes of obviating more overt interethnic conflicts.

Neither federal agents nor missionaries had enough power to force
Paiutes to comply with these programs. Native people explored what was
offered, evaluated its usefulness for their lives and situations, and usually
soon drifted away. They experimented with casual, short-term labor for
immigrants, in mining towns, and on Mormon farms but continued to
travel to whatever native food sites still remained to gather wild plants seasonally and to hunt whenever possible. Paiutes' pacific response allowed
non-Indians to spread out from prime, well-watered townsites to remote
rangelands and mineral outcrops. Only when Euro-Americans filled the
landscape in the early years of the twentieth century were Paiutes compelled
to come in to towns for permanent if marginal employment and to make
sustained efforts at earning a living out of the few resources of the tiny and
inadequate reservations.

Once in these towns and reservations, Paiutes continued to manage
their interethnic relations through mechanisms that had served them so
well for so long. Whenever they could, they avoided direct conflict and ac-

commodated rather than challenged non-Indians. When this proved impossible, they moved from one reservation jurisdiction to another, one state to another, to evade demands that they formally marry, work at low wages, or pay back impossible federal loans. Employers and the BIA demanded contracts with specific repayment schedules, state marriage licenses, enlistment on single reservation rolls, a whole series of rigid rules to surround and bind Paiutes' behaviors and actions. Paiutes responded with passive but persistent resistance.

Federal representatives were especially frustrated when so many of their assumptions about Indians, ossified into laws and regulations, failed to fit amorphous Paiute structures. Agents struggled to apply legal definitions of ward and non-ward Indian status to decide which Paiutes were eligible for financial help or required to register for the draft, but they became entangled in Paiute kinship networks and were defeated by Paiute mobility. When agents tried to regulate Paiute drinking, gambling, or hunting, the gaps between federal jurisdiction on the tiny reservations and state control everywhere else, the lack of federal personnel and interest of state officers, and the inexorable distances between reservations and courts assured their inability to constrain Paiute personal behavior for many years.

Because the federal government had not set aside reservations early during wars of conquest, it later had to carve out reserves from established non-Indian occupation. Under chronic budget constraints, the BIA looked for cheap land, which was necessarily of poor quality and short of water. When the agency tried to construct Paiute agricultural communities on these plots, it failed. Begrudgingly diverting funds from its primary program, the agency offered occasional short-term employment building roads, ditches, and fence lines. For the most part, Paiutes had to leave the reserves to find jobs with non-Indian landowners and businessmen. Persistently large numbers of Paiutes lived off-reservation, although they were enrolled on one, constituting, according to the BIA, an obligation that at the same time was beyond its jurisdiction.

When drought and the Great Depression dried up off-reservation jobs, these jurisdictional issues exacerbated Southern Paiute interethnic relations. The federal government was clearly responsible for welfare programs on the reservations, but were the states liable for relief of enrolled Paiutes actually living off the reserves? Did the money-short states have to pay for schooling Paiutes' children, regulating their marriage licenses, prohibiting their alcohol consumption, or policing their communities, as it did for non-Indian citizens? The same automobiles and new highways that enabled Paiutes to travel farther for jobs in these years also brought in competing job hunters from distant areas. Further, these transportation improvements allowed the BIA to consolidate several reservations into a single jurisdiction, which saved money but also made it more difficult for Paiutes to exploit the numerous agents' isolation and limited jurisdiction to evade federal demands.

Paiute leadership was strengthening at the same time. Early Mormon settlers had tried to suborn and manipulate headmen, miners had selectively shot and hanged them, and the BIA had ignored them. But in the 1930s, the Wheeler-Howard Act authorized any reservation population to set up a tribal council that would be federally recognized as the local governing body. Most Paiute groups seized this opportunity. The law itself grew out of Depression-era Washington politics that increased governmental manipulation of the economy, large-scale trends that originated far beyond the Paiute communities.[7]

Paiutes added their new tribal councils to more established political ' mechanisms that maintained social order internally within their communities and reached externally across the interethnic boundary with non-Indian neighbors. Both on reservations and in off-reservation towns, informal Paiute headmen discussed issues within their groups and voiced native opinion to non-Indian political and clerical bureaucracies. Shivwits people had a tribal court and judge for many years. Kaibab Paiutes met in irregular open tribal meetings to discuss cattle herds and land improvements. The avoidance of confrontation and active consensus building that characterized all these native political institutions was molded onto the new constitutional governments, creating a form of tribal council that was uniquely Paiute.

The vulnerability of Paiutes to external economic and political forces was demonstrated again shortly after World War II, when the government unilaterally refused to recognize some of their groups as tribal entities any longer and terminated them from federal administration. In an era rife with national-level pressures to reduce federal spending and suspicion of social collectivities, Utah Paiutes fell under the termination policy because of the sheer chance that the Senate Indian Affairs Committee was chaired by Arthur Watkins of their state; the debatably more eligible Nevada and Arizona Paiutes were left under federal management.

The federal government and its subsidiary BIA were not the only large external structures that pushed and shoved Paiutes during their history. From the days of early settlement to the present, the highly structured and regionally dominant Mormon Church has been heavily involved in Paiute affairs, especially in the Utah area. When Paiutes moved into towns, they often lived on land owned directly by the Mormon Church, as in Cedar City, where church influence successfully displaced the BIA for fifty years. When federal law authorized Indian land claims, it was a local Mormon missionary who first contacted the BIA on Paiutes' behalf; he recommended a prominent Mormon attorney, who handled their case. Missionaries guided Utah Paiutes' economic development efforts a generation after they were terminated while resisting the involvement of federal organizations with similar goals, such as VISTA. Those missionaries helped construct the tribal corporation whose structure was later mirrored by the reinstated tribe.

For the last 150 years Southern Paiutes have not only had to fend off external efforts from the federal government and clerical bodies to control them politically and manipulate them socially but have also had to cope with severe and immediate economic pressures. Surely loss of effective control over their territory and over the flora, fauna, minerals, and waters of that land generated the stubborn, disproportionate poverty that they have experienced for generations. Whether they were in remote remnant independent homesteads, inadequate federal reservations, mining and farming towns, or glittering urban areas, whether there were reservations or these were terminated, and even after a successful federal land claim suit, for generation after generation every record speaks of Paiutes' material deprivation, inadequate and crowded housing, and subminimal wages. Kin pooled whatever they had and used every means they could to make a living: time-consuming traditional crafts, migrant harvesting, hunting, federal job training, leaving for distant urban employment, and even collecting wild nuts and fruits.

Paiutes could only deal with symptoms on the local level, the end results of the actual large-scale causes of their poverty. It was not until the 1980s that they gained any leverage against the structural situation within which they were bound. Only then were they able to form new alliances with political organizations independent of and often opposed to the federal BIA, the Mormon Church, and local non-Indian society. The Utah Division of Indian Affairs helped pressure Congress to reinstate Utah Paiutes. The Native American Rights Fund threatened to sue Cedar City for denial of civil rights and public utilities. Paiute groups recruited funds to hire independent tribal attorneys to defend their legal rights and economic planners to design long-term fiscal growth from small industries to huge casino-resorts. They explored new sources of funding outside of federal budgets or the charity of local church groups; they competed for foundation grants, risked bank loans, and built a cautious pyramid of tribal enterprises. Although many Paiute groups are still frustrated by lack of infrastructure, little capital, and geographic isolation from the recreation-driven service industries that are the center of the regional economic boom, a few others benefit from their locations to sell tax-discounted cigarettes or build golf courses. Paiutes are restructuring their internal social relations in the direction of non-Indian norms as they select leaders for their youthful energy and skill at dealing with bureaucrats, define tribal membership as a singular identification set by formal criteria, and debate the distribution and investment of new wealth. It will be a challenge for future generations of tribal leaders to find creative ways through the labyrinths of economic growth and yet still maintain community cohesiveness.

The boundaries that lay between Southern Paiutes and non-Indians were thus institutionalized within both the native culture and the Euro-American culture. These boundaries were not only pervasive but persistent, shifting form through time but ever present and visible. Whether a particular group of Paiutes had a small reservation with a little water or had none, whether they were terminated, restructured, and reinstated as a tribal entity or had a more stable legal relation with the federal government, whether their territory was occupied by agriculturally based Mormons, individualistic miners, or land-consuming cattlemen, their diverse regional and chronological experiences encompassed a number of common themes, processes, and results. These similarities penetrated economic relations, were even more obvious in political relations, and were most apparent in social relations.

Economic issues pivoted around control of productive resources and labor. Non-Indians attempted to establish a geographic boundary with themselves holding the best and most productive resources and Paiutes being somewhere, almost anywhere, else. Mormon irrigation farmers came wanting arable land and took the best watered and most fertile places, spots that had previously supported Paiutes. Cattlemen came wanting pasturage and took over the grasslands that had formerly supplied the Paiute diet. Miners wanted mineral ores, which had not been directly used by natives, but even mining towns needed firewood, grazing for the horses and mules that pulled ore wagons, and food for miners from supportive farmers in the valleys.

Despite this economic variation among different groups of non-Indians, the ultimate result was identical. Paiutes, squeezed away from resources and places they had formerly used as their own, retreated into ever more remote areas until there were none left. Early nominal reservations, at Corn Creek and Moapa, were either sold off by the federal government or virtually forgotten. Later the BIA got a few unwanted scraps of minimal and marginal lands set aside for Paiute reservations. These never had adequate arable land, water, or other resources; they provided places to return to and foci for identification but not productive bases for viable communities. As the Utah Paiutes discovered when they were once again recognized as a tribe, attempts to chip loose any economically significant resources once those were held by Euro-Americans were essentially impossible. Las Vegas Paiutes succeeded in turning a dry, rocky hillside, added to their reservation in the 1980s, into a thriving commercial enterprise only through persistence, vision, and lucky proximity to a booming tourist economy.

Land and land-based resources, while an important element in Southern Paiutes' interethnic relations, were not the only economic component. Throughout the last century and a half, labor relations were an important mechanism of interaction. Paiute manpower constructed much of the infrastructure of Euro-American occupation, modifying the landscape previously harvested for its natural products. Paiutes occupied a distinctive niche in the regional economy, providing inexpensive, seasonal wage labor. Paiute men cleared fields and dug irrigation ditches for non-Indian farmers, cut firewood for ore smelters and built roads from mines to the towns, while Paiute women washed miners' dirty clothes. Together they harvested crops on Mormon farms and sought work in nearby towns. By the turn of the century Paiutes could not survive on the reservations without wage labor and the little hunting and gathering still possible between wage jobs. They faced the competition of new groups of poor non-Indians during the Great Depression, later of migrant Navajos and Hispanics, forcing them to readjust their ties with employers. They drove second-hand automobiles down the new highways to novel opportunities. By the Second World War they had extended their search for employment to distant urban areas, a hunt intensified by the erratic termination and cancellation of some reservations. For more than twenty-five years wage work has been Paiutes' most common means of support and most common forum of interaction with non-Indian society.

Many of the political mechanisms that composed the boundary between Paiutes and non-Indians were elements intrinsic to American nation building. Like all nation-states, the United States was culturally heterogeneous. In order to form a single national entity out of these diverse parts, component subcultural groups had to be made subordinate in at least some regard to the larger whole to become elements in a hierarchical, multilayered single system. This involved not only economic integration but also political domination and its converse, the subordination of ethnic peoples within external territorial limits to the decision-making authority of the nation-state.[8] In order to extend the control of its laws over them, the nation-state had to do such things as simply enumerate who lived where, hence the insistence on census taking, marriage and death records, and that Paiutes should have one permanent name for a lifetime with a "last" name to pass systematically through the father's line. The national government established reservations for Paiutes, not as a process of land acquisition for expanding frontiersmen but as an exercise in the consolidation of its power, demonstrated as much over those individualistic homesteaders, cattlemen, and dissident Mormons as over Indian people. It insisted that each Paiute be enrolled at one and only one of these reservations and, if they relocated, that they go through a formal procedure, so it would know under which jurisdiction each native resided.

The complex federal debate over legal jurisdiction constituted an attempt to dictate Paiutes' identity and envelop them in hegemonic regulation. Agencies of the federal government meticulously applied legal concepts of federal ward and non-ward status to separate which Paiutes would be subject to agents' regulations and which could be drafted for the army, who could receive a reservation land assignment and who could not, whose children could attend a reservation school and whose were the responsibility of public education. It ignored, suppressed, and manipulated native leaders and then seized for itself the power to approve written constitutions that itemized powers and procedures for tribal council structures, to terminate certain groups from federal relations, and then to rerecognize them in a new forms. Using these and many other mechanisms, the BIA and other federal agencies progressively consolidated their power over Paiutes and proceeded to exercise it.

Paiutes were vulnerable to these arbitrary impositions because they had no effective access to national political structures or leverage within the political process. They were progressively incorporated within and subordinated to the nation-state, not only to its bureaucratic structures but also to the larger sociocultural system that characterized that nation.

Southern Paiutes' interethnic social relations were not restricted historically to federal officeholders. Where some other tribes fought wars and then were militarily restricted on reservations, Paiutes lived among ordinary settlers. Paiutes' interethnic relations were not primarily with temporary agents who executed federal policies until they left for another assignment but with neighboring men, women, and children who stayed year after year, generation after generation. While these non-Indians pursued their own cultural and individual agendas, ambitious for position, growth, and wealth, Paiutes had to find a way to survive the demands placed upon them so that they could survive as a people both for today and for tomorrow.

To remain a separate people, Southern Paiutes had to establish and maintain a social boundary between themselves and the various groups of non-Indians who crowded around them. This separation appeared at the earliest period in the caution with which Paiutes approached trappers, explorers, and travelers, using the open spaces of their familiar countryside to buffer the unpredictable response of the strangers. Later Paiutes preferred to abandon rights to territory and political autonomy rather than force direct confrontation. Paiutes' efforts at social separation were enforced by the cultural disdain and violence of settlers, miners, and cattlemen. These lashed out at nearby Paiute encampments, with or without evidence of guilt, to intimidate, plunder, or kill natives whom they saw clearly as separate from the non-Indian community. The Paiute children bought by Mormons never became full members of non-Indian society, rarely married or had children of their own, and often lived only short lives. Children of mixed ancestry, whether products of casual or even violent liaisons or of the occasional marriage, were more readily absorbed by Paiute society than by non-Indian communities.

Once established, the social boundaries between Paiutes and non-Indians were maintained by a series of mechanisms. Paiutes were physically segregated in "Indian villages" on the geographic fringes of mining or agricultural towns. Later federal reservations were located at even greater distances—Shivwits well outside of St. George, Kaibab miles from Kanab, Moapa and Chemehuevi far out in the desert. Missionaries, Indian agents, and friends and advocates of various kinds who purported to speak for Paiutes mediated between the two separated groups.

Internally within their own community Southern Paiutes employed a repertoire of social mechanisms to maintain cohesion. They constantly visited kin in the various dispersed locales, cooperated on household and community projects, borrowed and lent economic aid, and intermarried. They wrote letters to one another and later telephoned. They drove hundreds of miles to express the loss of community members in elaborate funerals and memorial ceremonies and later prayed together in meetings of the Native American Church. They insisted that internal community decisions be made by consensus among a broad base of adult members.

Despite such distinctiveness from non-Indians and integration within their own community, Paiutes were not autonomous. Over the years they were drawn into a larger system of increasing scope and complexity. Local

Mormon settlers were components of a highly structured theocratic state; in dealing with local missionaries and bishops, Paiutes inevitably interacted with that larger leadership and reacted to its goals of expansion. Miners were not only individualists but part of a large regional network that shipped ore to San Francisco and New York where banks and entrepreneurs in turn invested in mines. Indian agents were the local arms of federal policy that was the response to political, economic, and social groups that dominated national life.

As the best land passed into Euro-American hands, Paiutes either could not or chose not to leave. They stayed or actually moved to non-Indian towns, often living on church-owned lands. They worked for non-Indian employers at low wages in subordinate positions without the likelihood of becoming economic competitors. Once native headmen were eliminated or suborned, Indian agents and church officials took it upon themselves to make decisions that affected native communities. State laws demanded marriage licenses, and Indian agents insisted on them. Federal regulations dictated residency requirements for "ward Indian" status. The BIA set up reservation courts, appointed judges, and approved written constitutions for reservation groups that institutionalized the federal veto over tribal council decisions and budgets.

Paiutes were not alone. Economically, politically, and socially, Paiute lives were progressively enmeshed by multiple inextricable webs to the larger structures and hegemony of the nation-state. They had become an ethnic group.

Southern Paiutes' primary strategy throughout this dynamic period of change was flexibility, molding themselves to changing circumstances.[9] Their hunting and gathering past had been adapted to an environment that had spotty resources, unpredictable from season to season. Their culture was underspecified, without fixed structures to hem them in or preempt otherwise viable alternatives. They were allowed choices among alternate campsites, foods to harvest, and kin to live with. Their life demanded that they be able to adapt and shift as each new situation demanded.

This flexibility has served Paiutes well over the last century and a half. Without rigid commitment to a single, proper way of doing things, Paiutes could and did accommodate the new demands brought by settlers, miners, cattlemen, reservationization, and urban growth. Camp groups shifted gathering grounds, combined membership, enrolled on reservations, moved to towns, reaffiliated, and formed new communities. Paiutes continued to hunt and gather but supplemented their economic repertoire with sedentary agriculture where they could and added in wage work, whether minor and casual, seasonal, or regular. While the BIA insisted that reservation groups were tribes and tribal councils were governments, Paiute leaders transmuted Indian courts into community meetings and decided council actions by covert consensus. They let missionaries baptize them or agents fill out their marriage certificates and then divorced, moved, and remarried as they pleased.

By avoiding direct conflict with non-Indians, by not challenging Euro-American power or cultural demands, Southern Paiutes have survived into the twenty-first century against overwhelming odds. Today, as Paiute tribal governments bow to pressures for formal membership criteria, as the people aspire to and achieve commercial success, as their leadership becomes hierarchical, centralized, and decision making, in short, as they become more like Euro-Americans not only in outward material ways but inner structure as well, only the future will tell whether Paiutes can continue to reconstruct their culture and to maintain their internal cohesion as a distinctive community for the generations to come.

NOTES

ABBREVIATIONS

ARCIA   *Annual Report of the Commissioner of Indian Affairs*, micro-fiche reprint ed. (Washington DC: Microcard Editions, n.d.)

BIA-CCF   BIA Central Classified Files, 1907–39, RG 75, USNA

BIA-LR   BIA Letters Received, 1824–81, microfilm M234, USNA

LDS-CHO   Church of Jesus Christ of Latter-day Saints, Church Historian's Office, Salt Lake City

LN   BIA, Phoenix Area Office Records, USNA, Laguna Niguel

OCC   Office of Community Development and Public Service, Southern Utah State College, Cedar City

SAN   Superintendents' Annual Narrative and Statistical Reports, 1907–38, microfilm M1011, USNA

UO-MC   Uintah-Ouray Agency, Miscellaneous Correspondence, BIA Records, RG 75, USNA, Denver

USGPO   U.S. Government Printing Office

USNA   U.S. National Archives (Washington DC, unless noted otherwise)

USR   Utah Superintendency Records, 1853–70, roll 1, Miscellaneous Sources, 1859–70, microfilm M834, USNA

1. QUESTIONS AND ISSUES

1. Kroeber, *Handbook*, 889.

2. Steward, *Theory of Culture Change*, 5.

3. White, *Evolution of Culture*, 33–57.

4. Harris, *Cultural Materialism*, 77–113.

5. For example, Olson and Wilson, *Native Americans in the Twentieth Century*.

6. Barth, introduction to Barth, ed., *Ethnic Groups*, 9–38.

7. Redfield, Linton, and Herskovits, "Memorandum." Edward Spicer's *Cycles of Conquest* is among the best in the acculturation genre because he overtly acknowledges power differentials between groups.

8. For example, Bunte and Franklin, *From the Sands*; Churchill, *Struggle for the Land*. There are, of course, numerous fine, sophisticated, and detailed analyses of Indian-white relations that use variations of this simple paradigm as well as others. See Krech, "The State of Ethnohistory."

9. Roosens, *Creating Ethnicity*. Paiutes' ethnic self-identity as an Indian tribe today is not the cause of their ability to retain a distinctive culture but an expression of their success in doing so. In this I fundamentally disagree with Barth, who says that ascriptive category, by the group or by external identification, is a critical feature of ethnic maintenance (introduction to Barth, ed., *Ethnic Groups*, 13). In contradiction, he later equates ethnic group identity with participation in the community, an empirical social measure, rather than a psychological or cognitive self-awareness (Barth, introduction to Barth, ed., *Ethnic Groups*, 26). I believe that social identification is not a cause but a result of ethnicity. If a group were not actually a distinctive body in some way, people could not think of themselves as members of that group. While self-definition feeds back into the system and reinforces the structure of that system, it cannot create social networks or hierarchies in opposition to reality.

10. Hall, *Social Change*; Jorgensen, *Sun Dance Religion*; Wallerstein, *Modern World-System*; White, *Roots of Dependency*; Wolf, *Europe and the People*, esp. chap. 6.

2. FROM THE BEGINNING

1. Madsen and Rhode, eds., *Across the West*.

2. Brown, *Climates of the States: Nevada*.

3. Fowler, *Native Americans and Yucca Mountain*, I-5.

4. Fowler, *Models and Great Basin Prehistory*; Fowler and Madsen, "Pre-

history of the Southeastern Area"; Madsen and O'Connell, *Man and Environment*.

5. Miller, "Classification."

6. Fowler, "Settlement Patterns," 130; Kelly, *Southern Paiute Ethnography*, 24–26.

7. Fowler, "Settlement Patterns," 127.

8. Kelly and Fowler, "Southern Paiute," 380; Kelly, *Southern Paiute Ethnography*, 23; Laird, *Chemehuevis*, 7–9.

9. Euler, *Southern Paiute Ethnohistory*, 111–12; Kelly, *Southern Paiute Ethnography*, 39–41; Kelly and Fowler, "Southern Paiute," 371.

10. Bye, "Ethnobotany"; Fowler, "Environmental Setting"; Fowler and Matley, "The Palmer Collection"; Fowler and Euler, eds., "Kaibab Paiute and Northern Ute Ethnographic Field Notes," 790–812; Kelly, *Southern Paiute Ethnography*, 41–55; Kelly, unpublished ethnographic field notes for Moapa, 37–39; Kelly and Fowler, "Southern Paiute," 370–71; Powell, "Means of Subsistence"; Stewart, *Culture Element Distributions*, 240–56; Train, Henrichs, and Archer, "Medicinal Uses of Plants."

11. In the order they are mentioned above, the more formal botanical identifications of these plants are *Scirpus* sp., *Agave utahensis*, *Yucca brevifolia* or *angustissima*, *Prosopis juliflora*, *Prosopis pubescens*, *Agave utahensis*, and *Opuntia* sp. These and subsequent plant identifications are from Bowers, *Shrubs and Trees*; Elmore, *Shrubs and Trees*; Fowler and Euler, eds., "Kaibab Paiute and Northern Ute Ethnographic Field Notes," 864–65; Jaeger, *Desert Wild Flowers*; Munz, *California Desert Wildflowers*. See also Stuart, "Southern Paiute Staff of Life," and Stuart, "Pug-a-roo Gathers Mescal."

12. Kelly and Fowler, "Southern Paiute," 370.

13. Kelly, *Southern Paiute Ethnography*, 22–24; Powell, "Means of Subsistence," 38–39; Steward, *Basin-Plateau*, 182–84.

14. *Calochortus nuttallii*, *Shepherdia argentea*, *Rhus trilobata*, *Lycium* sp., and *Vitis arizonica*.

15. *Prunus virginiana*, *Rubus leucodenmis*, *Ribes aureum*, *Ribes montigenum*, *Amelanchier utahensis*, and *Pinus edulis*.

16. *Oryzopsis hymenoides*, *Rumex hymenosepalus*, *Streptanthus inlatus*, *Yucca schidigera*, and *Yucca brevifolia*.

17. *Pinus monophylla*. See Lanner, *The Piñon Pine*, 56–81; Stuart, "Pug-a-roo Picks Pine Nuts."

18. *Achillean millefolium, Glycyrrhiza lepidota, Artemisia tridentata, Eriodictyon angustifolium*, and *Arctostaphylos pungens*. See Bye, "Ethnobotany"; Inter-tribal Council of Nevada, *Nuwuvi*, 15.

19. Fowler and Dawson, "Ethnographic Basketry," 724–26; Fowler and Matley, *Material Culture*, 11–23.

20. *Salix exigua, Pinus* sp., *Yucca elata, Yucca brevifolia, Cowania mexicana, Apocynum cannabinum, Asclepian fascicularis, Phragmites communis, Amelanchier utahensis, Rhus trilobata, Sarcobatus* sp., and *Phragmites communis*. See Kelly and Fowler, "Southern Paiute," 375.

21. Fowler and Euler, eds., "Kaibab Paiute and Northern Ute Ethnographic Field Notes," 790–99, 864–65; Kelly, *Southern Paiute Ethnography*, 43; Powell, "Means of Subsistence," 48.

22. Fowler, "Settlement Patterns," 127; Kelly, *Southern Paiute Ethnography*, 6–22. The total population of the bands varied, as did the size of their territories, but that difference in total band populations may have had less to do with the carrying capacity of their landscapes than with the practical limitations of pedestrian travel.

23. Kelly, *Southern Paiute Ethnography*, 24–26, 121–30; Kelly and Fowler, "Southern Paiute," 380; Lowie, *Notes*, 275, 283–88.

24. Kelly, *Southern Paiute Ethnography*, 10–21.

25. Kelly, *Southern Paiute Ethnography*, 99–100; Kelly and Fowler, "Southern Paiute," 377; Lowie, *Notes*, 275; Stewart, *Culture Element Distributions*, 296.

26. Kelly, *Southern Paiute Ethnography*, 26–30; Kelly and Fowler, "Southern Paiute," 380–81; Fowler and Euler, eds., "Kaibab Paiute and Northern Ute Ethnographic Field Notes," 827; Stewart, *Culture Element Distributions*, 300.

27. Kelly, *Southern Paiute Ethnography*, 29.

28. Kelly and Fowler, "Southern Paiute," 370; Stewart, *Culture Element Distributions*, 240.

29. Kelly reports that Kaibab antelope drives were under secular leadership (*Southern Paiute Ethnography*, 50), while Stewart says bands south and

west of Shivwits had a special "hunt chief" and ritual preparation (*Culture Element Distributions*, 241). Both of these sources agreed with Sapir that only men took part in the rabbit drives (Fowler and Euler, eds., "Kaibab Paiute and Northern Ute Ethnographic Field Notes," 791–92), while Powell suggests that women and children helped drive the animals, at least in his generic description of Numics ("Means of Subsistence," 48).

30. Bye, "Ethnobotany."

31. Kelly, "Chemehuevi Shamanism"; Kelly, "Southern Paiute Shamanism"; Kelly and Fowler, "Southern Paiute," 383; Laird, "Chemehuevi Religious Beliefs," 22–23.

32. Kelly and Fowler, "Southern Paiute," 380.

33. Kelly and Fowler, "Southern Paiute," 381–82.

34. Laird, *The Chemehuevis*, 138; Kelly, "Southern Paiute Bands," 560; Fowler and Euler, eds., "Kaibab Paiute and Northern Ute Ethnographic Field Notes," 785.

35. Kelly, "Southern Paiute Bands," 550. See also Kelly, "Band Organization."

36. Kelly and Fowler, "Southern Paiute," 368, 380; Kelly, *Southern Paiute Ethnography*, 26–28; Fowler and Euler, eds., "Kaibab Paiute and Northern Ute Ethnographic Field Notes," 827; Stewart, *Culture Element Distributions*, 299–300. Opinions differ on the issue of leadership, although the actual evidence cited by authors who posit a more or less elaborate, hierarchical, permanent political structure need not necessarily conflict with the more egalitarian process I suggest here. Robert Manners contends that any political linkages above the level of the residential group were posthistoric creations ("Southern Paiute and Chemehuevi," 135–50). Euler is cautious but less doctrinaire, saying that larger groups occurred only temporarily in certain places under particular historical pressures (*Southern Paiute Ethnohistory*, 99–104). In 1874 Powell and Ingalls declared that the "original political organization of the tribes [bands] under consideration had a territorial basis; that is, the country was divided into districts, and each district was inhabited by a small tribe, which took the name of the land, and had one principal chief. These tribes, or 'land-nameds,' as they are called in the Indian idiom, were the only permanent organizations, but sometimes

two or more of them would unite in a confederacy under some great chief" (*Report*, 10). Bunte and Franklin describe the San Juan Paiutes as strongly united in action under leadership that passed from generation to generation through family lines, with both features strengthening in historic times (*From the Sands,* 31–35). On the basis of work with a single informant, Laird's rather idiosyncratic work describes a ranked, inherited hierarchy of sacrosanct offices, including a high chief, war chief, and subordinate camp leaders who were ceremonially distanced from their followers by use of formal criers to announce chiefly decisions and a distinct "chiefs' language" unknown to commoners (*The Chemehuevis*, 24–29). Amateur ethnographer William Palmer was most extreme and envisioned, probably on an ethnocentric Mormon model, a permanent, multilayered trans-Paiute chieftainship, where power delegated from the "great chief" was exercised by subordinates in charge of territorial subdivisions. Further, he said Southern Paiutes were a client nation to the Utes: "The Ute Nation was presided over by a royal family, and so far as can be ascertained, the ruling heads of the five independent tribes were of the same royal stock. This at least was true as to the Pahutes" ("Pahute Indian Government," 37; see also his "Pahute Indian Homelands").

37. Kelly, unpublished ethnographic field notes for Chemehuevi, 76–78, 81, 86.

3. FATHERS, FUR TRAPPERS, AND TRAVELERS

1. Haines, "The Northward Spread"; Jorgensen, "Great Basin Language," 81; Jorgensen, "Synchronic Relations," 89–90.

2. Jorgensen, "Great Basin Language," 21–31.

3. Callaway, Janetski, and Stewart, "Ute"; Smith, *Ethnography*; Steward, *Basin-Plateau*, 223, 235–36; Steward, "Changes"; Stewart, *Culture Element Distributions*.

4. Jones, "A Reinterpretation."

5. Compare Secoy, *Changing Military Patterns*, 86–95.

6. Auerbach, "Father Escalante's Route"; Bolton, "Escalante in Dixie"; Bolton, "Pageant in the Wilderness"; Chavez and Warner, *Dominguez-Escalante Journal*.

7. Euler, *Southern Paiute Ethnohistory*, 32–36.

8. Chavez and Warner, *Dominguez-Escalante Journal*, 85.

9. Chavez and Warner, *Dominguez-Escalante Journal*, 89–90.

10. Coues, *On the Trail*; Galvin, trans., *Record of Travels*.

11. Galvin, trans., *Record of Travels*, 32.

12. Spicer, *Cycles of Conquest*, 211–12.

13. Forbes, *Apache, Navajo and Spaniard*, 254–69.

14. Snow, "Utah Indians," 68.

15. Hafen, "Armijo's Journal"; Warren, "Armijo's Trace Revisited."

16. Warren, "Armijo's Trace Revisited," 28.

17. Hafen and Hafen, *Journals*, 19, 21.

18. Frémont, *A Report of the Exploring Expedition to Oregon*, 160.

19. See, for example, Jones, *Forty Years*, 49–50; Smith and Walker, *Indian Slave Trade*, 11.

20. Farnham, *Life and Adventures*, 377; Jones, *Forty Years*, 50.

21. Hafen and Hafen, *Old Spanish Trail*, 273; Bailey, *Indian Slave Trade*, 147.

22. Howard L. Conard, quoted in Alley, "Great Basin Numa," 364–65; Preuss, *Exploring with Frémont*, 134.

23. Alley, "Prelude to Dispossession"; Malouf and Malouf, "The Effects of Spanish Slavery."

24. Jones, *Forty Years*, 50.

25. Garland Hurt, quoted in Simpson, *Report of Explorations*, 461–62.

26. "The Story of an Old Trapper: Life & Adventures of the Late Peg-Leg Smith," *San Francisco Evening Bulletin*, 26 October 1866.

27. Morgan and Wheat, *Jedediah Smith*, 62.

28. Both from Jedediah Smith to General William Clark, Superintendent of Indian Affairs, 15 November 1827, extract in *U.S. Gazette*, 15 November 1827, 2, cols. 3–4, copy in the Newberry Library, Chicago.

29. Daniel Potts, quoted in Hafen and Hafen, *Old Spanish Trail*, 121.

30. Alley, "Prelude to Dispossession."

31. Camp, "Chronicles," 39.

32. Camp, "Chronicles," 38; Camp, *George C. Yount*, 73.

33. Camp, "Chronicles," 38.

34. Euler, *Southern Paiute Ethnohistory*, 37–43.

35. "The Story of an Old Trapper."

36. Camp, "Chronicles," 73; Pattie, *Personal Narrative*.

37. Manly, *Death Valley*, 115.

38. Hafen and Hafen, *Journals*, 185.

39. Manly, *Death Valley*, 119.

40. Brown, ed., *Autobiography*, 111.

41. Manly, *Death Valley*, 119.

42. O. Pratt, quoted in Hafen and Hafen, *Old Spanish Trail*, 352; see also Nusbaumer, *Valley of Salt*, 36.

43. Manly, *Death Valley*, 116–17.

44. This was probably "bug sugar." See Harrington, "Bug Sugar." Quote from Manly, *Death Valley*, 126.

45. Manly, *Death Valley*, 133.

46. Hafen and Hafen, *Old Spanish Trail*, 185 (quote), 186.

47. Hafen and Hafen, *Old Spanish Trail*, 354.

48. John Brown, Journal, entry for 1 January 1850, copied into Church of Jesus Christ of Latter-day Saints, Journal History of the Church of Jesus Christ of Latter-day Saints, 1 January 1850, LDS-CHO. Hereafter cited as Church, Journal History.

49. Preuss, *Exploring with Frémont*, 130.

50. Hafen and Hafen, *Old Spanish Trail*, 355.

51. Preuss, *Exploring with Frémont*, 127–28.

52. Farnham, *Life and Adventures*, 378.

53. Hafen and Hafen, *Old Spanish Trail*, 351.

54. Nusbaumer, *Valley of Salt*, 44.

55. Frémont, *Report of the Exploring Expedition to the Rocky Mountains*, 267.

56. Manly, *Death Valley*.

57. Nusbaumer, *Valley of Salt*, 38.

58. Christopher Carson, quoted in Hafen and Hafen, *Old Spanish Trail*, 314.

59. Cronon's innovative ecological history of New England proposes that much interracial conflict stemmed from differing ideological conceptions of animals rooted in the Indian and non-Indian cultures (*Changes in the Land*, 127–56). He suggests that Indians without domesticated animals categorized them with deer, created by nature to be hunted equally by all. Left to run loose to forage in the woodlands, the stock was hunted by Indians, which Euro-Americans considered theft of private property. Cronon argues that these cross-cultural misunderstandings persisted for generations. Surely it would have soon become obvious to New England Indians, as it did to Paiutes, that Euro-Americans were willing to fight and even kill to retain the docile animals they brought with them. Even if they were themselves unwilling to accept livestock as personal property (and the record is silent on this point), they were not foolish enough to refuse to acknowledge that Euro-Americans did. To maintain otherwise shows a very low estimation of Indians' intelligence, flexibility, and sense of self-preservation.

60. Alley, "Prelude to Dispossession."

61. Inter-tribal Council of Nevada, *Nuwuvi*, 51, 70. This simply reverses the stereotyping process onto Euro-Americans.

4. MORMONS MEET PAIUTES

1. Hansen, *Mormonism*, 48; Vogel, *Indian Origins*.

2. Hansen, *Mormonism*, 8–9; Vogel, *Indian Origins*, 49–51.

3. Book of Mormon, 2 Nephi 5:21, 2 Nephi 30:5–6.

4. Book of Mormon, Enos 1:20.

5. McMurrin, *Theological Foundations*, 96–109.

6. Brigham Young, quoted in Church, *Journal of Discourses*, 7:336. See also Young, 9 April 1871, in Church, *Journal of Discourses*, 14:86–87.

7. Orson Pratt, "Salvation of the House of Israel to Come Through the Gentiles," in Church, *Journal of Discourses*, 9:174–79. See also Pratt, 7 February 1875, in Church, *Journal of Discourses*, 17:301; Whittaker, "Mormons and Native Americans," 38.

8. Church, Journal History, 30 December 1849.

9. George Washington Bean, "Report of Exploration in South Western Deserts of Utah Territory," 7 June 1858, typescript copy, Charles Kelly Papers, ms. no. B-114, Utah State Historical Society, Salt Lake City, 2; Little, *Jacob Hamblin*, 88, 92; Woolf and Grant, "Albinism."

10. Arrington, *Great Basin Kingdom*, 10–11.

11. Heinerman and Shupe, *The Mormon Corporate Empire*.

12. Arrington, *Great Basin Kingdom*, 84–95; Hansen, *Mormonism*; Stegner, *The Gathering of Zion*.

13. Brooks, ed., *Journal*, 2–4; Cleland and Brooks, eds., *A Mormon Chronicle*, 1:132–33.

14. Arrington, *Great Basin Kingdom*, 50–55, 96–130; Arrington, Fox, and May, *Building the City of God*; Nelson, *The Mormon Village*.

15. Mike Carter, "Mormon Church Runs Utah Behind Scenes," *Las Vegas Review Journal*, 22 March 1993, 1A, 2A; Larson, *The "Americanization" of Utah*. For a descriptive example, see Dalton, comp., *History*, 27–29.

16. Church, *Journal of Discourses*, 11:264. For the general application of this stance with regard to other tribes in Utah, see the discussion in Larson, "Land Contest," 313.

17. Brigham Young to H. S. Eldredge, 29 May 1857, quoted in Arrington, *Great Basin Kingdom*, 169.

18. Arrington, *Great Basin Kingdom*, 117.

19. Church, Journal History, 30 December 1849.

20. John D. Lee to Br. Richards, 7 August 1852, *Deseret News* (Salt Lake City), 4 September 1852.

21. Aroet Hale to "Dear Companion," 12 June 1855, ms. no. D 3212, folder 1, item no. 3, LDS-CHO.

22. Anson Call to George A. Smith, 25 December 1864, *Deseret Weekly News*, 18 January 1865. Much of that "use" was by Mormon-owned cattle.

23. Alley, "Great Basin Numa," 123. There are hints that Hopis too may have sought a Mormon alliance in their uneasy relations with neighboring Navajos (Cleland and Brooks, eds., *A Mormon Chronicle*, 2:295–96).

24. Jacob Hamblin to Editor, *Deseret News*, 4 April 1855, printed in *Utah Historical Quarterly* 5 (1934): 131–34.

25. Brooks, ed., *Journal*, 104.

26. Henry Lunt, Journal, typescript copy, Manuscripts and Archives Division, Brigham Young University Library, Provo, Utah, 152.

27. George Smith, Journal of George A. Smith, President of the Iron County Mission, typescript copy, Utah State Historical Society, Salt Lake City, 23.

28. James Wittaker, Diary, January 1851–July 1852, ms. no. 8189, LDS-CHO, entry for 11 March 1852.

29. The common usage of "Indian," with tribal identity unmarked, is very noticeable in the frontier period sources, even when they clearly conceived a distinction between pedestrian "local Indians" and mounted "foreign" ones.

30. Knack, "Political Strategies."

31. Arrington, *Great Basin Kingdom*, 195–244; Madsen, *Corinne*; Utah Territorial Legislature, "A Preamble and an Act for the Further Relief of Indian Slaves and Prisoners," 1852, reprinted in *Utah Historical Quarterly* 2 (1929): 84–86.

32. George A. Smith to all whom it may concern, 20 March 1851, reprinted in Brooks, "Indian Relations," 6.

33. Brigham Young, quoted in Brooks, "Indian Relations," 6. See also Brooks, *Dudley Leavitt*, 57.

34. Jones, *Forty Years*, 53.

35. Smith, Journal, 6–7.

36. Jacob Hamblin, Journal, 1854–57, typescript copy, Utah State Historical Society, Salt Lake City, 21. See also the violent intertribal warfare Iroquois and others engaged in to maintain their lucrative middleman positions in the beaver fur trade (see Fenton, "The Iroquois"; Ray, *Indians in the Fur Trade*; Trigger, "Early Iroquoian Contacts").

37. Hamblin, Journal, 6, 25.

38. Brooks, ed., *Journal*, 135.

39. Bonsel, ed., *Edward Fitzgerald Beale*, 141.

40. Brooks, *Dudley Leavitt*, 57.

41. Jorgensen, *Sun Dance Religion*, 34; Dalton, comp., *History*, 80.

42. Church of Jesus Christ of Latter-day Saints, "History of Brigham Young," n.d., ms., LDS-CHO, 140.

43. Bonsel, ed., *Edward Fitzgerald Beale*, 142.

44. Lunt, Journal, 136. Another observer of this same incident recorded that Utes killed or wounded twenty Paiute men and seized additional women and children (John D. Lee to Bro. Richards, 5 February 1853, *Deseret News*, 19 March 1853).

45. Henry Lunt to George A. Smith, 12 February 1853, Church, Journal History, 12 February 1853.

46. John D. Lee to Editor, 24 January 1854, *Deseret News*, 16 February 1854.

47. Christopher J. Arthur, Autobiography, n.d., typescript copy, ms. no. A 25–1, Utah State Historical Society, Salt Lake City, 18.

48. Cleland and Brooks, eds., *A Mormon Chronicle*, 1:167.

49. Cleland and Brooks, eds., *A Mormon Chronicle*, 1:168.

50. See, for example, Rachel Lee, Diary of February 1856–July 1860, typescript copy, ms. no. 918, LDS-CHO (original in Huntington Library), 9, 12, 72; Brooks, *Dudley Leavitt*, 57.

51. Brooks, "Indian Relations."

52. Knack, "Political Strategies."

53. King, "Millard County," 150. These assumptions continued historically; see, for example, Palmer, "Pahute Indian Government"; Palmer, "Pahute Indian Homelands."

54. See, for example, Jensen, ed., *History*, 228, 234, 279.

55. See, for example, Lorenzo Brown, Diaries, 1853–59, microfilm copy, ms. no. 1563, LDS-CHO, 5 June 1856, 22 February 1857.

56. For example, James Martineau, "An Indian Dinner," typescript in Dana

Roberts, comp., "Selected Parowan Ward Records," n.d., ms. no. 3346, LDS-CHO, n.p.

57. Brooks, ed., *Journal*, 24; Amasa Lyman, Journal no. 16, n.d., typescript copy, Public Library, St. George, Utah, 18; John Steele to George A. Smith, *Deseret News*, 30 November 1854.

58. Isaac C. Haight to Erastus Snow, 9 June 1855, *St. Louis Luminary*, 18 August 1855.

59. Anderson, "Apostle Lyman's Mission," 515.

60. Lee to Richards, 7 August 1852. See also Lunt, Journal, 93–94; a more colorful version is in Brooks, *John Doyle Lee*, 173–74. For similar incidents, most instigated by petty theft, see John Harris Henderson, Autobiography, 1909, microfilm copy, ms. no. 7253, LDS-CHO, 34; King, "Millard County," 29. See Brooks, ed., *Journal*, 100, for a reverse instance of a Mormon being whipped for beating a Paiute with his rifle barrel; and Brooks, *Dudley Leavitt*, 58–60, for Paiutes being urged to hang an Indian for stealing Mormon horses.

61. Arrington, "How the Saints Fed."

62. Knack, "Political Strategies."

63. For example, Ellen Bird, Indian Chief Kanosh, 1937, typescript, Works Projects Administration, Archival and Manuscript Records, Library of Congress, Washington DC; O. H. Irish to Commissioner of Indian Affairs D. N. Cooley, 9 September 1865, in ARCIA, 1865, 311–14; Melville, "Chief Kanosh."

64. Dimick B. Huntington to Church Historian, 1 September 1856, copied into Church, Journal History, 1 September 1856.

65. On visits, see Church, Journal History, 24 August 1853, 1 September 1857, 28 April 1876. For correspondence, see Kanosh to President Brigam [*sic*] Young, 13 December 1868, Brigham Young Collection, ms. no. 1234, reel 91, LDS-CHO, no frame numbers. On marriage, see Kane, *Twelve Mormon Homes*, 65, n. 38, 71; Carter, "Indian Women," 6–7, which also reproduces a photograph of the wife on the cover; Golden Buchanan, Interviews, December 1974–March 1975 with William Hartley, ms. no. 200/186/3, LDS-CHO, 28. On baptism, see Church, Journal History, 11 May 1874. On acculturation, see Brown, Diaries, 15 March 1857; photograph from National Anthropological Archives, Smithson-

ian Institution, printed in Fowler and Fowler, eds., *Anthropology of the Numa*, 17.

66. On treaty signings, see King, "Millard County," 153; "Treaty of Spanish Fork," 8 June 1865 (unratified), in usna, microfilm t494, Documents Relating to the Negotiation of Ratified and Unratified Treaties with Various Indian Tribes, 1801–69, roll 8, no frame numbers. On house, see Bailey, "Last Wife"; Kane, *Twelve Mormon Homes*, 71. On translator, see Dimik Huntington to the Editor, 8 February 1852 [*sic*], *Deseret News*, 19 February 1853. On land deed, see Church, Journal History, 20 March 1854; the irony of Young issuing a deed for land to an individual Indian man when tribal title had not yet passed out of Indian hands can only be explained by the Mormon theological assumption of divine ownership of the earth and hence its automatic stewardship by the church. On the presidential medal, see F. H. Head to D. N. Cooley, 13 August 1866, bia-lr, roll 902, no frame number.

67. Brigham Young, "Our Indian Relations—How to Deal with Them," 28 July 1866, Church, *Journal of Discourses*, 11:263.

68. Brigham Young, "Proper Treatment of the Indians, etc.," 6 April 1854, Church, *Journal of Discourses*, 6:329; Church, "History of Brigham Young," 51.

69. Dalton, comp., *History*, 29.

70. Brooks, ed., *Journal*; Jensen, ed., *History*.

71. Arrington, *Great Basin Kingdom*, 86.

72. Brigham Young to Hamblin, 4 August 1857, quoted in Brooks, "Indian Relations," 20.

73. John Steele, quoted in Jensen, ed., *History*, 171.

74. As quoted in Law, "Mormon Indian Missions," 6.

75. Brooks, ed., *Journal*, 25, emphasis in the original.

76. Jensen, ed., *History*, 159.

77. Lee, Diary, 8.

78. Aroet Hale, Reminiscences, c. 1882, microfilm copy, ms. no. 1590, lds-cho, 18.

79. Brigham Young to Rufus C. Allen, 1 March 1857, ms. no. 578, Manuscript Collection, Brigham Young University Library, Provo ut.

80. Young to Allen, 1 March 1857. See also Cleland and Brooks, eds., *A Mormon Chronicle*, 1:155, 160–63, 165, 169, 190–94, 206–7, 214; Knack, "Nineteenth Century," 145–62.

81. Brooks, ed., *Journal*, 103. Missionaries were also expected to discover and report exploitable resources as they moved through Indian territory. See, for example, Brigham Young to William Bringhurst, 4 August 1856, in Jensen, ed., *History*, 235–36.

82. Brooks, ed., *Journal*, 29–30.

83. Brooks, ed., *Journal*, passim; Jensen, ed., *History*, 17, passim.

84. Young to Allen, 1 March 1857, 2. See also Brooks, ed., *Journal*, 54, 59.

85. Young to Bringhurst, 4 August 1856, in Jensen, ed., *History*, 235.

86. Stucki, *Family History*, 53.

87. Knack, "Missionaries."

88. Hale, Reminiscences, 12.

89. Lee to Editor, 16 February 1854.

90. For examples of solicited curing, see Brown, Diaries, 9 June 1856; George Washington Bean, Diary, December 1854–March 1856, typescript copy, ms. no. A-68, Utah State Historical Society, Salt Lake City, 6, 27. For blessings, see Lee, Diary, 48. For burials, see Brown, Diaries, 28 February 1857.

91. Jensen, ed., *History*, 165–66.

92. Bean, Diary, 4, 16. One is reminded of the mass Catholic baptisms in early Spanish colonial days; see Spicer, *Cycles of Conquest*, 48, 88.

93. Jensen, ed., *History*, 166. See also Cedar Ward, Church of Jesus Christ of Latter-day Saints, Extracts from Ward History Record, 3 February 1875, typescript copy, Historical Digest Book F, William R. Palmer Papers, Southern Utah State University, Cedar City UT, n.p. Hereafter cited as Palmer Papers.

94. James G. Bleak, "Annals of the Southern Utah Mission," typescript copy, Utah State Historical Society, Salt Lake City, 2 vols., 1:114.

95. Huntington to Editor, 19 February 1853. See also Little, *Jacob Hamblin*, 113–18; Ida Chidester, Indian Tribe (Piute), c. 1930, Manuscript Collection, Daughters of the Utah Pioneers, Salt Lake City, 7.

96. Brooks, ed., *Journal*, 85–86.

97. Garland Hurt to Commissioner of Indian Affairs, 2 May 1855, in ARCIA, 1857–58, 593.

98. Brooks, "Indian Relations," 31.

99. Brooks, *Dudley Leavitt*, 45–48, 100; Brooks, "Indian Relations," 38–39, 42–43; Brooks, *Quicksand and Cactus*, 50; Little, *Jacob Hamblin*, 72.

100. Cleland and Brooks, eds., *A Mormon Chronicle*, 1:181, 184; Lee, Diary, 61–62.

101. Aroet Hale to "Dear Companion," 12 June 1855, ms. no. D-3212, item no. 3, 1–2, LDS-CHO.

102. Aroet Hale to "Dear Companion," 9 September 1855, ms. no. D-3212, item no. 9, LDS-CHO.

103. Hamblin, Journal, 33. The prevalent Western nineteenth-century use of the terms "buck," "squaw," and "papoose" to refer to Paiute men, women, and children clearly had the effect, if not necessarily the intentional purpose, of dehumanizing them. The popular use in Utah of the name of a game animal to refer to Indian males is neither accidental nor meaningless.

104. Jensen, ed., *History*, 170.

105. Stewart, "A Brief History," 20.

106. Brooks, "Indian Relations," 48.

107. Alter, ed., "Journal," 193; Brooks, *Quicksand and Cactus*, 43.

108. Brooks, *Jacob Hamblin*, 106; Little, *Jacob Hamblin*, 113–18.

109. Hamblin, Journal, 17–18.

5. PAIUTES MEET MORMONS

1. King, "Millard County," 148; Holt, *Beneath These Red Cliffs*, 154.

2. Sadly, the reverse is not true; numerous incidents of indiscriminate non-Indian attacks on native communities litter the documents, often told with pride in the intrepid ancestors who attacked with sometimes only trivial causes.

3. Arrington, *Great Basin Kingdom*, 50, 160–94, 437; Haynes, "Federal Government."

4. Jacob Holeman to Commissioner of Indian Affairs Luke Lea, 28 December 1851, quoted in Brooks, "Indian Relations," 15.

5. Jacob Holeman to Luke Lea, 29 February 1852, BIA-LR, roll 897, Utah 1846–55, no frame numbers.

6. Garland Hurt to Commissioner of Indian Affairs George Manypenny, 2 May 1855, BIA-LR, roll 897, Utah 1846–55, no frame numbers.

7. Thomas Flint, Diary, quoted in Brooks, "Indian Relations," 19. Tick-a-boo is the consistent frontier Mormon transliteration of the Paiute word *tïyvï*, "friend" (Sapir, *Southern Paiute Dictionary*, 682).

8. John Wesley Powell, "Las Vegas Vocabulary and Grammatical Notes," May 1873, in Fowler and Fowler, eds., *Anthropology of the Numa*, 152. "Mormoni" is still frequently asserted by twentieth-century Mormon historians to be a generic Paiute term for "white man."

9. Sylvester Mowry to Col. S. Cooper, 23 July 1855, War Department Records, Selected Letters of Sylvester Mowry, 1854–55, microfilm 106, Utah State Historical Society, Salt Lake City.

10. Lunt, Journal, 52. See also Cleland and Brooks, eds., *A Mormon Chronicle*, 1:iii; U.S. Congress, House of Representatives, *Investigation*.

11. Arrington, "Mormons and the Indians," 16; Brooks, "Indian Relations," 23; Joseph Clarke and John Pierce, Map of Corn Creek Reservation, 1 January 1867, USNA, Map Division, Alexandria VA; Jackson, "Mormon Indian Farms"; Royce, *Indian Land Cessions*, 830; Tyler, "The Indians in Utah Territory," 359; Brigham Young to Utah territorial observer in Congress John M. Bernhisel, 20 November 1850, copy in LDS-CHO; Brigham Young, Proclamation, 21 July 1851, BIA-LR, roll 897, Utah 1846–55, no frame numbers; Brigham Young to Garland Hurt, 23 November 1855, microfilm copy, ms. no. 1234, reel 93, Brigham Young Collection, LDS-CHO.

12. William Bringhurst to the Editor, 10 July 1855, *Deseret News*, 8 August 1855, parenthetical in the original. See also Bleak, "Annals," 1:116; Larson, "Brigham Young and the Indians"; Spencer, "The Development of Agricultural Villages."

13. Cohen, *Handbook*, 510–22.

14. A. W. Babbitt to the Editor, 28 November 1853, *Deseret News*, 4 December 1853; Church, Journal History, 25 October 1853; Gibbs, "Gunnison

Massacre"; Dimick B. Huntington to Brigham Young, 11 November 1853, copy in Brigham Young Collection, ms. no. 1234, reel 91, no frame numbers, LDS-CHO, abbreviated version published in *Deseret News*, 11 November 1853; Miller, "Impact of the Gunnison Massacre," 165–80; Stephen Rose to Brigham Young, 31 March 1854, Brigham Young Collection, ms. no. 1234, reel 93, no frame numbers, LDS-CHO. These clearly unlikely assassins were nonetheless tried, convicted, and sentenced, but they promptly escaped the territorial prison.

It is not insignificant that this railroad, when completed, would end Utah's isolation as an exclusive Mormon community. Because this high profile murder seemed to have served Mormon interests so well, and in light of the subsequent Mountain Meadows incident, there was considerable speculation in the East that Gunnison's killing had not been exclusively an Indian homicide (Fielding, *Unsolicited Chronicler*; Miller, "Impact of the Gunnison Massacre," 81–83; Simpson, *Shortest Route*, 45).

15. Israel Call, quoted in Miller, "Impact of the Gunnison Massacre," 36, see also 44, 51.

16. "We Stop the Presses to Announce," *Deseret News*, 11 November 1853.

17. Angel, *History of Nevada*, 45–46; Brooks, *The Mountain Meadows Massacre*; Church, Journal History, 21 September 1857; Penrose, *The Mountain Meadows Massacre*. Reasoned argument quickly gave way to diatribe against the Mormon Church; see, for example, Gibbs, *Lights and Shadows*. For the long-term effects of these suspicions of church involvement, see Larson, *The "Americanization" of Utah*; U.S. Congress, House of Representatives, *Mountain Meadow Massacre*. The suspicion of extensive church involvement persists; see, for example, Backus, *Mountain Meadows Witness*; Bigler, *Forgotten Kingdom*, 159–80; Quinn, *The Mormon Hierarchy*, 248–54, 260.

18. Brooks, *John Doyle Lee*; Lee, *Life and Confession*.

19. James H. Martineau, "Record: Parowan, 1855–1860," typescript, Palmer Papers, 26, 34. Other folkloric explanations, such as bullwhipping oxen addressed as "Joe Smith" and "Brigham" while moving down the main street of Cedar City, are harder to envision as causes of Indian wrath (Penrose, *The Mountain Meadows Massacre*, 8–10; Brooks, *The Mountain Meadows Massacre*, 44–52).

20. See contemporary but secondary accounts of native testimony in John

Cradlebaugh, "Utah and the Mormons, a Speech Given to U.S. House of Representatives upon Admission of Utah as a State," 7 February 1863 (privately printed, n.d.), Graff Collection, ms. no. 899, Newberry Library, Chicago; William Rogers to the Editor, *Valley Tan* (Salt Lake City), 29 February 1860, copy in Graff Collection, ms. no. 4453, Newberry Library, Chicago, 2–3. See also the oral history account of Frank Beckwith, *Indian Joe: In Person and in Background* (privately printed, 1939), copy in Utah State Historical Society, Salt Lake City, 69–71.

21. Kroeber and Kroeber, *Mohave War Reminiscence*, 13–14.

22. Brooks, *John Doyle Lee*, 224; Garland Hurt to Superintendent of Indian Affairs Jacob Forney, 4 December 1859, printed in U.S. Congress, Senate, *Message of the President*, 96. See, however, the very important accusation by J. D. Lee's disaffected wife, Rachel Lee (Diary, 40).

23. On the other hand, the case for Mormon culpability in the event is convincing, stemming from Mormons' fears of imminent attack by the U.S. Army because of Utah's separatism and practice of polygyny; a wave of religious fervor that swept the southern settlements that same autumn preaching "blood atonement" for heresy; and the recent murder of a very high church official, Parley Pratt, in Arkansas, the home state of the travelers (Brooks, *The Mountain Meadows Massacre*, 52–59, 211–22; Neff, *History of Utah*, 411–25; Bigler, *Forgotten Kingdom*, 159–80; Quinn, *The Mormon Hierarchy*, 248–54). Such arguments, however, lie in the area of historical quarreling between Euro-American populations and as such lie outside of our interests here. The relevant factor is that an attempt was made to pass off the event as an Indian massacre, with the assumption that this explanation would not be questioned by the American public. Such faith in the racist presumptions of native hostility reflects the frontier attitudes of the times, attitudes that the Mormons of Utah shared with their fellow Americans.

24. Ida Chidester, Indian Tribe (Piute), c. 1930, Manuscript Collection, Daughters of the Utah Pioneers, Salt Lake City, 1–3. Notice that this author again gives no reason, and does not apparently see the need for one, for Paiutes to "become very hostile" other than their inherent Indianness. See also Bradley, "The Whitmore-McIntyre Dugout," 41.

25. Mr. and Mrs. Higbee, Interview with Juanita Brooks, 19 June 1935, Juanita Brooks Papers, Utah State Historical Society, Salt Lake City, 1. Hereafter cited as Brooks Papers.

26. Church, Journal History, 10 March 1866. See also Dalton, comp., *History*, 97–101; Little, *Jacob Hamblin*, 109–18; David McMullin, Interview with Wilma Hartman, 20 June 1935, ms. no. B-103, Brooks Papers; Walter Clement Powell to Editor, *Chicago Tribune*, 12 June 1872, in Kelly, ed., "Journal," 420; Woodbury, "A History," 177–78.

27. Bunte and Franklin, *From the Sands*, 62–72.

28. Bleak, "Annals," 1:210, see also 268, 325.

29. Morton Brigham Cutler, Autobiography of Morton Brigham Cutler, c. 1940, ms. no. 4515, LDS-CHO, 3–4. See also George F. Fawcett, Memoirs of George W. Fawcett, of Lund, White Pine County, Nevada, 1936, Brooks Papers, 9–10.

30. For example, Dalton (comp., *History*, 101) accuses Navajos alone, while Bradley ("The Whitmore-McIntyre Dugout," 42) and Melinda P. Roundy (Indians in Kanab and Other Settlements, n.d., Manuscript Collection, Daughters of the Utah Pioneers, Salt Lake City, 2) accuse Navajos and Paiutes of working together.

31. Daniel McArthur, letter without addressee, 21 January 1866, copied in Bleak, "Annals," 1:204. See also Woodbury, "A History," 168.

32. McArthur, letter without addressee. See also family reminiscence versions in Woodbury, "A History," 168, and Etta H. Spendlove, Memories and Experiences of James Jepson, Jr., 1934, ms. no. A-31, Utah State Historical Society, Salt Lake City, 14–15.

33. Lydia Johnson and Martha Johnson, Biographical Sketch of Seth E. Johnson, n.d., typescript copy, ms. no. 4888, LDS-CHO, 28–30.

34. Bradley, "The Whitmore-McIntyre Dugout," 42.

35. Martha E. Averett, Memoirs, 1951, typescript copy, Brooks Papers, 3; George A. Smith, Journal, quoted in Church, Journal History, 14 February 1866.

36. Dalton, comp., *History*, 102; Woodbury, "A History," 170. See also John M. Berry to Apostle A. W. Ivans [*sic*], 8 March 1916, Anthony W. Ivins Papers, Utah State Historical Society, Salt Lake City (hereafter cited as Ivins Papers); Gottfredson, *Indian Depredations*, 181; Peterson, *Utah's Black Hawk War*.

37. Dalton, comp., *History*, 102.

38. Berry to Ivans, 2; Woodbury, "A History," 170. Why a whole Paiute family would be involved in an attack was never questioned. Although the bodies were not discovered for at least four days, and the Indians were never tracked, some sources firmly assert that the leader of the attack was the headman of the local Kaibab band, Timpenampats. One oral account asserts that the Paiute killed at the site was Timpenampats himself, that his sons swore revenge, murdered a white militiaman years later, and were themselves killed by John D. Lee in distant Beaver (Anthony W. Ivins, notes on conversation with Nephi Johnson, 1–2 September 1917, Ivins Papers). Another version specified, "One of the men who was responsible for this bloodshed was a Paiute called Cold Creek John [a headman near Cedar City]. On a number of occasions Berry [surviving brother William] tried to get in a position to kill this Indian, but the latter was always a little bit too wary" (John H. Davies, *Among My Memories* [privately printed, 1941], copy in Utah State Historical Society, ms. no. A-2461, 18).

39. B. A. Riggs, "The Life Story of Quag-unt, a Piute Indian," 11 June 1938, Works Project Administration, Folklore Manuscript Collection, box A686, Library of Congress, Washington DC, 1–2.

40. Higbee, Interview.

41. Woodbury, "A History," 170.

42. Winkler, "The Circleville Massacre."

43. Henderson, Autobiography, 47.

44. Henderson, Autobiography, 47.

45. Christian Larsen, "Biographical Sketch" ms., as quoted in Winkler, "The Circleville Massacre," 18. This section quoted from the manuscript source differs in the published version of Larsen's reminiscence. See also a native reminiscence in Martineau, *Southern Paiutes,* 58–59.

    The few young children allowed to live were presumably too young to remember or tell of the events. The similarity between this saving of the very young and the rationale for it is strongly reminiscent of the events and pronouncements following the Mountain Meadows Massacre, when a few young immigrant children were also allowed to live and fostered out to Mormon families (Brooks, *The Mountain Meadows Massacre,* 97–109).

46. Mrs. Gibbs Monsen to William Palmer, Jimmie Pete, "and all of you," 6 August 1936, Palmer Papers, 2–3.

47. Brooks, ed., *Journal*, 58.

48. Brooks, *Dudley Leavitt*, 38–39; Martha Cragun Cox, Autobiography, c. 1928–30, microfilm copy, ms. no. 1661, LDS-CHO, 155.

49. Caroline H. Behunin, Reminiscences, n.d., ms. no. 6649, LDS-CHO, 2–4.

50. Bean, Diary, 3.

51. Bean, Diary, 17. See also Jensen, ed., *History*, 169, 181.

52. Brown, Diaries, 18 June 1856.

53. Jensen, ed., *History*, 222, and compare 228, 234, 239, 246, 250.

54. Brooks, ed., *Journal*, 58, see also 41, 60, 87.

55. Jensen, ed., *History*, 178.

56. Brigham Young to William Bringhurst, 30 October 1855, copied in Jensen, ed., *History*, 179.

57. Bean, Diary, 23, see also 17, 18, 19, 22, 24; Jensen, ed., *History*, 175, 178, 198, 209, 222, 251.

58. Cleland and Brooks, eds., *A Mormon Chronicle*, 1:192. See also the incident described on page 190.

59. Little, *Jacob Hamblin*, 43.

60. John Wilbert Chamberlin to W. H. Chamberlin, 6 March 1863, microfilm copy, ms. no. 6510, LDS-CHO.

61. Martineau, "An Indian Dinner."

62. Perkins, *Pioneers of the Western Desert*, 16.

63. Lyman, *Indians and Outlaws*, 58.

64. Andrew Jensen, comp., "Manuscript History of the Muddy Mission," n.d., microfilm copy, ms. no. 4029/13/4, reel 8, LDS-CHO, entry for 15 February 1868.

65. William Foote, Journal, n.d., microfilm copy, ms. no. 42, LDS-CHO, 1:195–97.

66. Leo Thompson, Personal Pioneer History of His Mother, Mrs. James Thompson, n.d., typescript, Works Project Administration, Writers' Project, Utah State Historical Society, Salt Lake City, 1.

67. W. H. Crawford to the Editor, *Deseret News*, 25 February 1860, emphasis added.

68. Willis E. Robison, Pioneer Interview with Mary L. Reeve, 22 January 1937, McQuown Papers, Manuscripts Collection, University of Utah, Salt Lake City, 10–11.

69. Bleak, "Annals," 1:207. See also Jensen, comp., "Manuscript History," entry for February 1866. In the early twentieth century, Mouse and Avote were similarly hunted and killed by Paiutes, necessarily with the acquiescence, if not cooperation, of their relatives, probably in order to rid the community of a threat. That threat was not their own violent behavior but the potential of drawing the wrath of the Euro-American legal structure and of unofficial non-Indians down on the whole native community.

70. Little, *Jacob Hamblin*, 97–98.

71. Hamblin, Journal, 24.

72. Woodfield, "Initiation," 38.

6. THE MILITARY, MINERS, AND MOAPA

1. Arrington, *Great Basin Kingdom*, 241–43.

2. Spier, *Yuman Tribes*, 11–18; Kroeber, *Handbook*, 796–803.

3. Kroeber and Kroeber, *Mohave War Reminiscence*, 3, 84; Spicer, *Cycles of Conquest*, 267; Foreman, ed., *Pathfinder*, 232.

4. Galvin, trans., *Record of Travels*, 33; Kroeber, *Shoshonean Dialects*, 106; Kroeber, *Handbook*, 594. Compare Kelly, Unpublished Ethnographic Field Notes from Chemehuevi, 26–31.

5. Kelly, Unpublished Ethnographic Field Notes from Chemehuevi, 14–17; Laird, *The Chemehuevis*; Laird, *Mirror and Pattern*; Roth, "Incorporation and Changes," 85–89; Stewart, "Chemehuevi Culture Changes."

6. Kroeber and Kroeber, *Mohave War Reminiscence*, 13–14; Udell, *Journal*, 28, 32.

7. W. W. MacKall to Col. Hoffman, 31 January 1859, in U.S. Department of War, *Annual Report* (1860), 407–8.

8. Spicer, *Cycles of Conquest*, 269–70.

9. Kroeber and Kroeber, *Mohave War Reminiscence*, 57.

10. Charles Poston, "Treaty between Tribes of Mohaves, Pimos and Papagos, Maricopas, Yuma, Chemanowee, and Wallapyes," 9 April 1863, USNA, RG 279, Records of the U.S. Indian Claims Commission, docket 351, exhibit 28. The political support of individual enterprise through federal actions and expenditures for military force is exceptionally transparent here.

11. Pub. L. No. 38-127, 13 Stat. 541, 559 (1865).

12. Kroeber and Kroeber, *Mohave War Reminiscence*, 83–86. Chemehuevi oral history says the war originated when a Mohave man abused a Chemehuevi woman, which demanded vengeance; this may recall simply an immediate cause or a single, early incident in the conflict and need not contradict the existence of additional larger and more deeply rooted causes (Kelly, Unpublished Ethnographic Field Notes from Chemehuevi, 31–36). For subsequent events, see George Dent to Commissioner of Indian Affairs, 15 July 1867, in ARCIA, 1868, 154–58; Kelly, Unpublished Ethnographic Field Notes from Chemehuevi, 37; Kroeber, *Handbook*, 32, 37; Kroeber and Kroeber, *Mohave War Reminiscence*, 86–88; Stewart, "A Brief History," 21; Woodward, *Feud*, 116, 187–88.

13. James Leithead to Erastus Snow, 24 November 1870, copy in Jensen, comp., "Manuscript History."

14. "Indian Matters in Arizona," *Deseret News*, 10 December 1870; William E. Goodyear, "Narrative," in Abbott, *Christopher Carson*, 320; Kroeber and Kroeber, *Mohave War Reminiscence*, 45, 89; Roth, "Incorporation and Changes," 110.

15. Casebier, *Camp Rock Spring*, 2; Casebier, *The Mojave Road*, 126; Casebier, *The Mojave Road in Newspapers*, 32, 45.

16. James F. Curtis to Col. R. C. Drum, Assistant Adjt. Genl., Dept. of the Pacific, 2 March 1865, in Waitman, "The History of Camp Cady," 60–61.

17. Casebier, *Camp Rock Spring*, 2, 12–13, 16, 24, 56, 61–62, 84.

18. Dobyns and Euler, *Wauba Yuma's People*, 43.

19. "From Arizona—More Indian Outrages," *San Bernardino (CA) Guardian*, 9 March 1867, quoted in Casebier, *The Mojave Road*, 67–68.

20. *Arizona Miner* (Prescott), 15 December 1866, quoted in Casebier, *Camp El Dorado*, 24.

21. Charles Whittier to James Fry, 8 April 1868, quoted in Casebier, *Camp El Dorado*, 64. See also Irvin McDowell to Lt. Col. R. N. Scott, 18 October 1866, in U.S. Department of War, *Annual Report* (1866), 32–36.

22. Casebier, *Camp El Dorado*, 27, 33, 51, 52, 61–62. Survey ambiguities were rife. For years, many people thought all of southern Nevada was in Arizona Territory, while Mormons settling the Muddy Valley were convinced they were in Utah. See Arrington, *The Mormons in Nevada*, 42–43, 52; Bancroft, *History of Nevada*, 155–56; Elliot, *History of Nevada*, 75–77, 108–10.

23. William Redwood Price to Maj. John P. Sherburne, January 1868, in U.S. Congress, Senate, *Walapai Papers*, 62.

24. William R. Price, no addressee, 22 November 1867, quoted in Casebier, *Camp Rock Spring*, 64. Note here the recurrence of the same misconception of the headman's role as made by the Mormons.

25. *Arizona Miner* (Prescott), 23 November 1867, quoted in Casebier, *The Mojave Road in Newspapers*, 76.

26. "From the Muddy," *Pioche (NV) Daily Record*, 19 November 1872, 3; "From the Muddy," *Pioche Daily Record*, 28 May 1873, 3; Lt. William J. Ross, Muster Roll of Piute Indian Scouts, 30 April 1873, USNA, RG 393, Military Records.

27. Elliot, *History of Nevada*, 69–89; Larson and Poll, "The 45th State," 387.

28. Hulse, *Lincoln County*, 22.

29. Davis, *The History of Nevada*, 2:933.

30. Elliot, *History of Nevada*, 110; Hulse, *Lincoln County*, 22, 40, 49.

31. Angel, *History of Nevada*, 476, 485; "Fresh Search for the De La Mar Mine," *Denver Times*, 4 May 1902, 2.

32. "Indian Difficulty," *Pioche Daily Record*, 24 June 1874, 3.

33. Aubry, "Diaries," 360.

34. Bleak, "Annals," 1:209.

35. Bleak, "Annals," 1:209. The Danites were a shadowy enforcement arm of the Mormon Church presidency. See Hickman, *Brigham's Destroying Angel*.

36. Bleak, "Annals," 1:211.

37. "A Massacre Rumored," *Pioche Daily Record*, 17 December 1874, 3.

38. "Indian Troubles," *Pioche Daily Record*, 15 January 1875, 3.

39. "Indian Troubles," 1875.

40. David Krause to R. A. Hovell, 15 May 1875, BIA-LR, roll 541, 3. Compare an even bloodier and more crass oral history version that narrates that the vigilantes first killed an entire camp of eighteen Paiutes. They then captured a headman and declared, "We do not know who did it, so we will kill you all. We will not leave one of your tribe in Nevada unless you give us the men who killed our white brothers." He sent out some of his men, who handed Bill over to them. The end result was the same: "The court simply suspended the rules, declared the prisoner guilty by a unanimous vote of the house, and then suspended the prisoner" out the window of the county courthouse ("Fresh Search," 2).

41. Charles F. Ashley, note in the Colorado River Agency Census, 30 June 1886, microfilm M595, Indian Census Rolls, 1885–1940, roll 46, frame 33, USNA.

42. "Shooting Arrows," *Pioche Daily Record*, 14 July 1876, 3. Old photographs show the addition of novel canvas coverings and later stovepipes and milled-wood doorframes as Paiutes salvaged Euro-American building materials.

43. Casebier, *Camp El Dorado*, 4.

44. "Indian Fandango," *Pioche* (NV) *Weekly Record*, 7 April 1877, 3; "Indian Trouble," *Pioche Weekly Record*, 3 September 1887, 3; Sapir, "The Mourning Ceremony." Compare Clemmer, "Ideology and Identity."

45. "Fresh Search"; Arrington and Jensen, "Panaca"; Knack, "The Role of Credit"; Nye, "A Winter."

46. Knack, "Newspaper Accounts," 85; Daniel Lockwood to George Wheeler, 28 February 1872, in Wheeler, *Preliminary Report*, 74–75.

47. Wheeler, *Preliminary Report*, 28.

48. Piute Company, *The Piute Company*, 18.

49. Knack, "Nineteenth Century," 153–55.

50. "Old Piute Woman Left to Die," *Pioche Daily Record*, 23 March 1873, 3; "Indian Dead & Dying in the Sagebrush," *Pioche Daily Record*, 3 April

1873, 3; "Still Dying in the Sagebrush," *Pioche Daily Record*, 19 April 1873, 3; untitled, *Pioche Daily Record*, 17 August 1873, 3.

51. "Excitement over Shoshone Squaw," *Pioche Daily Record*, 25 March 1873, 3.

52. "Excitement," 1873.

53. "Indian Killed," *Pioche Daily Record*, 1 August 1875, 3, emphasis added.

54. "Mating," *Pioche Weekly Record*, 12 February 1881, 3.

55. "An Indian Love Scene," *Pioche Daily Record*, 21 March 1873, 3.

56. W. R. Bradfute to W. D. C. Gibson, 11 June 1887, USNA, BIA Letters Received, 1881–1907.

57. Lockwood to Wheeler, 75.

58. "Pinenut Gathering," *Pioche Daily Record*, 22 August 1875, 3; "In Demand," *Pioche Weekly Record,* 10 October 1885, 3.

59. Knack, "Newspaper Accounts," 87–90. Brigham Young instituted a ban on the Mormon faithful consuming liquor in 1867 in order to limit the outflow of scarce hard money from the religious community (Arrington, *Great Basin Kingdom*, 250). Most Mormons today consider this a tenet of faith based on revelation.

60. "Last Friday a Gala Day in Buillionville," *Pioche Weekly Record*, 7 April 1883, 3.

61. "Two Indians Shot and One Indian's Throat Cut," *Pioche* (NV) *Tri-Weekly Record*, 20 December 1876, 3.

62. "A White Outrage upon Indians," *Pioche Weekly Record*, 29 November 1890, 3.

63. "Presents to Indians," *Pioche Daily Record*, 15 December 1872, 3.

64. Knack, "Newspaper Accounts," 86.

65. "Another from Pahranagat," *Pioche Weekly Record*, 22 July 1882, 3.

66. "Canyon Tragedy," *Las Vegas Age*, 26 November 1910, 1; compare "Indian Justice," *Las Vegas Age*, 7 May 1910, 4, for a similar incident in the 1880s in Ivanpah.

67. "Gus Wilson," *Pioche Weekly Record*, 18 August 1888, 3; "Indian Buck's

Death," *Pioche Weekly Record*, 25 August 1888, 3; "Fatal Drunk among Indians of Pahranagat," *Pioche Weekly Record*, 16 August 1890, 3.

68. Weil, "Legal Status," 70.

69. "Disturbance at the Muddy," *Pioche Daily Record*, 20 August 1876, 3. A group of his relatives from the Muddy River area objected to such high-handed threats and promptly broke him out of jail.

70. A. W. Ivins to R. V. Belt, 20 September 1891, USNA, BIA Letters Received, 1881–1907, 1–2; A. W. Ivins to Thomas J. Morgan, 8 August 1892, USNA, BIA Letters Received, 1881–1907, 3; and A. W. Ivins to Thomas J. Morgan, 11 August 1892, USNA, BIA Letters Received, 1881–1907, 4–5.

71. "Complaint Was Made," *Pioche Daily Record*, 21 November 1872, 3; "Lichtenstein Trial," *Pioche Daily Record*, 27 November 1872, 3.

72. "Indian Killed," *Pioche Weekly Record*, 15 September 1888, 3.

73. "Death Sentence," *Lincoln County Record* (Pioche NV), 13 November 1903, 4. Segmiller was convicted, sentenced to hang, commuted to life in prison, and released in 1911 through the intercession of the sentencing judge and the regional BIA agent (C. A. Asbury to Commissioner of Indian Affairs, 7 February 1911, BIA-CCF).

74. "Buckboard and Harness," *Pioche Weekly Record*, 12 December 1895, 4.

75. "A Physician Killed," *Pioche Weekly Record*, 28 February 1885, 3.

76. Louis Stern, William H. Henderson, and Albert Barber to E. S. Parker, 26 December 1870, BIA-LR, roll 539, 3.

77. Charles Mix, "Narrative Report to Jacob Thompson, Secretary of the Interior," in ARCIA, 1858, 9.

78. Mix, "Narrative Report," 10.

79. William P. Dole, "Narrative Report," in ARCIA, 1863, 5.

80. Brigham Young, Proclamation to All Whom it may Concern, 21 July 1851, BIA-LR, roll 897. Another agency called the Parowan Agency was to include most of the other Paiutes in "all the country lying west of the eastern rim of the Great Basin and South of the South line of the Parvan Valley to the Western bounds of the Territory."

81. "Sketch of a Trip to Pauvan," *Deseret News*, 13 December 1851, 3. Potatoes were not an aboriginal crop in this area.

82. Garland Hurt to Brigham Young, 20 November 1855, ms. no. 1234, roll 93, LDS-CHO.

83. Brigham Young to Garland Hurt, 23 November 1855, ms. no. 1234, roll 93, LDS-CHO, 2.

84. Garland Hurt to Brigham Young, 31 December 1855, BIA-LR, roll 898, 2.

85. Garland Hurt to Commissioner of Indian Affairs, 30 June 1857, BIA-LR, roll 898, 2.

86. Garland Hurt, List of Agency Property, 30 November 1859, BIA-LR, roll 898.

87. Peter Boyce to Jacob Forney, 20 March 1859, USR.

88. Peter Boyce to Jacob Forney, 16 July 1859, BIA-LR, roll 899, 1–2.

89. Peter Boyce to Jacob Forney, 20 August 1859, USR, emphasis added.

90. A. Humphreys to A. B. Greenwood, 16 July 1860, BIA-LR, roll 899.

91. A. Humphreys to William P. Dole, Commissioner of Indian Affairs, 30 September 1861, in ARCIA, 1861, 441–43.

92. James D. Doty to William P. Dole, 12 September 1862, in ARCIA, 1862, 342.

93. Thomas Callister to D. J. Doty, 9 August 1863, USR. Kanosh, clearly in communication with native leaders throughout the territory and even across tribal boundaries, was here trying to extract gifts from the BIA the way he had from Brigham Young. Such a personal statement of need would, in the native society, have inevitably produced generosity.

94. Pub. L. No. 38-77, 13 Stat. 63 (1864).

95. A. P. Usher to William P. Dole, 6 February 1865, copied in Powell and Ingalls, *Report*, 20.

96. Joseph Clark and Frank Pierce, "Plat Map of Corn Creek Indian Reservation," approved by General Land Office, 1867, USNA, Arlington VA, Cartography Division, Central Map File, Utah no. 217.

97. Amos Reid to William Hooper, 18 January 1866, USR; J. C. Tourtellotte to E. S. Parker, 16 October 1869, BIA-LR, roll 902.

98. O. H. Irish, "Treaty of Spanish Fork," 8 June 1865, USNA, microfilm T494, Documents Relating to the Negotiation of Ratified and Unratified Treaties with Various Indian Tribes, 1801–69, roll 8.

99. O. H. Irish, "Articles of Agreement and Convention Made and Concluded at Pinto Creek, Utah Territory," 18 September 1865, USNA, microfilm T494, Documents Relating to the Negotiation of Ratified and Unratified Treaties with Various Indian Tribes, 1801–69, roll 8.

100. Irish, "Articles of Agreement."

101. J. E. Tourtellotte to E. S. Parker, 16 October 1869, BIA-LR, roll 902, 5–6.

102. Royce, *Indian Land Cessions*, 892.

103. F. H. Head to D. N. Cooley, 4 August 1866, BIA-LR, roll 902, 2–3.

104. William P. Dole to James D. Doty, 10 October 1862, USR, emphasis in the original.

105. William Raymond et al. to Superintendent of Indian Affairs, State of Nevada, 29 October 1865, BIA-LR, roll 538.

106. James Day to H. G. Parker, 13 January 1866, BIA-LR, roll 538; George Ingalls to E. P. Smith, 30 November 1873, in ARCIA, 1873, 327–31; Stern, Henderson, and Barber to Parker, 26 December 1870.

107. Erastus Snow to John Wesley Powell, 24 September 1872, copy in Bleak, "Annals," 2:150; Woodruff, "Remarks."

108. H. G. Parker to Commissioner of Indian Affairs, 15 June 1867, BIA-LR, roll 538; E. S. Parker to H. Douglas, 12 November 1869, USNA, microfilm M837, Records of the Nevada Superintendency, 1869–70, roll 1.

109. D. N. Cooley, "Narrative Report to the Secretary of Interior," in ARCIA, 1866, 29.

110. R. N. Fenton to H. Douglas, 28 April 1870, USNA, microfilm M837, Records of the Nevada Superintendency, 1869–70, roll 1.

111. C. A. Bateman to F. A. Walker, 26 October 1872, BIA-LR, roll 540, 3.

112. John Wesley Powell to G. W. Ingalls, 13 February 1873, BIA-LR, roll 540.

113. See map in Royce, *Indian Land Cessions*, plate 150.

114. George W. Ingalls to H. R. Clum, 7 March 1873, BIA-LR, roll 540. For house construction he included some high land with timber, which happened to be food-producing piñon pine.

115. Powell and Ingalls, "Report," 17.

116. L. A. Walker to C. Delano, 17 December 1872, USNA, microfilm M348,

Report Books of the Commissioner of Indian Affairs, 1838–85, roll 22; Royce, *Indian Land Cessions*, 862.

117. Powell and Ingalls, "Report," 15.

118. A. J. Barnes to E. P. Smith, 20 December 1874, BIA-LR, roll 541, 1–6; Elliot, *History of Nevada*, 107–10.

119. Powell and Ingalls, "Report," 16.

120. "The Threatened Outrage," *Pioche Daily Record*, 17 April 1873, 2.

121. "A Reservation on the Muddy," *Pioche Daily Record*, 18 July 1873, 3.

122. "Muddy Indians Wish to Speak in Pioche," *Pioche Daily Record*, 22 September 1874, 3; "From the Muddy and Los Vegas," *Pioche Daily Record*, 14 June 1873, 3; "St. George, 21 . . . ," *Deseret Weekly News*, 27 August 1873, 465.

123. George W. Ingalls to E. P. Smith, 1 June 1874, BIA-LR, roll 540.

124. George W. Ingalls to E. P. Smith, 16 July 1873, BIA-LR, roll 904, 4.

125. Powell, *Statement*, 6.

126. "Muddy," *Pioche Daily Record*, 22 September 1874.

127. John Wesley Powell and George W. Ingalls to Commissioner of Indian Affairs, 6 August 1873, BIA-LR, roll 904.

128. George W. Ingalls to E. P. Smith, 5 June 1874, BIA-LR, roll 540, 4, emphasis in original.

129. Ingalls to Smith, 16 July 1873, 2.

130. Ingalls to Smith, 16 July 1873, 2.

131. John Wesley Powell and George W. Ingalls to E. P. Smith, 7 February 1874, BIA-LR, roll 541, emphasis in original.

132. E. P. Smith to E. Delano, 10 February 1874, USNA, microfilm M348, Report Books of the Commissioner of Indian Affairs, 1838–85, roll 24; Royce, *Indian Land Cessions*, 870 and map plate 150.

133. Barnes to Smith, 20 December 1874, 9.

134. A. J. Barnes to Edward P. Smith, 11 September 1875, in ARCIA, 1875, 839; Edward P. Smith, "Narrative Report to Secretary of Interior," in ARCIA, 1874, 363.

135. Pub. L. No. 43-132, 18 Stat. 420, 445 (1875).

136. Royce, *Indian Land Cessions*, 882.

137. C. A. Bateman and A. J. Barnes to William Vandever, 7 June 1875, BIA-CCF, 3.

138. Bateman and Barnes to Vandever, 7 June 1875, 6.

139. Bateman and Barnes to Vandever, 7 June 1875, 11.

140. Ingalls to Smith, 20 July 1873, 3. See also "Statistical Summary," in ARCIA, 1874, 443.

141. Ingalls to Smith, 20 July 1873, 3, second emphasis in the original.

142. A. J. Barnes to Edward P. Smith, 11 September 1875, in ARCIA, 1875, 337.

143. Ingalls to Smith, 5 June 1874, 2–3.

144. Charles Powell to H. R. Clum, 2 October 1871, in ARCIA, 1871, 978; J. C. Tourtellotte to E. S. Parker, 10 May 1870, BIA-LR, roll 903.

145. Ingalls to Smith, 30 November 1873.

146. "Statistical Summary," ARCIA, 1875, 616–17, 632.

147. "Statistical Summary," ARCIA, 1877, 694.

148. W. R. Bradfute to James Spencer, 12 October 1879, BIA-LR, roll 544.

149. Bradfute to Spencer, 12 October 1879.

150. G. W. Ingalls to Edward P. Smith, 1 October 1874, in ARCIA, 1874, 283.

151. "Killed by Indians," *Pioche Weekly Record*, 25 October 1879, 3.

152. W. R. Bradfute to James Spencer, 29 November 1879, BIA-LR, roll 54, 4.

153. A. J. Barnes to Commissioner of Indian Affairs, 3 July 1877, BIA-LR, roll 542; E. C. Watkins, Report to J. C. Smith, 28 March 1877, USNA, microfilm M1070, BIA Inspection of the Field Jurisdictions, 1873–1900, roll 26, 17–20.

154. E. C. Watkins to E. A. Hayt, 16 February 1878, BIA-LR, roll 543.

155. Zanjani, "Totell Disregard"; James Spencer to W. R. Bradfute, 3 September 1880, USNA, BIA Letters Received, 1881–1907.

156. James E. Spencer to E. R. Trowbridge, 31 May 1880, BIA-LR, roll 545, 3.

157. W. R. Bradfute to James McMaster, 10 April 1884, USNA, BIA Letters Received, 1881–1907.

158. James E. Spencer to R. E. Trowbridge, 25 March 1880, BIA-LR, roll 545, 15, emphasis in original.

159. R. E. Trowbridge to James Spencer, 19 April 1880, BIA-LR, roll 545.

160. "Colonel Bradfute Writes," *Pioche Weekly Record*, 24 February 1883, 3.

161. "Indians," *Pioche Daily Record*, 7 September 1875, 2.

162. Cox, Autobiography, 159.

163. W. R. Bradfute to R. E. Trowbridge, 3 April 1880, BIA-LR, roll 545, 2.

164. J. D. C. Atkins to H. M. Welton, 20 September 1887, USNA, BIA Letters Sent, 1881–1907, Accounts Division, 4, emphasis added.

165. Henry Welton, Report on Closing out the Moapa Indian Reservation, 1 March 1888, USNA, BIA Letters Received, 1881–1907, 3.

166. Henry Welton to Commissioner of Indian Affairs, 2 November 1887, USNA, BIA Letters Received, 1881–1907.

167. George Segmiller, Affidavit, 12 December 1887, USNA, BIA Letters Received, 1881–1907.

168. Welton, Report, 2, emphasis in the original.

169. L. J. Harris, "Names of Indians to whom the several sub-divisions of land on the Moapa Indian Reservation had been allotted by L. J. Harris, Trustee," 29 September 1888, BIA-CCF.

170. Jones, "Notes"; Charles Powell to H. R. Clum, 2 October 1871, in ARCIA, 1871, 978; John Oakley to Brigham Young, 1 August 1875, microfilm copy, ms. 8828, LDS-CHO.

171. E. S. Parker to C. Delano, 23 February 1871, USNA, microfilm M348, BIA Report Books, 1838–85, roll 20; John Wesley Powell to Charles Powell, 16 January 1872, BIA-LR, roll 545.

172. Levi Chubbuck to Secretary of the Interior, 31 December 1906, USNA, BIA Letters Received, 1881–1907, 13.

173. Manly, *Death Valley*, 117, 119, 128, 132, 138, 139, 140; "Another from Pahranagat," *Pioche Weekly Record*, 22 July 1882, 3; "An Artist," *Pioche Weekly Record*, 24 February 1883, 3.

174. R. S. MacKenzie to Assist. Adjt. Genl. of Department of the Missouri, 26 September 1883, in U.S. Department of War, *Annual Report* (1883), 137–45.

175. Roth, "The Calloway Affair"; Jonathan Biggs to Commissioner of Indian Affairs, 25 August 1881, in ARCIA, 1881, 1–3.

176. Charles Ashley, Colorado River Agency Census, Note on Chimihuevis, 30 June 1886, USNA, microfilm M595, Indian Census Rolls, 1885–1940, roll 46.

177. George A. Allen, Colorado River Agency Census, 30 June 1893, USNA, microfilm M595, Indian Census Rolls, 1885–1940, roll 46.

178. Roth, "Incorporation and Changes," 115; J. A. Tonner to Commissioner of Indian Affairs, 25 September 1875, in ARCIA, 1875, 210–11.

7. LAND, WATER, AND THE FEDERAL GOVERNMENT

1. See, for example, Brandon, *American Heritage Book of Indians,* 403–17.

2. For example, Utley and Washburn, *The American Heritage History,* 194.

3. For example, Jorgensen, "A Century," 2.

4. "A Reservation on the Muddy," *Pioche Daily Record,* 18 July 1873, 3.

5. Ivins, "Traveling," 1021.

6. Anthony W. Ivins to John Caine, 31 June 1890, BIA-CCF.

7. Arrington, *Great Basin Kingdom,* 96; Arrington, *The Mormons in Nevada,* 26–31; Harper, "Historical Environments," 60–63; Woodfield, "Initiation," 51.

8. E. W. Penny to Department of Interior, 23 January 1891, USNA, BIA Letters Received 1881–1907, 2.

9. Woodbury, "A History," 191–92.

10. Joe Indian to Washington DC, 10 September 1916, BIA-CCF, 1, 3; E. D. Woolley to Senator Reed Smoot, 29 December 1905, USNA, BIA Letters Received, 1881–1907. Woolley's correspondence also suggested another motivation for the reversal of Utahans' historic antipathy to federal presence—desire for bureaucratic jobs. Sensitive to the pressure

of a burgeoning population amid an environmentally constricted agricultural economy, Woolley pointedly suggested that "we have suitable men and women here that have been aquainted or raised with the Indians, in whom they have explicit confidence, that would make suitable Superintendents or teachers."

11. Chubbuck to Secretary of the Interior, 31 December 1906, 7.

12. E. G. Murtaugh to Commissioner of Indian Affairs, 16 November 1912, BIA-CCF, 2.

13. E. G. Murtaugh to Commissioner of Indian Affairs, 15 December 1915, BIA-CCF, 2.

14. Joel Olive to Commissioner of Indian Affairs, 13 April 1897, USNA, BIA Letters Received, 1881–1907, 3–4.

15. Joe Norris, Report to Secretary of the Interior, 25 July 1910, BIA-CCF, 20–21.

16. Joe Norris to Secretary of the Interior, 5 November 1910, BIA-CCF, 10–12.

17. Ivins to Caine, 31 June 1890, and enclosure, 6.

18. R. V. Belt to George W. Parker, 26 September 1890, USNA, BIA Letters Sent, 1871–1907, Land Series—Letterpress, 3, 5–6.

19. George W. Parker to Commissioner of Indian Affairs, 18 October 1890, USNA, BIA Letters Received, 1881–1907, 7.

20. John Caine to Thomas J. Morgan, 9 March 1891, USNA, BIA Letters Received, 1881–1907, 2, 3.

21. Pub. L. No. 51-543, 26 Stat. 989, 1005 (1891); Thomas J. Morgan to Anthony W. Ivins, 28 April 1891, USNA, BIA Letters Sent, 1881–1907, Land Series, 2.

22. Anthony W. Ivins to Commissioner of Indian Affairs, 17 September 1891, BIA-CCF; John Noble to Commissioner of the General Land Office, 28 September 1891, BIA-CCF.

23. R. V. Belt to Anthony W. Ivins, 9 September 1891, USNA, BIA Letters Sent, 1881–1907, Land Series, 5.

24. A. W. Ivins to R. V. Belt, 20 September 1891, USNA, BIA Letters Received, 1881–1907, 2; Anthony W. Ivins to R. V. Belt, 25 January 1892, USNA, BIA Letters Received, 1881–1907, 2.

25. Anthony W. Ivins to Commissioner of Indian Affairs, 13 December 1892, USNA, BIA Letters Received, 1881–1907, 6.

26. T. J. Morgan to A. W. Ivins, 5 January 1893, USNA, BIA Letters Sent, 1881–1907, Land Series; D. N. Browning to Anthony W. Ivins, 25 September 1893, USNA, BIA Letters Sent, 1881–1907, Land Series.

27. James Andrus et al., Petition to Senator Joseph L. Rawlins, 10 September 1899, USNA, BIA Letters Received, 1881–1907; James Andrus et al., Petition to Joseph L. Rawlings, 22 November 1899, USNA, BIA Letters Received, 1881–1907; Charles Dickson to Commissioner of Indian Affairs, 13 June 1900, USNA, BIA Letters Received, 1881–1907, 7.

28. George Johnson et al., Petition to Senator Thomas Kearns, 14 March 1901, USNA, BIA Letters Received, 1881–1907.

29. C. D. Whittmore to Commissioner of Indian Affairs, 25 November 1901, USNA, BIA Letters Received, 1881–1907; E. A. Hitchcock to Commissioner of Indian Affairs, 10 December 1901, USNA, BIA Letters Received, 1881–1907; W. A. Jones to Secretary of the Interior, 31 October 1903, USNA, BIA Letters Sent, 1881–1907, Land Series.

30. Laura Work to Commissioner of Indian Affairs, 1 July 1904, in ARCIA, 1904, 346; Laura Work, "Report of Superintendent of Panguitch School," 31 July 1906, in ARCIA, 1906, 366; Frank C. Churchill to Secretary of the Interior, 30 August 1907, BIA-CCF, 2, 4.

31. F. E. Leupp to Superintendent of Panguitch Indian School, 13 January 1908, UO-MC, 1–2.

32. As a condition to the gift, Congress demanded that "Indian pupils shall at all times be admitted at such school free of charge for tuition and on terms of equality with white pupils" (William Spry to Commissioner of Indian Affairs, 15 May 1909, BIA-CCF), but the state never operated a school there, using it instead for agricultural extension work. When Utah wanted to close the aging facility in 1934, it offered title back to the BIA, which refused it (John Collier to P. V. Cardon, 7 January 1935, BIA-CCF).

33. Reed Smoot to Francis E. Leupp, 1 December 1905, USNA, BIA Letters Received, 1881–1907, 1–2.

34. Smoot to Leupp, 1 December 1905, emphasis added. Local citizens promptly offered to sell the entire "town" of Johnson for $45,000, with-

out mentioning that the single Johnson family could not make an adequate living there (H. S. Cutler to Senator Reed Smoot, 15 December 1905, USNA, BIA Letters Received, 1881–1907).

35. Laura Work to Commissioner of Indian Affairs, 2 December 1905, USNA, BIA Letters Received, 1881–1907, 2.

36. F. E. Leupp to Reed Smoot, 27 January 1906, USNA, BIA Letters Sent, 1881–1907, Land Series, 3.

37. Pub. L. No. 59-258, 34 Stat. 325, 376 (1906).

38. Chubbuck to Secretary of the Interior, 31 December 1906, 6–7, 9.

39. C. F. Larrabee to Secretary of the Interior, 15 October 1907, approved by Thomas Ryan, 16 October 1907, BIA-CCF.

40. Knack, "Interethnic Competition."

41. Work to Commissioner of Indian Affairs, 1 July 1904, 345.

42. Laura Work to Commissioner of Indian Affairs, 20 February 1906, USNA, BIA Letters Received, 1881–1907, 2.

43. F. E. Leupp to Secretary of the Interior, 20 March 1906, USNA, BIA Letters Sent, 1881–1907, Land Series, 2.

44. Pub. L. No. 59-258, 34 Stat. 325, 376 (1906).

45. Chubbuck to Secretary of the Interior, 31 December 1906, 29.

46. Chubbuck to Secretary of the Interior, 31 December 1906, 29.

47. Chubbuck to Secretary of the Interior, 31 December 1906, 30. A second agent, sent to confirm Chubbuck's observations, managed to contact two groups of San Juan people who "insisted from first to last that the Piutes needed nothing from the Government; that they were minding their own business and were contented and comfortable, and asked for nothing beyond being let alone" (Churchill to Secretary of the Interior, 30 August 1907, 5). He made the radical suggestion that "they should be encouraged to develop their own resources and work out the problem of comfortable existence along their own lines" (Churchill to Secretary of the Interior, 30 August 1907, 7–8). This contradicted the BIA's own bureaucratic self-interest, which was to increase its charge, staff, budget, and hence political power, and it also would leave Indians autonomous. They would stand in potential economic competition with the

powerful settler faction that had raised the cry of Paiute "need" in the first place. His recommendation was ignored.

48. C. V. Larrabee to Secretary of the Interior, 15 October 1907, approved 16 October 1907, BIA-CCF; Senator Reed Smoot to Secretary James Garfield, 9 October 1908, BIA-CCF; Reed Smoot to Secretary of the Interior, 8 February 1909, BIA-CCF; Francis Pierce to Commissioner of Indian Affairs, 7 June 1909, BIA-CCF.

49. Bunte and Franklin, *From the Sands*, 100–172; Euler, *Southern Paiute Ethnohistory*, 97–116.

50. Walter Runke to Commissioner of Indian Affairs, 3 August 1908, BIA-CCF, 2–3.

51. Byron A. Sharp to Commissioner of Indian Affairs, 2 June 1922, as quoted in Bunte and Franklin, *From the Sands*, 176.

52. Charles Burke to Secretary of the Interior via General Land Office, 10 July 1922, BIA-CCF; Bunte and Franklin, *From the Sands*, 174–90.

53. R. G. Valentine to Lorenzo D. Creel, 21 July 1911, USNA, BIA Special Agents Files.

54. Lorenzo D. Creel, "Narrative Report, Scattered Bands of Utah Agency," 21 July 1914, USNA, BIA Special Agents Files, 2.

55. Lorenzo D. Creel to Commissioner of Indian Affairs, 2 April 1915, BIA-CCF.

56. E. B. Meritt to Secretary of the Interior, 26 July 1915, USNA, RG 48, Secretary of the Interior Records, Indian Division; Woodrow Wilson, Executive Order, 2 August 1915, USNA, RG 48, Secretary of the Interior Records, Indian Division.

57. C. F. Hauke to Nick Conner, 28 July 1919, UO-MC.

58. Washington Endicott to Cato Sells, 27 March 1920, USNA, BIA Inspection Division Files, 3.

59. Pub. L. No. 66-3, 41 Stat. 3, 34 (1919); Pub. L. No. 68-164, 43 Stat. 246 (1924).

60. Pub. L. No. 43-131, 18 Stat. 402, 420 (1875); Pub. L. No. 49-119, 24 Stat. 388 (1887), as amended Pub. L. No. 51-383, 26 Stat. 794 (1891); Pub. L. No. 59-149, 34 Stat. 182 (1906); Pub. L. No. 61-313, 36 Stat. 855 (1910). On

the issue of tribal confusion, the BIA knew so little of Southern Paiutes that, as the Smithsonian's Bureau of American Ethnology and the Library of Congress still do, it used the name "Paiute" for both the Northern and Southern Paiute tribes despite their distinctive linguistic, cultural, geographic, and historical identities. In 1910 an inspector seriously proposed that Las Vegas, Tonopah, Kanab, and Kanosh "Paiutes" be given allotments at the big "Paiute" reservations in northwestern Nevada then scheduled for division, suggesting that "there is a sufficient amount of irrigable land and land suitable for grazing purposes, either one or the other or both, to eventually place all the Indians belonging to the bands located at these places in fairly comfortable financial circumstances" (Norris to Secretary of the Interior, 5 November 1910, 7). The Walker River (Northern Paiute) Reservation was allotted into twenty-acre pieces in 1902 (Johnson, *Walker River Paiutes*, 99–112) and Pyramid Lake (Northern Paiute) Reservation was under political pressure to be broken up into five-acre parcels in 1904 (Knack and Stewart, *As Long as the River Shall Run*, 201–2).

61. C. F. Hauke to Lorenzo Creel, 18 December 1911, BIA-CCF.

62. Lorenzo D. Creel to Commissioner of Indian Affairs, 15 December 1911, UO-MC; Lorenzo D. Creel to Commissioner of Indian Affairs, 6 September 1912, USNA, BIA Special Agents Files. Several of these applications were subsequently rejected by the BIA, particularly those of women, resulting in gaps within the Indian properties. See also Knack, "Utah Indians," 73–80; Cato Sells to Nick Conner, 3 July 1920, BIA-CCF; Cato Sells to Nick Conner, 14 December 1920, BIA-CCF.

63. Creel to Commissioner of Indian Affairs, 15 December 1911; Cox, Autobiography, 255; Knack, Field Notes, Utah Southern Paiutes.

64. Cox, Autobiography, 255.

65. Lorenzo D. Creel to Commissioner of Indian Affairs, 16 October 1911, BIA-CCF, 4–5. Perhaps this was related to the "epidemic" he mentioned that had killed off many of the Indian elderly the previous year and clearly pointed to health conditions, probably of economic origins, that differentiated Koosharem Paiutes from their neighbors.

66. Lorenzo D. Creel to Commissioner of Indian Affairs, 13 April 1915, BIA-CCF; Louis Hatch to A. R. Frank, 19 May 1917, UO-MC; Louis Hatch to A. R. Frank, 7 July 1918, UO-MC. Paiutes complained of coffins and services unequal to those of their neighbors, to which the commissioner

replied that the government provided only minimal care for the indigent and that the Paiutes were welcome to any additional funeral celebrations they thought necessary, but at their own expense (E. B. Meritt to Nick Conner, 21 March 1923, BIA-CCF).

67. Nick Conner to Commissioner of Indian Affairs, 10 January 1922, BIA-CCF. Three years later a Utah congressman pressed for and got a formal contract for this woman but was unsuccessful in obtaining physical improvements for the tiny school, as it was not a federally owned building (Charles H. Burke to Congressman Don Colton, 4 February 1924, BIA-CCF). See also C. F. Hauke to E. A. Farrow, 25 April 1924, BIA-CCF.

68. E. A. Farrow to Orson Bagley, 31 August 1930, BIA-CCF, 1–2.

69. E. A. Farrow to Commissioner of Indian Affairs, 5 August 1927, UO-MC.

70. Lorring Whittoldey to E. A. Farrow, 8 August 1927, UO-MC; C. F. Hauke to Edgar A. Farrow, 27 September 1927, UO-MC; Pub. L. No. 70-91, 45 Stat. 162 (1928).

71. H. H. Fiske to Commissioner of Indian Affairs, 14 August 1928, BIA-CCF, 3; Knack, Field Notes, Utah Southern Paiutes.

72. Edward S. Curtis to Francis Leupp, 17 November 1906, USNA, BIA Letters Received, 1881–1907, 1–2.

73. Francis E. Leupp to C. E. Kelsey, 8 December 1906, USNA, BIA Letters Sent, 1881–1907, Land Series.

74. C. E. Kelsey to Commissioner of Indian Affairs, 10 December 1906, BIA-CCF, 3. See also Kroeber, *Ethnography*, 33–34, 37.

75. C. E. Kelsey to Commissioner of Indian Affairs, 19 December 1906, BIA-CCF, 3, 2.

76. C. F. Larrabee to Secretary of the Interior, 31 January 1907, USNA, RG 49, General Land Office Records, Division E, Special Files.

77. F. H. Newell to Secretary of the Interior, 30 April 1907, BIA-CCF, 1–2.

78. C. F. Larrabee to Secretary of the Interior, 2 December 1907, BIA-CCF, 3.

79. F. H. Newell to Commissioner of Indian Affairs, 12 October 1909, BIA-CCF, 1, 2. See also Jesse E. Wilson to Commissioner of Indian Affairs, 26 February 1909, BIA-CCF, 3; BIA, Chief of Land Division to Education, memorandum, 28 August 1911, BIA-CCF, 1–2.

80. M. F. Holland to Commissioner of Indian Affairs, 27 December 1909, BIA-CCF, 3; BIA, Chief of Land Division, Memorandum for Education-Law and Order, May 1911, BIA-CCF, 2.

81. William Williams to Commissioner of Indian Affairs, 1 January 1910, BIA-CCF.

82. William Williams, Map of Chemehuevis Indian Allotment, Chemehuevi Valley, California, 16 April 1910, BIA-CCF.

83. C. M. Bruce to Registrar and Receiver at Los Angeles, 21 August 1915, USNA, RG 49, General Land Office Records, Letters Sent; Roth, "Incorporation and Changes," 161–62.

84. C. H. Gensler to Commissioner of Indian Affairs, 6 July 1927, BIA-CCF; C. H. Gensler to Commissioner of Indian Affairs, 14 April 1932, BIA-CCF; C. J. Rhoads to Secretary of the Interior, 16 August 1932, approved by Joseph Dixon, 23 August 1932, BIA-CCF.

85. T. J. Murphy et al. to Commissioner of Indian Affairs, 10 December 1896, BIA-CCF. See also George A. Allen, Report of the Superintendent of the Colorado River Reservation, in ARCIA, 1892, extract reprinted in U.S. Congress, Senate, *Walapai Papers*, 175.

86. D. M. Browning to John McKoin, 5 March 1897, USNA, BIA Letters Sent, 1881–1907, Financial Series, emphasis in the original.

87. John McKorn to Commissioner of Indian Affairs, 19 March 1897, BIA-CCF.

88. Leo Crane to Commissioner of Indian Affairs, 1 April 1924, BIA-CCF; E. B. Meritt to Leo Crane, 23 April 1924, BIA-CCF.

89. C. H. Gensler to Commissioner of Indian Affairs, 4 December 1926, BIA-CCF, 3, 2, 1.

90. Gensler to Commissioner of Indian Affairs, 4 December 1926. See also Charles Burke to Secretary of the Interior, 20 December 1927, BIA-CCF; C. H. Gensler to Commissioner of Indian Affairs, 9 March 1932, BIA-CCF; Mary McGair, Memorandum on Purchase of Land for Needles Colony of Indians, 4 June 1932, BIA-CCF; H. C. Weekley to "Mr. Monahan," memorandum, 25 November 1932, with attached note by "Daiker," BIA-CCF.

91. R. N. Fenton to Henry Douglas, 28 April 1870, USNA, BIA Nevada Superintendency Field Papers, Letters Received, 1870.

92. Catherine S. Fowler, telephone communication to the author, August 1987; Knack, "The Role of Credit."

93. Mary E. Cox to Commissioner of Indian Affairs, 20 June 1910, BIA-CCF, 2; C. L. Ellis, Report to Commissioner of Indian Affairs, 14 July 1911, BIA-CCF, 5–6; C. E. Kelsey to Commissioner of Indian Affairs, 12 May 1911, BIA-CCF; Daisy Sackett Mike, "Reminiscences," in Inter-tribal Council of Nevada, *Personal Reflections,* 18–19; Kenneth Anderson and Daisy Mike, "History of the Las Vegas Indian Colony," in Inter-tribal Council of Nevada, *Personal Reflections,* 19–20.

94. Cox to Commissioner of Indian Affairs, 20 June 1910; see also "Made Good: Indian Medicine Man Executed by Tribal Law," *Las Vegas Age,* 7 May 1910, 4; Elton Garrett, "Bad Medicine Man," *Las Vegas Journal,* 7 October 1931, 8.

95. James Cox, advertisement, *Las Vegas Age,* 17 June 1911, 4.

96. Francis Swayne to Commissioner of Indian Affairs, 6 November 1911, BIA-CCF, 3–4; see also C. L. Ellis to Commissioner of Indian Affairs, 14 July 1911, BIA-CCF, 6.

97. Ellis to Commissioner of Indian Affairs, 14 July 1911, 5; L. B. Sandall to Commissioner of Indian Affairs, 23 December 1918, BIA-CCF.

98. Francis Swayne to Commissioner of Indian Affairs, 7 September 1911, BIA-CCF.

99. Samuel Adams to Francis Swayne, 27 November 1911, USNA, RG 48, Secretary of the Interior Records, Indian Division; "Vegas Indian Reservation: Congressman Roberts Favors Tract Owned by Mrs. Helen J. Stewart," *Las Vegas Age,* 6 January 1912, 4; Francis Swayne to Helen J. Stewart, 6 July 1912, Nevada Historical Society, Las Vegas, Helen J. Stewart Papers; E. A. Farrow to Commissioner of Indian Affairs, 18 May 1931, UO-MC.

100. E. G. Murtaugh to Commissioner of Indian Affairs, 12 July 1912, BIA-CCF; John Francis, Memo of Justification, 23 September 1912, BIA-CCF, 1–2; "Indian Agent Here," *Las Vegas Age,* 11 January 1913, 1. Rather than selling land, the agent suggested the BIA invest $18,000 to buy land for an agricultural reserve near the town but was denied. Over the years, as he and others pointed to the increasingly overcrowded conditions on the ten-acre site (Edward G. Murtaugh to Commissioner of Indian Affairs, 16 November 1912, BIA-CCF, 4; C. H. Asbury to Commissioner

of Indian Affairs, 10 February 1915, BIA-CCF, 2; "Land Needed for Indians: Mrs. Stewart Writes to Senator Newlands for Help for Local Tribe," *Las Vegas Age*, 27 February 1915, 1), Washington suggested variously moving "excess" Southern Paiutes to the Northern Paiute reservation at Fallon where allotments were available (C. F. Hauke to Edward G. Murtaugh, 5 February 1913, BIA-CCF), to Winnemucca in northern Nevada (C. F. Hauke to Edward Murtaugh, 13 February 1917, BIA-CCF, 2), or out to Moapa (H. A. Meyer to Cato Sells, 23 December 1914, USNA, RG 48, Secretary of the Interior Records, Indian Division).

101. "For the Indians: Government Will Establish a School on Vegas Reservation," *Las Vegas Age*, 20 January 1912, 1; C. A. Thompson to Commissioner of Indian Affairs, 27 February 1912, USNA, RG 48, Secretary of the Interior Records, Indian Division; C. F. Hauke to Edward Murtaugh, 12 November 1912, BIA-CCF; Edward Murtaugh to Commissioner of Indian Affairs, 16 November 1912, BIA-CCF, 1–2; F. H. Abbott to Edward Murtaugh, 12 December 1912, BIA-CCF.

102. Edward Murtaugh to Commissioner of Indian Affairs, 20 February 1918, BIA-CCF; Otis Goodall, Inspection of Moapa Agency, 14 September 1913, BIA-CCF, 6.

103. Edward Murtaugh to Commissioner of Indian Affairs, 28 August 1913, BIA-CCF. See also Goodall, Inspection, 6; Knack, "Newspaper Accounts."

104. C. H. Asbury to Commissioner of Indian Affairs, 10 February 1915, BIA-CCF.

105. Walter Runke to Commissioner of Indian Affairs, 10 December 1907, BIA-CCF, 1–2.

106. Lorenzo D. Creel to Commissioner of Indian Affairs, 9 January 1913, USNA, BIA Special Agents Files, 4. See also Lorenzo D. Creel to Commissioner of Indian Affairs, 28 February 1916, BIA-CCF.

107. Edgar A. Farrow to Commissioner of Indian Affairs, 21 April 1924, BIA-CCF, 2.

108. Carl Stevens, Supplement to Goshute Report, 6 March 1923, USNA, BIA Inspection Division Files, 3.

109. William R. Palmer to Doctor Farrow, 21 April 1924, BIA-CCF, 2.

110. William R. Palmer to A. W. Ivins, 28 December 1925, copy in BIA-CCF, 1–2; Knack, "Church and State."

111. T. B. Roberts Sr. to Commissioner of Indian Affairs, 23 January 1926, BIA-CCF, 2.

112. E. A. Farrow to Commissioner of Indian Affairs, 27 January 1926, BIA-CCF.

113. E. B. Meritt to Edgar A. Farrow, 23 February 1926, BIA-CCF.

114. C. J. Rhoads to E. A. Farrow, 12 March 1931, UO-MC.

115. E. B. Meritt to John Perkins, 23 May 1921, BIA-CCF, emphasis added.

116. William Sharp, "Report of Farmer in Charge of Moapa Reservation," 15 August 1904, in ARCIA, 1904, 245; John R. Cox, Census of the Moapa Band of Paiute, 6 July 1910, USNA, microfilm M595, Indian Census Rolls, 1885–1940, roll 268; H. W. Hincks, List of Cultivated Land, Moapa River Reservation, April 1912, USNA, BIA Irrigation Division, Office of the Chief Engineer.

117. Laura Work, Census of Shebit Indians, 30 June 1900, USNA, microfilm M595, Indian Census Rolls, 1885–1940, roll 543; Laura Work, Census of Shivwits Indians, 30 June 1905, USNA, microfilm M595, Indian Census Rolls, 1885–1940, roll 543; John F. Wasmund to Commissioner of Indian Affairs, 11 August 1911, BIA-CCF; Uintah-Ouray Agency, Non-Taxable Lands under Jurisdiction, as of June 30, 1933, and Subsequent Acquisitions to 1939, BIA-CCF, n.p.

   Similarly, Kanosh began with 840 acres, of which 25 were judged arable by the BIA, a population of between 35 and 40 Paiutes registered, giving 0.7 acre or less per person, only the size of a good-sized kitchen garden (U.S. Department of Commerce, 13th Census of the United States Population, 1910, Utah, Millard County, Kanosh Precinct, USNA, RG 29, microfilm, roll 1604, sheets 14A, 14B; Lorenzo D. Creel to Commissioner of Indian Affairs, 9 January 1913, USNA, BIA Special Agents Files, 2; A. A. Kimball, Census of the Kanosh Indians, 11 February 1918, UO-MC).

   Koosharem had 240 acres, 25 were arable, a population of 35, leaving 0.7 acre per capita (A. R. Frank, Census of Piute Indians of Koosharem, 30 June 1918, USNA, microfilm M595, Indian Census Rolls, 1885–1940, roll 167; E. A. Farrow to Commissioner of Indian Affairs, 6 October 1927, BIA-CCF; U.S. Congress, Joint Committees on Interior and Insular Affairs, *Hearing on Termination*, 14).

   Most of Indian Peak's 10,240 acres were dry rangeland, but a tiny creek watered about 60 acres for the 25 people who lived there (2.4

acres apiece) (Nick Conner, Census of Paiutes Indians at Indian Peak, 30 June 1919, UO-MC; E. A. Farrow, Annual Narrative Report, SAN, roll 98, 17; Uintah-Ouray Agency, Non-Taxable Lands, n.p.).

Of Kaibab's 120,031 acres, only about 20 were considered arable, and yet 93 Paiutes were expected to live there (0.2 acre per person) (Laura Work, Census Roll of Kaibab Indians, 30 June 1910, USNA, microfilm M595, Indian Census Rolls, 1885–1940, roll 543; Ralph A. Ward to Commissioner of Indian Affairs, 15 December 1910, BIA-CCF, 2; Uintah-Ouray Agency, Non-Taxable Lands, n.p.).

Las Vegas's ten acres could hardly house the 50 people registered there, let alone support them on the scant acre or two that could be spared for garden use (L. B. Sandall, Census of the Las Vegas Paiute Indians, 30 June 1926, USNA, microfilm M595, Indian Census Rolls, 1885–1940, roll 268).

Of Chemehuevi Valley's 2,040 acres and San Juan's nearly half a million (Bunte and Franklin, *From the Sands*, 186), the BIA could not even guess how much was arable, acknowledging that only "isolated spots" near springs, creeks, or where the Colorado River overflowed were productive of crops.

118. It is often impossible to separate the issues of soil fertility and arability from the practical question of water supply for those lands in BIA records. If water was not available, agents often simply accepted that the land was not "suitable for farming."

119. W. A. Jones, "Narrative Report to the Secretary of the Interior," 16 October 1902, in ARCIA, 1902, 140. See also Laura Work to W. A. Jones, 10 June 1898, USNA, BIA Letters Received, 1881–1907, 1–2; Congressman William King to Commissioner of Indian Affairs, 27 June 1900, USNA, BIA Letters Received, 1881–1907.

120. W. B. Hill to Commissioner of Indian Affairs, 8 March 1912, USNA, BIA Irrigation Division Papers, 7; C. F. Hauke to Secretary of the Interior, 8 May 1912, USNA, RG 48, Secretary of the Interior Records, Indian Division, 6.

Under both Utah and Nevada state water laws, water and land are separate commodities, so the purchase of land does not automatically carry rights to use the water that rises in springs on that land, flows across it in rivers, stands in ponds on it, or can be pumped from beneath it. When making the separate purchase of water rights, the buyer acquires two things: the privilege of using a specified quantity of water and a priority date set at the time of purchase. In case of water shortage, the owner with the oldest priority date in the watershed or irrigation system has the right to use his full quantity of water. Only then can the second oldest draw his full amount, then the third, and so on until the supply has been exhausted. Recent claimants run the risk of receiving no water at all. In desert areas with fluctuating patterns of rainfall, the priority date attached to a water right can be more important than the amount of water owned. When the water owner sells his water right, the original priority date goes along with the purchase, so old water rights are of much greater value than younger ones.

121. John F. Wasmund to Commissioner of Indian Affairs, 11 March 1911, BIA-CCF; Oliver Humbarger to Commissioner of Indian Affairs, 13 August 1918, UO-MC; E. A. Farrow to Commissioner of Indian Affairs, 5 August 1927, UO-MC; C. A. Engle to E. A. Farrow, 13 August 1930, UO-MC.

122. Leo Snow, quoted in Hauke to Secretary of the Interior, 8 May 1912, 8.

123. Hill to Commissioner of Indian Affairs, 8 March 1912, 6.

124. Hauke to Secretary of the Interior, 8 May 1912, 11; A. C. Plake, Annual Narrative Report for Shivwits School, SAN, roll 137, 4.

125. Henry Dietz, Report on the St. George & Santa Clara Bench Irrigation Co. Furnishing Water for Certain Lands, Shivwits Indian Reservation, April 1917, USNA, RG 48, Secretary of the Interior Records, Indian Division, Special Irrigation Reports, 7. See also E. B. Meritt to Charles Wagner, 18 April 1918, UO-MC.

126. Henry Dietz to Charles Wagner, 11 September 1917, UO-MC.

127. Lorenzo D. Creel to Superintendent of Shivwits Indian School, 28 January 1915, UO-MC; Charles Wagner to H. W. Dietz, 28 June 1915, UO-MC.

128. Charles Wagner to Lorenzo Creel, 23 December 1915, UO-MC; Charles Wagner to Commissioner of Indian Affairs, 21 April 1916, BIA-CCF; Charles Wagner to Commissioner of Indian Affairs, 25 August 1916, BIA-CCF, 2.

129. E. B. Meritt to Oliver Humbarger, 27 December 1918, UO-MC; William Ray to Oliver Humbarger, 17 June 1919, UO-MC.

130. Oliver Humbarger to William Ray, 7 July 1919, UO-MC.

131. A. C. Plake to H. W. Dietz, 12 May 1921, UO-MC.

132. Henry Dietz to A. C. Plake, 8 June 1921, UO-MC; A. C. Plake to H. W. Deitz [sic], 9 June 1921, UO-MC.

133. A. C. Plake to H. W. Deitz [sic], 11 June 1921, UO-MC; Henry Dietz to A. C. Plake, 10 June 1921, UO-MC.

134. Fifth District Court, State of Utah, "Proposed Determination of Water Rights, St. George Clara Field Canal Co. et al. v. Newcastle Reclamation Company et al.," 6 November 1922, UO-MC, 4.

135. A. C. Plake to H. W. Deitz [sic], 9 July 1920, UO-MC; C. A. Engle to E. A. Farrow, 6 May 1925, UO-MC; C. A. Engle to E. A. Farrow, 26 October 1925, UO-MC; E. A. Farrow to W. E. Blomgren, 21 July 1927, UO-MC; Ambrose Cannon to Doctor [Farrow], 10 August 1927, UO-MC; George M. Bacon to Shivwits Indian School, 17 August 1927, UO-MC; E. A. Farrow to Commissioner of Indian Affairs, 18 August 1927, BIA-CCF; Ambrose Cannon to E. A. Farrow, 29 August 1927, UO-MC.

136. E. A. Farrow to W. E. Blomgren, 21 July 1927, UO-MC. The *Winters* decision came down in 1908.

137. *Winters v U.S.*, 207 US 564 (1908).

138. W. E. Blomgren to H. O. Davidson, 14 May 1928, UO-MC. Agency personnel protested (C. A. Engle to Commissioner of Indian Affairs, 6 July 1929, UO-MC, 3), but the decision not to pursue a further water claim remained unchanged (J. Henry Scattergood to C. A. Engle, 25 March 1930, BIA-CCF, 2).

139. Leo Snow to E. A. Farrow, 18 July 1933, UO-MC; L. M. Holt to Commissioner of Indian Affairs, 11 September 1933, UO-MC; L. M. Holt and John Hafen (signatories), Agreement between the U.S. Government and the Saint George and Santa Clara Bench Irrigation Company, 4 November 1933, BIA-CCF.

140. E. A. Farrow to A. C. Cooley, 14 February 1935, BIA-CCF; Geraint Humphreys to A. L. Wathen, 6 June 1935, BIA-CCF.

141. Knack, "Interethnic Competition," 227–33.

142. Chubbuck to Secretary of the Interior, 31 December 1906, 11; William Spry to the Commissioner of Indian Affairs, 22 May 1922, BIA-CCF. During my research in the Church Historian's Office of the Church of

Jesus Christ of Latter-day Saints in Salt Lake City, the normal repository of such a document, I could not discover any record or title of such a "gift" of water.

143. Joseph Maxwell to Commissioner of Indian Affairs, 24 August 1915, BIA-CCF; H. M. Dietz to Commissioner of Indian Affairs, 21 November 1921, BIA-CCF; Knack, "Interethnic Competition," 227–28.

144. E. C. Finney, Decision on Appeal from the General Land Office, Phoenix 04907-K, 6 June 1921, BIA-CCF.

145. Stephen Mather to Charles Burke, 6 June 1921, BIA-CCF; Warren G. Harding, Presidential Proclamation no. 1663, 31 May 1923, BIA-CCF.

146. E. A. Farrow, W. M. Reed, Frank Pinkley, Charles C. Heaton, and Randall L. Jones, Memorandum of Agreement, 9 June 1924, BIA-CCF.

147. L. M. Holt, Report on Water Supply Development, Kanosh Reservation, April 1936, BIA-CCF, 1–2.

148. Samuel Flickinger to Commissioner of Indian Affairs, 21 December 1927, BIA-CCF.

149. Joseph Pikyavit to Secretary of the Interior, 28 July 1922, BIA-CCF; H. H. Fiske to Commissioner of Indian Affairs, 11 August 1928, BIA-CCF.

150. Alice Ballerstein to E. A. Farrow, 15 September 1924, BIA-CCF, 2; Fifth District Court, State of Utah, "Proposed Determination of Water Rights on the Sevier River System, Richlands Irrigation Co. vs. Westview Irrigation Co., et al.," 21 February 1926, UO-MC, 8; affidavits by George Day et al., enclosed in E. A. Farrow to Edward Morrissey, 24 March 1928, BIA-CCF.

151. Charles Burke to Edgar A. Farrow, 18 February 1928, BIA-CCF. See also E. A. Farrow to Commissioner of Indian Affairs, 27 August 1927, UO-MC, 3–4.

152. Quoted in Geraint Humphreys to Edgar A. Farrow, 4 September 1930, UO-MC. See also Geraint Humphreys to Charles Hollingsworth, 30 June 1930, UO-MC.

153. Pub. L. No. 70-721, 45 Stat. 1161 (1929).

154. F. Earl Stott to Edgar A. Farrow, 19 July 1935, UO-MC; Utah State Engineer's Office, Certificate of Appropriation of Water by U.S. Indian Irrigation Service, 27 November 1937, BIA-CCF.

155. John Collier to Edgar A. Farrow, 21 February 1936, BIA-CCF; Holt, Report; C. A. Engle to A. L. Wathen, 14 May 1937, BIA-CCF; William Zimmerman to Congressman W. K. Granger, 19 October 1941, BIA-CCF; Knack, "Utah Indians," 78.

156. Creel to Commissioner of Indian Affairs, 16 October 1911, 5.

157. Lorenzo Creel to Horace Wilson, 24 January 1922, BIA-CCF, 1–2.

158. E. A. Farrow to Commissioner of Indian Affairs, 5 August 1927, UO-MC, 2; Earl Henderson, Report to Samuel Elliot, Board of Indian Commissioners, 24 February 1931, BIA-CCF, 29. My efforts to locate a formal trust deed issued by the church to designate the Koosharem people as recipients have been unsuccessful.

159. Creel to Wilson, 24 January 1922, 1; Fiske to Commissioner of Indian Affairs, 14 August 1928, 2.

160. Nick Conner to Commissioner of Indian Affairs, 22 November 1921, BIA-CCF.

161. Edward Bagley to A. E. [*sic*] Farrow, 17 June 1935, UO-MC. See also Fiske to Commissioner of Indian Affairs, 14 August 1928, 2.

162. Edward Bagley to O. R. Michelsen, 30 April 1936, UO-MC.

163. Pub. L. No. 75-125, 50 Stat. 241 (1937); E. A. Farrow, Superintendent's Annual Narrative Report, Kaibab Agency, 1937, SAN, roll 99, 8; E. A. Farrow to Commissioner of Indian Affairs, 3 August 1937, UO-MC.

164. Jack Steinberg to Commissioner of Indian Affairs, 23 September 1948, BIA-CCF.

165. Lorenzo D. Creel to Commissioner of Indian Affairs, 8 May 1913, BIA-CCF, 1–2.

166. George A. Mitchell to W. D. Beers, Utah State Engineer, 24 March 1913, BIA-CCF; Nick Conner to Commissioner of Indian Affairs, 23 June 1919, BIA-CCF.

167. Caleb Tanner to G. A. Mitchell, 31 March 1913, BIA-CCF.

168. [Nick Conner] to G. A. Mitchell, 23 June 1919, carbon copy in BIA-CCF. See also A. R. Frank to Commissioner Sells, telegram, 20 September 1916, UO-MC.

169. Hauke to Conner, 28 July 1919.

170. C. A. Engle, Report to Commissioner of Indian Affairs, 12 May 1924, UO-MC, 2, emphasis added. By May the Paiutes had already decided not to cultivate these patches that year, because "the water supply is very deficient and the snow was practically all off the surrounding mountains." See also Charles M. Morris to Nick Conner, 8 October 1923, UO-MC.

171. Engle, Report, 3–4, emphasis added.

172. F. M. Goodwin to U.S. Attorney General, 5 June 1924, BIA-CCF, 2, emphasis added.

173. Harlan Stone to Hubert Work, 10 September 1924, BIA-CCF.

174. E. B. Meritt to Edgar A. Farrow, 18 August 1927, UO-MC, 1–2.

175. A. J. Barnes to E. P. Smith, 20 December 1874, BIA-LR, roll 541, 5–6.

176. Fred Spriggs to Commissioner of Indian Affairs, 7 July 1899, USNA, BIA Letters Received, 1881–1907; E. E. Jones to Secretary of the Interior, 27 July 1901, USNA, RG 48, Secretary of the Interior Records, Letters Received, 2–5, 9.

177. V. S. Barber to E. W. Casson, 21 April 1902, BIA-CCF; A. C. Tonner to Secretary of the Interior, 18 June 1902, USNA, BIA Letters Sent, 1881–1907, Land Series.

178. The secretary did originally approve the survey (W. A. Richards to Commissioner of Indian Affairs, 7 July 1902, BIA-CCF) but later rescinded that approval (E. A. Hitchcock to Commissioner of Indian Affairs, 12 June 1903, USNA, BIA Irrigation Division, Office of the Chief Engineer, General Correspondence, 1901–31, 5).

179. A. C. Tonner to Secretary of the Interior, 11 July 1902, BIA-CCF, 7; A. C. Tonner to Secretary of the Interior, 28 July 1903, BIA-CCF; Theodore Roosevelt, Executive Order, 31 July 1903, in ARCIA, 1903, 480.

180. Samuel Flickinger to Mr. Miner, memorandum, 7 February 1928, BIA-CCF; E. B. Meritt to E. A. Farrow, 5 May 1928, BIA-CCF.

181. E. E. Jones to W. H. Code, 9 February 1908, BIA-CCF, 6.

182. W. H. Code to Secretary of the Interior, 11 March 1908, BIA-CCF, 2–3; H. W. Hincks to John Granville, 25 April 1912, USNA, BIA Irrigation Division, Office of the Chief Engineer, General Correspondence, 1901–31, 1–2.

183. Levi Chubbuck to Secretary of the Interior, 16 December 1907, BIA-CCF, 2–3; "Big Irrigation Project by Muddy Valley Co.," *Clark County Review* (Las Vegas NV), 27 January 1912; Francis A. Swayne to H. W. Hincks, 8 May 1912, USNA, BIA Irrigation Division, Office of the Chief Engineer, General Correspondence, 1901–31.

184. Frank Nichols to E. E. Jones, 12 June 1908, USNA, BIA Irrigation Division, Office of the Chief Engineer, General Correspondence, 1901–31. See also C. F. Larrabee to Industrial Teacher in Charge, Moapa River Indian Reservation, 28 March 1908, BIA-CCF; William C. Sharp, Application for Permit to Appropriate Public Waters of the State of Nevada, 1 May 1908, USNA, BIA Irrigation Division, Office of the Chief Engineer, General Correspondence, 1901–31.

185. John Granville to Secretary of Interior, 25 June 1912, USNA, RG 48, Secretary of the Interior Records, Indian Division, 5.

186. E. B. Meritt to H. W. Dietz, 23 May 1914, USNA, BIA Irrigation Division, Office of the Chief Engineer, General Correspondence, 1901–31. Such a claim anticipated the Supreme Court's later decision in *Arizona v California* (373 US 546 [1963]). See also C. F. Hauke to Commissioner of the General Land Office, 26 July 1912, USNA, BIA Irrigation Division, Office of the Chief Engineer, General Correspondence, 1901–31; Senator Key Pittman to Cato Sells, 26 September 1913, BIA-CCF; Cato Sells to Senator Key Pittman, 17 October 1913, BIA-CCF, 4; E. B. Meritt to William Woodburn, 1 March 1915, BIA-CCF; E. B. Meritt to Superintendent Murtaugh, telegram, 3 July 1915, BIA-CCF.

187. H. W. Dietz to Commissioner of Indian Affairs, 10 May 1919, BIA-CCF.

188. E. B. Meritt to J. G. Schrugham [*sic*], 24 June 1919, BIA-CCF, 1–2.

189. E. B. Meritt to Henry W. Dietz, 15 March 1920, BIA-CCF, 2; S. G. Hopkins to U.S. Attorney General, 10 January 1921, BIA-CCF.

190. John Truesdell to Col. J. G. Scrugham, 1 April 1921, BIA-CCF, 9, 11.

191. Charles Burke to Governor J. G. Scrugham, 15 October 1926, BIA-CCF, 1–2. See also Henry Albert and W. Mendelsohn, Report, 25 April 1925, BIA-CCF; L. B. Sandall to Commissioner of Indian Affairs, 28 October 1925, BIA-CCF.

192. H. T. Johnson to Henry W. Dietz, 24 May 1917, BIA-CCF; Henry W. Dietz to R. M. Reed, 20 November 1917, USNA, BIA Irrigation Division,

Office of the Chief Engineer, General Correspondence, 1901–31; W. E. Blomgren to Commissioner of Indian Affairs, 8 March 1928, BIA-CCF, 3; E. A. Farrow to Commissioner of Indian Affairs, 9 April 1929, BIA-CCF.

193. L. M. Holt to A. L. Wathen, 23 March 1935, BIA-CCF; "White Narrows Dam to Be Built," *Las Vegas Review-Journal*, 6 November 1937, 8.

194. E. C. Fortier, Report on White Narrows Project, Moapa Indian Reservation, Nevada, November 1941, USNA, BIA Irrigation Division, Special Reports, 3; E. C. Fortier to Geraint Humphreys, 23 May 1944, BIA-CCF; Geraint Humphreys to Director of Irrigation, memorandum, 24 August 1944, BIA-CCF, 8, 12; Walter Woehlke to Geraint Humphreys, 13 October 1944, BIA-CCF, 1, 5.

195. Rulon Earl to Burton Ladd, 19 May 1954, BIA-CCF; C. Tyndall to Ralph Gelvin, 23 July 1954, BIA-CCF; Evan Flory to Leonard Nelson, 10 December 1954, BIA-CCF; Burton Ladd, Report on Trip to Moapa to Negotiate with Muddy Valley Irrigation Company, 19 April 1955, BIA-CCF. See Martha C. Knack, "Another Decade of Pyramid Lake Paiutes' Pursuit of 'Wet Water,'" in Knack and Stewart, *As Long as the River Shall Run*, 359–76, for summary discussion of and citations on policy and strategy of negotiating water settlements for Indian tribes rather than litigating.

196. Carson Indian School Agency, Irrigation Report, Moapa Reservation, Fiscal Year 1942, USNA, San Bruno, Carson School Agency, Coded Files, 152.

197. Moapa Tribal Council, Minutes of Council Meeting, 19 April 1953, BIA-CCF; Knack, Field Notes, Moapa Southern Paiutes.

198. C. H. Gensler to Commissioner of Indian Affairs, 4 May 1934, BIA-CCF, 4.

199. A. J. Wirtz to Los Angeles Metropolitan Water District, 9 October 1940, LN, General Files; Roth, "Incorporation and Changes," 194.

200. Edward G. Murtaugh to Commissioner of Indian Affairs, 16 November 1912, BIA-CCF, 4.

201. E. A. Farrow, Superintendent's Annual Narrative Report, 1932, SAN, roll 98, 3; E. A. Farrow to Commissioner of Indian Affairs, 8 August 1932, BIA-CCF; G. E. Lindquist, Report on the Paiute Indian Agency,

Utah, 7 April 1932, USNA, BIA, Board of Indian Commissioners, Special Reports, 20; George LaVatta, Mark Radcliffe, John Montgomery, and J. E. White, Findings and Recommendations with Reference to Reorganization Activities for the Paiute Jurisdiction, 30 September 1936, USNA, BIA Indian Organization Division, General Records, 8.

202. A. R. Trelease to A. H. Kennedy, Las Vegas City Manager, memorandum, 1 September 1955, BIA-CCF; Inter-tribal Council of Nevada, *Nuwuvi*, 126.

203. U.S. Department of Agriculture, Bureau of Agricultural Economics, "Water Facilities Area Plan for the Upper Virgin River Area, Utah and Arizona," mimeographed, 1940, 37.

204. Ralph A. Ward to Commissioner of Indian Affairs, 31 January 1910, BIA-CCF, 2.

205. A. C. Plake, Annual Report for Shivwits School, July 1920, SAN, roll 137, 4, emphasis in original.

206. Frank A. Virtue to Commissioner of Indian Affairs, 15 March 1912, BIA-CCF.

207. E. A. Farrow to J. Harvey Pocock, 30 August 1935, BIA-CCF, 2.

208. Joseph Maxwell to Commissioner of Indian Affairs, 28 December 1912, BIA-CCF, 6.

209. E. G. Murtaugh to Commissioner of Indian Affairs, 10 September 1914, BIA-CCF.

210. L. B. Sandall, Annual Narrative Report of Moapa River Reservation, 16 June 1920, SAN, roll 87, 12.

211. E. G. Murtaugh to Commissioner of Indian Affairs, 29 November 1913, BIA-CCF, 3.

212. William Sharp to Commissioner of Indian Affairs, 4 January 1908, BIA-CCF.

213. E. G. Murtaugh to Commissioner of Indian Affairs, 1 July 1917, SAN, roll 87, 2.

214. James A. Brown, "Report of Special Agent for Kaibab Indians," 15 August 1903, in ARCIA, 1903, 329. See also M. F. Holland to Commissioner of Indian Affairs, 26 November 1909, BIA-CCF, 2; Rider and Paulson, *The Roll Away Saloon*, 60.

215. W. R. Bradfute to W. D. C. Gibson, 22 July 1886, USNA, BIA Letters Received, 1881–1907, 4.

216. Ralph A. Ward to Commissioner of Indian Affairs, 31 January 1910, BIA-CCF.

217. Robert Pikyavit to Commissioner of Indian Affairs, 6 December 1909, BIA-CCF, 1–2.

218. Carl Stevens, Report on the Cedar City Indians, 6 March 1923, USNA, BIA Inspection Division Files, 2.

219. Grey Duclos to C. L. Ellis, 6 July 1911, BIA-CCF, 2.

220. William Sharp to Commissioner of Indian Affairs, 1 October 1907, BIA-CCF.

221. Lorenzo D. Creel to Commissioner of Indian Affairs, 16 October 1911, BIA-CCF, 5.

222. E. G. Murtaugh to Commissioner of Indian Affairs, 15 July 1913, SAN, roll 87, 3.

223. William Sharp to Commissioner of Indian Affairs, 1 July 1907, BIA-CCF.

224. William Sharp, "Report of Industrial Teacher in Charge of Moapa River Reservation," 1 August 1906, in ARCIA, 1906, 271. See also Walter Runke to Frank C. Churchill, 8 July 1907, BIA-CCF, 4; E. A. Farrow to Commissioner of Indian Affairs, 5 August 1927, BIA-CCF; E. A. Farrow to C. E. Faris, 10 September 1927, UO-MC.

225. Frank Virtue, Authorization Request for Irrigation Ditch Work, Shivwits Reservation, 6 September 1911, BIA-CCF; Joseph Maxwell to Commissioner of Indian Affairs, 1 January 1913, UO-MC; Otis Goodall, Report of Inspection, Shivwits Indian School, 18 September 1913, BIA-CCF, 8; E. A. Farrow to Commissioner of Indian Affairs, 18 November 1930, UO-MC; E. A. Farrow to Commissioner of Indian Affairs, 15 May 1935, BIA-CCF.

226. John Granville to Commissioner of Indian Affairs, telegram, 22 January 1912, USNA, BIA Irrigation Division, Office of the Chief Engineer, General Correspondence, 1901–31, 2. See also E. A. Farrow, Annual Report of the Paiute Agency for 1931, SAN, roll 98, 25.

227. Frank Virtue, Annual Report of the Shivwits Indian School for 1912, SAN, roll 87, 2.

228. E. A. Farrow to Louis Mueller, 14 February 1935, USNA, BIA Education Division, Chief of Law and Order, General Correspondence Files.

229. Joseph Murtaugh to Commissioner of Indian Affairs, 25 November 1913, BIA-CCF.

230. Pub. L. No. 63-160, 38 Stat. 582, 583 (1914); E. B. Meritt to Charles Wagner, 28 April 1915, UO-MC.

231. Joe Smith to President Calvin Coolidge, 5 September 1925, BIA-CCF.

232. Cato Sells to Edward G. Murtaugh, 18 December 1913, BIA-CCF, 1, 2.

233. E. G. Murtaugh to Commissioner of Indian Affairs, 15 April 1914, BIA-CCF.

234. E. B. Meritt to Edward G. Murtaugh, 30 January 1917, BIA-CCF.

235. E. G. Murtaugh to Commissioner of Indian Affairs, 2 February 1917, BIA-CCF, 2.

236. E. G. Meritt to Edward Murtaugh, 15 February 1917, BIA-CCF.

237. E. A. Farrow, Annual Narrative Report of Kaibab Agency for 1927, SAN, roll 68, 9.

238. E. A. Farrow to Commissioner of Indian Affairs, 14 January 1929, BIA-CCF.

239. Henry Albert and Isador Mendelsohn, Report on Muddy River Sanitation, 25 April 1915, BIA-CCF, 3. Only after fully four generations of intense and radical ethnohistorical change did the first ethnographers come along these improved roads to study Southern Paiute culture. Robert Lowie visited Moapa and Shivwits briefly in 1912 (*Notes*, 191–314); Samuel Barrett photographed in Cedar City, Shivwits, Kaibab, and Moapa in 1916 but never published any ethnographic observations (Samuel A. Barrett, Field Notes, 1916, Milwaukee Public Museum, Milwaukee WI); and Isabel Kelly's systematic fieldwork with all groups in 1932–33 was the basis for the accepted baseline ethnography (*Southern Paiute Ethnography*, 3). All these scholars were aware that they were not actually observing anything that approached an undisturbed "aboriginal" culture, despite their efforts to describe a truly indigenous lifestyle. Much of the work of Lowie and Kelly was based on oral native recall of former conditions no longer observable. Edward Sapir's dictionary and ethnographic notes were based on one infor-

mant in absentia (Fowler and Euler, eds., "Kaibab Paiute and Northern Ute Ethnographic Field Notes," 779–922; Sapir, *Southern Paiute Dictionary*, 537–730).

240. E. H. Hammond to Commissioner of Indian Affairs, 28 August 1926, BIA-CCF, 4.

241. E. A. Farrow to Commissioner of Indian Affairs, 23 October 1926, BIA-CCF, 1, 2.

242. Charles H. Burke to Edgar A. Farrow, 14 December 1926, BIA-CCF.

243. Joe Norris to Secretary of the Interior, 5 November 1910, BIA-CCF, 10–12.

8. SOCIAL AND POLITICAL RELATIONS

1. William Thackrey to Paul Popenoe, 10 November 1921, BIA-CCF. See also U.S. Department of Commerce, Bureau of the Census, Thirteenth U.S. Census, 1920, USNA, microfilm copy, roll 41, Arizona, Mohave County, Enumeration District 37.

2. "Trailing Queho: Systematic Search Being Made," *Las Vegas Age*, 14 January 1911, 1; S. E. Yount to Moapa Indian Agent, 21 March 1911, BIA-CCF; C. E. Miner to Commissioner of Indian Affairs, 1 February 1922, BIA-CCF; L. B. Sandall to James Jenkins, 26 November 1923, BIA-CCF; Madeline Thompson to Superintendent Farrow, 2 January 1933, BIA-CCF.

3. Helen Stewart to Agent Murtaugh, 17 January 1913, BIA-CCF, 2; Charles Wagner to Commissioner of Indian Affairs, 8 February 1917, BIA-CCF, 2; Goshute Agency, Annual Narrative Report for 1921, SAN, roll 57, 1; Washington Endicott, Report on Moapa Agency, 27 September 1921, BIA-CCF, 3; Nick Conner to Commissioner of Indian Affairs, 13 October 1922, BIA-CCF; Freudrichal and Grace Bonnau to Moapa Agent, 15 April 1924, BIA-CCF.

4. Wagner to Commissioner of Indian Affairs, 8 February 1917, 2; Charles Wagner to Commissioner of Indian Affairs, 7 June 1917, BIA-CCF.

5. Clark Alvord to Samuel Arentz, Congressman, c. September 1927, BIA-CCF.

6. Knack, *Life Is with People*, 16.

7. E. B. Meritt to Leo Crane, Colorado River Agency, 23 April 1924, BIA-CCF.

8. C. J. Rhoads to E. A. Farrow, 28 August 1930, BIA-CCF.

9. Cohen, *Handbook*, 207–28.

10. L. B. Sandall to Superintendent Snyder, Reno Agency, 21 December 1925, BIA-CCF.

11. E. A. Farrow to Commissioner of Indian Affairs, 23 May 1931, BIA-CCF.

12. C. J. Rhoads to Edgar A. Farrow, 11 June 1931, BIA-CCF.

13. C. J. Rhoads to John F. Brown, 15 April 1932, BIA-CCF, 1–2. Similar logic presumably applied to all the Paiutes who had enrolled on one or the other reserves but had moved elsewhere for wage labor.

14. C. J. Rhoads to O. M. Boggess, 29 May 1931, BIA-CCF.

15. C. J. Rhoads to Carl Moore, Supervisor of Indian Education, 3 August 1932, BIA-CCF.

16. Nick Conner to Commissioner of Indian Affairs, 13 March 1922, BIA-CCF, 2.

17. Ambrose Cannon to E. A. Farrow, 24 October 1933, UO-MC.

18. Washington Endicott, Report of Inspection of Shivwits Agency, 1 September 1920, BIA-CCF, 8.

19. Charles Wagner, Annual Narrative Report of Shivwits Indian School, 30 June 1918, SAN, roll 137, 1.

20. Charles Wagner to U.S. Attorney for Utah, 15 November 1917, BIA-CCF.

21. E. M. Sweet, Report of Inspection of Moapa Agency, 26 August 1916, BIA-CCF, 10.

22. For example, at Cedar City (F. J. Franklin to Commissioner of Indian Affairs, 22 June 1922, BIA-CCF), Kanosh (William R. Palmer to A. W. Ivins, 17 August 1925, ms. no. B-2, Ivins Papers), and Kaibab (E. A. Farrow to J. Harvey Pocock, 9 June 1927, UO-MC).

23. "Episcopal Services Held for Dead Indian Boy," *Las Vegas Age*, 7 May 1927, 5.

24. Sapir, "The Mourning Ceremony"; E. A. Farrow, Annual Report of

Kaibab Agency for 1924, SAN, roll 68, 24. On the other hand, Carobeth Laird considers the Cry aboriginal among the Chemehuevis (*The Chemehuevis*, 25–26, 41–43).

25. "Piute Indians Install New Chief at Ceremony," *Las Vegas Age*, 7 September 1933, 1.

26. Nick Conner, Annual Report of the Goshute Agency, 1 July 1919, SAN, roll 57, 4.

27. H. H. Fiske to Commissioner of Indian Affairs, 14 August 1928, BIA-CCF, 5.

28. James McGregor to Commissioner of Indian Affairs, 8 December 1921, BIA-CCF.

29. Nick Conner to Commissioner of Indian Affairs, 12 January 1924, BIA-CCF.

30. Washington Endicott to Cato Sells, 5 August 1920, BIA-CCF.

31. J. Harvey Pocock to E. A. Farrow, 20 September 1933, UO-MC.

32. J. S. Maxwell to Lornzo [*sic*] Creel, 16 November 1915, UO-MC.

33. E. A. Farrow to Commissioner of Indian Affairs, 29 September 1920, BIA-CCF, 2; E. A. Farrow to Nick Conner, 26 March 1923, UO-MC; L. B. Sandall, Annual Report of Moapa River Agency, 30 June 1925, SAN, roll 88, 2; L. B. Sandall to E. A. Farrow, 13 April 1926, UO-MC; E. A. Farrow to Commissioner of Indian Affairs, 4 September 1928, BIA-CCF; E. A. Farrow to Commissioner of Indian Affairs, 11 October 1928, BIA-CCF; E. A. Farrow to Commissioner of Indian Affairs, 10 January 1930, BIA-CCF.

34. E. G. Murtaugh to Commissioner of Indian Affairs, 20 October 1913, BIA-CCF, emphasis in the original.

35. E. A. Farrow to Commissioner of Indian Affairs, 28 May 1918, BIA-CCF.

36. Laura Work to Commissioner of Indian Affairs, 1 July 1902, USNA, BIA Letters Received, 1881–1907, 3. See also Joseph Maxwell to Commissioner of Indian Affairs, 20 December 1914, BIA-CCF.

37. C. J. Rhoads to Edgar A. Farrow, 3 November 1932, BIA-CCF; Stuart, "Old John's Ford."

38. E. A. Farrow to Commissioner of Indian Affairs, 8 May 1928, BIA-CCF.

39. L. B. Sandall to Commissioner of Indian Affairs, 9 September 1919, BIA-CCF.

40. Charles Wagner to Cedar Lumber & Commission Co., 11 April 1918, BIA-CCF.

41. Charles Wagner to Commissioner of Indian Affairs, 20 October 1916, BIA-CCF, 3.

42. C. F. Hauke to Edward G. Murtaugh, 21 November 1915, BIA-CCF. The regulation cited dealt with treaty rights, which were not at issue in the Paiute case. It said, "An Indian holding equal rights in two or more tribes can share in the annuities of but one, and will be required to elect with which tribe to be enrolled, and relinquish in writing his claims to annuities with all others before receiving any payment" (Bureau of Indian Affairs, *Rules and Regulations*, 85).

43. Washington Endicott to Cato Sells, 21 July 1920, BIA-CCF.

44. Charles Wagner to Joseph Maxwell, 16 November 1915, UO-MC.

45. Superintendent of Shivwits School to L. B. Sandall, 24 June 1921, carbon copy, UO-MC.

46. Superintendent of Moapa to Superintendents of Scattered Bands of Utah, Shivwits, and Kaibab Agencies, 1 December 1915, carbon copies, UO-MC.

47. E. A. Farrow to Superintendent of Shivwits Reservation, 7 June 1917, BIA-CCF.

48. E. B. Meritt to E. A. Farrow, 22 September 1921, BIA-CCF.

49. Meritt to Farrow, 22 September 1921.

50. E. A. Farrow to Commissioner of Indian Affairs, 3 September 1921, BIA-CCF, emphasis added.

51. E. G. Murtaugh to Commissioner of Indian Affairs, 5 February 1917, USNA, microfilm M595, Indian Census Rolls, 1885–1940, roll 268; E. A. Farrow to Commissioner of Indian Affairs, 29 September 1920, BIA-CCF.

52. E. G. Murtaugh to Commissioner of Indian Affairs, 9 March 1918, BIA-CCF; E. B. Meritt to L. B. Sandall, 12 December 1918, BIA-CCF.

53. Murtaugh to Commissioner of Indian Affairs, 9 March 1918.

54. L. B. Sandall to Commissioner of Indian Affairs, 5 April 1919, BIA-CCF.

55. Fanny Adair to F. A. Virtue, 16 December 1913, enclosure in E. G. Murtaugh to Commissioner of Indian Affairs, 8 June 1914, BIA-CCF.

56. C. F. Hauke to Secretary of the Interior, 19 November 1914, USNA, RG 48, Secretary of the Interior Records, Indian Division; L. B. Sandall to Commissioner of Indian Affairs, 2 June 1919, BIA-CCF.

57. E. A. Farrow, Annual Narrative Report of Kaibab Agency for 1922, SAN, roll 68, 11; Farrow, "Kaibab Indians," 59. Although they gave lip service to such egalitarianism, agents also tried to instill into Paiute gender roles the inequality familiar to larger American society. When a married woman got an allotment, her current husband's name was automatically inscribed on the deed; the reverse was not true for a married man (C. J. Rhoads to E. A. Farrow, 15 November 1932, BIA-CCF). Men, it was demanded, should be the breadwinners and "support their children," even when it was acknowledged that women often were "capable of work in the fields and gardens along with the men" (Farrow, "Kaibab Indians," 59).

58. Ralph Ward, Annual Narrative Report of Kaibab Agency, 12 July 1910, SAN, roll 68, 4.

59. John Wasmund, Annual Narrative Report of Shivwits Indian School for 1911, SAN, roll 68, 1–2; Francis Swayne to Commissioner of Indian Affairs, 27 April 1912, BIA-CCF.

60. E. A. Farrow, Annual Narrative Report of Kaibab Agency for 1917, SAN, roll 68, 2.

61. John Wasmund, Annual Narrative Report of Shivwits School, 8 July 1910, SAN, roll 137, 4.

62. The agent incorrectly suggested that inconvenience was the reason that even "the white people round about usually go to one of the Mormon temples in Utah to marry and do not secure a license in Arizona" (Joseph Maxwell, Annual Narrative Report of Kaibab Agency for 1914, SAN, roll 68, n.p.).

63. Nick Conner to Commissioner of Indian Affairs, 11 October 1923, BIA-CCF. Agents who themselves stocked state forms to issue to Indians were not authorized state employees, acted illegally, and made Paiutes' resulting marriages questionable under state law.

64. Rusco, "The Status of Indians," 78.

65. Robert N. Newborne to Commissioner of Indian Affairs, 5 September 1922, BIA-CCF, 7.

66. Frank Virtue, Annual Narrative Report of Shivwits Indian School for 1912, SAN, roll 137, 10; E. A. Farrow, Annual Narrative Report of Kaibab Agency for 1923, SAN, roll 68, 2.

67. Susie Grayman to A. C. Plake, 6 January 1920, BIA-CCF.

68. E. B. Meritt to Charles Wagner, 17 May 1915, BIA-CCF, 1–2.

69. Because both Indians had already formed new unions and the state judge had abjured jurisdiction, the commissioner went on to say that he "believed that you [the agent] are justified in recognizing the parties in question as free from their former alliances" (E. B. Meritt to Charles Wagner, 17 August 1915, BIA-CCF, 2–3). State courts rather consistently denied their own jurisdiction in cases of marriage, thus cutting off the commissioner's preferred venue for divorce. See also Charles Wagner to Commissioner of Indian Affairs, 20 July 1915, BIA-CCF.

70. Frank Virtue, Annual Narrative Report of Shivwits Indian School for 1914, SAN, roll 137, 10.

71. E. A. Farrow, Annual Narrative Report of Kaibab Agency for 1921, SAN, roll 68, 2. See also A. C. Plake, Annual Narrative Report of Shivwits Indian School for 1921, SAN, roll 137, 1; John W. Atwater, Inspection Report of Moapa River Indian Agency and School, 1–5 September 1923, BIA-CCF, sec. 2, 1. Later reports show that such sanguine hopes were premature.

72. E. M. Sweet, Report of Inspection of Moapa River Agency, 20 December 1919, BIA-CCF, 26.

73. E. B. Meritt to L. B. Sandall, 13 February 1920, BIA-CCF.

74. E. A. Farrow, Annual Narrative Report of Paiute Agency for 1929, SAN, roll 97, 2.

75. A. C. Plake, Annual Narrative Report of Shivwits Indian School for 1920, SAN, roll 137, 1.

76. E. A. Farrow to Commissioner of Indian Affairs, 23 June 1924, BIA-CCF. See also E. A. Farrow to Commissioner of Indian Affairs, 30 August 1923, BIA-CCF; E. A. Farrow to United States District Attorney, 30 Au-

gust 1923, BIA-CCF; E. A. Farrow to Commissioner of Indian Affairs, 9 May 1924, BIA-CCF; L. C. Wheeler to E. A. Farrow, 16 June 1924, BIA-CCF.

77. E. A. Farrow to Commissioner of Indian Affairs, 8 March 1930, BIA-CCF.

78. E. A. Farrow to Commissioner of Indian Affairs, 3 March 1932, BIA-CCF.

79. Walter Harrington to E. A. Farrow, 3 February 1930, UO-MC.

80. A. C. Plake to Commissioner of Indian Affairs, 27 August 1920, BIA-CCF.

81. A. C. Plake to Commissioner of Indian Affairs, 16 February 1920, BIA-CCF.

82. William Orr, Lincoln County District Attorney, to Charles Wagner, 20 August 1917, BIA-CCF; Charles Wagner to Commissioner of Indian Affairs, 24 August 1917, BIA-CCF; William Thackrey, Superintendent Fort Mohave Indian School, to Commissioner of Indian Affairs, 28 February 1918, BIA-CCF.

83. John Cox to Commissioner of Indian Affairs, 28 June 1910, BIA-CCF. See also E. A. Farrow to Roy Madsen, 20 August 1931, UO-MC, for a similar case at Shivwits.

84. A. C. Plake to H. B. Peairs, Supervisor of Haskell Indian Institute, 26 July 1921, UO-MC.

85. James McGregor to Commissioner of Indian Affairs, 4 January 1922, BIA-CCF.

86. John Perkins to Dr. Sandall, 10 December 1920, BIA-CCF.

87. E. B. Meritt to L. B. Sandall, 28 August 1921, BIA-CCF. The BIA used a variety of other institutions to remove the physically or mentally handicapped from the reservations. In 1911 a Shivwits boy, "since birth simple minded," living with his elderly parents, was sent to an insane asylum after a report "that he once attempted to choke his father, and it is certain that he is a dangerous character. . . . All the Indians fear him and never cross him in any way" (Francis Swayne to Commissioner of Indian Affairs, 9 January 1911, BIA-CCF). At Kaibab in 1914 lived "Mrs. Neil Samson who is not only totally blind, but in my opinion, is insane, also. Her son Major Powel Samson is also affected in the mind. . . . They have

no near relatives and have been kept on Government rations during the past winter" (Joseph Maxwell to Commissioner of Indian Affairs, c. 6 July 1914, BIA-CCF). Both were institutionalized. The BIA was so effective in removing the handicapped from Paiute communities that in the early 1970s, when new federal legislation mandated equal public access for the handicapped, I was told by at least two informants that Paiutes had never had such people in their society. Their presence in the Euro-American population, I was told, was evidence of the degeneracy and moral inadequacy of, among other things, American kinship behavior (Knack, Field Notes, Utah Southern Paiutes).

88. E. A. Farrow to Commissioner of Indian Affairs, 11 May 1917, BIA-CCF.

89. E. B. Meritt to Arthur C. Plake, 17 February 1920, BIA-CCF, 2.

90. E. B. Meritt to L. B. Sandall, 24 May 1919, BIA-CCF.

91. Washington Endicott to Commissioner of Indian Affairs, 10 September 1920, USNA, BIA Inspection Division Files, 6–7.

92. Laura Work, "Report of School Superintendent among the Shivwits Indians," 30 June 1903, in ARCIA, 1903, 330.

93. Mary Cox to Commissioner of Indian Affairs, 20 June 1910, BIA-CCF.

94. "Some time back a Muddy Indian came . . . ," *Lincoln County Record*, 29 August 1902, 4.

95. "Shot Squaw," *Las Vegas Age*, 18 June 1910, 1; John Cox to Commissioner of Indian Affairs, 20 June 1910, BIA-CCF.

96. John Cox to Commissioner of Indian Affairs, 31 March 1911, enclosure no. 3, BIA-CCF. This was said even though Paiutes had never all been on reserves and had never been under legal or military compulsion to do so. See also "Canyon Tragedy: Indian Kills Watchman of Mine near Nelson," *Las Vegas Age*, 26 November 1910, 1.

97. John Riggs to Commissioner of Indian Affairs, 12 March 1919, BIA-CCF, 5.

98. E. B. Meritt to John Riggs, 26 March 1911, BIA-CCF, 2. The posseman saw the commissioner's letter as "a piece of droll humor" and replied that no sane man could actually take the accidental killing of an Indian so seriously (John Riggs to E. B. Meritt, 1 April 1919, BIA-CCF, 6).

99. "Not Killed: James Patterson Insists that He Is Alive in Spite of Queho,"

Las Vegas Age, 4 March 1911, 1; Cox to Commissioner of Indian Affairs, 31 March 1911, with enclosures; "Mysterious Murder in El Dorado Canyon," *Las Vegas Age*, 25 January 1919, 1; "Two Skeletons Found at Forlorn Hope Spring: Trailers of Queho Unearth New Mysteries in Fastnesses of the Desert," *Las Vegas Age*, 15 February 1919, 1; L. B. Sandall to Commissioner of Indian Affairs, 12 April 1919, BIA-CCF; Balknap, "The Saga of Queho," 28.

The well-known Willie Boy case of 1909 also resulted in a large-scale manhunt. Originally from Pahrump and not enrolled on any reservation, he killed a Chemehuevi on a ranch near Banning CA, ran off with the victim's daughter, and was pursued by a posse in cars across the Mojave Desert before dying in a shoot-out (Carling, "On the Trail"; Lawton, *Willie Boy*; Lawton, *The Last Western Manhunt*; made into the film *Tell Them Willie Boy Is Here* [1969], directed by Abraham Polonsky and starring Robert Redford and Katherine Ross).

Like Queho, Cochie Segmiller from Moapa quarreled with his rancher boss concerning $6 in wages and killed him in 1903, but unlike Queho, he was peacefully taken into custody in Las Vegas, admitted to the murder in state court, and was sentenced to hang. The sentence was commuted to life in prison. Segmiller was paroled, but he broke parole and was rejailed a number of times before being released to the custody of a retired BIA legal investigator on condition they leave the state. "Death Sentence," *Lincoln County Record*, 13 November 1903, 4; "Sentence Commuted to Life," *Lincoln County Record*, 24 January 1904, 4; William Johnson to Commissioner of Indian Affairs, 5 January 1911, BIA-CCF; C. H. Asbury to Commissioner of Indian Affairs, 29 June 1914, BIA-CCF; E. G. Murtaugh to Commissioner of Indian Affairs, 18 November 1914, BIA-CCF; W. E. Johnson to Cato Sells, 20 May 1917, BIA-CCF.

100. Claude Covey to Commissioner of Indian Affairs, 18 May 1914, BIA-CCF; Claude Covey to Commissioner of Indian Affairs, 26 September 1914, BIA-CCF, 3; James Jenkins to Commissioner of Indian Affairs, 23 March 1915, BIA-CCF. Tse-ne-gat was also known to non-Indians as Hatch. The historical documents in this area are complicated by local non-Indians' habit of translating the term "Paiute" as "renegade Ute" and using it for any off-reservation Indians they felt were hostile, regardless of ethnic background or language spoken. While it is unquestionable that some ethnic Paiutes were in the area, they practiced a lifestyle of horse nomadism and cattle raising like Utes and sheep rais-

ing and wearing, according to Scott's photographs, high-crowned, black, broad-brimmed Stetsons like Navajos. The ethnic affiliations of particular individuals and proportions of Paiutes in the Allen Canyon interethnic community can only be authoritatively established by very careful genealogical ethnohistory, which, to the best of my knowledge, has not been done.

101. "Conquering Indians with Kindness: General Hugh L. Scott Tells Secret of His Remarkable Mastery of Red Men," *Colorado Springs Gazette*, c. April 1915, undated clipping in Topical Clipping Files, Western History Department, Denver Public Library; General Hugh Scott to *Sunset Magazine*, c. April 1923, Hugh L. Scott Papers, National Anthropological Archives, Smithsonian Institution, 2–3.

102. "Piutes Penned in by Posses after Furious Night Attack," *Washington Times*, 23 February 1915; "Troopers Back to Posse's Aid: Cavalry on Way across the Desert Where Piutes Are on Warpath," *Washington Herald*, 23 February 1915; Lyman, *Indians and Outlaws*, 161.

103. Lorenzo D. Creel to Commissioner of Indian Affairs, 13 April 1915, BIA-CCF, 2. See also James Jenkins to Commissioner of Indian Affairs, 1 March 1915, BIA-CCF, 6; Scott to *Sunset Magazine*, c. April 1923, 3.

104. "Conquering," n.p.; Scott to *Sunset Magazine*, c. April 1923, 3–4; Jenkins to Commissioner of Indian Affairs, 23 March 1915; Lyman, *Indians and Outlaws*, 160–67.

105. James Jenkins to Commissioner of Indian Affairs, 15 April 1915, BIA-CCF, 2; David Cook to U.S. Attorney General, 22 April 1915, BIA-CCF; Laura Holderby to Arthur Horn, 25 April 1915, BIA-CCF.

106. Lyman, *Indians and Outlaws*, 164. See also Harry Tedrow to U.S. Attorney General, 6 May 1915, BIA-CCF, 3; W. W. McConihe to Commissioner of Indian Affairs, 22 October 1915, BIA-CCF.

107. Jenkins to Commissioner of Indian Affairs, 1 March 1915, 7–9; McConihe to Commissioner of Indian Affairs, 22 October 1915, 6; Scott to *Sunset Magazine*, c. April 1923, 4.

108. Lyman, *Indians and Outlaws*, 192, see also 194–95.

109. Kelly, "Southern Paiute Shamanism," 155, 159, 160, 162.

110. "Made Good: Indian Medicine Man Executed According to Tribal

Law," *Las Vegas Age*, 7 May 1910, 4; John Cox to Commissioner of Indian Affairs, 3 June 1910, BIA-CCF.

111. E. G. Murtaugh to Commissioner of Indian Affairs, 25 September 1916, BIA-CCF, 2. See also E. G. Murtaugh to Commissioner of Indian Affairs, telegram, 25 December 1914, BIA-CCF; "Indian Held for Murder: Indian Fred Ben Must Answer before District Court for Killing Bismark," *Las Vegas Age*, 9 January 1915, 1; "Murder Trial in Progress," *Las Vegas Age*, 25 September 1915, 1; "Fred Ben Is Not Guilty," *Las Vegas Age*, 2 October 1915, 1; E. G. Murtaugh to Commissioner of Indian Affairs, 6 November 1915, BIA-CCF. See another witchcraft accusation that Posey brought to state officers after his own trial for attempted murder of a federal marshal ("Piute Indians Appeal to Attorney for Aid in Getting Rid of Tribesman Practicing Magic," *Salt Lake Tribune*, 31 October 1921, copy in Church, Journal History).

112. Robert George and Yellowjacket, Minutes of Shivwits Court of Indian Offenses, 11 April 1906, UO-MC, 6.

113. Charles Wagner to Commissioner of Indian Affairs, 27 November 1915, BIA-CCF, 1–2.

114. Joseph Maxwell to Commissioner of Indian Affairs, 22 October 1915, BIA-CCF. Paiute traditional community decisions took into account the entire life history of the accused; the American political insistence that a case be limited to only the one single event isolated from its biographical context was undoubtedly considered short-sighted by the Shivwits community.

115. E. B. Meritt to Charles Wagner, 1 May 1916, BIA-CCF, 2.

116. C. F. Hauke to Edward G. Murtaugh, 27 August 1912, BIA-CCF; E. G. Murtaugh to Commissioner of Indian Affairs, 26 April 1916, BIA-CCF, 2; Pub. L. No. 362-341, 23 Stat. 362, 385 (1885). The child developed a venereal disease.

117. E. G. Murtaugh to Commissioner of Indian Affairs, 15 June 1916, BIA-CCF, 2. See also Murtaugh to Commissioner of Indian Affairs, 26 April 1916.

118. E. G. Murtaugh to Commissioner of Indian Affairs, 25 September 1916, BIA-CCF, 2; E. B. Meritt to E. G. Murtaugh, 11 October 1916, BIA-CCF. Jim Henry reappeared in agency records in 1920 as remarried at Shivwits, Utah. He reportedly "deserted Serena Snow, to whom he is

legally married, deserting also their infant child, and is living with another woman at Moapa Reservation, Nevada" (Washington Endicott to Cato Sells, 21 July 1920, BIA-CCF), hence breaking his oath to the county attorney. Like Mericats, he was simply chastised for desertion by the Moapa Court of Indian Offenses (E. B. Meritt to Arthur Plake, 19 October 1920, BIA-CCF).

119. "Piute Indians on Warpath," *Caliente (NV) Prospector*, 27 March 1909, 1.

120. "'Alex,' the Indian 'Cop,'" *Caliente (NV) Express*, 15 March 1906, 1. See also "Aristocratic Squaws," *Caliente Express*, 4 January 1906, 1; "Good Indians Now: Because Justice Maynard Coralls [*sic*] Them Together at 9 O'Clock," *Caliente Express*, 4 January 1906, 1.

121. "'Frank' and 'Monshan' . . . ," *Las Vegas Age*, 8 June 1907, 5; "Nice Mixture," *Las Vegas Age*, 13 May 1911, 4.

122. E. G. Murtaugh to Commissioner of Indian Affairs, 5 July 1913, BIA-CCF, with enclosed clipping; E. G. Murtaugh to Commissioner of Indian Affairs, 6 December 1913, BIA-CCF.

123. "Busy Times in Justice Court," *Las Vegas Age*, 12 June 1915, 1.

124. T. E. James to Commissioner of Indian Affairs, 12 March 1917, BIA-CCF, 2. See also E. G. Murtaugh to Commissioner of Indian Affairs, 5 April 1917, BIA-CCF.

125. H. S. Cutler to Reed Smoot, 15 December 1905, BIA-CCF, with enclosure; Joe Indian to Commissioner of Indian Affairs, 10 September 1916, BIA-CCF; E. B. Meritt to Joe Indian, 26 September 1916, BIA-CCF.

126. Mable Wall to [Church President] Grant, 11 September 1935, Palmer Papers, 4.

127. "Indians Sentenced for Killing Deer," *Iron County (UT) Record*, 1 November 1934, 1.

128. L. B. Sandall to Commissioner of Indian Affairs, 30 December 1925, BIA-CCF; L. B. Sandall to Commissioner of Indian Affairs, 1 April 1926, BIA-CCF.

129. Conyers Hedge to E. A. Farrow, 29 September 1932, BIA-CCF.

130. E. A. Farrow to Commissioner of Indian Affairs, 14 May 1927, BIA-CCF; E. A. Farrow to Commissioner of Indian Affairs, 13 July 1927, BIA-CCF.

131. C. N. Jensen to T. E. Bartlett, 22 September 1932, BIA-CCF, emphasis added.

132. L. B. Sandall, Annual Narrative Report of Moapa River Agency for 1923, SAN, roll 88, 5.

133. L. B. Sandall to Commissioner of Indian Affairs, 28 October 1925, BIA-CCF, 2. As late as 1930 not a single Indian had registered to vote in Clark County, Nevada, which contained both the Las Vegas and the Moapa reservations (*Las Vegas Review-Journal*, 5 August 1930, 6).

134. Editorial, "Laws, Not Courts, Keep Indians Voting," *Las Vegas Review-Journal*, 5 December 1930, 8; U.S. Supreme Court, docket 534, *Allen v Merell*, "Stipulation of Parties," 1956, copy in BIA-CCF. This is, of course, precisely the same argument that Indians eventually turned to their advantage in the 1980s to evade state restrictions against casino gambling.

135. Laura Work to Commissioner of Indian Affairs, 11 October 1904, USNA, BIA Letters Received, 1881–1907, 2; E. A. Hitchcock, Secretary of the Interior to Commissioner of Indian Affairs, 6 April 1904, USNA, BIA Letters Received, 1881–1907. Seventy years later, this issue would become famous in a series of cases from the Navajo Reservation.

136. For instance, consider the federal conviction of a Kaibab man for raping a minor on the reservation, followed by a petition by Shivwits men for his release after one year because "we feel that he has been in there long enough and want him to come home" (Yellowjacket et al., Petition to Commissioner of Indian Affairs, 22 March 1915, BIA-CCF; see also Frank Virtue to Commissioner of Indian Affairs, 25 March 1914, BIA-CCF; E. B. Meritt to Yellow Jacket, 7 May 1915, BIA-CCF). Compare Arizona's attempts to control Paiute marriage customs by using state rape laws against men at Kaibab (C. J. Rhoads to E. A. Farrow, 30 November 1932, BIA-CCF).

Concerning other areas of Paiute behavior, federal law was invoked against a Kaibab man who served over a year at Leavenworth for forging a check (R. A. Ward to Commissioner of Indian Affairs, 1 July 1910, BIA-CCF). A Shivwits man drew thirteen months hard labor for burglarizing the St. George post office (U.S. District Court for Utah, Judgment, docket 479, 1902, USNA, Denver, RG 21, U.S. District Court, Utah, Combined Case Files, 1896–1938). In 1930 a Shivwits man was convicted by a federal grand jury for the interstate theft of a

Moapa man's car (E. A. Farrow to Commissioner of Indian Affairs, 10 June 1930, BIA-CCF).

137. Prucha, *The Great Father*, 2:653–55, 783–85.

138. William Sharp to Commissioner of Indian Affairs, 10 August 1905, in ARCIA, 1905, 256; C. F. Larrabee to Secretary of the Interior, 17 March 1906, USNA, RG 48, Secretary of the Interior Records, Indian Division, Letters Received, 1906; William Sharp to Commissioner of Indian Affairs, 17 June 1909, BIA-CCF; L. B. Sandall to Commissioner of Indian Affairs, 23 December 1918, BIA-CCF; E. M. Sweet, Report of Inspection of Shivwits Reservation, 18 December 1919, BIA-CCF, 15.

139. C. L. Ellis to Commissioner of Indian Affairs, 14 July 1911, BIA-CCF, 7.

140. R. A. Ward, Annual Narrative Report of Kaibab Agency, 1911, SAN, roll 68, 1–2.

141. L. B. Sandall, Annual Narrative Report of Moapa River School, 1 July 1918, SAN, roll 87, 2.

142. Hagan, *Indian Police*, 104–24.

143. Anthony W. Ivins to Commissioner of Indian Affairs, 24 August 1891, USNA, BIA Letters Received, 1881–1907, 4. As late as 1924 churchmen engineered the naming of a single "chief" to represent the Paiutes at Cedar City to serve as a conduit for information into and out of that nonreservation community (William Palmer to Anthony W. Ivins, 20 January 1924, Palmer Papers, 2).

144. R. V. Belt to Anthony Ivins, 9 September 1891, USNA, BIA Letters Sent, 1881–1907, Land Division, 5.

145. E. A. Farrow, Annual Narrative Report of Kaibab Agency, 1924, SAN, roll 68, 15.

146. E. M. Sweet, Kaibab Inspection Report, 16 December 1919, BIA-CCF, 10. See also, on Kanosh, William Penny to "Indian Agent," 18 December 1918, BIA-CCF; Joseph McGregor to Commissioner of Indian Affairs, 8 December 1921, BIA-CCF. On Cedar City, Carl Steven, Supervisor of Schools, Supplement to Goshute Report, 6 March 1923, BIA-CCF, 2; William Palmer to Anthony Ivins, 21 October 1924, Ivins Papers, 2; Knack, "Church and State."

147. E. B. Meritt to Carl Boyd, 16 October 1922, BIA-CCF. See also M. F.

Holland to Commissioner of Indian Affairs, 28 March 1901, BIA-CCF, 2.

148. Mabel Jarvis, "Essay no. 220 Indians," 4 March 1936, Federal Writers' Project Collection, Manuscript and Archive Division, Library of Congress, Washington DC. Elsewhere in the Great Basin native leadership on the local level similarly survived BIA persecution. See Clemmer, "Differential Leadership Patterns"; Lewis, "Reservation Leadership"; Crum, *The Road*, 49–50, 65–66, 75–84.

149. Pete, Peach, Squint, John, and Blueshirt to Anthony Ivins, 18 March 1923, Ivins Papers, published in *Salt Lake Tribune*, 28 April 1923.

150. Laura Work to Commissioner of Indian Affairs, 30 June 1902, in ARCIA, 1902, 473; R. A. Ward, Annual Narrative Report of Kaibab Agency, 1914, SAN, roll 68, sec. 8.

151. First Shivwits reference, Otis Goodall, Report of Inspection of Shivwits School and Agency, 5 December 1915, BIA-CCF, 2; for Moapa, C. D. Munroe to Commissioner of Indian Affairs, 10 January 1921, BIA-CCF; second Shivwits item, Harwood Hall, Report of Inspection of Shivwits Indian Day School, 24 April 1916, BIA-CCF, sec. 4.

152. E. A. Farrow to Isabel Allardyce of *Western Story Magazine*, 4 December 1923, UO-MC, 2.

153. L. B. Sandall to Commissioner of Indian Affairs, 22 July 1925, BIA-CCF.

154. E. A. Farrow to Commissioner of Indian Affairs, 11 March 1919, BIA-CCF. Note the recurrence of the idea that Paiutes had one "proper" place where they "belonged."

155. L. B. Sandall to Commissioner of Indian Affairs, 15 April 1921, BIA-CCF.

156. L. B. Sandall, Annual Narrative Report of Moapa River Agency, 16 June 1920, SAN, roll 87, 2. Note that, contrary to common U.S. practice, the arresting officer was part of the decision structure.

157. Francis Swayne to Commissioner of Indian Affairs, 26 February 1912, BIA-CCF, 1–2. The commissioner refused to overturn the Indian court in this case.

158. Robert George and Yellowjacket, Minutes, 11 April 1906, UO-MC; Laura Work to Commissioner of Indian Affairs, 1 March 1907, USNA, BIA Letters Received, 1881–1907.

159. [Signed with the initials R. A. M.], "Writes of an Indian Court He Witnessed," *Millard County (UT) Chronicle*, c. 13 February 1931, clipping in Palmer Papers. From internal evidence, this reminiscence is of an event c. 1905.

160. Lincoln Silver to Lizzie Segmiller, 29 January 1920, BIA-CCF.

161. "Writes," c. 13 February 1931.

162. A. C. Plake to Commissioner of Indian Affairs, 3 November 1920, BIA-CCF; L. B. Sandall, Annual Narrative Report of Moapa River Agency, 30 June 1925, SAN, roll 88, 1.

163. E. A. Farrow, Annual Narrative Report, Paiute Agency for 1933, SAN, roll 98, 32.

164. Their salary was $20 per month, one fifth that of the Indian agent (F. M. Goodwin to Commissioner of Indian Affairs, 25 October 1921, BIA-CCF).

165. W. A. Jones to William Sharp, 30 December 1902, USNA, BIA Irrigation Division, Office of the Chief Engineer, General Correspondence, 1901–31, 11.

166. Emily Day to Washington DC, 9 March 1909, BIA-CCF.

167. L. B. Sandall to Commissioner of Indian Affairs, 3 February 1920, BIA-CCF.

168. E. A. Farrow to Commissioner of Indian Affairs, 21 April 1927, BIA-CCF; E. A. Farrow to Commissioner of Indian Affairs, 15 November 1929, BIA-CCF.

169. E. A. Farrow to Commissioner of Indian Affairs, 15 December 1922, BIA-CCF.

170. L. B. Sandall to Commissioner of Indian Affairs, 19 November 1920, BIA-CCF.

171. Walter Runke to Commissioner of Indian Affairs, 10 December 1907, BIA-CCF, 3.

172. John Wasmund, Annual Narrative Report of Shivwits Indian School for 1911, SAN, roll 137, 1.

173. "Bad Injun," *Las Vegas Age*, 22 August 1908, 6; William Sharp to Commissioner of Indian Affairs, 5 September 1908, BIA-CCF; Day to Wash-

ington DC, 9 March 1909; Swayne to Commissioner of Indian Affairs, 26 February 1912.

174. A. R. Frank to M. J. Macfarlane, 30 October 1918, UO-MC. See also Amos Frank to Bishop Kimball, 8 January 1918, UO-MC; Amos Frank to Commissioner Sells, telegram, 9 February 1918, BIA-CCF; E. B. Meritt to E. A. Farrow, 15 February 1918, UO-MC; M. J. Macfarlane to A. R. Frank, 19 September 1918, UO-MC.

175. Wood, "Gosiute–Shoshone Draft Resistance."

176. Emily Workie née Day, for Lincoln Silver, to Maud Russell, 29 May 1917, BIA-CCF, 1–4.

177. William Johnson to Emily and John Workie, 11 June 1917, BIA-CCF.

178. E. B. Meritt to Emily D. Workie, 28 June 1917, BIA-CCF.

179. Captain Pete to Charles Wagner, c. October 1917, UO-MC.

180. Amos Frank to Captain Pete, 19 March 1918, UO-MC.

181. Charles Wagner to Cedar Pete, 3 March 1918, UO-MC.

182. "Indian Uprising Tickles Pioche," *Pioche Daily Record*, c. 1917–18, clipping in USNA, San Bruno, RG 75, BIA Special Agents Files, L. A. Dorrington Files.

183. E. B. Meritt to E. A. Farrow, 20 July 1918, BIA-CCF. See also E. A. Farrow to Commissioner of Indian Affairs, 21 June 1918, BIA-CCF.

184. The Las Vegas newspaper did report in 1919 the death of one hometown serviceman identified as an Indian ("Another Vegas Boy Was Killed in Action," *Las Vegas Age*, 18 January 1919, 1). His name did not appear in any of the Paiute records, so he may have been Shoshoni, from one of the Arizona tribes, or unenrolled. Two columns away the headline read, "Articles Are Signed Extending Armistice."

9. THE GREAT DEPRESSION AND WORLD WAR II

1. Washington Endicott, Report of Inspection of Goshute Agency, 27 March 1920, USNA, BIA Inspection Division Files; Cato Sells to Secretary of the Interior, 8 July 1920, USNA, RG 48, Secretary of the Interior Records, Indian Division; Woodrow Wilson, Executive Order, 12 July 1920, USNA, RG 48, Secretary of the Interior Records, Indian Division.

2. C. J. Rhoads to Secretary of the Interior, 16 August 1932, approved by secretary 23 August 1932, BIA-CCF.

3. Pub. L. No. 66-3, 41 Stat. 3, 34 (1919).

4. L. B. Sandall, Annual Narrative Report of Moapa River Agency, 30 June 1924, SAN, roll 88, 5. See also E. B. Meritt to L. B. Sandall, 7 June 1924, BIA-CCF; E. B. Meritt to Leo Crane, 23 April 1924, BIA-CCF.

5. Charles Burke to Secretary of the Interior, 10 July 1922, approved by secretary 17 July 1922, BIA-CCF.

6. A. C. Plake, Annual Narrative Report of Shivwits School, 1 July 1920, SAN, roll 137, 5. See also John Atwater, Report of Inspection of Kaibab Agency, September 1922, BIA-CCF, 1.

7. E. A. Farrow to Commissioner of Indian Affairs, 29 September 1920, BIA-CCF, 2; James MacGregor to Commissioner of Indian Affairs, 9 December 1921, BIA-CCF, 2; Charles Burke to Arthur C. Plake, 2 March 1922, BIA-CCF.

8. H. H. Fiske to Commissioner of Indian Affairs, 24 July 1928, BIA-CCF, 6; E. A. Farrow, Annual Narrative Report of Paiute Agency for 1935, SAN, roll 98, 11; C. Cope, Annual Narrative Report of Moapa River Agency for 1947, USNA, Laguna Niguel, BIA-CCF, 3; Knack, Field Notes, Moapa Southern Paiutes.

9. Washington Endicott to Cato Sells, 21 July 1920, BIA-CCF, 2; E. A. Farrow, Annual Narrative Report of Kaibab Agency for 1922, SAN, roll 68, 16; E. A. Farrow, Annual Narrative Report of Paiute Agency for 1928, SAN, roll 97, 3.

10. Carl Boyd to Commissioner of Indian Affairs, 25 March 1922, BIA-CCF; John Atwater, Inspection of Moapa River Agency, 1–5 September 1922, USNA, BIA Special Agents Files, Investigative Records of Col. L. A. Dorrington, 1913–23, 7; L. B. Sandall to Commissioner of Indian Affairs, 21 April 1925, BIA-CCF; G. A. Trotter to Commissioner of Indian Affairs, 19 October 1938, BIA-CCF.

11. Lonnie Kouchomp for Kanosh Band of Paiute Indians to E. A. Farrow, 2 May 1938, BIA-CCF.

12. W. Greenwood to C. C. Wright, 26 April 1940, BIA-CCF.

13. E. A. Farrow to Commissioner of Indian Affairs, 28 February 1927, BIA-CCF; E. A. Farrow to R. B. Millin, 12 January 1937, LN, Forestry and Grazing Development Division; C. C. Wright to Commissioner of Indian Affairs, 15 February 1940, BIA-CCF; C. C. Wright to Commissioner

of Indian Affairs, 2 January 1943, LN, Forestry and Grazing Development Division; J. E. White to Commissioner of Indian Affairs, 14 November 1945, BIA-CCF, 2.

14. E. A. Farrow to E. H. Hammond, 13 October 1926, BIA-CCF.

15. Knack, "Interethnic Competition."

16. E. A. Farrow to Commissioner of Indian Affairs, 20 August 1923, BIA-CCF; E. A. Farrow to Commissioner of Indian Affairs, 25 August 1924, BIA-CCF, 1–2; Charles Heaton to E. A. Farrow, 1 December 1924, BIA-CCF.

17. E. A. Farrow, Annual Narrative Report of Paiute Agency for 1937, SAN, roll 99, 1; Knack, "Interethnic Competition," 228–32.

18. E. A. Farrow to Commissioner of Indian Affairs, 29 September 1925, BIA-CCF; E. A. Farrow, Annual Narrative Report of Kaibab Agency for 1929, SAN, roll 97, 19; E. A. Farrow to Commissioner of Indian Affairs, 5 June 1929, BIA-CCF.

19. Farrow, Annual Report for 1937, 2; E. A. Farrow to Commissioner of Indian Affairs, 3 February 1926, BIA-CCF.

20. John T. Montgomery to A. C. Cooley, 10 January 1931, BIA-CCF; E. A. Farrow to Commissioner of Indian Affairs, 26 February 1937, BIA-CCF; P. E. Church, Kaibab Indian Cattle Operations, in Annual Extension Report of Paiute Jurisdiction for 1948, BIA-CCF, 93–96.

21. Edwin Drye, Julian Bulletts, and Xavier Vigeant, For the Use of the Rehabilitation Grant—Fiscal Year 1941, 4 June 1941, BIA-CCF; Uintah-Ouray Agency, Suggested Plan of Investment of the $15,000 Tribal Fund of Kaibab Reservation, 28 October 1941, BIA-CCF.

22. Richard Millin to Commissioner of Indian Affairs, 26 January 1943, BIA-CCF; E. K. Douglass, Kaibab Reservation Utilization Study, May 1943, BIA-CCF; Forrest Stone and Albert Huber to A. C. Cooley, 19 May 1945, BIA-CCF.

23. L. M. Holt to Commissioner of Indian Affairs, 4 January 1935, BIA-CCF; Thomas Guyn to Don Foster, 6 August 1942, BIA-CCF.

24. BIA Irrigation Division, Report on White Narrows Project, Moapa Indian Reservation, Nevada, November 1941, USNA, BIA Irrigation Division, Special Reports Files, 5.

25. S. M. Dodd to E. A. Farrow, 11 November 1937, LN, CCC Indian Division Files; U.S. Attorney General to Secretary of the Interior, 25 June 1940, LN, Land Operations/Land Acquisitions Files; Douglas Clark to Don Foster, 2 December 1943, LN, Land Operations/Land Acquisitions Files.

26. E. A. Farrow to Commissioner of Indian Affairs, 7 August 1934, BIA-CCF; E. A. Farrow to A. C. Cooley, 14 February 1935, BIA-CCF.

27. E. B. Meritt to Secretary of the Interior, 22 October 1928, BIA-CCF; Pub. L. No. 70-721, 45 Stat. 1161 (1929).

28. L. M. Holt to H. E. Adams, 20 April 1935, BIA-CCF; T. H. Humpherys, Utah State Engineer to E. A. Farrow, 18 July 1935, BIA-CCF; L. M. Holt, Water Supply Development, Kanosh Reservation, April 1936, BIA-CCF, 5; A. L. Wathen, Work Program, Irrigation District 4, Garden Tracts—Utah, 30 October 1936, BIA-CCF; William Zimmerman to Congressman W. K. Granger, 19 October 1941, BIA-CCF.

29. E. A. Farrow to Commissioner of Indian Affairs, 3 August 1937, BIA-CCF; Jacob Steinberg to Commissioner of Indian Affairs, 23 September 1948, BIA-CCF.

30. W. H. Zeh and Richard Millin, Report on Kaibab Reservation, 27 July 1935, LN, Forestry and Grazing Development Division, 20–24.

31. John Collier to Purchasing Office, memorandum, 28 July 1933, LN, CCC Indian Division Files; E. A. Farrow, Annual Narrative Report of Kaibab Agency for 1936, SAN, roll 99, 6; Uintah-Ouray Agency, Road Survey, Fiscal Year 1937, UO-MC.

32. Secretary of the Interior to Senator Elmer Thomas, July 1935, BIA-CCF; Guy Hafen, E. S. Gardner, J. R. Fawcett, J. H. Schmutz, and George Seegmiller to Congressman Abe Murdock, 11 August 1935, BIA-CCF; Laron Andrus to Congressman Abe Murdock, 20 August 1935, BIA-CCF; E. A. Farrow to Commissioner of Indian Affairs, 23 September 1935, BIA-CCF; Pub. L. No. 75-124, 50 Stat. 239 (1937).

33. J. L. Bennett to Indian Field Service, Salt Lake City, 20 October 1941, LN, BIA-CCF, 2. See also C. C. Wright to Kenneth Green, 29 October 1941, LN, BIA-CCF.

34. Pub. L. No. 74-155, 49 Stat. 393 (1935); Pub. L. No. 75-123, 50 Stat. 239 (1937).

35. L. L. Nelson to Forrest Stone, 17 February 1948, BIA-CCF.

36. William Eddy to Commissioner of Indian Affairs, 1 August 1936, USNA, BIA Indian Organization Division, General Records; A. J. Wirtz to Metropolitan Water District of Southern California, 9 October 1940, LN, BIA-CCF.

37. J. Henry Scattergood to E. A. Farrow, 14 October 1929, BIA-CCF.

38. Farrow, Annual Report for 1928, 10.

39. E. A. Farrow to Commissioner of Indian Affairs, 2 August 1930, UO-MC.

40. E. A. Farrow, Annual Narrative Report of Paiute Agency for 1933, SAN, roll 98, 4.

41. Farrow, Annual Report for 1933, 6.

42. E. A. Farrow to J. F. Worley, 26 February 1934, BIA-CCF.

43. George Hedges, Report of Reimbursable Accounts and Leases of Paiute Agency, 16 December 1938, BIA-CCF, 4; A. C. Cooley to E. A. Farrow, 30 August 1937, BIA-CCF.

44. K. A. Perkins to Commissioner Collier, 24 August 1936, BIA-CCF.

45. Carson Agency, Total Individual Income—Moapa River, 1942, BIA-CCF; Uintah-Ouray Agency, Total Individual Income—Kaibab, Shivwits, Kanosh, Koosharem, 1942, BIA-CCF.

46. Robert N. Newborne, Report of Kaibab Consolidated Agency, 5 September 1922, USNA, BIA Inspection Division Files, 9–10.

47. For example, "Deer," 1 November 1934. Adding insult to injury, at the same time Utah was hiring non-Indian hunters to cull deer herds north of Shivwits in order to reduce grazing competition for non-Indian stockmen, the venison was donated to the Paiutes because of their poverty (Ambrose Canon to E. A. Farrow, 7 September 1935, UO-MC).

48. E. A. Farrow to Commissioner of Indian Affairs, 8 January 1931, BIA-CCF, 2.

49. Nick Conner to Commissioner of Indian Affairs, 13 October 1922, BIA-CCF; L. B. Sandall, Annual Narrative Report of Moapa River Agency for 1923, SAN, roll 88, 6; L. B. Sandall to Commissioner of Indian Affairs, 5 October 1923, BIA-CCF; L. B. Sandall to James Jenkins, 26 November 1923, UO-MC; Sandall, Annual Report, 30 June 1924, 5.

50. William Palmer to A. W. Ivins, 17 August 1925, Ivins Papers.

51. L. B. Sandall to Commissioner of Indian Affairs, 5 June 1923, BIA-CCF.

52. Sandall, Annual Report, 30 June 1924, 5; J. Harvey Pocock to E. A. Farrow, 15 September 1934, BIA-CCF, 6; H. J. Doolittle to Commissioner of Indian Affairs, 24 May 1939, UO-MC. As late as the 1970s, several Las Vegas and Moapa men still formed a highway maintenance crew and were among the highest paid and most steadily employed men on those reserves (Knack, Field Notes, Moapa Southern Paiutes).

53. L. B. Sandall to Commissioner of Indian Affairs, 23 November 1925, BIA-CCF.

54. E. A. Farrow, Annual Narrative Report of Kaibab Agency for 1927, SAN, roll 68, 25.

55. Helen Stewart, Account Books and Ledgers, University of Nevada, Las Vegas, Library, Special Collections; J. Dalley, Indians, c. 1930, Library of Congress, Works Projects Administration, Archival and Manuscript Records, 6; E. A. Farrow and P. E. Church, Annual Extension Report for Paiute Jurisdiction, Fiscal Year 1935, 16 April 1936, BIA-CCF, n.p.; "Pah Ute Indians Appear to Have Found New Interest," *Deseret News*, 1 January 1937, 4–5; Fowler and Dawson, "Ethnographic Basketry," 730–34; Franklin and Bunte, *The Paiute*, 102.

56. L. B. Sandall, Annual Narrative Report of Moapa River Agency, 30 June 1926, SAN, roll 88, 17; "Willis, Oliver Evans, Nevada Indians Sit in Dim Light Circle in Cave Digging Out Relics Which Will Make History," *Las Vegas Age*, 15 February 1930, 1; C. C. Wright to Commissioner of Indian Affairs, 21 October 1940, BIA-CCF; Pervis E. Church to Forrest Stone, 5 August 1945, UO-MC.

57. E. A. Farrow to Commissioner of Indian Affairs, 15 November 1929, BIA-CCF, 2. See also Roy Madsen to E. A. Farrow, 1 December 1932, UO-MC.

58. Mabel Wall to [Church President] Grant, 11 September 1935, Palmer Papers, 5–6.

59. E. A. Farrow to Commissioner of Indian Affairs, 3 March 1932, BIA-CCF.

60. Walter Harrington to E. A. Farrow, 12 August 1930, UO-MC; E. A. Farrow to Commissioner of Indian Affairs, 1 December 1930, UO-MC; Board of Washington County Commissioners, Tony Tillohash, Brig George, and Charley Grayman, Agreement for Construction of Fence, 12 March

1931, BIA-CCF; E. A. Farrow to Roy Madsen, 6 February 1933, UO-MC; E. A. Farrow to Commissioner of Indian Affairs, 22 June 1934, UO-MC; William Zeh and Richard Millin, Report on the Kaibab Reservation, 27 July 1935, BIA-CCF, 17–21; Richard Millin and Paul Krause, Report of Physical Survey of Kaibab Reservation Range Land, October 1942, LN, Soil Conservation Service Files.

61. Farrow to Madsen, 6 February 1933; Shivwits Agency, Weekly Payroll Records for 6 June 1933, 8 December 1933, 12 January 1934, 12 February 1934, 3 November 1934, 5 December 1934, UO-MC.

62. E. A. Farrow, Annual Narrative Report of Paiute Agency for 1931, SAN, roll 98, 25; E. A. Farrow to Shivwits Farmer, 5 January 1934, UO-MC.

63. Farrow and Church, Annual Extension Report, passim.

64. E. A. Farrow to Roy Madsen, 19 April 1933, UO-MC; Roy Madsen to E. A. Farrow, 29 April 1933, UO-MC. Two generations later, at least one Paiute man at Cedar City was still doing very similar work on a federal labor program (Knack, Field Notes, Utah Southern Paiutes).

65. J. Harvey Pocock to E. A. Farrow, 20 September 1933, UO-MC; E. A. Farrow to Commissioner of Indian Affairs, 2 October 1933, BIA-CCF, 2; F. A. Gross to Thomas Mayo, 15 December 1933, UO-MC; J. Harvey Pocock to E. A. Farrow, 15 September 1934, BIA-CCF, 6.

66. Walter Lewis and Harold Wheeler to Louis Mueller, 15 February 1935, USNA, BIA Education Division, Chief of Law and Order, General Correspondence Files.

67. Julian H. Steward, "Shoshonean Tribes: Utah, Idaho, Nevada, Eastern California," 1936, University of Nevada, Reno, Special Collections, 14.

68. Pocock to Farrow, 15 September 1934, 6.

69. E. A. Farrow to J. Harvey Pocock, 30 August 1935, BIA-CCF. See also Patterson, "The New Deal."

70. Alter, *Indian Joe*, 74.

71. Stewart Snow and Tony Tillohash to Commissioner of Indian Affairs, 13 May 1940, BIA-CCF.

72. Farrow and Church, Annual Extension Report, passim.

73. G. E. Lindquist, Report on the Paiute Indian Agency, Utah, 7 April 1933,

USNA, BIA, Records of the Board of Indian Commissioners, Special Reports, 20, emphasis added. See also E. A. Farrow, Annual Narrative Report of Paiute Agency for 1932, SAN, roll 98, 5; G. E. Lindquist to Samuel Elliot, Chairman, Board of Indian Commissioners, 7 April 1933, BIA-CCF, 5.

74. L. B. Sandall to Commissioner of Indian Affairs, 22 November 1924, USNA, BIA Irrigation Division, Office of the Chief Engineer, General Correspondence, 1901–31; L. B. Sandall, Annual Narrative Report of Moapa River Agency, 30 June 1925, SAN, roll 88; J. Harvey Pocock to E. A. Farrow, 15 July 1932, UO-MC; Russell, "A Fortunate Few."

75. "Tecope Guilty: Will Get Life Term," *Las Vegas Review-Journal*, 11 November 1931, 1; Alfred M. Smith to E. C. Fortier, 14 April 1942, BIA-CCF; E. C. Fortier to Alfred Smith, 18 April 1942, BIA-CCF.

76. Sandall to Commissioner of Indian Affairs, 23 November 1925, emphasis in original. See also Sandall, Annual Report, 30 June 1926, 14.

77. Grant Magleby to P. E. Church, 6 July 1943, UO-MC.

78. Ida Chidester, Indian Tribe (Piute), c. 1930, Manuscript Collection, Daughters of the Utah Pioneers, Salt Lake City; Uchendu, "Seasonal Agricultural Labor," 14, 147, 159–61; Heinz, "Origin and Development," 38, 85–92.

79. Charles Buell to Moapa Tribal Council, memorandum Re: Death of Tapio Williams, June 1945, BIA-CCF; Knack, Field Notes, Moapa Southern Paiutes; Roosevelt Fitzgerald, "The Evolution of a Black Community in Las Vegas, 1905–1940," n.d., University of Nevada, Las Vegas, Library, Special Collections.

80. John Collier to Edgar A. Farrow, 9 September 1933, LN, CCC Indian Files, Correspondence Paiute Agency.

81. E. A. Farrow, Questionnaire on Shivwits Tribal Organization, 6 August 1934, USNA, BIA Indian Organization Division, 2, 5, 6.

82. For example, E. A. Farrow to Commissioner of Indian Affairs, 3 April 1933, LN, Forestry and Grazing Development Division.

83. C. C. Wright to P. E. Church, 18 February 1942, UO-MC. See also Parvin Church to C. C. Wright, 1 March 1941, BIA-CCF; Grant Magleby to C. C. Wright, 8 March 1941, BIA-CCF; C. C. Wright to Commissioner of Indian Affairs, 3 April 1941, BIA-CCF.

84. 48 Stat. 984.

85. For example, for Shivwits, Fred Daiker to Coulsen C. Wright, 14 August 1939, USNA, BIA Indian Organization Division.

86. E. A. Farrow to Commissioner of Indian Affairs, 6 August 1934, BIA-CCF.

87. Toney [*sic*] Tillohash and James Yellowjacket to E. A. Farrow, 17 January 1935, USNA, BIA Indian Reorganization Act Records; E. A. Farrow to Commissioner of Indian Affairs, 13 January 1936, BIA-CCF.

88. F. A. Gross to E. A. Farrow, 11 April 1935, USNA, BIA Indian Organization Division, General Records.

89. William Zimmerman to Edgar A. Farrow, 22 April 1936, USNA, BIA Indian Organization Division, General Records. Like Shoshones, Southern Paiutes often prefer to avoid taking public negative postures and frequently abstain from voting, trusting that their withholding of approval will be interpreted as disapproval.

90. George P. LaVatta to Commissioner of Indian Affairs, 17 May 1939, USNA, BIA Indian Organization Division, General Records; George P. LaVatta to Commissioner of Indian Affairs, 13 May 1940, BIA-CCF.

91. Carson Agency, Annual Narrative and Statistical Report of Moapa Reservation for 1942, USNA, San Bruno, BIA, Carson Indian School Records, Coded Subject Files, 152.

92. Moapa Tribal Council, Minutes of Council Meeting, 3 December 1942, BIA-CCF; Moapa Business Council, Ordinance I, 14 February 1944, BIA-CCF; Paul Flickinger to Ralph Gelvin, 14 June 1945, USNA, RG 48, Secretary of the Interior Records, Indian Division.

93. Allan Harper to William Zimmerman, memorandum, 25 February 1943, BIA-CCF.

94. Walter Woehlke to C. C. Wright, 22 April 1943, BIA-CCF.

95. George P. LaVatta to Commissioner of Indian Affairs, 15 March 1942, BIA-CCF.

96. Don C. Foster to Commissioner of Indian Affairs, 28 January 1942, BIA-CCF.

97. A. C. Cooley to E. A. Farrow, 25 May 1938, BIA-CCF; M. J. Armstrong to

C. L. Lynch, 1 April 1939, BIA-CCF, 3; Will Bolen, Supervisor's Report of Extension and Industry Division, 11 May 1939, BIA-CCF.

98. C. L. Lynch to Commissioner of Indian Affairs, 3 January 1939, BIA-CCF, 2; Forrest Stone to Commissioner of Indian Affairs, 12 March 1946, LN, Land Operations and Acquisitions Series, 1935–49. BIA efforts to get Kanosh people to diversify with cattle jointly with Indian Peak Paiutes, using each reservation in season, were met unenthusiastically.

99. J. E. White to Commissioner of Indian Affairs, 10 April 1946, BIA-CCF; Kanosh Business Council, Minutes of Special Meeting, 10 August 1949, BIA-CCF; Forrest Stone to A. C. Cooley, 31 August 1949, BIA-CCF; Kanosh Business Committee, Minutes of Special Meeting, 11 January 1950, BIA-CCF.

100. Kanosh Business Committee, Application for Federal Revolving Credit Loan, 13 January 1950, BIA-CCF, 8–13.

101. Forrest Stone to Joe Pikyavit, 21 August 1950, UO-MC.

102. Albert Huber to Ralph Gelvin, 21 January 1953, BIA-CCF, 2. See also Forrest Stone to Will Bolen, 21 August 1950, BIA-CCF; Axahel [*sic*] Perry and Paul Krause to Forrest Stone, memorandum, 24 May 1951, BIA-CCF.

103. P. E. Church to Harry Gilmore, memorandum, 11 July 1952, UO-MC; Robert Cole to Harry Gilmore, 14 July 1952, BIA-CCF; Ralph Gelvin to Harry Gilmore, 22 July 1953, BIA-CCF.

104. L. L. Nelson to Commissioner of Indian Affairs, 17 February 1953, BIA-CCF, 2.

105. Wilson Gutzman and Asahel Perry to Harry Gilmore, memorandum, 13 March 1953, BIA-CCF; Kanosh Business Committee, Resolution Requesting Modification of Contract I-109-IND-5364, 22 April 1953, BIA-CCF.

106. Wilson Gutzman to Harry Gilmore, 5 May 1953, BIA-CCF, 5; P. E. Church, Programming Report for Federal Withdrawal from Kanosh Indian Reservation, 2 September 1953, BIA-CCF, 12.

107. Forrest Stone to Commissioner of Indian Affairs, 3 September 1946, BIA-CCF. See also Shivwits Tribal Council, Minutes of Special Meet-

ing, 31 May 1940, BIA-CCF; W. B. Greenwood to C. C. Wright, 20 June 1940, BIA-CCF.

108. Will Bolen to Forrest Stone, 29 March 1949, BIA-CCF. See also Shivwits Paiute Tribal Council, Application for Federal Revolving Credit Loan, 6 August 1946, BIA-CCF, 48–52; W. R. Bolen, Report of Jurisdiction Visit of Agricultural Extension Agent, 23 April 1949, BIA-CCF; Forrest Stone to Commissioner of Indian Affairs, 14 November 1949, BIA-CCF; Forrest Stone to Parvin Church, 9 July 1951, UO-MC.

109. E. J. Utz to Ralph Gelvin, 28 February 1952, BIA-CCF; Forrest Stone, Lucille Jake, and Robert Cole, Annual Credit Report of Kaibab Tribal Herd Enterprise, 1 July 1952, BIA-CCF, n.p.; Forrest Stone, Lucille Jake, and Robert Cole, Annual Credit Report of Kaibab Tribal Herd Enterprise, 30 June 1953, BIA-CCF, n.p.; Forrest Stone, Lucille Jake, and Robert Cole, Annual Credit Report of Kaibab Tribal Herd Enterprise, 1 July 1954, BIA-CCF, n.p.; Forrest Stone, Lucille Jake, and Robert Cole, Annual Credit Report of Kaibab Tribal Herd Enterprise, 30 June 1956, BIA-CCF, n.p.

110. Moapa Paiute Business Committee and Walter Woehlke, Agreement, 4 April 1942, LN, Extension Division, Audit Reports; Walter Woehlke to John Pohland, 11 April 1942, LN, Extension Division, Audit Reports; William Zeh to E. Morgan Pryse, 1 March 1948, LN, Land Operations and Acquisitions Series, 1935–48; Burton Ladd, Advertising Restricted Indian Lands for Farming and Grazing Purposes Permit, 26 June 1953, BIA-CCF; Moapa Paiute Business Committee and Ken Searles, 1 August 1953, BIA-CCF.

111. Arvilla Benson to William Palmer, 26 September 1941, Palmer Papers, 5.

112. Shivwits Tribal Council, Minutes of Special Meeting, 19 January 1943, BIA-CCF, 2. See also Lila Frank to "Dearest Auntie," 7 May 1942, Palmer Papers; Grant Magleby to P. E. Church, 5 December 1942, BIA-CCF; Clyde W. Pensoneau, Annual Extension Report for Calendar Year 1942, 14 January 1943, BIA-CCF, 25; Yetta McFee to William Palmer, 10 January 1946, Palmer Papers; Knack, Field Notes, Utah Southern Paiutes.

113. L. J. Arnold to Parvin Church, 2 October 1944, UO-MC; P. E. Church to Forrest Stone, 25 July 1946, UO-MC; P. E. Church to Forrest Stone, 26 March 1947, UO-MC.

10. LAND CLAIM AND TERMINATION

1. Fixico, *Termination and Relocation*, 21–31; Holt, *Beneath These Red Cliffs*, 109–12.

2. Pub. L. No. 79-726, 60 Stat. 1049 (1946); Pub. L. No. 84-767, 70 Stat. 624 (1956), as amended, Pub. L. No. 87-48, 75 Stat. 92 (1961); Pub. L. No. 90-9, 81 Stat. 11 (1967).

3. Forrest Stone to D. S. Myer, 12 February 1952, BIA-CCF.

4. William R. Palmer to Ernest L. Wilkinson, 31 December 1946, Palmer Papers.

5. Kanosh Band of Paiute Indians, Minutes of Special Meeting, 27 March 1951, Palmer Papers; Minutes of Meetings at Cedar City, Kaibab, Richfield, and Kanosh, 5–6 June 1951, BIA-CCF.

6. Indian Peaks Paiute Indians, Paiute Indians of Cedar City, Paiute Indians of Koosharem, Kaibab Indians of Arizona, Kanosh Band of Paiute Indians, and John S. Boyden, Attorney Contract, 9 June 1951, BIA-CCF. This was approved by the commissioner of Indian affairs on 10 July 1951 (Fred Daiker to General Accounting Office, 11 July 1951, BIA-CCF).

7. Forrest Stone to Commissioner of Indian Affairs, 20 July 1951, BIA-CCF, 2.

8. H. Rex Lee to Forrest Stone, telegram, 26 July 1951, BIA-CCF. See also Dillon S. Myer to A. Devitt Vanech, 16 April 1951, BIA-CCF; Will L. Hoyt to Forrest Stone, 17 July 1951, BIA-CCF; Parvin E. Church to Forrest Stone, 7 August 1951, BIA-CCF. The local agency preferred Wilkinson because he had met with Paiutes personally and had advised Kanosh people on water rights (Harry W. Gilmore to Douglas McKay, 14 September 1953, BIA-CCF). Curry was both distant and under investigation by the powerful Nevada senator Patrick McCarren, chair of the Indian Affairs Subcommittee, who accused him of soliciting more tribal contracts than he had staff to complete (Patrick McCarren, Speech before the Senate, *Congressional Record,* 82nd Cong., 2nd sess., 1952, 98, 6, 7889–7900). Eighty percent of the contracts that failed approval under the new BIA regulations that resulted from the Senate investigation were Curry's (Dillon S. Myer, "Statement on Proposed Attorney Contract Regulations," February 1951, BIA-CCF). In late 1951 and again in 1954 the Shivwits contract was renegotiated to meet agency objections (James Yellowjacket and Stewart Snow for Shivwits Band of Paiute In-

dians, and Hoag, Edwards, Lindquist, Cobb, Weissbrodt and Weissbrodt, Attorney Contract, 11 May 1954, BIA-CCF).

9. Carl S. Hawkins to Omer C. Stewart, 18 August 1953, University of Colorado–Boulder, Library, Special Collections, Omer C. Stewart Papers; John Boyden to Glenn Emmons, 20 August 1956, BIA-CCF. The Wilkinson claim was originally docket #330 and Curry's #88; the Chemehuevi docket was #351. Efforts to merge the Paiute into the larger Ute case and the Chemehuevi into the mammoth collective California case were successfully evaded, so eventually two Southern Paiute suits were heard by the U.S. Indian Claims Commission.

10. William R. Palmer to John Boyden, 12 July 1951, Palmer Papers.

11. *McKay Pikyavit et al. v Uintah Ute Indians of Utah and Stewart L. Udall,* U.S. District Court for Utah, civil case no. C-79-63.

12. U.S. Indian Claims Commission, "Findings of Fact," dockets 88, 330, and 330-A, 18 January 1965, 14 Ind. Cl. Comm. 618, at 620; U.S. Indian Claims Commission, "Findings of Fact," dockets 351 and 351-A, 18 January 1965, 14 Ind. Cl. Comm. 651, at 653.

13. Kroeber, "Coefficients."

14. Jones, "A Reinterpretation."

15. Kelly, "Southern Paiute Bands"; Park et al., "Tribal Distribution"; Steward, *Basin-Plateau,* 180–85.

16. Kroeber, "The Nature."

17. U.S. Indian Claims Commission, "Findings of Fact," dockets 88, 330, and 330-A, 14 Ind. Cl. Comm. 618–20. The law, of course, did allow individual bands to file claims, but such small groups would most likely have been unable to mobilize the finances needed to pursue a successful suit. Although claims attorneys routinely worked on a contingency basis, the amounts of land involved in a band-level case would be too small to repay the expenses of the necessary years of scholarly evidence building. Besides, the deadline to file was long past by the time of these Paiute hearings, so had the U.S. Indian Claims Commission ruled in favor of this legal objection, Southern Paiutes would have been locked out of the claims process.

18. Manners, "Southern Paiute and Chemehuevi"; "Petitioner's Proposed

Findings of Fact and Brief," U.S. Indian Claims Commission, dockets 88, 330, and 330-A, 11 December 1963.

19. U.S. Indian Claims Commission, "Opinion of the Commission," dockets 88, 330, and 330-A, 18 January 1965, 14 Ind. Cl. Comm. 618; U.S. Indian Claims Commission, "Findings of Fact on Award of Attorneys' Fees," dockets 88, 330, and 330-A, n.d., 15 Ind. Cl. Comm. 433. The unproven estimate of 30 million acres for Paiute territory was used in the negotiations.

20. U.S. Indian Claims Commission, "Findings of Fact," dockets 88, 330, and 330-A, 622–30.

21. U.S. Indian Claims Commission, "Findings of Fact," dockets 88, 330, and 330-A, 630.

22. Pub. L. No. 90-584, 82 Stat. 1147 (1968).

23. U.S. Congress, Joint Resolution no. 108, 1 August 1953, 83rd Cong., 1st sess., reprinted in Washburn, ed., *The Indian and the White Man*, 397.

24. American Indian Policy Review Commission, *Final Report*, 1:477.

25. Orfield, "Study"; Watkins, "Termination." Even Watkins's hometown newspaper resisted his glib assurances and recommended a gradual "approach to avoid chaos" (Editorial, "Making Indian Responsible Citizen Not Easy," *Salt Lake Tribune*, 15 April 1952, n.p., clipping in BIA-CCF).

26. Glenn Emmons to All Bureau Personnel, memorandum, 1 December 1954, USNA, BIA General Services Accreted Files, 1940–56; American Indian Policy Review Commission, *Final Report*, 1:447.

27. U.S. Congress, House of Representatives, *Report with Respect to House Resolution*, 3–4, 17, 29, 158–60.

28. H. W. Gilmore and L. L. Nelson, Summary of Accomplishment in Withdrawal by Termination or Transfer of Bureau Services to Other Auspices and Withdrawal Planning Report for Kanosh, 27 August 1952, BIA-CCF; H. W. Gilmore and L. L. Nelson, Summary of Accomplishment in Withdrawal by Termination or Transfer of Bureau Services to Other Auspices and Withdrawal Planning Report for Indian Peak, 2 September 1952, BIA-CCF; H. W. Gilmore and L. L. Nelson, Summary of Accomplishment in Withdrawal by Termination or Transfer of Bureau Services to Other Auspices and Withdrawal Planning Report for

Koosharem, 2 September 1952, BIA-CCF; H. W. Gilmore and L. L. Nelson, Summary of Accomplishment in Withdrawal by Termination or Transfer of Bureau Services to Other Auspices and Withdrawal Planning Report for Shivwits, 2 September 1952, BIA-CCF; H. W. Gilmore and L. L. Nelson, Summary of Accomplishment in Withdrawal by Termination or Transfer of Bureau Services to Other Auspices and Withdrawal Planning Report for Kaibab, 5 September 1952, BIA-CCF; Agent Walters and L. L. Nelson, Summary of Accomplishment in Withdrawal by Termination or Transfer of Bureau Services to Other Auspices, and Withdrawal Planning Reports for Las Vegas, 5 September 1952, BIA-CCF; Agent Walters and L. L. Nelson, Summary of Accomplishment in Withdrawal by Termination or Transfer of Bureau Services to Other Auspices, and Withdrawal Planning Reports for Moapa, 5 September 1952, BIA-CCF.

29. BIA Phoenix Area Office, Conference Agenda for 19–26 August 1953 Meeting, USNA, BIA General Services Accreted Files, 1940–56.

30. H. M. Critchfield to William Seagle, memorandum, 4 December 1953, USNA, BIA General Services Accreted Files, 1940–56.

31. G. Warren Spaulding to William Gilbert, 25 January 1954, USNA, BIA General Services Accreted Files, 1940–56; Schedule of Joint Hearings of Senate and House Committees on Indian Affairs, 25 January 1954, USNA, BIA General Services Accreted Files, 1940–56.

32. William Zimmerman to Forrest Stone, 29 December 1949, BIA-CCF; Minutes of General Council of Indian Peaks Paiutes, 18 June 1952, in Forrest Stone to Commissioner of Indian Affairs via Ralph Gelvin, 18 June 1952, BIA-CCF. The group signed a separate contract with John Boyden, one of the attorneys representing them to the U.S. Indian Claims Commission, to handle the sale. Interestingly enough, twenty years later the man whose court case instigated the vote told this anthropologist that he was the only member of the band who had not favored selling the reservation (Knack, Field Notes, Utah Southern Paiutes). The Indian Peak Paiutes' request to sell was eventually subsumed into the termination bill.

33. Gilmore and Nelson, Summary—Kanosh, n.p., items 11, 19, 27, and pt. C, sec. 5; Harry Gilmore, Questionnaire on Tribal Organizations—Kanosh Tribe, 22 June 1953, BIA-CCF, 4.

34. Harry Gilmore, Questionnaire on Tribal Organizations—Shivwits

Tribe, 22 June 1953, BIA-CCF, 3. See also Gilmore and Nelson, Summary—Shivwits, n.p., items 1, 11, 19, and pt. C, 29.

None of the six families enrolled at Indian Peak lived on the reserve, which had been leased to non-Indians for years and was up for sale. Fully 25 percent of adults could neither read nor write; only one man supported his family through wages, while the rest depended on unearned income. Average family income was only $1,500 in a county where the mean was $4,200; "no individual in the group has ever engaged in a successful business enterprise"; and the agent stated, "Indian Peak Paiute Indians are not competent to manage their own affairs" (Gilmore and Nelson, Summary—Indian Peak, 1, 10, 16, 18). Nevertheless, on the very next page, he wrote, "The Indian Peak Band of Paiute Indians are ready for complete Bureau withdrawal as soon as the reservation is sold and the Indians completely established on individual homesites within good labor-market areas" (Gilmore and Nelson, Summary—Indian Peak, 19).

At Koosharem, seven of the nine families were adjudged "surplus." Ten percent spoke no English; 20 percent were illiterate. Only two families supported themselves on the reservation, three depended totally on welfare, and the rest combined some wage work and unearned income in distant Richfield. Together this averaged them an estimated $1,500 per year per family, about two fifths the $3,900 made by local non-Indian households (Gilmore and Nelson, Summary—Koosharem, items 1, 11, 19, and p. 29).

35. Gilmore and Nelson, Summary—Kanosh, Summary—Koosharem, Summary—Indian Peak, and Summary—Shivwits, n.p., item 7. The agency reported to Congress that the overall costs of all four reservations plus Kaibab was $7,000 per year (U.S. Congress, Joint Committees on Interior and Insular Affairs, *Hearing on Termination*, 76). Compare Holt's more comprehensive calculation that more than $21,600 in federal funds subsidized the still floundering Paiute economy in 1953, including those from agencies outside the BIA, in the form of Johnson-O'Malley Act school tuition payments, Soil Conservation Service programs, and other services (*Beneath These Red Cliffs*, 71). These monies would, of course, be lost upon termination. How this rate of expenditure compared on a per capita basis with federal subsidies of neighboring non-Indian communities in the form of farm price supports, irrigation project construction and management, conservation and agricultural extension services, farmers' home loans, highway con-

struction, and other federal programs that were not historically available to reservation populations is unknown. See also E. M. Axtell, Irrigation Project Proposal, Fiscal Year 1952, n.d., BIA-CCF.

36. H. W. Gilmore and L. L. Nelson, Progress Report on Reduction of Bureau Services—Kanosh, 1 December 1953, BIA-CCF; H. W. Gilmore and L. L. Nelson, Progress Report on Reduction of Bureau Services—Indian Peak, 1 December 1953, BIA-CCF; H. W. Gilmore and L. L. Nelson, Progress Report on Reduction of Bureau Services—Shivwits, 1 December 1953, BIA-CCF; and H. W. Gilmore and L. L. Nelson, Progress Report on Reduction of Bureau Services—Koosharem, 1 December 1953, BIA-CCF.

37. Harry Gilmore, Questionnaire on Tribal Organization—Shivwits Tribe, 22 June 1953, BIA-CCF, 3.

38. BIA, Background Data on Shivwits, Koosharem, Indian Peak, and Kanosh Bands of Paiute Indians, in U.S. Congress, Joint Committees on Interior and Insular Affairs, *Hearing on Termination*, 13–16. The sole exception concerning readiness was Indian Peak as quoted supra fn. 34, based on Paiutes' own request to sell the reserve.

39. Arthur V. Watkins, Speech before the U.S. Senate, *Congressional Record*, 83rd Cong., 2nd sess., 1954, 100, 5, 5925.

40. U.S. Congress, Joint Committees on Interior and Insular Affairs, *Hearing on Termination*, 41.

41. Shivwits Business Committee, Minutes of Meeting, 9 February 1954, BIA-CCF. By the next meeting a week later the Shivwits council was already diverted into preparations of the final membership roll demanded by the bill. See also U.S. Congress, Joint Committees on Interior and Insular Affairs, *Hearing on Termination*, 51, 61, for Watkins's accounts of these meetings; compare Holt, *Beneath These Red Cliffs*, 73–77.

42. Knack, Field Notes, Utah Southern Paiutes; a lengthy quote from this man appears in Holt, *Beneath These Red Cliffs*, 75. Watkins expressed on the public record his patronizing disdain of Paiute opinion in the termination hearings that he chaired in Washington: "I think they are going to feel all right about it [termination] if we could do two or three little things which they want to have done" (U.S. Congress, Joint Committees on Interior and Insular Affairs, *Hearing on Termination*, 49).

43. A generation later, Paiutes were still commonly referring to the land claim settlement payments as "termination money" (Knack, Field Notes, Utah Southern Paiutes). See also Paul White, VISTA Survey Summary Report, c. 1970, copy in possession of the author; Dale Lambert to Joseph Brecher, memorandum, August 1971, copy in possession of the author, 2; Holt, *Beneath These Red Cliffs*, 119.

44. Knack, Field Notes, Utah Southern Paiutes. Paiutes from Cedar City and Shivwits remember Watkins's meeting as dominated by Kanosh people who lived closest to Fillmore and apparently were present in large numbers. Those descendants of transitional Ute/Paiutes, historically always seen by people farther south as to some extent different and only recently adjudged to be "really" Paiutes by federal U.S. Indian Claims Commission ruling, are blamed by some as having caused the termination of other Utah Paiutes. A generation later, several people, perhaps seeking a scapegoat for subsequent events, blamed the single politically active family, who had initiated the suit for Kanosh inclusion in the Paiute land claim case and was still very active in Paiute politics, for championing termination and persuading others to comply. It was apparently at this same meeting that a shadowy bribe was extended to Kanosh people. A letter in the files of the commissioner of Indian affairs states that "verbal commitment was made [by a BIA employee] to the [Kanosh] Band that the outstanding indebtedness of $10,000 of revolving credit funds would be cancelled" (Ralph M. Gelvin to Commissioner of Indian Affairs, 8 April 1954, BIA-CCF, 2).

45. Orem Lewis to Senator Hugh Butler, 15 February 1954, in U.S. Congress, Joint Committees on Interior and Insular Affairs, *Hearing on Termination*, 9. Fellow congressmen were told on the floor that two Shoshone groups, Washakie and Skull Valley, were dropped from the bill at House members' insistence during the conference committee stage because of Indian letters of opposition (*Congressional Record*, 83rd Cong., 2nd sess., 1954, 100, 8, 10905, and 100, 11, 14874). The report of that committee, however, gave different reasons—that those two groups were too remote for full consultation to have been possible, that it was unlikely they clearly understood the full implications of termination, and that additional time was needed to inform them of the import of being terminated (U.S. Congress, House of Representatives, *Conference Report*, 2). Surely, exactly the same could have been said of Southern Paiutes, who were nonetheless terminated.

46. Quoted in full in W. B. Greenwood to Senator Guy Cordon, 9 August 1954, USNA, RG 46, Records of the U.S. Congress, 83rd Cong., Senate, Files of the Committee on Interior and Insular Affairs, Bill Files. See also U.S. Congress, Joint Committees on Interior and Insular Affairs, *Hearing on Termination*, 52, 84.

47. U.S. Congress, Joint Committees on Interior and Insular Affairs, *Hearing on Termination*, 50, 61. See also Holt, *Beneath These Red Cliffs*, 76–80.

48. U.S. Congress, Joint Committees on Interior and Insular Affairs, *Hearing on Termination*, 64; Norman G. Holmes to Executive Director, Association on American Indian Affairs, 28 January 1954, BIA-CCF, 2. Senator Watkins misrepresented these agency contacts as having been accomplished independently by eager Paiutes themselves (*Congressional Record*, 83rd Cong., 2nd sess., 1954, 100, 5, 5925).

49. Robert L. Bennett, Field Trip Report to C. Warren Spaulding, 10 April 1953, BIA-CCF, 5. Such a program would hardly have been necessary if Paiutes were truly "ready" for termination. From the beginning of the termination process, the BIA knew that most Paiutes were by then living on lands owned by the Mormon Church in Richfield and Cedar City, and this residence pattern entered prominently in agency calculations (Frank Scott, Termination Paiute Band of Indians, 14 November 1956, BIA-CCF, 2). The BIA knew it was releasing Paiutes from federal supervision into reliance on private charity.

50. Governor J. Bracken Lee to Senator Hugh Butler, 16 February 1954, in U.S. Congress, Joint Committees on Interior and Insular Affairs, *Hearing on Termination*, 52–53.

51. Pub. L. No. 83-762, 68 Stat. 1099 (1954). Cedar City and San Juan Paiutes, although in Utah, had never been recognized as tribes by the federal government, held no land in federal trust, and were receiving no federal services. Not federally recognized as "tribes," they were not included in the legislation and, therefore, were not technically terminated.

52. U.S. Congress, Joint Committees on Interior and Insular Affairs, *Hearing on Termination*, 20. The local agent in charge of termination procedures estimated that if all group lands and property were successfully liquidated at fair market value and the proceeds divided per capita, each Koosharem enrollee would receive $91, Shivwits $543, Indian Peak

$1,385, and Kanosh $2,059. If not sold but divided into individual property holdings, he said that "in no event does the enrollee's share in tribal assets . . . constitute an economic farm unit" (Scott, Termination, 1). Thus neither by liquidation and financial investment nor by division of the land itself could Paiutes become economically self-sufficient.

53. L. L. Nelson to Commissioner of Indian Affairs, 9 November 1954, BIA-CCF; T. W. Tylor to Program Coordination Staff, memorandum, 21 December 1954, BIA-CCF; F. M. Haverland to Commissioner of Indian Affairs, 19 March 1956, BIA-CCF, 3.

54. A. A. Perry and F. L. Howard to Harry Gilmore, memorandum, 24 November 1954, BIA-CCF; H. W. Gilmore to F. M. Haverland, 30 June 1955, BIA-CCF; Harry Gilmore to F. M. Haverland, 26 July 1955, BIA-CCF; Commissioner of Indian Affairs to Solicitor of the Department of Interior, 29 August 1955, BIA-CCF; *Federal Register* 21 (14 April 1956): 2453–55.

55. Glenn Emmons to chairmen of Kanosh Indian Community Council, Shivwits Business Council, Koosharem Band of Paiute Indians, and Indian Peaks Band of Paiute Indians, 29 May 1956, BIA-CCF.

56. Wesley Bobo, Summary Report of Action Taken by Cedar City Termination Office, 6 September 1956, USNA, BIA General Services Accreted Files, 1940–56.

57. A. Huber to Office 500, memorandum, 20 April 1954, BIA-CCF; Commissioner of Indian Affairs to L. L. Nelson (draft not sent), c. November 1954, BIA-CCF.

58. U.S. Congress, Senate, *Report to Accompany H. R. 9828*, 1. See also Harry W. Gilmore to F. W. Haverland, 17 May 1955, BIA-CCF; W. Barton Greenwood to Legislative Counsel, 23 November 1955, BIA-CCF; U.S. Congress, Senate Bill 3385, 84th Cong., 2nd sess.; Pub. L. No. 84-696, 70 Stat. 528 (1956).

59. Wesley Bobo to F. M. Haverland, 30 April 1956, USNA, RG 49, Secretary of the Interior Records, Central Classified Files, 1954–58; F. M. Haverland, Memorandum for the Record, 5 July 1956, LN, General Classified Files, 1936–59; Kanosh Band of Paiute Indians, Resolution K-4, 10 July 1956, BIA-CCF; Kanosh Band of Paiute Indians, Resolution K-5, 18 July 1956, LN, General Classified Files, 1936–59; Earl Pikyavit, Lonnie Kochoump, Johnson Levi, and Fred Levi, Agreement Granting Life Estate

to Thirty-Eight Members of Kanosh Band of Indians, 18 July 1956, BIA-CCF; James Ring to Commissioner of Indian Affairs, 23 August 1956, BIA-CCF; Bobo, Summary Report, 2, 4.

60. U.S. Department of Interior, Schedule of Lands to Be Sold, Kanosh Indian Reservation, Utah, 10 July 1956, LN, General Classified Files, 1932–48; F. M. Haverland to John O. Crow, 12 July 1956, LN, General Classified Files, 1932–48; A. L. Hook to L. L. Nelson, memorandum, 24 July 1956, LN, General Classified Files, 1932–48.

61. F. M. Haverland, Memorandum for the Record—Koosharem Termination, 6 July 1956, LN, General Classified Files, 1936–59; Wesley Bobo to E. M. Bagley, 13 July 1956, LN, General Classified Files, 1936–59; Koosharem Band of Paiute Indians, Resolution KO-3, 14 July 1956, LN, General Classified Files, 1936–59; U.S. Department of Interior, Schedule of Lands to Be Sold, 16 July 1956, LN, General Classified Files, 1932–48; Koosharem Band of Paiute Indians, Resolution KO-5, 17 July 1956, BIA-CCF. None of the bids for the land met the minimum appraisal, so it went under management by Walker Bank. After five years, title to the four hundred acres was returned to the Koosharem people, who could not meet the tax assessments. The land was eventually seized by the state and auctioned (Jacobs, "Termination," 37).

62. Indian Peaks Band of Paiute Indians, Resolution IP-4, 20 July 1956, BIA-CCF; W. B. Greenwood to Indian Peaks Band Tribal Council, telegram, 26 July 1956, LN, General Classified Files, 1932–48.

63. Each enrolled man, woman, and child netted $1,374.11 for the complete liquidation of their last remaining collective economic assets (Walker Bank, Indian Peaks Piute Indians Trusteeship Account, 12 December 1957, BIA-CCF).

64. Perry and Howard, memorandum, 24 November 1954; Haverland to Commissioner of Indian Affairs, 19 March 1956, 2.

65. F. M. Haverland, Memorandum for the Record—Shivwits Termination, 5 July 1956, LN, General Classified Files, 1936–59; U.S. Department of Interior, Schedule of Land to Be Sold—Shivwits Indian Reservation, 10 July 1956, LN, General Classified Files, 1932–48; Shivwit[s] Band of Paiute Indians, Resolution S-1, 14 July 1956, LN, General Classified Files, 1936–59; H. M. Molony to BIA Branch of Realty, memorandum, 10 August 1956, LN, Land Operations—Allotment Transactions Files; Bobo, Summary Report, 4; H. Rex Lee to Director, Bureau of Land Manage-

ment, memorandum, 10 September 1956, LN, General Classified Files, 1936–59; Scott, Termination, 2.

66. F. M. Haverland to Commissioner of Indian Affairs, 19 March 1956, BIA-CCF, 3.

67. Thomas Reid to Fredrick M. Haverland, 25 June 1956, BIA-CCF, 2.

68. Indian Peaks Band of Paiute Indians, Minutes of Meeting, 5 August 1956, BIA-CCF; W. B. Greenwood to Fredrick M. Haverland, 29 October 1956, LN, Land Operations Files; Holt, *Beneath These Red Cliffs*, 85–87.

69. Sophie Aberle, "Termination and Its Effect on the Shivwits, Koosharem, Indian Peaks, and Kanosh Bands of Indians in Utah," report for Commission on the Rights, Liberties, and Responsibilities of the American Indian, 10 July 1958, quoted in Jacobs, "Termination," 39.

70. Darell Fleming to Phoenix Area Director, 25 March 1959, LN, General Classified Files, 1936–59.

71. The other "two or three little things" Paiutes requested from Watkins at the Fillmore meeting were outstanding federal loans to be canceled, which was done; subsurface mineral rights to pass to Indian control along with the land, which was denied; and Indian custom marriages be recognized by the state (U.S. Congress, Joint Committees on Interior and Insular Affairs, *Hearing on Termination*, 51). Utah, as had Nevada before 1945 (Rusco, "The Status of Indians," 78), refused to accept Indian custom marriages. This implied that virtually all Utah Paiute adults were living in extralegal unions and that their offspring were therefore illegitimate. Once final probates of intestate estates were completed as part of termination, inheritance would thereafter follow state law. The legal status of their parents' marriages would have substantial impact on Paiute children's rights to property. Utah refused to budge on this issue.

72. *Congressional Record*, 83rd Cong., 2nd sess., 1954, 100, 5, 6253.

73. Orem Lewis to Chairman Hugh Butler, 15 February 1954, in U.S. Congress, Joint Committees on Interior and Insular Affairs, *Hearing on Termination*, 9.

74. Hildegard Thompson to Code #105 via Mr. Nishimoto, memorandum, 22 September 1955, BIA-CCF; Carl Cornelius to Commissioner of Indian Affairs, memorandum, 29 September 1955, BIA-CCF; Osborn, "Evaluation of Counseling," 26.

75. Charles F. Miller to Assistant Commissioner for Community Services, memorandum, 2 November 1954, BIA-CCF; Osborn, "Evaluation of Counseling," 25.

76. T. Witherspoon to John Crowe, 22 March 1956, BIA-CCF; Glenn Emmons to Fredrick M. Haverland, 1 June 1956, BIA-CCF, 3; H. Rex Lee to Fredrick M. Haverland, 11 September 1956, BIA-CCF.

77. C. E. Hazard, Report of Relocation and Vocational Training for Utah Paiute Indians, 3 August 1956, USNA, BIA General Services Accreted Files, 1940–56.

78. Knack, *Life Is with People*, 42.

79. *Federal Register* 22 (1 March 1957): 1301.

80. BIA, "Press Release—Four Paiute Indian Bands Given Full Autonomy," 1 March 1957, BIA-CCF. The commissioner of Indian affairs congratulated his bureaucratic staff for Paiute termination: "Its successful carrying-out reflects on the enterprise and perseverance of the men, particularly in the field who administered it" (W. B. Greenwood to All Area Directors, memorandum, 28 October 1957, BIA-CCF). In a self-critique, the Washington office admitted that "future terminal acts should provide more time after tribes make elections to carry out the trusts or transfers they desire" and that the enrollment lists had been rushed and bungled by overworked Washington bureaucrats, but nowhere did it challenge the concept of termination or its application to Utah Paiutes in the first place (Greenwood to All Area Directors, 14, 16). During the debriefing, the only person who asked this fundamental question was the man who had headed the temporary Cedar City office. He listed as the first question to ask of future termination legislation, "Are the Indians prepared for a withdrawal program?" (Scott, Termination, 5).

81. The senator publicly acknowledged his promise (U.S. Congress, Joint Committees on Interior and Insular Affairs, *Hearing on Termination*, 51). See the coinciding remembrance of the tribal negotiator, quoted from Aberle, "Termination," in Jacobs, "Termination," 29; also Frank Scott to F. M. Haverland, memorandum, 9 October 1956, BIA-CCF; E. J. Utz to Fredrick M. Haverland, 4 February 1957, BIA-CCF; Holt, *Beneath These Red Cliffs*, 76–77.

82. Brophy and Aberle, *The Indian*, 195.

83. Uintah-Ouray Agency, Listing and Description of Tasks Remaining to Be Done to Effect Complete Withdrawal of Bureau Services—Kaibab, 25 August 1952, BIA-CCF, sec. C-5; Harry W. Gilmore, Questionnaire of Tribal Organizations—Kaibab Tribe, 22 June 1953, BIA-CCF.

84. Nevada Agency, Questionnaire of Tribal Organizations—Moapa Tribe, 23 June 1953, BIA-CCF; Nevada Agency, Listing and Description of Tasks Remaining to Be Done to Effect Complete Withdrawal of Bureau Services—Moapa, 5 September 1952, BIA-CCF, sec. C-5; Phoenix Area Office, Summary Statement of Withdrawal Status—Moapa, April 1956, BIA-CCF, 2.

85. A. R. Trelease to A. H. Kennedy, City Manager, memorandum, 1 September 1955, BIA-CCF; D. D. Carr to Mayor C. D. Baker, 6 September 1955, BIA-CCF, 2. See also George Kyle to A. H. Kennedy, memorandum, 6 September 1955, BIA-CCF.

86. F. Rittenhouse to Deputy U.S. Attorney General Joseph Lesh, 3 February 1956, BIA-CCF.

87. Anderson and Mike, "History," 20–21.

88. Nevada Agency, Listing and Description of Tasks Remaining to Be Done to Effect Complete Withdrawal of Bureau Services—Las Vegas, 5 September 1952, BIA-CCF, sec. C-5; Robert L. Bennett, Field Trip Report to G. Warren Spaulding, 14 April 1953, BIA-CCF. Interestingly, the Nevada agency perhaps inadvertently admitted the totally arbitrary nature of the statistics that were central to termination planning, specifically, those concerning "competence to handle own affairs" and of population "surplus" to reservation resources. Just after the war, Las Vegas and Moapa had been shifted to the Truxton (Hualapai) Agency jurisdiction in Arizona because some bureaucrat had looked at a map and decided it would save fuel to place them with the "nearest" agency, not noticing the deep and unbridged Grand Canyon in between. The preliminary planning estimates, done by the Truxton agent, were disproportional to those for all the other Nevada reserves and so were "adjusted" before being sent to Congress (Nevada Agency, Remarks and Observations of a General Nature Relative to the Report on Withdrawal of the Indian Service From Nevada, in U.S. Congress, House of Representatives, *Report on House Resolution Authorizing Congress*, 64).

89. Pub. L. No. 83-280, 67 Stat. 588 (1953); Pub. L. No. 47-198, Nev. Stat. 297 (1955).

90. R. K. Sheffer, Las Vegas Chief of Police, to A. H. Kennedy, memorandum, 2 September 1955, BIA-CCF.

91. A. H. Kennedy to Franklin Rittenhouse, 10 January 1956, BIA-CCF.

92. Homer Jenkins to Commissioner of Indian Affairs, memorandum, 8 March 1956, BIA-CCF, 2.

93. Glenn L. Emmons to Joseph Lesh, 13 April 1956, BIA-CCF, 2.

94. *Congressional Record*, 84th Cong., 1st sess., 1955, 101, 1, 888. While that legislation was still pending, the BIA began construction of water and sewer systems, which would not be completed and connected to the city network for many years (Jenkins, memorandum, 8 March 1956, 2). In this tourist mecca of neon and stage lights, Paiutes did not get electricity or telephones until 1965 or paved streets until 1970 (Intertribal Council of Nevada, *Nuwuvi*, 126; Anderson and Mike, "History," 20).

95. Pub. L. No. 90-584, 82 Stat. 1147 (1968).

96. Hill, "Social and Economic Survey," 22.

97. Hill, "Social and Economic Survey," 13.

98. Hill, "Social and Economic Survey," 22.

99. Inter-tribal Council of Nevada, *Nuwuvi*, 107.

100. Euler, *Southern Paiute Ethnohistory*, 94.

101. Peter Brill, as quoted in Holt, *Beneath These Red Cliffs*, 120.

102. Knack, Field Notes, Utah Southern Paiutes.

103. Knack, Field Notes, Utah Southern Paiutes; Knack, *Life Is with People*, 92–96. See also Orfield, "Study," 17 et seq., for comparable posttermination data for Klamath; Jorgensen, *Sun Dance Religion*, 151–56, for comparable postdistribution data on the Northern Ute land claim.

11. NEGLECT AND REINSTATEMENT

1. Hill, "Social and Economic Survey."

2. Douglas Braithwaite, "Resume: Cedar City Community," n.d., mimeographed, n.p., copy in possession of the author; Knack, *Life Is with People*; U.S. Congress, Joint Committees on Interior and Insular Affairs, *Hearing on Termination*.

3. Knack, *Life Is with People*, 32–44, 50–90; Knack, "Church and State."

4. Lawyers working on efforts to restore federal recognition claimed evidence that Paiute income was less than one third that of local non-Indians (Holt, *Beneath These Red Cliffs*, 134).

5. Knack, "Beyond a Differential."

6. Some Paiutes sought connection with Indians elsewhere and resolution of their personal difficulties through membership in the Native American Church (Stewart, *Peyote Religion*, 291–92).

7. Pub. L. No. 83-762, sec. 17, 68 Stat. 1099 (1954).

8. Pub. L. No. 83-280, 67 Stat. 588 (1953), as amended Pub. L. No. 90-284, sec. 2, 82 Stat. 73 (1968); Pub. L. No. 47-198, Nev. Stat. 297 (1955), as amended Pub. L. No. 57-601, Nev. Stat. 1051 (1973).

9. Grant W. Magleby to the Phoenix Area Director, memorandum, 23 April 1955, USNA, Denver, Phoenix Area Office Records. The BIA contracted for town jail space as needed, and as late as 1960 accused Kaibab Paiutes were tried before the non-Indian justice of the peace in Fredonia, largely for public drunkenness and domestic disputes (Grant W. Magleby to the Phoenix Area Director, memorandum, 9 June 1960, USNA, Denver, Phoenix Area Office Records).

10. R. K. Sheffer to A. H. Kennedy, memorandum, 2 September 1955, USNA, BIA-CCF.

11. Franklin Rittenhouse to Joseph Lesh, 3 February 1956, USNA, BIA-CCF.

12. Paul Fickinger to Division Directors, memorandum, 27 June 1945, USNA, BIA-CCF; Walter Woehlke to Commissioner of Indian Affairs, 20 February 1950, USNA, BIA-CCF.

13. Euler, *The Paiute People*, 91.

14. Bunte, "Ethnohistory," 12.

15. Knack, Field Notes, Utah Southern Paiutes.

16. VISTA, Minutes of Meeting of 31 March 1971, VISTA Files, OCC. He was opposed by many other Mormons at the meeting, who, although subject to his rulings, worked to have him replaced. Scott Urie, the subsequent head of the Cedar City Paiute mission, told another volunteer that "he wouldn't have agreed to talk with them if he had known they

had anything to do with VISTA" and closely quizzed this ethnographer about any VISTA affiliations she might have before he agreed to be interviewed (Kathy Schuler, Paiute and VISTA Resources and Interaction, 12 March 1973, VISTA Files, OCC, 3).

17. Braithwaite, "Resume," 2. See also Donna Kunitz, Cedar City VISTA Report, 9/1/70–7/20/71, VISTA Files, OCC, 23; Faye Price, Report of VISTA Activities, 1971–1972, 12 July 1972, VISTA Files, OCC, 9.

18. Holt, *Beneath These Red Cliffs*, 128; Knack, Field Notes, Utah Southern Paiutes; Kunitz, Report; Price, Report.

19. Daniel Taaffee to Faye Price, 22 November 1971, VISTA Files, OCC.

20. Price, Report, 7, 1.

21. Charles Wilkinson for Yetta Jake, Draft to Richard G. Kleindienst, 11 September 1972, VISTA Files, OCC. See also Dale Lambert to Native American Rights Fund, 23 August 1971, VISTA Files, OCC; Charles Wilkinson to Yetta Jake, 11 September 1972, VISTA Files, OCC.

22. Price, Report, 6.

23. Bruce Parry to Native American Rights Fund, 19 May 1972, VISTA Files, OCC, emphasis added.

24. Daniel J. Taaffee to Faye Price, 5 July 1972, VISTA Files, OCC.

25. "Benefit Dinner Supports Indian Village Projects," *Iron County Record*, 27 May 1971; Kunitz, Report, 11.

26. Holt, *Beneath These Red Cliffs*, 128; Knack, Field Notes, Utah Southern Paiutes; Price, Report, 1.

27. State of Utah, Office of Secretary of State, Certificate of Incorporation of Paiute Tribal Corporation, 17 July 1972, copy in possession of the author; also Knack, Field Notes, Utah Southern Paiutes.

28. "Utah Indians Get EDA Grants," *Iron County Record*, 16 November 1972; Knack, Field Notes, Utah Southern Paiutes; Paiute Tribal Corporation, Minutes of Meeting of the Board of Directors, 7 October 1972, copy in possession of the author.

29. Knack, Field Notes, Utah Southern Paiutes; Paiute Tribal Corporation, Minutes of Meetings of Board of Directors, 22 January 1973 and 16 March 1973, copy in possession of the author; Paiute Tribal Corpora-

tion, Organizational Chart, April 1973, copy in possession of the author. The Koosharem/Richfield director was a woman, Vera Charles.

30. Church of Jesus Christ of Latter-day Saints, Deed of Land to Utah Paiute Tribal Corporation, 7 December 1973, copy in possession of the author; Knack, Field Notes, Utah Southern Paiutes.

31. Knack, Field Notes, Utah Southern Paiutes.

32. "Paiutes Open Store in New Building," *Iron County Record*, 24 October 1974; Knack, Field Notes, Utah Southern Paiutes; Turner, "Utah Paiute Tribal Governance," 30–31.

33. Knack, Field Notes, Utah Southern Paiutes. This was not an isolated incident; other non-Indian shysters defrauded federal minority business programs aimed at helping Paiutes. For six years during the 1980s, for instance, a Kaibab woman was persuaded to front a dummy corporation for an Arizona construction firm that employed her husband; the dummy company received federal minority-preference contracts and funneled inflated invoices for materials to the parent company (U.S. Congress, Senate, Select Committee on Indian Affairs, *Final Report*, 71–73).

   Paiutes are singularly forgiving of their leaders, who have remarkable resilience and public dedication. Pikyavit's daughter won election to chair the interim government and sat on the first tribal council after restoration to federal recognition only six years later. Within a decade, Pikyavit himself had been reelected to the local band chairmanship. Paiute Indian Tribe of Utah, *Newsletter*, no. 2, 6 March 1981, 4; no. 9a, 29 October 1981, 1; no. 43, 19 April 1984, 7.

34. "Woman Embezzled from Paiutes," *Las Vegas Review-Journal*, 13 July 1979, 5B; Charles Zobell, "Indian Colony Funds Focus of FBI Probe," *Las Vegas Review-Journal*, 9 February 1978, 1A, 4A. As with the Pikyavit family, this did not prevent her daughter from being politically active, although she did have to relocate to Cedar City, where she had relatives, in order to win the election to chairmanship of the restored Utah Paiute Tribal Council. Such suspicions and the resulting gossip actively reinforced traditional ethics of reciprocity and served as an effective leveling mechanism (Knack, *Life Is with People*, 86–90).

35. Knack, Field Notes, Utah Southern Paiutes.

36. Price, Report, 7.

37. "Cedar City Corporation, Piutes Sign Cooperative Housing Agreement," *Iron County Record*, 26 September 1974, n.p.; Loraine Juvelin, "Cedar's Indian Village Finally Puts Housing Funds to Work," *Color Country Spectrum* (Cedar City UT), 24 July 1975, n.p.; Knack, Field Notes, Utah Southern Paiutes. The tax status of this land, church-owned but essentially leased to a private corporation, remained ambiguous.

38. "Indians to Build Twenty-five Homes," *Iron County Record*, 25 June 1974, n.p.; Lois Linford to Martha Knack, 27 March 1975, in possession of the author. Later grants further expanded federally funded houses to more than fifty by 1989 (Holt, *Beneath These Red Cliffs*, 129, 151).

39. Arizona Department of Commerce, "Kaibab-Paiute Indian Reservation: Community Profile" (Phoenix: Department of Commerce, June 1991); Knack, Field Notes, Moapa Southern Paiutes; Mark Shaffer, "Paiutes' Waste-site Plan Alarms Neighbors," *Arizona Republic* (Tucson), 28 January 1990, B1, B4, B5; Preston Tom to Dale Bumpers, 12 October 1979, in U.S. Congress, Senate, Committee on Energy and Natural Resources, *Hearing*, 122–23.

40. Prucha, *The Great Father*, 2:1133–35.

41. Paiute Tribal Corporation, Board of Directors, Minutes of Meeting of 5 October 1973, copy in possession of the author. Note how he was treating a state corporation as though it were a representative tribal government. See also Holt, *Beneath These Red Cliffs*, 129; Turner, "Utah Paiute Tribal Governance," 31–32.

42. Holt, *Beneath These Red Cliffs*, 130–31; Caryn Ochse, "Restoration of Pauite [*sic*] Tribe Sought," *Deseret News*, 27 September 1979, Z-2, Z-4.

43. Holt, *Beneath These Red Cliffs*, 132; U.S. Congress, Senate, Select Committee on Indian Affairs, *Hearing on Paiute Restoration Act*, 6–7.

44. "Paiutes Plead Tribal Case," *Deseret News*, 27 April 1978, B2; Holt, *Beneath These Red Cliffs*, 133–34; Yvette Miles, "Piute Indians: Officials Debate Tribal Status," *Salt Lake Tribune*, 31 August 1979, n.p.

45. Frank Hewlett, "Seek Return to BIA: Paiute Indians' Request Studied by Committee," *Salt Lake Tribune*, 27 October 1979, n.p.; George Raine, "Paiutes Finally Regaining Status, Self-Sufficiency," *Salt Lake Tribune*, 20 September 1981, B-1, B-2; U.S. Congress, Senate, Select Committee on Indian Affairs, *Hearing on Paiute Restoration Act*, 21–56. Only local

advocate Blomquist had not been properly rehearsed; he praised Paiutes for the success of their recent corporate and housing efforts to better their own condition, contradicting the image of a helpless and poor minority desperately needing federal protection that the lobbyists had wanted to project (U.S. Congress, Senate, Select Committee on Indian Affairs, *Hearing on Paiute Restoration Act*, 55).

46. George Raine, "Paiute Indians Seeking Tribal Status," *Salt Lake Tribune*, 17 September 1979, B1; Raine, "Paiutes Finally Regaining Status," B-1, B-2.

47. U.S. Congress, Senate, Select Committee on Indian Affairs, *Hearing on Paiute Restoration Act*, 25–27. Like the termination hearings before them, the congressional restoration hearings were a forum not only for political posturing and blame casting but also for the overt reconstruction of history. Congressmen virtuously accused the BIA of supporting Utah Paiutes' termination when they did not meet the agency's own administrative standards; the BIA blamed Congress for terminating them against its own criteria; they both agreed that Senator Watkins had played politics with a sacrificial tribe from his home state (U.S. Congress, Senate, Select Committee on Indian Affairs, *Hearing on Paiute Restoration Act*, 12–14, 56–62). Only Hatch stood up for his fellow Utahan, whom he characterized as a "sincere" man who honestly "thought he was doing them a favor" by getting Paiutes terminated (U.S. Congress, Senate, Select Committee on Indian Affairs, *Hearing on Paiute Restoration Act*, 29). Parry asserted that posttermination federal neglect had escalated so that the plans of the BIA-authorized trustee bank to sell the former Shivwits Reservation proceeded without Paiute knowledge and was forestalled only by chance, thus denigrating years of anxious innovations by the Shivwits land committee to meet their tax bills; he asserted that Indian Peak was sold against the wishes of the group, completely ignoring their specific request for its sale in 1954 (U.S. Congress, Senate, Select Committee on Indian Affairs, *Hearing on Paiute Restoration Act*, 21).

48. U.S. Congress, Senate, Select Committee on Indian Affairs, *Hearing on Paiute Restoration Act*, 18.

49. Congressman Dan Marriott, *Congressional Record*, 96th Cong., 2nd sess., 1980, 126, 29, 1207; U.S. Congress, Senate, Select Committee on Indian Affairs, *Hearing on Paiute Restoration Act*, 13, 15, 62–63.

50. U.S. Congress, Senate, Select Committee on Indian Affairs, *Hearing on Paiute Restoration Act*, 28. Notice that by implication the state of Utah's programs or their historic delivery were declared inadequate. The rhetorical resemblance to Watkins's protermination speeches here is striking.

51. Senator Robert C. Byrd for Senator Melcher, *Congressional Record*, 96th Cong., 2nd sess., 1980, 126, 39, 2369.

52. U.S. Congress, Senate, *Report to Accompany S. 1273*, 6–10.

53. *Congressional Record*, 96th Cong., 2nd sess., 1980, 126, 29, 1209, and 126, 39, 2369.

54. Pub. L. No. 96-227, 94 Stat. 317 (1980).

55. Richard Stoffle has argued that the creation of the amalgamated tribe was an indigenous Paiute movement striving toward reconstruction of the indigenous, precontact native nation that had formerly united into a single structure and consciousness all the Paiute bands from the Four Corners, across Utah, Arizona, southern Nevada, and the Mojave Desert. That nation, Stoffle declared, had been destroyed by the advent of "the white man" ("American Indians and Nuclear Waste Storage," 6). See also Palmer, "Pahute Indian Government."

56. Paiute Indian Tribe of Utah, Constitution, in CH2M Hill, "Proposed Paiute Indian Tribe," D-1–D-19.

57. Knack, "Contemporary Southern Paiute Women"; Paiute Indian Tribe of Utah, *Newsletter*, no. 4, 1 May 1981, 2; no. 5, 8 June 1981, 1; no. 8, 9 October 1981, 2; no. 9b, 1 December 1981, 1–2; no. 23, 10 February 1983, 4; no. 40, 5 March 1984, 2. The first election for tribal chair saw only sixty-four of approximately three hundred qualified voters participate. Chairman Benioh was soon to follow his predecessor McKay Pikyavit in political appointment to the governor's advisory board of Indian affairs.

58. For example, Paiute Indian Tribe of Utah, *Newsletter*, no. 23, 10 February 1983, 4; no. 24, March 1983, 4. Perhaps due to the new chairman's status as the only Utah Paiute to serve as a Mormon missionary, or perhaps due simply to the overwhelming local influence of the Mormon Church, several of these projects took on a decided sectarian slant. At the first meeting of the interim council, alcohol was banned from the tribal government building in conformity to the church's dictates (Pai-

ute Indian Tribe of Utah, *Newsletter,* no. 9b, 1 December 1981, 4). Within the year the church organized and paid for the first Paiute Conference (*Newsletter,* no. 17, 10 August 1982, 2). Brigham Young University was invited to present its generic "Indian" cultural festival, the Lamanite Generation (*Newsletter,* no. 37, 16 January 1984, 3).

59. CH2M Hill, "Proposed Paiute Indian Tribe," 18, 22, 77.

60. Raine, "Paiutes Finally Regaining Status." See also "Public Hearing Set on Paiute Land," *Emery County Progress,* 12 May 1982, n.p.; George Raine, "Paiute Indians to Acquire BLM Acreage?" *Salt Lake Tribune,* 5 July 1982, B-1, B-3.

61. CH2M Hill, "Proposed Paiute Indian Tribe," 3–4; U.S. Congress, Senate, Select Committee on Indian Affairs, *Hearing on Trust Lands,* 33–90.

62. "Paiute Bands List Acreage They Prefer," *Deseret News,* 9 February 1982; Holt, *Beneath These Red Cliffs,* 138–39, 141, 149; Raine, "Paiutes Finally Regaining Status"; U.S. Congress, Senate, Select Committee on Indian Affairs, *Hearing on Trust Lands,* 18, 89–90.

63. Quoted in Raine, "Paiute Indians to Acquire," B-3.

64. J. Elmer Collings, Sevier County Commissioner for Monroe, quoted in George Raine, "Rich Land 'Not Available' to Paiutes," *Salt Lake Tribune,* 13 May 1982, B-2. Note the implications: should Paiutes develop those same resources, it would not constitute regional development; Paiute actions were separate and not part of the whole. Further, there is the unsubtle racism that non-Indians would not "sit" if they became wealthy. See also Pat Thorne, "Paiute Land Deal May Be Back to Ground Zero," *Cedar City (UT) Spectrum,* 19 May 1982, n.p.

65. "Matheson Asks Energy Firm to End Opposition to Paiute Land Selection," *Salt Lake Tribune,* 27 January 1983, A11; CH2M Hill, "Proposed Paiute Indian Tribe," 8, 129; Editor, "Only the Players Will Change," *Salt Lake Tribune,* 28 January 1983, copy in U.S. Congress, Senate, Select Committee on Indian Affairs, *Hearing on Trust Lands,* 116; Scott Matheson to J. Elmer Collings, 21 October 1982, copy in U.S. Congress, Senate, Select Committee on Indian Affairs, *Hearing on Trust Lands,* 110–12; Paiute Indian Tribe of Utah, *Newsletter,* no. 21, December 1982, 3.

66. U.S. Congress, House of Representatives, *Report to Accompany H.R. 2898,* 10; U.S. Congress, Senate, Select Committee on Indian Affairs, *Hearing on Trust Lands,* 62–63, 117–20.

67. CH2M Hill, "Proposed Paiute Indian Tribe," 115; Patrick Charles, "Statement before the U.S. House of Representatives, Interior and Insular Affairs Committee on H.R. 2898," 14 July 1983, in U.S. Congress, Senate, Select Committee on Indian Affairs, *Hearing on Trust Lands*, 26; Pikyavit, "Use of Fish Lake"; U.S. Congress, House of Representatives, *Report to Accompany H.R. 2898*, 2–3. Compare Taos Pueblo's greater concessions from the Forest Service for religious use of Blue Lake in the 1970s, but their ceremonies were far better documented and stood within a cultural tradition of secrecy from the uninitiated.

68. "Paiute Land Proposal Still under Study," *Cedar City Spectrum*, 3 March 1982, 1; "Tribe Want Input," *Cedar City Spectrum*, 24 March 1981, 1; Mary Finch, "Lands Hold Tribe's Future," *Deseret News*, 10 March 1982, B-1, B-2; Holt, *Beneath These Red Cliffs*, 143, 146; U.S. Congress, Senate, Select Committee on Indian Affairs, *Hearing on Trust Lands*, 76, 123–28; U.S. Congress, Senate, *Report to Accompany S. 1273*, 14; U.S. Congress, Senate, Select Committee on Indian Affairs, *Hearing on Paiute Restoration Act*, 15, 39.

69. Paiute Indian Tribe of Utah, *Newsletter*, no. 14, 14 May 1982, 3. For examples of programs, see no. 12, 12 March 1982, 7; no. 14, 14 May 1982, 7; no. 18, 10 September 1982, 3; no. 21, December 1982, 1.

70. Beaman, "The Canon," 624; Bleak, "Annals," 2:231; Cleland and Brooks, eds., *A Mormon Chronicle*, 2:266–68; Little, *Jacob Hamblin*, 112, 114.

71. Bunte and Franklin, *From the Sands*, 17–99; Shepardson and Hammond, *The Navajo Mountain Community*, 27–42.

72. Prucha, *Great Father*, 2:1195–96.

73. Bunte and Franklin, *From the Sands*; Eddie F. Brown, "Summary under the Criteria and Evidence for Final Determination for Federal Acknowledgment of the San Juan Southern Paiute Tribe," 20 December 1989 (Washington DC: U.S. Department of Interior, 1989); *Federal Register* 54, pt. 240 (29 December 1989): 51502; Mark Shaffer, "Paiutes to Celebrate Own Identity," *Arizona Republic*, 3 June 1990, B1, B6.

74. "Paiute Unit on Navajo Land Seeks Tribal Rank," *Arizona Republic*, 18 November 1985, n.p.

75. "Court Can't Carve Paiute Area from Navajo Land," *Arizona Republic*, 19 March 1992, B5.

76. Shaffer, "Paiutes to Celebrate." In 1985 Kaibab was transferred from the Hopi Agency jurisdiction and added to Cedar City too (Mark Shaffer, "Identity Crisis: Isolated Tribe Faces Hardships on Fringe of Arizona Fold," *Arizona Republic*, 13 October 1985, n.p.). In addition to San Juan, another little-known group of Paiutes traditionally centered at Pahrump, Nevada, filed for federal recognition in the early 1990s. Their appeal is still pending at the time this goes to press.

77. Euler, *The Paiute People*, 91; Turner, "Adaptive Continuity," 48.

78. Euler, *The Paiute People*, 94; Turner, "Adaptive Continuity," 48–52.

79. Turner, *The Kaibab Paiute Indians*, 55, 77, 87–89; Shaffer, "Identity Crisis"; Mark Shaffer, "Farming Failure Heightens Craving by Paiutes for Moccasin's Water," *Arizona Republic*, 13 October 1985, n.p.; Turner, *The Kaibab Paiute Indians*, 19, 78, 80–81.

80. Turner, "Adaptive Continuity," 49; U.S. Department of Interior, *Pipe Spring National Monument*.

81. Euler, *The Paiute People*, 92–93; Shaffer, "Identity Crisis"; Turner, "Adaptive Continuity," 45.

82. Euler, *The Paiute People*, 91; Turner, *The Kaibab Paiute Indians*, 77.

83. Arizona Department of Commerce, "Kaibab-Paiute Indian Reservation," 1; Shaffer, "Identity Crisis." Of course, such high levels of unemployment would never be tolerated politically should they appear in the non-Indian sector.

84. With an equipment grant from the EDA, Moapa Paiutes also bought two hundred head of tribal cattle and planted alfalfa. The new tribal farm generated five jobs for members, but by the late 1980s the elderly farmer in charge was despairing of being able to interest any young man in an agricultural career and feared the farm would fold upon his retirement (Knack, Field Notes, Moapa Southern Paiutes).

85. Moapa Paiute Tribe, *Moapa Band of Paiute Indians*, c. 1979; Preston Tom to Senator Dale Bumpers, 12 October 1979, in U.S. Congress, Senate, Committee on Energy and Natural Resources, *Hearing*, 122–23.

86. James Wright to Charles Wilkinson, memorandum, 18 April 1975, in U.S. Congress, Senate, *Hearing on Miscellaneous Public Lands*, 123–27.

87. Thomas Fredericks to Senator Henry Jackson, 9 September 1980, in

U.S. Congress, Senate, Committee on Energy and Natural Resources, *Report*, 5–8; *Congressional Record*, 96th Cong., 2nd sess., 1980, 126, 22, 29818–19; Jimmy Carter, "Statement on Signing S. 1135 into Law," *Weekly Compilation of Presidential Documents* 16 (5 December 1980): 2780; Pub. L. No. 96-491, 94 Stat. 2561 (1980).

88. Dolores Wood, "Hail Damages Paiute Indians' Tomato Crop," *Las Vegas Review-Journal*, 9 September 1980, 10A.

89. "Bureau Overrides Moapa Paiute Plan for Brothel," *Las Vegas Review-Journal*, 2 October 1982, 1C; "Paiutes Sue Feds for OK to Build Brothel," *Las Vegas Review-Journal*, 13 August 1983, 1A; "The Paiute Social Club: Beleaguered Tribe May Open Brothel," *Arizona Republic*, 28 October 1984, n.p.; "Brothel Ban for Moapas Is Upheld," *Las Vegas Review-Journal*, 17 November 1984, 9C; Knack, Field Notes, Moapa Southern Paiutes.

90. "Bingo Games under Way at Moapa Indian Reservation," *Las Vegas Review-Journal*, 16 March 1985, 2B; "Moapa Bingo Workers Payroll Checks Bounce," *Las Vegas Review-Journal*, 5 April 1985, 4B; "Bingo Games Canceled at Reservation," *Las Vegas Review-Journal*, 6 April 1985, 12A; Jane Ann Morrison, "Indian Bingo Has Shaky Start: Legal Questions Hang over Moapa Game," *Las Vegas Review-Journal*, 19 March 1985, 1C, 3C.

91. Lisa Friedman, "Trailers Full of Fireworks Go up in Smoke," *Las Vegas Review-Journal*, 29 June 1995, 1B, 7B. In 2000, Moapa Paiutes were approached by Calpine Corporation, a California-based energy company, that proposed construction of an electricity generating plant on the new land that would feed the demand for power by the explosive growth of Las Vegas and southern California (Michael Weissenstein, "Proposed Power Plant Could Spark Local Tribe's Economy," *Las Vegas Review-Journal*, 3 September 2000, 1B, 6B).

92. *Washington v Confederated Tribes of the Colville Indian Reservation*, 447 US 134 (1980).

93. "Cigarette Tax Starts State 'Indian War,'" *Las Vegas Review-Journal*, 13 December 1977, 1; "Commission to Review Revised 'Smoke Shop' Rule," *Las Vegas Review-Journal*, 8 March 1978, 9A; "State Taxes Indian Cigarette Sales," *Las Vegas Review-Journal*, 3 July 1980, 4A; Ed Vogel, "State Eyes Indian Cigarette Vendors," *Las Vegas Review-Journal*, 11 June 1980, 1B.

94. "Access Road Planned to LV Paiute Colony," *Las Vegas Review-Journal*, 27 August 1981, 2B; "Paiute Center Readied," *Las Vegas Review-Journal*, 2 September 1981, 14B.

95. U.S. Congress, Senate, Select Committee on Indian Affairs, *Hearing on S. 2931*, 70–88; U.S. Congress, Senate, Select Committee on Indian Affairs, *Hearing on Las Vegas Paiute Tribe Trust Lands*; Pub. L. No. 98-203, 97 Stat. 1383 (1983).

96. Phil Pattee, "Paiutes Plan Development of Newly Acquired Lands," *Las Vegas Review-Journal*, 8 December 1983, 4B.

97. Mary Hynes, "Paiutes Seek Ground Water for Project," *Las Vegas Review-Journal*, 18 May 1994, 1A, 3A; Warren Bates, "State Files Federal Suit against Paiutes," *Las Vegas Review-Journal*, 23 November 1994, 1A, 3A; Warren Bates, "Paiutes, Water District Reach Pact," *Las Vegas Review-Journal*, 2 December 1994, 1B, 6B.

98. Mary Hynes, "Paiutes Charge Racism in Water Denial," *Las Vegas Review-Journal*, 25 August 1995, 1B, 2B; Mary Hynes, "Deal Reached in Paiute Water Battle," *Las Vegas Review-Journal*, 1 September 1995, 1B; Shaun McKinnon, "Water Settlement Reached with Las Vegas Paiutes," *Las Vegas Review-Journal*, 13 April 1996, 1A, 2A.

99. Roth, "Incorporation and Changes," 156–221.

100. Marian Green, "Protesters Fight to Remove Tribe's Chief," *Las Vegas Review-Journal*, 23 March 1992, 1B, 2B.

101. Green, "Protesters"; Marian Green, "Chemehuevi Indians to Appeal for New Leaders," *Las Vegas Review-Journal*, 12 April 1992, 1B, 8B; Marian Green, "Woman Plans to Reclaim Tribal Leadership," *Las Vegas Review-Journal*, 11 June 1992, 8B.

102. Marian Green, "Chemehuevi Eye Constitution: Bureau of Indian Affairs Plans Jan. 9 Vote," *Las Vegas Review-Journal*, 6 December 1992, 7B. See also Green, "Woman"; Marian Green, "Indian Tribe Votes to Oust Ruling Council," *Las Vegas Review-Journal*, 26 April 1992, 1B, 3B.

103. Green, "Chemehuevi Eye Constitution"; Marian Green, "Chemehuevis Enact Revisions Aimed at Ousting Tribal Council," *Las Vegas Review-Journal*, 12 January 1993, 1B, 3B. As tribal governments increasingly controlled significant economic resources, rights to vote and

share in the proceeds became more valuable. Both Chemehuevi and Las Vegas tribal rolls were increasingly contested. For instance, after the Las Vegas woman was convicted of embezzlement, her kinsmen had to sue in federal court for recognition of their tribal rights (Warren Bates, "LV Man, Sons Sue for Admission to Tribe," *Las Vegas Review-Journal*, 24 January 1995, 2B; Alan Tobin, "LV Paiute Tribe Sues Own Court," *Las Vegas Review-Journal*, 13 July 1990, 6F). As profits from corporate developments rose, Las Vegas Paiutes were again embroiled in membership disputes when nine people with long-standing ties to the community were dropped from the rolls in 1999 (George Knapp, KLAS-TV [Las Vegas NV] News, 2 November 1999). In 2000, when tribal distributions reached a purported $100,000 per capita per year income, tribal membership rolls were pared down fourteen more through challenges to people's ancestry and historic residence to only forty persons (Greg Tuttle, "Blood Fight Splits Tribe," *Las Vegas Sun*, 3 September 2000, 1J, 5J). Katherine Verdery has generalized, "Such [ethnic] identities will be less flexible wherever the process of modern nation-state formation has the greatest longevity and has proceeded the furthest" ("Ethnicity," 37).

104. Marian Green, "Chemehuevi Indians Elect New Leaders," *Las Vegas Review-Journal*, 29 April 1993, 7B. FBI investigation of the seized documents did not result in any formal charges or arrests.

105. Mark Shaffer, "Few Oppose New Strip Uranium Mine," *Arizona Republic*, 24 March 1987, n.p.; Mark Shaffer, "Paiutes' Waste-site Plan Alarms Neighbors," *Arizona Republic*, 28 January 1990, B1, B4, B5; Thomas Graf, "Tribal Showdown over Incinerator: Proposed Project a Blessing or Curse," *Denver Post*, 22 July 1990, 1A, 15A; Mark Shaffer, "Tribe Approves Plan for Waste Incinerator," *Arizona Republic*, 9 October 1990, n.p.; "Arizona Tribe Accepts Huge Incinerator," *Denver Post*, 10 October 1990, 1B, 5B; "Kaibab-Paiute Council Ends Talks for Sludge Incinerator," *Arizona Republic*, 1 February 1991, n.p.

106. "Kaibab-Paiute Tribe to Close Troubled Casino in Arizona," *Las Vegas Review-Journal*, 23 September 1996, 3D.

107. Holt, *Beneath These Red Cliffs*, 135; Paiute Indian Tribe of Utah, *Newsletter*, no. 17, 10 August 1982, 4; no. 27, 14 June 1983, 2.

12. BOUNDARIES AND TRANSITIONS

1. For acculturation theorists, see Spicer, "Types of Contact"; Tax, ed., *Acculturation*; Walker, ed., *Emergent Native Americans*. For a summary of sociological approaches, see Yinger, "Ethnicity."

2. Bennett, ed., *The New Ethnicity*; Plattner, ed., *Prospects*.

3. Compare Anderson, *Imagined Communities*.

4. Barth, introduction to Barth, ed., *Ethnic Groups*; Barth, "Enduring and Emerging Issues."

5. Historians and archivists occasionally still ask in puzzlement where this band or that group of Paiutes "disappeared" to and ask whether they died off or moved away, when all that had happened was that writers simply stopped bothering to mention them.

6. Cornell, *Return of the Native*; Jorgensen, "A Century." I suspect a non-military context similar to that of Southern Paiute ethnohistory was far more common than is usually acknowledged, particularly in such areas as the Arctic, Subarctic, and Northwest Coast, where hunting and gathering economies also prevailed.

7. See Biolsi, *Organizing the Lakota*.

8. This internal neocolonialism is, of course, just as much a case of colonialism as it is when native populations and territories abroad are subjected to political control and seizure of economic resources (Jorgensen, *Sun Dance Religion*, 1–13). Ironically revealing is the local use of the term "colony" to describe the small residential sites that were set aside as reservations in Las Vegas, Reno, Ely, Elko, Battle Mountain, and other places across Nevada. For diagnostic features of nation-states, see Kottak, *Mirror for Humanity*, 157–63.

9. Such flexibility seems to have been a general characteristic of Great Basin native cultures. See for Western Shoshones, Crum, *The Road*; Steward, *Basin-Plateau*, esp. 239–46, 257. For Northern Utes, see Lewis, *Neither Wolf nor Dog*, 22–70. Even Numic Comanches were notably flexible when compared to other tribes of the Great Plains (Foster, *Being Comanche*, 22, 171–73). Greatest contrast may be with Pueblos, whose carefully structured and defended culture is obviously also a source of strength (e.g., Clemmer, "Directed Resistance").

   I suspect that this adaptability has aided the survival of many hunting-gathering peoples, from Eskimos of Arctic North America to !Kung San of south-central Africa. Shostok, for instance, says of the latter group, "Adaptability is the key to their success" (Nisa, 8). Years ago Elman Service proposed his Law of Evolutionary Potential: "Specific evolutionary progress is inversely related to general evolutionary potential" ("The Law of Evolutionary Potential," 97).

BIBLIOGRAPHY

ARCHIVES

*All citations to manuscript correspondence are to page 1, unless speci-
fied otherwise.*

Bancroft Library, University of California, Berkeley

Brigham Young University, Provo UT

Church Historian's Office, Church of Jesus Christ of Latter-day Saints, Salt
Lake City

Denver Public Library

Library of Congress, Archival and Manuscript Records, Washington DC

Milwaukee Public Museum, Library, Milwaukee WI

Nevada Historical Society, Las Vegas

Newberry Library, Chicago

Smithsonian Institution, National Anthropological Archive, Washington
DC

St. George (UT) Public Library

Southern Utah State University, Special Collections, Cedar City UT

      William R. Palmer Papers

U.S. National Archives, Washington DC

      RG 29 Department of Commerce

      RG 46 U.S. Congress, Senate

      RG 48 Secretary of the Interior

      RG 75 Bureau of Indian Affairs

      RG 279 Indian Claims Commission

RG 393 U.S. Army, Continental

U.S. National Archives, Arlington VA

Cartography Division

U.S. National Archives, Denver

RG 21 Judiciary, U.S. District Court Records

RG 75 Bureau of Indian Affairs

U.S. National Archives, Laguna Niguel CA

RG 75 Bureau of Indian Affairs

U.S. National Archives, San Bruno CA

RG 75 Bureau of Indian Affairs

U.S. National Archives, Suitland MA

RG 49 Bureau of Land Management/General Land Office

University of Utah, Manuscript Collection, Salt Lake City

Utah State Historical Society, Salt Lake City

Anthony Ivins Papers

Juanita Brooks Papers

NEWSPAPERS

Arizona Republic (Tucson)

Caliente (NV) Express

Caliente (NV) Prospector

Cedar City (UT) Spectrum

Clark County Review (Las Vegas NV)

Color Country Spectrum (Cedar City UT)

Colorado Springs Gazette

Denver Post

Deseret News (Salt Lake City)

Deseret Weekly News

Iron County (UT) Record

Las Vegas Age

Las Vegas Review-Journal

Lincoln County Record (Pioche NV)

Pioche (NV) Daily Record

Pioche (NV) Tri-Weekly Record

Pioche (NV) Weekly Record

Salt Lake Tribune

Washington Herald

BOOKS, ARTICLES, AND OTHER SOURCES

Abbott, John S. C. *Christopher Carson: Familiarly Known as Kit Carson.* New York: Dodd & Mead, 1873.

Alley, John R. "Great Basin Numa: The Contact Period." Ph.D. diss., University of California, Santa Barbara, 1986.

———. "Prelude to Dispossession: The Fur Trade's Significance for the Northern Utes and Southern Paiutes." *Utah Historical Quarterly* 50 (1982): 105–23.

Alter, Cecil. *Indian Joe: In Person and in Background.* Delta UT: Privately printed, 1939, copy in Utah State Historical Society, Salt Lake City.

———, ed. "Journal of Priddy Meeks." *Utah Historical Quarterly* 10 (1942): 145–223.

American Indian Policy Review Commission. *Final Report.* 2 vols. Washington DC: USGPO, 1977.

Anderson, Benedict. *Imagined Communities: Reflections on the Origin and Spread of Nationalism.* London: Verso, 1991.

Anderson, Edward H. "Apostle Lyman's Mission to the Indians." *Improvement Era* 3 (1899–1900): 510–16.

Anderson, Kenneth, and Daisy Mike. "History of the Las Vegas Indian Colony." In Inter-tribal Council of Nevada, *Personal Reflections of the Shoshone, Paiute, and Washo,* 20–21. Provo: University of Utah Printing Service, 1974.

Angel, Myron. *History of Nevada*. Oakland: Thompson & West, 1881. Reprint, Berkeley CA: Howell-North, 1958.

Arrington, Leonard J. *Great Basin Kingdom: An Economic History of the Latter-day Saints, 1830–1900*. Cambridge MA: Harvard University Press, 1958. Reprint, Lincoln: University of Nebraska Press, 1966.

———. "How the Saints Fed the Indians." *Improvement Era* 57 (1954): 800–801, 814.

———. "Mormons and the Indians: A Review and Evaluation." In *The Record*, 5–29. Pullman: Friends of the Library of Washington State University, 1970.

———. *The Mormons in Nevada*. Las Vegas: Las Vegas Sun, 1979.

Arrington, Leonard J., Feramorz Fox, and Dean May. *Building the City of God: Community and Cooperation among the Mormons*. Salt Lake City: Deseret Book Co., 1976.

Arrington, Leonard J., and Richard L. Jensen. "Panaca: Mormon Outpost among the Mining Camps." *Nevada Historical Society Quarterly* 18 (1975): 207–16.

Aubry, Francois. "Diaries of 1853–1854." In Ralph Bieber, ed., *Exploring Southwestern Trails, 1848–1854*, 351–83. Glendale CA: Arthur H. Clark Co., 1938.

Auerbach, Herbert S. "Father Escalante's Route." *Utah Historical Quarterly* 9, nos. 1–2 (1941): 73–80.

Backus, Anna Jean. *Mountain Meadows Witness: Life and Times of Bishop Philip Klingensmith*. Spokane WA: Arthur H. Clark Co., 1995.

Bailey, Alice M. "Last Wife of Chief Kanosh." *Frontier Times* (March 1980): 16–22, 50–51.

Bailey, L. R. *Indian Slave Trade in the Southwest*. Los Angeles: Westernlore Press, 1966.

Balknap, William. "The Saga of Queho: The Paiute Renegade." *Arizona Highways* 17, no. 9 (1941): 28–29, 33.

Bancroft, Hubert H. *History of Nevada, 1540–1888*. San Francisco: History Co., 1890. Reprint, Reno: University of Nevada Press, 1981.

———. *History of Utah, 1840–1886*. San Francisco: History Co., 1889. Reprint, Las Vegas: Nevada Publications, 1982.

Barth, Fredrik. "Enduring and Emerging Issues in the Analysis of Ethnicity." In Hans Vermeulen and Cora Govers, eds., *The Anthropology of Ethnicity: Beyond Ethnic Groups and Boundaries*, 1–32. Amsterdam: Het Spinhuis, 1994.

———. Introduction to Fredrik Barth, ed., *Ethnic Groups and Boundaries*, 9–38. Boston: Little, Brown, 1969.

Beaman, O. E. "The Canon of the Colorado and the Moqui Pueblos." *Appleton's Journal* 11, old series (1874): 481–84, 513–16, 545–48, 590–93, 623–26, 641–44.

Bennett, John, ed. *The New Ethnicity: Perspectives from Ethnology*. St. Paul MN: West, 1975.

Bigler, David L. *Forgotten Kingdom: The Mormon Theocracy in the American West, 1847–1896*. Spokane WA: Arthur H. Clark Co., 1998.

Biolsi, Thomas. *Organizing the Lakota: The Political Economy of the New Deal on the Pine Ridge and Rosebud Reservations*. Tucson: University of Arizona Press, 1992.

Bolton, Herbert E. "Escalante in Dixie and the Arizona Strip." *New Mexico Historical Review* 3 (1928): 41–72.

———. "Pageant in the Wilderness: The Story of the Escalante Expedition to the Interior Basin, 1776, Including the Diary and Itinerary of Father Escalante." *Utah Historical Quarterly* 18 (1950): 1–265.

Bonsel, Stephen, ed. *Edward Fitzgerald Beale: A Pioneer in the Path of Empire, 1822–1903*. New York: Knickerbocker Press, 1912.

Bowers, Janice E. *Shrubs and Trees of the Southwest Deserts*. Tucson: Southwest Parks and Monuments Association, 1993.

Bradley, Zorro A. "The Whitmore-McIntyre Dugout, Pipe Spring National Monument: Part I: History." *Plateau* 33, no. 2 (1960): 40–45.

Brandon, William. *American Heritage Book of Indians*. New York: American Heritage Publishing Co. and McGraw Hill, 1961.

Brooks, Juanita. *Dudley Leavitt: Pioneer of Southern Utah*. St. George UT: Privately printed, 1942.

———. "Indian Relations on the Mormon Frontier." *Utah Historical Quarterly* 12 (1944): 1–48.

———. *Jacob Hamblin: Mormon Apostle to the Indians*. Salt Lake City: Westwater Press, 1980.

———. *John Doyle Lee: Zealot—Pioneer Builder—Scapegoat*. Glendale CA: Arthur Clark, 1962.

———. *The Mountain Meadows Massacre*. Stanford CA: Stanford University Press, 1950. Reprint, Norman: University of Oklahoma Press, 1970.

———. *Quicksand and Cactus: Memoir of the Southern Utah Frontier*. Salt Lake City: Howe Brothers, 1982.

———, ed. *Journal of the Southern Indian Mission: Diary of Thomas D. Brown*. Western Text Society Monograph no. 4. Logan: Utah State University Press, 1972.

Brophy, William A., and Sophie D. Aberle. *The Indian: America's Unfinished Business*. Norman: University of Oklahoma Press, 1966.

Brown, John Z., ed. *Autobiography of Pioneer John Brown, 1820–1896*. Salt Lake City: Stevens and Wallis, 1941.

Brown, Merle. *Climates of the States: Nevada*. U.S. Department of Commerce, Weather Bureau, *Climatography of the United States* no. 60–26. Washington DC: USGPO, 1960.

Bunte, Pamela A. "Ethnohistory of the San Juan Paiute Tribe." In Susan Brown McGreevy and Andrew Hunter Whiteford, eds., *Translating Tradition: Basketry Arts of the San Juan Paiutes*, 9–13. Santa Fe: Wheelwright Museum, 1985.

Bunte, Pamela A., and Robert J. Franklin. *From the Sands to the Mountain: Change and Persistence in a Southern Paiute Community*. Lincoln: University of Nebraska Press, 1987.

Bye, Robert A. "Ethnobotany of the Southern Paiute Indians in the 1870s." In Don D. Fowler, ed., *Great Basin Cultural Ecology: A Symposium*, 87–103. Publications in the Social Sciences no. 8. Reno: Desert Research Institute, 1972.

Callaway, Donald G., Joel C. Janetski, and Omer C. Stewart. "Ute." In Warren L. d'Azevedo, ed., *Great Basin*, 336–68. Vol. 11, *Handbook of North American Indians*, gen. ed. William Sturtevant. Washington DC: Smithsonian Institution Press, 1986.

Camp, Charles L. "The Chronicles of George C. Yount: California Pioneer of 1826." *California Historical Society Quarterly* 2 (1923): 3–66.

———. *George C. Yount and His Chronicles of the West.* Denver: Old West Publishing Co., 1966.

Carling, James L. "On the Trail of Willie-boy." *Desert Magazine* 5, no. 1 (November 1941): 6–9.

Carter, Kate B. "Indian Women of the West: Lessons for April 1938." Salt Lake City: Daughters of the Utah Pioneers, 1938.

Casebier, Dennis. *Camp El Dorado, Arizona Territory: Soldiers, Steamboats, and Miners on the Upper Colorado River.* Arizona Monographs no. 2. Tempe: Arizona Historical Foundation, 1970.

———. *Camp Rock Spring California.* Norco CA: Tales of the Mojave Road Publishing Co., 1973.

———. *The Mojave Road.* Norco CA: Tales of the Mojave Road Publishing Co., 1975.

———. *The Mojave Road in Newspapers.* Norco CA: Tales of the Mojave Road Publishing Co., 1976.

CH2M Hill. "Proposed Paiute Indian Tribe of Utah Reservation Plan—Draft." Washington DC: U.S. Department of Interior, 1982.

Chavez, Angelico, and Ted J. Warner. *The Dominguez-Escalante Journal.* Provo UT: Brigham Young University Press, 1976.

Churchill, Ward. *Struggle for the Land: Indigenous Resistance to Genocide, Ecocide, and Expropriation in Contemporary North America.* Monroe ME: Common Courage Press, 1993.

Church of Jesus Christ of Latter-day Saints. *Journal of Discourses.* 26 vols. Liverpool: E. D. and S. E. Richards, 1854–86.

Cleland, Robert Glass, and Juanita Brooks, eds. *A Mormon Chronicle: The Diaries of John D. Lee, 1848–1876.* 2 vols. Salt Lake City: University of Utah Press, 1983.

Clemmer, Richard O. "Differential Leadership Patterns in Early Twentieth-Century Great Basin Indian Societies." *Journal of California and Great Basin Anthropology* 11 (1989): 35–49.

———. "Directed Resistance to Acculturation: A Comparative Study of the Effects of Non-Indian Jurisdiction on Hopi and Western Shoshone Communities." Ph.D. diss., University of Illinois, 1972.

———. "Ideology and Identity: Western Shoshoni 'Cannibal' Myth as Ethnonational Narrative." *Journal of Anthropological Research* 52 (1996): 207–23.

Cohen, Felix S. *Handbook of Federal Indian Law.* Rev. ed. Charlottesville VA: Bobbs-Merrill, 1982.

Cornell, Stephen. *Return of the Native: American Indian Political Resurgence.* New York: Oxford University Press, 1988.

Coues, Elliot. *On the Trail of a Spanish Pioneer.* New York: F. P. Harper, 1900.

Cronon, William. *Changes in the Land: Indians, Colonists, and the Ecology of New England.* New York: Hill and Wang, 1983.

Crum, Steven J. *The Road on Which We Came: A History of the Western Shoshone.* Salt Lake City: University of Utah Press, 1994.

Curtis, James F. Letter to Col. R. C. Drum, Assistant Adjt. Genl., Dept. of the Pacific, 2 March 1865. In Leonard Waitman, "The History of Camp Cady: The Early History of a Desert Water Hole." *Historical Society of Southern California Quarterly* 36, no. 1 (1954): 49–91.

Dalton, Luella Adams, comp. *History of the Iron County Mission and Parowan, the Mother Town.* Parowan UT: Privately printed, 1963.

Davis, Sam. *The History of Nevada.* 2 vols. Reno: Elms Publishing Co., 1913.

Dobyns, Henry F., and Robert C. Euler. *Wauba Yuma's People: The Comparative Sociopolitical Structure of the Pai Indians of Arizona.* Prescott AZ: Prescott College Press, 1970.

Elliot, Russell R. *History of Nevada.* Lincoln: University of Nebraska Press, 1973.

Elmore, Francis. *Shrubs and Trees of the Southwest Uplands.* Globe AZ: Southwest Parks and Monuments Association, 1976.

Euler, Robert C. *The Paiute People.* Phoenix: Indian Tribal Series, 1972.

———. *Southern Paiute Ethnohistory.* University of Utah Anthropological Papers no. 78. Salt Lake City: University of Utah Press, 1966.

Farnham, Thomas J. *Life and Adventures in California and Scenes of the Pacific.* New York: Graham Publishing, 1846.

Farrow, E. A. "The Kaibab Indians." *Utah Historical Quarterly* 3 (1930): 57–59.

Fenton, William. "The Iroquois in History." In Eleanor B. Leacock and Nancie O. Lurie, eds., *North American Indians in Historical Perspective*, 129–68. New York: Random House, 1971.

Fielding, Kent. *Unsolicited Chronicler: Account of the Gunnison Massacre.* Brookline MA: Paradigm Press, 1993.

Fixico, Donald L. *Termination and Relocation: Federal Indian Policy, 1945–1960.* Albuquerque: University of New Mexico Press, 1986.

Forbes, Jack D. *Apache, Navaho and Spaniard.* Norman: University of Oklahoma Press, 1960.

Foreman, Grant, ed. *Pathfinder in the Southwest: The Itinerary of Lt. A. W. Whipple during His Explorations for a Railway Route from Ft. Smith to Los Angeles in the Years 1853 & 1854.* Norman: University of Oklahoma Press, 1941.

Foster, Morris W. *Being Comanche: A Social History of an American Indian Community.* Tucson: University of Arizona Press, 1991.

Fowler, Catherine S. "Environmental Setting and Natural Resources." In Robert C. Euler, *Southern Paiute Ethnohistory*, 13–31. University of Utah Anthropological Papers no. 78. Salt Lake City: University of Utah Press, 1966.

———. *Native Americans and Yucca Mountain: A Summary Report.* State of Nevada, Nuclear Waste Project Office Report no. NWPO-SE-026-90. Carson City NV: N.p., 1990.

———. "Settlement Patterns and Subsistence Systems in the Great Basin: The Ethnographic Record." In David B. Madsen and James F. O'Connell, eds., *Man and Environment in the Great Basin*, 121–38. Society for American Archaeology Papers no. 2. Washington DC: Society for American Archaeology, 1982.

Fowler, Catherine S., and Lawrence Dawson. "Ethnographic Basketry." In Warren d'Azevedo, ed., *Great Basin*, 705–37. Vol. 11, *Handbook of North American Indians*, gen. ed. William Sturtevant. Washington DC: Smithsonian Institution Press, 1986.

Fowler, Catherine S., and Robert C. Euler, eds. "Kaibab Paiute and Northern Ute Ethnographic Field Notes." In *Southern Paiute and Ute Linguistics and Ethnography*, 779–922. Vol. 10, *The Collected Works of Edward Sapir*, gen. ed. William Bright. Berlin: Mouton de Gruyter, 1992.

Fowler, Catherine S., and Don D. Fowler. "Notes on the History of the Southern Paiutes and Western Shoshonis." *Utah Historical Quarterly* 39 (1971): 95–113.

Fowler, Don D., ed. *Models and Great Basin Prehistory: A Symposium.* Publications in the Social Sciences no. 12. Reno NV: Desert Research Institute, 1977.

Fowler, Don D., and Catherine S. Fowler, eds. *Anthropology of the Numa: John Wesley Powell's Manuscripts on the Numic Peoples of Western North America, 1868–1880.* Smithsonian Institution Contributions in Anthropology no. 14. Washington DC: Smithsonian Institution Press, 1971.

Fowler, Don. D., and David B. Madsen. "Prehistory of the Southeastern Area." In Warren d'Azevedo, ed., *Great Basin,* 183–93. Vol. 11, *Handbook of North American Indians,* gen. ed. William Sturtevant. Washington DC: Smithsonian Institution Press, 1986.

Fowler, Don D., and John F. Matley. *Material Culture of the Numa: The John Wesley Powell Collection, 1867–1880.* Smithsonian Institution Contributions to Anthropology no. 26. Washington DC: Smithsonian Institution Press, 1979.

———. "The Palmer Collection from Southwestern Utah, 1875." In C. Melvin Aikens et al., *Miscellaneous Collected Papers, nos. 19–24,* 19–42. University of Utah Anthropological Papers no. 99. Salt Lake City: University of Utah Press, 1978.

Franklin, Robert A., and Pamela A. Bunte. *The Paiute.* New York: Chelsea House, 1990.

Frémont, John C. *A Report of the Exploring Expedition to Oregon and North California, in the Years 1843–'44.* New York: A. Appleton & Co., 1846.

———. *Report of the Exploring Expedition to the Rocky Mountains in the Year 1842.* Washington DC: Gales and Seaton, 1845.

Galvin, John, trans. *A Record of Travels in Arizona & California, 1775–1776 by Fr. Francisco Garces.* San Francisco: John Howell Books, 1965.

Gibbs, Josiah. "Gunnison Massacre; 1853; Millard County, Utah; Indian Mareer's Version of the Tragedy." *Utah Historical Quarterly* 1 (1928): 65–75.

———. *Lights and Shadows of Mormonism.* Salt Lake City: Salt Lake Tribune Publishing Co., 1909.

Goodyear, William E. "Narrative." In John S. C. Abbott, *Christopher Carson: Familiarly Known as Kit Carson*. New York: Dodd & Mead, 1873.

Gottfredson, Peter. *Indian Depredations in Utah*. Salt Lake City: Skeleton Publishing, 1919. Reprint, Salt Lake City: Merlin Christensen, 1969.

Hafen, LeRoy. "Armijo's Journal." *Huntington Library Quarterly* 11 (1947): 87–101.

Hafen, LeRoy, and Ann Hafen. *Journals of Forty-niners*. Glendale CA: Arthur H. Clark Co., 1954.

———. *Old Spanish Trail: Santa Fe to Los Angeles*. Glendale CA: Arthur H. Clark Co., 1954.

Hagan, William T. *Indian Police and Judges*. New Haven CT: Yale University Press, 1966. Reprint, Lincoln: University of Nebraska Press, 1980.

Haines, Francis. "The Northward Spread of Horses among the Plains Indians." *American Anthropologist* 40 (1938): 429–36.

Hall, Thomas D. *Social Change in the Southwest, 1350–1880*. Lawrence: University Press of Kansas, 1989.

Hansen, Klaus J. *Mormonism and the American Experience*. Chicago: University of Chicago Press, 1981.

Harper, Kimball T. "Historical Environments." In Warren d'Azevedo, ed., *Great Basin*, 51–63. Vol. 11, *Handbook of North American Indians*, gen. ed. William Sturtevant. Washington DC: Smithsonian Institution Press, 1986.

Harrington, Mark R. "Bug Sugar." *Masterkey* 19 (1945): 95–96.

Harris, Marvin. *Cultural Materialism: The Struggle for a Science of Culture*. New York: Vintage, 1979.

Haynes, Alan E. "Federal Government and Its Policies Regarding the Frontier Era of Utah Territory, 1850–1877." Ph.D. diss., Catholic University, 1968.

Heinerman, John, and Anson Shupe. *The Mormon Corporate Empire*. Boston: Beacon Press, 1985.

Heinz, Lyle S. "Origin and Development of the San Juan Mission in Southeastern Utah in Its Work with Indian People (Principally since 1940)." M. A. thesis, Brigham Young University, Provo UT, 1976.

Hickman, Bill. *Brigham's Destroying Angel: Life and Confession of a Danite*. New York: George Crofutt, 1872.

Hill, Leonard. "Social and Economic Survey of Shivwits, Kanosh, Koosharem, Indian Peaks and Cedar City Bands of Paiute Indians." Washington DC: Bureau of Indian Affairs, 1968. Mimeograph.

Holt, Ronald L. *Beneath These Red Cliffs: An Ethnohistory of the Utah Paiutes*. Albuquerque: University of New Mexico Press, 1992.

Hulse, James W. *Lincoln County, Nevada, 1864–1909*. Nevada Studies in History and Political Science no. 10. Reno: N.p., 1971.

Inter-tribal Council of Nevada. *Nuwuvi: A Southern Paiute History*. Provo: University of Utah Printing Service, 1976.

———. *Personal Reflections of the Shoshone, Paiute, Washo*. Provo: University of Utah Printing Service, 1974.

Ivins, Anthony W. "Traveling over Forgotten Trails: A Mystery of the Grand Canyon Solved." *Improvement Era* 27 (1924): 1017–25.

Jackson, Richard H. "Mormon Indian Farms: An Attempt at Cultural Integration." In Jerry N. McDonald and Tony Lazewski, eds., *Geographical Perspectives on Native Americans: Topics and Resources*, 41–54. Associated Committee on Native Americans Publications no. 1. N.p.: Association of American Geographers, 1976.

Jacobs, Mary Jane. "Termination of Federal Supervision over the Southern Paiute Indians of Utah." M. S. thesis, University of Utah, 1974.

Jaeger, Edmund C. *Desert Wild Flowers*. Rev. ed. Stanford CA: Stanford University Press, 1941.

Jensen, Andrew, ed. *History of the Las Vegas Mission*. Nevada Historical Society Papers no. 5. Reno: Nevada Historical Society, 1926.

Johnson, Edward. *Walker River Paiutes: A Tribal History*. Salt Lake City: University of Utah Printing Service, 1975.

Jones, Daniel W. *Forty Years among the Indians*. Salt Lake City: Church of Jesus Christ of Latter-day Saints Juvenile Instructor's Office, 1890.

Jones, J. A. "A Reinterpretation of the Ute-Southern Paiute Classification." *Anthropological Quarterly* 27 (1954): 53–58.

Jones, Volney H. "Notes of Frederick S. Dellenbaugh on the Southern Paiute from Letters of 1927 and 1928." *Masterkey* 22 (1948): 177–82.

Jorgensen, Joseph G. "A Century of Political Economic Effects on American Indian Society, 1880–1980." *Journal of Ethnic Studies* 6 (1978): 1–82.

————. "Great Basin Language, Culture and Environment." Manuscript. 1984. Copy in possession of the author.

————. *The Sun Dance Religion: Power for the Powerless.* Chicago: University of Chicago Press, 1972.

————. "Synchronic Relations among Environment, Language, and Culture as Clues to the Numic Expansion." In David B. Madsen and David Rhode, eds., *Across the West: Human Population Movement and the Expansion of the Numa,* 84–102. Salt Lake City: University of Utah Press, 1994.

Kane, Elizabeth Wood. *Twelve Mormon Homes Visited in Succession on a Journey through Utah to Arizona.* Philadelphia: Privately printed, 1874. Reprint, Salt Lake City: University of Utah Library, 1974.

Kelly, Charles, ed. "Journal of Walter Clement Powell." *Utah Historical Quarterly* 16–17 (1948–49): 257–478.

Kelly, Isabel T. "Band Organization of the Southern Paiute." *American Anthropologist* 40 (1938): 633–34.

————. "Chemehuevi Shamanism." In Robert Lowie, ed., *Essays in Anthropology Presented to A. L. Kroeber,* 129–42. Berkeley: University of California Press, 1936.

————. "Southern Paiute Bands." *American Anthropologist* 36 (1934): 548–60.

————. *Southern Paiute Ethnography.* University of Utah Anthropological Papers no. 69. Salt Lake City: University of Utah Press, 1964.

————. "Southern Paiute Shamanism." University of California Anthropological Records 2, no. 4 (1939): 151–67.

————. Unpublished Ethnographic Field Notes from the Southern Paiute and Chemehuevi, 1932–34. University of California Archives Microfilm no. 138.1, Anthropology Document no. 17. Original manuscript in University Archives, Bancroft Library, University of California, Berkeley.

Kelly, Isabel T., and Catherine S. Fowler. "Southern Paiute." In Warren d'Azevedo, ed., *Great Basin,* 368–97. Vol. 11, *Handbook of North American Indians,* gen. ed. William Sturtevant. Washington DC: Smithsonian Institution Press, 1986.

King, Volney. "Millard County, 1851–1875." *Utah Humanities Review* 1 (1947): 18–37, 147–65, 261–78, 378–400.

Knack, Martha C. "Beyond a Differential: An Inquiry into Southern Paiute Indian Experience with Public Schools." *Anthropology and Education Quarterly* 9 (1978): 59–66.

———. "Church and State in the History of Southern Paiutes in Cedar City, Utah." *Journal of California and Great Basin Anthropology* 19 (1997): 159–78.

———. "Contemporary Southern Paiute Women and the Measurement of Women's Economic and Political Status." *Ethnology* 28 (1989): 233–48.

———. Field Notes, Moapa Southern Paiutes, Nevada, 1983.

———. Field Notes, Utah Southern Paiutes, Terminated Bands, 1973–76.

———. "Interethnic Competition at Kaibab during the Early Twentieth Century." *Ethnohistory* 40 (1993): 212–45.

———. *Life Is with People: Household Organization of the Contemporary Southern Paiute Indians*. Ballena Anthropological Papers no. 19. Socorro NM: Ballena Press, 1980.

———. "Missionaries as Shamans." Paper read at the annual meeting of the American Society for Ethnohistory, Bloomington IN, November 1993.

———. "Newspaper Accounts of Indian Women in Southern Nevada Mining Towns, 1870–1900." *Journal of California and Great Basin Anthropology* 8 (1986): 83–98.

———. "Nineteenth Century Great Basin Wage Labor." In Alice B. Littlefield and Martha C. Knack, eds., *Native Americans and Wage Labor: Ethnohistorical Perspectives*, 144–76. Norman: University of Oklahoma Press, 1996.

———. "Political Strategies without Political Power: Thoughts on How Headmen Work." Paper read at the annual meeting of the American Society for Ethnohistory, Minneapolis MN, 14 November 1998.

———. "The Role of Credit in Native American Adaptation to the Great Basin Ranching Economy." *American Indian Culture and Research Journal* 11 (1987): 43–65.

———. "Utah Indians and the Homestead Laws." In George Pierre Castile and Robert L. Bee, eds., *State and Reservation: New Perspectives on Federal Indian Policy*, 63–91. Tucson: University of Arizona Press, 1992.

Knack, Martha C., and Omer C. Stewart. *As Long as the River Shall Run: An*

Ethnohistory of Pyramid Lake Indian Reservation. Berkeley: University of California Press, 1984. Expanded ed., Reno: University of Nevada Press, 1999.

Kottak, Conrad. *Mirror for Humanity,* 2nd ed. New York: McGraw Hill, 1999.

Krech, Shepard, III. "The State of Ethnohistory." *Annual Review of Anthropology* 20 (1991): 345–75.

Kroeber, Alfred L. "Coefficients of Cultural Similarity of Northern Paiute Bands." In A. L. Kroeber, *Ethnographic Interpretations, 1–6,* University of California Publications in American Archaeology and Ethnology 47, no. 2: 209–14. Berkeley: University of California Press, 1957.

———. *Ethnography of the Cahuilla Indians.* University of California Publications in American Archaeology and Ethnology 8: 1–68. Berkeley: University of California Press, 1908.

———. *Handbook of the Indians of California.* Smithsonian Institution, Bureau of American Ethnology Bulletin no. 78. Washington DC: USGPO, 1925. Reprint, New York: Dover Publications, 1976.

———. "The Nature of the Land-holding Group." *Ethnohistory* 2 (1955): 303–14.

———. *Shoshonean Dialects of California.* University of California Publications in American Archaeology and Ethnology 3, no. 4: 66–170. Berkeley: University of California Press, 1907.

Kroeber, Alfred L., and C. B. Kroeber. *A Mohave War Reminiscence, 1854–1880.* University of California Publications in Anthropology no. 10. Berkeley: University of California Press, 1973.

Laird, Carobeth. "Chemehuevi Religious Beliefs and Practices." *Journal of California Anthropology* 1 (1974): 19–25.

———. *The Chemehuevis.* Banning CA: Malki Museum Press, 1976.

———. *Mirror and Pattern: George Laird's World of Chemehuevi Mythology.* Banning CA: Malki Museum Press, 1984.

Lanner, Ronald M. *The Piñon Pine: A Natural and Cultural History.* Reno: University of Nevada Press, 1981.

Larson, Gustive O. *The "Americanization" of Utah for Statehood.* San Marino CA: Huntington Library, 1971.

————. "Brigham Young and the Indians." In Robert Ferris, ed., *The American West: An Appraisal*, 176–87. Santa Fe: Museum of New Mexico Press, 1963.

————. "Land Contest in Early Utah." *Utah Historical Quarterly* 29 (1961): 309–25.

Larson, Gustive, and Richard Poll. "The 45th State." In Richard Poll, ed., *Utah's History*, 387–404. Provo UT: Brigham Young University Press, 1978.

Law, Welsey R. "Mormon Indian Missions—1855." M. S. thesis, Brigham Young University, 1959.

Lawton, Harry. *The Last Western Manhunt: Riverside County Sheriff Frank Wilson's Official Report on the Willie Boy Manhunt of 1909*. San Diego: Privately printed, 1966.

————. *Willie Boy: A Desert Manhunt*. Banning CA: Malki Museum Press, 1960.

Lee, John D. *Life and Confession of John D. Lee, the Mormon*. Philadelphia: Barclary & Co., 1877.

Lewis, David Rich. *Neither Wolf nor Dog: American Indians, Environment, and Agrarian Change*. New York: Oxford University Press, 1994.

————. "Reservation Leadership and the Progressive-Traditional Dichotomy: William Wash and the Northern Utes, 1865–1928." *Ethnohistory* 38 (1991): 124–49.

Little, James. *Jacob Hamblin: A Narrative of His Personal Experience*. Salt Lake City: Church of Jesus Christ of Latter-day Saints Juvenile Instructor's Office, 1909.

Lowie, Robert H. *Notes on Shoshonean Ethnography*. American Museum of Natural History Anthropological Papers 20, no. 3: 185–314. New York: N.p., 1924.

Lyman, Albert. *Indians and Outlaws: Settling of the San Juan Frontier*. Salt Lake City: Bookcraft, 1962.

Madsen, Brigham D. *Corinne: The Gentile Capital of Utah*. Salt Lake City: Utah State Historical Society Press, 1980.

Madsen, David B., and James F. O'Connell. *Man and Environment in the Great Basin*. Society for American Archaeology Papers no. 2. Washington DC: Society for American Archaeology, 1982.

Malouf, Carling, and A. Arline Malouf. "The Effects of Spanish Slavery on the Indians of the Intermountain West." *Southwestern Journal of Anthropology* 1 (1945): 378–91.

Manly, William Lewis. *Death Valley in '49.* San Jose: Pacific Tree and Vine Co., 1894. Reprint, Bishop CA: Chalfant Press, c. 1978.

Manners, Robert A. "Southern Paiute and Chemehuevi: An Ethnohistorical Report." U.S. Indian Claims Commission, Docket 88–330, Defendant's Exhibit no. 113. Published in *Paiute Indians: I,* series ed. David Horr. American Indian Ethnohistory Series. New York: Garland, 1974.

Martineau, LaVan. *Southern Paiutes: Legends, Lore, Language, and Lineage.* Las Vegas: KC Publications, 1992.

McMurrin, Sterling M. *The Theological Foundations of the Mormon Religion.* Salt Lake City: University of Utah Press, 1965.

Melville, Maud C. "Chief Kanosh, the Peacemaker." In Kate B. Carter, ed., *Indian Chiefs of Pioneer Days,* 16–18. Salt Lake City: Daughters of the Utah Pioneers, 1937.

Miller, David. "The Impact of the Gunnison Massacre on Mormon-Federal Relations: Colonel Edward Jenner Steptoe's Command in Utah Territory, 1854–1855." M. A. thesis, University of Utah, 1968.

Miller, Wick. "Classification of the Uto-Aztecan Languages Based on Lexical Evidence." *International Journal of American Linguistics* 50 (1984): 1–24.

Moapa Band of Paiute Indians. *Moapa Band of Paiute Indians.* N.p., n.d. (c. 1979).

Morgan, Dale L., and Carl I. Wheat. *Jedediah Smith and His Maps of the American West.* San Francisco: California Historical Society, 1954.

Munz, Philip A. *California Desert Wildflowers.* Berkeley: University of California Press, 1962.

Neff, Andrew L. *History of Utah, 1847–1869.* Salt Lake City: Deseret News Press, 1940.

Nelson, Lowry. *The Mormon Village: A Pattern and Technique of Land Settlement.* Salt Lake City: University of Utah Press, 1952.

Nusbaumer, Louis. *Valley of Salt, Memories of Wine: Journal of Death Valley in 1849.* Berkeley: University of California Press, 1967.

Nye, William. "A Winter among the Piutes." *Overland Monthly* n.s. 7 (1886): 293–98.

Olson, James S., and Raymond Wilson. *Native Americans in the Twentieth Century.* Urbana: University of Illinois Press, 1984.

Orfield, Gary. "A Study of the Termination Policy." Denver: National Congress of American Indians, 1965. Mimeograph.

Osborn, Harold Wesley. "Evaluation of Counseling with a Group of Southern Utah Paiute Indians." Ph.D. diss., University of Utah, 1959.

Paiute Indian Tribe of Utah. *Newsletter.* Cedar City UT: Paiute Indian Tribe of Utah, 1981–87.

Palmer, William R. "Pahute Indian Government and Laws." *Utah Historical Quarterly* 2 (1929): 35–42.

———. "Pahute Indian Homelands." *Utah Historical Quarterly* 6 (1933): 88–102.

Park, Willard Z., et al. "Tribal Distribution in the Great Basin." *American Anthropologist* 40 (1938): 622–38.

Patterson, James T. "The New Deal in the West." *Pacific Historical Review* 38 (1969): 317–27.

Pattie, James O. *Personal Narrative of James O. Pattie.* Cincinnati: John Wood Co., 1831.

Penrose, Charles. *The Mountain Meadows Massacre.* Salt Lake City: Church of Jesus Christ of Latter-day Saints Juvenile Instructor's Office, 1884.

Perkins, George Elwood. *Pioneers of the Western Desert: Romance and Tragedy along the Old Spanish or Mormon Trail and Historical Events of the Great West.* Los Angeles: Wetzel Publishing Co., 1947.

Peterson, John Alton. *Utah's Black Hawk War.* Salt Lake City: University of Utah Press, 1998.

Pikyavit, Rick. "Use of Fish Lake by Native People: A Personal Perspective." Paper read at Great Basin Anthropological Conference, Lake Tahoe CA, 12 October 1996.

Piute Company. Prospectus of *The Piute Company of California and Nevada.* San Francisco: Edward Bosqui & Co., 1870.

Plattner, Stuart, ed. *The Prospects for Plural Societies.* Washington DC: American Ethnological Society, 1984.

Powell, John Wesley. "Means of Subsistence." In Don D. Fowler and Catherine S. Fowler, eds., *Anthropology of the Numa: John Wesley Powell's Manuscripts on the Numic Peoples of Western North America, 1868–1880.* Smithsonian Institution Contributions to Anthropology no. 14, 39–50. Washington DC: Smithsonian Institution Press, 1971.

———. *Statement Made before Committee on Indian Affairs, on Indians of the Rocky Mountains.* U.S. Congress, House of Representatives, Executive Document no. 86, 43rd Cong., 1st sess. Washington DC: USGPO, 1874. Serial Set no. 1618.

Powell, John Wesley, and George W. Ingalls. *Report on the Condition and Wants of the Ute Indians of Utah, the Pai-Utes of Utah, Northern Arizona, Southern Nevada, and Southeastern California.* U.S. Congress, House of Representatives, Executive Document no. 157, 43rd Cong., 1st sess. Washington DC: USGPO, 1874.

Preuss, Charles. *Exploring with Frémont: Private Diaries of Charles Preuss.* Norman: University of Oklahoma Press, 1958.

Price, William Redwood. Letter to Maj. John P. Sherburne, January 1868. In U.S. Congress, Senate, *Walapai Papers*, 55–65. Executive Document no. 273, 76th Cong., 2nd sess. Washington DC: USGPO, 1936.

Prucha, Francis Paul. *The Great Father,* 2 vols. Lincoln: University of Nebraska Press, 1984.

Quinn, D. Michael. *The Mormon Hierarchy: Extensions of Power.* Salt Lake City: Signature Books, 1997.

Ray, Arthur J. *Indians in the Fur Trade: Their Role as Hunters, Trappers, and Middlemen in the Lands Southwest of Hudson Bay, 1660–1870.* Toronto: University of Toronto Press, 1974.

Redfield, Robert, Ralph Linton, and Melville Herskovits. "Memorandum on the Study of Acculturation." *American Anthropologist* 38 (1936): 149–52.

Rider, Rowland W., and Deirdre M. Paulson. *The Roll Away Saloon: Cowboy Tales of the Arizona Strip.* Logan: Utah State University Press, 1985.

Roosens, Eugene. *Creating Ethnicity: The Process of Ethnogenesis.* Newberry Park CA: Sage Publications, 1989.

Roth, George E. "The Calloway Affair of 1880: Chemehuevi Adaptation and Chemehuevi-Mohave Relations." *Journal of California Anthropology* 4 (1977): 273–86.

————. "Incorporation and Changes in Ethnic Structure: The Chemehuevi Indians." Ph.D. diss., Northwestern University, 1976.

Royce, Charles C. *Indian Land Cessions in the United States*. Smithsonian Institution, Bureau of American Ethnology Eighteenth Annual Report, pt. 2. Washington DC: USGPO, 1900.

Rusco, Elmer R. "The Status of Indians in Nevada Law." In Ruth Houghton, ed., *Native American Politics: Power Relationships in the Western Great Basin Today*, 59–97. Reno: Bureau of Governmental Research, University of Nevada, 1973.

Rusco, Elmer R., and Mary K. Rusco. "Tribal Politics." In Warren L. d'Azevedo, ed., *Great Basin*, 558–72. Vol. 11, *Handbook of North American Indians*, gen. ed. William Sturtevant. Washington DC: Smithsonian Institution Press, 1986.

Russell, Andrew. "A Fortunate Few: Japanese Americans in Southern Nevada, 1905–1945." *Nevada Historical Society Quarterly* 31 (1988): 32–52.

Sapir, Edward. "The Mourning Ceremony of the Southern Paiutes." *American Anthropologist* 14 (1912): 168–69.

————. *Southern Paiute Dictionary*. American Academy of Arts and Sciences Proceedings 65, no. 3. Boston: American Academy of Sciences, 1931.

Secoy, Frank R. *Changing Military Patterns on the Great Plains*. American Ethnological Society Monographs no. 21. Locust Valley NY: J. J. Augustin Publishing, 1953.

Service, Elman R. "The Law of Evolutionary Potential." In Marshall D. Sahlins and Elman R. Service, eds., *Evolution and Culture*, 93–122. Ann Arbor: University of Michigan Press, 1960.

Shepardson, Mary, and Blodwen Hammond. *The Navajo Mountain Community: Social Organization and Kinship Terminology*. Berkeley: University of California Press, 1970.

Shostok, Marjorie. *Nisa: Life and Words of a !Kung Woman*. New York: Vintage, 1981.

Simpson, J. H. *Report of Explorations across the Great Basin of the Territory of Utah for a Direct Wagon-Route from Camp Floyd to Genoa, in Carson Valley in 1859.* Washington DC: USGPO, 1876.

―――. *Shortest Route to California, Illustrated by a History of Explorations of the Great Basin of Utah.* Philadelphia: J. B. Lippincott & Co., 1869.

Smith, Anne M. *Ethnography of the Northern Utes.* Museum of New Mexico Papers in Anthropology no. 17. Albuquerque: University of New Mexico Printing Plant, 1974.

Smith, Gerald, and Clifford Walker. *Indian Slave Trade along the Mojave Trail.* San Bernardino CA: San Bernardino County Museum, 1965.

Smith, Jedidiah. Letter to General William Clark, Superintendent of Indian Affairs, 17 July 1827. In Harrison Clifford Dale, *The Ashley-Smith Explorations and the Discovery of a Central Route to the Pacific, 1822–1829,* 186–94. Cleveland: Arthur H. Clark Co., 1918.

―――. Letter to General William Clark, Superintendent of Indian Affairs, 15 November 1827. Extracted in *U.S. Gazette,* 15 November 1827, 2. Copy in the Newberry Library, Chicago.

Snow, William J. "Utah Indians and Spanish Slave Trade." *Utah Historical Quarterly* 2 (1929): 67–90.

Spencer, Joseph E. "The Development of Agricultural Villages in Southern Utah." *Agricultural History* 14 (1940): 181–89.

Spicer, Edward H. *Cycles of Conquest: The Impact of Spain, Mexico, and the United States on the Indians of the Southwest, 1533–1960.* Tucson: University of Arizona Press, 1962.

―――. "Types of Contact and Processes of Change." In Edward H. Spicer, ed., *Perspectives in American Indian Culture Change,* 517–44. Chicago: University of Chicago Press, 1961. Reprint, Chicago: Midway, 1975.

Spier, Leslie. *Yuman Tribes of the Gila River.* Chicago: University of Chicago Press, 1933. Reprint, New York: Cooper Square, 1970.

Stegner, Wallace. *The Gathering of Zion.* New York: McGraw-Hill, 1964.

Steward, Julian H. *Basin-Plateau Aboriginal Sociopolitical Groups.* Smithsonian Institution, Bureau of American Ethnology Bulletin no. 120. Washington DC: USGPO, 1938. Reprint, Salt Lake City: University of Utah Press, 1970.

———. "Changes in Shoshonean Indian Culture." *Scientific Monthly* 49 (1939): 524–37.

———. *Theory of Culture Change.* Urbana: University of Illinois Press, 1955.

Stewart, Kenneth. "A Brief History of the Chemehuevi Indians." *Kiva* 34, no. 1 (1968): 9–27.

———. "Chemehuevi Culture Changes." *Plateau* 40 (1967): 14–21.

Stewart, Omer C. *Culture Element Distributions: XVIII: Ute-Southern Paiute.* University of California Anthropological Records 6: 231–355. Berkeley: University of California Press, 1942.

———. *Peyote Religion: A History.* Norman: University of Oklahoma Press, 1987.

Stoffle, Richard. "American Indians and Nuclear Waste Storage: The Debate at Yucca Mountain, Nevada." Paper read at the meeting of the American Anthropological Association, Chicago, 19 November 1987.

Stuart, Bradley. "Old John's Ford." *Masterkey* 19, no. 1 (1945): 28.

———. "Pug-a-roo Gathers Mescal." *Masterkey* 19, no. 3 (1945): 79–81.

———. "Pug-a-roo Picks Pine Nuts." *Masterkey* 19, no. 5 (1945): 155.

———. "Southern Paiute Staff of Life." *Masterkey* 19, no. 4 (1945): 133–34.

Stucki, John S. *Family History Journal of John S. Stucki.* Salt Lake City: Pyramid Press, 1932.

Tax, Sol, ed. *Acculturation in the Americas.* Chicago: University of Chicago Press, 1952. Reprint, New York: Cooper Square, 1967.

Train, Percy, James Henrichs, and W. Andrew Archer. *Medicinal Uses of Plants by Indian Tribes of Nevada.* U.S. Department of Agriculture, Bureau of Plant Industry Contributions toward a Flora of Nevada no. 33. Washington DC: Department of Agriculture, 1941. Mimeograph.

Trigger, Bruce G. "Early Iroquoian Contacts with Europeans." In Bruce G. Trigger, ed., *Northeast,* 349–56. Vol. 15, *Handbook of North American Indians,* gen. ed. William Sturtevant. Washington DC: Smithsonian Institution Press, 1978.

Turner, Allen C. "Adaptive Continuity and Cultural Development among the Paiute Indians of the Grand Canyon's North Rim." *Tibewa* 22 (1985): 28–53.

———. *The Kaibab Paiute Indians: An Ecological History.* New Haven CT: HRAFlex Books, 1985.

———. "Utah Paiute Tribal Governance: A Study in Political Persistence." Manuscript in possession of the author. C. 1984.

Tyler, S. Lyman. "The Indians in Utah Territory." In Richard Poll, ed., *Utah's History,* 357–69. Provo UT: Brigham Young University Press, 1978.

Uchendu, Victor Chikezie. "Seasonal Agricultural Labor among the Navajo Indians: A Study in Socio-Economic Transition." Ph.D. diss., Northwestern University, 1966.

Udell, John. *Journal of John Udell, Kept during a Trip across the Plains, Containing an Account of the Massacre of a Portion of His Party by the Mohave Indians in 1858.* Suisun CA: Solano Country Printers, 1859. Reprint as Yale University Library Western Historical Series no. 1. New Haven CT: Yale University Library, 1952.

U.S. Congress, House of Representatives. *Conference Report to Accompany S. 2670.* House Report no. 2661, 83rd Cong., 2nd sess. Washington DC: USGPO, 1954.

———. *Investigation of the Accounts of Brigham Young, Superintendent of Indian Affairs, Utah Territory.* Executive Document no. 29, 37th Cong., 2nd sess. Washington DC: USGPO, 1862.

———. *Mountain Meadow Massacre.* Executive Document no. 605, 57th Cong., 1st sess. Washington DC: USGPO, 1902.

———. *Report on House Resolution Authorizing Congress to Investigate the Bureau of Indian Affairs, Pursuant to House Resolution 89.* House Report no. 2680, 83rd Cong., 2nd sess. Washington DC: USGPO, 1954.

———. *Report to Accompany H. R. 2898,* House Report no. 98-414, 98th Cong., 1st sess. Washington DC: USGPO, 1983.

———. *Report with Respect to House Resolution Authorizing the Committee on Interior and Insular Affairs to Conduct an Investigation of the Bureau of Indian Affairs, Pursuant to H. Res. 698.* House Report no. 2503, 82nd Cong., 2nd sess. Washington DC: USGPO, 1953.

U.S. Congress, Joint Committees on Interior and Insular Affairs, Joint Subcommittees on Indian Affairs of Committees on Interior and Insular Affairs. *Hearing on Termination of Federal Supervision over Certain Tribes of*

Indians, on S. 2670 and H. R. 7674, Part I, Utah. 83rd Cong., 2nd sess. Washington DC: USGPO, 1954.

U.S. Congress, Senate. *Message of the President of the United States, Communicating in Compliance with a Resolution of the Senate, Information in Relation to the Massacre at Mountain Meadows and Other Massacres in Utah Territory.* Executive Document no. 42, 36th Cong., 1st sess. Washington DC: USGPO, 1860.

———. *Report to Accompany H. R. 9828.* Senate Report no. 2279, 84th Cong., 2nd sess. Washington DC: USGPO, 1956.

———. *Report to Accompany S. 1135.* Senate Report no. 96-951, 96th Cong., 2nd sess. Washington DC: USGPO, 1980.

———. *Report to Accompany S. 1273.* Senate Report no. 96-481, 96th Cong., 1st sess. Washington DC: USGPO, 1979.

———. *Walapai Papers.* Executive Document no. 273, 76th Cong., 2nd sess. Washington DC: USGPO, 1936.

U.S. Congress, Senate, Committee on Energy and Natural Resources. *Hearing on Miscellaneous Public Lands, National Forest, and Park Related Proposals, Held 15 October 1979.* 96th Cong., 1st sess. Washington DC: USGPO, 1980.

———. *Report to Accompany S. 1135, Expansion of Moapa Indian Reservation, Nevada.* Senate Report no. 96-951, 96th Cong., 2nd sess. Washington DC: USGPO, 1980.

U.S. Congress, Senate, Select Committee on Indian Affairs. *Hearing on Las Vegas Paiute Tribe Trust Lands, 16 September 1983.* 97th Cong., 2nd sess. Washington DC: USGPO, 1983.

———. *Hearing on Paiute Restoration Act, S. 1273, Held 8 November 1979.* 96th Cong., 1st sess. Washington DC: USGPO, 1979.

———. *Hearing on S. 2931, S. 2998, and S. 1893, 7 December 1982.* 97th Cong., 2nd sess. Washington DC: USGPO, 1983.

———. *Hearing on Trust Lands for the Paiute Tribe of Utah, H. R. 2898, Held 2 November 1983.* 98th Cong., 1st sess. Washington DC: USGPO, 1983.

U.S. Congress, Senate, Select Committee on Indian Affairs, Subcommittee on Investigations. *Final Report and Legislative Recommendations.* Senate Report no. 101-216, 101st Cong., 2nd sess. Washington DC: USGPO, 1989.

U.S. Department of Interior, Bureau of Indian Affairs. *Rules and Regulations*. Washington DC: USGPO, 1904.

U.S. Department of Interior, National Park Service. *Pipe Spring National Monument*. Washington DC: USGPO, 1994.

U.S. Department of War. *Annual Report of the Secretary of War*. U.S. Congress, House of Representatives, Executive Document vol. 1, no. 2, 36th Cong., 1st sess. Washington DC: USGPO, 1859.

———. *Annual Report of the Secretary of War*. U.S. Congress, House of Representatives, Executive Document vol. 1, no. 2, 39th Cong., 2nd sess. Washington DC: USGPO, 1866.

———. *Annual Report of the Secretary of War*. U.S. Congress, House of Representatives, Executive Document vol. 1, no. 2, 48th Cong., 1st sess. Washington DC: USGPO, 1883.

Utley, Robert M., and Wilcomb E. Washburn. *The American Heritage History of the Indian Wars*. New York: American Heritage Publishing Co. and Simon and Schuster, 1977.

Verdery, Katherine. "Ethnicity, Nationalism, and State-making: Ethnic Groups and Boundaries, Past and Future." In Hans Vermeulen and Cora Govers, eds., *Anthropology of Ethnicity: Beyond Ethnic Groups and Boundaries*, 33–58. Amsterdam: Het Spinhuis, 1994.

Vogel, Dan. *Indian Origins and the Book of Mormon*. N.p.: Signature Books, 1986.

Waitman, Leonard. "The History of Camp Cady: The Early History of a Desert Water Hole." *Historical Society of Southern California Quarterly* 36 (1954): 49–91.

Walker, Deward, ed. *Emergent Native Americans*. Boston: Little, Brown, 1972.

Wallerstein, Immanuel. *The Modern World-System: Capitalist Agriculture and the Origins of the European World-Economy in the Sixteenth Century*. New York: Academic Press, 1974.

Warren, Elizabeth V. "Armijo's Trace Revisited: A New Interpretation." M. A. thesis, University of Nevada, Las Vegas, 1974.

Washburn, Wilcomb, ed. *The Indian and the White Man*. Documents in American Civilization Series. Garden City: Doubleday, 1964.

Watkins, Arthur V. "Termination of Federal Supervision: The Removal of Restrictions over Indian Property and Person." In George E. Simpson and J. Milton Yinger, eds., *American Indians and American Life*. Special issue, *American Academy of Political and Social Science Annals* 311 (1957): 47–55.

Weil, Robert. "The Legal Status of the Indian." Ph.D. diss., Columbia College, 1888.

Wheeler, George. *Preliminary Report Concerning Explorations and Surveys Principally in Nevada and Arizona*. U.S. Congress, Senate, Executive Document no. 65, 42nd Cong., 2nd sess. Serial Set no. 1479. Washington DC: USGPO, 1872.

White, Leslie A. *The Evolution of Culture*. New York: McGraw-Hill, 1959.

White, Richard. *The Roots of Dependency: Subsistence, Environment, and Social Change among the Choctaws, Pawnees, and Navajos*. Lincoln: University of Nebraska Press, 1983.

Whittaker, David J. "Mormons and Native Americans: A Historical and Bibliographical Introduction." *Dialogue: A Journal of Mormon Thought* 18, no. 4 (1985): 33–64.

Winkler, Albert. "The Circleville Massacre: A Brutal Incident in Utah's Black Hawk War." *Utah Historical Quarterly* 55 (1987): 4–21.

Wolf, Eric R. *Europe and the People without History*. Berkeley: University of California Press, 1982.

Wood, David L. "Gosiute-Shoshone Draft Resistance, 1917–1918." *Utah Historical Quarterly* 49 (1981): 173–88.

Woodbury, Angus M. "A History of Southern Utah and Its National Parks." *Utah Historical Quarterly* 12 (1944): 111–223.

Woodfield, John K. "The Initiation of the Range Cattle Industry of Utah." M. S. thesis, University of Utah, 1957.

Woodruff, Wilford. "Remarks in the Bowry, 15 July 1855." Church of Jesus Christ of Latter-day Saints, *Journal of Discourses* 9 (1855): 221–33.

Woodward, Arthur. *Feud on the Colorado*. Los Angeles: Westernlore Press, 1955.

Woolf, G. M., and R. B. Grant. "Albinism among the Hopi Indians of Arizona." In Jack Kelso and G. Lasker, eds., *Yearbook of Physical Anthropology, 1962*, 13–22. Boulder CO: N.p., 1962.

Yinger, J. Milton. "Ethnicity." *Annual Review of Sociology* 11 (1985): 151–80.

Young, Brigham, Heber Kimball, and Jedidiah Grant. "Eleventh General Epistle of the Presidency." 1854. In James R. Clark, ed., *Messages of the First Presidency of the Church of Jesus Christ of Latter-Day Saints, 1833–1964*. Salt Lake City: Bookcraft, 1965.

Zanjani, Sally S. "'Totell Disregard to the Wellfair of the Indians': The Longstreet-Bradfute Controversy at Moapa Reservation." *Nevada Historical Society Quarterly* 29 (1986): 241–53.

INDEX

acculturation, Paiute. *See* Indian policy, federal: acculturation in; Paiute traditional culture: absorption of traits into

acculturation theories: description of, 1–2; inadequacy of, 4, 5–6, 297

Adair, Fanny: enrolled at Moapa, 193–94

adaptation: in Paiute interethnic relations, 311–12; to physical environment, 2, 10–29; to social environment, 6–7

adoption. *See* interethnic relations with the federal government: enrollment issue in

affinal kinsmen. *See* Paiute social organization: affinal obligations in; Paiute social organization: marriage

agriculture: in Mormon missionary program, 64, 76; Paiute, compared to non-Indian, 163–64, 171, 362 n.170; as unprofitable on reservations, 177. *See also* Indian policy, federal: agriculture in

alcohol: access limited by federal law, 211; access opposed by BIA, 175, 200, 217; Mormons reject, 339 n.59; purchase of, 142, 149–50; purchased in mining towns, 106; relation to wage labor of, 172. *See also* interethnic relations with federal government: alcohol regulated in; interethnic relations with miners: and alcohol; Kaibab Reservation: alcohol on; Moapa Reservation: alcohol access on; state jurisdiction: over alcohol

alcoholism: ridiculed in press, 208

Allen, Jim (Ute guide), 205

Allen, R. C. (Mormon missionary), 64

Allen Canyon Paiutes: ethnic identity of, 203, 204, 376–77 n.100

allotment of Northern Paiute reservations, 351 n.60. *See also* General Allotment Act; Indian policy, federal: allotment in

allotments from public lands, 143. *See also* Chemehuevi Valley Reservation: allotted; Fort Mohave Reservation: allotted

American Indian Religious Act: invoked by Paiutes, 286

Ammon, 56–57

annual cycle: impact of travelers on, 35, 39; traditional subsistence, 14–20, 29

antelope drives: leadership of, 316 n.29; technique of, 17

Apache wars: Paiutes in, 99

archaeology of Paiute culture, 13–14

Armijo, Antonio: expedition of, 34

Armstrong, Martha: in Los Angeles, 210

Arrow Canyon: water storage planned for, 168, 226

arrows, compound, 19

Ash Meadows NV: Paiutes living in, 44

Association of American Indian Affairs: in Paiute termination, 254

attorneys, disputes over, in land claim, 245–46, 395 n.8

automobiles: death of Paiute by, 210; expenses of, 233; Paiute views on 232; as social integration mechanism, 301; theft of, 380–81 n.136; used for job access, 177, 231, 304, 308

Avote: death of, 108, 335 n.69

Bagley, Orson: and Koosharem water rights, 144, 161–62

bands: characteristics of, 28; cultural variation among, 247; location of, *11*; membership (*see* interethnic relations with federal government: enrollment issue in); names for, 28; in reinstated tribe, 279; relation to reservation group, 191; residence areas as, 274, 275; size of, 316 n.22; structure of, 78, 317–18 n.36. *See also* Kaibab band; Kanosh band; Las Vegas band; Moapa band; Paiute political organization; San Juan band; Santa Clara band

baptism, Mormon: of headmen, 61, 67; as method of cure, 67; performed, 69, 298